Recharting the Black Atlantic

Routledge Research in Atlantic Studies

William Boelhower, Louisiana State University
Stephen Fender, University of Sussex
William O'Reilly, University of Cambridge

Recharting the Black Atlantic

Modern Cultures, Local Communities, Global Connections

Edited by
Annalisa Oboe and Anna Scacchi

Routledge
Taylor & Francis Group
New York   London

Transferred to digital printing 2010

First published 2008
by Routledge
270 Madison Ave, New York, NY 10016

Simultaneously published in the UK
by Routledge
2 Park Square, Milton Park, Abingdon, Oxon OX14 4RN

Routledge is an imprint of the Taylor & Francis Group, an informa business

© 2008 Taylor & Francis

Typeset in Sabon by IBT Global

Library of Congress Cataloging in Publication Data
Recharting the Black Atlantic : modern cultures, local communities, global
  connections / edited by Annalisa Oboe and Anna Scacchi.
      p. cm. — (Routledge research in Atlantic studies)
  Includes bibliographical references and index.
  ISBN-13: 978-0-203-92958-2
  ISBN-10: 0-415-96111-4
  1. Blacks—Atlantic Ocean Region—Civilization. 2. Atlantic Ocean Region—
Civilization—African influences. 3. Blacks—Race identity—Atlantic Ocean Region.
4. Blacks—Atlantic Ocean Region—Intellectual life. 5. African diaspora.
6. Hybridity (Social sciences)—Atlantic Ocean Region. I. Oboe, Annalisa.
II. Scacchi, Anna.
  CB235.R43 2008
  909'.0496075—dc22
  2007037751

ISBN10: 0-415-96111-4 (hbk)
ISBN10: 0-415-88393-8 (pbk)
ISBN10: 0-203-92958-6 (ebk)

ISBN13: 978-0-415-96111-0 (hbk)
ISBN13: 978-0-415-88393-1 (pbk)
ISBN13: 978-0-203-92958-2 (ebk)

for Oyekan Owomoyela

Pípé là ńpé gbón
A kì í pé gò

Assembling is what we do in order to be wise
(Yoruba proverb)

Contents

viii *Contents*

PART III
Black Bodies, Global Voices

List of Figures

Acknowledgments

This book records the final stage of a research project called "Sea Changes: Bodies, Practices and Discourses around the Atlantic," which began at the University of Padua, Italy, in 2004. It is particularly indebted to all the scholars from Europe, Africa and the U.S. who over the years have contributed to set up and develop a productive multi-disciplinary, circumatlantic dialogue—both those whose contribution appears in the present collection and those who generously collaborated in the earlier stages of the research: cultural critics Tim Brennan, Alfred Hornung and Roger Bromley, whose intellectual passion has been contagious; philosopher V. Y. Mudimbe, for his inspiring theoretical inputs; and our colleague Bill Boelhower, who first introduced transatlantic studies at the University of Padua. Our gratitude also goes to all the promising younger academics from the three continents who enthusiastically worked with us. With Dorothea Fischer-Hornung, Patrick Williams and Richard Follett we shared all the way—a special thank you for your friendship.

We wish to thank the University of Padua for funding the Sea Changes project and for its financial support to the colloquiums of the research group—these encounters have been essential in promoting exchange of ideas and fertile debate. Numerous colleagues and friends helped at various stages of our collective venture. We are especially grateful to Giuseppe Brunetti, Head of the Department of Anglo-Germanic and Slavic Languages and Literatures at the University of Padua, for his encouraging presence at the colloquiums; Carol Taylor, who gave us access to the technical resources of the University Language Center; Paola Bottalla, for her precious advice; Jozef Falinski, who helped at various stages of the editing process; Mariella Veronese, for her administrative capacities; Davide Marangon and Filippo Boscariol, whose patience and technical competence in all things 'digital' never failed us.

The volume is dedicated to the memory of our Yoruba friend, Oyekan Owomoyela, whose wisdom we all miss.

Introduction
Black Bodies, Practices and Discourses around the Atlantic

It may appear that seas put nations out of all communion with each other. But this is not so; for by means of commerce, seas form the happiest natural provision for their intercourse. And the more there are of neighbouring coastlands, as in the case of the Mediterranean Sea, this intercourse becomes the more animated. And hence communications with such lands, especially where there are settlements upon them connected with the mother countries giving occasion for such communications, bring it about that evil and violence committed in one place of our globe are felt in all. Such possible abuse cannot, however, annul the right of man as a citizen of the world to attempt to enter into communion with all others, and for this purpose to visit all the regions of the earth.

> I. Kant, "Nature and Conditions of Cosmopolitical Right."[1]

Chart—a map for the use of navigators; a delineation of a portion of the sea, indicating the outline of the coasts, the position of the rocks, sandbanks, channels, anchorages, etc.

> *Oxford English Dictionary*

A sea-chart draws attention to local details in relation to the wider expanse of seawater and the intricate circuits of flows. The idea of *re-charting* suggested in this volume refers both to the aim of studying the specificities of black cultures, histories, arts, and ideologies against the larger background of diasporic movements around the Atlantic, and to the necessity of revisioning the theoretical cartography of the "Black Atlantic." It highlights an interest in mapping the uprooting and re-routing of the "translated" cultures of the modern world,[2] and the impact of such movements on location.

Committed to a cross-cultural vision, the research project "Sea Changes: Bodies, Practices and Discourses around the Atlantic," from which this book stems, is the expression of an international community of scholars that started to gather at the University of Padua in October 2004, to engage in a complex and polysemic dialogue on questions of identity, social memory, literary and artistic expression, and global/local tensions in a circumatlantic perspective.

Growing out of an awareness that there is no single "Atlantic" culture and that the ocean has, in fact, given way to a network of discrete but related, and inherently polymorphous, socio-political contact zones, the circumatlantic perspective is able to generate any number of productive lines of inquiry. It converses with the expanding plethora of descriptive/interpretive terms that in recent years have sought to name the sites of interaction between nations, cultures, and regions: terms such as *creolization, transculturation, hybridity, migrancy, diaspora,* and *globalization.*[3] All of these terms point to an area of shared and discrepant meanings, neighboring maps, and tangential histories—a fluid domain that is often a palimpsest of places and times, of different seas that are separate and yet flow into each other, and that are being explored from different theoretical perspectives, so that the ocean has emerged as a truly interdisciplinary field of inquiry.

As cultural historian Donna Gabaccia observes, the Atlantic today comes in many colors, which signal various forms of allegiance determined by political, economic, social, and cultural interests and exchanges between the continents on either side: the White Atlantic of Euro-America, the Red Atlantic of rebellious and egalitarian movements, the Black Atlantic of the African slave trade and diaspora.[4] Each of these narrative frameworks has been in place for quite some time, and all of them, although they set up cultural scenarios with very different priorities, detect something cohesive about the Atlantic zone.

In the Sea Changes project the Atlantic is a heuristic tool, a space for scholarly discovery which starts from the basic assumption that the sea as culture does not exist without the people that inhabit its shores. In other words, the Atlantic becomes a discursive space of interesting perspectives because it is crisscrossed and traveled in ways that speak of exchanges among the cultures that define its borders, or of modes in which the cultures of Europe, Africa, and the Americas respond to one another, collide, or converge. This viewpoint has the advantage of allowing the tensions between the local/national and the global/transnational to come into sharper focus. In fact, it turns the circumatlantic zone into a signifier not simply of transnationality and movement but, particularly, of the cultural, political, and literary need to rethink the local, a distinctive community or an individual identity, in historical contexts of displacement or of globalizing tensions. This is accomplished in the belief that global phenomena cannot be studied apart from the politics of location they disrupt and are contested by. From this position, the Black Atlantic presented in this volume does not overlap with Paul Gilroy's: it becomes a space where a multiplicity of research/cultural paradigms coexist, and where various locally inflected approaches confront one another.

When Gilroy appeared on the scene of Atlantic studies in 1993, with his influential *The Black Atlantic,* the global dynamics of slavery and racism and the worldwide interactions of local discourses on race had already been studied by a number of great twentieth-century intellectuals—among them W.E.B. Du Bois, C.L.R. James, and Frantz Fanon—while the idea of approaching the sea as a single unit of analysis had been eloquently advanced in Fernand Braudel's magisterial work on the Mediterranean. Gilroy's book, however, had the merit of focusing on the Black Atlantic as a "contact zone," to use Mary Louise Pratt's term indicating "the space of colonial encounters":[5] that is to say, as a "system of cultural exchanges,"[6] defined by flows and contingent exchanges—rather than by national constituencies and racial authenticity—both central and marginal to the contemporary hegemonic discourses of modernity. Gilroy thus provided a liberating example, capable of illuminating new terrains of research and of giving visibility to cultural processes to which nation-based approaches were blind. The incredible popularity of his book probably capitalized on the growing discomfort of many critics with excessively dichotomous, crystallized analyses of power relationships.

The concept of the Black Atlantic as a unifying site of hybridization, linking together Africa, Europe, and the Americas, and joining in critical dialogue with the West both the Africans transported in the slave ships to the plantations of the New World and their nationally diverse descendants, bound by their common history of enslavement, racial oppression, and double consciousness, has opened up new analytical possibilities and incredibly enriched our archives, especially in regard to eighteenth- and early nineteenth-century black writing. The sheer number of volumes, journal articles, anthologies, conferences, seminars, and academic programs that have employed the Black Atlantic as an identifying tag since the publication of Gilroy's book—either because they applied it as an analytical tool to read cross-cultural exchanges among diaspora blacks, or because they argued against its validity or usefulness, or simply because it has rapidly become an effective marketing strategy—attests to the impact that the notion of the Atlantic Ocean as a site of transnational affiliation and cultural dialogue, transcending "the structures of the nation state and the constraints of ethnicity and national particularity,"[7] has had on cultural and postcolonial studies, on African diaspora studies in general, and on African American studies in particular.

The Black Atlantic has forcefully impacted the discipline of American studies, which in the early 1990s was busy questioning American exceptionalism and consequently remapping American culture beyond and across national borders, with the purpose of revising the monologic, self-referential approach that remains dominant. This may help explain the ready acceptance of Gilroy's work in U.S. universities and academic publishing beyond the field of African American studies and the proliferation, in the 1990s, of studies questioning Anglocentric ideas of nation and national tradition and advocating the advent of a postnational, comparative turn in American studies that would bring into focus the complex web of cultural strands making up the United States. The "Black Atlantic" field, as Brent Hayes Edwards remarks, has been rapidly canonized and institutionalized in the U.S. academy, where it threatens to become the equivalent of diaspora and has been concretized as a formalized space, in spite of Gilroy's efforts to propose it as a provisional term of analysis.[8]

The reconceptualization of "America" in transnational terms, however, has not failed to raise doubts as to its possibly unconscious collusion with worldwide corporate capitalism, which needs to replace nation-states with a borderless space allowing the free flow of capital, or, especially on the part of non-U.S. Americanists, to provoke criticism of what looks like U.S. imperialism under new clothes. In a similar fashion, in regard to *The Black Atlantic*, many scholars of the African diaspora have commented negatively on the book's Americocentrism and the paradox of an effort to debunk African American parochialism that ends up taking the African American experience as paradigmatic of the black diaspora. Gilroy and the scholars influenced by his study have been taken to task for homogenizing the complexities of the diaspora on the model of black America or, at best, of the Anglophone Black Atlantic. This is in spite of the fact that, contrary to what happens in other nations of the Americas, such as the Caribbean and Brazil, in the U.S. blacks are a minority and racial relations are framed in a black/white opposition that erases the visibility of mixed-heritage people.

Moreover, it should be observed that the concept of the "Black Atlantic" circulating in the academic world is largely a product of American research and of its "version" of Gilroy's proposition. As Pierre Bourdieu and Loïc Wacquant have argued, while commenting on the tendency of the American worldview to impose itself as a universal perspective, especially when it comes to such issues as "race," "the dehistoricization that almost inevitably results from the migration of ideas across national boundaries is one of the factors contributing to derealization and false universalization."[9] It is quite understandable, then, that the universalizing of the (black) American experience appears as just another instance of U.S. imperialism and its drive to turn the globe into "McWorld."

In addition, as many have pointed out, the Black Atlantic paradigm is exceedingly pliable in Gilroy's use and above all in its practitioners': it seems to apply indifferently to all historical epochs, from the slave trade era to contemporary patterns of migration, and consequently fails to account for the complexities and historical specificities of the connections between Africa and its diasporas. With a panorama of case studies focusing predominantly on middle-class male intellectuals born in the U.S., such as Alexander Crummell, Martin Delany, and W.E.B. Du Bois, moreover, Gilroy also fails to take into proper consideration important identity markers such as class and gender. He makes of a few African American men the representatives of the diasporic experience and the black counterculture of modernity that it generates, and seems oblivious to the problematic collusion between black American nationalism and patriarchy. The idea that traveling and crossing the sea produce a cosmopolitan perspective on the world, besides, is in itself a gender-specific reading of the black diaspora, since it gives primacy to experiences that have been and still are the prerogative of bourgeois men and obscures the importance of women, land, and local agency.

The major shortcoming in Gilroy's book, however, according to scholars such as Ntongela Masilela, Simon Gikandi, Laura Chrisman, Joan Dayan, Paul Zeleza, and others, is one that seriously impairs the validity of the Black Atlantic epistemology: locating a black counterculture of modernity in the Atlantic and finding its genealogy in the slave trade, in fact, is complicit with the familiar stereotyping of Africa as the primitive "dark continent." The Black Atlantic proposition has indeed limited its investigative horizons to the Anglophone Atlantic, or better, to the American (and to some extent black British) branch of the African diaspora, and there is wide agreement on the need to expand it in order to track multidirectional cultural exchanges not only across and around the Atlantic rim, but also between Africa and Europe, between the Atlantic and the Mediterranean, across the Pacific and the Indian Oceans, and within the Americas. This enlarged recharting of the Black Atlantic would not be blind to the interplay between the local and the global, the national and the transnational, and would alert us to the fact that locating modernity in the West is a problematic act, to say the least.

Since its publication *The Black Atlantic* has generated a flow of studies aiming to critique the validity of Gilroy's epistemology of the African diaspora, to investigate areas that have remained peripheral to Gilroy's perspective, and to counter an emphasis on the interconnections of slavery and the Western discourse of modernity which threatens to erase Africa and its many diasporas from the remapping of black cultures. Our volume adds up to this intense debate and is motivated by the same desire to extend and revise Gilroy's work.

Thus, when we speak of the Black Atlantic as a field of inquiry, we choose to use a concept which we know is inherently flawed, a term designating the difficulty of what needs to be studied by positing what is *not* studied. That is, the "Atlantic" is, precisely, not the focus: the study of culture, particularly in the context of imperialism and globalization, is always an exercise in tangents, evasions, and absences. Seen from its borders, and from the crisscrossing or circular routes that link them, the ocean keeps changing; it ebbs and flows, and also (geography tells us) spreads into other oceans. There is a sense of dispersion, caused by the infinite possibilities of such a fluid landscape, as well as a sense of closure in the option of selecting one "ocean" from among, or in contrast to, the others.

In an effort to counter the surface fragmentation of the Caribbean archipelago, the Barbadian writer Kamau Brathwaite once suggested the idea of an underwater coming together of the disparate histories, languages, and communities of the Caribbean islands, pointing to a potential under-the-surface connectedness among them. This worldview, expressed in his assertion that "the unity is submarine,"[10] may be extended to our multi-layered oceanic venture, to describe the status of research in the present volume, which shows an adaptive constellation of responses to black cultures in the Atlantic world. The connecting platform may indeed appear to be underwater, but a unity is certainly visible, since a set of shared subtexts clearly informs our idea and study of cultures—first and foremost, a politics of knowledge involving a postcolonial stance and a cultural studies and new historical approach.

Research on Black Atlantic cultures is necessarily multi-disciplinary. The field radically advocates a liberating interplay of disciplines, an exploding of various parochialisms, so that scholars in the literatures and the arts of Europe, Africa, and the Americas may dialogue not only with each other but also with practitioners of diaspora studies, international relations, history, cinema, and popular culture. In recharting the Black Atlantic, the volume presents a plurality of voices and histories, all aimed at disrupting the Euro-American sense of where the center lies. It engages mainly with the black Anglophone cultures of Africa, Europe, and the Americas, but also sets up a dialogue with the Francophone (Caribbean) and particularly Lusophone (Brazil, Guinea Bissau) Black Atlantic; and a brand new route that connects the Black Atlantic and the "Black" Mediterranean is also investigated, which focuses on the recent production of Italophone writers. The black circumatlantic vision offered here thus opens up to a multiplicity of aesthetic, ideological, historical, linguistic, and geographical constituents, giving birth to a plurality of coexisting and often related Black Atlantics.

While the three sections that make up this volume share much thematic and theoretical ground, each is devoted to recharting a specific morphological aspect of Black Atlantic cultures. The first section, "Circumatlantic Connections, Local Lives," collects essays that investigate the interplay between grand transnational ideologies and movements, like Négritude and Pan-Africanism, and local experiments in black individual and collective self-creation on the three continents. It problematizes the assumptions that the relationship between Africa and its Atlantic diasporas is one of imitation or dependence and that nationalism is an obsolete political practice and should be replaced by hybrid transnationalism, thus showing the coexistence of cross-cultural and "strategic essentialist" impulses in African, Brazilian, Caribbean, and North American contexts. The essays locate artistic and literary practices (black installation art, romance fiction, neo-slave narratives, theater, satire), political projects (South African proto-nationalism, Afro-Brazilian cultural identity and racial politics, Canadian multiculturalism), tortured and splintered black bodies (in a variety of diasporic milieus), and popular cultural forms (like football) in socially and spatially defined communities that contextualize subjectivity in spite of the eradicating pull of oceanic flows. Ideas, texts, discourses, space, and time are socialized and localized through complex and deliberate practices of performance, representation, and action.

The section on "Modern Societies, Ancient Routes" traces connections between contemporary art forms (cinema, hip-hop, dance, African American autobiography, black European literature, and architecture) and forceful acts of rememorying, where "modernity" emerges as inextricably linked to "tradition," both local and diasporic. The present rememories portions of the past so that it comes to shape not only today's African and Black Atlantic cultures, but also the "modernity" of Europe. Africa figures here as both "resistance" to Gilroy's model for re-reading modernity, which drowns the Dark Continent in the trench of the Atlantic, and as a proposal for re-viewing the concept of "the modern." Modernity is not, as Arjun Appadurai insists,[11] the end of the local, the national, the traditional, nor does it necessarily imply dramatic global changes; it is rather a way of "doing tradition differently," of articulating experiments in contemporary living through (non-essentialized) re-articulations of inheritance—national, ethnic, local. "Doing tradition differently" thus becomes a key for reading contemporary African art forms as well as African American or black European cultural productions. More importantly, from this viewpoint slavery and the Atlantic slave trade—as both history and icon of a counterculture of modernity—can be turned into a reference point (an inheritance) for today's phenomena of global dislocation. For many black British or black Italian writers, the contemporary passage from Africa or the Caribbean to Europe implies re-enactments of the self that go through rememoryings of the by-now "traditional" Middle Passage. The "ghosts" of the African slaves, severed from home, buried at sea, or working in the southern plantations, haunt the present of migrants and their own painful efforts to do tradition "differently."

In the third part, "Black Bodies, Global Voices," the terms *black* and *global* need qualification. We see "black" here—and throughout the volume—as a loosely defined, adaptive signifier, disconnected from essentialized notions of "race," African diaspora, or African American culture: it is a useful label to be negotiated and opportunely filled in a variety of ways, so as to include diverse marginal subjects. And "global" does not unproblematically stand for borderless transnationalism, nor is it a decontextualized given, inevitably deriving from displacement and exile and the overcoming of racial and national absolutism; rather, it refers to historically specific discourses on the "politics of identity," enabling black bodies to become voices for adversarial cultures within and across ethnic, racial, and national borders. Cross-culturality, as well as the necessity of problematizing what links minority cultures, is foregrounded in this section, so that the emphasis is on subjective attempts at recharting Atlantic relations from the perspective of representative black voices in writing, music, performance, and politics, who daily experience the devastating pressure but also the potentialities of modern/global capitalism.

Annalisa Oboe and Anna Scacchi
May 2007

NOTES

1. From *The Philosophy of Law* (1796).
2. See Salman Rushdie's remarks on the postcolonial condition in *Imaginary Homelands*, 17.
3. See Clifford, "Diasporas," 303.
4. Gabaccia, "A Long Atlantic in a Wider World," 2.
5. Pratt, *Imperal Eyes*, 6.
6. Gilroy, *The Black Atlantic*, 14.
7. Gilroy, *The Black Atlantic*, 19.
8. Edwards, "The Uses of Diaspora," 45, 61.
9. Bourdieu and Wacquant, "On the Cunning of Imperialist Reason," 51.
10. Brathwaite, *Contradictory Omens*, 64.
11. Appadurai, *Modernity at Large*.

Part I
Circumatlantic Connections, Local Lives

1   David Hammons's *Sheep Raffle* at Dak'Art 2004

Reading Black Art through Léopold Sédar Senghor's Négritude

Manthia Diawara

PRELUDE

> No sooner did Sango enter the town than he demanded the sacrifice of a ram.
>
> Yoruba saying

In March 2004, I was invited by my friend Salah Hassan to write an article on David Hammons's contribution to the Dak'Art Biennale.[1] I then invited the artist to lunch in the Village, in New York City, to talk about his installation. Soon after we sat down in Il Buco restaurant, David informed me that he was going to do a sheep raffle as his contribution to Africa's biggest art show.

"A Sheep Raffle?" I asked. "But why?"

"Oh, for no reason in particular," he said.

Knowing David, I told myself that I must remain cool; that it would serve no purpose to push him to say more, right away, about his project. So I told him that it was a great idea, and changed the subject of the conversation. Fortunately, it did not take David too long to return to the topic.

"You know," he said, "people in Dakar do not go to exhibitions. They think that the Dak'Art is for white people. And, considering the state of the art world today, I can't blame them for not showing up. At least with the Sheep Raffle, I'll give them something that they can relate to. They'll come, and at the end of the day, the lucky winners will take home a sheep."

I asked David if he had any idea of both the symbolic and literal significance of the ram in West African cultures—from the Yoruba to the Baule and the Dogon. In my desire to impress David, I said that the ram was central to life in West Africa, whether one looked at it from an Islamic point of view or an Animist system of thought. At the end of the Ramadan fast—a tradition emanating from Abraham and Isaac—the ram is the most important sacrifice for every Moslem household. Still today, in many villages in Mali and Senegal, one can see a white ram roaming around. It is considered a kind of safeguard from evil spirits, a sort of *pharmakon* or caretaker that keeps an eye on the village. The ram is the symbol of purity, of innocence, and it is therefore sacred.

In the West African spiritual imaginary, the ram is both Moslem and Animist. It has survived in many cultures as both a totem of the ancestors and a metaphor for human sacrifice in monotheism. More importantly, it is a signifier of religious syncretism and cultural hybridity. As more and more Africans migrate from the village to the city, the ram has also become cosmopolitan. For example, in the Medina districts of such capital cities as Dakar and Bamako, the traffic often stops to let a herd of white sheep—wearing gris-gris on their necks—cross the street. I have often wondered, why the gris-gris? To protect the rams, or to scare taxi drivers from running over them? But it is clear that while these sheep wait for the Tabaski feast, a Moslem holiday, to be slaughtered, they receive special treatment in the city. In Dakar, they are well fed and bathed in the ocean by young men.

Could David Hammons's *Sheep Raffle* be a signifyin' practice on some of these uses of the ram? I reminded him of the sheep symbolism behind his own name. The Bible says that King David returned to caring for the sheep and "The Spirit of The Lord came upon [him] . . . from that day forward."[2] It was also the same David who challenged Goliath the Philistine,[3] just as he, David Hammons, is now challenging the art world. Finally, I asked, is David signifyin' on Picasso's *The Man with a Lamb* (1943)? A friend of Léopold Sédar Senghor's—poet and first president of Senegal—Picasso had once visited Dakar. David said that he did not know about all of that. All he wanted to do was to be useful while in Africa. He wanted to communicate with the people at a spiritual level. That was what mattered to him. The art world did not matter to him.

Left on my own, I went over my conversation with David, attempting to give meaning to the silences, David's body language, and how many times he had repeated the words—*the art world, art and politics, spirituality, emotion, secrecy,* and *the arbitrariness of the market value of a work of art.* I knew the anarchic side of David—one who was always testy and provocative. The seeming banality of the *Sheep Raffle* calls to mind Gianni Vattimo's concept of weak thought, or what David himself calls the art of "dumbing down."

But I also knew that he was working within a tradition; that everything he did was a commentary on a stereotype or a piece of common sense into which he invested new and provocative signifiers. More than any other contemporary artist's, David Hammons's work questions the mode of existence of African American art; its relations to the art of the black diaspora and of Africa; and its capacity to transform people spiritually. I believe therefore that whatever David does, in spite of his critique of art and the art world, is strongly grounded in black aesthetics. By that, I mean that his work sets in motion the essential elements of black aesthetics—collective memory, vital force, emotion, rhythm, image, recognition of pleasure and terror, and the disposition of the black body. So, given this definition of black art, what could a performance of a David Hammons *Sheep Raffle* at the Dak'Art tell me? To be more precise, what else could it signify in both the Saussurian and the Black Vernacular senses of the term?

THE DAK'ART BIENNALE: MAY 2004

I arrived in Dakar on the night of the eighth of May, a full day after the opening ceremony of the official Biennale. The catalogue was still not out, and many of the installations were not ready at the main sites: the Foire Internationale des Expositions, the Chamber of Commerce, and the Musée de l'IFAN. I had therefore the time to go and see the secondary shows called the "Off Biennale." David Hammons's *Sheep Raffle* was part of an "Off Show," entitled *3x3,* and curated by Salah Hassan and Cheryl Finley.

The *Sheep Raffle,* or *Tombola de moutons,* took place outdoors by the main street going past the Sumbejun fish market and toward the university Cheick Anta Diop. It was like a typical crowd gathering around a platform with drummers, singers, and dancers. The master of ceremonies, with a loudspeaker in his hand, announced the sheep raffle and enunciated the rules for participants. At the sound of the drums, the local crowd gathered spontaneously. There were also David Hammons fans who had come from America and Europe, as well as curious foreigners who were attracted by what seemed to be a strange and incomprehensible event.

There were banners and flyers advertising both the event and a brand of soy sauce called Maggi, with which the Senegalese like to season their favorite dish, Cebu Jen. The sheep were tied to a pole nearby, and David himself sat on top of the platform, surveying the performance, or came down the ladder to film certain scenes with a small digital camera. Every once in a while there was a winner—a man or a woman—who pulled the sheep away with a rope tied on its neck. Then a taxi was hailed and a fare negotiated, whereupon the lucky winner put the sheep in the trunk and said goodbye to the envious crowd. David then returned to the drummers and singers to watch over the proceedings of the last raffle of the day. All in all, he gave away twelve sheep in six days.

The *Sheep Raffle* contrasted nicely with everything going on in the official Biennale. The more the one was popular and grounded in the tradition of West African masquerade and performance, the more the other was steeped in the contemporary fashion of video and sculpture installations. The installations, paintings, and sculptures in the official show mimicked sheepishly, excuse the pun, the conceptual artists in London, New York, and Berlin. Okwi Enwezor put it aptly in a talk he delivered at the Dakar Conference Center, when he compared the official selection to a second dance in the Yoruba tradition. According to Enwezor, the first dance was the best for the Yoruba. Any performance that was cutting edge belonged to this category, in contradistinction to diluted performances, mimicry, and repetitions, which are called second dances.

I realize that I may be taking Enwezor's nice metaphor of the first dance out of context here, by linking it to the literal and essentialist meanings of such words as mimicry and repetition. For we all know what original thought a Homi Bhabha or James Snead is capable of deriving from these concepts. In Négritude aesthetics, there is also Senghor's notion of a repetition that does not repeat itself, or what Amiri Baraka calls the changing same in the Black Arts movement.

My point is that David Hammons's return to African ritual practices through the *Sheep Raffle* constitutes an important critique of the limits that the art world has put on artistic productions in Africa and the world. A similar critique was voiced at the École des Beaux Arts of Dakar during the Biennale. A student whose submission to the Biennale was rejected complained that he could not afford a digital video camera, and therefore could not compete with African artists living in Europe and America. The student echoed a general feeling at the École des Beaux Arts of Dakar, when he stated that the future of African art was no longer based in Africa, but rather in Europe and America. "Every artist must do a video installation or be excluded," he said. It is in this sense that I quoted Enwezor's statement about first and second dances among the Yoruba.

For me, the *Sheep Raffle* by David Hammons, a project produced in Africa with local material, provides an invaluable instruction not only to the students at the Beaux Arts, but also to the Dak'Art Biennale as a whole. How can African art find a relative autonomy vis-à-vis the tyranny of the art world, curators, and cultural imperialists? How might one use art at the Dak'Art Biennale to say that there is no art here? In other words, David Hammons's ambition, in the battle between David and Goliath, is to save the soul of Black Art. He had come with the sacrifice, as an ancestor figure, to exorcize the Biennale, to give it strength, and to make it universal, instead of the product of a second dance. If performance art can be compared to a sacrificial object and to a masquerade, then let's look for a moment at the sacrificer and the sacrificed in David Hammons's *Sheep Raffle*.

THE SACRIFICED

> The sacrifice creates a relationship between the Ancestor and the sacrificer; it is the dialogue between the You and the I.
>
> L.S. Senghor, *Présence Africaine*, 1956

In some sense, the sheep is literally the signified in Hammons's performance. If you take part in the commerce of the *Sheep Raffle*, you may win a sheep; but also you may not. Either way, you have participated in the performance and you know the rules of the game. Similarly, the one who

accepts the sacrifice carries with her/him the burden of the sacrificer—she/
he becomes the scapegoat. But as the Senghor quote above shows, the sacrifice is a means to enter a relation with the Ancestor. The sheep is therefore
a way to communicate with the Ancestor, and to bring change in the lives of
the living. The first purpose of the David Hammons *Sheep Raffle* was to use
art and bring people to have confidence in themselves. Hammons accomplished this by grounding it in a public space, for collective participation.
Every time there is a winner, the sacrificed brings the sacrificer closer to
the ancestors. According to the rules of ritual performance, somebody wins
when the ancestors have accepted the sacrifice. Otherwise, the whole afternoon will be spent without a winner. This reminds me of a scene of sacrifice
in Chinua Achebe's *Arrow of God* (1964). In this masterpiece of African
literature there is a sacrifice ritual carried out before the yam harvest and
the priest must accept the gift before the farmers can begin to harvest. In
this particular scene, Ezeulu, the priest who is the link between the ancestors and the living, refuses to take the sacrifice. The yams lie rotting until a
Christian priest comes to receive the gift in Ezeulu's stead. And this leads the
farmers to choose Christianity over the tradition of their ancestors.

David Hammons's *Sheep Raffle*, and the significance of the sacrifice,
recall other representations of the sheep for similar purposes in African
art, literature, and film. For me, one of the most memorable scenes in African literature concerns the battle between Ramatoulaye and Vendredi, the
white ram, in Sembene Ousmane's *God's Bits of Wood* (1960). Vendredi is
described as a robust ram belonging to El Hadji Mabigué, a collaborator for
the French in the battle that pitted the colonial administration against the
striking railroad workers. The book depicts Mabigué as a pseudo-commu-
nity and -religious leader who participates in the oppression of the people.
Vendredi, the ram, is a signifier for Mabigué's wealth, arrogance, yet powerlessness in front of the colonizer. Vendredi is fat, white, and castrated. It
roams freely in the neighborhood, from compound to compound. It goes
into peoples' kitchens and bedrooms and, like its owner, it feeds off the
people, without fear of retribution. Its whiteness and castrated state represent Mabigué's own assimilation into the white colonial system, which
occurs without the acquisition of real power.

In contrast to Vendredi and its owner, there is Ramatoulaye, who supports the strike and works in solidarity with the community. One day, as
Ramatoulaye returns home from the store where she was turned down for
credit, she is told that Vendredi has gone to her kitchen and eaten the only
rice left for her famished family. At that moment, Vendredi emerges from
her bedroom with pieces of cloth in its mouth. Ramatoulaye meets it with a
knife in her hand and they engage in an epic battle. It is a battle of life and
death: who will be sacrificed for the strike—the community or the ram? The
sacrificial battle between Ramatoulaye and Vendredi is therefore a battle
for the success or failure of the strike and the survival of the community.
To put it in Ramatoulaye's own words, "When we know that the life and

courage of others depend on our lives and courage, we no longer have the right to be afraid."⁴ Thus, Ramatoulaye defeats Vendredi. She slaughters it and distributes the meat among the strikers. The sacrifice of Vendredi becomes a moral and literal victory for the spouses of the men on strike. The whole community comes to realize, through this ritual of sacrifice, that they can defeat colonialism if they have confidence in themselves.

Another great moment of political and aesthetic representation of the sacrifice of a ram in African art occurs in Souleymane Cissé's award-winning film *Finyé* (*The Wind*, Mali, 1982). The story of *The Wind*, like that of *God's Bits of Wood*, revolves around a strike. The film depicts the conflict between the student resistance movement and the military dictatorship in Mali in the 1970s. When students go on strike to protest against corruption and the soldiers' abuse of power, the soldiers beat them up and throw them in jail. The colonel of the army, who is also the governor, threatens that the students must return to school or be killed.

In the film, the students' resistance is defined through the character of a young man, called Bah, whose innocence and love for democracy contrast with the dictatorship of the colonel/governor. Bah defies him by choosing to die in prison. Bah's grandfather, a traditional figure in the film, then decides to confront the colonel/governor. However, before the confrontation, Kansaye, the grandfather, goes to the shrine and offers a ram as sacrifice to his ancestors in return for advice and protection. But, soon after the ritualistic greetings, the ancestors advise Kansaye to listen to the winds of change; to find new ways of handling the present situation; to follow the stars and the youth. At that point in the film, we see a magnificent-looking white ram running toward Kansaye, who waves at the animal to keep going. The ram's horns match the shape of the hat Kansaye is wearing, creating an identification between the two, the human and the animal. There is no doubt at that moment in the film that Kansaye and the ram, sacrificer and sacrificed, have become one with the ancestors. Now they must all fight together to survive in a modern world. The film implies that the message of the ancestors is that Kansaye must have confidence in the youth. Thus he returns to the city and follows the youth in their civil disobedience, which eventually brings down the military dictatorship.

The political and aesthetic lessons we learn in all these performances in literature and film concern the transformative power and modernity of the sacrifice in contemporary African art. Far from being static and primitive, the purpose of sacrifice is to teach people the modern techniques, the new aesthetic languages and political strategies that enable the sacrificer to transcend obstacles in her/his environment. In *God's Bits of Wood*, the sacrifice of Vendredi enables women to acquire agency, and transform their role in the struggle for self-determination. In *The Wind*, the sacrifice of the ram is seen as a sign that the old generation should give way to the young.

To return again to the Senghor quote above, the sacrifice is a means to enter a relation with the ancestors, a dialogue between the "You" and the

"I." The radical emotional and terrifying moment in *The Wind* comes when the ancestors follow the youth, instead of guiding them, as we are used to seeing in traditional African society. Similarly, in David Hammons's *Sheep Raffle* the sacrificed brings more vital force from the ancestors to the art world at Dak'Art. As Senghor puts it, in Baule ritual, the dancer who is wearing the ram mask, and the audience in attendance, identify with the ram-symbol of Nyamie, the Sun King. It is through this identification that the spirit of the ancestors finds an outlet and then flows in the bodies of the audience attending the ritual.[5] David Hammons's *Sheep Raffle* therefore provides a new energy to the Dak'Art Biennale through the sacrificed.

THE SACRIFICER

> Everything sacred, that intends to remain so, must cover itself in mystery.
>
> L.S. Senghor, *Liberté 5*, 1993

> I once saw the Sun-King-Ram dance in Côte d'Ivoire. The dancer expressed with his steps the sacred furor of the Ram, and the orchestra followed with musical phrases.
>
> L.S. Senghor, *Présence Africaine*, 1956

One way of reading David Hammons's *Sheep Raffle* is to look at it through a detour to Léopold Sédar Senghor and the Négritude movement. It is well known that when the movement was under attack in the 1950s and 1960s by such young Turks as Frantz Fanon, Wole Soyinka, and Ezekiel Mphahlele, Senghor defended himself by hiding behind the writers of the Harlem Renaissance. For example, when Wole Soyinka brashly dismissed Négritude in a now famous statement—"The tiger does not go about boasting of its tigritude"—Senghor's response was both surprising and revealing. He stated that if Négritude's poems were perceived as self-celebratory, it was because they were influenced by the poets of Harlem. He cited Langston Hughes, who said: "We younger Negro artists, who create now, intend to express our individual dark skinned selves without fear and shame."[6]

Unfortunately for Senghor, most people, including this author, preferring to see Négritude only as an instance of Francophone imperialism and assimilation, did not hear or see the strong echoes of the Harlem Renaissance in the definition of the movement. We also missed the strong racial consciousness in black poetry from America to France and Africa which today defines the African diaspora aesthetics. In retrospect, one can see that Soyinka's position was more appealing as a critique of the Négritude movement not only because of the pun which linked Négritude to Tigritude, but also because Soyinka had dismissed the essentialist claim to racial solidarity that was at the core of the Négritude movement and the Harlem Renaissance.

But if we were to take Senghor seriously today, and consider the influence of Harlem on Dakar, then the David Hammons's *Sheep Raffle* becomes more relevant at the Dak'Art Biennale. Senghor was the translator into French of the poetry of Langston Hughes. In the work of Hughes and other Harlem Renaissance writers like Claude McKay and Countee Cullen, Senghor and his Négritude peers discovered "a whole network of ties and relations, images and archetypes that had been dormant at the bottom of memory."[7] The deep-seated memory in question is that of Africa before slavery and colonialism. Islam and Christianity combined forces to destroy its social, religious, and economic systems. When Harlem comes to Dakar, it brings back to life this memory, it awakens the gods and the ancestors for the homecoming ceremony.

David Hammons, the sacrificer, knows his role in the dance of this homecoming. According to Senghor, "the sacrificer as the oldest member of the community is closest to the ancestors, can even be considered as part of them. He is the one who offers the sacrifice to the Ancestor. In exchange the latter makes the vital force flow through the sacrificer to the entire participating community."[8]

I attended several performances of the *Sheep Raffle* in Dakar. I tried to observe from distance as much as I could. But one day I could not resist the temptation to interview David. After all, I felt confident of our friendship in New York. I was also feeling confident that I had a privileged relationship with David and I knew that he was pleased that I was writing this article on him. But he completely ignored my presence and continued with his performance. Surely, David must have incarnated the body of the Ancestor in Dakar during the Biennale. I felt that he was not himself in the way that he was relating to people.

It is important to return to Senghor's theory of African art to make my point here. It is well known that Senghor's theory of Négritude was more drawn toward the primacy of "emotions," "feelings," "rhythms," and "repetitions." For him African art, unlike Western art, was not "a discourse with a beginning, middle and end."[9] So, instead of being an art of imitation, African art is an art of invention, and a visionary art; instead of an art of re-presentation, it is a production, a spiritual transference that "guides the creator all along her/his performance."[10] It was for this reason that Senghor believed that African art obtains its full meaning only during performance. He writes: "Hence, these rituals or prayers and sacrifices, music and song, dance and masquerade are at the same time artistic manifestations. It is the way they partake of art that they are meaningful."[11]

When I met David during his *Sheep Raffle*, he was possessed by the performance, and therefore was not himself. He had, as Senghor puts it,

> taken hold of the world outside and made it respond to him. He was one with the world he had created, with its shapes, colors, movements, sounds, and rhythms—both musical and plastic—taste and smell. . . .

He had begun to live at the pace of this world, beyond the pleasure of the sensory systems. He had identified with the object, and had became the Other [creator, ancestor, God?] in the happiness of communion, a feeling of total presence, of beyond-being.[12]

What could one say about David Hammons's sheep raffle, by way of conclusion? Some people thought that it was arrogant on the part of a black American to come to Africa and make fun of African art. A *Sheep Raffle* during Africa's most prestigious art meeting is a kind of Afro-pessimism that foreigners project onto the African landscape. In this sense David's *Sheep Raffle* resumes recent racist representations of Africa by journalists such as Keith Richburg's *Out of America* (1998) and Stephen Smith's *Négrologie* (2003). It is also possible to see the exotic side of the *Sheep Raffle* that is so much a part of tourist art. Many African artists, for this reason, stayed away from the performance. They argued that it was not art, and that David was able to get away with it only because he is David. In fact, some found the whole thing misleading and dangerous because the craft of art was missing in it. Even as I write this last sentence, I am still thinking about all these assessments of David Hammons's *Sheep Raffle*. But, putting aside the artist's mastery of modernism, the place of blackness in the Western imaginary, the art market, the minstrelsy of contemporary black artists, and my own fascination with the artist—I wonder?

NOTES

1. David Hammons (born in Springfield, Illinois, in 1943) is a well-known African American installation artist. His works can be found at the Museum of Modern Art in New York and in most contemporary art galleries in the U.S. and Europe. Salah Hassan is Chair of the Department of History of Art and Professor of African and African Diaspora art history and visual culture in the Africana Studies Department at Cornell University. He is also a curator and art critic, and founder and editor of *NKA: Journal of Contemporary African Art*.
2. 1 Samuel, 16:13.
3. 1 Samuel, 17:1–58.
4. "Quand on sait que la vie et le courage des autres dépend de votre vie et de votre courage on a plus le droit d'avoir peur." Sembene, *God's Bits of Wood*, 117.
5. Senghor, "L'esprit de la civilisation," 56.
6. Senghor, *Liberté 5*, 15.
7. Senghor, *Liberté 5*, 18.
8. Senghor, *Liberté 5*, 19.
9. Senghor, *Liberté 3*, 326.
10. Senghor, *Liberté 3*, 327.
11. Senghor, *Léopold Sédar Senghor et la revue* Présence Africaine, 126.
12. Senghor, *Léopold Sédar Senghor et la revue* Présence Africaine, 123.

2 From South Africa to Europe to North America and Back
Sol Plaatje, W.E.B. Du Bois, and the Routes of Romance

Annalisa Oboe

In 1904 a South African student at Lincoln University in Pennsylvania sent home, to Sol Plaatje's newspaper *Koranta ea Becoana,*[1] a poem about Africa's relationship with America. In its lines the old continent asks her black children on the other side of the Atlantic to return, so that they can bring light back to their "dark" homeland.

> Come to me, oh, ye children
> For I am old and out of date,
> Bring with you the wisdom
> Whence it may be obtained;
> Tell me not of Socrates and Plato
> For their words are old and gray,
> But your youngest infant state.
>
> I have worried long without you
> For a thousand years or so;
> Come and put us "in the know";
> I have sat in the quiet cloister
> My light behind a bush,
> And I need your kind assistance
> In the modern game of push.[2]

This invitation to Africans abroad, sent more than a century ago, reflects the early attraction of South African educated people and intellectuals to the young American nation, which was perceived as a more feasible model for Africa's modernization than the ancient civilization, philosophy, and culture of imperial Europe. This pull was only partly a result of the formative experience of the first African intellectuals in American schools; it was also due to the prior existence of a bond between southern Africa and black America, forged through a long history of exchanges that goes back to at least the eighteenth century—a two-way Atlantic flow, largely motivated by shared experiences with white domination and similar efforts to overcome discrimination. Links between the black communities on either side of the ocean were established quite permanently through education, religion, newspapers, music—there was a famous tour of the Jubilee Singers in 1895 which introduced many "Negro spirituals" to South African audiences—but also through literature, cinema, and, of course, politics.

For black South Africans, African Americans—who had survived slavery and were moving forward in an industrialized society (potentially) similar to their own—became an early icon of progress and success.[3] The South African writer Peter Abrahams's discovery of American Negro thought and literature through the work of W.E.B. Du Bois has somehow become paradigmatic of what black America could mean to South African culture. From the library of the Bantu Men's Social Centre in Johannesburg, in the early 1930s, Abrahams took out *The Souls of Black Folk* and read:

> "For this much all men know: despite compromise, war, struggle, the Negro is not free."
>
> The Negro is not free. . . . I remembered those "Reserved For Europeans Only" signs; . . . I remembered spittle on my face. . . . The Negro is not free.
>
> But why had I not thought of it myself? Now, having read the words, I knew that I had known this all along. But until now I had had no words to voice the knowledge. Du Bois's words had the impact of a revelation. . . .
>
> For all the thousands of miles, for all the ocean, between the land and people of whom he wrote and my land, Du Bois might have been talking about my land and people. The mood and the feeling he described was native to me. . . . Du Bois had given me a key to the understanding of my world. The Negro is not free.[4]

Abrahams's autobiography acknowledges the huge debt that South African culture owes Black America, a debt that accrued through the darkest years of apartheid and the various American campaigns against the white racist regime. It is clear that black South African and American cultures have functioned as powerful geopolitical frames of reference for each other, and literature has been a constitutive and emblematic strand of this web of transnational, cross-cultural exchanges.

This complex circuit of intellectual, cultural, and political "materials," however, deserves further investigation, particularly in view of the fact that while the impact of African American culture on black South Africa has gained recognition by a number of comparative scholars (Rob Nixon, Ntongela Masilela, and Tim Couzens, among others), who have variously stressed Africa's "dependence" on African American models and often upheld the primacy of an African American "modern vanguard" over a more passive and "un-modern" African landscape, very little attention has been paid to the reverse cultural and political movement, or to the

African "declinations" of Atlantic, pan-Africanist inputs. This chapter, which looks comparatively at the work of Sol Plaatje (1876–1932) and W.E.B. Du Bois (1868–1963), is part of an effort to uncover the range of dialectical experiences positioned between localism/nationalism on the one hand, and cosmopolitanism/transnationalism on the other, that make up the archives of contemporary African life and knowledge,[5] and also chart less traveled routes around an Atlantic ocean that divides, just as much as it links, the black cultures that inhabit its rim.

Through his writing and political activism Sol Plaatje challenged the cultural, political and economic inequality of early twentieth-century settler colonialism in South Africa, engaging in a tireless confrontation with his country's white government, and in direct dialogue with the British imperial authorities and the great African American political and intellectual figures of his time. In 1919 Plaatje left South Africa and started on a long journey, his second to Europe and his first to North America (Canada and the U.S.), that would keep him away for over four years and during which he worked hard to present the South African situation to the world and to raise political and economic support for the black community back home. It was during his 1920s travels—from South Africa, to England, to North America, and back—that he drew a revised cultural cartography of the relationships between the three continents: the triangulation of his movements physically sketches a network of inextricable relationships on the Atlantic map, which is essentially aimed at demarginalizing South Africa by connecting it to transatlantic flows, but which also articulates a critical distance both from European imperial policies and from black American racial pan-Africanism, in ways that tell of a complex use of transnational elements and national or local assertion. Plaatje's travels, as well as his writings, in fact offer a paradigm for the investigation of the zones of interaction, dependence, and distance between Africa and the Atlantic world—an interaction which went on to include the growing presence of "democratic" North America after a failed confrontation with the European imperial power. But, Plaatje's intensely dialogic American experience suggests, the coalescence of local and national interest into transnational, global concerns did not imply forgetting the specificities of African roots, nor the global weight of empire and capital on (still colonial) Africa—*pace* Paul Gilroy, who mystifies modernity as the primary object of Black Atlantic critique, barring from his anti-nationalist vision questions of imperialism and capitalism, and losing sight of Africa in the process.

THE ROUTES TO WISH FULFILLMENT

Traveling across the Atlantic with Plaatje in 1920 was his manuscript of *Mhudi*, the first black South African novel in English, which he described as "a love story after the manner of romance . . . but based on historical facts,"[6] and which he hoped to publish with the help of W.E.B. Du Bois, whose works he had been reading since the beginning of the century and with whom he was in contact.

According to Brian Willan's groundbreaking research, *Mhudi* was begun at the same time as Plaatje's *Native Life in South Africa*, while Plaatje was part of a South African Native National Congress[7] delegation in England during World War I, petitioning the British government to repeal the Natives Land Act of 1913, which removed land ownership and share-cropping rights from rural Africans, and forced them into native reserves. *Mhudi* was apparently intended as a "companion volume" to *Native Life*, a unique travelogue recording the consequences of the 1913 Act and exploring the wretched lives of black South Africans under white control. Willan observes that "parts of [*Mhudi* and *Native Life*] appear in draft form in the same notebook. And whilst it is not possible to establish exactly how each developed in relation to the other, it does seem reasonable to assume that the question Plaatje posed for himself [in *Native Life*] . . . provided something of a starting point for him in *Mhudi* as well." There is evidence, however, that Plaatje "felt he had said what he wanted to far more effectively in *Mhudi*," as shown by subsequent elaborations and his extensive efforts to have it published.[8]

In 1921, a few months after Plaatje's arrival in the States, Du Bois arranged for his journal, *The Crisis*, to bring out an American edition of the already published *Native Life* (1916), but, strangely enough, he did not provide the same opportunity for *Mhudi*, whose publication remained an unfulfilled wish till the South African Lovedale Press accepted it in 1930. If it is understandable that the African American intellectual found *Native Life*'s explicit references to his own *The Souls of Black Folk* appealing, and that it was easy for him to foretell the impact that Plaatje's black political statement would have on the American community, it is hard to explain why *Mhudi* did not elicit as much attention. This is surprising because *Mhudi* deals creatively and originally with questions relating to imperialism, racism, the place of blacks in the South African nation and in the modern world, which one would expect to be of interest to the black editor and his public. But it is even more puzzling for the simple fact that the book holds a place in Plaatje's oeuvre that is in many ways similar to and as special as that occupied in Du Bois's own canon by *Dark Princess: A Romance*, written in the mid-1920s and published in 1928. Both authors in fact ransacked the Western romance tradition to produce, within a few years from one another, intensely visionary statements of their life projects: for a long time Du Bois thought of *Dark Princess* as his "favorite" book,[9] while Plaatje's determination to have *Mhudi* published at all costs proves the great worth he attributed to his bold "Native venture."[10]

The two authors' research, political work, and thinking of the previous decade are clearly recognizable in both romances, which nevertheless represent a step ahead in the elaboration of their views. *Mhudi* moves beyond

Native Life's appraisal of the South African situation, toward historical and cultural revisionism, feminism, and proto-nationalism; *Dark Princess* enlarges the discourse of *Souls* on "race" and double consciousness to include an understanding of the roles of gender, material conditions, and labor in the fight against white supremacy. And there is an added visionary value in these works, which comes from the imaginative freedom allowed by the choice of expressive medium and from the passionate intensity of utopian desires.

Both romances, moreover, share to some extent similar fortunes: highly treasured by their authors and underestimated by critics, they remained somewhat isolated achievements in their time, owing to the lack of a literary market for blacks in South Africa, and to the aesthetic requirements of modernist realism in the United States. Their histories differ, however, in the present, for while it is still debatable whether *Dark Princess* can be considered more than an eccentric jump into creative romanticizing and artistic propaganda on the part of the black American thinker, *Mhudi* was successfully rediscovered in the 1970s and has since gained the status of a canonical founding text in South African literature and post-apartheid culture.

Whatever the two romances' respective fates, I am advocating the possibility of setting them side by side in a comparative reading which starts from their surface similarities in the use of literary genre, themes, and concerns, and takes into account the intense intellectual trafficking connecting their authors for decades.[11] I am not suggesting a case of intertextual cross-fertilization that would see Plaatje's romance, which subtly and obliquely incorporates Black Atlantic ideas, become in its turn a sort of subtext for *Dark Princess*, but rather arguing that a joint examination may clarify Plaatje's and Du Bois's respective projects, and reveal both the intersections and the oceanic distances between Black transatlanticism and African nationalism—two practices which often interrogate one another from the perspective of largely different cultural and historical experiences.[12]

I intend romance here in Northrop Frye's sense of a "literature of wish fulfillment," in which the "might have been" intrudes into the "it was," dissolving the boundaries between the actual and the potential to offer a vision of "the possible or future or ideal."[13] The driving force of "desire" forms an essential part of this utopian dimension. At the root of romantic mythology is the ideal of the pursuit of the unobtainable, the quest for the infinitely desirable and beautiful which stands outside human rational and linguistic faculties, although romances are also about "desire" in young heroes for beautiful heroines—a yearning that is usually frustrated by social or historical impediments, the overcoming of which hopefully produces the desired end.

The romantic love story in Plaatje's and Du Bois's novels is modeled on the essential stereotypical fable of romance, summarized by Leslie Fiedler in ways that particularly fit the story of Mhudi and Ra-Thaga, and of the Dark Princess with her African American lover:

> Initially confused about his own ambitions or the true identity and character of those who surround him . . . the hero is forced to flee—usually in the midst of some famous historic conflict just then conveniently approaching its climax. The heroine meanwhile has been abducted or is off on some private evasion of her own. . . . The two are kept apart as long as possible, but are finally joined . . . their problems resolved, their enemies discomfited, all confusions cleared up.[14]

With its desire-motivated, forward-looking movement, the love story contributes to enhance the "projective" character of quest narratives, and is also an essential feature of the wish fulfillment dimension of foundational fictions.[15] The passionate sentiments of loving couples help to "correct" unsatisfactory or controversial circumstances by supplying ideal stories in which love is able to provide dynamic solutions whenever "the real" gets stuck in the mire of unsolvable problems or non-productive events. In other words romance, a genre of excess with a limit-breaking quality, is able to exceed cultural prescriptions and historical determinism. It knows how to turn desire into the motivation for literary, historical, and political projects and, by urging the readers to read on—following the lovers' drive towards union, marriage, family, prosperity—forces them to become partisans.

Although both *Mhudi* and *Dark Princess* are much more than romances, being highly hybrid texts and showing considerable traces of realist influence in keeping with the development of the genre in the nineteenth and twentieth centuries, a comparative analysis of their "structures of wish fulfilment" may help us approach the two authors' respective worlds.

Plaatje sets up a critical dialogue with the imperial romance tradition of South Africa,[16] revises it by means of parodic interventions, and places it in complex dynamics with history, exploiting to his advantage the possible intersections between romantic and historical "desires." In *Mhudi* history and romance effectively trope each other, exchanging expectations and purposes, sharing languages, creating the metaphors that hold cultures, families, and individuals together (or drive them apart). Du Bois taps into a well-established practice in American fiction of rejecting the limits of verisimilitude, or the confines of the real, in favor of the mysterious, masculine, quest-adventure type of story, combining it with a sort of Orientalist political romance that constitutes the utopian frame of reference of the narrative and provides the ideological interpretive key to the hero's adventures and the author's political message. If the requirements of a new literary and historiographic enterprise are met by means of genre hybridity and heteroglossia in *Mhudi,* in *Dark Princess* the alternation between realist and romantic narrative modes and registers is dictated by the configuration of a new global political geography. In each case the works' physiognomy is determined by their being comparative projects: Plaatje needs to search literature and history for a kind of writing that may inscribe the intersections of time, place, and "difference" that constitute the (modern) experience of the nation in Africa, while Du Bois has to decide what linguistic and stylistic modes and analytical frame to use in presenting the history, geography, and culture of a black diasporic world. Their novels, therefore, require an approach that is both literary and historical, and one that considers together the histories of imperialism and pan-Africanism, combined, in Plaatje's case, with the South African resistance to white domination and, in Du Bois's, with the emergence of black radicalism in the U.S., communism, and exile Indian nationalism. In spite of their respective idiosyncratic choices, both novels come closer than any of the two intellectuals' scholarly works to explaining to the reader their life desires.

What follows is a contrastive analysis of the beginning of each romance, of the meeting of the lovers, the description of the heroine, and the climactic ending—in search of the routes to wish fulfillment that Plaatje and Du Bois devised to mediate their messages. The reading suggests unstable analogies and diverging paths and is aware that it runs the risk of any comparative project: namely, that the categories under consideration will not translate neatly into each other.

MAPS AND BEGINNINGS

In *Mhudi* and *Dark Princess* real and imagined geographies support the movements of personal, domestic, and national desires. At the beginning of Du Bois's book, the African American (ex)student Matthew Towns is fleeing from 1920s America's racism, while in Plaatje's novel Ra-Thaga, a youth belonging to the Rolong clan of the Tswana people (Plaatje's own group), is running away from the Ndebele's destruction of the city of Kunana at the beginning of the 1830s. Both romances open with a map of conflict that sets the tone and scope for the adventures that follow.

The descriptive-topographical opening of *Mhudi* is concerned not only with fixing the geographical limits of the novel, but also with establishing that ideal center of the crossroads where the present can meet and recognize the past that is going to be reconstructed. "Two centuries ago the Bechuana tribes inhabited the extensive areas between Central Transvaal and the Kalahari Desert" (25). This is exactly the space where the story takes place, the delimitation of a region whose significance is not so much geographical as historical and anthropological, as illustrated by the description of the precolonial Tswana society in the first pages of the text. Space, time, and human life are intimately interwoven in the oral tale once told by a "hoary octogenarian," which the author now puts on paper. Through this oral narrative Plaatje recovers a whole world of social and political events, customs, linguistic peculiarities and human passions which allow him to construct an African location which is knowable and very much alive, in spite of the initial pastoral mode. This anthropological narrative line is important in that it specifies the function of the historical one: to rehabilitate the Africans by rescuing them from a century of Eurocentric historiography (and historical fiction) in which they were (re)presented as savages.

At the very beginning of the book, the communal values of the pastoral Rolong society are conveniently set against its later transformations under the impact of Ndebele imperialism and white settlement, and also against the new knowledge, economy, and culture the African people would soon have to relate to and come to terms with:

> These peasants were content to live their monotonous lives, and thought nought of their oversea kinsmen who were making history on the plantations and harbours of Virginia and Mississippi at that time; nor did they know or care about the relations of the Hottentots and the Boers at Cape Town nearer home. . . .
>
> Strange to relate, these simple folk were perfectly happy without money and without silver watches. Abject poverty was practically unknown; they had no orphanages because there were no nameless babies. (27)

The narrative and historical movement traced by Plaatje's romance transforms the ancient Rolong map into the complex chart of the present, where continental wars, the consequences of European colonialism, a new economy, the slave trade, and the African American experience on the other side of the Atlantic are simultaneously acknowledged. Complexity is forced onto the simple pastoral world which is being celebrated, but which will be destroyed (perhaps inevitably, given the tone of the narration) by local conflicts and global phenomena that it will not be allowed to (and should not) overlook. If the topography is carefully delimited and local, the story that Plaatje's narrative inscribes on it is wide-ranging: it locates the region in a discursive space which is contiguous to Europe and America, a site of intersection between colonialism and slavery. Though this is now part of a conventional reading of South African history, the connection between empire and slave trade was not obvious when Plaatje wrote *Mhudi*.[17] The unique reference to black America, which comes so early in the narrative and is the only explicit one in the text, is extremely relevant as it draws the Tswana into the racial and economic map of modern times, and signals that in 1920 Plaatje had definitely left behind his staunch pro-British imperialist stance and was moving toward an understanding of Africa's position and role in the Atlantic world. To see nineteenth-century South Africa as a palimpsestic or stratified crossroads of black and white cultures, ethnic groupings, economies, and stories—conflicting or interacting on the vast southern tip of the continent—means for Plaatje to imagine a history which is at the same time more complex and less definitive than most historians and novelists at the beginning of the twentieth century would allow. In that history he singles out moments of contact between tribe and tribe, people and people—a choice which requires a shift of focus from the relatively easy singling out of binary oppositions (which is a typical colonial formula), to the individuation of chiasmatic intersections where alliances are more meaningful than conflict and wars. In the novel the chronotope of the crossroads becomes a spatial and temporal empowering metaphor for (trans)national cultural, historical, and political change, which has the power to criticize the all-pervasive imperial thrust operating both in literature and in society. The protagonists of the romantic love story, who are forced to leave the ordered and peaceful Tswana society, who get to know the Ndebele's fury, and are later involved in the relationship with the Boers, move through this changing space of contact, following their desire for survival and love, and play out the discourse of cultural and racial dialogue in South Africa in terms that point to an extensive pan-ethnic southern African nationalism.

Mhudi's well-defined (though shifting) landscape contrasts sharply with *Dark Princess*'s geopolitical map, which spreads widely over the globe, and whose prominent sites are the United States, Berlin, Moscow, China, and India. Such an extensive topography allows Du Bois to discuss the role and function of the nation and radical political questions on a global scale, although the scope and depth of African American participation in these international debates are undeniably centralized. In fact most of Matthew's and Kautilya's adventures take place in the U.S., portrayed as a site of class and race confrontation that metonymically stands for the world: "There was war in Chicago—silent, bitter war. It was part of the war throughout the whole nation; it was part of the World War."[18] This conflict-ridden American milieu, which hosts the trials of the romance protagonists, is juxtaposed to the crucible from which new solutions to world problems may emerge: the black South of the U.S. in fact allows a topical moment of theoretical and geographical rapprochement of the aspirations of nationalist anti-colonialism and communist anti-capitalism that the novel allegorizes.[19]

The divergent concerns of Plaatje and Du Bois are clearly reflected in the organizing tropes of their novels: whereas the South African writer plots story and history through the crossroads chronotope, Du Bois combines race theory, politics, and geography to concoct the metaphor of the "Black Belt," which transforms socio-historical events into magical processes of black American-African-Asian connectedness. The Black Belt metaphor refers both to the U.S. southern region of Matthew's birth[20] and, borrowing Du Bois's own words, to *the color line* that *belts the world*.[21] It is a real place of black experience, and at the same time the origin of a sensual, warm, and radiating bond connecting the darker races of the world, which proves effective when both diplomatic and revolutionary maneuvers have failed. The belt circumscribes a realm of romantic imagination, where domesticity and procreation take over from unsuccessful politics and provide an alternative model, a synthesis based on love and reproduction.[22] The space that makes this possible is neither a European capital like Berlin nor a modern American city like Chicago, but the fertile terrain of the black American South, which emerges as a *locus amoenus* of infinite possibilities and indissoluble connections of bodies, minds, and future liberation plans. Du Bois's exceptionally talented hero and heroine, his black vanguard, will change the world from here.

At the beginning of *Dark Princess* the would-be hero of this ante-litteram globalized romance is fleeing from the all-pervasive unjust control of what he calls "the White Leviathan," the white racist society that has just denied him a profession because of his dark skin. The young man takes leave of his old mother, who still works on the farm in Prince James County, Virginia, and jumps on the first ship to Europe, so that the book opens, as Gilroy has noted,[23] with a transatlantic crossing to Antwerp, away from penalizing white America toward romance and possibility. Matthew finds momentary refuge in the relative anonymity and indifference of Europe, where "he was treated as he was dressed, and . . . could at least eat where he wished so long as he paid" (7).

This passage into some sort of "neutral ground" is the precondition—for Du Bois's dandyish Matthew as for Plaatje's war-shocked Ra-Thaga—to the meeting of the heroine, who appears as a safety anchor at a moment of distress: the European metropolis in *Dark Princess* and the South African wilderness in *Mhudi* become the place of chance encounter, far from the circumstances that determined the initial catastrophe but, as we shall see, able to reproduce, symbolically or metonymically, the same antagonistic conditions. The encounter episodes of Ra-Thaga with Mhudi, the Rolong girl, and of Matthew Towns with the Indian princess in fact follow an escapist movement into the territory of romance while reasserting the main real-life preoccupations of the authors.

The Rolong youth wanders alone through the African forest, totally confused as to his own identity and unable to foresee his future. At the height of despair, Mhudi appears; she has survived the same bloody destruction of her people, met almost as many lions as Ra-Thaga, and undergone the same kind of initiatory ritual in the wilderness. When she stumbles upon her future husband she is running once again from the king of the forest, but instead of imploring the youth "to take her far away from the man-eater," she guides him against his will to where the lion is, and is as much an active participant in the chase as the young man. Surprised, Ra-Thaga reflects that in his country "lions are usually hunted by large companies of armed men aided by fierce mastiffs, and not by one badly armed man guided by a strange girl" (35). These thoughts provide an image that becomes a textual motif: the woman is referred to as "strange" not just because she is still a foreigner at this stage, but because she is novelty, she goes against expected codes of gender behavior, and she is a leader. The beginning is only one example in the book in which Mhudi forces her frightened and cowardly man to be "manly," to face troubles and, by extension, history, if the lion they fight together is to be read as a symbol of imperialism or a challenge of the times.[24] Right from the beginning, the unromantic romance heroine sets the reader on the track of Plaatje's revisionist routes.

In a Berlin café, a beautiful woman of color who sits alone at one of the tables is also in danger: a white American tourist is proffering his advances to her, and Matthew Towns is filled with anxiety and disgust as he witnesses the diffusion, even on European soil and in a cosmopolitan context, of what Plaatje would call the "White Peril."[25] The woman's cool obliviousness to the man's intrusion, however, incites Matthew to manly action, and he knocks the American down once out in the street. Emasculated by his rejection from the medical profession in the States the American Negro, whom D.L. Lewis describes as "a man of feminine sensibilities who defers to women and finds himself alternately manipulated and wonderfully improved by them,"[26] is restored to manhood by his reaction, provoking the woman's interest in him and the romance that follows. Commenting on the coincidence of their meeting and on Matthew's performance, the woman, who turns out to be the Princess Kautilya of Bwodpur, India, says: "it had never happened before that a stranger of my own color should offer me protection in Europe. I had a curious sense of some great inner meaning to your act—some world movement" (17). In Kautilya's words Matthew's exploit is given cosmic overtones that anticipate the unfolding of the couple's ambitious project, while the connection between gender and race discrimination is firmly inscribed on the world geopolitical map. In both romances, then, the providential meeting with an exceptional woman opens up the protagonist's horizon to new ideas and unexpected developments.

CHOOSING A BLACK HEROINE

The heroines of Plaatje's and Du Bois's romances, their physical and mental traits and behavior, offer an index of the male protagonist's wishes and of the two narratives' aims. Though we see less of them than their male counterparts, we know right from the book titles that the two female characters are assigned a vital role in the narrative: they downplay the traditional romance emphasis on masculine action and are pervading presences even when they are not on stage. The reader's first view of the two women, through their prospective lovers' first reactions, sheds light on the ways identity expresses itself in, and a life's project can coalesce around, the choice of a love partner. This is clear in both texts, which exploit one of the devices responsible for the popular appeal of romance: the narrative of why and how a man and a woman choose each other is interesting because it expresses and plays out forms of desire, identity, and difference.[27]

Here's youthful and charmingly African Mhudi in her future husband's (decidedly male) gaze:

> Her curly hair was as carefully trimmed as though she had come from her mother's house that morning . . . Mhudi had a magnificent figure. . . . the colour of her skin was a deep brown that set off to advantage her brilliant black eyes. A pretty pair of dimples danced around her cheeks when she smiled; and the smile revealed an even set of ivories as pure as that of any child. Her bewitching mouth and beautiful lips created a sense of charm . . . In front she wore an apron of thin twisted strips, suspended evenly from a belt round her waist, reaching just above the knees, while a springbuck skin drooping from her hips downward formed the kirtle that matched her beautiful form. Round her shoulder hung a furry rug of speckled lamb-skins very carefully tanned. . . . He thought she had above her beaded anklets the most beautiful limbs he had ever seen. (37–38)

Mhudi appears as deeply local, a rustic girl dressed in typical African garb, and full of the beauty of youth and womanliness. "Charmed" and "charming" in spite of the recent ordeal, all is as it should be in her figure and behavior, described earnestly with sporadic recourse to simile and metaphor. She infuses a special sense of ecstasy and hope in the young hero, who notices with satisfaction the deep brown color of her skin (an anachronism that signals how shades of color matter in the present of the narration) and the overall sense of order and propriety that emanates from her beautiful figure. No strange woman this Mhudi, after all, but a respectable girl from home, who fits the young Rolong's need to overcome the present impasse, his loneliness, his sense of bereavement.

This description, however, follows the lion chase episode, and the reader is already aware that the girl is special. She in fact takes a leading role in the relationship with Ra-Thaga, who is called "the bird man" in the list of the novel's characters at the beginning of the book—a label that is probably motivated by the character's (unmanly) instability, curiosity for anything new, and often naive trust of others. Plaatje is clearly playing with gender stereotypes, but in ways that add to rather than detract from his characters' humanity, and that reinforce his intent to revise traditional patriarchal codes and possibly transform southern African society. So if Mhudi's main qualities are active determination and courage, which are traditionally considered masculine, in the characters' list she is glossed as "harvester," which links her to the fruitful soil of Africa, to fertility, maternity, and care. She is also therefore "conventional" as an allegory of Africa, but the character herself in turn modifies this traditional connection between woman and continent and, quite importantly, comes to signify an Africa on the brink of change.

Du Bois's princess, when we first meet her, appears as an exotic, magical and difficult-to-place creature in a dynamic passage which is full of mystery even as it conveys a lot of information:

> First and above all came that sense of color: into this world of pale yellowish and pinkish parchment, that absence or negation of color, came, suddenly, a glow of golden brown skin. It was darker than sunlight and gold; it was lighter and livelier than brown. It was a living, glowing crimson, veiled beneath brown flesh. It called for no light and suffered no shadow, but glowed softly of its own inner radiance.
>
> Then came the sense of the woman herself: she was young and tall even when seated, and she bore herself above all with a singularly regal air. She was slim and lithe, gracefully curved. . . . she was looking with eyes that were pools of night—liquid, translucent, haunting depths—whose brilliance made her face a glory and a dream. . . . There was a hint of something foreign and exotic in her simply draped gown of rich, creamlike silken stuff and in the graceful coil of her hand-fashioned turban. Her gloves hung carelessly over her arm, and he caught a glimpse of slender-heeled slippers and sheer clinging hosiery. There was a flash of jewels on her hands and a murmur of beads in half-hidden necklaces. . . . Who was she? What was she? . . . Was she American? (8)

This vibrant portrait, whose suggestiveness derives from the insertion of actions and the use of metaphor, is an active display of the workings of desire filtered through Matthew's chain reactions. The woman's rich clothes have an indefinite quality ("creamlike silken stuff" vs. Mhudi's recognizable "furry rug of speckled lamb-skins very carefully tanned"), her jewels are veiled by their own brightness ("flash of jewels"), murmuring necklaces are "half-hidden": a mysterious halo surrounds her.

In spite of the intense scrutiny of his mesmerized gaze, Matthew is unable to locate Kautilya; he is uncertain of her provenance. For, what could be American about her—her color, her black eyes, the softness and warmth of her figure that in Matthew's experience are linked to memories of his mother and his birthplace—is in fact belied by her exotic attire, her half-glimpsed extraordinary ornaments, her being in Berlin. Compared with Mhudi, whose "curly hair was as carefully trimmed as though she had come from her mother's house that morning," Kautilya is as much an alien as the Rolong girl is an assurance of common origin and shared experience.

What sort of desires do these women speak to and eventually fulfill? What sort of black aesthetics is at work here? In the first instance we have recognition and a promise of sameness, roots, and steadiness in uncertain times, as Ra-Thaga struggles for survival and the recovery of his own place in the world. There is neither exoticism in the description of Mhudi, nor concessions to the idea of the primitive or to the supposed black physicality of the Dark Continent—the viewpoint is that of the insider, the points of reference are deeply localized. And although Plaatje's intention is to stress Mhudi's beauty and propriety, his modes express the need to communicate comprehensible feelings rather than an ideological adherence to some aesthetic canons, as happens for example in the work of the Négritude writers later in the century, and in Du Bois's own portrait of the princess. This is a moment in Plaatje's romance in which aesthetics turns into ethics and, possibly, politics; where individual desire is transformed into a signifier of Plaatje's particular brand of African humanism.

In *Dark Princess* we find Matthew's fascination—at a time of dissatisfaction with his own culture—for mysterious and exotic difference, which is deeply Orientalist in thrust. This perception of difference, however, is coupled with emotional hints at potential similarities that increase as the novel progresses. The woman is in all ways exceptional for what we later get to know as an extraordinary combination of Indian sovereignty, proto-feminist attitudes, and Bolshevik inclinations. But being of color, a potential victim of white men's will, and a visionary seeker, she is also very similar to Matthew. The gap between her uniqueness and her shareable traits is covered in the course of the narration by the man's process of internationalization, a personal growth combined with a global quest that will eventually land him back in his home country. In the movement, an image of Matthew's mother comes to the foreground, which eases the tension between the local (his African American birth and experience) and the global (Kautilya's work for the union of the darker races), further diluting the initial difference: through the recognition of a mythical common origin via the old black ex-slave mother, the princess offers the first allusion to an American reconciliation of Africa and Asia: "Oh, Matthew, you have a wonderful mother. Have you seen her hands? Have you seen the gnarled and knotty glory of her hands? . . . Your mother is Kali, the Black one; wife of Siva, Mother of the World!" (220). Kautilya's own movement toward Matthew will then lead her to identify with the black mother and to accept her African inheritance as part of her worldwide status by giving birth to Matthew's son.

The choice of Mhudi and Kautilya as love partners for the two heroes clearly speaks of largely different projects. The African author uses European romantic conventions ironically and points to the existence in the African world of a new kind of men and women endowed with all the "qualities" and "virtues" that are necessary to give birth to a solid modern nation. Plaatje's couple need to prove that where they come from is a place of dignified living and long-standing tradition, that they are reliable people who, through their ability to face the upheavals of the times, are open to encounter and (ex)change: the novel will trace their growth in terms of education, understanding of gender roles, religion, economy, and technological knowledge. Together Mhudi and Ra-Thaga will fight for self-determination and the recognition of the right to their land as

Africa enters modern history, and will counter the ideology of imperialism and white supremacy by behaving as active historical subjects in their own environment. If, in so doing, Plaatje downplays racial difference, stressing traits common to all humanity, in *Dark Princess* Du Bois counters that same imperial ideology with compelling examples of black exceptionalism. Matthew and Kautilya trespass upon the boundaries of class, race, and nation, and disregard conventional institutions like marriage, in search of a new connection that might solve their respective predicaments and fulfil their dreams. Together, as Claudia Tate has stressed, they outline the formation of a *heroic* black psyche that Du Bois sees as essential for the defeat of the White Leviathan and the advancement of world culture.[28] On the contrary, Plaatje locates in a kind of heterosexual love bond essentially coinciding with monogamous marriage the possibility for a new African society. In his view, going beyond the limits of tradition and the male-dominated past (exemplified by the quarreling wives of tyrannical Mzilikazi's polygamous household) is the necessary step forward which guarantees the emancipation of black women and, consequently, of black people. The change in man-woman patterns of relation would modify the social structure of the nation and ensure its place among the "civilized" people of the twentieth century through a concurrent movement out of patriarchal and imperial control. In the register of ideology the structures of heterosexual union, that combine individual and collective yearnings, project Plaatje's and Du Bois's decidedly different notions of humanity, identity, and culture, as well as a preoccupation for the destiny of black people in their own respective countries.

But just as heterosexual love is functional to the schemes of each author, so is the role of a new kind of woman in (the narration of) history, politics, and nation. Kautilya and Mhudi are their men's muses and inspiration, as well as the loves of their lives. As romance heroines, both women are complicit in the patriarchal world they move in, which they nonetheless contribute to modify if not dismantle. Though endorsing the patriarchal codes of male heroic narratives, *Mhudi* and *Dark Princess* show the limit-breaking potential of romance by putting forward an innovative idea of woman.

In *Mhudi*, the female protagonist has great courage, independence, wisdom, and determination, qualities that stand in sharp contrast to those of white romance heroines, while her husband admits, without shame, his deep love and respect for the woman who "made me what I am" (158). According to Plaatje, only by recognizing this strength and this link of interdependence can black men and women find their true nature. The novel, however, points beyond this, in the direction of a new cross-cultural vision signified by the women's ability to establish liaisons which bypass ethnic boundaries, political factions, and, possibly, race. The female characters in the novel in fact set up with one another ties of love and reciprocal trust. This happens with the friendship between Mhudi and Umnandi, the Ndebele queen; between the latter and her Rolong girl; and to some extent with the close bond between Mhudi and Hannetjie, the young Boer girl whose disposition seems to the Rolong woman "a shining contrast to the general attitudes of the Boers." Although these women profess absolute fidelity in regard to their respective people (a principle which applies to all the characters in the novel), this does not prevent them from helping each other, thus anticipating the workings of a cross-ethnic South African community. The inclusion of the whites in this community, however, as Mhudi's resistance to become an "ayah" for the De Villiers shows, will only take place (the narration seems to imply) when the economic inequality that accompanies the construction of race difference is overcome.[29]

Plaatje's women appear as positive examples of the idea of a new womanhood propounded by early twentieth-century feminism. An example of the debt to the feminist/pacifist perspective of Olive Schreiner's 1911 manifesto, *Woman and Labour,* is provided by the following passage: "'How wretched,' cried Mhudi sorrowfully, 'that men in whose counsels we have no share should constantly wage war, drain women's eyes of tears and saturate the earth with God's best creation—the blood of the sons of women. What will convince them of the worthlessness of this game, I wonder?'" (165). If linked to Plaatje's somewhat humorous and often ironic play with male/female stereotypes and to his foundational discourse, the image of the female as maker and preserver of life—which might seem a patriarchal commonplace—reveals an unusual early insight into the parallels between racial and sexual discrimination, and assigns women a special role in bringing a more just and non-violent society into existence. Plaatje thus extends Schreiner's vision to include African women's gender subjectivity and social role, and his proto-feminism, that was sneered at by the same missionaries who first published the text in 1930 and more recently by the South African ANC (male) intelligentsia,[30] appears successfully functional to his emancipatory vision. The feminine, the domestic, but also the participation of women to the public sphere, versus masculinist assumptions and myopic power, was a highly provocative plan.

In his rendering of a strong female self Plaatje was certainly inspired by the women in his family, but also by the group of British women who "adopted" him during his 1920 sojourn in London, while the book was being written,[31] and by American black women. Tim Couzens and Stephen Gray, who rescued Plaatje's text from oblivion in the 1970s, state that *Mhudi* was revised in 1921 (Plaatje arrived in the U.S. in February that year) in order to give the heroine a more prominent role than she had had in the earlier version,[32] and a letter the writer sent from New York to his English friend Mrs. Colenso shows that a new black woman's world had in fact been revealed to him while in the States: "And oh, the women! They are progressive educationally, socially, politically, as well as in church work, they lead the men."[33]

These are the years of Du Bois's own thinking on "the damnation of women," and one wonders whether Plaatje did read his *Darkwater,*[34] where the relationship between the self-determination of black women and the uplift of the race (which is romanced in *Mhudi*) is debated in political terms through sociological analysis. In *Darkwater*, "a sort of semi-biography," Du Bois presents the plight of women in labor terms, revealing that, as he moved toward a transnational understanding of race and class, he placed greater emphasis on gender, making the reproduction of labor and the labor of reproduction central concerns.[35] As such, the transformation that Kautilya undergoes in *Dark Princess*—from princess to manual worker, to trade unionist and mother—is crucial, and helps to correct (intermittently and not always successfully) the male Orientalist gaze of the romantic narrative.

Two conflicting (progressive vs. conservative) trends coexist both in *Dark Princess* and in *Darkwater*, and the conservative one is mainly predicated through the evocation of mythicized Africa, exactly the myth Plaatje intends to deconstruct in *Mhudi*. In "The Damnation of Women" Du Bois recovers what he calls "the African mother-idea" that will help him to center African America (hence his own personal story) in the global family tree descending from a primal moment of Afro-Asian commingling: "The father and his worship is Asia; Europe is the precocious, self-centred, forward-striving child; but the land of the mother is and was Africa. In subtle and mysterious way, despite her curious history, her slavery, polygamy, and toil, the spell of the African mother pervades her land."[36] A privileged biological and cultural link with this (imagined, ancient, and uncritically ascribed) generative power is passed on from Mother Africa to her black American children and to the author himself: "I honor the women of my race. Their beauty,—their dark and mysterious beauty of midnight eyes, crumpled hair, and soft, full-featured faces—is perhaps more to me than to you, because I was born to its warm and subtle spell."[37] In the novel, this same dark, warm, mysterious spell emanates from Matthew's black mother and from Kautilya, whom Du Bois fuses into a single image of the pan-Africanist identification of the female as repository of race and national culture. Recent criticism has remarked on Du Bois's ascription of images of black maternity to both the hero's biological mother and the princess, which reveal his vulnerability to a tradition of what might be called "Afro-Orientalism," generally depending on "an exotic essentializing of Afro-Asian vitality, usually associated with the feminine, and an uncritical glorification of black antiquity."[38] But it is exactly this primitive vitality of black culture as female, rather than its intellectual or political development predicated through Kautilya's experiments, that becomes functional to the portrayal of the possible unification of the double consciousness of African Americans in the novel. The sexual union of this feminine ideal with its masculine complement serves as a metaphor for the formulation of a superior black personality that will effect the cultural synthesis of peoples of color. The configuration of the feminine in *Dark Princess* is indeed a complex attempt to combine intellectual, political, and emotional desires.

As we will see, however, the woman figure elaborated in the novel, in spite of its apparent far-sightedness, still conveys a patriarchal prioritizing of male needs; it perpetuates stereotypical views of Africa and, as D.L. Lewis appropriately remarks, it remains subordinate, in Du Bois's thinking and in the romantic denouement of the novel, to the problem of the color line.

DREAMS AND PROPHECIES

At the end of *Mhudi*, the cycle of events reaches its happy conclusion and order is (at least momentarily) restored. Having obtained their revenge and removed the Ndebele's imperial presence forever, Ra-Thaga and Mhudi's wish is fulfilled, so they leave their white friends and allies and go back home. Their contact with the whites has not been destructive: they retain an entirely African identity, and have in addition acquired deeper human experience, wider linguistic knowledge, and more sophisticated techno-logical means, like the wagon they now travel in and a musket they can go hunting with. The old days are gone, an epoch is finished, Ra-Thaga muses, and the future in view has the dream-like quality of romance:

> Gone were the days of their primitive tramping over long distances, with loads on their heads. For them the days of the pack-ox had passed, never to return again. The carcase of a kudu or any number of bles-buck, falling to his musket by the roadside, could be carried home with ease, leaving plenty of room in the vehicle for their luggage. Was it real, or was it just an evanescent dream? (187)

Tension between tradition and modernity, a transitional stage of develop-ment, rather than success and closure, are signified at the end of the novel. Critics have remarked that for Ra-Thaga and Mhudi, trekking across the empty veldt in a dilapidated wagon, which the only man among the Dutch who treats blacks with some respect has given Mhudi as a souvenir for her part in the defeat of the Ndebele, can hardly be considered a reassuring achievement.[39] But this closing image must be read in the romantic mode which throughout the narrative has served to combine the good of tradi-tion with positive novelty, and understood also in the light of the author's own belief in "progress." Steeped in the British nineteenth-century cul-tural tradition, Plaatje regarded technological and economic advancement (alongside cultural education) as the necessary starting point for a "mod-ern" African life. This is one of the reasons why he was a keen admirer of Booker T. Washington in the States, and his *Bechuana Gazette* did much to publicize Washington's philosophy and the Tuskegee Institute among black South Africans. During his American tour Plaatje visited Tuskegee and acquired some film footage of the college that he later showed to African audiences who, besides being fascinated by what was likely to be their first exposure to motion pictures, were shown what Plaatje regarded as a daz-zling example of black achievement.[40] As a black South African, he could not afford to take sides in the early Washington–Du Bois controversy about the competing claims of political action and economic self-help.[41] Acquir-ing technology, skills and capital, for Plaatje and the founding members of the SANNC, went hand in hand with Duboisian agitation for equal consti-tutional rights.[42] Much as he admired Du Bois, the comments on the Afri-can American way of life in letters from the U.S. and in his final account of the North American tour all stress the modern advantages, the wealth and the educational facilities of the black communities, which he distressfully compares to the "wretched backwardness" of blacks "in our part of the empire."[43] Plaatje sees the role of economy and access to work and career as essential to the blacks' advancement, though this is no unproblematic endorsement of capitalism on his part.[44] It is rather an acknowledgment that the "modernity" represented by capital can be disconnected from whiteness, and it subsumes the matter-of-fact recognition that a destitute, hungry, and landless people can hardly fight for freedom.

In *Mhudi*, the characters have proved their value, won their battle, and gained a compensation—all of which places them squarely inside moder-nity. The incredulity that goes with such achievement—"was it reality or dream?"—is far from implying a naive acceptance of the gifts and of the presence of the white Voortrekkers in South Africa. It is rather accompa-nied by Mhudi's distrust of them (which is a constant in the book) and by the couple's relief at going back to their family and "kind" again. The parting of the ways after the fruitful meeting indicates the spirit of indepen-dence with which the Africans have lived the encounter, and the conscious-ness that the allies may represent a potential danger, now that the common enemy has been removed.

It is only at the end of the story, then, that "race consciousness" is openly signified. It appears forcefully in the famous speech by the villain of the story, King Mzilikazi, who utters a prophecy which mars the vision of future harmony projected by the narrative at a superficial level, offering a more complex political view of Plaatje's utopian credo: alliances work only when the parties involved are consistently honest toward each other. The king's curse uncovers and prophetically anticipates the dishonesty of the "marauding wizards from the sea" (the Europeans) and its consequences for their black "friends" (175). Although Mzilikazi's passionate Shake-spearean monologue explains why he is incapable of entering the new era of modernity,[45] the angry power of his warning words dispels any false illu-sions concerning the untroubled nature of racial encounters on the South African crossroads.

As Chennells has noticed, no voice is silenced at the end of *Mhudi*: the lesson of the past, the possibilities and the perils of the future, divergent ethnic African stories, race differences, white colonialism, female emanci-pation, tradition, and modernity are simultaneously offered to the reader's consideration. I believe that Plaatje's far-sightedness can be seen in this complex multi-vocal synchrony: his novel anticipates the post-civil rights, post-Cold War, post-apartheid era in stating that the potential for black advancement and for positive (trans)national interactions may derive not so much (or not only) from shared race consciousness but also from other social, cultural, and historically specific factors, including gender politics, political economy, and (perhaps) strategic pacifism[46]—meaning that actors may not always view racial pan-Africanism as the most efficient way to "imagine" an African national community. *Mhudi* thus interrogates African American race-based solidarity, and the critique becomes even clearer when we recall that for Du Bois, as D.L. Lewis usefully points out, pan-Africanism "meant enormously more than the ethnic romanticism of roots traced and celebrated. It signified the militant, anti-capitalist solidarity of the darker world."[47] Plaatje's vision, grounded in the non-racial inheritance of nineteenth-century Cape liberalism, could endorse Du Bois's emphasis on race consciousness only up to a point; he subordinated it to a stronger cross-cultural/national drive, to earnest inter-cultural cooperation, to a recognition of the underlying common humanity of individuals belonging to a different race (or sex), and the right to land, capital, and self-improvement.

While *Mhudi*'s romantic ending is imprinted with the text's heteroglossia, *Dark Princess* is an example of how the politics of romance may dwarf the greatness of an ambitious, multifaceted project. In the last part of the novel, when Kautilya is finally allowed to come into her own voice and narrate her life adventures, she writes to Matthew from Virginia of what she has learned through the trials they have both suffered:

> to be in the center of power is not enough. You must be free and able to act. You are not free in Chicago nor in New York. But here in Virginia you are at the edge of a black world. The black belt of the Congo, the Nile, and the Ganges reaches by way of Guiana, Haiti, and Jamaica, like a red arrow, up into the heart of white America. Thus I see a mighty synthesis: you can work in Africa and Asia right here in America if you work in the Black Belt. . . . You may stand here, Matthew—here, halfway between Maine and Florida, between the Atlantic and the Pacific, with Europe in your face and China at your back; with industry in your right hand and commerce in your left and the Farm beneath your steady feet; and yet be in the Land of the Blacks. (286)

In her words the Black Belt emerges as an extension of a belt encompassing much of the world, so that the New World African, a special nation within a nation, can become the centerpiece in Du Bois's interpretation of the political cosmology of the twentieth century. The African American's history and inner moral fiber will allow him to advance the world culture by combining black culture and Western civilization. As the romantic ending implies, he will be able to guide his people and the new miscegenated humankind in general. It is only right, then, that Matthew should conclude his quest in the Black Belt. After Kautilya summons him to his mother's place in James County, he discovers not only that he is to be married to the princess, but that he is already a father. So the two lovers are happily and doubly (re)united by their love and its newly born "golden" fruit.

Matthew and Kautilya's physical and theoretical coming together is meant to represent an answer to the problem of how to combine in one movement labor and race. The princess had written to Matthew: "Workers unite, men cry, while in truth always thinkers who do not work have tried to unite workers who do not think. Only working thinkers can unite thinking workers" (286). As black thinking workers of the wide world—the new "Talented Tenth" appraised of the condition of laborers—Kautilya and Matthew can now fuse the formula of Du Bois's Afro-Asian internationale with the potential of proletarian internationalism and lead social change. Their relationship therefore becomes an allegory for the changing world that Du Bois believed would emerge from global anticolonialism and in the face of capitalism's collapse. [48] This is what the text communicates on a discursive level. According to Gilroy, the union of Matthew and Kautilya, in this conclusion that particularly suits his politics of the Black Atlantic, would represent "a meeting of two heterogeneous multiplicities that in yielding themselves up to each other create something durable and entirely appropriate to anti-colonial times."[49] Unfortunately the message becomes distorted in the final wedding ceremony and in the messianic pageantry in which their son is to be crowned the Maharaja of Bwodpur, through an exotic hybrid ceremony including Christian, Buddhist, Hindu, and Muslim ritual references: though in tune with the love plot and the projective character of the romance narrative, an international line of descent, signified in the birth of the golden child, is only imperfectly consistent with Du Bois's complex message.

Critics have observed that *Dark Princess*'s melodramatic and sentimental climax, offering a miscegenated messiah as the birth of a new international world order, renders visible the patrician paternalism of Du Bois's Asian romance.[50] "With its hallucination of Brahamin royalty, royal blood, and its vision of the golden child as the incarnation of a new interracial alliance," notes Alys Weinbaum, "*Dark Princess* reinscribes the Orientalism we might expect it to challenge, while simultaneously making what may be called a 'racial original mistake,' an essentializing argument about racial genealogy and belonging that is on a structural level a mere revamping of that made by advocates of racial nationalism in the U.S. context."[51] This comment perhaps disregards the fact that the ending is inscribed in romance rhetoric, not history, and that procreation here should stand for cultural formation and transformation, but it is a fact that Du Bois's effort of redefining the discourse of race in terms of culture rather than biology, particularly in *Souls*, is somehow thwarted by the birth of the royal male heir in *Dark Princess*. It is therefore worthwhile to briefly draw attention to the limits of this wish-fulfilling conclusion, which may convey a cosmic vision, but sidelines the cultural, feminist, and anti-capitalist concerns that the novel discursively supports.

What is most evident in the novel's concluding scenes is that they are steeped in heavy religious tones, which contrast sharply with the intensely "worldly" and political quests of the protagonists; linguistic choices convey an emphasis on wealth, superiority and elitism in contrast to the narrative's opening on the common people and the workers' experience; masculinity is celebrated, and female characters (both Kautilya and Matthew's mother) are empowered only as bearers of exceptional sons, so that Du Bois's romance finally leads to the kind of female self-image that romance traditionally promotes, "the self-in-relation demanded by patriarchal parenting arrangements."[52] The only female "labor" acknowledged in the last ceremony is in fact that of reproduction, which is rated successful in so far as it produces a *male* heir. Resplendent in her full regalia, no trace of the factory worker detectable in her, Kautilya dons an unexpected "new humility" (307), and her words are infused with submission to the rules of royal and patriarchal descent. Explaining to Matthew her silence about the recent pregnancy she confesses: "had it been a girl child, I must have left both babe and you. Bwodpur needs not a princess, but a King" (308). So the princess sacrifices her woman's rights and complies with the request of a male heir for her Asian kingdom, and the mission of "Messenger and Messiah to all the Darker Worlds" is naturally handed over to her son. The global union of the darker races is safe in the symbol of his miscegenated blood, but the fate of black female workers seems to have no place in his future. The understanding of the interconnected dimensions of gender, class, and race systems of exploitation is somehow lost in the eroticized fantasy of romance.

It is with this image of brilliant dissonance that I wish to conclude. For all its supposed globality, Du Bois's project in *Dark Princess* remains deeply rooted in the exceptional history of southern slavery, and the defeat of the White Leviathan seems to depend (as Kautilya's own story shows) on the rest of the colored world's acceptance of its exclusive experience. Exclusivity and exceptionality characterize *Dark Princess* at various levels—cultural, national, sexual—so that in the end the future may rest in the hands of a talented black American man.

The textual discussion of Plaatje's and Du Bois's romances has hopefully provided an example of the contrastive framework that is needed to discuss black transatlantic relations. The flows of ideas, narratives, and projects between Plaatje and Du Bois do reveal points of contact, as does their use of the white romance tradition for "black ends," but there is no doubt that the two followed largely independent routes. A comparative reading of *Mhudi* and *Dark Princess* evidences the outline of specific national projects, the urgency of alternative ideological trajectories, and divergent practical solutions. Just as Plaatje's travels to England and America were undertaken with the aim of putting an end to the fatal isolation of black South Africans, and his work connected the plight of his fellow countrymen to global anti-racialism mainly to promote local disenfranchisement, so his creative writing—by drawing on and elaborating a variety of experiences and ideas—endeavored to conjure up an inclusive and modular response to the prospect of building the South African modern nation. Du Bois's *Dark Princess*, on the other hand, shows all the utopian self-absorption of the diasporic American thinker, whose opening, welcoming gestures toward all people of color—and toward his intellectual peer from across the Atlantic—could not go so far as to include the possibility of lifting the veil from over his romantic ideas of the Dark Continent. Nor could he effectively imagine a black ideology separated from a specifically androcentric American racial environment, and go beyond ritual gestures to gender to coherently produce a contemporary black woman as his Dark Princess. Going back to the question of why Du Bois did not publish an American edition of *Mhudi*, it seems possible to state that Mhudi and Ra-Thaga's African story was—perhaps and paradoxically—too "modern" for this American intellectual, at least at this stage of his long, productive life, which appropriately ended in Africa thanks to the hospitality of Kwame Nkrumah's postcolonial Ghana.

NOTES

1. The *Bechuana Gazette*, which Plaatje edited from 1902 to 1909, was a path-breaking Tswana/English newspaper.
2. J. Msikinya, "Africa's Tears," *Koranta ea Becoana*, 7 September 1904.
3. One of the most popular figures was Marcus Garvey, with his message of race pride, unity, and self-determination for Africa. After World War I, Garvey's Universal Negro Improvement Association set up branches around South Africa and the Garvey message took on a life of its own as African politicians shaped it to serve their local needs.
4. Abrahams, *Tell Freedom*, 192–194.
5. Among African intellectuals A. Mbembe, in "Ways of Seeing," encourages this same effort.
6. Plaatje to Silas Molema, quoted in Willan, *Plaatje*, 349.
7. SANNC, later the African National Congress.
8. Willan, *Plaatje*, 255–256.
9. Du Bois, *Dusk of Dawn*, 751.
10. This is how the author defines his literary enterprise in his Preface to *Mhudi* (1930). Further references to the novel are from the 1978 Heinemann edition and are included in the text.
11. *Mhudi*'s intertextual relationships with the European literary tradition and political culture, which are its immediate reference points, have been repeatedly highlighted in a number of critical studies and are taken for granted here.
12. On this point see Chrisman, "Black Atlantic Nationalism," in *Postcolonial Contraventions*, 89–103.
13. Frye, *The Secular Scripture*, 58, 179ff.
14. Fiedler, *Love and Death*, 166.

15. Sommer, "Irresistible Romance," 84–85.
16. For the connection between *Mhudi* and the imperial romance see my *Fiction, History and Nation*, 115–121; and Chrisman, *Rereading the Imperial Romance*, 163–166.
17. Plaatje must have been aware of Du Bois's view on this question, expressed in his 1915 article "The African Roots of War." Du Bois contended that the British Empire had been built on the slave trade, so that by the 1870s England was in Africa, cleaning away the debris of the slave trade and half-consciously groping toward the new imperialism. Plaatje, who before the Act of Union had been a supporter of British rule in the Cape, started to reconsider the role of the empire after 1910 and in the aftermath of World War I.
18. Du Bois, *Dark Princess*, 168. Further references to the novel are included in the text.
19. Mullen, "Du Bois," 230.
20. In Chapter 7 of his 1901 autobiography, *Up from Slavery*, Booker T. Washington wrote of the Black Belt:
    The term was first used to designate a part of the country which was distinguished by the colour of the soil. The part of the country possessing this thick, dark, and naturally rich soil was, of course, the part of the South where the slaves were most profitable, and consequently they were taken there in the largest numbers. Later and especially since the war, the term seems to be used wholly in a political sense—that is, to designate the counties where the black people outnumber the white. (108)
21. Du Bois, "The Color Line," 30.
22. See Ahmad, "More Than Romance," 775–803.
23. Gilroy, *The Black Atlantic*, 140.
24. See Gray, "Sources of the First Black South African Novel," 23.
25. In *The Mote and the Beam* (1921), published while in the States, Plaatje discusses the question of sex across the color bar and deconstructs the white man's claim that the black man is such a scoundrel that he cannot trust him with his wife behind his back. What white South Africans called the "Black Peril" (assaults by black men upon white women) is exposed as hypocrisy and reversed.
26. Lewis, *The Fight for Equality*, 215.
27. Strehle and Paniccia Carden, Introduction to *Doubled Plots*, xv.
28. Tate, Introduction to *Dark Princess*, xviii.
29. See *Mhudi*, 183–184.
30. See Kunene, "Review Article on Sol Plaatje," 244–247. Also Chrisman, *Rereading*, 177–178.
31. Willan, *Plaatje*, 360.
32. Couzens and Gray, "Printers and Other Devils," 202.
33. Plaatje, "Letter to Mrs. Sophie Colenso," in *Selected Writings*, 288.
34. There is indirect evidence that Plaatje at one time possessed a copy of the book. After the publication of *Mhudi* he sent copies to friends and acquaintances in the hope of receiving in exchange books to add to his library. To Du Bois he wrote: "I should be glad to receive in exchange any Negro book—particularly *Darkwater* or *The Quest of the Silver Fleece*, as some sinners have relieved me of those two." Quoted in Willan, *Plaatje*, 364.
35. See Lewis, *The Fight for Equality*, 11–12.
36. Du Bois, "The Damnation of Women," 954.
37. Du Bois, "The Damnation of Women," 967–968.
38. Mullen, "Du Bois," 223.
39. See Chennells, "Narrative," 47–48.
40. See Willan, *Plaatje*, 278–279.

41. Du Bois's aversion to Washington's pragmatic program is expressed in *Dark Princess* through Matthew's narration of his unhappy experience at the Hampton Institute, the first model for Tuskegee, a place that would prevent utopian possibility.
42. See Fredrickson, *Black Liberation*, 119–120.
43. Plaatje, "Letter to Mrs. Sophie Colenso," in *Selected Writings*, 288.
44. For a reassessment of Plaatje's position in relation to capital and labor see Limb, "The 'Other' Sol Plaatje."
45. Masilela, "New Negro Modernity," 15.
46. For the possible intersections between Plaatje's political ethics and Ghandi's pacifism see Boehmer, *Empire*, 158–166.
47. Lewis, *Biography of a Race*, 9.
48. Gregg and Kale, "The Negro and the Dark Princess," 148.
49. Gilroy, *The Black Atlantic*, 144.
50. See Mullen, "Du Bois," 234.
51. Weinbaum, "Reproducing Racial Globality," 36, 37.
52. Radway, *Reading the Romance*, 147.

3   Négritude as Performance Practice
Rio de Janeiro's Black Experimental Theater

Judith M. Williams

> To ransom the dignity of the black man and his culture—to verify and proclaim black beauty from its intimate nature; to consider its intrinsic values as its only foundation and parameter would not, we knew, be an easy job. For black beauty as a value in itself implies a new perspective for the spectacle, involving the consideration of a black esthetics—parallel, in interaction, or even opposed to the white esthetics prevalent until our inception. Black beauty advocates a transformation in the structure of dramaturgical creativity for, from our point of view, the existing theater of white exclusivism had to be disdained or destroyed. In reality, we proposed a true revolution.
>
> Abdias do Nascimento, "Sortilege (Black Mystery)"

As the curtain rose on the stage of the Teatro Municipal in Rio de Janeiro on May 8, 1945, for the opening of the Teatro Experimental do Negro's first full-length production the streets of Rio were exploding with the celebration of V-E Day. Unlike the carnivalesque scene unfolding outside the theater, where the rhythms of the Afro-Brazilian music of samba reenacted the pre-Lenten carnival festival, the mood inside the Teatro Municipal was somber and even confrontational. Rather than choose a Brazilian author who might have celebrated the congenial race-mixing that Brazil reputedly maintained in the 1940s, the Teatro Experimental do Negro (TEN) chose Eugene O'Neill's *Emperor Jones* for its debut. The play had premiered in 1920 in New York City, with Charles Gilpin in the leading role, and was captured in celluloid with the 1933 film starring Paul Robeson. The tortured devolution of a Pullman porter would seem to have little to do with the situation of the black man in Brazil. However, in choosing this play TEN showed at its inception an awareness of transnational connections among blacks in the diaspora and affirmed the congruency of their material and psychic conditions.

When TEN founder Abdias do Nascimento requested the rights to translate and perform the play O'Neill responded positively:

You have my permission to produce "The Emperor Jones" without any payment to me, and I want to wish you all the success you hope for with your Teatro Experimental do Negro. I know very well the conditions you describe in the Brazilian theatre. We had exactly the same conditions in our theatre before "The Emperor Jones" was produced in New York in 1920—parts of any consequence were always played by blacked up white actors. (This, of course, did not apply to musical comedy or vaudeville where a few Negroes managed to achieve great success). After "The Emperor Jones," played originally by Charles Gilpin and later by Paul Robeson, made a great success, the way was open for the Negro to play serious drama in our theatre. What hampers him most now is the lack of plays, but I think before long there will be Negro dramatists of real merit to overcome this lack.[1]

Emperor Jones was an interesting choice. Although Du Bois called it a "wonderful play," since its appearance in 1920 many blacks had objected to its depiction of a brutish black hero. Yet, black theater in the United States grew from the interest of white authors like Eugene O'Neill in creating complex, even if stereotyped black characters, and TEN's interest in it illustrates the ways that TEN trafficked more in an international discourse of blackness than with the criticisms of these discourses in the United States.

Founded in 1944, TEN challenged the notion of Brazilian racial democracy when its founders asserted a distinct racial identity for blacks and demanded equal access to the privileges of Brazilian national identity. Racial democracy was built on the idea that there were no color barriers to success and that individuals had the mobility to improve their status regardless of race. If, in fact, there were no laws preventing their advancement, then what were these black Brazilians fighting against? TEN founder, Nascimento, argued that the emphasis on the possibility of individual success, or the creation of a "mulatto escape hatch" which allowed mixed-race individuals, obscured the racial realities of Brazil's society. He contends: "It is not enough that one black—exceptional or under paternalistic protection, gains a place of projection, elevates himself above the general median of his people."[2] Instead Nascimento remained adamant in his advocacy of both a specific black ethnic identity that rejected the idea of mulatto exceptionalism and an emphasis on communal racial uplift, rather than individual success. In this Nascimento recalls W.E.B. Du Bois, who in his famous "Talented Tenth" essay describes "the function of the college-bred Negro," arguing that "he is, as he ought to be, the group leader, the man who sets the ideals of the community where he lives, directs its thoughts and heads its social movements."[3] Nascimento and Guerreiro Ramos, another of TEN's intellectual leaders, embraced the idea of an elite activism and Ramos suggested that, because of TEN's efforts "to elevate the cultural level" of Brazilian blacks, "in this sense . . . the Black Experimental Theatre is forming itself an intelligentsia, an elite."[4] The first step for this new elite was to establish an understanding of the idea of "blackness." In a country where "whitening" had been the entrenched route toward privilege and advancement, and a factor that limited race-based activism, this remedy to promote racial equality forced Brazilian society to consider blacks as a separate and disadvantaged group. Despite research findings that point to racial inequalities in Brazilian society, Brazil has long denied that racial prejudice is a part of Brazilian society, and has labeled black attempts to mobilize against discrimination as importing racism.

TEN asserted blackness first through theatrical practice and second through the dissemination of an alternate discourse of blackness. Ramos, in fact, called TEN's theater the practice for his social theories, and argued: "To reveal blackness in its intrinsic validity, to dissipate with one's luminary focus the darkness which resulted from our total possession by whiteness is one of the heroic undertakings of our epoch."[5] TEN's theorists looked not only at their material conditions in the formulation of their ideas of blackness, but participated in a network of transnational exchange—illustrated by their use of O'Neill's play in their first production. TEN's strategies for racial uplift were informed by its vision of the Francophone movement, Négritude. Marc Caplan has called Négritude "the first effort by black artists, primarily poets, to create an aesthetic that was both explicitly black, pan-African and at the same time modernist."[6] All three of these aspects were key components of TEN's project. Their appropriation of the discourse and aesthetics of Négritude illustrates a version of the Black Atlantic that moves away from a distinctly Francophone or Anglophone vision. Like many Brazilian intellectuals, TEN's founders looked to Paris for inspiration and for expressions of the modern. Négritude placed TEN within the cultural exchange between Rio and Paris, while allowing them to connect their project to a larger pan-African cultural practice and to articulate Afro-Brazilian culture within a modernist transnational ideological flow.

TEN's work illustrates the local employment of Négritude's transnational ideology. I define this local employment of Négritude's discourse, as well as other ideas and tropes that seemed alien to Brazil's ideological vision, as "sampling." Within rap, "the art of digital sampling in (primarily) African American hip-hop is intrinsically connected to an African American/African diasporic aesthetic which carefully selects available media, texts, and contexts for performative use."[7] Like the technology employed by rappers of varying national origins, TEN's sampling allows the incorporation of ideas, texts, and tropes from a wide range of sources into a distinctly new context to produce art and discourse that reflect the situation of its producers. TEN continually sampled ideas, plays, and performance tropes to create its own uniquely Brazilian discourse.

Although critics credit Os Comediantes, another Brazilian amateur theater group, with bringing modernist theater to Brazil with its debut of Nelson Rodrigues's play, *The Wedding Gown*, in 1943, TEN's use of Négritude to articulate blackness added another element of modernism to

Brazilian theater. TEN wanted to show in theatrical practice and in discourse that blacks were not the folklore of the country tied to a mythical past, but were modern subjects who were conversant with both the contemporaneous modernist discourses that had emerged within the theater, and the transnational dynamics of cultural exchange. Furthermore, TEN's choice of O'Neill's plays for its first productions was a clear attempt to stake a claim to modernism. Nascimento's correspondence with Eugene O'Neill also created a legitimating performance and such extra-theatrical performances were equally part of TEN's arsenal. TEN's long-standing collaboration with Os Comediantes also illustrated that the Teatro's project was as much a part of the modernist revision of the Brazilian theater as Os Comediantes.

In Brazil it was absolutely essential for Afro-Brazilians to proclaim their blackness so that they might find acceptance as blacks, or a recognition that there were particular cultural features that were not simply Brazilian, but black and *essentially* African. The terms of acceptance into the formation of national identity were predicated on the idea that race-mixing produced a new race that was superior to those that created it. However, that superiority in terms of culture had everything to do with European influences and very little to do with its African influences. Instead the influx of African culture was a folkloric or picturesque element. Nascimento deplored both the essentialism and chauvinism implicit in such claims about black Brazilian culture. Thus he emphasized the dignity and beauty of the black experience and its heritage (and invoked another type of essentialism), as he demanded an aesthetic reassessment and reconstruction of Brazilian theater. Darien Davis has argued that, whereas mainstream discourse wanted to assert the primacy of mulattoes as able to make a contribution because of their European heritage, TEN wanted to recover the black heritage of mulattoes and the importance of African intellectual and aesthetic contributions.[8] Négritude provided a discourse for articulating this vision.

In the 1961 prologue to an anthology of plays that TEN produced, called *Dramas para Negros, Prólogo para Brancos*, Nascimento outlined his specific vision of Négritude. In this volume he links TEN's political project and their employment of the discourse of Négritude together with their aesthetic project. In his words:

> our anthological work for the black Brazilian drama reveals another dimension, in which surges the authentic black voice, as a race and as a man of color: the social life. Living as a black man is not a common perception of the western mind. Race and color differentiate themselves and turn to a specific sensibility that developed a new creative dimension in the century of Négritude.[9]

TEN had been proclaiming its connections to Négritude since the 1940s. For example, in every issue of *Quilombo*, its short-lived magazine, there appeared an ad for the Francophone magazine *Présence Africaine*. TEN also recorded in *Quilombo* the triumphs of blacks through the diaspora and capitalized on the presence of any Afro-descended visitors in Brazil, trying to make use of their appearances as legitimating vehicles for TEN's own project.[10]

TEN's project, to reveal the everyday lives of black Brazilians, falls in sharp contrast to the idea that race is not a marker of difference in Brazil. Nascimento positions Négritude as an alternate racial vision to racial democracy, which does not create more opportunities for blacks in Brazil but rather erases the presence of blacks and blackness. Négritude becomes a mirror that allows Afro-Brazilians to see themselves, an ideology that accepts and recognizes some essential black essence that has value for its blackness. Nascimento argues that, since there are no models in Brazil that allow him to do this, he looks to Négritude as the creative force that guides the theatrical work of TEN. In his discussion of Négritude he quotes Sartre, when he suggests that "Négritude is something that a white cannot speak conveniently about, because he does not have the interior experience of it."[11] Nascimento emphasizes that Négritude is something that is both essentially black and unintelligible to whites. This reference is a specific dig at white Brazilian intellectuals like Gilberto Freyre, who through their conferences in the 1930s spoke about the inner lives of blacks without allowing actual blacks a voice. TEN's vision of Négritude was distinct and separate from the Francophone movement that informed it, because the articulation of race and the conditions of blacks were different from those in the Paris of the 1930s, where Négritude was born. Caplan has argued that Négritude was never a single manifestation but diverged from its origins and "came to signify quite distinct aesthetic and political perspectives."[12] In Brazil, where blacks were not limited by a colonial system, Négritude provided a point of departure for TEN to dissent from the trope of mulatto exceptionalism. Returning to the earlier discussion of "sampling," we should consider TEN's employment of Négritude as akin to the sampling prevalent in hip-hop. The riffs that DJs sample are revised and changed so that they are often unrecognizable and bear little resemblance to what came before. What I want to claim is that, while Négritude arose from its own specific historical context, and one that was foreign to Brazil, TEN's local employment of those ideas was distinctly Afro-Brazilian.

TEN's appearance on the stage of the Teatro Municipal was a first for black Brazilians—the first black theatrical troupe to perform on the boards of Brazil's most esteemed theater—and was debated in the mainstream press. One finds in the reviews of TEN a discussion of its work as both aesthetic process and political project. The reviews of their first production were all quite positive, with particular praise for Aguinaldo Camargo, who played Emperor Jones. Each of the reviewers pays attention to the difference between the physical size of the actor Camargo, and the size of the character as established by the U.S. black actors, especially Paul Robeson, who had taken the role before him. Despite being small of stature, Camargo receives strong accolades from reviewers, such as this one: "He does not have the 'métier,' he has little notion of theatrical 'time,' but he is a great actor in the sense of obtaining in the audience a determined state of the soul through the force of his rustic instinct for humanization. He grows word after word—and it is easy to follow that phenomenon of growing vision . . . in the religious and avid silence of the audience."[13] In another review of the play, Vera Pacheco observes: "Aguinaldo Camargo was plainly up to the height of the role, adapting his interpretation to his own personal resources as an intelligent actor does without losing his nature."[14]

Camargo's performance functions on two levels here—it showcases his power as an actor, but also calls attention to the legitimacy of a black man playing a tragic role. Although critics were receptive to Camargo's performance, there were those who took offense at the idea of a black theater. TEN's ideas challenged the mythological ideal of a racially inclusive Brazil and despite the stage absences of blacks the intelligentsia and the press accused TEN's founders of importing racism into the Brazilian discourse of racial democracy. The newspaper *O Globo* criticized TEN's project: "It is clear that there exists nothing among us [Brazilians] that justifies distinctions between the scenes of blacks and whites."[15] Instead Brazil, unlike the United States, is

> without prejudice, without stigmas, mixed and in fusing the crucibles of all bloods we are constructing the nationality and affirming the race of tomorrow . . . to speak of defending the theatre of blacks among us is the same as stimulating the sports of blacks when the pictures of our Olympiads, even though strange, mix everything, and end creating schools and universities of blacks, black regiments and thus forward.[16]

Here we see a strident defense of the racial democracy myth and the anxieties that TEN provoked in whites. The writer seems to say that the theatrical spaces of Brazil are open to blacks, yet when Nascimento, Camargo, Ramos, and others founded the Teatro Experimental do Negro, blacks appeared on stage only in menial and comic roles. Furthermore, black characters were usually portrayed by white actors in blackface. To say that there is no need to change what appears on the stage is also to say that there is no need to upset the social order or the ways that Brazil chooses to represent itself to itself. The terms that TEN used, those of Négritude, may have indeed emerged from an external source, but Nascimento applied them to the particular Brazilian situation.

TEN's early work was largely about legitimating itself as a theater, and as such it chose texts by foreign authors. With its second and third productions TEN continued to sample from the work of playwright Eugene O'Neill, and they also rehearsed, but did not produce, Langston Hughes's *Mulatto*. Furthermore, Nascimento claimed that foreign plays were necessary because

Brazilian authors did not write roles for black characters that would show the dignity that TEN wanted to display. Creating a dramaturgy that was more representative of Afro-Brazilian characters was part of TEN's agenda and, after a number of short works and festival presentations, TEN's first full-length production by a Brazilian author, *O Filho Prodigo*, opened on December 5, 1947, at the Teatro Fenix in Rio de Janeiro. This play provided the first of TEN's national plays with mythic themes. *O Filho Prodigo* uses the biblical story of the prodigal son as a basis to explore issues of racial discrimination and self-hatred. The play opens in a remote area with a black family, whose members have not seen individuals of any other color. When a white female pilgrim arrives, she challenges the vision that the family members had had of themselves, and when she leaves the middle son, in an act of rebellion and self-abnegation, follows her. The isolated characters are attracted to whiteness only because it is white. In this play TEN takes on the idea of prejudice against skin color without the negative stereotypes that come with it and seeks to show the absurdity of the privileging of a white appearance or white skin over the black on aesthetic grounds alone.

The subsequent three plays that TEN chose can be described, in Paul Carter Harrison's words, as "innovative theatrical exercises of ritual reenactment of experience," in which "a mystery unfolds through a narrative fueled by the imagination of a 'mythic consciousness'; it reenacts ritually an 'ahistorical inner reality' that expands the boundaries of time and space."[17] Each of the plays uses a *terreiro*, the sacred space of the Afro-Brazilian religion *candomblé*, as its setting and its mythical and thematic locus. The three plays employ the music and drums of the *candomblé* to support the narrative of the plays. They include ritualized elements but tend to be realistic in their basic form. With these plays TEN was attempting to adapt the serious dramatic form to the traditional rituals and folk life of Afro-Brazilians. Like *O Filho Prodigo*, they are also concerned with biases for those who are white or mulatto over those who are black. It is in these plays, however, that TEN's aesthetic practice of Négritude emerges.

Of these three mythic plays, the last of them and TEN's last full-length production, *Sortilégio*, created the most controversy. *Sortilégio*, by founder and artistic director Abdias do Nascimento, shows the mental dissolution and sacrifice of the assimilated Dr. Emmanuel. Initially censored when written in 1952, it was not produced until 1957, when TEN returned to the stage of the Teatro Municipal, and it was accused of being racist in content. Nascimento reports: "Police censorship prohibited it under the allegation of pornographic language. This was merely an excuse. In reality, what was intended was to veto the subject of the work; that is, to prevent black and white from coming face to face on stage, in terms of social interaction, of race and of cultural confrontation."[18] Nelson Rodrigues makes a similar claim when he says: "*Sortilégio*, classified by its author as a 'black mystery,' is a bold work for its theme, as well as its form. For this it provoked heated discussion in the Rio press, and Mr. Abdias do Nascimento merited the severe criticism of some, that accuse him of racism, while receiving the enthusiastic applause of others."[19] The play was a direct challenge to ideas of peaceful race-mixing, because in *Sortilégio* the cross-racial pairing ends in murder and death.

The play opens in the *terreiro*, the sacred home of the syncretic religion *candomblé*, with three *filhas de santo*, or priestesses of the *candomblé*, who are anticipating the arrival of Dr. Emmanuel. Augusto Maurício reports in the *Jornal do Brasil* that "the presentation of the *terreiro* is curious and has the matrix of authenticity."[20] The *terreiro* is one location of the symbolic Africa present in Brazil. Unlike African Americans who were implicated in the U.S.'s own imperial project in their anthropological and creative appropriations of Brazil voodoo, Brazilians did not need to leave their country to find a surreal space or a spiritual link to African deities. In describing the setting, Nascimento highlights the uniqueness of this African space in Brazil: "It is essential to accentuate the phantasmagorical unreality of the environment."[21] The priestesses of the *candomblé* commune with one another and the *orixas* as they provide essential exposition for the audience. They predict Dr. Emmanuel's eventual fate:

I FILHA DE SANTO
Is color a destiny?
III FILHA DE SANTO
(With conviction)
Destiny is in color. No one flees from his destiny.
II FILHA DE SANTO
A black man when he denies Exu . . .
I FILHA DE SANTO
Forgets the orixas . . .
II FILHA DE SANTO
Dishonors Obatala . . .
III FILHA DE SANTO
(Vigorous)
Deserves to die. To disappear.[22]

Emmanuel's tragic fate is foreordained and the action of the play simply fulfills the will of the Orixa Exu. When Emmanuel arrives he is on the run from the police. He has fled the white world beyond the *terreiro* because he has murdered his white wife, Margarida, and fears for his life. He is an educated black man who has attempted to leave behind his African roots. However, his connection to the cultural space of the *terreiro* is clear the moment he steps on the stage. He instantly recognizes the accoutrements of the deities even as he denies their power:

Ah, it's an offering. A black rooster even. Then it's for Exu. What bullshit. (He looks at the pegi.) That's the pegi. . . . (He returns to the great tree.) . . . the sacred tree . . . The terreiro ought to be over there. (worried) But . . . why did I stop here? This is dangerous. And unwise. The police are always raiding the terreiros. They take the sacred drums, daughters and fathers of the saint.[23]

He is like Aimé Césaire's narrator in *Cahier d'un retour au pays natal*, "a lone man imprisoned in whiteness/ a lone man defying the white screams of white death."[24]

Like Césaire's unnamed hero in the *Cahier*, Emmanuel undergoes a spiritual journey that allows him to recover his African or Afro-Brazilian roots. Césaire's poem articulates the tragic state of the black man, exactly as Nascimento chooses to do in *Sortilégio*. According to Keith Walker:

> To Césaire, loss of self esteem, alienation, a complex of inferiority, a retreat to the solitude of the self often carry with them a linguistic impoverishment. There is a progressive inability to articulate one's agonies except through a shout, a shriek or whimpering in the night. The self is immured in a state of mutism. Agonizing mutism, the self walled up, speechless and silence are the ultimate enslavement. If there is speech in such a state, it is usually as wretched and humiliated as the Black man's condition. The joyous song of self is lost.[25]

Emmanuel's spiritual journey does not end in a muted state, but he increasingly abandons the speech of the educated and assimilated black Brazilian for the language of the Afro-Brazilian *candomblé*, crying out in agony to Exu. Alienation from the religious practice of *candomblé* serves as a sign of Emmanuel's futile assimilation and attempt to escape his own blackness. Nascimento, like Césaire, suggests that the tragic state of the black man crosses national boundaries and, like Négritude, forges a link across the diaspora. As the non-African or diasporic African in the triumvirate of Léopold S. Senghor, Léon G. Damas, and himself, Césaire articulates the position of the colonized other outside of Africa and he makes clear that he considers New World Africans like those of the United States as part of that colonized America.[26] In his prologue Nascimento makes the correlation between the situation of the black man in Brazil and that in the United States explicit by his transposition of O'Neill's tragic hero, Brutus Jones, to a Brazilian context and his articulation of a genealogy for black Brazilian theater that includes the cultural production of blacks in the United States. It is Nascimento's appropriation of the term *Négritude* that allows him to tie these two neocolonial situations together.

The drums, the journey, the dissolution, and the unraveling and undressing of the assimilated hero signify revolt in *Sortilégio*. As the play continues we see his dissolution and the story of his life is revealed. Eventually, the rhythms of the *candomblé* overtake him, and he recalls the loves of his life, Margarida, his white wife, and Ifegenia, his black sweetheart. By the end of the play Emmanuel has shed his clothing and reclaimed his black identity and his African heritage. Whereas prior to the stripping away of the veneer of white culture he had refused his crime, at the end, when he stands before the audience dressed only in a loincloth, he embraces his actions. He speaks a litany to Exu and then exclaims: "I killed Margarida. I am a free black man."[27] The *filhas do santo* then run to impale him on Exu's lance. Emmanuel is a tragic hero, like Brutus Jones or Césaire's own King Christopher, who must be killed to escape his tragic fate.

In his "Notes of a Director of *Sortilégio*," Augusto Boal writes: "Emmanuel is, above everything, a black alienated from his own condition of blackness. He was educated in a white society and he learned that he has the same right and prerogatives as white men."[28] It is the failure of the society to fulfill those prerogatives that leads to Emmanuel's destruction. He is forced back to the spiritual space that he left behind and his divided soul is made whole. Boal remarks that in the battle between Christianity and *macumba*, white privilege and black unity, it is the African heritage that wins: "Exu wins. Emmanuel will be happy in Aruanda." Boal views the play as part of the overall struggle for blacks. He concludes:

> The liberation of the blacks of Brazil will not occur in a single sudden strike. First came the law of the sextagenarians, after that the free womb, after that the abolition of physical slavery. Spiritual slavery still persists and I believe that *Sortilégio*, in spite of its small technical dramaturgical defects, will be for sociological motives, not less than dramatic ones, a decisive step in the spiritual emancipation of the black Brazilian man.[29]

The spiritual emancipation that Boal locates is the same spiritual emancipation that Césaire advocates in the *Cahier* when he speaks of "the nigger seated nigger scum/ unexpectantly standing."[30] The rhythms of the *candomblé* and the hypnotic dance that it includes overtake Nascimento's hero. At the climax of the play, the *candomblé* provides a physical embodiment of Césaire's call from the *Cahier*:

> Rally to my side dances
> you bad nigger dances
> the caracan-cracker dance
> the prison-break dance
> the it-is-beautiful-good-and-legitimate-to-be-a-nigger dance
> Rally to my side and let the sun bounce on the racket of my hands.[31]

The same dances that were criminalized and denigrated become the sign of liberation. The dance, like *candomblé*, serves as the sign of the repossession and glorification of the African practices present in the Afro-diasporic culture.

Not all who viewed the production were as favorably inclined toward it as its director. Nelson Rodrigues, pivotal Brazilian modernist playwright and cultural critic, anticipates these critics when he says:

> I already imagine what three or four critics of the new generation will say—that the problem does not exist in Brazil, etc., etc., etc. But it exists. And only stony obtuseness or cynical bad faith could negate it. We don't hunt blacks in the middle of the street with blows like in the United States. But what we do might be worse. The life of the black Brazilian is full of humiliations. We treat him with a cordiality and a pusillanimous disguise of a depression that ferments in us, day and night. I think the white Brazilian is one of the most racist people in the world.[32]

In Rodrigues's opinion *Sortilégio* deals with real problems of race in Brazil that cannot be denied even though many whites make the attempt. Furthermore, like Nascimento and O'Neill, he sees parallels between the racial situation in Brazil and in the United States. Implicit in his argument is the idea that the overt racism that blacks in the United States experience is less dangerous to the black psyche than the polite dismissals that Brazilian blacks receive and internalize daily. Like Rodrigues, in his review José Paulo Moreira da Fonsêca addresses the play's relevance to Brazilian society, although he comes to a different conclusion. Fonsêca is disappointed with the resolution of the play, which he considers to be advocating segregation, rather than the truthful racial critique that Rodrigues sees. Fonsêca resorts to the conception of Brazilian society articulated by Gilberto Freyre in *New World in the Tropics* as his solution and his defense. Invoking Freyre's cosmic race, Fonsêca argues: "We formed ourselves with the amalgam of three races—the Iberian, the African, and the Aboriginal; it would not be the negation of the roots of these lines if we arrive at a Brazilian solution (the only valid one) to a Brazilian problem."[33] Despite such criticisms of the larger political aims that underlie the play, Fonsêca praises the work of Nascimento and TEN: "Abdias do Nascimento gets it right many times, as a writer and as an actor. He executes, we register what he says with a staging and a set well skilled, both mythical, conformed to the wide and occult tenor of the work. The cast in general performed well."[34] Fonsêca's two lines of argument reflect the uncomfortable fissure that TEN created. As an aesthetic movement that upheld the essential beauty and racial essence of blacks it could be accepted, albeit uncomfortably. But when the group strayed into the realm of societal or racial critique, and tried to move its aesthetic practice into a more political arena, it found approbation, or accusations of reverse racism.

Rather than accept the terms of Brazilianness as spelled out by white intellectuals, TEN attempts to redefine Brazilianness through the terms of blackness. Although the theatrical work of TEN begins with the transnational translation of *Emperor Jones*, in its later plays it shows that the circumstances of the black man in the mulatto nation create a fractured psyche, what Wole Soyinka calls "the fragmentation of essence from self."[35] TEN stakes the terrain of tragedy for the black man in Brazil and rescues him from the margins of the popular and the comic. Négritude becomes the intellectual foundation for this process. The Francophone movement, with its debt to surrealism and its focus on an aesthetic valorization of blackness as part of a political process, provided a distinct appeal to TEN, and also provided an international language of blackness that TEN could appropriate. TEN's local adaptation of the terms of the movement had little to do with the movement itself and very few of the currents that created the French movement were at play in Brazil, but Négritude, the idea of Africa as a spiritual and artistic source, inspired TEN. Rather than to the triumphant national discourse of hybridity, it looked to Négritude as an essentialist base from which to launch its own project.

NOTES

1. O'Neill, letter to Abdias do Nascimento, 6 December 1944.
2. Nascimento, *O Negro Revoltado*, 52. All translations from the Portuguese, unless otherwise stated, are mine.
3. Du Bois, "The Talented Tenth," 851.
4. Ramos, "O Museu como sucedâneo da violência," 49.
5. Ramos, "O Negro desde dentro," 130.
6. Caplan, "Nos Ancêtres, Les Diallobés," 936.
7. Bartlett, "Airshafts, Loudspeakers, and the Hip Hop Sample," 639.
8. Davis, *Avoiding the Dark*, 80.
9. Nascimento, "Prólogo para brancos," 9–10.
10. These visitors include Marian Anderson, Irene Diggs, Katherine Dunham, and George Schuyler.
11. Nascimento, "Prólogo para brancos," 10.
12. Caplan, "Nos Ancêtres, Les Diallobés," 936.
13. Nascimento, *Teatro Experimental do Negro*, 16.
14. Nascimento, *Teatro Experimental do Negro*, 1.
15. Nascimento, *Teatro Experimental do Negro*, 1.
16. Nascimento, *Teatro Experimental do Negro*, 11–12.
17. Harrison, "Form & Transformation," 323–334.
18. Nascimento, Preface to "Sortilege," 822.
19. Rodrigues, "Será racista Abdias do Nascimento?" 194.
20. Maurício, "Sortilégio," 224.
21. Nascimento, "Sortilege," 823.
22. Nascimento, "Sortilege," 829.
23. Nascimento, "Sortilege," 832.
24. Césaire, *Cahier*, 47.
25. Walker, "In Quest of the Lost Song of Self," 125.
26. For a discussion of Césaire's speech to the First International Conference of Negro Writers and Artists, organized by *Présence Africaine* in Paris (September 19–22, 1956), where he makes this contention, see Julien, "Terrains de Rencontre."
27. Nascimento, "Sortilege," 861.
28. Boal, "Notas de um diretor de Sortilégio," 150. In his autobiography, *Hamlet and the Baker's Son*, Boal credits Nascimento, and by extension TEN, with

leading him to understand just who was oppressed in Brazilian society and what types of characters might succeed in overcoming that oppression. Boal is arguably the most influential theorist of the Brazilian theater, especially outside of Brazil. Boal, *Hamlet and the Baker's Son*, 112.

29. Boal, "Notas de um directo de Sortilégio," 150.
30. Césaire, *Cahier*, 81.
31. Césaire, *Cahier*, 85.
32. Rodrigues, "Abdias: O Negro autêntico," 11.
33. Fonsêca, "Nota sôbre 'Sortilégio,'" 160.
34. Fonsêca, "Nota sôbre 'Sortilégio,'" 160.
35 Soyinka, "Appendix: The Fourth Stage," 145.

4   *The Book of the Dead*
Inscribing Torture into the Black Atlantic

Nicole Waller

In Edwidge Danticat's book *The Dew Breaker* (2004), a Haitian man working as a *Tonton Macoute* and torturer for the Duvalier regimes which controlled Haiti from 1957 to 1986 talks to a woman he has taken to bed. He describes to her how he first heard the president give a long speech, which the man had been forced to attend. After the fifth hour of the speech, the man had fancied seeing "a flock of winged women" of all skin colors circling the palace, hissing at the president angrily. He imagined, he tells his lover, that they were caryatids, originally the name for Greek classical architectural statues of women (sometimes thought to have been of slave origin and associated with spiritual power) holding up a superstructure as pillars, or perhaps angels functioning as additional souls for the listeners standing beneath the palace. The woman's reply to him is simple: "You can't afford to be a spiritual man."[1]

   In its linking of the theme of torture, political power structures, and the question of spirituality, Danticat's scene outlines many of the issues I am concerned with in this chapter. While scholars of the Atlantic world have established the space of the circumatlantic as marked by the historical breaks imposed through conquest, the Middle Passage, enslavement, and other dislocations, I am setting out, in this larger general context, to examine two Caribbean and circumatlantic depictions of torture: first, the "philosophy of torture," which the Martinican psychiatrist Frantz Fanon describes as a French colonial strategy used against the Algerian struggle for independence in the 1950s; secondly, Haitian writer Edwidge Danticat's fictionalized account of torture in postcolonial Haiti during the Duvalier regimes.[2] I am interested in the way these accounts attempt to "read" torture, thus to symbolize and historicize events. This becomes particularly crucial since torture, in the context of theories on trauma, is said to destroy in its victims precisely the ability to symbolize and historicize. As a related point, I will also explore the ways in which Fanon's and Danticat's texts envision possibilities for agency and healing. In Fanon's context, where French doctors were treating Algerian patients as mere bodies, and in the historical context of Caribbean slavery, which attempted to reduce human beings to their physicality, it remains important, as Édouard

Glissant has pointed out, to insist on the connection of the body to some form of subjecthood. While most contemporary theories on torture have discarded the notion of healing torture victims by restoring to them an "undamaged" or "unquestioned" subjectivity, the subject position remains a crucial factor in envisioning a healing process. However, as Glissant has argued for Caribbean literary production, the subject position is frequently reinscribed within communal structures. "The collective 'We'," Glissant states, "becomes the site of the generative system and the true subject."[3] Such collectivity, I will argue, is precisely where the notion of healing is grounded for both Fanon and Danticat. While both authors, in vastly different contexts, make visible the ruptures which threaten subjectivity, both render these ruptures less constraining through the employment of group dynamics.

My reading of these communal strategies of healing will evolve via an interrogation of the concept of nationhood in a circumatlantic context. Despite the current disillusionment with the concept of the nation-state, the nation emerges as a crucial category for the analysis of Fanon's and Danticat's work because the collective structures described by both writers surpass categories such as "community" in their political orientation. Fanon developed his theories of healing torture victims during the heyday of anticolonial nationalism, which evolved as a counterreaction to colonization but, in its employment of strategies of "reverse-discourse," ran the danger of remaining caught in older colonial structures.[4] As Kobena Mercer points out, the anticolonial nationalist project seems to have created its own share of hierarchies and exclusions, leading to what Mercer calls our contemporary awareness of "the failures of revolutionary nationalism— the political failure of the radical humanist utopian vision associated with Fanon's name in the past."[5] Nevertheless, the nation envisioned by Fanon was never quite a North African mirror image of European nationhood, which drew on elements such as territorial borders, a standardized language, a historical master narrative, and firmly defined ethnic or "racial" categories.[6] Neither did Fanon advocate a complete return to precolonial structures. Rather, Fanon's theory of nation is marked by his own position as a newcomer to the colonial struggle in Algeria and his experiences in the Caribbean, where both indigenous and African languages could no longer be reconstructed to a precolonial state, where the notion of territory frequently delineated sea instead of land, and where historical master narratives had to contend with the fact that almost all groups, including those fighting the colonizers, originated in an "elsewhere." Fanon did not have to address such perplexing multiplicity in championing the Algerian peasantry as the time-tested guardians of precolonial Algerian culture. In Glissant's words, African opposition to colonialism could frequently draw on "[t]he ancestral community of language, religion, government, traditional values—in brief, a worldview" to create homogeneous historical counternarratives.[7] Nevertheless, Fanon began, through the analysis of torture, to envision a slightly different narrative of nation that attempted to integrate an array of "broken voices" without pretending to an original wholeness.

Influenced by Western psychiatry, Fanon's text establishes torture both as an actual event and the main metaphor of French colonialism in Algeria. In reading torture explicitly on two levels, the literal and the figurative, Fanon supplies his patients with an exemplary discourse that creates what torture is said to destroy, namely a network of symbolization. This becomes possible because Fanon acknowledges his patients' inability to symbolize but reads this breakdown as the collapse of *colonial* structures of communication, a breakdown which can be overcome by moving beyond personal dimensions into the realm of politics through the creation of an independent postcolonial nationhood. In Danticat's more contemporary work, situated in a time of disillusionment with such revolutionary acts of nation-building, the postcolonial nation itself has become the agent of torture. Unlike Fanon, who was critical of European thought but equally wary of Algerian or Caribbean spirituality as useful tools either in the anticolonial struggle or in his attempts at healing his patients, Danticat creates agency and the hope for healing by drawing on various forms of spirituality. In my analysis I will thus also move from considerations of Western theories of trauma—via Fanon's critique of the collusion of psychiatry and the colonial project—to an examination of forms of spirituality which insist on being philosophically, politically, and medically relevant. In this way, the postcolonial nation itself is rethought with new underpinnings.

In using spiritual symbolism, Danticat draws on political philosophies and strategies of healing which were originally created, in the Caribbean, to work through the trauma of the Middle Passage by employing African-based religion to move beyond the conceptualization of slaves as persons without agency. In Haitian history, religion had proved to be a crucial force already by the late eighteenth and early nineteenth centuries, during the struggle for independence. Nevertheless, over the course of Haitian history, both voodoo and Christianity became the battlegrounds of various political interests and were frequently exploited by rulers. This is perhaps why Danticat has one of her characters, as quoted above, critique the conflation of the spiritual and the political, and why *The Dew Breaker* ultimately does not merely employ established modes of spirituality for a description of Haiti, but widens the circle to draw on a combination of Haitian, West African, Ancient Egyptian, Greek, and Christian spirituality in order to approach the subject of torture.

These additional spiritual systems also become formative for Danticat's rethinking of the nation. Danticat's work addresses another dimension of the circumatlantic by tracing the patterns of circular migration between the Caribbean and the United States and exploring how the Atlantic World has prepared Haitians for mapping such movement. Some of Danticat's earlier writing sought to interpret the sea journeys of Haitian refugees to the U.S. in terms of the historical Middle Passage from Africa to the Americas and in terms of voodoo concepts of journeys between life and death, material and spiritual realms.[8] These interpretive patterns are retained in *The Dew Breaker* but are, as in Danticat's larger model of spirituality, interspersed with the Ancient Egyptian and Greek cosmologies which her expatriate characters encounter in the form of artifacts in American museums and which they claim and infuse with new life. Such borrowing becomes what Edward Said has called "travelling theory," setting the tone for Danticat's project of addressing the trauma of torture: "The Ancient Egyptians, they was like us," one of the characters tells his daughter, who in turn observes: "The Egyptians worshipped their gods in many forms, fought among themselves, and were often ruled by foreigners. . . . But what he [her father] admires most about the Ancient Egyptians is the way they mourn their dead" (12). In *The Dew Breaker*, the characters and the narrative itself move back and forth between Haitian and U.S.-American spaces, and these journeys become associated with multidirectional movements across the boundaries of life and death. The various spiritual systems which mark such movements thus can also serve as models for comprehending Danticat's conception of contemporary Haitian nationhood.

In Western psychology, the trauma of torture is understood to tear what specialists have called a "black hole" or an "empty circle" into the psyche, a rupture which cannot be integrated into the usual networks of signification.[9] As a result, traumatized persons can often no longer trust their own perceptions and memories, let alone speak of them. As Sverre Varvin has argued, this erasure of symbolization can also include the ability to evoke images, sounds, smells, dynamic memory, and social relations.[10] While the traumatic instances must be integrated into symbolic structures in order for healing to take place, integrating trauma into webs of signification paradoxically works to create an almost unbearable malignant reality both for speakers and listeners, a reality which in turn unsettles the trust in both language and community and thus delineates the margins of the symbolic system.

If this process describes most instances of trauma, torture as a traumatic event is most intricately tied up with the act of communication, designed to pressure the victim into speech. This is the situation encountered by Frantz Fanon, who was trained in France and sent to Algeria as a psychiatrist in 1953. Fanon, who had himself grown up in the colonial structures of Martinique, soon realized that there were not only two opposed political and cultural codes at work in Algeria—one French colonial, one Algerian—but that there were also two different philosophies and sites of medical treatment and healing. One of Fanon's tasks was to treat French policemen and soldiers who were suffering from psychological symptoms resulting from their torturing of Algerians. For a time, Fanon, who had secretly begun to link up with the Algerian Liberation Front (FLN), was treating the French torturers by day and their Algerian former prisoners at night. As a cultural outsider, a black Frenchman with two radically different lives, Fanon occupied the quintessential position in between.

This position determined Fanon's point of entry into the conflict. His treatment of French patients, who were restored in order to be able to resume their work in the prisons, highlighted his and his profession's collaboration with colonialism and led him to abandon his post at Blida and join the Algerian struggle, as well as to theorize the entire French colonial endeavor in Algeria via an analysis of what, in "Algeria Face to Face with the French Torturers" (1957), he termed the French "philosophy of torture." Fanon claims that "[t]orture in Algeria is not an accident, or an error, or a fault. Colonialism cannot be understood without the possibility of torturing, of violating, or of massacring. Torture is an expression and a means of the occupant-occupier relationship."[11]

Fanon attempts to deconstruct the French "philosophy of torture" by claiming that torture attests to the breakdown of any regular form of communication between colonizer and colonized. Drawing on the reports of his patients and on secret material written by the French police and intercepted by the FLN, Fanon claims that from a certain point on, torture was no longer used to elicit information about the FLN through direct questioning, but to terrorize an entire population: for the French, torture was becoming the main "mode of contact" with Algerians. Fanon writes: "The questioning is deferred. In this perspective, in which the excuse of the end tends more and more to become detached of the means, it is normal for torture to become its own justification."[12]

Fanon underscores this breakdown of communication by relating an instance in which a French policeman, whom Fanon was treating for symptoms of "overwork" in the torture room, encountered another patient of Fanon's, an Algerian who had been tortured by this very policeman. The encounter left both men completely shaken. The Frenchman, who was suffering from hearing endless screams in his mind, experienced a breakdown. The Algerian, who thought that the Frenchman was coming to resume the torture, attempted to kill himself. Fanon "saved" the man, sadly and ironically, by persuading him that the Frenchman was an apparition of his torture-wrecked imagination. For both men, communication with the other had become utterly impossible, lost in endless screams and a labyrinth of visions which could no longer be trusted as real.

Fanon's analysis and attempts to heal his patients in many ways foreshadow the insights of contemporary psychoanalysis, where torture is seen as an act which replaces a person's "good inner object," thus the networks for symbolization or even language itself, with a damaging internalization of the torturer.[13] Fanon struggled to deny the torturers such permanent access to their victims' psyches. To Fanon, the only possible response to torture was an equally violent rupture on the part of the colonized, which also entailed what he called an "overwhelming silence," a refusal to encounter the torturer on a psychological level. Writing about the scene of torture, Fanon advocates "weigh[ing] as heavily as [one] can on the body of [one's] torturer." Following directly upon the envisioned rupture, however, Fanon's text calls our attention to the creation of an alternative communal structure, which Fanon identifies as nationhood: "And then there is that overwhelming silence—but of course the body cries out—the silence that overwhelms the torturer. Let us admit that here we find again that very ancient law which forbids any element whatsoever to remain unmoved when the nation has begun to march."[14]

As a psychiatrist, Fanon realized that although silence could be turned against the torturer in order to renounce the colonial relationship, healing his Algerian patients necessitated finding new conceptualizations of speaking and listening. As the last quote indicates, Fanon envisioned the postcolonial Algerian nation as the "good inner object" which would occupy the space claimed by the French torturers. As critic Nigel Gibson has observed, this healing nationhood is most powerfully constructed in Fanon's work as a web of signification, a communal weaving of voices against an imposed silence.[15] In an article entitled "This Is the Voice of Algeria," Fanon describes how the radio, introduced to Algeria mainly as a French colonial tool, was radically reinvented during the Algerian struggle for independence. Whereas Algerians had at first resisted French radio programs by a refusal to listen, this situation changed when the Algerian revolutionaries created their own radio program, *The Voice of Algeria*. Whereas the rebel station initially told Algerians, in an official voice, how the liberation was progressing, polyphony developed as the French detected *The Voice of Algeria* and attempted to jam its broadcasts, forcing the Algerian station onto various other wavelengths in an auditory mirroring of the actual guerrilla combat. As a result, *The Voice of Algeria* did not become a new national master narrative but, in Fanon's words, instead became a "choppy, broken voice."[16] In Fanon's description, this broken voice, like the voices of the torture victims, was communally accepted and restored by the Algerian listeners, who congregated in order to hear the interrupted broadcasts and to make up for the silence imposed by the jammed airwaves through supplying their own versions of the interrupted narratives. "The listener," Fanon observes, "would compensate for the fragmentary nature of the news by an autonomous creation of information."[17]

In his seminal essay on Fanon's radio article, Nigel Gibson claims that "[i]n this context it was not the actual sounds of *The Voice* but the people's collective interpretation that represented the creative moment."[18] Fanon thus locates the creation of the postcolonial nation not only on the battlefield, but in the radio room, characterizing it as a "vast network of meanings born of the liberating combat."[19] The silence of the torture chamber is overcome through communal renderings of *The Voice*. As Gibson argues, this communal structure can even create a new space and function for the language of the colonizer once the revolutionary moment has sparked an awareness which breaks through the older patterns of colonial collaboration.[20] In this way, communal speaking and listening become the main qualifications for a nationhood that accommodates multiple and broken voices and includes even those who had formerly been positioned at the margins of ancestral culture like Fanon himself.

Despite this hopeful image, both the concept of a creative, communal, multilingual listening act in the radio room and Fanon's polyphonic work itself foreshadow the limits of nationhood. At the boundaries of the post-colonial nation, Fanon suggests, there remain many victims who cannot be healed, as well as many militants who cannot completely be absolved of the violence they resorted to in order to break the nation out of the torture chamber.[21] It is precisely these limits which Edwidge Danticat's novel *The Dew Breaker* examines further. Haiti, where nationhood was likewise attained through violent struggle, shook off its colonizers in 1804 but has since then frequently been caught in a string of violent governments. Danticat's book takes its title from a Haitian term for torturers, those who stomp on the morning dew to prolong the night. Whereas Fanon, who is caught in the colonial struggle, begins treating his patients in the gray area between torturer and tortured but ultimately comes to insist on the political difference between the two sides, Danticat begins her book with clearly delineated sides and proceeds to interrogate the boundaries. Whereas Fanon saw spirituality, such as the voodoo belief in Legba which he uses as an example, as a force which sidetracked the revolution and deterred believers from the task at hand, Danticat insists on rethinking both healing and the concept of nationhood in spiritual terms. This reappraisal of the nation has become necessary not only, in Haiti's case, because of the disappointments of independence, which created a nation whose postcolonial political practice has included torture, but also because a large part of the Haitian nation is now located in yet another diaspora in the United States.

The central character of Danticat's book is a Haitian Dew Breaker who emigrates to the United States, where he marries and raises a daughter. The Dew Breaker legitimizes his new life in the U.S. by suggesting that he was a victim of torture, a fact taken for granted by his daughter because of the large scar he bears on his face. When he finally admits to her that he was, in his own words, "the hunter, . . . not the prey," his daughter's entire version of her father's life is reversed (21). The scar on her father's face, his marker of victimization, is revealed to have been inflicted by one of his victims in a desperate but Fanonian attempt to assume agency in the torture chamber.

The moment in which the scar and the father's life turn into their opposite meaning for his daughter is marked both as a spiritual and a discursive event. The Dew Breaker's daughter recalls how her father frequently read to her from the Ancient Egyptian *Book of the Dead*, a collection of spells and texts meant to accompany and protect the dead on their passage through the underworld—and through sessions of examination by the gods—into a happy afterlife:

> I think back to "The Negative Confession" ritual from *The Book of the Dead*, a ceremony that was supposed to take place before the weighing

of hearts, giving the dead a chance to affirm that they'd done only good things in their lifetime. It was one of the chapters my father read to me most often. Now he was telling me I should have heard something beyond what he was reading. I should have removed the negatives.

"I am not a violent man," he had read. "I have made no one weep. I have never been angry without cause. I have never uttered any lies. I have never slain any men or women. I have done no evil." (22–23)

In *The Dew Breaker*, torture leaves both torturer and tortured without the proper language to speak about the past. The ritualized confession can communicate meaning about the past only at the moment in which it turns into its opposite, the moment in which we "remove the negatives." Similarly, the scar, inflicted by a preacher before being shot to death by the Dew Breaker, was meant by the preacher to ensure that every time his torturer was asked about the scar on his face, "he would have to tell a lie, a lie that would further remind him of the truth" (228). This structure, however, is more than a juxtaposition of negatives and positives. By focusing on the point of reversal, Danticat situates her characters in between, in the very position abandoned by Fanon because he needed to choose his sides in a war. Returning to this position in between, a position Édouard Glissant would term the "point of entanglement,"[22] the torturer's daughter sets out to uncover a past which, in her words, "offer[s] more choices than being either hunter or prey" (24).

The stories that unfold in Danticat's book are filled with muted characters haunting the spaces between Haiti and the U.S. As in Fanon's work, we witness the collapse of communication between torturer and tortured. Danticat describes a scene of torture in which the Dew Breaker attempts to terrorize but not kill one of his victims. The interaction ends with the death of the victim precisely because torturer and tortured cannot trust the meaning of each others' words, because the kind of violence initiated by the act of torture cannot be controlled within the bounds and assumptions of ordinary communicative acts, because "truth" can, at any moment, revert into its opposite. In another instance, Dany, a young man whose parents were killed by the Dew Breaker years ago, encounters the torturer in the United States and, one night, creeps into the apartment where he is asleep. Standing face to face with the Dew Breaker, Dany finds he can neither speak to nor kill him. Having brought about the crucial moment in which he could reverse the roles of torturer and tortured, of interrogator and interrogated, Dany finds it impossible to fit the Dew Breaker's and his own parents' lives and deaths into a meaningful pattern, realizing that he will "never know why . . . one single person had been given the power to destroy his entire life" (107).

Nevertheless, both torturer and tortured find indirect ways of expressing their past. In the nighttime, Dany and his aunt, sole survivors of a destroyed family, talk in their sleep. "They were both palannits, night talkers, people who wet their beds, not with urine but with words" (98). Whereas Dany's and his aunt's night talk never becomes an act of speaking to another, Dany's acquaintance with the young man Claude suggests a move from the nocturnal realm of the Dew Breaker into daylight and from solitary speech to communication: "Claude was a palannit, a night talker, one of those who spoke their nightmares out loud to themselves. Except Claude was even luckier than he realized, for he was able to speak his nightmares to himself as well as to others, in the nighttime as well as in the hours past dawn, when the moon had completely vanished from the sky" (120).

The Dew Breaker, on the other hand, attempts to connect to and express his past through Ancient Egyptian rituals of mourning, "marveling at the mummification process that went on for weeks but resulted in corpses that survived thousands of years" (13). The notion of "corpses" that "survive" situates the Dew Breaker precisely at the point where death turns into life, the space between the poles of life and death. Before the Dew Breaker reveals his past as a torturer to his daughter, she attempts to "tell [her] father's story" by making a sculpture of him as a prisoner (6). This statue, offered to him as a double, an expression of what cannot be voiced about his past, is rejected and destroyed by the Dew Breaker because, as he admits, it fails to tell the story in a relevant way. Instead of accepting the simple lines of good and evil expressed by the statue, the Dew Breaker asks his daughter to become his double and to take responsibility for his past. For the torturer and his wife, their daughter becomes "an orator at a pantomime" (241). They name her Ka, an Ancient Egyptian term for the double of the body, a companion guiding the body through life and after-life (17). The Ka as a concept ties body and spirit together, being a spirit-double which nevertheless depends for its existence on the proper burial and preservation of the body after death. For her father, the daughter Ka is a mask "against his own face," a responsibility which the young woman first rejects and then begins to embrace (34).

Whereas European and American psychology has repeatedly shown the damaging consequences of trauma for succeeding generations and attempted to shield children from the effects produced by both perpetrator and victim parents, *The Dew Breaker* critiques but ultimately accepts the burden of the children not simply as a personal, but as a political task. This task, in Danticat's work, is performed mostly by women. The woman Ka has counterparts in the figures of other young women of the Haitian community, who assume responsibility not just for the perpetrators, but especially for those who have been tortured. In several instances, these characters offer to act as a Ka, a guide and double for the bodies of the dead and maimed. For example Aline, a young Haitian woman who grew up in the United States, decides to listen to and write about the Haitian victims of torture she encounters. Like Fanon, Danticat portrays the survivors of torture as unsure about their own perceptions, hunted people who feel the presence of their torturer everywhere. Those who decide to listen to them and to write their stories must learn to perceive in a new way and offer their own bodies and minds as sources of solace. This task, Danticat suggests, requires an immense effort at balancing. As Aline begins to share the world of the survivor she writes about, her own perceptions are altered not to the point of disorientation, but to the point of ambivalence. Beatrice, the survivor she interviews, claims that her torturer lives in her street and follows her wherever she goes. Aline attempts to monitor the torturer's house but learns that it belongs to a single woman who does not fit the description of a Haitian Dew Breaker. In one scene, Aline sits in her car simultaneously observing Beatrice's street and Beatrice looking out over her street. For a very short moment, aspects of the two women's visions overlap:

> From the front seat of her car, Aline could see the Roman shades on the barber's front window and the green ash shedding more leaves on Beatrice's porch in one glimpse. . . . Beatrice was sitting on the steps in front of her house, watching the street, but mostly watching the leaves drop. It was an odd yet beautiful sight, the leaves seemingly suspended in the air, then falling ever so slowly as cushioned by air bubbles. (133)

The short glimpse during which Aline sees the ash and the barber's window simultaneously suggests the intrusion of Beatrice's haunted vision, because, despite the fact that the house Beatrice associates with her torturer is inhabited by someone else, we learn elsewhere in the narrative that the Dew Breaker is now working as a barber.

In a related conceptualization, Danticat imagines a generation of caryatids. Suzanne Blier has pointed out that in central African Luba culture caryatids were carved from wood to support the seat of a ruler at his investiture. They are thus the symbolic pillars of the political superstructure but are also quite practically associated with a line of female ancestors.[23] In this way, they can signify, in Danticat's work, not just a future generation of politically significant women, but also the necessity of interacting with the past. As Danticat makes clear via the image of the caryatids hissing at the president, these women cannot help the tortured to regain full speech. Nevertheless, they make visible their own connectedness to those trapped in the dungeons.

In Fanon's work, the new nation leaves the torture chamber and progresses to a communal speech act through the radio. In Danticat's work, we follow a preacher who is arrested for speaking too critically on the radio and who is subsequently forced to descend into the torture chamber. The prison he enters is guarded by a man named after Legba, the West African god of the crossroads who mediates between humans and gods, the living and the dead. Placing Legba at the gate of a prison certainly does not constitute a glorification of spirituality. Nevertheless, Legba can serve to highlight both Fanon's insistence on choosing direction, on reaching a decision at the crossroads, and Danticat's insistence on allowing for a world of fluid boundaries as a space of negotiation between present and past, living and dead. The Dew Breaker, after having shot and killed the preacher, exits through this very gate at a pivotal moment which marks the end of his career as a torturer. The preacher, however, is never given the chance to exit through the gate. When he is initially delivered into the dungeon, he is severely bruised and collapses in his cell, where his prison mates do not find words to soothe him but nevertheless perform an act of love: they soak his wounded body in their urine to cure the pain. The preacher experiences his cell mates as existing in a realm between life and death, frozen at the crossroads: "Many of them were forgotten by the world outside, given up for dead. For indeed they had died. They were being destroyed piece by piece, day by day, disappearing like the flesh from their bones" (225). These figures are mirrored in others, like a little boy who drowns in the ocean and is doomed to wander the earth to find his grave, and like the body of the preacher himself after his murder, burned to leave no trace.

Like Fanon, Danticat acknowledges the horrors of the space in between. But the prisoners are also, more hopefully, part human, part angel, "man-angels who saw in [the preacher's] survival hope for their own" (226). Their existence in the dungeon is, albeit only symbolically, brought into relationship with the young women who have not forgotten them in Danticat's work. It is significant that the new political structures which emerge from the pages of *The Dew Breaker* move back and forth between Haiti and the United States, with various characters undertaking journeys in either direction. While many of the young women in the book are situated in the United States, their engagement with Haiti reveals them to be what Danticat has elsewhere called citizens of the "tenth department": "Haiti has nine geographic departments and the tenth was the floating homeland, the ideological one, which joined all Haitians living in the *dyaspora*."[24] The idea of a "tenth department" emphatically retains the notion of a Haitian nationhood with its own political organization and thus differs from ideologies calling for Haitian immigrants' assimilation into U.S.-American political structures. Simultaneously, however, the "floating homeland" becomes a drifting zone in between Haiti and the United States that functions in analogous ways to the characters' positioning between hunter and prey, life and death. It marks the movement of reversal, evoking both the horror of deadly boat journeys across the sea and the solace of multidirectional travels between the living and the dead.

In the final analysis, the shift from Fanon's to Danticat's writing about torture marks a decisive aspect of the historical shift from anticolonial to postcolonial visions of nationhood, namely a shift in the way in which we have begun to rechart the Atlantic world as a site of what Vine Deloria has called "world views in collision."[25] In Fanon's work, which sets out to inscribe coloniality into history and medicine and calls for a change in perception, we see the seeds of a process described by Walter Mignolo as the creation of "neither (or at least not only) revisionist narratives nor narratives that intend to tell a different truth but, rather, narratives geared toward the search for a different logic," changing "the terms of the conversation as well as its content."[26] Nevertheless, Fanon's writing, influenced as it is by theories of psychoanalysis, Marxism, and French literary movements, could still be read as what Mignolo labels a critique of dominant forms of knowledge from *within* a Western hegemonic logic. While Legba, a key figure in West African, African American, and Caribbean theorizing about signification,[27] does make an appearance in Fanon's work, he appears in *The Wretched of the Earth* only to be rejected as an interruption of the necessary revolutionary work at hand. In Danticat's more contemporary work, Lebga and the spirituality represented by him do not suggest an ancestral, slightly suspicious interruption of the progress towards nationhood, but alternative cosmologies at work. In *The Dew Breaker*, Legba as the guardian of the gates that demarcate the entrance of the torture chamber marks the crucial movement of Danticat's text itself, the pivotal moment in which meaning is fixed or reversed, in which the living connect with the dead, in which interpretive communities take shape. Danticat's use of Ancient Egyptian and Greek spiritual systems likewise works to create such charged spaces and to envision torture, healing, and nationhood in larger geographical and historical contexts.

Ultimately, Danticat can offer no complete language for speaking about torture, but she offers a web of signification which allows for a communal approach toward healing, making room for both the living and the dead in a new attempt at postcolonial nationhood. Whether the caryatids have enough strength to support the political structure remains open. But if the woman in my initial quote told the Dew Breaker that he could not afford to be a spiritual man, Danticat's book seems to insist that we must take her words and "remove the negatives."

NOTES

1. Danticat, *The Dew Breaker*, 193. Further references are included in the text.
2. For an earlier version of my work on Fanon, see Waller, *Contradictory Violence*, 61–114.
3. Glissant, *Caribbean Discourse*, 149.
4. For a discussion of "reverse-discourse" and its possibilities, see Parry, "Resistance Theory."
5. Mercer, "Decolonisation and Disappointment," 116.
6. See Anderson's classic analysis of the creation of national structures in *Imagined Communities*.
7. Glissant, *Caribbean Discourse*, 62–63.
8. See, for example, Danticat, "Children of the Sea."
9. See Bohleber, "Die Entwicklung der Traumatheorie in der Psychoanalyse," 823, 831.
10. Varvin, "Extreme Traumatisierung und Psychotherapie," 916.

11. Fanon, "Algeria Face to Face," 68, 66.
12. Fanon, "Algeria Face to Face," 69.
13. See Bohleber, "Die Entwicklung der Traumatheorie in der Psychoanalyse," 822–823; see also Varvin, "Extreme Traumatisierung und Psychotherapie," 908.
14. Fanon, *The Wretched of the Earth*, 295.
15. See Gibson, "Radical Mutations," 408–446.
16. Fanon, "This Is the Voice of Algeria," 86.
17. Fanon, "This Is the Voice of Algeria," 86.
18. Gibson, "Jammin' the Airwaves and Tuning into the Revolution," 279.
19. Fanon, "This Is the Voice of Algeria," 94.
20. Gibson, "Jammin' the Airwaves and Tuning into the Revolution," 281.
21. See Fanon, *The Wretched of the Earth*, 253.
22. Glissant, *Caribbean Discourse*, 26.
23. Blier, "African Art and Architecture."
24. Danticat, Introduction to *The Butterfly's Way*, xiv.
25. Deloria, "Civilization and Isolation," quoted in Mignolo, *Local Histories*, 8.
26. Mignolo, *Local Histories*, 22.
27. See, for example, Gates, *The Signifying Monkey*.

5 The Spirit of Brazil
Football and the Politics of Afro-Brazilian Cultural Identity

Richard Follett

The airwaves popped and hissed as Decio de Almeida Prado, a twenty-one-year-old university student in São Paulo who would later become a leading essayist and public intellectual, listened attentively to the crackling radio commentary from Bordeaux as Brazil and Sweden clashed in the 1938 World Cup. It was an inauspicious year; the forces of National Socialism in Germany reigned triumphant as fascist Europe carved up the continent, Austria and the Sudetenland were annexed, and the storm clouds of war gathered. In the sporting world, Hitler had drawn an immutable color line through the Olympic movement two years earlier, while in the United States racial segregation dictated the lives of American athletes, infamously so in the segregated baseball leagues. Sprinter Jesse Owens and boxer Joe Louis—both sons of southern sharecroppers—bucked the racial essentialism of 1930s America, but despite their successes white supremacy continued to flourish in their homeland. But over the airwaves came a different story from France. Huddled around a radio set in a São Paulo coffeeshop, Decio de Almeida Prado "suffered," he recalls, through the "interminable match" before the score-line was finally broken with the news of a Brazilian goal in extra time. It was the player soon to be named Black Diamond, Leônidas da Silva, who slotted it home past the outstretched Swedish goalkeeper.[1]

The 1938 World Cup was the first time Brazil had entered a team of professional players featuring two black athletes (Leônidas da Silva and Domingos da Guia). It was, moreover, the first opportunity international critics had to view an authentically Afro-Brazilian footballing style—a cultural aesthetic that confounded the opposition and that spectators marveled at both in Europe and Latin America. Earning the epithet "Rubber Man," Leônidas was the "incarnation of skill," Almeida Prado explains—he was a juggler and acrobat, an individualist who played with the ball as if it were his personal possession. Reputedly inventing the bicycle kick, where the ball is kicked while the player's body is horizontal in the air, Leônidas, Prado recalls, was the "spirit of Brazil," an unparalleled striker whose magical artistry created panic among the opposition and whose exploits few could predict or defend against. His style on the ball disorientated defenders, his sly bodily moves giving an "air of prodigious muscular coordination" and of balanced movement. Leônidas's agile callisthenics gave a singularly Brazilian style to international football, one that sociologist Gilberto Freyre described as a confluence of samba, capoeira (an Afro-Brazilian martial art), wiliness, chicanery, bohemianism, and urban hustling. Applying Nietzsche to contrast the classic Apollonian ethos of the European football (where boundaries are maintained and order, reason, self-control and perfection are celebrated) with the more tropical Dionysian aesthetic of Brazilian soccer (where the dissolution of boundaries, intoxication, celebration of nature, music, dance, and passion are definitional), Freyre concluded that his nation's footballing style might best be described as a dance. Indeed, the "irrational surprises and Dionysian variation" that he characterized as emblematic of Brazilian football were, Freyre argued, an improvisational dance performed most animatedly by Afro-Brazilians in the 1938 World Cup. In Brazil's first game of the competition against Poland, Leônidas gave physical form to the Freyrean choreography, tricking opponents, magically weaving through the defense, and scoring four goals in the 6-5 victory. His final goal, the winner, was struck barefoot after his boot came off. "The shot, strong and unexpected, left everyone in Strasbourg's small stadium open-mouthed," wrote one witness. "People were stunned. Europe's sports press, who thought they had already seen everything on a football pitch, reacted with fright, confusion and shouts of 'bravo!, bravo!, bravo.'" As one Brazilian reporter summed up, Leônidas was "simply amazing. He was our stick of dynamite. He did the impossible."[2]

Despite being dismissed by Italy in the semi-finals, Brazil proved to be the competition's real sensation. Leônidas was voted best player, he was the top scorer, and when he returned to his homeland, Brazilians of every color fêted their national team and star player as a potent symbol of nationhood. With his biracial identity (he had a black mother and white Portuguese father), Leônidas's instant celebrity reaffirmed Brazil's relatively urbane racial order, while his footballing artistry drew attention as an embodiment of the true and distinct essence of Brazil, a postcolonial nation no longer imitating Europe but crafting its own authentic and unique national style. A style, moreover, that was harmonious with Brazil's definitively cross-cultural and racial landmarks—samba, capoeira, and carnival. To be sure, Europeans were familiar with the evolving power of Latin American football; Uruguay defeated Argentina in the inaugural FIFA world cup of 1930 and had twice won Olympic gold in the 1920s, but Brazil's 1938 squad mystified Europeans with their innovation, flamboyance, audacious technique, and spontaneity. Distinct from the football brought across the Atlantic by the British in the 1890s, Brazilian soccer was inherently performative, Gilberto Freyre later observed, a sport played as a dance, one that united the country, and showed its greatness. With its cultural aesthetic of artistic hedonism, trickery, and subtle guile, Brazil's multiracial team darted through opposition defenses, forging a style of play that mirrored perceived national traits and characteristics. The beguiling feints and ball-play of the Brazilian team, for instance, wove the subtle, ironic art of *malícia* or slyness into football. Such audaciousness on the pitch, moreover, choreographed the antics of the roguish, cunning, streetwise hustler or *malandro*, who by guile and wit challenged his more powerful opponent, humbling him with quick-witted stratagems that obeyed no structural rules. As Roberto DaMatta observes, such principles are fundamental to Brazilian society where "relational power," or "the power of the weak," is invoked to challenge normative structures of domination. Through the guile of *futebol-arte* (art football), Leônidas accordingly satirized and mocked European *futebol-força* (power football) and inverted the pyramid of rational authority with his unconventional bicycle kicks, skilful dribbling, and body sway or *ginga*. *Futebol-arte* thus choreographed major themes within Brazilian society and as such proved to be a potent symbol of national identity and a shared idiom for exploring community consciousness. Furthermore, as sociologist DaMatta argues, football (like carnival) served as a canvas for the multiple dramatizations of society and a vernacular through which Brazilians perceived and invented themselves. The football commentary that Decio de Almeida Prado so attentively listened to ultimately enabled him and fellow listeners to actualize their national characteristics and sense their "specific continuity as a distinct social and political entity through and over time." By dramatizing "a vision of ourselves through a confrontation with others (our adversaries)," DaMatta concludes, football evolved as a vehicle by which Brazilians reveled in "their differentiated collectivity, as a unity that perceives itself as unique." The acrobatic and wily style of Leônidas da Silva and Domingos da Guia affirmed Brazilian distinctiveness and provided the basis of an internationally recognized footballing style that reflected, and constructed, Brazilian identity.[3]

This chapter explores the role of football in shaping mid-twentieth-century Brazilian culture and examines in the first instance how the exploits of the multiracial national team served to dramatize the Brazilian myth of racial democracy. Scholars of Brazilian soccer and society, from Gilberto Freyre to José Sergio Leite Lopes and most recently José Miguel Wisnek, have long recognized the sport's central role in national self-imagining. While accepting that for much of Brazil's population, soccer has served to propagate nationalist leanings, the second half of this chapter breaks with established scholarship to suggest that black Brazilian football proved to be a crucial political and social site where Afro-Brazilians spoke out, not in celebration of the racial democracy thesis, but celebrating the roguish *malandro*, a figure from the slave quarters and urban slums who pitted his wits against authority and who challenged his former masters by cunning, contrivance, and uncontrollable spontaneity. On a soccer pitch, Afro-Brazilians choreographed these skills and wove football into a longer tradition of black, working-class resistance where oppositional politics have frequently taken popular cultural forms like in samba and capoeira. Like the latter, which whites long mistook to be little more than a dance, football ultimately served two broadly coeval functions: on the one hand, I suggest, soccer expressed the inner tensions, anger, and aspirations of Afro-Brazilians in the *favelas* or slums, while on the other it simultaneously served as an effective device for national cohesion and patriotic verve.[4]

Leônidas's footballing skills, his "silent language" as poetess Gilka Machado wrote in celebratory verse following the World Cup,[5] served to convey a vibrant sense of national and cultural identity, one that was essentially masculine, yet concurrently served as a catalyst for social cohesion. As sociologists Janet Lever, Pablo Alabarces, and above all Eduardo Archetti observe, the social function of football—in Brazil, Argentina, or elsewhere—is toward social integration and for the invention and subsequent consolidation of national identity. The success of the national team ritualizes mass-identification and serves as a lexicon through which society perceives itself. Mass spectator sport, Lever observes, paradoxically brings society together by "emphasizing the conflict between the parts." Indeed, she adds, "sport is the perfect cultural reflection of our Janus-headed existence; it becomes the arena for displaying allegiance to competing groups while cultivating a shared outlook as a basis for order." Nowhere is this truer than Brazil, where success or failure of the national squad has led to fervent patriotism and ethno-racial pride in Brazilian masculinity (as Machado underscores) or, alternatively, to deep introspection over the perceived genetic and racial shortcomings of Brazilian people in relation to Europeans. Brazilians accordingly celebrated the ultimately fruitless campaign of 1938 as a heroic manifestation of aesthetically superior football, and they fêted the team's leading performers as emblems of Brazilian culture. Twelve years later, however, when Brazil failed to secure the World Cup on home soil, the defeat galvanized racist and eugenicist concerns that the multi-ethnic nature of Brazilian society was ultimately culpable for the latest disappointment. Brazilians consequently freighted the performance of the national squad with ethnocultural significance. They celebrated the Afro-mulatto *malandro* in 1938 yet denigrated him in 1950 and 1954 for lacking the discipline, teamwork, and emotional balance required for victory against gritty, spirited, and imposing opposition. The very fact that Brazil exited the 1954 World Cup after a physically violent encounter with Hungary, during which three players were sent off the field and fighting continued in the players' dressing rooms following the match, indicated to some critics—such as Joãs Lyra Filho—that the national team lacked the necessary emotional and psychological mettle for competition and that this derived from the ethnoracial composition of Brazilian people and the mixed race players within the national squad.[6]

If moments of defeat provided occasion to inspect the national character for its flaws (and obfuscate the reality that Brazil was occasionally beaten

by superior teams), the 1938 World Cup and the campaigns from the 1950s
to the 1970s offered Brazilians the chance for more positive introspection
and self-affirmation. The artistry of Leônidas, the audaciousness of Didi
with his *folha seca* or "falling leaf" free kicks, and the irrepressible dribbling of Garrincha confirmed the aesthetic majesty of *futebol-arte* and validated Brazil's national and multiracial distinctiveness. As Gilberto Freyre
observed, the Brazilians' characteristics included:

> surprise, craftiness, shrewdness, readiness, and I shall even say, in-
> dividual brilliance and spontaneity, all of which expresses our *"mu-
> lattoism."* Our passes, our tricks, that *something* which is related to
> dance, to capoeira, mark the Brazilian style of football, which rounds
> and sweetens the game the English invented, the game which they and
> other Europeans play in such an acute, angular way—all this seems to
> express . . . the *flamboyant* and at the same time shrewd (*malandro* or
> hustler) *mulattoism*, which today can be detected in every true affirma-
> tion of Brazil.[7]

Journalist Mário Filho—perhaps one of the most insightful commentators
on the sport—concurred with Freyre, observing that *futebol-arte* derived
from the African and mulatto Brazilian's bodily techniques. Emerging first
among the predominantly black neighborhoods of Rio de Janeiro, Brazilian
football—Freye and Filho argued—was a form of evolutionary dance, one
which expressed national, though principally Afro-Brazilian, characteristics such as cunning, art, musicality, spontaneity, and *ginga* (swing/sway).
Although modern scholars now see Filho's scholarship as a compilation of
oral testimony on the national game and a period product of mid-century
nationalism where soccer evolved as a heuristic device for envisioning Brazilian identity, Filho's work continues to animate scholarship and proffers
a compelling narrative for the racial origins of Brazilian football.[8]

By concentrating on a series of racial traits within early Brazilian soccer, Filho nonetheless celebrated Afro-Brazilian play as an embodied practice that ritualized aesthetic pleasures and emphasized agility and virtuoso
movement, in strict contrast to the phlegmatic, disciplined "machine" football of the European nations. On the field of play, Brazilians choreographed
this distinction in visible and palpable ways. Whereas late nineteenth-century European football was played by overwhelmingly attacking formations, by the 1920s and the 1930s club and national teams adopted more
defensive formations, notably that developed by Herbert Chapman at the
London club, Arsenal. Chapman initiated a footballing system known as
the "W-M" that broke down opponents by force and method, yet simultaneously cramped his own players' creative potential. While Arsenal was
at the vanguard of creating a defensively minded playing style, other European nations also developed tactical formations that attempted to nullify
the opposition. The successful Hungarian squad of the early 1950s, for

instance, withdrew the attacking center-forward into midfield, ensuring a robust defensive line. Austrian Karl Rappan similarly developed the elaborate *verrou* or "bolt" system in the 1930s. It was among the first formations to use four players in defense with one of them (the *libero*) employed as a "security-bolt" behind the other three defenders and just ahead of the goalkeeper. Rappan's "bolt" formation created one interlinked, compact defensive block and relied on teamwork, discipline, and organization ahead of individual skill. Although versions of the bolt formation continued into the 1970s, it was the Italian *catenaccio* system developed by Helenio Herrera at Milan-based Inter in the 1960s that perfected a highly organized and effective backline defense that closed down opponents with man-to-man marking and systematically checked attacking flair.[9]

In Brazil, by contrast, tactics evolved quite differently and in accordance with Freyre's and Filho's nomenclature of ethno-racial traits. Indeed, the "diagonal" formation developed by Flávio Costa, initially at the Rio club Vasco da Gama, but subsequently as national coach in the early 1950s, relied on the players' individual skill and initiative. Critiquing modern football for its lack of improvisation, Costa's diagonal formation exploited his players' fitness and skill and placed specific focus on fluidity, rapid movement, and cooperation. By encouraging defensive players to tackle, hold, and then initiate counterattack, Costa's formation linked defensive cover with the forward line, drawing defenders into the midfield and unlocking the potential for attack in depth and number. Inherently offensive and flexible in its formation, Costa's system necessitated great tactical awareness and improvisation as players interlinked between roles. Simultaneously, the "diagonal" provided scope for greater freedom and individuality, but not at the cost of team play; six men defended, six, or seven, attacked. Gradually evolving into the 4–2–4 formation that Brazil would apply in the victorious World Cup campaigns of 1956, 1962, and 1970, Costa's diagonal emerged initially from the multiracial Vasco team, a squad that included Barbosa, Danilo, and the legendary Ademir, a striker and unrivaled ball juggler whose deceptions and rapid changes in tempo mystified opposing defenders. Appropriately too, it was Costa's Vasco team with its "swinging passes" and his developmental formation that humbled the visitors from Arsenal 1–0 with its Chapmanesque W-M formation in May 1949. These Brazilian victories and the introduction of Dutch "Total Football" in the 1970s (a style that expanded upon Costa's philosophy over space and movement) would alter the trajectory of the European game from its defensive predilections, but in the two decades following World War II, Brazil's attacking soccer formations collectivized episodes of individual skill and dramatized the deceptive discourse of Brazilian society. Writing through this period of evolutionary play, Mário Filho and Gilberto Freyre feverishly associated soccer with Brazilian identity, conflating a player's *ginga* within a lexicon of national distinction, converting the sport into a potent symbol of nationhood and social integration.[10]

In Brazil, football has been appropriated for "imagining the national" since the professionalization and massification of the sport in the 1930s. The Rio de Janeiro playwright Nelson Rodrigues may not speak for every Brazilian, but his work *A pátria em chuteiras* (The Nation in Football Shoes) speaks to the conflation of sport, nation, and identity. Given Brazil's vast size, its limited communications network, its marked regionalism, and its ethnic, racial, and cultural diversity, mass culture—be it spiritualism, football, or samba—has served a particularly important role in providing a national lexicon of wholeness and patriotism. The inherently gendered nature of soccer, moreover, reinforced the misogynistic character of Brazilian culture and ritualized masculinity for the larger goal of communal identity. Brazil's political leaders from the 1930s to the 1970s eagerly exploited the integrationist dynamic within football, particularly with regard to the exploits of the national team, and utilized the sport's mass following to subordinate ethnic, racial, and class differences to national unity. As Eduardo Archetti observes, albeit writing on Argentinean football where a similarly nationalistic dynamic was underway in the mid-twentieth century, ideologies of nationalism have been integrated into social practices that create, over time, a powerful sense of identity from what is, in many cases, an imagined political community. If nationalism can be conceived as a cognitive and social arena for integration, Archetti concludes, it is vital to locate those social practices that reflect versions of self and national identity and investigate the "content" of these practices, both for the actors involved, but more broadly for the values conveyed. In Brazil, as in Argentina, those integrative and totalizing social practices included aspects of performative and embodied culture, among them the national style of football.[11]

Brazilian soccer, however, was not always the domain of the streetwise trickster or *malandro*. Indeed, the functional democratization and proletarianization of Brazilian football in the 1930s was preceded by three decades of amateur football, racial exclusion, and elite control. Introduced by British and German migrants in the 1890s, early Brazilian soccer was dominated by the new urban elite in aristocratic clubs who opposed the participation of the popular classes, particularly blacks and mestizos. The popularity of the game, however, swiftly spread to factories throughout Rio de Janeiro and as it did, a few teams—notably the Bangú Athletic Club, a team serving the English managers and multiracial Brazilian employees of the textile factory town—began to draw on blacks and mulattoes both for players and as a fan base. It was not until the early 1920s, however, that the elite amateur clubs of Rio de Janeiro began to loosen their grip over the city league. Vasco da Gama, a club belonging to the bourgeois sons of Portuguese immigrants, initiated the transformation of Rio football winning the state *Carioca* championship in 1923 with a team that drew upon the wealth of multiracial and proletarian talent emerging on the improvised football fields or *peladas* of the working-class suburbs. The larger clubs attempted to stymie Vasco, investigating the players' "true" amateur status and introducing exclusionary measures such as literacy tests for the players. Vasco evaded such class and color prejudice, however, presaging the democ- ratization and professionalization of the game in the early 1930s. Although the elite teams continued to dominate the *Carioca* league, the mass depar- ture of white players, to Italy above all, left the Brazilian game in black and mestizo hands. Blocked from playing in Mussolini's Italy, mixed-race and Afro-Brazilians such as Arthur Friedenreich, Leônidas da Silva, and Domingos da Guia (who began his career at Bangú) were effectively fated to local success. European racial exclusion accordingly drew a color line through the Brazilian game as skilful and talented black individuals, Leite Lopes concludes, "were seeking their ethnic emancipation but condemned to succeed exclusively in their homeland." Professionalization of the leagues further ensured that football became a means of social emancipation for black athletes. By the mid-1930s, Leônidas and Domingos da Guia joined Flamengo as the once-elitist team emerged from the shadows of Vasco to become Rio de Janeiro's primary mixed-race, proletarian club, a position it retains to the present day. Nearby adversaries Fluminense attempted to sustain a broadly Caucasian team in counterpoint to the broader devel- opments within Rio, but the racial democratization of the game ensured that *Carioca* football remained an essentially black and mestizo arena. The departure of Leônidas and Domingos to join São Paulo and city-rivals Cor- inthians in 1942 and 1943 accelerated the process of integrating black play- ers into leading football clubs and hastened the creolization of the national team, both in terms of players and the footballing style.[12]

By the late 1940s, mulattoes like Zizinho had supplanted Leônidas and Domingos as the principal emblems of Brazilian multiracial football and by the eve of the 1950 World Cup, the audacious skills of Ademir and Zizinho served as a potent symbol of Brazil's comparatively advanced and sophisticated race relations. The 1950 World Cup provided Brazil with the opportunity to display the functional democratization of race relations within their own nation. Hosting the first World Cup since the exploits of Leônidas before the war, they built the Maracanã, a stadium—though more like a cathedral—big enough to match their expectations and those of the 180,000 screaming fans within it. Having swept aside their opponents with such brilliance that it reminded Milan journalist Giordano Fattori of a "Da Vinci painting[,] something rare," Brazil faltered and lost 2–1 in the final to a technically inferior Uruguay team. It was a devastating loss that unleashed a litany of racial accusations against the black players, but one that piqued national pride because Brazilians associated the dif- ferent socio-racial groups in the national team with the Freyrean goal of unity. Although the culpability of miscegenation and the perceived geneti- cal deficiencies of black and mestizo players resurfaced in 1950 and 1954, Brazilians endeavored to retrieve a semblance of national harmony not- withstanding the defeat at the Maracanã. Even the blue and white team shirts worn by the 1950 squad were deemed responsible for the unbearable loss. As one Rio newspaper observed, the national jerseys were lacking in "psychological and moral symbolism." Working with the Brazilian Sports Confederation, the *Correio da Manhã* launched a competition to design a football kit utilizing the four colors of the national flag—green, blue, white, and yellow. The winning design by Aldyr Garcia Schlee was selected as the most "harmonious" combination—yellow shirts with green trim, blue shorts, and white socks. The new kit was unveiled in March 1954 just prior to the World Cup campaign in Switzerland; it failed to have its talismanic effect that year, but the national team with the "universalist image of mixture" imprinted upon their shirts proved triumphant in 1958 and 1962. They were the first mestizo teams featuring black, white, and mixed-race players to win a World Cup at a time when their European competitors were uniformly white. These two titles checked any lingering reservations over national or racial inferiority and consolidated a positive national self-image with football and Brazil's peculiarly democratic and multiracial style of playing the game as its national emblem.[13]

Since the 1930s, Brazilian governments—notably the administration of Getúlio Vargas—have stressed national integration, economic and political nationalism, and state-guided modernization. Academics, particularly social scientists, contributed to these debates by stressing the hybrid and syncretic nature of Brazilian national identity and the nation's history of racial mixture and democracy. Brazilians were not alone in placing the *mestizo/mestiço* at the heart of nationalist thought within Latin America, though theorists such as Gilberto Freyre positively underscored *mestiçagem* as the foundation of Brazilian distinctiveness. To be sure, some public intellectuals continued to preach the doctrine of racial hierarchy, warning against the dangers of miscegenation, and parading broadly eugenicist arguments, but the democratic tone of Brazilian popular culture led toward the affirmation of greater racial pluralism. The success of Bangú, Vasco, and Flamengo placed multiracial football at the axis of Brazilian vernacular culture. The emergence of professional samba and the carnival traditions of Rio de Janeiro further ritualized racial mixture in the nation's leading multiracial city. In these discrete, yet semiotically linked cultural forms, the powerless—da Matta observes—are temporarily empowered, normative structures of authority are suspended and subverted, and the individual is liberated to perform freely without reference to blood, race, gender, or, to a lesser extent, class. The functional democratization and racial egalitarianism of Brazilian popular culture by the 1930s provided scholars like Freyre with the cultural bricolage to assemble his cosmopolitan thesis on the organic nature of Brazilian society and accentuate its relative racial sophistication, in contradistinction to the segregated and racist United States.[14]

Freyre rejected the prevailing current of promoting European imitation, scientific racism, and racial whitening within Brazilian nationalist thought.

By contrast, he exploited the syncretic constructiveness of Brazilian race relations to suggest that miscegenation produced a *"moreno* meta-race," Rebecca Reichmann observes, "who would unify the country." In his landmark 1933 study, *Casa Grande e Senzala (The Masters and the Slaves),* Freyre positively reassessed the role of miscegenation in Brazilian history and argued that nineteenth-century plantation communities were extended families in which slaves and masters were interdependent and even interrelated—a patriarchal system much more benign and attenuated, he argued, than other enslaved societies. Race mixing prompted a "democratizing" and "interpenetration" of African, European, and indigenous societies, and the creolized culture that emerged from the interstices of the plantation world had advantageous consequences for the Brazilian character and sensibility. As Freyre candidly observed, miscegenation and "Brazilianization" unleashed a profound and "fraternal association of values and sentiments" among those in the Big House and in the slave huts. The cultural enrichment derived from such episodes of racial mixing created a "new world in the tropics," a distinct civilization—Freyre later concluded—whose cultural perspectives were "extra-European." Although his scholarship subsequently underwent withering assault and problematic exaggeration, Freyre's notion of racial democracy rooted in this agrarian culture captured the national imagination from the 1930s to the 1950s and became the hallmark of national identity and the essence of national meaning. The reality of growing black urban poverty suggested otherwise, but the idea of racial democracy proved nonetheless resilient and politically progressive for the 1930s. The cult of *morenidade* or the celebration of the light-brown *mestizo* as the synthesis of the "Brazilian race" thus became a foundational myth within Brazilian society. Creating a national and ethnic "self" through racial mixing served the integrationist agenda of the mid-twentieth century, and although his work was subsequently appropriated by the military dictatorship of the 1970s to provide a scholastic justification for their disregard of the mounting problems of endemic poverty, notably among Afro-Brazilians, Freyre's principal contribution lay in resuscitating the role of the African in Brazilian society and underscoring the pluralistic consequences of *mestiçagem.* Freyre, moreover, valorized the notion of racial democracy and wove a social construction of national identity from the mythically harmonious threads of Brazilian culture.[15]

If we understand the formation of ethnic and national identity to be a process where borders and markers are constantly shifting—a dynamic Alejandro Frigerio calls "ethnicization"—then the exploits of the national football team can be seen as a socio-cultural space for the construction and modification of that identity. Whether watched from the terraces or listened to on the radio, football evolved as a social practice for national integration and social cohesion—it enabled mid-twentieth-century Brazilians to gloss over the class and ethnic divisions of society in favor of a mythic national consciousness. Football thus united Brazilians in a cognitive celebration of self and group identity and it served as a public mirror for national consciousness. To be sure, soccer is fundamentally a leisure pursuit and one must guard against reifying the sport as philosophy and its practitioners as self-conscious ideologues for, in the most part, they are not. But, as Noel Dyck and Eduardo Archetti observe, sport possesses its own ontological function; it serves as a prime location for "the production, reproduction and contestation of identities"—identities that are simultaneously "frivolous and serious, categorical yet personal, ephemeral yet abiding." Every footballing nation, of course, shares its own abiding memories, be they club rivalries, national triumphs (or defeats), or episodic instances (flashes of brilliance, moments of despair); yet in the case of Brazil, soccer evolved as a central component of the public narrative, a universal icon within the language of national distinction. Virtuoso movement, cunning passes, shrewd feints, and complex stratagems to outwit one's adversary ritualized and validated the national character, testing the agility of the Brazilian *malandro* against burly overseas opposition. Soccer victories affirmed national distinctiveness and in its kinesthetic action and wide popular support, football emerged as a shared cultural lexicon where the national self was embodied in the performance of the team, just as the team embodied "the people," *o povo*. As Richard Giulianotti observes in his sociological analysis of football rivalry, social groups adopt both semantic and syntactic forms to define "what they are" and "what they are not," often by reference to the soccer pitch, though frequently to express a more poignant sense of community or identity among groups of supporters. Nowhere was this truer than in the 1950s, when, despite marked racial inequalities, the fictive idea of racial democracy and the totemic Freyrean vocabulary of national character and cultural essence remained wedded to the embodied identities of the racially mixed, artistic football teams that Brazil fielded at each World Cup. So impressed was author José Lins do Rego with the visible representation of Freyre's logic within Brazilian football that he celebrated the national team as "a portrait of our racial democracy" where blacks, whites, and Brazilians of every socio-economic class battled in unison for the national flag with its commanding patriotic motto ORDEM E PROGRESSO (Order and Progress).[16]

Brazilian politicians have thus long harnessed the totalizing nationalist power of football and its mass crowds to further, Rowe and Schelling contend, "the hegemonic interests of the government in power and the respective model of development it sought to actualize." Getúlio Vargas, like Juan Perón in Argentina, sponsored stadium construction, not only to export a positive national image but additionally to address mass crowds with his propagandistic, corporatist oratory. The monumental Maracanã stood as fitting testimony to Vargas's patriotic agenda and the celebration of the fourth World Cup in 1950 on home soil provided an apt moment for insurgent Brazilian nationalism. The symbiosis of politics and sport continued under the military regimes of the 1970s, which harnessed the popular appeal of football in order to advance their own political projects. The military government of Emílio Garrastazú Médici (1969–74), for instance, used the marching tune "*Pra Frente Brasil*" (Forward Brazil)—written to inspire the 1970 World Cup Team—as the regime's theme song and plastered the nation with posters juxtaposing an image of Pelé in midair after scoring a goal with their nationalistic slogan "No one will hold Brazil back now." Unquestionably sport—especially the mass size of football crowds—was used, Matthew Karush argues, "as a step in the process of hegemonic nation building." But to view the massification of spectator sport as an opiate for the socially manipulated masses would overlook a dissident African streak in the cultural politics of football, a streak moreover which consciously and unconsciously questioned the progressive identity and harmonious values of mid-twentieth-century Brazilian society. To the contrary, Afro-Brazilian football served as an arena for "speaking out" and positing a more defiant agenda for those in the urban slums.[17]

If we decode the stylistics of football—just as one might do for dance—as a dynamic and dialogic form for expressing both the individual self and collective identity, then within the symbolic world of culture performative acts such as soccer embody multiple identities with heterogeneous axes of signification. As Helen Thomas observes, bodily movement and motion have been deciphered as a form of pseudo-linguistics, a discrete channel of communication with its own scriptural terminology reflecting institutionalized social contexts and experimental responses to "deployments of power," as Michel Foucault described them in reference to bodily practice. Whereas sociologists and historians have focused on the Afro-Brazilian footballing style as a choreographed emblem of national identity, freighting black performativity with the burden of nationality, we can alternatively read soccer as an embodied script that challenged the culture of racial power and the discourse of harmonic nationhood. As such, the creativity and dribbling brilliance of early mulatto and African Brazilians evolved as a form of creative and, by implication, political intervention. An intervention and aestheticization, moreover, that was carried out socially from below by the poorest and most racially marginalized. By examining Brazilian football through the lens of recent cultural studies, notably dance, alternate possibilities emerge where the bodily "habitus" choreographs an autobiographical "first person" or "I," which in turn allows for self-invention and the embodiment of difference or political struggle. As Ann Cooper Albright suggests, embodied practice serves as a form of communal autobiography that enables the marginalized to "hold onto the experience of their own body while reclaiming their history," an act that transmits though alters the signification—Jane Desmond reasons—of the danced form. If black performativity gestures toward multiple signification and ambivalence of identification, as Homi Bhabha implies, then soccer as an expression of an embodied practice commands attention for its transgressive potential. Indeed, if we accept Albright's injunction toward the formal hybridity of autobiography as a genre, and view autobiographical consciousness "not as a discourse of individual authorship," Caren Kaplan writes, but "as a discourse of situation—a politics of location," we can begin to examine expressive culture as a signpost of collective and individual expression, a cultural marker no less significant than individual acts of speaking and writing. By extending this conclusion to the symbolism of culture, performative acts (such as soccer and dance) can be read as dynamic and dialogic forms of expressing individual and communal consciousness, an autobiographical "I" or "we" that by implication stretches textual forms and serves as a resource for cultural memory and, Laura Marcus concludes, as a site for "speaking out" and "authorising identity."[18]

The opportunities for Afro-Brazilians to "speak out" and reclaim a distinct authorial voice were, of course, highly limited. From the 1940s to the 1960s, Brazilian leaders and academics preached the gospel of racial harmony, nationalism, and Freyrean integration; culturally, black Brazilian soccer was reappropriated within the modernist agenda and players like Leônidas and Zizinho were fêted for their mastery of the nationally/integrationally defined footballing style. Freyre, Filho, and Vargas successively exploited football as an emblem for imagining Brazilian nationalism, and they imposed this social inscription not only upon the black players, but additionally upon the discrete Afro-Brazilian voice. The "overwriting" of the specifically black body by Brazilian nationalism, however, did not erase its symbolism or silence the creative expression of Afro-Brazilians. By contrast, black football evolved as a performative script where Afro-Brazilians reaffirmed their history of cultural resistance and their hostility to white racial power. The democratization of the Brazilian game in the 1940s and its affirmation of an essentially Afro-mulatto style provided an arena for the free descendants of Brazilian slavery to employ generations of socially encoded practice; through guile, wit, and cunning, they had occasionally outwitted their erstwhile owners and had mastered the art of hustling to improve their lives and challenge the dominant structures of power and authority in post-emancipation Brazil. By celebrating the rascalesque, bohemian, *malandro* figure, black Brazilians on a football pitch and in the stadiums appropriated soccer as a cultural site to celebrate individuality and disorder against the hegemonic and hierarchic structures of mid-twentieth-century society. Much like the irreverence of carnival and samba, football was "resistance in motion," an aesthetic of the possible in contradistinction to the social realities of proletarian improbables and a ritualized site to safely challenge the social and political hierarchies of Brazilian society.[19]

In Brazil as elsewhere in the Black Atlantic, the African body proved a peculiarly contested or conflicted site and icon. Slavery reduced the African, in white colonial eyes, to productive and reproductive capital, while economic discrimination, combined with informal and formal structures of racial inequality, further limited opportunities in post-emancipation societies. To be sure, race relations in Latin America proved singularly more ambiguous than those in the United States, but the processes of class and racial marginalization have particularly encumbered those of African descent. As Livio Sansone recently argued, given prevailing somatic norms that place Afro-Brazilians toward the bottom of social hierarchies, the construction of black identity has often been associated with specific uses of the black body. On the one hand, blackness was encoded into discrete jobs, ranks, and behaviors, while on the other, physical appearance, demeanor, and gestures have been the means by which black people—a racialized people—recognize themselves and attempt to regain dignity and status. As anthropologist James Scott observes, albeit for peasant culture in southern India, oppressed groups challenge those in power by constructing a hidden transcript, a dissident political culture that manifests itself in cultural practices. One also finds the hidden transcript emerge "on stage" in spaces controlled by the extant hegemony, though almost always in disguised forms. The submerged social and cultural worlds of oppressed people—the infrapolitics of working-class resistance—Scott observes, are like "infrared rays, beyond the visible end of the spectrum." The Brazilian mantra of racial democracy leaves little scope for Scott's argument, but, as Robin Sheriff among others has recently argued, public denial of racism cannot mask the realities of racialized prejudice and discrimination within Brazilian society. Despite the palpable shortcomings of the "racial democracy" thesis, the myth nonetheless retains currency; although blackness is still equated with sloth, deceit, hypersexuality, and waste, the terms *preto* or *negro* are rarely used in daily life—Sheriff observes—they are subsumed within Brazil's silent racial consciousness. Such silence is dictated, as Gayatri Spivak has argued, by dominant social groups, who ultimately control and sanction many of the narrative strategies available for oppressed groups. Given the overwhelming silencing of a working-class black commentary on the construction of Brazilian identity from the 1930s to the 1960s and the muting of any populist, vernacular challenge to the mythic model of racial harmony, it remains vital to examine the counter-possibilities and racially encoded counter-narratives even in situations of relative constraint. Indeed, as Michael Hanchard contends, marginalized groups create territorial and epistemological communities that critique the bourgeois public sphere and its societal and political norms. Brazilian soccer, being essentially black and mestizo at its professional inception in the 1940s, evolved into such an epistemological community, one that valorized a discrete Afro-Brazilian aesthetic in counterpoint to the modernist and nationalist rhetoric of the Vargas regime. Football thus served as a counter-hegemonic gesture—an infrapolitical statement that was "on stage" at the Maracanã.[20]

   If Brazilian football was essentially a valorization of black working-class culture and a form of coded political and social resistance, then the origins of such activism unquestionably lay in the slave communities of the Brazilian past. Syncretism and creolization altered the cultures of the slave diaspora, but along the Northeastern shore of Brazil, West African cultural patterns persisted and continue to do so. The Afro-Brazilian religion *candomblé*, for instance, derives its divination and scarification from a syncretic blend of monotheistic Roman Catholicism with polytheistic West African beliefs in spiritual intermediaries or *orixás* (orishas). Within the pantheon of *orixás* are divinities who dialogue with every aspect of life: *yemanja* proffers fertility and abundance, the warrior *ogun* is the divinity of war, *ewa* is the queen of metamorphosis, while *exú* is the divine trickster and messenger, the master of the improbable, uncertainty, and disruption. Performed within a circle, *candomblé* dances mimetically choreograph the *orixás* and commemorate the West African ring, a ring which encircles the community, encompasses the renewal of life, and embodies a "deep-seated cultural memory" of movement and sound upon which diasporic Africans have long drawn. As Barbara Browning contends, *orixá* choreography constitutes "a form of writing—writing through motion" in which the dancer becomes the text, an emblem of the *orixás* mythic drama. Such mimetic incorporation is also true of samba, a vernacular pun on *candomblé,* performed in the circle or *roda*, but where the cult of the body is in ascendancy. Artistry in samba lies with the individual's *axé*, a talent possessed by the orisha *exú* and which translates as potentiality or invention, "the force to make things happen," as Robert Farris Thompson observes. *Axé,* like the orisha, are derivatives of Yoruba culture and appear in various guises throughout the Black Atlantic; in samba the dancer's *axé* is measured by his or her capacity to balance the multiple rhythms within the samba beat and respond corporally and imaginatively to the various instruments and patterns being played within the *roda*. The volatile potential of *axé* where invention and creativity are valorized, however, literally exploded "on stage" in the most culturally forceful artefact of the Afro-Brazilian triad, capoeira.[21]

Whether capoeira originated in Brazil or Africa remains unclear, though it undoubtedly shares an African aesthetic with samba and *candomblé*. Appearing to the white masters of the Big House as a dance, capoeira was in fact a martial art developed within the slave communities by Afro-Brazilian slaves who used the sport to develop the skills necessary for life in bondage, namely deception, cunning, and guile—attributes that enabled bonded people to challenge the hegemony of the master class, albeit temporarily, and eke out a modest existence through trickery and wiliness. These "weapons of the weak," as James Scott observes, constituted the infrapolitics of daily black resistance as the enslaved manipulated the planter's production system by direct opposition or by trickery. Traditional capoeira celebrates the essence of guile or *malícia*, a shrewdness and wariness that enables the capoeira player to anticipate his opponent's moves and prepare for a counterattack. Central to this process is the art of deceiving or faking and, like *axé, malícia* exploits creative responses for exhibiting one's mastery of the game. Performed to polyrhythmic music within the *roda* or ring, capoeira offered culturally encoded lessons for the slave community and, as Afro-Brazilians emerged from beneath the shadow of slavery and migrated to the emerging cities at the turn of the twentieth century, the skills learned in capoeira proved a valuable resource for urban survival. The roguish *malandro* who hustled in the cities exercised *malícia* with aplomb and like a savvy feint in capoeira, he dodged the exploitative structures that hampered the Brazilian working classes. *Malícia* thus evolved as a compensatory tool within the arsenal of black resistance, a weapon of cultural resistance that emerged from the plantation complex and was refined on the urban streets to combat the racial, economic, and class dependencies of Brazilian culture. Despite police efforts for its repression, capoeira proved one of the "most persistent and perhaps most successful efforts to establish a social 'space' on the part of urban Afro-Brazilians—an area of activity which they controlled, used for their advantage largely on their terms," historian Thomas Holloway observes, and "from which they could exclude outsiders." Capoeira thus reaffirmed group solidarity within the *roda* but simultaneously challenged the rigidity of social rules by the bending and twisting implicit in the players' acrobatic moves. Equally significantly, capoeira gave those chained to the base of the socioeconomic pyramid the opportunity to meet force with force and through deception and dissimulation muddy the hegemonic contours of Brazilian society.[22]

Brazilian football emerged from the working-class black *peladas* of Rio and like samba, capoeira, and *candomblé*, it *choreographed* the collective cultural memory of the Afro-Brazilian experience. The basic movement in capoeira features body sway or *ginga* and it is from this constant and improvised movement that subsequent deceit derives; from it, the skilled *capoeirista* can "hide, dodge, feint and attack." *Ginga* incorporates three basic aspects—the *passada* or footwork, the *balanço* or bobbing of the body, and the *jôgo do corpo* or body play, where the player twists, turns, and sways his torso from side to side to distract and disorientate the opponent while protecting himself from attack. Although regional styles alter the form and nature of capoeira, *ginga* provides the basis for the physical agility and sudden changes of speed required to deceive opponents or evade their attack. Beyond the *capoeirista*'s *ginga*, the complex floor moves, kicks, and takedowns within the sport serve to lay traps, dazzle the opponent, and lure him into a false sense of security and dominance. As noted performer Nestor Capoeira observes of the *aú*, a defensive formation known as the cartwheel, it is "part of the web of unexpected movements which encircles your opponent and leaves him dizzy, making him hesitate, lose his center of balance, and even open his guard." Once rhythmically compromised, the master *capoeirista* unleashes a series of kicks both from the ground and while in midair, often upside down. The skilled artist executes such kicks in perfect balance and under full control, swiftly assuming a position of defense in preparation for the counterattack. In every move, be it *ginga* which adds a basic rhythmic cadence to the bodily moves or the specific kicks and defensive movements, capoeira exploits balance, agility, improvisation and mobility, and it seeks to unbalance the opponent leaving space and time to exploit counterattacks. It is the maintenance of this rhythmic give and take, call and response, escape and counterattack which sustains the flow of the game and provides interludes for improvisation, indirection, and guile, the bodily encoded aesthetic of *malícia*. The parallels to the evolution of the Brazilian footballing style are axiomatic as black players used invention, body swing, suppleness, and flexibility to trick, deceive, and outwit the opposing players. In their *ginga* or feints on the ball, footballers like Leônidas fused *axé* and *malícia* within their ball-control skills and launched overhead bicycle shots, so similar to the spinning, jumping moves of capoeira's *parafuso* and *armada pulada* kicks. Likewise, the counterattacking elegance of the Brazilian "diagonal" sprung from the capacity of the players to win the ball quickly, make a counterturn, and unbalance opponents with rapid movement, a dynamism stemming from their "swinging passes," individual *axé*, and capricious *ginga*.[23]

Brazilians call Pelé the king and view him with almost regal deference, but their idol remains Mané Garrincha—a midfielder of prodigious talent who died young and penniless in an alcoholic coma after decades of drinking and womanizing. In contrast to the ascetic and politically savvy Pelé, who rose from humble origins himself, the mestizo Garrincha (part American Indian and part Afro-Brazilian) demonstrated with acuity that there was no safety net in Brazilian society, not even for a world champion. Systematically underpaid, exploited by his club chairman, and frequently negligent in his professional duties beyond the football field, Garrincha was a metaphor for those in the *favelas* and an exemplar of the working-class *malandro* tradition within professional soccer. To be sure, Garrincha enjoyed substantial fame and his twenty-year on-off relationship with samba star Elza Soares gained him additional notoriety, but unlike Pelé, who harnessed his exceptional talents with aptitude, Garrincha impatiently squandered his. Physically diminutive with crooked legs, Garrincha nonetheless became the greatest dribbler of a football in the 1950s; he swerved his body and ball past defenders, confounding them with feints and unbalancing them with his *ginga*. The poet Paulo Mendes compared him to an artistic genius: "Like a poet touched by an angel, like a composer following a melody that fell from the sky, like a dancer hooked to a rhythm, Garrincha plays football by pure inspiration and magic, unsuffering, unreserved, and unplanned." On a summer afternoon in Gothenburg, as Brazil and the Soviet Union clashed in the 1958 World Cup, Garrincha seized the opportunity to display his talents against a team that announced itself the masters of "scientific football." To challenge the infamously larger, fitter Soviet team who had won Olympic gold in 1956, coach Vicente Feola concluded that an early goal and rapid movement within Brazil's 4–2-4 "diagonal" formation was essential. Armed with the offensive flexibility and fluidity of such a tactical schema, Feola turned to Garrincha in the final team talk, urging him "to throw them off balance right from the start." And so he did; after just twenty seconds, Garrincha took the ball, he dribbled—mesmerizingly so—through the Soviet defense, pulling them one way and then the other, before unleashing a shot at the post. Not even a single minute had elapsed before Pelé also hit the woodwork from a Garrincha pass. "The pace was mind-boggling," journalist Ney Bianchi wrote, "as is Garrincha's rhythm." The onslaught continued until Vavá finally smashed home a goal on three minutes. In just 180 seconds Brazil had shown the world such audaciousness and skill, it was a master-class in *futebol-arte* and prefigured Brazil's dominance from 1958 to 1970.[24]

But Garrincha's appeal was greater still. He was famously lazy and relaxed yet irreverent of authority; his gamesmanship was legendary, as was his amateuresque abuse of every vice he encountered. But, above all, he was a *malandro*, a bohemian rascal who with skill and savoir faire exploited order and disorder in society and on the pitch. As Decio de Almeida Prado recalls, Garrincha would advance with the ball, swaying his body seductively as if in a dance; when he felt his marker was unbalanced, with his weight on the wrong leg, Garrincha would launch past him throwing his opponents into disorganization and panic. Garrincha's moves, of course, his virtuoso dribbling, body sway, and explosive acceleration combined aspects of capoeira and samba with the ball control of soccer. From a tactical perspective, his dribbling created space and time for his teammates to move into position, but Garrincha's ball work was that of an urban hustler who employed his guile or *malícia* to humble his foe. For contemporaries like Prado and Nelson Rodrigues, the infectious rhythm of Garrincha's play celebrated the ludic, but it also improvised upon the polyrhythmic meter of Afro-Brazilian music and dance. Musicologists refer to this as a "metric mosaic" of rhythms, some of which are audible, whereas others are not. The good dancer "tunes his ear to hidden rhythms, and he dances to the gaps in the music." To achieve that end, dancers had to respond to and critically balance the complex multiple-meter structure. Above all, such dance requires guile, evasion, deception, balance, and above all a coolness of mind. Balance, Robert Farris Thompson argues, is "the aesthetic acid test" of West African dance and of its New World derivatives in which samba, capoeira, and arguably Afro-Brazilian football may be included. Faced by multiple rhythms, the weak dancer, Thompson continues, "soon loses his metric bearings in the welter of competing counter meters and is, so to speak, knocked off balance." Garrincha received his orders well—knock the Soviets off balance from the opening whistle, fluster them until their coolness breaks, cut back, dribble, and shoot, all at contrasting rhythms. The polyrhythmic mosaic of Garrincha's play danced literally to the gaps within the Soviet defense as the deceptive discourse of *futebol-arte* demolished the rigid scientific lines of *futebol-força*. Discipline, order, physical force, teamwork, the essential values that modernizing nations (be it the Soviet Union or Vargas's Brazil) sought to instill lay in tatters as Brazil's black players performed to an alternative rhythm, one that celebrated the individual, the cunning *malandro* whom modernity could not capture and who mischievously dethroned the Olympic champions.[25]

For millions of working-class Brazilians who faced a highly structured, hierarchical society, and the twin forces of industrialization and proletarianization, Garrincha's exploits underscored that at least in football, samba, and carnival individualism, instinct, and spontaneity are possible, as is a temporary assault (albeit solely for 90 minutes on a grassy pitch) upon the class and racial hierarchies of Brazilian society. However attractive these insurgent and creative values appeared to those in the *favelas*, they clashed directly with the mores of industrializing society. As Matthew Shirts observes on Brazil, "modernization translated into an emphasis on discipline and obedience to the detriment of improvisation, on teamwork in place of individual expression, on physical force instead of art, and on imported technocratic jargon where popular wisdom had previously prevailed." Yet if football served as a vehicle for dramatizing society, then *futebol-arte* articulated a discrete, gendered, working-class black identity in counterpoint to the nationalist, modernist tradition of the mid-twentieth century. To be sure, football has been a powerful mechanism for consolidating and "imagining" the multiracial nation, but Garrincha's *ginga* typified the Afro-Brazilian *geist*. The dribbling and artistry both confirmed and questioned the racial democracy thesis, posing the question, but not fully answering it: what is our collective, communal consciousness and who are we as a people and as a multiracial post-emancipation society? Theorists like Freye and Filho and politicians such as Getúlio Vargas believed football might help answer those questions, affirming the nationalist myth of multiracial equality but, on the *peladas* of the Rio shanty towns that swelled in size as employment opportunities lured black Brazilians from the countryside, soccer evolved as a cultural site for self and collective definition, a space for authorising black working-class identity, and a location for "speaking out," albeit in a relatively confined sociocultural space. Excluded from established political channels, Afro-Brazilians nonetheless converted performative activities, such as capoeira and football, into platforms for subtly critiquing the national narrative of racial harmony. From the black *peladas* emerged a different narrative form, one that celebrated *malandragem*, the cunning, double-dealing, streetwise hustling of the Rio *favelas* where racial power and control is tested often by surreptitious means.[26]

In Brazil's context, of course, such episodes of black activism and insurgency failed to reverse the process of economic deprivation in the slums, nor did they profoundly alter the nation's political map until the 1980s. Soccer may well have been an autobiographical site, but the extent to which Brazilian elites listened to or heard Afro-Brazilians "speaking out" on a soccer pitch remains an open question. Indeed, by effectively isolating the infrapolitics of resistance to expressive and performative culture, black Brazilians situated ideological and cultural concerns above more fundamental structural, economic, and class issues. The very centripetal forces that expelled the black working class into the ghettos were thus not fundamentally challenged by soccer and the prospect of defying racial and class hierarchies remained elusively bound to the football pitch. For many Brazilians of all racial types, however, soccer and the national football team served as little more than icons for national identity. If the sport contained a transgressive agenda, for millions of radio listeners and armchair supporters, black politics like the terms *preto* or *negro* were concealed within Brazil's unspoken racial consciousness. To a very real extent, Brazilians in the mid-twentieth century employed soccer as a symbol of racial democracy and they consciously manipulated the sport for nationalist agendas. But on the essentially black and mixed-race soccer pitches of Brazil's burgeoning cities, *futebol-arte* in its style and performativity proffered a somewhat dissident, counter-hegemonic narrative that re-"imagined" national identification and wove the black insurgent *malandro* into a social construction of Brazilian identity.

NOTES

1. Prado, *Seres, Coisas, Lugares*, 203. Brazil won the match 6–5, Leônidas da Silva scored his final two goals in the 93rd and 104th minutes, respectively. On race in American sport, see Miller, *Sport and the Color Line*, and McRae, *Heroes without a Country*.
2. Prado, *Seres, Coisas, Lugares*, 191, 194; Freyre, *Interpretação do Brasil*, 173; Freyre, "O negro no futebol brasilero," in Filho, *O Negro no Futebol Brasilero*, xi; Bellos, *Futebol*, 39. On the Apollonian-Dionysian contrast, see Nietzsche, *The Birth of Tragedy*.
3. DaMatta, *Carnivals, Rogues, and Heroes*, 15–16, 262–263. See also DaMatta and Neves, *Universo do Futebol*, 21; and Kuper, *Football against the Enemy*, 197.
4. On Brazilian soccer style see Leite Lopes, "The Brazilian Style of Football and Its Dilemmas," 86–87; Leite Lopes, "Success and Contradictions in 'Multiracial' Brazilian Football," 54; Wisnek, "The Riddle of Brazilian Soccer," 198–209; Helal and Gordon, "Sociologia, história e romance na construção da identidade nacional através do futebol," 64–70; Soares, "História e a invenção de tradições no futebol brasiliero," 30–36; Rosenfeld, *Negro, Macumba e Futebol*, 101–103.
5. Machado quoted in Bellos, *Futebol*, 40–41.
6. On football in national consciousness see Lever, *Soccer Madness*, 6; Lever, "Sport in a Fractured Society," 86; Leite Lopes, "A vitòria do futebol que incorporou a *pelada*," Leite Lopes, "Brazilian Style of Football," 86, 90, 95; Gordon, "História Social dos Negros no Futebol Brasileiro," 71–76; Alabarces, "Boundaries and Stereotypes," 1–12; Archetti, *Masculinities*.
7. Freyre in *Diário de Pernambuco*, 17 June 1938, quoted in Soares, "História e a invenção de tradições no futebol brasiliero," 31.
8. Leite Lopes, "Success and Contradictions in Multiracial Brazilian Football," 72–75.
9. Lutz, "The 'Bolt'—Never Fully Understood by Many People"; Lutz, "Playing Systems"; Kuper, *Football against the Enemy*, 76–84; Toledo, *Lógicas no futebol*, 27; Giulianotti, *Football*, 127–134.

The Spirit of Brazil 91

10. Toledo, *No País do Futebol*, 36–48; Lutz, "The 4-2-4 System"; C.R. Vasco da Gama, "História, 1944–1852: Quebrada a invencibilidade inglesa," http://www.netvasco.com.br; Hamilton, *An Entirely Different Game*, 195–201; Winner, *Brilliant Orange*, 28–66.
11. Archetti, "Masculinity and Football," 225; Archetti, *Masculinities*, 161–179; Lever, *Soccer Madness*, 48–69; Ronsbo, "The Embodiment of Male Identities," 157–175. See also Anderson's classic study on the concept of the national community, *Imagined Communities*.
12. Lopes, "Multiracial Brazilian Football," 55–70; Soares, "O Racismo no Futebol do Rio de Janeiro nos anos 20," 101–122; Herschmann and Lerner, *Lance de Sorte*, 42–56; Taylor, *The Beautiful Game*, 81–84; Lacey, *God Is Brazilian*.
13. Giordano Fattori, quoted in *Gazetta dello Sport*, 13 July 1950. See also http://www.bangu.net/informacao/cronicas/20060208.php; Bellos, *Futebol*, 64–66; Bellos, "The Golden Years," *The Observer*, 18 January 2004; Soares, "História e a invenção de tradições no futebol brasileiro," 39–43; Leite Lopes, "Multiracial Brazilian Football," 70–75.
14. Cleary, "Race, Nationalism, and Social Theory in Brazil"; DaMatta, *Carnivals, Rogues, and Heroes*, 60–115.
15. Freyre, *The Masters and the Slaves*, xvi, 372, 376; Freyre, *New World in the Tropics*, 146; Reichmann, Introduction to *Race in Contemporary Brazil*, 8; Skidmore, *Black into White*, 183–218; Schwartz, *Misplaced Ideas*, 1–17; Marx, *Making Race and Nation*.
16. Frigerio quoted in Sansone, *Blackness without Ethnicity*, 3; Dyck and Archetti, "Embodied Identities," 2, 4–5, 10, 18; Giulianotti and Armstrong, "Constructing Social Identities," 267–297; Giulianotti, *Football*, 14–22; Gordon and Helal, "The Crisis of Brazilian Football," 146.
17. Lever, "Sport in a Fractured Society," 91–93; Gordon and Helal, "The Crisis of Brazilian Football," 145–148; Duke and Crolley, "*Fútbol*, Politicians, and People," 103; Karush, "National Identity in the Sports Pages," 13; Rowe and Schelling, *Memory and Modernity*, 141.
18. Thomas, *The Body, Dance, and Cultural Theory*, 26–28, 45–46; Foucault, *The Will to Knowledge*, 151; Albright, *Choreographing Difference*, 120, 149; Desmond, "Embodying Difference," 34; Bhabha, *The Location of Culture*, 42; Gates, *Figures in Black*, 63–89; Kaplan, "Resisting Autobiography," 119; Marcus, *Auto/biographical Discourses*, 9, 289.
19. Smith, *Subjectivity, Identity, and the Body*, 188, 130; Gordon and Helal, "The Crisis of Brazilian Football," 139–158; Archetti, "Playing Football and Dancing Tango," 217–229; Browning, *Samba*; Fair, "Ngoma Reverberations," 109.
20. Sansone, *Blackness without Ethnicity*, 11; Reichmann, Introduction to *Race in Contemporary Brazil*, 1–13; Skidmore, "Bi-Racial U.S.A. vs. Multi-Racial Brazil," 373–386; Spivak, "Can the Subaltern Speak?" 82; Hanchard, "Black Cinderella," 61; Scott, *Domination and the Arts of Resistance*, 183; Scott, *Weapons of the Weak*; Kelley, "'We are Not What We Seem,'" 75–112; Sheriff, *Dreaming Equality*, 29–58.
21. Matory, "The English Professors of Brazil," 72–103; Gates, *The Signifying Monkey*, 6–10, 21; Stuckey, *Slave Culture*, 25; Browning, *Samba*, 28, 43–44, 50; Thompson, *Flash of the Spirit*, 18.
22. Lewis; *Ring of Liberation*, 18–50, 188–208; Capoeira, *The Little Capoeira Book*, 33–34; Holloway, "'A Healthy Terror,'" 646.
23. Lewis, *Ring of Liberation*, 98–100; Capoeira, *Little Capoeira Book*, 61–84; Brennecke, Amadio and Serrao, "Parâmetros dinâmicos de movimentos selecionados da Capoeira," 153–159.

24. Nascimento, *Pelé*, 84–95; Mendes in Bellos, *Futebol*, 95–120; Bianchi in Castro, *Garrincha*, 209–214; Rodrigues, *A Pátria em Chuteiras*, 186–187.
25. Prado, *Seres, Coisas, Lugares*, 216–217; Chernoff, *African Rhythm and African Sensibility*, 144–151; Thompson, "An Aesthetic of the Cool," 85–102, especially 91; De Frantz, *Dancing Many Drums*.
26. Shirts, "Sócrates, Corinthians, and Questions of Democracy and Citizenship," 104; Hanchard, Introduction to *Racial Politics in Contemporary Brazil*, 14; on the continuing relevance of *malandragem* see Helal, "Idolatria e Malandragem," 225–240.

6 *Black Man and White Ladyship* (1931)
A Manifesto

Renata Morresi

It was 1931, the year of the Colonial Exposition. Paris inaugurated *l'Exposition Coloniale et Internationale* in the Bois de Vincennes. With its display of colonial paraphernalia, exotic foods and perfumes, raw materials, and hand-made artifacts, and its pavilions of religious missions and the imposing reconstructions of Cambodian temples, the human zoos, and the circular train carrying visitors around, the exhibit intended to testify the grandeur of the colonial enterprise, celebrating its accomplishments and potentials and boasting of its civilizing function. The setting was designed to enhance the visitors' privileged panoptical stance, to allow them to enjoy a kaleidoscope of exotic difference without being contaminated by it: the "authentic" experience of the colonized, his/her "real" presence, but seemingly ages behind the colonizer's fellow citizens, constituted one of the main attractions of the exposition.[1] That no such stable, fixed, unassailably separate identities could exist has been amply demonstrated by later cultural criticism. That the exhibition's claims hid the inherent iniquity and degenerations of colonialism was evident to few contemporary opponents.

Among them the Surrealist group produced two manifestos, "Ne visitez pas l'Exposition Coloniale" and "Premier Bilan de l'Exposition Coloniale," denouncing the "carnaval de squelettes" staged in Vincennes.[2] The Surrealists had already expressed contempt of the *mission civilisatrice* in 1925, when another manifesto was issued, "La révolution d'abord et toujours," in favor of Abd-el-Krim's insurrection against French dominance in Morocco. In 1931, with the help of friends and companions and the Communist *Ligue anti-impérialiste*, they organized a counter-exhibition, "La vérité aux colonies," using as location the Soviet pavilion of the 1925 Decorative Arts Exposition. André Thirion, George Sadoul, and Louis Aragon were the principal organizers of the event. Where the official exhibition presented benefits and progress, the counter-exhibition bore evidence of miserable living conditions, forced labor, armed repression, and cultural subjugation. Christian devotional ornaments were used as samples of European fetishes; stories, statistics, photographs, art and sculptures were put on display for everyone to know "la vérité." Although their interest in the exposition's subjects was tainted by ideological and primitivistic strains, undeniably, in the intellectual history of anti-imperialism, the Surrealists' prolonged, flamboyant, and sustained opposition has given them legendary status.

It was 1931: young men in search of work were hoboing on a freight train to Memphis. Some were black, some white, riding the same train. Somewhere also on the train were two women dressed in overalls. When a fight broke out some of the white boys were forced to leave the train. They called the police and reported that they had been assaulted by a gang of blacks. The train was stopped near Paint Rock, Alabama, and Olen Montgomery, Clarence Norris, Haywood Patterson, Ozie Powell, Willie Roberson, Charlie Weems, Andy and Joy Wright, and Eugene Williams, aged 12 to 21 years old, were arrested and taken to jail to Scottsboro. Their arrest was meant to punish their transgression of the Jim Crow laws; when the officers discovered that two white women had been in their vicinity the official allegation became rape. After a first hasty trial, characterized by the incompetence of the defense, the intimidating presence of racist mobs and the gross racist bias of the jury and the prosecutor, the "Scottsboro boys" were sentenced to death, with the exception of 12-year-old Andy Wright, who received a life sentence.[3] The case would last for decades.

In 1931 Michel Leiris left for the mission Dakar-Djibuti, the expedition that produced the scenario of his famous self-ethnographic writings. Moreover, 1931 was also the year of Nancy Cunard's *Black Man and White Ladyship*, a text where self-ethnography intersects with avant-garde poetics and anti-imperialist discourse, crossing continents, challenging the British ruling class's amnesia, exposing the illegitimacy of the Scottsboro trial, confronting the historical legacy of exploitation inscribed in her surname.

Cunard, who at that time was Sadoul's employer at her Hours Press and had been Aragon's companion for some years, was among the unacknowledged friends who contributed to the organization of the counter-exposition. In that very year she began her research for the *Negro* anthology, a sort of portable counter-colonial exhibition that would be published three years later: in this massive work ironic reversal, the same strategy at the heart of the Surrealists' counter-exhibit, was the instrument to organize the anti-colonialist and anti-imperialist frame. Less studied and renowned than her male counterparts, Cunard was inspired by the same comparative yearning and inflammatory attitude, thus realizing a counter-colonial forum, a "solarized"[4] version of the traditional, paternalistic representations displayed at colonial expositions. Against the primitive in the hut she put the Marxist intellectual or the refined artist; instead of reassuring views and exotic landscapes she presented statistics on voting in the United States, a surrealist manifesto denouncing "Murderous Humanitarianism," the proclamation of emancipation in Uruguay, extracts from a pamphlet circulating in Belgian Congo. The common trait was not race per se, as a biological or cultural category, but the opposition to white racism and its colonialist civilization. The heterogeneity and discontinuity of its contributions demonstrated not so much the "editorial naiveté or overambitiousness"[5] of its editor, as critics like Michael North have implied, but rather the schizophrenic nature of racism itself.[6]

Zulu songs, Uruguayan *candombes*, the *soucouyan*, Baronga proverbs, magic in the Ubanghi-Shari, the *biguine* of the French Antilles, and a letter on the social role of the half-caste in Brazil were traces of overlapping histories and sophisticated cultures scattered across continents. Her "reading back" of historical documents—such as her "Proclamation of Emancipation of the Slaves," where she presents Abraham Lincoln as a cynical statesman indifferent to the institution of slavery and to the destiny of ex-slaves—was part of an epistemological attempt to recover "the underneath of history,"[7] hidden in archives or simply unnoticed, a project which was intertwined with the effort to give the status of cultural texts to objects that till then had been considered culturally irrelevant. Cunard's objective was to expose the responsibilities of colonialism and imperialism, and their destructive tools of subjugation, in suffocating peoples and cultures, but also to suggest a strategy to counteract them. Thus her extraordinary collection of contributions celebrated the global and indisputable significance of the black presence and its multifarious expressions, presenting a history written by black people themselves and not by colonial statistics. She did so by means of specific modernist devices: surrealist estrangement and the modernist fascination for the fragment as a repository of revelation.[8]

It seems to me that *Negro*, which was made by more than 150 contributors of different racial, ethnic, and national origins, demonstrates that the grammar of interracial relationship included more than neurotic fascination, consumption, or disguised contempt. And, as George Hutchinson has underlined, it is inadequate and unilateral to reduce all relations between races "under the single heading of white folks' sexual and racial neuroses."[9] Friendship was one of the great unacknowledged forces connecting people and at the basis of the politics of affectivity underrepresented by longtime privileged, dichotomous pairs of cultural discourse, such as black/white, man/woman, modern/primitive, colonial/postcolonial. Thus, while much white modernists' interest in "blackness" has been amply unmasked as a primitivist discourse of ahistorical formal affinity, of therapy against the evil of modernity or metaphorical artifice to represent it, in short as "a conduit to understanding 'civilized' man, art, and poetry, not an endpoint in itself,"[10] we have not sufficiently explored the engagement across races that could and did evolve into forms of partnership and networking, despite frictions and misunderstandings obviously fueled by painful social imbalances. It is not a matter of adding a name to the list of "good whites," but of taking seriously the effort to build a pacifist, interracial, transcultural discourse against the hegemony of colonialist discourse and racism. Despite the fact that Cunard's countercultural community of disparate intellectuals and radicals may today seem awkward, not informed by any theory of difference, quite unaware of their rich creolizing agency, often deluded by Soviet propaganda, quarrelsome, and frequently in disagreement as to means, methods and motives, from the pages of *Negro* they set up a process of "rememory," to use Toni Morrison's neologism, that can be considered as an attempt to deal with experience and complexity, where dissonance is not only a physiologic but even a creative factor.[11]

Nevertheless, commentators and scholars are still embarrassed by Cunard's militant and impassionate advocacy, her credentials as revolutionary activist being quite compromised by her matching too aptly the figure of the "Imperial Lady." Sexually ambiguous, a radical questioned for the aristocratic origins she publicly disowned, politically utopian and socially improper, a poet, editor, publisher, and journalist writing across genres, languages, and traditions, Cunard was fighting for the overturn of white hegemony, to reestablish the truth against the "scandaleux détournement de sens"[12] of white supremacists, undeterred by the plain evidence that seemed to include her among them. As a very white British Lady who exposed the responsibilities of whiteness (and white women); as a very rich heiress who rejected the wealth her great-grandfather had built on, among other things, slavery; as a bohemian who wrote and rallied against imperialism but did not renounce her public, empowering image of assertive eroticism; she shocked people and disoriented possible allies. Critics often find her intellectual motives compromised by her excessive and politically incorrect sexuality.[13] Cunard's racial and cultural trespassing hasn't been forgiven: despite her enormous effort to cherish and preserve black cultures she is still considered a radical-chic vulture, or she is dismissed as a victim of "interracial ontological incommunicability," the "perfect" interracial relationship obviously remaining a dream deferred.

The question with Cunard is that every time, entering the subject, one has first to wonder (at) how it could happen that an enormous amount of scattered knowledge and history concerning black cultures was collected precisely by such a "white lady," who alarmingly reminds us of Amiri Baraka's Lula and other such white female vultures. The question itself stems from a limited perspective that either makes her two positions—political activist, female bohemian—mutually exclusive or reduces her to a "brave" isolated exception, erasing the ways in which at that time women poets and authors like Cunard were actually asserting themselves as modern subjects—that is, by claiming their right to be public women intellectuals, by disidentification from given traditions and affiliations, and by the challenging self-positioning against Imperial culture and its traditional femininity, inspired by "the dream of an affective rather than an elective community."[14] As Marina Camboni has pointed out, reconstructing women's cultural presence in the modernist age means confronting the elusive traces of their historical talent to weave relations across national, racial, ethnic, and gender barriers.[15]

The next question usually regards her real motives. Notably the first and most pervasive explanation was Claude McKay's: "In her pamphlet *Black*

Man and White Ladyship the reader gets the impression that the Cunard daughter enjoys taking a Negro stick to beat the Cunard mother."[16] Reducing her manifesto to a *querelle* between silly female aristocrats, he dislodged her as an associate in the discourse against colonialism and racism. Portraying her as a bizarre radical chic, he took revenge for the incident that had put an end to their friendship. The *Negro* anthology was published as a collective self-production, no publishing house being willing to bear the costs: when he realized that Cunard couldn't afford to pay her contributors McKay, who was in desperate need of financial support and had broken his ties with most African American intellectuals, became furious and accused her of exploiting his work. None of McKay's exasperated invectives against W.E.B. Du Bois and Alain Locke have ever been taken so seriously in the analyses of their work as happened with Cunard's. It seems to me that McKay's rage has been used to erase her discourse by later commentators, who could take her seriously as a patron and sponsor, even as an inspiring model, but not as a cultural agent. The problem in the McKay-Cunard case was precisely their weakness in the cultural field: neither of them had the cultural or financial power to establish themselves as producers of literary and intellectual work. Their friendship was crushed by the double grip of an editorial market and a cultural sphere unable to acknowledge the value of their projects.

At the time of their correspondence McKay was living in Tangier, Morocco, while Cunard was constantly on the move between Provence and Normandy, where her little publishing house was settled; London, where she was desperately looking for a publisher; Belgium and Germany, where she traveled to visit a number of ethnological museums; and, in 1932, the United States and the Caribbean, where she went to collect first-hand materials for the volume. The Jamaican writer, a driving force of the Harlem Renaissance and on bad terms with most of its central exponents, a radical communist who couldn't bear the prescriptions of Soviet art, proud and oversensitive, aware of the rich and multifarious Afro-Caribbean culture and impatient with the excessive respectability of the black intelligentsia, declared that he was "very excited" about Cunard's project, and precisely because of her distance from the political complexities of the North American "racial" publishing market, from the intellectual rivalries among black writers, and from the hysterical atmosphere around the issues of interracial partnership and collaboration.[17] Cunard wrote to McKay as a master of black forms who could decisively contribute to her current effort: how to imagine and organize a transnational interracial forum against the forces of racial fascism and colonialism, and moreover in a single book.[18]

In December 1931, in the attempt to avoid the label of patronizing philanthropist and get "authorization" as a partner in the struggle for resistance and emancipation, Cunard sent McKay a copy of her *Black Man and White Ladyship*, which, she pointed out, was thought of as an introduction for an all-British audience. McKay acknowledged that the piece must have incensed the British ruling class, and its conflation of anti-imperialism and radical racial politics did constitute an innovative perspective, especially bold for the American scene of racial relations and therefore most likely subject to opposition and censorship by reactionaries and liberals alike.

Black Man and White Ladyship was a letter-manifesto Cunard addressed to her own mother, Lady Cunard, who opposed her daughter's love affair with an African American musician and eventually disinherited her. Combining private life and public discourse, showing how racism and sexism intersect and sustain each other and how desire molds politics, the text is an exercise of proto-feminism in claiming that "the personal is the political." *Black Man and White Ladyship* was a manifesto in that it established a new, progressive, and assertive subject exposing the responsibilities of "white womanhood" and setting for the *Negro* anthology a cultural agenda that included rewriting history, revising stereotypes, opposing legal (and physical) lynching, and studying black cultures as contemporary crucibles of an alternative modernity.

In what follows I explore how her pamphlet, reduced to a hysterical burst by former friends and later commentators, was actually the founding act of a political voice and a program, a manifesto exposing the horrors of colonialism and segregation and proposing an epistemological alternative, laying the foundations of the interracial cooperation necessary to produce the *Negro* anthology and support the dream of a "New Abolitionism."[19] In Nancy Cunard's work the surrealist lesson conflates with the conquests of the New Woman, modernist ethnography with the tradition of the first feminist activism within abolitionism, the fight for civil rights with modernist fascination for the borderline, where hypotheses of univocal positioning waver on the verge of new alienations and new negotiations, putting into question the very possibility of one core of essential truth. Cunard's experiments with her own public image, her ironic deconstruction of (white) gender and (gendered) race, are openly pursued in the writing of *Black Man and White Ladyship*.

The pamphlet had two editions: the first was privately published by Cunard in Toulon, the second was issued by Utopia Press, both in 1931. By mistake the second edition left out the title of the second part of the pamphlet, "Black Man," which is the counterpoint to the title of the first, "White Ladyship," and crucial to the formal structure of the piece. Opening the pamphlet an attached sheet reads "Address signatures and funds to Nancy Cunard Co *Everyman*, 66 Chandos Street, Strand, London, who will forward both to the Scottsboro Defence." *Everyman*, a periodical published by Purdom, employed Louise Morgan, the American journalist and wife of Otto Theis, the literary agent. What did the Scottsboro case have to do with what to many looked like an angry daughter's nasty trick on a popular socialite mother?

The flier that follows, which was printed in red ink, includes a short account of "the Scottsboro case in Alabama, U.S.A., the most outstanding and appalling example of race hatred and white prejudice against Negroes," giving some details of the "farcical trial" and the intimidating atmosphere surrounding it: "The 9 lads have been in jail since then, facing the electric chair—and facing it in a literal sense too. For several times during the different stages and successive appeals in the case (all rejected by Southern courts) the chair has been wheeled in front of their cells and left there as each new date set for execution approached." The flier then relates how the increasing mass protest throughout the world helped to raise the funds to support the boys' defense, how the defense won the appeal brought before the Supreme Court and how eventually the Supreme Court ruled that the defendants were entitled to a new trial.

> The appeal has been won—and this means? It means that the whole case will be re-tried in the same violently prejudiced Southern State lynch atmosphere. It means that every voice of protest is of imperative urgency and necessity to free the 9 innocent working class victims of American race hatred. If you are against the lynching and terrorisation of the most oppressed race in the world, if you have any innate sense of justice,
>   sign this protest
> and contribute towards the defence funds.

The Scottsboro case aroused global indignation. The mothers of the Scottsboro boys traveled around the world in a long series of rallies, speeches, and campaigning, the popular Leadbelly dedicated a song to them, graphic novels were printed to denounce the injustice,[20] authors wrote poems and pleas—among them Langston Hughes, who wrote the play *Scottsboro Limited*, and the poems "Christ in Alabama," "Scottsboro," "The Town of Scottsboro," and "Justice"—and public meetings, appeals and fund-raising events were organized to support their defense. The *British Scottsboro Defence Committee*, a group formed by the association of the *League Against Imperialism* and the *Negro Workers Association*, had as presidents Eleanor Rathbone and Naomi Mitchinson, and as secretaries Jomo Kenyatta and Gladys White. Nancy Cunard, honorary treasurer of the committee, contributed to arouse the interest of intellectuals, writers and artists, helped by an assorted group of volunteers.[21] Moreover, she dedicated to the Scottsboro boys a dramatic monologue, *Rape*, published on the pages of *The Afro-American*: giving voice to a southern farmer's wife who lusts after a black convict forced to work for her husband and charges him with rape when refused, the piece staged white women's complicity with the exploitation of the black working class. The monologue deconstructed white women's "inherent" purity and exposed the violence imbuing gender relations, across *and* within races, "dislodging the (white) woman as a privileged signifier of 'otherness.'"[22]

The Scottsboro appeal, with its emphasis on the international visibility of the case, was an attention-catching tool devised for mass circulation.

Inviting "non-racial" subjects to intervention in an episode of "racial violence," it exploded the notion of the case as a problem of U.S. interior politics and made it a global concern for civil rights. Thanks to her networks of friends and associates in Europe and the U.S., Cunard was able to collect the signatures and support of a vast array of personalities: Alastair Crowley, Stephen Spender, John Rodker, André Gide, Alberto Giacometti, René Crevel, Salvador Dalì, Samuel Beckett, Bronislaw Malinowski, Beatrice Hastings, Dorothy and Ezra Pound, Rosamund Lehmann, Laura Riding, Barbara Ker-Seymern, Elsa Hahn, Sinclair Lewis, George Antheil, Janet Flanner, Solita Solano, Bryher, H.D., Robert Macpherson, Norman Douglas, and Pino Orioli were some of the intellectuals, writers, and cultural agents who, moved by the injustice or out of sympathy for Cunard, signed the petition and contributed a short message of protest.

In 1932 the Scottsboro appeal and the request for contribution were thus included in the pamphlet and sent to influent friends and rivals, writers and intellectuals, politicians and aristocrats attending Lady Cunard's salon. Her circle gathered a variety of prominent personalities, such as Lord Chancellor R.E. Smith, Prime Minister Herbert Asquith, Lord Napier Alington, poet laureate Alfred Austin and the Prince of Wales; in short, exponents of the British intelligentsia willing to discuss openly the season at the Old Vic, not the issues of interracial encounter, desegregation, colonial exploitation, homosexuality, and Communism raised by the piece, and still less the trial of nine black Alabamian workers charged with rape. All the paratextual elements considered, attributing the pamphlet to the mere scheming of an angry daughter was a misunderstanding of its political positioning. The text had an assertive, sardonic, modernist spirit, but as a manifesto, as a cultural statement, it remained unfathomable to those who were expressly addressed, the imperial class of British higher-ups, who dismissed the piece as an embarrassing bad joke.[23]

Considered an impulsive and ungrateful attack against her mother, the pamphlet's most controversial and political aspects were either unconsciously removed by commentators, who were not able to read the piece within its transnational context of race and gender politics, or voluntarily suppressed by later editors.[24] Cunard's scornful assault at the racism of the British upper classes was imbued of a definite modernist stance, evident in the rejection of the "feminine" as an icon of domesticity and tradition that annihilates women's agency; in the use of montage as a narrative strategy; and in the focusing on "irregular" people and desires, criticizing the exoticization of black bodies, black women's sexual exploitation, the prejudice of "the pore ole down-trodden canticle-singing nigger daddy who used to be out to clown for the whites," and describing instead the advancement of "the very much up to date, well educated, keen, determined man of action" and introducing questions of cultural relativism: "How come, white man, is the rest of the world to be re-formed in your dreary and decadent image?"[25]

In the unacknowledged tradition of modern women's manifestos (and I think of H.D.'s *Borderline* and Marita Bonner's *To Be Young—a Woman—and Colored*, for example), issues of women's liberation, racial discrimination, and class struggle intersect, showing, as Ann McClintock underlines, that "race, gender and class are not distinct realms of experience, existing in splendid isolation from each other; nor can they be simply yoked together retrospectively like armatures of Lego. Rather, they come into existence in and through relation to each other—if in contradictory and conflictual ways."[26] Cunard's perspective, contiguous with the Surrealists' subversive spirit, sharing African American authors' vocation to the intersection of aesthetics and politics, following a genealogy of feminist self-fashioning, was devoted, among other things, to exposing the repressive function of conventional representations and to deconstructing the stereotyping device.

Modernist manifestos differ in intention, structure, and reception: some, like "Bondwomen" by Dora Marsden, were reserved to a small coterie; others, like Mina Loy's *Feminist Manifesto*, have remained unpublished for decades; yet others, like futurist manifestos, which expressed the highest point of the movement's literary production, have constituted the exemplar texts of a group.[27] *Black Man and White Ladyship*, despite being published as a pamphlet, starting as a letter to the mother and ending up addressing "the white man," shares with more formalized models of the genre the same programmatic, emphatic, epigrammatic tone vindicating a new assertive subject that publicly opposes and distances itself from an old, base, anachronistic one:

> The nigger Christy Minstrel conception prevails—to be fair, mainly with the older generation—as does the Pip and Squeak Daily Mirror children's page idea of the Bolshevik, all beard and bombs. So perhaps in London's high social circles of supposedly well educated arts-and-letters-appreciating aristocrats and hostesses it is a thing of age. It is certainly a thing of ignorance. (10)

Like other manifestos, this text cannot be interpreted out of context: the revolutionary import is informed by the conditions of its reception. "I have a Negro friend, a very close friend (and a great many other Negro friends in France, England and America). Nothing extraordinary in that" (1): statements like these, pronounced by a white woman in a segregated society, can have a shocking value. In such a case "la parole réprimée prend valeur insurrectionnelle."[28]

Cunard's heated argument is set in motion by the association of two unexpected and usually antithetical elements: the black man, that conservatives and supremacists would see as a figure of savagery, naiveté, and backwardness, and the worthy white woman, the lady, incarnation of angelical virtues and personification of the Empire. The parataxical structure of the title, alluding to a scandalous and illicit coupling, is meant to shock the conventional audience whom the pamphlet is addressed to and becomes the instrument of a chiasmus that is central to the structure of the text. The double reversing of stereotypes is charged with implications, since each element is deconstructed and reimagined within this "oxymoronic" relation between "black man" and "white ladyship." The same chromatic chiasmus and opposition between identity and representation would be taken up by Fanon, years later, in his well-known *Peau noire, masques blancs* (1952). Cunard's text instead is structured on the sexual and racial intersection given by that "and."

The pamphlet opens on "Her Ladyship": in her description of Lady Cunard in her familial/imperial setting (the house of Grosvenor Square she rented from Lord Asquith), Cunard focuses on the icon of the "White Lady," de-raced and asexual body, moral champion of domestic virtues and patriotic superiority, revealing its conflation of class privilege, imperial arrogance and racist bias. "Hello Maud, what is it now—drinks, drugs or niggers?" (1): this is the challenge addressed to Lady Cunard by a rival socialite lady, and it sets the tone of the following reactions. The response to the author's relationship with a black man ranges from fainting spells, embarrassed circumlocutions, and petty expedients to patent slandering and racial slur and culminates in Thomas Beecham's exclaiming that she "ought to be tarred and feathered!" (3). The reference to the infamous practice of lynching shows how Cunard's trespassing of the color line was in the first place perceived as a sexual transgression. Aware of it, Cunard used her mother's American origins to set off a scornful attack against the American dread of miscegenation that here intersects British high society's obsession for rank:

> But, your Ladyship, you cannot kill or deport a person from England for being a Negro and mixing with white peoples. You may take a ticket to the cracker southern states of U.S.A. and assist at some of the choicer lynchings which are often announced in advance. You may add your purified-of-that-horrible-american-twang voice to the yankees outbursts: America for white folks—segregation for the 12 million blacks we can't put up with—or do without. . . . No, with you it is the other old trouble—class. Negroes, besides being black (that is, from jet to as white as yourself but not so pink) have not yet "penetrated into London Society's consciousness." You exclaim: they are not "received." They are not found in the Royal Red Book. Some big hostess gives a lead and the trick is done! (2)

In his autobiography McKay wrote that Cunard was here ridiculing her mother's American accent, "[y]et the American Negroes she professes to like speak the same language as her mother, with slight variations" (345). But at a closer reading it is evident that the operation was quite the opposite: in fact,

Cunard was making fun of the Lady's obsession for "purity," of her refusing to admit that she did share an American accent with black Americans. Cunard thus denounces the social construction of whiteness, the notion of whites as morally superior, their effort to "transcend their raced bodies"[29] at the other's expense. Cunard collates apparent disparate sketches from the Lady's everyday life in a list that serves to shed light on the way white women are especially busy performing their whiteness: obsessed by the outer image; pretending ignorance in matter of sexuality and politics; compulsively accumulating commodities, either art objects or clothes; abusing servants; becoming the moral controllers of a racist order. Staging the "White Lady" is here inescapably intertwined with serving capitalism. Lady Cunard is thus shown in a series of farcical sketches: while she details to the *Sunday Express* the fortune she spends on clothes, while she leaves through the pages of a book where her photographs appear, busy at "the Art game of Picture racket" (4), during a discussion on "the tabooed subject of pederasty . . . frequently introduced and worried like a fox in death-throes by a whole pack of . . . allusions" (5), or during a scene to the butler. The mocking tone emphasizes the blind conformism to prescribed social rituals, and the Lady and her circle are thus observed, like "the savages" in Colonial Exhibits, under a scrutinizing light, while the observer poses herself at a distance: "They move and shift together in a crazy blur of dixhuitième, gold-plate and boiserie, topped with the great capital C, Conversation, rounded off with snobbery and gossip. The company has got mixed up with the background and the savonnerie it all makes waves for a moment in the wind of this distant and real place where I find myself suddenly wondering if it all still goes on" (7).

The practice recalls the "ethnographic surrealism" described by Clifford:

> The ethnographic label suggests a characteristic attitude of participant observation among the artifacts of a defamiliarized cultural reality. The surrealists were intensely interested in exotic worlds, among which they included a certain Paris. Their attitude, while comparable to that of the fieldworker who strives to render the unfamiliar comprehensible, tended to work in the reverse sense, making the familiar strange. The contrast is in fact generated by a continuous play of the familiar and the strange, of which ethnography and surrealism are two elements.[30]

Making the familiar strange: the Lady and the upper class surrounding her are mercilessly inspected through a deforming lens that shatters abstract ideals of culture and civilization under whose headings grim colonial ventures are pursued. In the second part of the pamphlet, "Black Man," what is strange and apparently far becomes familiar: instead of the close and scornful examination offered in the first part the author travels back in time to recover a repressed space and a distant episode: the Atlantic passage and slavery. The text here leaves the elitist, metropolitan, private space of Cunard's imperial family to enter the uncomfortable recess of the Middle Passage. Myth gives way to history and Cunard's interest in blackness turns away from mere aesthetic primitivism and enters a new political positioning. If her contemporaries' fascination for *art nègre* often ran parallel to obliterating the memory and history of those who had produced it, in *Black Man and White Ladyship* the author abandons primitivism as a formal device or as a longing for primeval origins and introduces the reality of black subjects, the way they have been discarded both by history and from slave ships, hinting at the debt her shipping family still has toward them. Her revisionary urge leads to the critique of modernity later effected in *Negro* from multiple African diasporic viewpoints. The figure of the ship, "a living, micro-cultural, micro-political system in motion," is here central, as in Gilroy's Black Atlantic, as an element to represent and expose the asymmetrical connections, veiled recurrence and unspeakable transactions of modern history.[31]

> Consider the following extract of what happened. From 1619 to after the middle of the 19th century hundreds of thousands of Negroes, men, women and children, were sold, stolen and torn out of Africa. They were herded into boats at one time especially built for their transport. The trade prospered; more profits were made at it, and more quickly, than at any other trade in history. Its apex, in number of slaves shipped from Africa to the New World, was the last two decades of the 18th and the first two of the 19th centuries—about the time there was most agitation for its abolition. An estimate puts the figure at over 100,000 slaves a year. On the special boats the slaves were manacled to each other two by two and to the ship itself; a space of 6 ft. by 1 ft. 4 was allotted each on the deck for the many weeks of the voyage. At night they were stuffed into the hold. Many would be found dead in the morning. Those that looked for death from starvation were forcibly fed—many hanged themselves, leapt overboard, died of the flux and of despair. They were made to jump up and down in their irons after eating; this was called "dancing," to obtain exercise. They were flogged, tortured and maimed. After three or four of such passages the slave ships had to be abandoned—having become unusable from filth. The stench of them spread some four miles out of sea. Once landed the slaves were sold by auction. Everyone knows how things went for them till 1863. 244 years of slavery in America, and Charles Lynch existed—a Virginian *Quaker*. For the first six months of this year, 1931, 30 cases of Negro lynching are reported. (7)

In a dizzy synthesis Cunard travels from the "unreal," artificial world of British aristocracy through the exposition of historical facts concerning the Middle Passage to the harsh reality of lynching and the urgency of the

Scottsboro case, "this distant and real place where I find myself" (7), the crossroads where history, aesthetics, and identity meet. Slavery, the mothers of black soldiers segregated in a special ship to visit the graves of their sons in France, the sexual and economic exploitation of black women in the plantation system, the stereotype of the black minstrel, Harlem and the Renaissance, African sculptures and the British Museum: in a juxtaposition of sketches resembling a modernist montage Cunard condemns whites' ignorance of their historical faults and lays the bases of her research project to record black cultures and their voices.

Once again reversal is the formal organizing principle at the heart of Cunard's strategy for raising awareness:

> Now how does it seem to you put this way: several hundreds of thousands of whites have been torn from their country, chained in pairs to boats, flogged across the Atlantic, flayed at work by a nigger overseer's whip, hunted and shot for trying to get away, insulted, injured, thrown out, emprisoned, threatened with lynching if they dare ride in the black man's part of the train, their houses burned down, if, despite everything, they seem to get too prosperous, their women spoken of as "dirty white sluts" and raped at every corner by a big Negro buck, told there's no job in the office for anyone with a bleedin' white mug and that their stinking white bitches needn't go on trying to "pass" nor hope to send their white vermin to any decent school—Over 300 years of it in all its different phases, substituting white for black all along the line. . . . You would say Justice was strangely absent. You would say the hell of a lot more than that. (8)

In this passage Cunard exposes the brutal fiction of the color line to her conservative audience: the unexpected reversal is meant to produce the sudden recognition of the violence of what is implicit, unspoken, and taken for granted. The encounter of disparate objects, usually alien to each other—the white body and racial violence, the black body and racial privilege—generates the sense of displacement and prodigious epiphany experienced in front of surrealist involuntary sculptures. What seems "natural," race with its destiny and consequences, explodes and reveals its artificial construction. The myth of the "100 per cent supreme examples of white womanhood" (8) is unmasked as an expedient to hide a history made of slave trade, exploitation, and abuse of black women. Brutally describing the white woman as the victim of rape is here a device to shock Cunard's aristocratic audience and reveal what has been the rule of the slave system, where black women were abused and moreover used as a foil to the fictional ideal of purity for white ones. When the author mimics a white racist Virginian who claims "d'black women 'r allright separately," she points out that "d'black women 'r allright, were very much allright for breeding bastards as new hands on the master's plantation," showing how his yearning for purity is betrayed by (and based on) a history of exploitation: "the fathers and mothers and ancestors of this superlative womanhood (as well as the manhood that so superlatively 'protects' it) were in a very great number suckled at the black breast" (8). A history inscribed even in his accent.[32]

Rewriting and montage were Cunard's favorite exercises in criticism: the practice became an epistemological strategy to read and expose the past and present infamous contradictions of whiteness. In *Black Man and White Ladyship* avant-garde poetics and racial politics conflate to produce a manifesto against racism, where a feminist vision is central, not only as defense of women's rights and integrity, but also as deconstruction of interiorized stereotypes and celebration of interconnections free from pre-arranged labels. If, as Rosi Braidotti writes, "[p]olitics in this framework has as much to do with the constitution and organization of affectivity, memory and desire as it has with consciousness and resistance,"[33] it is precisely the reorganization of Cunard's personal and intellectual alliances outside the spaces allotted to a white woman of her social class that leads her to a reassessment of spatial and temporal racial relationships, putting the Middle Passage at the center of contemporary cultural discourse, as one of the founding events of (counter)modernity.

The intertwining of personal passion and ideological commitment may seem politically incorrect, but it is precisely at this moment of contiguity, of shared political stance, acknowledgment of debt and loss of familiar bonds that her engagement in black culture stopped being mere "political tourism" or "Negrophilia' and became an attempt at collaboration *within* difference.[34]

NOTES

1. "Natives were the necessary supplement that ensured the authenticity of the Exposition and brought a 'savage' aspect to it. . . . The organizers went to lengths to prevent assimilated natives from appearing in Western dress, except in carefully controlled circumstances: in those few cases, the point of the display was the inappropriateness of natives in such clothes, 'en travesti.'" Morton, *Hybrid Modernities*, 112–113. Patricia Morton has explored the inescapable hybrid quality of the Colonial Exposition. On the 1931 Paris Exposition see also the extensive bibliography edited by Geppert, Coffey, and Lau, *International Exhibitions, Expositions Universelles and World's Fairs*.
2. In Nadeau, *Histoire du surréalisme*, 325–326, 330–333.
3. See Carter, *Scottsboro*; Kelley, *Hammer and Hoe*; Goodman, *Stories of Scottsboro*; Lee, *Scottsboro Alabama*.
4. In photography solarization there is a reversal of tones caused by prolonged exposure to a bright light; it turns the whole or part of the negative image into a positive. Cunard's own solarized photographs taken by Barbara Ker-Seymer are examples of playful (and disquieting) subversion of race and gender limits. Jane Marcus offers an interpretation of the photographs in her *Hearts of Darkness*, 132–137.
5. Edwards, *The Practice of Diaspora*, 316. Edwards argues that the book demonstrates "the impossibility of anthologizing blackness" and acknowledges

Negro's aspiration to posit itself between the archive, the census, the map, and the museum.

6. Michael North defines *Negro* as a "miscellaneous, collective, disorganized, supergeneric sprawl of a book," and adds: "too heavy to lift comfortably, the anthology is global in reach, miscellaneous as to contributors, and generically indiscriminate in the extreme." North, *The Dialect of Modernism*, 177, 189. North suggests as prototypes of "the black anthology" Jean Toomer's *Cane* and Du Bois's *The Souls of Black Folk*, which are undoubtedly modern masterpieces, but hard to reconcile to the notion of a collective work. It seems to me that what North indicates as the anthology's shortcomings are signs of a new historiographic perspective, an attempt to write history "from the bottom up," where contradictions and fragmentation are inevitable, that is comparable to archival projects such as the Works Progress Administration Slave Narratives Project. It is, in other words, "a new kind of history, a history in which the people are the historians as well as the history, telling their own story in their own words." Botkin, *Lay My Burden Down*, 5.

7. Cunard, "Proclamation of Emancipation of the Slaves," in Cunard, *Negro*, 15.

8. During the revision of this essay, I came across the work of Laura Winkiel, who similarly explores the relation between Surrealism and the making of *Negro* in "Nancy Cunard's *Negro*."

9. Hutchinson, *Harlem Renaissance in Black and White*, 110.

10. Gikandi, "Picasso, Africa and the Schemata of Difference," 458.

11. See the concept of *décalage* as crucial discrepancy, "a necessary haunting," and a difference "that allows movement," as explored by Edwards in *The Practice of Diaspora*, 14–15.

12. "Premier bilan de l'Exposition coloniale," in Nadeau, *Histoire du surréalisme*, 330.

13. Ann Douglas, for example, portrays Cunard as "a glamorous, alcoholic, British heiress, poet, rebel and profligate." Douglas, *Terrible Honesty*, 272.

14. Gandhi, "Sketch for an Ethics of Cosmopolitanism," 51.

15. See Camboni, "Networking Women."

16. McKay, *A Long Way from Home*, 344.

17. McKay, "Letter to Nancy Cunard."

18. Elsewhere I have explored their correspondence, which in the course of two years, between 1931 and 1933, displaced the traditional cartography of modernist relations and discourses on race. Morresi, "Racial Shake, 'Jagged Harmony' and Circum-Atlantic Networks."

19. Nancy Cunard elaborated the notion in "White Lies," 3.

20. See the graphic book recently rediscovered and edited by Lee, *Scottsboro Alabama*.

21. "[A]n unemployed or itinerant pedlar-newspaper seller, who became so interested in the case that he volunteered to get signatures in pubs, etc. and sell the Scottsboro postcard. . . . Bob Scanlon, ex-boxing champion of Colour, and Norah Andrews, English wife of Gordon Andrews, then secretary to Paul Robeson, also had lists . . . Protests were later sent to American authorities, and Funds to William Patterson, Sec. of Scottsboro Defence, I.L.D., New York." Cunard, "Scottsboro appeal and petition with signatures."

22. Sharpe, "The Unspeakable Limits of Rape," 226.

23. In the copy of the second edition kept in London at the British Library there is a short note signed "TmB" (supposedly Thomas Beecham): "Dear John, many thanks for this regrettable work, Edith says she can detect the hand of Wyndham Lewis." Beecham came from a family that had made a fortune in pharmaceutical products and, also thanks to Lady Cunard's sponsorship,

he had become the conductor who gave an important impulse to the British Opera scene. It is strange that "TmB" could suppose that the misogynist, anticommunist, self-centered Lewis was an accomplice in Cunard's operation, unless we consider what Lewis had published in *Blast* among the list of things he hated: "Beecham (pills, opera, Thomas)."

24. The pamphlet's most controversial passages were bowdlerized in Ford, *Nancy Cunard*, 103–108. Unaware of the fact, subsequent editor Bonnie Kime Scott published the same abridged version in *The Gender of Modernism*, 68–92. The original edition is now available in Moynagh, *Essays on Race and Empire*, 181–196.

25. Cunard, *Black Man and White Ladyship*, 11. Further page references to this work are included in the text.

26. McClintock, *Imperial Leather*, 5.

27. See Lyon, *Manifestoes*, and Caws, *Manifesto*.

28. Abastado, "Introduction à l'analyse des manifestes," 7.

29. Dyer, *White*, 25.

30. Clifford, *The Predicament of Culture*, 121.

31. Gilroy, *The Black Atlantic*, 4.

32. See Hurston, "Characteristics of Negro Expression": "it has often been stated by etymologists that the Negro has introduced no African words to the language. This is true, but it is equally true that he has made over a great part of the tongue to his liking and has had his revision accepted by the ruling class. No one listening to a Southern white man talk could deny this" (24–25).

33. Braidotti, *Metamorphoses*, 20.

34. See Moynagh, "Cunard's Lines: Political Tourism and Its Texts," 70–90, and Archer-Shaw, *Negrophilia*.

7 "What We All Long For"
Dionne Brand's Transatlantic Metamorphoses

Franca Bernabei

In her beautifully wrought non-fiction work *A Map to the Door of No Return*, which bears the provocative subtitle *Notes to Belonging*, the Trinidad-born Canadian writer Dionne Brand has her first-person narrator tell about an unexpected illumination she receives during a casual encounter with an African parking-lot attendant in Toronto. "What's happening?" she asks in a hurried act of recognition prompted more by the need to speed up the formalities of parking her car than by the obligation she feels to "preserve the thin camaraderie of the Diaspora." "Look," he says, "I come from one of the oldest cities in the world. The oldest civilization. They build a parking lot and they think that it is a civilization."[1] Shaking with laughter—which the African promptly adds to—Brand envisions this man surveying "their" civilization while spending most of his days squeezed into a parking-lot attendant's booth. She guesses that he was probably dislocated up by a war and must now be brooding over the luck of his landing in "this unending parking lot, which is the sum of its civilization, laughing sardonically at himself."[2] As to her own location, she ponders over the fact that she does not come from any old city and her civilization is indeed represented by the parking lot. And yet, for a flashing moment she recognizes the implication of the African's "they."

The non-place of the Toronto parking lot, a provisional and relatively anonymous transit point, but still requiring that one follow a set of unavoidable procedures in order to gain entry, becomes the terrain of the "thin camaraderie of the Diaspora"—a terrain already cultivated by the narrator's resort to "a language from another time," a common language which she uses to address her interlocutor: "give me a break, bro."[3] This camaraderie, however brief, leads to their rehearsing an exemplary script of Geertzian thick description followed by a "grim" but ultimately liberatory overturning of the notion of modernity as a manifestation of the West's cultural if not ontological priority. Indeed, since macrosociologists have recently argued that modernity is a distinct type of civilization marked by a recognizable social *imaginaire*,[4] it is perhaps the concept of civilization in the singular, with its accumulated heritage of competitive meanings and demarcating strategies,[5] that is finally subjected to the scathing, historicizing critique of these reluctant citizens of the North American parking lot.

Brand is a black, lesbian, (crafts)woman who, in her own words, was originally "exported" from the Caribbean to Canada "on the wings of international capital" with the unfulfilled intention of going back.[6] Her work is firmly based not only on the diasporic habit of surveying the hegemonic program of modernity but also on the relentless questioning of her geo-historical location in relation to it. Her polyhedric writing, in the form of prose and poetry, fiction and non-fiction, has multiplied the ways in which she is present on the Canadian scene[7] and suggests her ongoing effort to make sense of—and give sense to—the complexities of her heritage, world historical contingencies and her problematic, dissenting relation to the "civilization of the parking lot."

Brand's investigations range from an initial concern with oral history, documentary film and sociological reporting to autobiographical and composite non-fiction. They have evolved through a constant digging into the linguistic/expressive possibilities of both poetry and prose. One should not forget, however, that her investigations also represent a continuous sequence of "repositionings" which respond to the need to keep her voice sounding: a voice which is "constantly recalibrating its register against social forces as well as against the internal stagnation of community in the face of those forces."[8] In addition, Brand's appeal to the sonorities of the voice, with its implications of corporeality, vocal distinctiveness, and pluralistic relationality,[9] aptly underlines her aesthetic desire for beauty and her love for and faith in the liberatory and redeeming power of language.

She deeply believes in the performative nature of writing and reading as acts of desire, "of wanting to be wanted, to be understood, to be seen, to be loved," and these are equally acts "of translation, of succumbing or leaning into another's body idiom."[10] There is, in Brand's work, a confluence of political/social responsibility and belief in human, affective and aesthetic involvement in the condition of those excluded from the main narrative of Western civilization and in that of the (im)possible citizens of contemporary globalization. This confluence "voices" or "multi-voices" the interpretive translations and transatlantic passages which configure what has been variously defined as Brand's "grammar of dissent,"[11] her "dialogic of differences,"[12] and her "antisystemic"[13] writing, if not "transwriting."[14]

Indeed, the notion of the Caribbean as a crucible of different kinds of modernity finds in Brand a significant, and perhaps unique, rerouting.[15] The Caribbean stands for many things: an "inter-American contact zone *par excellence*,"[16] the paradigmatic archipelago of contemporary urban syncretic cultures or, rather, the last of the great meta-archipelagoes, lacking either a boundary or a center.[17] Her itinerary strictly entwines her "writing story" and her "life story" and, it should be said, has not only followed the propensity of the Caribbean to extend itself "past the limits of its own sea,"[18] but has also stretched its aquatic borderlessness to include multiple forms of landfalls and cross-cultural and civilizational passages careening from sea to land, from land to sea, from sea to ocean, and from ocean to ocean (the Indian, the Atlantic, and, recently, the "Canadian" Atlantic and the Pacific).

While the author's liquid and gendered imagery/imaginary, as well as her politics/poetics of "drifting" (rather than "flowing"), have already been subjected to close scrutiny,[19] in this chapter I will focus on her latest investigation of the nature of locality and community in Canada and, I should add, the globalized, multidimensional "modernity-world"[20] at large. In her previous work Brand has shown a strong concern with colonial, neocolonial and patriarchal structures of oppression. She has also exposed the ambivalence of decolonized nationalisms[21] and embraced the Maurice Bishop's New Jewel Movement in Grenada.[22] Subsequently, she has grieved over the wounds of its failure. But in her current work she has increasingly focused on the conflictual tensions which now beset both local and global realities and embrace the transformations and possibilities of becoming, which this new compression of life-worlds entails.[23]

ATLANTIC RUPTURES: THE DOOR OF NO RETURN

A Map to the Door of No Return represents a significant move in this direction and is centered on the conditions of blacks in the New World diaspora. Here the different forms and genres which have marked Brand's writing so far seem to crisscross or blend in one single text, so that its intentionally designed structural fragmentation is both counterpointed and underpinned by the fluidity of a prose in which narration and meditation, essay and poetry, life-writing and historical/archeological/geographical probing harmoniously flow into each other. Personal memories and musings—brief recollections about childhood, travel impressions, anecdotes about casual encounters, descriptions of global cities and Canadian suburbs, the evocation of the revolutionary experience of Grenada and its shattering consequences for her life and politics—entwine with excerpts from colonial documents, letters and reports, map books, newspaper articles, and writers she loves or with whom she engages in a critical confrontation (for example, Césaire, Rhys, Walcott, Naipaul, Neruda, Galeano, Glissant, Morrison, Coetzee).

In this way, the act of writing (or should we say translating?) the self is inseparable from the contingencies of its contradictory location and locatability in the world, while the "private act of self-writing" becomes "the cultural act of the self reading."[24] Moreover, the writer's existential and discursive itinerary appears not as a linear sequence of events, but as a series of positions (positionings) distributed on that map which is announced in the paratext, a map which they themselves actually make up and, at the same time, make out. In light of the cartographic model so openly evoked and interrogated, we might also say that through this spatializing dissemination of "notes" or "signposts," as she herself defines them elsewhere,[25] the writer's chorographic map, by definition concerned with the specific and the particular, bifocally reflects itself on the synoptic, more extensive and measurable cartographic scale of the globe.[26]

This chorography, however, is more metaphorical and imaginative than strictly disciplinary. The more so because Brand is fully aware of the narrative/cognitive rather than descriptive impulse which underlies cartography: "The book is a map. The form, the sketches and ruminations, as early maps were, allowed me the freedom to pick up an idea and examine it in different ways. The way it travelled was in some ways the way a poem travels. I could reach out and follow an idea. I could drop one thread and then pick up another one."[27]

It is evidently this "undisciplined" imaginative freedom of movement, this meandering, anti-systemic and thoroughly multidirectional probing of an idea that—in spite of Brand's propensity to consider cartographers mostly as "artists and poets," "dreamers and imaginers"[28]—finally explodes their synthesizing, pre-established geography and knowledge of an order of places as well as their disengagement from the itineraries that were initially the very condition of the map's possibility.[29] Concurrently, Brand intends that this same freedom of movement critically reflect on its own epistemic accountability.

This is the figurative method Brand has chosen to pursue her inquest, and it enables her to interact, from the outset, with the topos which is its paradoxical goal and the very ground of its vexed topological hermeneutics. The author describes "the door of no return" as "a collective phrase for the places, the ports, where slaves were taken to be brought to the Americas."[30] It is, therefore, a geohistorical site of forced departures which provoked psychic tearing, the unmeasurable attrition of enslaved labor, the humiliations of colonialism and racism, and which, in its concrete referentiality, still causes inconsolable grief to the descendants of the slaves who visit it. But being "a place where a certain set of transactions occurred, perhaps the most important of them being the transference of selves," this site which still affects the diasporic condition of blacks in the New World is also construed as a spiritual location, both real and metaphoric, imaginary and imagined, and ultimately "mythic."[31]

In the final count, Brand's mapping of the region is based on "random shards of history and unwritten memoir"; it relies on "sound or intuition, vision or aesthetic," on "any wisp of a dream," as evidence.[32] As she herself points out, it is not aimed at defining a place, but pursuing the intricate ways in which "those places, those ports, had metamorphosed" into a lingering metaphor for black uprooting.[33] And since to "have one's belonging lodged in a metaphor is voluptuous intrigue; to inhabit a trope; to be a kind of fiction," to live in the black diaspora is "to live as a fiction—a creation of empires, and also self-creation." As chronotope and trope founded on the violent erasure of origins and on a "million exits multiplied," the door is therefore "a site of belonging or unbelonging." It is, in a desolate sense, a "creation place . . . at the same time that it signified the end of traceable beginnings."[34] And it is exactly because she relies so persistently on this logic of inclusive distinction that Brand can state, in an interview, that her intention in the book was to chart a journey to a new kind of identity and existence in an attempt to challenge all sorts of identitarian fixations: in short, "to live in another kind of world."[35]

Such an aspiration to detour[36] the consequences of that inaugural oceanic rift and give a new twist to received notions of continuity and belonging is clearly manifested when Brand firmly impugns any revendication of origins. She opposes both those configurations conceived by nation-states as "exclusionary power structures which have legitimacy based solely on conquest and acquisition" and that weak gesturing at inclusion "used by the powerless to contest power in a society," which ends up setting "calcified hyphenated narratives" against the "calcified Canadian nation narrative." This critique of the "complicated juxtapositions of belonging and not belonging, belonging and intrabelonging" which underlie the relationship between immigrant minorities and the nation-state, is also extended to include the so-called romance of Africa as the lost matrix to which it is still possible to go back. As she reflects while on her first transatlantic flight to Africa, "Why do I slip into the easy-enough metaphor of Africa as body, as mother? . . . But this is not return. I am not going anywhere I've been, except in the collective imagination . . . I cannot go back to where I came from. It no longer exists. It should not exist."[37]

And yet, Africa, with its looming absent presence, haunts the recollections of Brand's childhood in Guayguayare, the place where she was born and which, as Brand would probably say, choreographed her beginnings. In tracing her younger self's perception of place, the autobiographical I remembers how it was territorially constituted: "to the south . . . on a clear day, you could see the mainland of South America. . . . To the north was the hinterland of Trinidad . . . To the west was the bird's beak of Venezuela and to the east, the immense Atlantic gaping to Africa." The pervasiveness of the ocean, its uncontrollable sovereignty and self-sufficiency, its originating "ownership" of the islanders, both insulating and suggestive of the magnificent and terrifying largeness of the world, framed and "reduced . . . to its unimportant random meaning" the life of a people marked by brutality, self-hatred, and disaffection. On the other hand, Brand experienced the ocean, her first memory, not only in terms of its immediate, all-encompassing, contextually informing, and internally historicized impact, but also according to its mythic construction as filtered through the conditioning perspective of an outside: "a full unending gasp of water called ocean or the savage sea which has shipwrecked you on this island, and which is the barrier between you and civilization."[38]

The ambivalence of that "you" signals the dislocation or mislocation of the colonial "inside" and is finally resolved when it is made clear that the feeling of being shipwrecked applies to the child's grandparents who are waiting for the BBC news to be rescued. Indeed, this narrative moment pivots around the lopsided relationship between the local and the global as symbolized by the role of the radio in opening a door "over there," in bringing the world to the island, along with "the strange intimacy of coveted estrangement, of envied cosmopolitanism." This listening was suspended only on Sundays and at Christmas, when through the relatives' voices (the voices of those "gone a foreign," as they say in the Caribbean) it was now the island that entered the world, "listening for itself." This presence of the radio proved that the people were shaped by British consciousness. On the other hand, they were also shaped by "an unknown self. The African" and this duality—this sense that "some being had to be erased and some being had to be cultivated"—was fought every day. So that the "'Dark Continent' was a source of denial and awkward embrace . . . No amount of denial, however, dislodged this place, this self, and no amount of forgetting obscured the Door of No Return."[39]

The theme of forgetting trenchantly inaugurates Brand's speculative route thanks to the opening evocation of the figure of her grandfather who was unable to satisfy his grandchild's desire to know who his ancestors were. His inability to remember and, concurrently, his unwillingness to invent a genealogy to appease the child, reveals that this memory gap didn't just concern family bonds, but "was a rupture in history, a rupture in the quality of being. It was also a physical rupture, a rupture of geography." At the end, however, her grandfather's forgetting of places and names is perceived not as a personal failure but as a gift passed on from generation to generation: "The only gift that one, the one bending reluctantly toward the opening, could give." The opening, of course, is that of the "Door of No Return" and the elision of the name seems to stress not so much the departure as the singularly performed, and collectively repeated, recalcitrant act of entrance of the blacks into the New World. After this, Brand concludes, "a map was only a set of impossibilities, a set of changing locations." Indeed, "a map, then, is only a life of conversations about a forgotten list of irretrievable selves."[40]

This ambivalent line of thought is further probed in the part dedicated to the genesis of her novel *At the Full and Change of the Moon* (1999), whose title, as she explains, is taken from Thomas Jefferys's observations regarding the best time and the most favorable locations ("At the full and change of the moon the sea will rise four feet perpendicular") to land the ships bringing slaves to the island of Tobago. In underlining the unintended irony of the piece written by the geographer to King George III, which she extensively reports, Brand also comments on the dissembling qualities of its erudite, gorgeous prose.[41] As she so cogently highlights, this passage proves, firstly, the radical revolution in the concept of space as global, homogeneous, and undifferentiated, which was brought about by the paradigm shift of modernity. Secondly, it reveals how the new image of the world as circumnavigable and the Ocean as main conduit of unhindered access and communication triggered a "catastrophe of local ontologies" which metamorphosed life-worlds into ubications.[42] Thirdly, and closest to the writer's concerns, this "sublime narrative" stands next to the images and drawings which accompanied cartographers' maps of the Antilles ("angels, or cherubs, mouths pursed, blowing the trade winds west on the Atlantic"), elegantly glossing over the link between geography and empire and, in particular, the traffic in human beings ("People are to be lost here, drowned here; people are to be sold, backs and hearts broken"),[43] which was the very reason which prompted its writing.

Determined to detour this palimpsestic inscription of place, with its "erasures and overwritings which have transformed the world,"[44] and to re-route the charted crossings of the slave ships, Brand will "sail" her characters, descendants of Marie Ursule, a rebel slave in Trinidad, into the late twentieth century and the metropoles of Europe and the Americas. Differently from the British traders, though, these characters "can only deliberately misplace directions and misread observations. They can take north for south, west for east. . . . They can in the end impugn the whole theory of directions."[45] Theirs is a willful impugning of the "westernization" of the globe and its Atlantic "tendency"[46] which mirrors the "unending and . . . inevitably futile search for a homeland" pursued by Kamena, an escaped slave who saves Marie Ursule's child Bola, thereby giving rise to the future scattering of generations. As a matter of fact, the "unraveling" of Jefferys's cartographic theory of directions and its final "bursting out" was triggered by the woman's decision to rescue her daughter from the mass suicide she had planned for herself and her companions: a decision based on a "whim," a "theory of nothing" which "opened up the world."[47]

As a whole, we might say that in spite of its displacing (or misplacing) civilizational critique, Brand's discursive itinerary in the book is finally oriented toward creation. The creation, that is to say, of those complex "webs of significance"[48] which in the last pages of her novel are sorted out and "tidalectically" elaborated.[49] This sorting out, as we have already seen, also points to the existential and extratextual creation of a new, transnational and highly reflexive way of being in the world. But Brand's attention seems primarily caught by the "nervous temporariness" and lack of destination which is "one of the inherited traits of the Diaspora" and leads to an always momentary and deferred location of the self. As she notes, "I am simply where I am; the next thought leads me to the next place." At least in one specific instance, her polyvalent I/we even appears to blend and share with her fugitive, deterritorialized characters their sense of being "marooned in outposts and suburbs and street corners anywhere in the world."[50]

In a later interview Brand more explicitly shifts her focus to the concept of rootedness itself, which, in her view, should not be considered "a given, or a wanted state." Actually, in light of its impossibility "after that door," rootlessness "would be the best starting place. . . . If we were to use it well . . .

it would be an incredibly starting point for relocating selves in the world."[51] The terrain of definition and negotiation of this impossible possibility of relocation is now Toronto itself, the cosmopolitan, global, Canadian city that comes to be perceived as the potential site of infinite transformations. Toronto is a city which "has never happened before because all of these different types of people, sharing different kinds of experiences, or what we call identities, have just not been in the same place together before."[52] It is a "yet-to-become" condition, which she first explored in the long poem *thirsty* (2002) and further sounds in her latest novel *What We All Long For* (2005), where the issues of origins and the traumatic spectrality of the past, of generational continuity, community, and (un)belonging, are recontextualized in a fresh but certainly not surprising way.

"IN THE MIDDLE OF WHIRLING PEOPLE"

As a matter of fact, the germ of the story lies in the figure of a girl who already appeared in *thirsty*: a girl who goes for a ride on her bicycle and suddenly "vanishes/as light" while fleeing from her mother and grand-mother, whose lives totally gravitate around her presence.[53] Youth symbolically embodies new, yet-to-become transatlantic hybridizations and the need ("longing") for alternative, transforming, and dynamic figurations of the self and the society with which it interacts. Emblematically, youth is the absolute protagonist of this challengingly "Canadian" city novel. Centered around four young people from Toronto, each of whom belongs to a different ethnic background (Vietnamese, Italian and Jamaican, Nova Scotian, Jamaican), *What We All Long For* significantly reconfigures the relationship between the local and the global. It also marks a transition from Brand's previous interest in "how to write passages"—"how to write what looks like journeys across water, across mind, space"[54]—to the consequences which these passages have had for the families who made them. The novel especially focuses on the children who reject their parents' ethnic memory and legacy of hardship, duty and binding love. "[B]orn in the city from people born elsewhere," they feel as if they were living in two dimensions, "as if they inhabited two countries—their parents' and their own," and have been clinging together since their school days, held together by a "friendship of opposition to the state of things, and their common oddness." This need to distance themselves "from the unreasonableness, the ignorance, the secrets, and the madness of their parents," to stave off talk about how life used to be back home and seek their own way in life, definitely leads them to alternative passages, journeys, and border crossings, projected as they are towards the outside, towards that city which they claim as their birthplace. Thus we read: "Each left home each morning as if making a long journey, untangling themselves from the seaweed of other shores wrapped around their parents. Breaking their doorways, they left the sleepwalk of their mothers and fathers and ran across the unobserved borders of the city, sliding across ice to arrive at their own birthplace—the city."[55] In Brand's previous novel Toronto was viewed through the eyes of one of its diasporic characters as a container of human wreckage, while in *thirsty* the city was seen as a complex, polycentric, and intersecting social context. Here it becomes the main vehicle and site of hope both for the older generations of immigrants and for their children, albeit for different reasons and with different results.

For the older generation, it offers the prospect of a "happening town" (as in the case of Jackie's Nova Scotian parents) which gradually fails their buoyant expectations and leads them to gambling, jail, and prostitution. In the case of Angie, Carla's Italian mother, it provides the allure of ethnic border crossing (she falls in love with a married man from Jamaica), which brings her to suicide. For Fitz, Oku's Jamaican father, it means toiling hard and feeling "oppressed, ground down by the system." As to Tuyen's Vietnamese parents, they are defined by the city without being able to "be who they were, or at least who they had managed to remain." Tuyen's father, a civil engineer, and her mother, a doctor, end up opening a "hole-in-the-wall restaurant off Spadina," although neither of them cooks very well. Ultimately, they see themselves "the way the city saw them: Vietnamese food."[56] Indeed, the notion of receding homes and identities is repeatedly stressed in the novel.

In spite of troubles of their own, it is up to the restless, mobile, and transgressive children to assert their belief in the feasibility of their desires as they skate over the constantly shifting, disordered, osmotic and impenetrable territory of the metropolis. In their haste, and "always trying to find something tingling on the skin," they inevitably and unwittingly overlook the social, racial and territorial borders that (de)limit the lives of the city's inhabitants. A case in point is Oku, the poet and storyteller of the group who, being black, tries not "to get involved in the ordinary and brutal shit waiting for men like him in the city. They were in prison, although the bars were invisible." Oku's strategy is to live in his head, to play it cool, not to "react reflexively to the stimuli of the city heading toward him with all the velocity of a split atom." After being momentarily detained by the police when he was eighteen and found to be high on marijuana, he has learned his lesson. "Whenever he encountered them, he simply lifted his arms in a crucifix, gave up his will and surrendered to the stigmata." Some years later, his symbolic gesture of sacrificial surrender doesn't prevent him from demonstrating with the black anarchists against globalization and being arrested again.[57]

Notwithstanding his sporadic surrender to the romance of dangerousness as an emblem of black masculinity and his recurrent feeling of "heading nowhere," Oku succeeds in avoiding the call of "the guys in the jungle"[58] thanks to his love for music and poetry and his close attachment to his friends. On the contrary, Jamal, Carla's brother, is always in trouble.

He hangs around with the wrong sort of people and ends up in a correctional institute. According to his sister, he sees the city "as something to get tangled in," while the girl, a postal courier who rides "through the neck of it" on her bicycle, sees it as "a set of obstacles to be crossed and circled, avoided and let pass." One particular day she even feels she is "slipping through the city on light."[59]

As a whole, the four friends experience Toronto not so much as a policed space but as a chaotic spectacle, a source of violence and ardor which is their only hope. But above all, it makes them feel alive. Fully embracing "the raw openness" of their living in all its liquid formlessness, these young people actually feel "borderless" as they chase headlong after freedom, or rather liberation from the solidity and "fatalism gathered in close houses."[60] And they would prefer not to see the established fate of their lives already turned into destiny, relying as they do on their individual self-assertion. Especially for Tuyen, the artist and the most daring of the four, the city represents escape from the "un-touch" of her family, their hold based on duty, obligation, honor, and "an unspoken but viselike grip of emotional debt." In order to feel that she is in the world, she wants "the alien touch of sidewalks, the hooded looks of crowds. She loved the unfriendliness, the coolness. It was warmer than the warmth of her family in Richmond Hill."[61]

Richmond Hill is indeed one of those "lookalike desolate suburbs" settled by "giant houses" where newly rich immigrants like the Vus have moved, looking for space and distance from their humiliations and "running away from themselves—or at least running away from the self . . . that can't fit in because of color or language, or both." To fit in is exactly what their daughter and her friends, who not only wish "not to be them" but have "never been able to join in what their parents called 'regular Canadian life,'" firmly oppose. On the other hand, Tuyen and her brother Binh "were born under the assumption that simply being born counted for something." Their Canadian-born status is symbolically appropriated by their mother and father, "as if their umbilical cords were also attached to this mothering city, and this made Binh and Tuyen not Vietnamese but that desired ineffable nationality: Western."[62]

The more this affiliative identity is internalized as being "ineffable," the more the newly born citizens—who in their childhood were "required to disentangle puzzlement" and translate "any idiom, or gesture or word"— are naturally invested with expectations. Thus the children become for their parents their cross-civilizational mediators, "their interpreters, their annotators and paraphrasts, across the confusion of their new life." Borderless as they now feel, within their families they represent the semiotic border where translation takes place, the very sum of the semiotic filters of translation, where negotiations are made and unmade, where similarities and differences must be confronted and where meanings tend to explode when no shared referent is available. They translate the untranslatable, the "ineffable," and this always arduous and inevitably frustrating process of explaining the West to the East, and the East to the West entails outwitting and misrepresenting their parents as well as outsmarting the authorities whose requests and rules they are supposed to explain. All this leads to their decision to "set off to live another life outside the knowledge or apprehension of Tuan and Cam."[63]

It is through her art, her installations, that Tuyen most radically expresses her ethnic distancing and strives to capture the shifting ground of transcultural passages and transformations determining Toronto's "polyphonic, murmuring" beauty. In this perspective, being a city-dweller means being exposed to a dynamic plurality of contingent encounters, to a network of chance implications in someone else's life which prove the interdependencies of urban figurations and that "anonymity is the big lie of a city." On the contrary, "You're common, really, common like so many pebbles, so many specks of dirt, so many atoms of materiality." This immanent, impersonal and transindividual condition of the city-dweller, in which inside and outside abruptly blend into each other, can lead to unexpected metamorphoses: "It's like this with this city—you can stand on a simple corner and get taken away in all directions . . . this all sums up into a kind of new vocabulary. No matter who you are, no matter how certain you are of it, you can't help but feel the thrill of being someone else." But it also determines the peculiar nature of urban risk: "Any minute you can crash into someone else's life, and if you're lucky, it's good, it's like walking on light."[64]

This authorial statement appears right after the narrative's incipit, which is a riveting description of the city waking up in the spring and brilliantly proceeds to introduce its young protagonists who, after having been out all night, get on the subway train and disrupt the silence of the commuters with their early morning laughter. Literally and metaphorically, the train becomes the vehicle for breaking into people's private sphere and its supposed inviolability. It triggers those "permutations of existence" which, "after being sandpapered by the jostling and scraping that a city like this does," also take place at the urban crossroads. "People turn into other people imperceptibly, unconsciously, right here in the grumbling train," the narrator says.[65]

The Toronto which is about to become the novel's focus of spatial attention is of course not an "anglicized" city at all, but the cosmopolitan recipient of people from all the world, and the "spillage" from the train to the pavement and the sidewalks is that of a "heterogeneous baggage" full of "all the lives they've hoarded, all the ghosts they've carried, all the inversions they've made for protection, all the scars and marks and records for recognition." The point is, individual lives are affected both by one's contingent proximity to others and by one's personal (whether chosen or imposed) shedding of identity: "Lives in the city are doubled, tripled, conjugated" and these complex, problematic, and sometimes untruthful or deceiving identitarian transactions—which can turn a former torturer into a totally benign taxi driver—seem to match the mutant topography of

growing ethnic neighborhoods and concomitant disappearing sites, buildings and popular haunts.[66]

An observer and a bricoleur who collects fragments of city life with the
purpose of reconstructing their "origins" or "flights," as well as a "Dadaist" who makes "everything useful useless and vice versa in her chaotic
apartment," Tuyen is particularly responsive to the city's heterogeneity
which, "like some physical light," can be found "[o]n any given day, on
any particular corner, on any crossroads." She aims at "the representation
of that gathering of voices and longings that summed themselves up into a
kind of language, yet undescribable."[67] In order to capture this polyphonic
murmur, she decides to work on a project she calls a *lubaio* (originally a
Chinese signpost on which people would pin messages). At the installation
she expects the viewers to post messages on it. Meanwhile, she goes about
collecting in a notebook (her "book of longings") stories she gathers from
people with the intent to make them public. Actually, what she wants to
create is "alternate, unexpected realities, exquisite corpses." In her wish to
give voice to this complex and multilingual vortex and reservoir of "parallel," "possible" stories, dreams and aspirations—where diverse people
from different countries interact with each other in unpredictable ways and
in so doing, transform the public sphere—she finally writes down the longings she has collected (even the "hideous" ones) on a drape of cloth. As we
might expect, these messages also include translations and different linguistic idioms. Her final version envisages three cylindrical curtains through
which the audience can pass: "At the center of one cylinder would be the
lubaio with all the older longings of another generation. . . . In another
cylinder there would be twelve video projections, constantly changing, of
images and texts of contemporary longing. . . . The last cylinder would be
empty. . . .She still wasn't quite certain what she was making; she knew she
would find out only once the installation was done."[68]

Here, clearly, Tuyen's dadaist and surrealist vision, rooted as it is in the
"hybrid cosmopolitanism of contemporary metropolitan life,"[69] seeks to
transform all these diverse human experiences into an installation. Evidently this vision is a (trans)cultural or supersyncretic act of "articulating
different kinds of times, spaces, ideas, and values," which has always represented for her "the unseen" and "the un-understood"[70] and, for her parents, a constant cause of grief, reciprocal blame, and remorse from which
they cannot recover.

The disconcerting story of this loss or rather mutilation (a loss which lin-
gers as a missing part of herself) started years before, outside the time frame
of the novel, in which the "struggle and the context of translation" are "part
of the form of the work itself."[71] Translation, however, must always reckon
with "the reality of what's missed and distorted in the very act of understanding, appreciating, describing."[72] But in her effort to create spaces that
express the untellable,[73] Tuyen is deeply influenced by the ghostly absent
presence of a lost brother. When the Vus were fleeing Vietnam during the

1970s and owing to a momentary oversight, they lost track of their beloved son, Quy, meaning "precious." In the rush and confusion of their escape, the little boy was set down on the ground and ended up following not his father's but someone else's legs. Tuyen has gathered this haunting story in fragments more sensed than overheard (she willfully has a limited knowledge of Vietnamese), a story that was never fully spoken: a "vulnerable spot" which in the course of years of interpreting she has been unable and unwilling to translate. Quite unexpectedly, rather than remaining confined to the past, this story "comes back with all it has stored up, to be resolved and decided, to be answered."[74]

Actually, what comes back to Tuyen is first of all a visage, which emerges from its effacement during the turmoil of the World Cup. The girl loves being "in the middle of whirling people" and while clicking her camera she sees her brother Binh in the company of a stranger. His face appears "ridiculous" and out of tune with the rest of his body: "the face of a boy, a baby, innocent and expectant." When she develops her film, she realizes that the face was the one "her mother, Cam, had coveted and sent all over Southeast Asia and Europe." If this sudden apparition brings apprehension and plunges her back into the ordeals of her childhood, on the other hand the reason she loves snapping photographs is precisely because she wants to catch and preserve what is not seen, to exorcise that moment in which Quy, "unseen," "floated away" from his family "without a trace."[75] Until now, Tuyen has been both fascinated and repelled by sentiment because it was always located in a sense of absence.[76] But Quy's return leads her to protect her parents from any possible harm this ghost might cause.

She and Binh also resume their old roles of interpreters in order "to translate now the years between that man and their parents. They must stand between them to decode the secret writing of loss and hurt." The difficulty here is how to mediate between a face which has oddly preserved its innocence as a plea to recognition and a body "springy as violence"[77]— how to reconcile strangeness and familiarity, their parents' vulnerability and the face's precarious right to exist, as well as representation and the incommensurability of the face to whatever it represents.[78] But in assuming this task and feeling ethically responsible for the "specialness"[79] and the sense of difference that binds her to Binh, Tuyen now is able to clarify to herself the purport of her art. She is also able to envisage her final version of the installation, which will also include among its records of longing Quy's photographs: the one she herself took and two old ones which portray him as a baby and a child, respectively, and which kept appearing and disappearing on the mantel of the Richmond Hill house.

Quy's experience has indeed been singularly marked by that original rupture, that originating moment of oversight which has rerouted the course of his life. It is Quy himself (the only character to do so) who narrates in his own voice how his life was shaped. And while his voice, addressed to an ideal listener, alternates with that of the narrator, his diegetic silent presence also frames the movement of the plot. In truth, he is one of the travelers who watch the giggling trio of friends in the novel's opening scene, and we find him again at the end when he is casually assaulted by two young delinquents, one of whom is Jamal. He is left half-dead on the road in front of his parents' house. This might be the ultimate landfall of an existence juggled around the Malaysian refugee camp at Pulau Bidong—where the boy spent seven years—and Singapore and Thailand, which he reached as the acolyte of an "ascetic," opium-addicted monk with a fuzzy past and a rather disreputable lifestyle. He finally abandons this monk only to join up with another one, "a high-tech monk"[80] with a laptop computer, a website, a cell phone, partners on every continent, and a dream of expanding into America.

Under this new direction, all the previous local repertoires of illegal traffic, quick gains, and petty acts of exploitation, brutality and violence, shifting identities, lies, strategies for survival aimed at grabbing all that you can and taking people for what they got, acquire a more globally sophisticated twist. Technology enables the monk and his followers to control "the unofficial refugee trade from Malaysia and Thailand to China and out" and hack into offshore bank accounts. There are also more ordinary forms of gain, such as exporting the *I Ching* "for idiots" or trading "in everything from plastic hair combs to liberated Ford Broncos from New York" that are available in that "dim corner of the world." More than that: "the world came to us and we ate."[81] In this interpenetrating world-system, goods, people and ideas circulate as commodities and different life worlds are united through compression.[82] The East and the West, the local and the global, and the part and the whole cut across each other and complicate their respective social spaces and civilizational assumptions.

As a result of this homogenizing and heterogenizing implication of the culturally local in the techno-economic and financial global realms, Quy (who as a monk has assumed the name of Loc Cuoi) flees to Canada after stealing the cell phone and the precious laptop. He confides in the latter as his capital, and after being jailed and subsequently escaping, he reaches Toronto in the company of "two girls worth eighteen thousand dollars apiece." There he meets Binh, whose name has appeared in his former boss's computer mailbox. The paradox is that there he had also found the correspondence between Cam, his mother, and the monk, who for ten years had been deceiving the woman and drawing money from her with false promises and news of her child. If by now the lost son no longer cares about finding his parents again, what he expects from his brother is the possibility "to take him for everything he's got. It's the things that were mine, and he got them double." [83]

The already mentioned final scene shows him waiting in the car while Binh and Tuyen are preparing their parents for the great moment of the family reunion. When Quy is beaten up by Jamal and his friend in an attempt to steal Binh's Audi, he at first reacts, "insulted and stunned" for having ended up in this way. According to the thugs who assault him, "the man is stupidly fighting as if he has a life that's precious." When he finally realizes that what they want is the car, he tells them in Vietnamese to take it. But, of course, translation requires knowledge and, since they do not understand him, "they beat him and kick him beyond recognition."[84]

The isotopies of chance, contingent history, immanent life, and total vulnerability find in this character their main vehicle of expression. At a certain point in his ruminations or "declensions on fate," Quy renounces belief in sentimental attachments, forgiveness, and redemption and trusts nobody. He feels both "innocent of all things" and "guilty of all things" and argues that it is probably useless to blame others and quibble over the circumstances that led to his getting lost. Previously, he had mused, "Perhaps this was my fate . . . I didn't have a hard life. It was simply a life. A life like millions of lives." And yet, on this occasion, contrary to other explanations he has tried to give of his experience, he rejects the notion of fate, believing that it is possible to gain control of things and choose one's own path in life. As he puts it elsewhere in the narrative, quoting from one of Lao Tzu's poems: "I look stupid, I play dumb, but I'm working. *Penetrating as the winter wind*—that's me." It is this circumstantial intelligence, also evident in his face, that has guided him since he was removed from his family and that is unexpectedly baffled in the car in Toronto, when we are made to realize that "to crash into someone else's life" is not at all "like walking on light." At the same time, it is while he is lying on the road, unrecognizable and waiting for his mother and father to "grab him as they should have,"[85] that chance and contingency come to be replaced by a sense of restoration and closure, albeit precarious. Invoking a powerful aquatic image, Brand reconnects this final passage to an earlier one in which an expectant Quy, now in a boat, sights the island of Pulau Bidong convinced that his family would be there, waiting to be reunited with him.

We are back to a face, then: one that has been defaced and, as Levinas would say, reveals a disjunction that makes representation impossible and qualifies the human as "that which limits the success of any representational practice."[86] Or we might also argue from a more immanent perspective that what is at stake here is the conferral of a subjectivity (Quy's recognition) which is itself the devious matrix of its de-subjectification.[87] But since the act of defacement has been brought about by gratuitous violence, it also shows that the human (the precious?) in and of itself is what is vulnerable and exposed to the other in its vulnerability.[88] A life: a life which might have been different "if . . ." and which is now contemplating itself as originated by and contained in that primal scene of rescue which did not occur when it should have. A life, finally, which is now suspended between life and death, beyond good and evil, subjectivity and objectivity, and which constitutes itself as desire or, if you will, as the immanence of desire to itself.[89]

Meanwhile, in another part of town Carla has finally made up her mind to free herself from Jamal's pain and is lazily looking out of the window, watching the people on the street and planning indifferently for tomorrow. According to the *I Ching,* evoked several times in the text, what counts is the synchronic coincidence of events rather than their causality, and everything that happens at a given moment inevitably possesses the peculiar qualities of that moment. And this, as C.G. Jung argues in his preface to the book, is something more than mere chance, inasmuch as the only criterion for judging the validity of this synchronic configuration of accidental events is the observer's opinion.[90]

In *What We All Long For* Brand is both a disillusioned and impassioned observer of the converging and diverging routes of the cosmopolitan city. She actually appeals to another way of confronting the notion of life based on the radical contingency of each situated existence and on a notion of chance that seems to belie the Chinese book of changes. Actually, Quy's disfigured face and body suggest that the bare life of Brand's protagonists is ambivalently played out against the biopolitical body of a fractured and irradiating globalized world.[91] Brand is also suggesting that Toronto, as the site of cross-civilizational erasures, collusions and transactions, provides a dynamic, risky plurality of points of contacts. According to Michel Serres, there is contingency when two varieties, two temporalities, touch each other. And since temporality can be thought of in terms of both order and disorder, contingency appears on the shared borders of order and disorder.[92] Indeed, the young Torontonians' turbulent, chaotic and antisystemic longings contingently situate them in between and beyond "the dying poetics of the anglicized city"[93] and the ghostly relics of a missing past which must finally be confronted and translated "to begin to know what you are missing."[94]

In Etienne Balibar's view, *civilité,* which is closely related to *civilitas, politeia* (the government of a community) and public and private manners, should be understood as politics, or even as art *tout court.* This insofar as it oversees the conflict between the impossible extremes of the macropolitics of social citizenship and the micropolitics of desire, which imply, respectively, a total identification and a fluctuating identification with the nation-state. *Civilité* does not suppress violence but gives space to emancipation and transformation and allows societies to historicize violence itself. The question concerns the conditions and the limits within which the state can contribute to its constitution.[95] In the final count, Brand's latest set of borderless, "post-ethnic" characters inhabit, as the author herself puts it, "a moment of upheaval"[96] which has yet to be unraveled: its unforeseen developments suggest that in the author's ongoing efforts to comprehend the world in which we live, modernity and its social imaginary, understood as a distinct type of civilization (*civilité?*), are indeed "on endless trial."[97]

NOTES

1. Brand, *A Map,* 102.
2. Brand, *A Map,* 109.

3. Brand, *A Map*, 102.
4. Eisenstadt, "The Civilizational Dimension of Modernity," 48.
5. Arjomand and Tiryakian, "Introduction," 5.
6. Daurio, "Writing It," 32.
7. As also pointed out in Wild, "Overhearing Dionne Brand," 159.
8. Olbey, "Dionne Brand in Conversation," 91.
9. Cavarero, *A più voci*, 228.
10. Brand, *A Map*, 193.
11. This is the title of a study which also includes poets Claire Harris and M. Nourbese Philip. See Morrell, *Grammar of Dissent*.
12. Zackodnik, "'I Am Blackening in My Way,'" 206.
13. Wiens, "'Language Seemed to Split in Two,'" 87.
14. Walter, "Between Canada and the Caribbean," 38.
15. Wright, "Interview," 41. This is Susheila Nasta's remark.
16. Walter, "Between Canada and the Caribbean," 24.
17. Clifford, *The Predicament of Culture*, 173; Benítez-Rojo, *The Repeating Island*, 4.
18. Benítez-Rojo, *The Repeating Island*, 4.
19. See Garvey, "'The Place She Miss,'" and Goldman, "Mapping the Door of No Return."
20. Marramao, *Passaggio a occidente*, 23.
21. Wiens, "'Language Seemed to Split in Two,'" 83.
22. The New Joint Endeavor for Welfare, Education, and Liberation, or New JEWEL Movement, was a Marxist populist political movement in the Caribbean island of Grenada and the ruling organization of that country from 1979 to 1983. The NJM had its intellectual and political roots in the local black power movement and was led by Maurice Bishop, a charismatic young lawyer who came to power in Grenada in 1979 following a period of instability which had occurred under the previous regime.
23. Marramao, *Passaggio a occidente*, 38.
24. Gunn, *Autobiography*, 8.
25. M. Mavjee, "Opening the Door. An Interview with Dionne Brand." *Read Magazine*, 27 November 2002. Available from http://www.Randomhouse.Ca/readmag/page28.htm, 1. Accessed: 21 October 2006.
26. Boelhower, *Through a Glass Darkly*, 51.
27. Mavjee, "Opening the Door," 1.
28. Brand, *A Map*, 200.
29. De Certeau, *The Practice of Everyday Life*, 119, 121.
30. Mavjee, "Opening the Door," 1.
31. Brand, *A Map*, 18.
32. Brand, *A Map*, 19.
33. P. da Costa, "An Interview with Dionne Brand," *Ciberkiosk*. http://www.Ciberkiosk.pt/entrevista/brand.html.
34. Brand, *A Map*, 18, 19, 6, 5.
35. Mavjee, "Opening the Door," 1.
36. With this term, originally used by Édouard Glissant with reference to the Caribbean propensity to wander, Brydon points to Brand's "oblique strategy" of reconfiguring "the concept of belonging within Canada and the world." Brydon, "Detour Canada," 110.
37. Brand, *A Map*, 64, 69, 70, 71, 90.
38. Brand, *A Map*, 7, 11, 13.
39. Brand, *A Map*, 14, 15, 17.
40. Brand, *A Map*, 5, 224.
41. Brand, *A Map*, 200–202.

42. Marramao, *Passaggio a occidente*, 19.
43. Brand, *A Map*, 201, 200.
44. Ashcroft, *Post-Colonial Transformation*, 132.
45. Brand, *A Map*, 203.
46. Marramao, *Passaggio a occidente*, 19.
47. Brand, *A Map*, 202, 207, 208.
48. Inglis, *Clifford Geertz*, 113. I adopt this term that in the text refers more specifically to Geertz's notion of culture as concerned with the definition of those "webs of significance" which mankind spins for itself.
49. Her "detouring" hermeneutic strategy also operates at this point, since she locates the genesis of her work in two different circumstances although she then proceeds to disclaim both. As far as "tidalectics" is concerned, this concept was originally developed by the Caribbean critics Kamau Brathwaite and Édouard Glissant. It suggests a circular and repetitive, rather than linear and progressive, movement. See also Deloughrey, "Tidalectics," and Pulitano, "'I Am of, and Not of, This Place.'"
50. Brand, *A Map*, 61, 150, 211.
51. da Costa, "An Interview with Dionne Brand," 2.
52. Mavjee, "Opening the Door," 1.
53. Brand, *thirsty*, 30.
54. Walcott and Sanders, "At the Full and Change of Can. Lit.," 23.
55. Brand, *What We All Long For*, 20, 19, 20.
56. Brand, *What We All Long For*, 265, 86, 66, 67.
57. Brand, *What We All Long For,* 204–205, 166, 165.
58. Brand, *What We All Long For*, 164, 166. By "the jungle" Brand refers to an area in Toronto situated at Laurence and Bathurst. This is where, in *A Map*, she presumes the African parking lot attendant lives (109).
59. Brand, *What We All Long For*, 32, 30.
60. Brand, *What We All Long For*, 212, 213, 61–62.
61. Brand, *What We All Long For*, 61, 62.
62. Brand, *What We All Long For*, 54–67.
63. Brand, *What We All Long For*, 67, 294.
64. Brand, *What We All Long For*, 149, 3, 154, 4.
65. Brand, *What We All Long For*, 5.
66. Brand, *What We All Long For*, 134, 5.
67. Brand, *What We All Long For*, 142, 68, 142, 149.
68. Brand, *What We All Long For*, 151, 224, 225, 158, 309.
69. Bhabha, "The Manifesto," 38.
70. Brand, *What We All Long For*, 267.
71. Bhabha, "The Manifesto," 40.
72. Clifford, *Routes*, 42.
73. Bok, "An Untellable Desire," G.3.
74. Brand, *What We All Long For*, 69, 301.
75. Brand, *What We All Long For*, 204, 208, 227, 206.
76. Bok, "An Untellable Desire," G-3.
77. Brand, *What We All Long For*, 308, 227.
78. Butler, *Precarious Life*, 144.
79. Brand, *What We All Long For*, 308.
80. Brand, *What We All Long For*, 285, 286.
81. Brand, *What We All Long For*, 285, 286.
82. Marramao, *Passaggio a occidente*, 38.
83. Brand, *What We All Long For*, 288, 311.
84. Brand, *What We All Long For*, 318.
85. Brand, *What We All Long For*, 4, 288, 200, 215, 4, 318.

86. Butler, *Precarious Life*, 144.
87. Agamben, *La potenza del pensiero*, 403.
88. Cavarero and Butler, "Condizione umana contro 'natura,'" 137.
89. Agamben, *La potenza del pensiero*, 399.
90. C.G. Jung, "Prefazione," 17–19.
91. Agamben, *La potenza del pensiero*, 404.
92. Serres, *Passaggio a nord-ovest*, 105.
93. This is the way in which their friends, graffiti artists bearing the names of Kumaran, Keeran, Abel and Jericho, envisage the city. They represent the "spiritual presences of Tuyen, Oku, and Carla's generation" and keep spray-painting the city's outlines with their tags and signatures, exhibited as "radical images" which actually inscribe, as the narrator points out, "their emblems of duality, their dangerous dreams" (134–135).
94. Clifford, *Routes*, 39.
95. Balibar, *La crainte des masses*, 47–53.
96. Bok, "An Untellable Desire," G. 3.
97. Eisenstadt, "The Civilizational Dimension of Modernity," 64. Indeed, this civilization is even more drastically questioned in Brand's latest book of poetry (*Inventory*), where she implacably denounces the ideological and cultural spectrality of a "sick modernity" which has brought about a polycentric and molecular dissemination of violence and death throughout the world.

8   Slavery, History, and Satire
The Legacy of Gilberto Freyre

Marcus Wood

He constructs a black ethos out of scraps of information taken from the days of slavery, and juxtaposed with observations on modern blacks. In fact, he is curiously lax about the normal scholarly procedures, be they historical, anthropological, or psychological.

David H. P. Maybury Lewis[1]

Gilberto Freyre remains a Colossus who transformed Brazilian understanding of what slavery, and its inheritance, means to that vast nation. He also provided a panoramic vision of the development of the slave cultures of Brazil, and of their cultural fallout in post-emancipation Brazil, which was adopted and adapted in various ways in Euro-American scholarship in the latter half of the twentieth century. Yet it is fair to say that his major work has not easily been understood by, or assimilated within, Anglo-American diaspora studies, where he remains an ambiguous presence.[2]

However, there is no point rehearsing the reactions of his critics at any length, as they are to a large extent irrelevant to what I am trying to draw attention to.[3] The following discussion seeks to change the terms of cultural negotiation with regard to reading Freyre both inside and outside Brazil. Analysis will consequently focus upon Freyre's masterpiece *Casa Grande e Senzala* and, rather than trying to read him through the conventional filters of slave historiography or postcolonial theory, Freyre will be considered on his own terms as an artist, an aesthete, and above all a satirist.

It should be noted that *Casa Grande* constitutes only the first book in a mighty trilogy upon which Freyre's reputation principally rests. The second volume was *Sobrados e Mocambos* (1936), translated as *The Mansions and the Shanties: The Making of Modern Brazil* (1962), and the third was *Ordem e Progresso* (1959), translated as *Order and Progress: Brazil from Monarchy to Republic* (1970). These books take the central insights of *Casa Grande* and follow them through Brazil's subsequent development. I am concentrating here fairly exclusively upon *Casa Grande* because the first part of the trilogy has generated by far the greater part of writing about Freyre in Europe and America. Given my focus on Freyre as a satirist it is also relevant that *Casa Grande* is formally, stylistically, and technically the most experimental of the volumes.

The intermittent enthusiasm and exasperation which have greeted *Casa Grande* were inevitable, given the ways in which processes of translation, retranslation, distortion, and ludic mayhem were inbuilt into the book from the beginning. Freyre was acutely—indeed, on the evidence of his unending prefaces and introductions to editions of *Casa Grande*, extravagantly—aware of his book as protean text, as paradigm bender, and as theatrical display. He did not see his work as history, sociology or anthropology, in any academically accepted definition of the fields, and it is wise not to approach his writings as such now. Freyre was making something new, unbalanced, not so much interdisciplinary as extradisciplinary.

I will also be gesturing toward another argument, which cannot be fully developed here. There is increasingly sophisticated work on Freyre's place in Brazilian race studies, yet what I want to draw attention to is a wider political context. Freyre's *Casa Grande*, when put in historical perspective, should be seen as a hymn of joy in denial of the brutal dogma of race which found its fullest expression in Germany in the years 1930–1945, the period when Freyre's masterpiece was conceived, researched, written, published, and first widely read.

CASA GRANDE: AN ACADEMIC *LUSUS NATURAE* OR A CRAFTY SATIRE?

Let it be freely admitted that Gilberto Freyre appears methodologically bizarre, indeed crazily inappropriate, if set against the norms of contemporary slavery scholarship. Freyre continues to trouble and annoy those American-based academics who would categorize him. American scholars still tend to view Freyre's patrician background, his private wealth, and his unconcern with academic institutions or their methods with a certain sniffiness. David Cleary is as bemused as any other commentator on where to place Freyre in terms of the forms and disciplines his work straddles, stating that the major work falls into "the grey area between social history, anthropology and sociology." He also comments on the wildly swinging nature of Freyre's critical reception inside and outside Brazil. Cleary suggests that Freyre is a decayed aristocrat writing unrigorously about the decay of the slave aristocracy: "Freyre's temperament was not suited to the kind of long-term primary research typical of the orthodox academic world he kept at arm's length all his life . . . he wrote about aristocracy, patriarchy and decline from the inside."[4] There is no way of gainsaying Freyre's flagrant unrespectability; yet the fact that he is not really an historian, in any accepted sense, must surely force us to ask: *what is he?* I will be arguing that if we desire to categorize Freyre in terms of genre and methodology, the most useful way to approach him is as a satirist and parodist. These are elements almost wholly lacking from analysis of him to date, yet central to his method and Brazilian cultural context. When Freyre was maturing as a writer in the 1920s and 1930s, Brazil was developing a celebratory and satiric cultural environment which stood out against extant white elitist traditions of racism. The strong institutional, political and intellectual traditions of eugenics and scientific racism had generated a counterculture: a celebratory popular culture, where the flourishing forms of music, votive art, *capoeira*, football, costume, and cuisine prioritized Afro-Brazilian culture in the ways we are now familiar with, globally, as essentially Brazilian. Freyre is to be understood as a satirist of the Brazilian slave patriarchy, who absorbed and contributed to contemporary emergent popular anti-authoritarian forms and who set these off against more elevated literary satire.

The Europhile and North-American educated Freyre amalgamated these Brazilian contexts with the traditions of Anglo-American satiric literature in which he was deeply versed. Freyre, very much a Brazilian of his time, also demands to be seen as, and succeeds in being, a Modernist. Freyre writes with a consciousness that could not have come into existence without Proust's *Recherche*, Joyce's *Ulysses,* or Picasso's *Desmoiselles d'Avignon*, and Freyre is very precise and insistent about the influence which European modernism had upon his formal approach to writing and structuring *Casa Grande*.[5] Finally, however, it is Freyre's full frontal celebration of Africanism, and his insistence on saturating his text with a weird and wonderful gallimaufry of Afro-Brazilian contributions to the national culture, which set him fundamentally apart from the monuments of European modernism, as well as the Anglo-American historiographies of the slave diaspora. And his reason for embracing this Luso-Africanist aspect of Brazilian culture, so neglected when he wrote, and so patronized when it was not neglected, had a noble and global justification. Which is to say, one way of reading Freyre is as a satirist of German Fascism.

THE NAZI CONTEXT FOR BRAZILIAN SLAVERY STUDIES

Freyre's *Casa Grande*, published amid fairly general unconcern in Brazil in 1933, the year Hitler came to power as chancellor in Berlin, was never, in terms of its interpretation or reception, a stable phenomenon. Its English language publication in 1945, at almost the precise moment of Hitler's death, saw the book assimilated into a European consciousness forced to fuse trauma and race theory in humbled, raw, and terrified ways. Freyre's book had a unique timeliness which gave it a cultural charge that it is now probably beyond the power of any single reader to recapture, or even comprehend. What did Auschwitz mean to Brazil, and what did Brazilian slavery mean to Europe after the Jewish Holocaust? The recent activities within Nazi Europe, and their global fallout, meant that in 1945 academic historians across central Europe and America were forced to think about race, and the sexual processes related to imperial formation, by using utterly new approaches. The old rulebooks of scientific racism had led directly to the crematoria of the lagers. The period 1945–50 saw intellectuals in Europe shattered—for the most part intellectually destabilized, if not paralyzed—over the whole miasma of race.

Because of his background and training Freyre had fascinating, probably unique, intellectual credentials when it came to writing about race theory and its relation to Europe, America, and Brazil. While studying at Columbia under Franz Boas, Freyre would have gained an unusual perspective on anti-black and anti-Semitic Anglo-American traditions of racist thought. Boas was a long-term enemy of German racism during, and well before, World War II. Yet Boas was also a committed critic of American racial theory. As early as 1894 Boas spoke out against racial prejudice. He was a personal victim of anti-Semitism, and he thought deeply about the comparative relation of anti-black and anti-Jewish systemic and institutional racisms in America.[6] Yet it was finally Boas's assimilationist arguments regarding, and celebrating, the ex-slave populations of North America which would have the greatest impact on Freyre's approach to black populations in Brazil, and to the overall strategy of *Casa Grande*. Although there is not enough space to go through Freyre's methodological debt to Boas in detail here, it might be forcefully argued that Freyre transported the central tenets of Boas's anti-racist anthropology, focused upon the achievements of African American cultures, to his study of Brazilian slave societies.[7] Boas provided Freyre with the beginnings of a model for thinking about the cultural construction of the fallout of slavery in ways that valued black culture. Back in Brazil Freyre was able to look down upon both the European and North American racist traditions, and their vulgar but influential manifestations in his homeland.

Freyre's reading of slavery was shamelessly amalgamatory. He believed that the intimate social lives of blacks and whites under slavery constituted a cultural revolution growing richer over three hundred years. In celebrating the evolutionary positives of miscegenation Freyre was taking on Hitler, and the European racist codes he had fed off. Hitler's race theory was founded in the false, and ridiculously crude, assumption that Nature operates a total ban on sexual miscibility: "All the innumerable forms in which the life-urge of Nature manifests itself are subject to one fundamental law—one may call it an iron law of Nature—which compels the various species to keep within the definite limits of their own life-forms when propagating and multiplying their kind. The titmouse cohabits only with the titmouse . . . the house-mouse with the house-mouse, the wolf with the shewolf etc."[8] From this position Hitler developed his thesis that any form of hybridizing has only one result, namely the sterility and degeneration of the offspring. If they interbreed, the strong and beautiful (Aryans) are always adulterated and ultimately destroyed by the weak and ugly, which in Hitler's analysis of human types are constituted by the Jew and the black.

The conviction that interracial sexual unions were fundamentally unnatu-
ral and led to the production of degenerate humans remained at the fore-
front of European and American, and indeed Brazilian, race theory in the
first half of the twentieth century.[9]

Freyre, of course, not only defied the obscene Nazi dogma of race, but
he provided a powerful theoretical counter to the orthodoxies of race and
eugenic theory in his own country. The most influential figures to write on
race in the context of Brazilian nation formation were Nina Rodrigues, in
Os Africanos no Brasil (The Africans of Brazil, 1905) and Oliveira Viana,
in *As Populações Meridionais do Brasil* (The Southern Populations of Brazil, 1920).[10] Yet it is important to see how far beyond this now relatively
familiar Brazilian context Freyre was operating. Freyre suggests a Brazilian
history of social and cultural formation in fundamental opposition to the
inheritance of the entire European tradition of Aryan racism. He storms a
phenomenal edifice, finally inhabited by Nazi Germany, but built by French,
English, and German intellectuals since the late eighteenth century. Freyre
opens *Casa Grande* by celebrating the mingling of black ("Saracen") and
Jewish peoples within the ethnographic mix of pre-Imperial Portugal. He
continues by celebrating every aspect of interethnic hybridity within Brazil
during the period of colonial slavery.

According to Freyre the relations between masters and mistresses, white
children and their black slave playmates, white boys and girls and their
black wet-nurses and maids (who so often took the emotional place of
the biological mother), white mistresses and their mulatto or *cafuso* servants, white males and their varied female slave partners all resulted in the
development of bonds of love and trust. Freyre argues that these emotional
bonds often went beyond the artificial dynamics of European racist codes,
codes which certainly were transplanted to the Brazilian intellectual elite,
but according to Freyre never took root. For Freyre the great cities and
plantations of the Atlantic seaboard constitute a finally triumphant social
experiment which never stopped growing. What should be emphasized at
this point is the historical context of *Casa Grande*. Scholars now acknowledge that Freyre was setting his stall out against early twentieth-century
race theory in Brazil. What has not been seen is that, more importantly, his
work had a global relevance, in that it was a passionate assault on Fascist
race theory and its all too practical results in Europe.

The extent to which Brazilian culture has elsewhere defined itself through
its miscibility as a triumphant refutation of Hitler's race theory is worth
emphasizing. Consider for example Pedro Archanjo, the black autodidact
cultural theorist, *capoeirista*, woman chaser, and devotee of *candomblé* in
Jorge Amado's novel *Tent of Miracles*, first published in 1969 as *Tenda dos
Milagres*. This tremendous satire is devoted to the ridicule of North American humanities scholarship on slavery and to the celebration of racial and
cultural fusion in Salvador Bahia, for over a century the world's biggest slave
port. Yet the book is also a committed assault on institutionalized white

Brazilian racism and its explicit links to Nazi race dogma. In 1942 Brazil first became seriously aware of the implications which World War II might have for it. Up until this point the dictatorship of Vargas had attempted to remain neutral, despite populist support for the Allies. German U Boats began sinking shipping off the Brazilian coast. Vargas gave permission for Allied bases to be built on the Brazilian coast closest to Africa, and German submarines then began serious assaults on Brazilian shipping, killing over six hundred Brazilians. In August 1942 Vargas's government declared war on the Axis Powers. It is within this context that Amado's analysis of race theory needs to be read.

In *Tent of Miracles*, as Archanjo collapses he has one thing on his mind: remembering a statement made that night in a bar by a huge blacksmith, as they listened to the American radio giving details of the defeat of the Nazis. In this deeply tolerant and inspiringly Brazilian vision of progress, all humans are part of humanity and Brazilian racial miscibility stands up in all its beauty as a triumphant antithesis of the Nazis' dream state. Freyre adopts such an approach wholeheartedly and transplants it back to the history of the plantations, and his method has great advantages over the Anglo-American interpretative traditions used to remember Atlantic slavery.

FREYRE AND BRAZIL AS A SATIRIC CONTINUUM

Consideration of Freyre the satirist can take him, and us, into spaces hitherto neglected by Anglo-American scholarship. The dual characteristics of intimacy and satiric exaggeration lie at the heart of Gilberto Freyre's vision. He can come at slavery and sexual corruption from a variety of standpoints that are shocking and educative. Take for an opening example the following, where Freyre seeks to articulate the fertility of the *massapé* of the Northeast, the region that generated the first rush of sugar plantations. The effect is that of a caricature seemingly aware of its absurdity—celebratory and simultaneously self-deflating.

Freyre desires to destabilize the clichéd view of the Northeast badlands of Brazil as an inhospitable and arid desert, the agonized and challenging symbolic landscape so typically the creation of Euclides da Cunha, and still a central cultural myth of Bahia. Freyre's first move is to provide a distillation of da Cunha's vision, a parody of the first hundred pages of his masterpiece *Os Sertões*. The summation of da Cunha's landscape aesthetic takes three sentences: "Droughts and dry sands of the *sertões* crunching beneath one's feet; the harsh landscape of the *sertões* making one's eyes ache; the cactuses, the bony cattle and horses; the tenuous shadows like ghosts from another world fearful of the sun."[11] Freyre wittily described da Cunha as "The El Greco of Brazilian Prose," a fanatic who transformed landscape into spiritual torture.[12] If the essential quality of this land is its dryness, it repulsiveness and its infertility, then Freyre will set his alternative vision of the other Northeast, the *massapé*, in precise and exaggerated opposition to these terms. He will obliterate one extreme with another, a land saturated with moisture, fertility, a land of sucking, womb-like longing. "In this Northeast you can always see a patch of water: an arm of the sea, a river, a stream, a greenish lagoon, in this Northeast the water does what it will with the soft yielding earth."[13]

Freyre takes a simple cliché, the idea of a "fertile mother earth," and runs with it in weird directions. The descriptive compounds "mother-earth" and "fertile-soil" are exhausted metaphoric currency, yet Freyre brings them violently back to linguistic life via outrageous literalization. His vision of the earth as black, female, and fertile rapidly becomes sexual: this mother earth is a voracious woman demanding sexual fulfillment and sexual relationships. Freyre's *massapé* becomes an oleaginous and saccharine landscape where plants people and earth drip with oil and sugar juices: "This is an oily Northeast where, on moonlit nights, a rich oil seems to stream from people and things; from the earth, from the black hair of mulattoes and caboclos, from the trees dripping with resin, from the water, from the brown bodies of men who work . . . pressing the sugar cane." Colonization, and all that it has created, is presented as involved in a prolonged act of intercourse with the soil it both penetrates and is consumed by: "For four hundred years the *massapé* of the Northeast has been pulling into itself the sugar cane stalks, men's feet, the hoofs of oxen . . . mango and jack-tree roots, the foundations of houses and churches; allowing itself more than any other land in the tropics to be penetrated by the agrarian culture of the Portuguese."[14]

In Freyre's intensely eroticized vision the land is not merely sweet and fertile, it is positively vaginal, and the mere act of walking on the moist black soil of the *massapé* becomes intimately sexual. The soil exists in a state of perpetual excitation and lubrication: "Nothing could be more different from the Northeast of hard-baked earth and arid sand than the other Northeast with its *massapé*, its spongy clay, its fatty humus. Here the earth is as sticky as honey, clinging to a man like a woman aroused."[15] How many English or American slavery historians have ever thought or written about the soil which sustained slavery in such terms? Freyre seems to have moved to a world of shifting realities more akin to Alejo Carpentier or the tropical visions of Bunuel's *Death in the Garden*, than to the canonic works of Anglo-American slavery historiography. This is quintessential Freyre, combining distortion with a disturbing and explicit naturalism, bringing his argument home through a visual and tactile prose that carries a forthright, even indecently direct, erotic charge. But in this context it is essential to emphasize that for Freyre the satiric impulse in Brazil is not casual or eccentric: it lies at the heart of his own art, and also informs his main themes as an historian of slavery and of the society which it generated.

If one takes, for example, Freyre's prophetic early analyses of the great mulatto sculptor Aleijadinho, Freyre's revelation of the political critique of slavery at the heart of this sculptural aesthetic is carefully evolved out of an extended satiric theory. Freyre begins by stating that Aleijadinho was the first great Brazilian artist to "appear with a socially significant artistic message and a technique distinguished by creativeness, audacity and non-European Characteristics." Born a cripple, the offspring of a white father and a black slave mother, for Freyre Aleijadinho seizes Luso-baroque sculptural tradition and exaggerates it into a ferocious anticolonial satire: "If I rightly interpret his work it was and remains the expression of social revolt and of the Brazilian native and mestizo wish for independence from white European masters and exploiters of slave labour."[16]

At the heart of this political critique Freyre isolates "a satirical or sarcastic way of brutally exaggerating, in the Roman officers and soldiers and in the Jewish high priests who persecuted Jesus, their noses and other racial characteristics . . . [This is an] expression of his revolt against the domination and exploitation of a rich country like the gold-mine country of Brazil by arrogant Portuguese colonials."[17] For Freyre the essence of Aleijahdinho's

Figure 8.1 Antônio Francisco Lisboa, O Aleijadinho, *Cristo Ultrajado* (eighteenth century). Polychromed wood sculpture, Congohnas do Campo, Minas Gerais.

satiric vision lies in the way he infuses popular satiric arts of Brazil into the high-art of the Brazilian baroque. For Freyre all Brazilian art and literature exists close to great popular art traditions which are saturated in distortion, caricature and satiric impulses. The creation of ex-votos, whether paintings or sculptures, is for Freyre "the great popular art of colonial Brazil and in their naïve exaggeration and belief in magic transformation they float in and out of satiric impulses."[18] Freyre even goes so far as to envision the popular confectionery of the Northeast as a satiric art form: "Even native pastry and Brazilian popular confectionary had an element of caricature in them, caricature of such sacred things as rosaries and such respectable beings as nuns . . . the name of one cake, 'nun's bellies' is a terribly sacrilegious name . . . sacred and worldly things were mixed in many ways, as if caricature were ubiquitous in Brazilian life."[19]

Freyre argues that an analogous and potent satiric impulse exists at the heart of Brazilian popular song and the *cordel* literature, a view which has been confirmed and expanded by subsequent scholarship.[20] His crucial point is that the satiric distortions upon which all these artistic media are built do not turn from the truth. The intimate caricature at the heart of Brazilian art is not related to escapism but to the brutal revealed truths of a savage satire: popular art "often tends to exaggerate and distort personalities and facts—not in an effort to hide the truth, but rather to make clear, violently and brutally clear, the most important characteristics of a fact or a personality . . . this is also the technique of caricature."[21] I want to stress, at this point, that this strangely intimate and brutal satiric impulse is frequently the technique of Gilberto Freyre himself, when writing at his most extravagantly effective, as a critic of the plantation systems of the northeast of Brazil. This takes us full circle to my opening contention that intimate satire is one quality which lies at the heart of Brazilian cultural fictions of slavery and which one seeks in vain to find replicated or echoed in the slavery archives of England and North America.

MASTERSHIP AND THE PITFALLS OF PORTABILITY: HAMMOCKS, PALANQUINS AND THE SERPENTINA

Freyre mercilessly satirizes the slave power throughout his book. He presents a vision of the white master class that bounces between a stupendous virility and an abject impotence. Part of the debunking of Brazil's planter class is done through the subtle and emphatic reiteration of criticisms which had long been a part of the Eurocentric denigration of the slave-power elites throughout the diaspora. The stereotypes of the planters as violent, sensual, indolent, decadent, enfeebled, and corrupt, a staple of abolition rhetoric in England and North America from the late eighteenth century, are reiterated by Freyre. What is new in Freyre's narrative is the manner in which he layers odd and intimate details onto the rather ungainly satiric models he has inherited. These details are not merely dressing up an old model, but have the capacity to transform it. It is one of Freyre's great moral dicta that "there is no slavery without sexual depravity" and this mounting up of a sea of evidence describing the peculiarities, anxieties, and inadequacies of white slave owners with regard to their own sexuality is one of the great original contributions of Freyre to the understanding of Brazilian slave culture.[22]

There is not space to run in detail through Freyre's intense and sustained evocations of the erotic life in the great houses of the plantations. I want to end this meditation on Freyre's method with a single example, which indicates two qualities above all: the first is the humor which, as has been indicated, runs in various forms throughout the text; the second is Freyre's sustained ability to take on Anglo-American abolition stereotypes, and go beyond them into a form of satiric cultural anthropology which is quite unique.

The example I want to take to elaborate Freyre's satiric ambition is that notorious symbol of planter decadence, the hammock. "The hammock is a fitting symbol of tropical lassitude. The first time I climbed into one, at that moment, I began going native . . . When I found myself taking to the hammock before lunch or even directly after breakfast, I had to admit to myself that I was succumbing to the inertia of the *vida tropical*."[23] Either stationary or carried by slaves, this tropical, or subtropical accessory had come to stand as a sign of white slave-owning lassitude and depravity. Within the travel

Figure 8.2 Anon. *Slaves Bearing a Hammock* (1717). Copper engraving from Amadeu François Frézier, *A Voyage to the South Sea and along the Coasts of Chile and Peru.*

literatures and abolitionist propaganda of England, devoted to denigrating the luxury of the slave power, the image of the planter reclining in typical costume in his hammock or palanquin, borne by slaves, was central.[24]

Freyre takes up this iconographic inheritance and moves it into a world of hyperbole and metaphoric literalization of almost Dickensian proportions. If the planter is carried everywhere, the logical way of articulating his relation to the slaves who carry him is to see them as a surrogate body. Starting with this idea Freyre moves beyond a tedious reiteration of a notion of dependency and into a world which again borders on the surreal:

> It was the slaves who literally became their masters' feet. Running errands for them and carrying them about in the hammock or palanquin. They also became their masters' hands; at least right hands, for it was they who dressed them, drew on their trousers and their boot for them, bathed and brushed them, and hunted over their persons for flees. There is a tradition to the effect that one Pernambucan planter even employed the Negro's hand for the most intimate details of his toilet; and von den Steinen tells us that a distinguished nobleman of the Empire was in the habit of having a slave girl light his cigars for him and then pass them to the old fellow's mouth.[25]

In this remarkable writing the slave body is metamorphosed into the master's. The notion of the trusted slave becoming the "right-hand man" is literalized, and then dirtied. Within a healthy social dynamic total dependency, what we might term "intimate dependency," is the prerogative of the helpless—the baby, the idiot, the senile. To care for the helpless is a noble and sacrificial calling reserved for the doctor, the nurse, the nun, the parent. Freyre gives us a shocking definition of the absolute nature of the slave power by conjuring up a vision of volitional dependency on the master's side. This detail of the slave hand forced to wipe the master's arse is introduced as "a tradition" with absolutely no scholarly credentials. Yet somehow this adds to, and does not detract from, its mythic status, as a symbol of utter depravity. This is a vision of the slave becoming the master or mistress not through some abstract power struggle, as in the Hegelian model, let alone through rebellion, but as a demonstration of absolute white power. Power is expressed through a self-imposed and celebratory enfeeblement, a literal self-effacement. Power is manifested as the capacity to be completely inactive.

The intimate satire focused on the hammock runs on and on. Freyre goes on to do remarkable things in analyzing connections between the backsides of the masters and their hammocks and palanquins. How many studies before Freyre's really thought about the relation between the hammock and hemorrhoids? Freyre seems to take an amused delight in suggesting that the mass occurrence of hemorrhoids in the ruling classes of Brazil over three centuries can be put down to the operations of the "palanquin de luxe":

Like a lord, or like those learned doctors and gentlemen of colonial times who lived in dread of haemorrhoids when they were not already suffering from the accursed malady, which ever since the sixteenth century seems to have persecuted the rich or educated Portuguese and their descendants in Brazil. This is not to be wondered at seeing that the colonists of the sixteenth seventeenth and eighteenth century . . . went out in palanquins that were also of silk, velvet, or damask on the inside. These palanquins de luxe were, without exaggeration, ambulating furnaces being covered with heavy blue, green, and scarlet drapes, or with thick curtains. Within their hammocks and palanquins the gentry permitted themselves to be carried about by Negroes for whole days at a time . . . when acquaintances met, it was the custom to draw up alongside one another and hold a conversation, but the masters would always remain seated, or stretched out on a pile of steaming cushions. In the house they were likewise always seated, or lay at full length in their hammocks, stuffed with insufferably hot pillows.[26]

Again Freyre seems to be entering a satiric domain, based in intimate physical detail that has the amused mock-horror of Swift about it. Freyre is getting down and dirty with the masters, and the mistresses. What sort of history is this? Apart from mentioning one Dutch source not a single reference is given to substantiate any of these assertions, from the very first claim that the white Brazilians have been uniquely afflicted with piles for three hundred years. Freyre has moved effortlessly into a purely satiric mode, and works through the imagined sufferings of his privileged victims in order to take vengeance upon them for their decadent cruelty towards their slaves. What saves Freyre's writing from becoming banal or even voyeuristic projection, is the extremity of the style, its metaphoric ambition.

As his chapter on "The Negro Slave" progresses, the hammock takes an ever more central semiotic role, until finally it seems elevated into a microcosm for the enclosed, idle, overerotic world of the slave masters:

Slothful but filled to overflowing with sexual concerns, the life of the sugar-planter tended to become a life that was lived in a hammock. A stationary hammock, with the master taking his ease, sleeping, dozing. Or a hammock on the move, with the master on a journey or a promenade beneath the heavy draperies or curtains. Or again, a squeaking hammock, with the master copulating in it. The slave master did not have to leave his hammock to give orders to his Negroes. . . . nearly all of them travelled by hammock, having no desire to go by horse; and within the house they permitted themselves to be jolted about like jelly in a spoon. It was in the hammock that, after breakfast or dinner, they let their food settle, as they lay there picking their teeth, smoking a cigar, belching loudly, emitting wind, and allowing themselves to be fanned or searched for lice by the pickaninnies, as they scratched their feet or genitals—some of them out of vicious habit, others because of a venereal or skin disease.[27]

In a book otherwise so swamped with learned citations and gargantuan footnotes this passage is again innocent of a single scholarly reference to back up the glorious word picture that has been painted. Again one has to ask, what is a conventional historian supposed to do with such writing? Rhetorically we are in the domain of prose poetry, this time a sort of Rabelasian or maybe Jonsonian satire, the planter almost glorious in his overblown lust-filled inactivity. The passage reminds me of nothing so much as the wealth fantasies of Sir Epicure Mammon in *The Alchemist*, and here Freyre's satire shares with that of Ben Jonson a sort of delighted awe for the sheer enormity of the sins of indulgence which it describes. Freyre here composes an elaborate prose which comes from another era. He is rhetorically Baroque in the wonderful use of the repeated initial clauses which provide the hammock with a life of its own as it progresses, like some strange animal, through the compound adjectives enacting its life cycle—"a stationary hammock," "a hammock on the move," "a squeaking hammock" ("rede parada," "rede andado," "rede rangedo"). What economic brilliance lies within that one perfectly judged simile, "like a jelly in a spoon," which in Portuguese sounds so guttural and glutinous: "como geléia por uma colher." The tense curve of the hammock under the bulk of the planter suggests the polished arc of the spoon, the only hard edge in this pneumatic world. The rotting planter in his magnificent corpulence is transformed into one of the preserves made with his own plantation sugar, and so celebrated elsewhere as the special preserves of the black slave-woman in the kitchen.

Freyre's ballooning digressions upon the palanquin de luxe take us to the heart of the Luso-Brazilian baroque. Without the necessity of elaborate historical parallels, or an elaborate art-historical descriptive superstructure, Freyre captures the exorbitant ostentation with which slave-evolved luxury flaunts, in its modes of transport, a capacity for sybaritic exhibition, which is also a definition of power. The idea of a vehicle, especially from the perspective of utilitarian design in the twenty-first century, is to get from A to B as quickly and efficiently as possible. Yet Freyre describes a world where the idea of a vehicle, whether a state coach in colonial Lisbon or a Palanquin de Luxe in late eighteenth-century Rio, is to express power. This expression of power takes every element connected with efficient movement—speed, strength, elegance, grace, economy—and turns them into a vehicular topos of topsyturvydom which celebrates slowness, incapacity, over-laboration, stasis, and luxury.

Freyre is talking about a certain style of palanquin, not the streamlined boxes which came to predominate in the nineteenth century, but the vast, heavy, shell-like creations of the eighteenth century. In these elaborate structures, known as *serpentines*, an outer housing hung with heavy drapes

Figure 8.3. Jean Baptiste Debret, *Lady in Serpentina* (1834). Copper engraving from *Voyage pittoresque et historique au Brésil*.

provided a cover for a hammock slung within, upon which the white master or mistress could lie or sit. If one looks at the surviving sketches of these "ambulatory furnaces," they prioritize weight, showiness, elaboration, inefficiency, and above all the performance of inactivity as spectacle.

Yet I cannot leave Freyre and the palanquin without emphasizing that, as ever, his construction of the hammock in *Casa Grande* is multifaceted. The excesses of his satiric construction of the hammock must be set off against an entirely different discourse which turns away from this extravagant manifestation of planter luxury. Freyre thinks deeply about the origins of the hammock in indigenous culture. The simple Indian hammock gets its own space in *Casa Grande* and is set out as a mysterious point of fusion between the bodies of the white, the black, and the Indian. The first section of *Casa Grande* analyzes with great delicacy and profundity the manner in which the hammock of the *cunha* women was adapted by whites and blacks in the plantations. Consequently the hammock becomes a rich symbol of cultural hybridity. Freyre talks of the fact that for children the hammock was a magical and protected space: "Many an illustrious person from the Northeast, today a made man, must have been reared in a hammock rocked by his negro nurse. Many times as an infant he must have dropped off to sleep listening to the mournful creak of the hammock-hook."[28] And Freyre goes on to point out that the hammock hook had magical properties for the Indians and was the site for displaying impromptu offerings to protect newborn children. The

I — CARACTERISTICAS GERAES
DA COLONIZAÇÃO PORTUGUESA DO BRASIL:
FORMAÇÃO DE UMA SOCIEDADE AGRARIA,
ESCRAVOCRATA E HYBRIDA

Figure 8.4 Cicero Dias, *Ladies in a Hammock* (1933). Colored lithograph from Gilberto Freyre, *Casa Grande e Senzala.*

hammock is further elaborated in a series of footnotes as central to the social history of Brazil, figuring "as a bed, as a means of conveyance or travel, and as a means of transport for the sick and the dead."[29]

If one turns back to the very first page of the very first edition of *Casa Grande,* Freyre's book begins with the hammock as the central symbol of Brazilian hybridity. It functions as both an intimate space, and as an indicator of the sybaritic tendencies of the planter class. Above the famous opening title, "General characteristics of the Portuguese Colonization of Brazil: The formation of an agrarian society, a hybrid slaveocracy," is a large colored plate by Freyre's friend, the proto-surrealist painter Cicero Dias. Dias complements Freyre in his ability to seamlessly fuse European high modernism with the Brazilian vernacular.[30] Executed in his uniquely playful and faux naïve style, which combines knowledge of Matisse and Modigliani with the art of the black Brazilian ex-voto painters of the Northeast, Dias gives a vision of hybridity which turns around the hammock. Two white women lie asleep in the same fringed hammock. One old, fat and supine, hands crossed over her chest, huge belly resplendent in the air, is asleep in a red dress. The other younger, her hips turned over the edge of the hammock, her legs dangling down, her dainty feet crossed, wears a light blue patterned skirt with scarlet trimmings and a bow. She lies asleep with her head inclined on the hammock, and the long braids of her hair dangling down. While she sleeps a black slave shown in profile stares intently at her head, while her hands search through the young mistress's hair looking for lice. Sitting above them a bird sings in a cage, its song indicated by the charming convention of floating musical notes. This magical picture somehow sums up the combination of humor and precise social observation which allows Freyre to see into the symbolic depths of social existence under slavery.

Even this, however, is not the first hammock in *Casa Grande*.

The elaborate folding frontispiece, nearly two feet square, which Dias worked up from a sketch by Freyre for the first edition and which still adorns the Brazilian editions of the book, gave an overview of life on the Noruega slave estate in Pernambuco. The design was elaborated out of a detailed pencil sketch now preserved in the Gilberto Freyre Museum. Outside the *casa grande* the uppermost slave huts (*senzala de cima*) are shown. Outside the huts slaves drum, and dance, while a white child carrying a whip plays with his black slave, who has been harnessed like a horse. A

Figure 8.5 Cicero Dias, *Noruega Estate* (detail, 1933). Coloured lithograph, frontispiece to Gilberto Freyre, *Casa Grande e Senzala*.

single slave lies stretched out in a hammock slung under the eaves, a slave who occupies a strange space in relation to the later constructions of the hammock. Is this sleeping black figure, rocked slowly in his simple Indian hammock, complicit in his relaxation? Does his contented slumber indicate a state of protected happiness, and consequently approval of his lot as a slave? Is he mimicking the behavior of the masters? The discussion of this one symbol, the hammock, and its contradictory functioning within the layered text of *Casa Grande* reveals Freyre as a visionary; his insights set the mind racing. There is, as yet, no equivalent for the range of this exuberant satiric voice within the historiographies of Anglo-American slavery.

NOTES

1. Lewis, Introduction to *The Masters and the Slaves*, lxxxviii.
2. Cleary, "Race, Nationalism and Social Theory in Brazil."
3. Andrews, *Blacks and Whites*; Fernandes, *Negro in Brazilian Society*; Needell, "History, Race, and the State"; Needell, "Identity, Race, Gender, and Modernity"; Degler, *Neither White nor Black*, 110–173; Skidmore, *Black into White*.
4. Cleary, "Race, Nationalism and Social Theory in Brazil."
5. Lewis, Introduction to *The Masters and the Slaves*, xxi–iii, xliii–iv.
6. Hyatt, *Boas*, 90–130.
7. Hyatt, *Boas*, viii–x, xli, 87–138; Stocking, *Boas*, 6–12, 310–330.
8. Hitler, *Mein Kampf*, "XI: Nation and Race." Electronic text available from http://www.hitler.org/writings/Mein_Kampf/. Accessed: 3 March 2007.
9. Adams, *Wellborn Science*; Kuhl, "Eugenics in Brazil, 1917–1940," 110–152; Kuhl, *Hour of Eugenics*.
10. Skidmore, "Biracial USA vs. Multiracial Brazil"; Twine, *Racism*, 30–57.
11. Freyre, *Reader*, 16.
12. Freyre, *Vida, Forma*, 62.
13. Freyre, *Reader*, 17.
14. Freyre, *Reader*, 17.
15. Freyre, *Reader*, 18.
16. Freyre, *Brazil*, 156; Bittencourt, *Ouro Preto*, 109–36.
17. Freyre, *Brazil*, 156.
18. Bercht and Frota, *House of Miracles*, 10–140.
19. Freyre, *Brazil*, 160–161.
20. Slater, *Stories on a String*, 1–80.
21. Freyre, *Reader*, 161–162.
22. Freyre, *The Masters and the Slaves*, 324.
23. N. Weeks, "Brazilian Names and Faces." *Brazil Magazine*, 1 November 2002. Available from http://brazzil.com/content/view/7048/73/. Accessed 24 April 2007.
24. Conrad, *Children*, 127–130.
25. Freyre, *The Masters and the Slaves*, 428.
26. Freyre, *The Masters and the Slaves*, 409–410.
27. Freyre, *The Masters and the Slaves*, 429.
28. Freyre, *The Masters and the Slaves*, 143.
29. Freyre, *The Masters and the Slaves*, 142.
30. Tribe, *Heroes and Artists*, 92–94.

Part II
Modern Societies, Ancient Routes

9 Return to the Source
Amilcar Cabral and Flora Gomes

Patrick Williams

Traditions inspire us, but we must not let ourselves be imprisoned by them.

Flora Gomes

One must have tradition in oneself, to hate it properly.

Theodor Adorno, *Minima Moralia*

This chapter focuses on the ideas and texts of two men from the small West African state of Guinea-Bissau: the well-known revolutionary theorist and activist Amilcar Cabral, leader of his people's fight for independence from the Portuguese; and virtually the only filmmaker from that country (and certainly the only one with an international reputation), Flora Gomes. Although both men were, and in different ways still are, strongly rooted in Guinea-Bissau, at the same time they both display important elements of a circumatlantic disposition, thereby occupying both sides of Paul Gilroy's "routes and roots" dyad. Both were educated abroad: Cabral studied in Portugal, becoming one of only three university graduates from Guinea-Bissau (after four centuries of Portuguese "civilization"), and his country's first agronomist, while Gomes studied at secondary school and the prestigious ICAIC film school in Cuba. Cuba was also an important site for Cabral, as he attended the first Tricontinental Conference in Havana in 1966, delivering his seminal paper "The Weapon of Theory." Traveling in order to speak became a central feature of Cabral's "routes," as his journeying took him to Europe and the U.S., both to encourage practical support for his people's struggle, and to argue the justice of their case at the United Nations Assembly. In Flora Gomes's films, journeys—diasporic and other—are structurally and thematically important, with the conditions and consequences of return variously unpredictable, challenging, or problematic.

The aim of what follows is simple, but one of the lessons of Cabral is that things are not always as simple as they seem. The discussion might also be regarded as repetitious, given that it offers yet another revisiting of the overworked—and in certain respects unworkable—pairing of tradition and modernity, but another of the lessons of Cabral, as we shall see, is that certain repetitions are essential, indeed, inescapable. It is, of course, important to emphasize that the idea that "modernity equals Western equals dynamic and progressive," while "tradition equals non-Western equals static and conservative" is a colonialist ideological construct. Such a construct ignores the existence of both modernity and tradition in both the West and non-West (though not in the same way, or to the same extent). It also ignores the (potentially) radical or progressive nature of tradition—something that has always been clear to Marxists, even if the epigraph from Adorno appears to construe tradition as simply something to be rejected. For Walter Benjamin, for example, tradition was to be understood in opposition to history: the latter first and foremost the preserve of official or dominant knowledge; the former above all the repository of the experiences of the oppressed in society, and as such the basis for their oppositional, or ultimately revolutionary, activity. For Trotsky, it was simply the case that: "We Marxists have always lived in tradition."[1] Nevertheless, tradition is neither an unproblematic given, nor simply and straightforwardly radical. For Benjamin, again, "the danger affects both the content of the tradition and its receivers. The same threat hangs over both: that of becoming a tool of the ruling classes. In every era the effort must be made anew to wrest tradition away from a conformism that is about to overpower it."[2]

The relationship between tradition and modernity, and the awareness that the former is constantly menaced by the powers of conformism, continue to be useful for Flora Gomes. It is an integral aspect of the structuring of his films and as necessary to his view of the world as the similarly "old-fashioned" theories of his fellow-countryman Cabral, and to that extent its use requires close critical examination. Although it seems that returning to these apparently passé topics can only be done apologetically or dismissively, there is an important sense in which the opposite is, or should be, the case, given that "those who cannot defend old positions will never conquer new ones,"[3] and it is this movement to defend the "old" positions which the films of Flora Gomes instantiate.

In certain contexts, of course, the "old-fashioned" carries very different implications, and for a great many postcolonial writers and theorists the moment of historical reclamation represents something like, to borrow Fredric Jameson's formulation, a "transhistorical imperative": Chinua Achebe's stated determination to use his novels to counter the prevailing racist image of his people and their past offered by Western texts is just one of many famous examples of anticolonial resistance at the level of history. For Cabral, too, "the foundation for national liberation rests in the inalienable right of peoples to have their own history."[4] The search for an acceptable national past is often intimately linked to the search for cultural authenticity, particularly via the ("old-fashioned") category of tradition. Here again, the understandings, effects, and political valencies of the traditional and the authentic vary enormously: cultural nationalists—Chinweizu and his co-authors in *Toward the Decolonisation of African Literature* might serve as representative examples—are typically criticized for essentializing and de-historicizing the authentic and the traditional. A progressive like Cabral, on the other hand, can fully understand the impetus behind a cultural nation-alist movement aiming at an ahistorical version of tradition and authenticity such as Négritude, but simultaneously consider it to be theoretically deeply flawed. For him, culture can only properly be understood historically, which also means politically and economically: "Whatever may be the ideological or idealistic characteristics of cultural expression, culture is an essential element of the history of a people. . . . Like history, or because it is history, culture has as its material base the level of the productive forces and the mode of production."[5]

For some, cultural nationalism or nativism remains profoundly prob-lematic, however hard one tries to understand or explain it. In *Culture and Imperialism* Said writes:

[To say that the nativist enterprise] is incoherent and yet, by its nega-tion of politics and history, also heroically revolutionary seems to me is to fall into the nativist position as if it were the only choice for a resist-ing, decolonising nationalism. But we have evidence of its ravages: to accept nativism is to accept the consequences of imperialism, the racial, religious, and political divisions imposed by imperialism itself. To leave the historical world for the metaphysics of essences like *négritude*, Irishness, Islam, or Catholicism is to abandon history for essentialisa-tions that have the power to turn human beings against each other; often this abandonment of the secular world has led to a sort of mil-lenarianism if the movement has had a mass base, or it has degenerated into small-scale private craziness, or into an unthinking acceptance of stereotypes, myths, animosities, and traditions encouraged by imperi-alism. Such programmes are hardly what great resistance movements had imagined as their goals.[6]

In this view, nativism, far from representing a return to indigenous authen-ticity, actually involves the acceptance of the thoroughly inauthentic—and alien—ideas, images, and identities put forward by imperialism in the pur-suit of its own ends. There is the profound (historical) irony that the move-ment which aims to leap out of the clutches of imperialism unwittingly reproduces a range of profoundly imperialist categories. (This, it should be noted, is not the same as the pointlessly self-defeating argument which says that if anticolonial movements use, for example, Marxist arguments to attack colonialism they remain trapped within Eurocentric categories.)

In the search for authenticity, the image of the "return to the source" is fundamental, and it is this image which the remainder of this chapter will examine: in relation to film studies, via the work of Manthia Diawara; in relation to political struggle, via Cabral; and in relation to both, via the films of Flora Gomes. In Diawara's book *African Cinema: Politics and Culture*, the "return to the source" is one of the three categories taken to constitute contemporary African filmmaking, the others being "social realism" and "colonial confrontation." Films in this category are concerned above all with articulating African identity, and doing so in a manner which prioritizes filmic style and form over politics and content. For Diawara, "there are at least three reasons why filmmakers turn to this genre: 1) to be less overt with the political message in order to avoid censorship, 2) to search for pre-colonial African traditions that can contribute to the solution of contemporary problems, and 3) to search for a new film language."[7] As far as Diawara is concerned, and other critics such as Melissa Thackway, the "return to the source" is an altogether positive movement:

> Unlike the films about historical confrontation that are conventional on the level of form, these films are characterised by the way the director looks at tradition. It is a look that is intent on positing religion where anthropologists only see idolatry, history where they see primitivism, and humanism where they see savage acts. . . . Pointing to their aesthetic appeal, some filmmakers and critics have acclaimed the return to the source movement as the end of "miserablism" in African cinema and the beginning of a cinema with perfect images, perfect sound and perfect editing.[8]

Although there are a number of problems with this, not least the claims for perfection and the assertion that "historical confrontation" films are formally conventional whereas "return to the source" films are not, the emphasis on a different directorial "look" at the question of tradition is important. Not everyone is as enthusiastic, however: while acknowledging the improved production values of these more recent works other critics, such as Clyde Taylor, have expressed anxiety over the ways in which, in an apparent bid for international acceptance, they effect "an abandonment of the original mission of presenting reflective and self-empowering narrative to African audiences—the only mission that justifies treating African cinema as a movement."[9] More importantly, filmmakers, including Med Hondo, Haile Gerima, and Férid Boughedir, have strongly criticized "return to the source" films for peddling precisely the kind of timeless, exoticized, "authentic" Africa that appeals to Western audiences and avoids the contemporary realities of the continent. Boughedir does at least acknowledge, in addition, that the pressure exerted by the Western audience and its tastes can distort the aims or effects of African films:

> *Yeelen*, which shows (with great talent) a timeless, "mysterious and haunting" Africa (to use terms from reviewers of the time) or, in short,

escapism for Europeans, was a brilliant commercial success in France in 1987–8. . . . Following *Yeelen*, numerous African films systematically integrated into their stories scenes where African magic is shown as a working reality. So what started as a return to African spirituality in order to differentiate itself from Western models and affirm an African specificity has become, through some strange perversion in the system, an object of consummation [*sic*] for Western audiences in need of escape.[10]

In the face of these somewhat polarized positions, it is important to appreciate Cabral's understanding of the concept, which is simultaneously more nuanced, wider-ranging, and more political. The first thing to emphasize is that, for Cabral, culture is anything but simple, static, "authentic," or racial: "From this we see that all culture is composed of essential and secondary elements, of strengths and weaknesses, of virtues and failings, of positive and negative aspects, of factors of progress and factors of stagnation or regression. From this also we can see that culture . . . is a social reality, independent of the will of men, the colour of their skins or the shape of their eyes."[11]

The complex nature of culture requires a correspondingly complex approach, both to understand it and to interact with it. (The absence of this is one reason why colonialists have, in Cabral's eyes, been unable either to control or to eradicate African culture as completely as they would have wished.) Unlike cultural nationalist commentators, for whom the return to the source is something incumbent on all formerly colonized individuals, communities, and cultures, Cabral is acutely aware of the profound difference that location—both in class terms and in spatial ones—makes:

> Repressed, persecuted, humiliated, betrayed by certain social groups who have compromised with the foreign power, culture took refuge in the villages, in the forests and in the spirit of the victims of domination. Culture survives all these challenges and through the struggle for liberation blossoms forth again. Thus the question of a "return to the source" or of a "cultural renaissance" does not arise and could not arise for the masses of these people, for it is they who are the repository of the culture and at the same time the only social sector who can preserve and build it up and *make history*.[12]

Among the important aspects to highlight here is the fact that the oppressed colonized culture may be forced to retreat or hide, but it is never destroyed. As a result of this, significant sections of the population—above all, the rural masses—never lose their culture, and therefore have no need to rediscover it in the movement of the return to the source. The corollary of this is, however, that other sections of the population do indeed need to make the movement of return.

But the "return to the source" is not and cannot in itself be an *act of struggle* against foreign domination (colonialist and racist) and it no longer necessarily means a return to traditions. It is the denial, by the petite bourgeoisie, of the pretended supremacy of the culture of the dominant power over that of the dominated people with which it must identify itself. The "return to the source" is therefore not a voluntary step, but the only possible reply to the demand of concrete need, historically determined, and enforced by the inescapable contradiction between the colonised society and the colonial power, the mass of the people exploited and the foreign exploitative class, a contradiction in the light of which each social stratum or indigenous class must define its position.[13]

One of the problems that Cabral, like Frantz Fanon, wrestled with was the question of who would govern the liberated postcolonial nation. The situation in Guinea-Bissau was even worse than that in Algeria in terms of the absence of a broad educated class capable of occupying positions of power in the new government, and, above all, there was nothing like an oppositional intelligentsia. What there was, was a petty bourgeoisie, assimilated as far as the Portuguese colonialists had managed (which was not very far at all), and whose involvement was essential for the future of the country. In Cabral's terms, they needed to commit "class suicide"—in other words, to renounce the status, privilege, ideologies, and assumptions acquired from their position in the colonized state, and to join with the mass of their fellow citizens in creating the new, liberated society. This, then, is the full meaning for Cabral of the return to the source: it is the return of the alienated and the inappropriately westernized to the place where they belong—side by side with their fellow countrymen and women, not distanced from them and harboring false ideas of superiority toward them. In addition, the importance of the historical situation, of the need of the new nation, is such that the return almost ceases to be a question of choice, and becomes rather something required as a matter of historical necessity. As such, the culturally and politically progressive nature of the return places it in stark contrast to that other form of "back to the roots," which is motivated by the West's desire for an appropriately "authentic," consumable, non-threatening indigeneity.

Flora Gomes is—inescapably—one of Cabral's indigenous, variously alienated, petty bourgeois individuals, and as such required to make his own return to the source. The ways in which he does this in his films are both varied and fascinating, comprising what one might call "doing tradition differently," or even perhaps, in an echo of the quote from Adorno above, "doing tradition properly," since there is an important sense in which you need to have tradition within yourself to do it properly, as well as to hate it properly. Here again, the lessons from Cabral are both simple and far-reaching. Firstly, tradition *looks* fixed and immutable (that is why it *is* tradition); the lesson of Cabral is that it is neither of these things. Secondly, tradition *looks* like the essence of authenticity (what could be more authentic?); the lesson of Cabral is that the more it tries to be immovably, essentially traditional, the less actually authentic it is. "Doing tradition differently" is an important trope in Flora Gomes's films, even those which, on the face of things, seem to be little concerned with the traditional. Gomes's first feature film, *Mortu Nega* (Those whom Death refused), is the story of Guinea-Bissau's fight for independence from the Portuguese and for survival after independence, struggles personified in the central character Diminga and her husband, Sako, the wounded guerrilla fighter. Diawara classes *Mortu Nega* as a film of "colonial confrontation," and that is certainly true of the first part, which concentrates on the fight for national liberation led by Cabral, but its final minutes contain a powerful example of the complexity of a return to the source.

Among the variety of problems facing the newly independent nation is that of drought (both real and symbolic), and Diminga has a disturbing dream which is interpreted as requiring that the ancestors be consulted. Accordingly, the ceremony is held and the ancestors and the deity Djon Cago (more usually known as Diancongo) are invoked, their instruction and guidance asked for. On the face of it, this looks like a society which, after painfully fighting for its place in the modernity of independent nation states, and buttressing that independence through progressive social policies—such as the radical democratic education we see being enacted in the post-independence section of the film—does what, after all, the West expects of Africa, rapidly slipping back into "primitivism." In fact, something very different is happening here: although the structure of the ceremony is traditional, the discourses and procedures employed are modern. For instance, there is a fundamental shift in gender roles, and a ceremony at which men usually preside is organized and conducted entirely by women. Also, the purpose of the gathering is political, not mystical or spiritual as one might expect from a conversation with the ancestors; the help of the latter is sought for in order to unmask the enemies within, those who "desire the death of the baobab." Once again, as with the drought, the simple, natural, "traditional" image serves a modern political purpose, as the baobab, the tree of life, represents the young, growing nation and its revolutionary struggle, which, as the film's audience is by now well aware, is under threat from a range of enemies. To counter that, the inclusive, multiethnic image of the nation—which was, above all, the one for which Cabral fought, and which is fundamentally opposed to the divisiveness of ethnicity as "traditionally" understood—is reaffirmed.

The relationship here is, significantly, tradition *and*—or, even more so, *as*—modernity, and categorically not, as it is usually represented, tradition *versus* modernity. In this respect, Flora Gomes's work figures as an example of the way in which, as Paul Gilroy argued in *The Black Atlantic*, the histories of black people and their modes of cultural production require at the very least a reevaluation, if not a fundamental restructuring, of typical conceptions of modernity. For Gomes, modernity and tradition are inseparable: "Nous ne pouvons comprendre la société moderne qu'en tenant compte de ses bases culturelles traditionnelles. Le retour au village que j'opère est une recherche d'inspiration. Nous n'avons pas de littérature écrite ancienne mais les statues, les tissages de nos pagnes portent également à réfléchir. Les morts restent proches de nous. L'aller-retour est permanent. L'intérrogation des ancêtres est possible."[14] Significantly, fifteen years after making *Mortu Nega*, Flora Gomes continues to stress the importance and, indeed, the living presence of the traditional and the spiritual at the heart of the modern. As he goes on to say, however:

> Il ne faut pas que cela nous empêche de nous développer ni de maîtriser la science et la technique. Nous faisons partie du monde d'aujourd'hui et devons profiter de ses progrès, mais le fait d'utiliser une caméra, un travelling ou une table de montage, ne doit pas m'empêcher de m'interroger sur mon origine. Notre inspiration doit venir des aspects positives de notre société, comme le disait Amilcar Cabral.[15]

In this case, the return to the source, the positive aspects of traditional practices applied in pursuit of progressive political aims, yields positive results: Diminga and Sako awaken to the sound of rain, marking the end of the (multilevel) drought. Doing tradition differently works.

Three points remain to be made briefly. Firstly, it is worth noting that, despite Manthia Diawara's claim in *African Cinema* that, during the invocation of Djon Cago, Diminga prays for rain, she does not: the purpose of the ceremony is, as already indicated, something other than this altogether traditional one. Secondly, while the film does not portray on screen a return to the source in the sense in which Cabral articulates this, given that the characters belong to the rural masses rather than to the assimilated/alienated petty bourgeoisie, it clearly nevertheless represents such a movement on the part of the (notionally assimilated/alienated) filmmaker. Finally, although the film ends on an optimistic note, the fact that those alienated individuals who are in positions of authority in the post-colonial state show no signs of making the necessary return to the source points toward future problems for Guinea-Bissau, problems which Gomes's subsequent films address.

Gomes's later film, *Po di Sangui*, released in 1996, presents an entirely different cinematic approach to traditional Africa and its cultural heritage, although many of the basic issues remain the same as in earlier films: "Avec [*Po di Sangui*] j'ai voulu . . . poser des questions. Est-ce que nous voulons continuer en gardant toutes nos traditions? Est-ce que nous voulons sacrifier une partie de nous-mêmes qui fait partie de notre tradition et rejoinder la pensée occidentale, celle des pays que l'on appelle développés?"[16] *Po di Sangui* is simultaneously more modern (in terms, particularly, of higher

cinematic production values) and more traditional (the film is set in a deliberately allegorically stylized African village, whose name means "tomorrow
is far away"). More important, however, is the weight given to traditional
culture: if *Mortu Nega* offered something in the way of balance or equiva-
lence between tradition and modernity in its final scene, *Po di Sangui* is
tilted very strongly in the direction of the traditional. At that level, the film
could hardly be more of a return to the source.

As we have already seen, however, it is not the simple fact of representing
traditional Africa in a return to the source which is crucial, but the nature
(political/ideological) of the representation. On one level, the village in *Po
di Sangui,* in its (apparently) timeless simplicity, is strikingly reminiscent of
that in Idrissa Ouedraogo's *Yaaba* (1989), one of the paradigmatic "return
to the source" texts. However, whereas the latter film has been criticized
for presenting a romanticized idyll of rural African life, that is something
of which *Po di Sangui* is clearly not guilty, based as it is on a narrative of
exile and catastrophe. In addition, if the idyll represents something like
a flight from the real, then *Po di Sangui* might be seen as simultaneously
more and less culpable. On the one hand, its (deeply traditional) mythic
dimension—anthropomorphized narratives of the Sun falling in love with
a beautiful young woman, for example—is both more powerful and more
persistent than anything in *Yaaba*; on the other, Ouedraogo's film has
nothing to compare with *Po di Sangui*'s critique of rapacious capitalism
masquerading as benevolent development, making the latter film arguably
more real, more political, and more modern.

The impact of capitalism means that, rather than working or negotiating with modernity, in *Po di Sangui* tradition finds itself reluctantly in
the position of having to fight modernity—at least insofar as capitalism
and modernity are synonymous. The "modern" attempt to work with the
modern world—cutting down the all-important trees in order to sell them
off as charcoal—fails, and tradition remains as the only available site and
means of resistance to the forces which then threaten the village of Amanha
Lundgu. Although this might look regressive—a retreating into the archaic
rather than an embracing of the modern—it is probably better understood
as another example of the kind of necessary cultural resistance to imperialism theorized by Cabral. Indeed, it is interesting to note how "development" in the film follows an archetypal colonialist/imperialist pattern:
beginning with "progressive" information gathering—the cataloguing of
the natural world presented as nonthreatening or even straightforwardly
beneficial—the process of knowledge formation rapidly shifts to enable
invasion of the people's territory, undesired commercial exploitation and
ultimately destruction of the environment.

If, as suggested by the quote from Flora Gomes above, signing up for
modernity comes at a price—giving up a part of ourselves, in the shape of
traditional culture and beliefs—then resisting it may come at an even higher
price. In *Po di Sangui,* as the unseen but all-too-audible and seemingly

apocalyptic threat draws near (the screeching chainsaws of the logging company, felling the village's sacred trees—simultaneously very real and presented as almost supernatural), the people of Amanha Lundgu are instructed by their wise man Calacalado to leave, while he will stay to defend the village on their behalf against the encroaching menace. The inhabitants then set off on a journey of exile and wandering, from which they eventually return (to their source, as it were) to discover the village reasonably intact—though looking somewhat like a battle-zone—and Calacalado dead.

There are a number of possible ways of interpreting the villagers' journey. One, perhaps not the most fully convincing, would be to see it as a form of collective alienation from which they must collectively return. Another would be to regard it as a sort of pedagogical space, a series of lessons from Calacalado. Among these would be a "back to the future" combination of regression as intimation of things to come: here, the return to a kind of absolute source—absolutely denuded nature, harsh, threatening, and unsupportive, a nature without human beings—which represents one possible future if things continue as they are at present. Alongside this is a lesson about the importance of human solidarity. Calacalado sends the villagers away as a united group: "All one. No one apart." This is severely tested by the rigors of their travels; then, when their journey is at its harshest, they meet another wandering, searching group, whose members, despite being strangers, treat them kindly. Perhaps the highest form of solidarity, however, is the one exhibited by Calacalado: to give your life for others, though a final lesson contained in his actions is that his death is only necessary because the rest of the community have forgotten how to behave appropriately towards one another and toward the natural world.

Calacalado's heroic and self-sacrificial fight is at one and the same time the defense of traditional culture, the traditional way of life, and the natural environment, since in the perspective embodied here all of these are indistinguishable or inseparable. Flora Gomes here suggests an ecology of liberation, or, indeed, ecology *as* liberation (liberation ecology, as opposed to liberation theology, perhaps), but the symbolic, and real, importance of the natural world has been present in all his films, as witnessed, for instance, in the significance of the drought in *Mortu Nega*. In *The Blue Eyes of Yonta*, a similar parallel between problems in the natural world and those in human society is expressed by the central character Vicente, as he is forced to realize that even his partially positive assessment of the state of postcolonial Guinea-Bissau is overoptimistic: "See the town? How it is dying? It weeps over its divorce from the River Geba. Now, it is married to the container ships. And the huge mango trees along the streets are gone; they reminded us of the jungle."

Cabral, too, as his country's first agronomist, had a very clear understanding of the importance of the natural world, again ranging from the symbolic/metaphorical—for example, his use of the (nonexistent) mountains of Guinea-Bissau in a series of political images—to the fundamentally real, as in the countryside's potential as the source of food for his people, or as camouflage for his fighters. Among Cabral's mountain images is, for example, the idea of "mountaintop-ism," where individuals elevate themselves to positions of actual or assumed superiority over their fellow citizens, as we see in the film with one of Sako's former comrades in arms. The assumed superiority is a mark of their alienation (the kind that would require exorcism via a return to the source); the absence of any actual mountain tops in Guinea-Bissau is a mark of the absence of any actual superiority. (The particular degree of perversion which "mountaintop-ism" represents can be seen from the fact that in one of his analyses of the conditions of the struggle, Cabral had referred to the lack of mountains—the typical source of support, refuge, etc. for the guerrillas—and said that in the case of Guinea-Bissau, the ordinary people were the mountains.)

In *Culture and Imperialism*, Said talks about the idea of "third nature," where an approach to the natural world which is non-essentializing, historically informed, and progressive is articulated:

> Following Hegel, Marx, and Lukacs, Smith calls the production of this scientifically "natural" world [of imperialism and expansionist capitalism] a *second* nature. To the anti-imperialist imagination, our space at home in the peripheries has been usurped and put to use by outsiders for their purpose. It is therefore necessary to seek out, to map, to invent, or to discover a *third* nature, not pristine and pre-historical . . . but deriving from the deprivations of the present.[17]

Importantly, Said recognizes the extent to which the reclamation of the natural world still involves the question of authenticity:

> One of the first tasks of the culture of resistance was to reclaim, rename, and reinhabit the land. And with that came a whole set of further assertions, recoveries, and identifications, all of them quite literally grounded on this poetically projected base. The search for authenticity, for a more congenial national origin than that provided by colonial history, for a new pantheon of heroes and (occasionally) heroines, myths, and religions—these too are made possible by a sense of the land reappropriated by its people.[18]

A range of complex and potentially contradictory or conflictual articulations of relationships to the land/nature within notionally postcolonial space is involved here. The second quotation outlines a classic anti-postcolonial stance, whose potential weakness lies in an oversimplified appropriativeness: as far as this approach is concerned, reconquest is all. That oversimplification may be compounded by a similar lack of self-reflection in relation to the notion of the authenticity being claimed. In contrast to that, the elaboration of a concept of "third nature," while also postcolonial, presents fewer problems in terms of foundationalist or originary claims, and operates within the space of a Cabralian emphasis on the real, constituted, in Said's words, by "the deprivations of the present." The sobering facts of deprivation make any slippage into romanticised notions of natural plenitude all the more unlikely, while a concentration on the present avoids problematic returns to the timelessness of the "pre-historical."

The self-reflexiveness involved in the articulation of a concept of third nature aligns it with the potentially more oppositional form of liberation ecology. Although a concern with ecology may look to some like modernity gone soft—in particular, the middle classes of the overdeveloped world getting oversensitive or sentimental about nature—it in fact involves a significant "return to the source." Whereas modernity is characterized by an increasingly intensive, capitalist-driven, and exploitative stance toward the natural world, one which grows ever more rapacious and destructive—and is therefore the complete antithesis of the ecological—traditional societies have, of necessity, lived in a relationship with nature which is more sparing, respectful, or harmonious; in other words, ecological. In that respect, a postcolonial politics of a "third nature" will involve a conscious return to tradition-as-ecology as part of the formulation of a more liberated, and liberating, relationship with the natural world. Among the best-known examples of recent ecological interventions characterized by an oppositional political stance are the Chipko movement in India, famous for its protective encircling of trees by women, and the Narmada Dam movement, also in India. In turn, Chipko has inspired, and is echoed by, the Green Belt movement of recent Nobel Peace Prize winner Wangari Maathai, involving Kenyan women fighting in similar ways to protect trees in Africa.

If *Mortu Nega* represents a classic example of the people, in the shape of the armed liberation struggle, fighting, as Said expressed it, "to reclaim, rename, and reinhabit the land," then *Po di Sangui* offers a different perspective on the relationship between humanity and nature, one which is more intimate and more mythic (but not, therefore, necessarily de-realized). At the heart of this is the symbiotic connection between people and trees, indicated in the film's title, variously translated as *Tree of Blood*, or, in the French version, *Tree of Souls*. In the culture of Amanha Lundgu, at the birth of a member of the community a tree is planted which is then seen as intimately connected to, and in some ways mirroring, the life of the human being. (It is a mark of the fact that the world of the village is moving dangerously out of kilter that when, at the opening of the film, the wanderer Dou returns to the village, he finds that his twin brother, Hami, is dead, he also finds that his own tree, not his brother's, has died.) As Calacalado later explains, the reason why the charcoal-making venture fails is because the men who have embarked upon it have perpetrated a kind of murder—turning living trees into dead wood—and have done so for money. One of these men was Dou's twin, Hami, and his death is a consequence of the "deaths" he has caused. In that context, Calacalado's fight is more than just to protect trees from the logging company: it represents quite literally a battle for the soul(s) of his people and their culture. It is also a battle whose lines extend far beyond the lands around Amanha Lundgu; writing about the stories of Mahasweta Devi from Bengal, Gayatri Spivak comments:

> In this context, it is important to notice that the stories in this volume are not only linked by the common thread of profound ecological loss, the loss of the forest as foundation of life, but also of the complicity, however apparently remote, of the power lines of local developers with the forces of global capital. This is no secret to the initiative for a global movement for non-Eurocentric ecological justice. But it is certainly a secret to the benevolent study of other cultures in the North.[19]

Notwithstanding the ramifications of this global battle, the implication, in Flora Gomes's typically quietly optimistic ending, is that Calacalado's fight has been successful. The villagers have returned to their place of origin. A new baby is born, and a new tree will be planted for it. The story, like a good traditional mythic tale, has returned to its starting point. Neither the people nor the narrative are quite the same, however, and it is this difference which is significant. The film begins with the "once upon a time" real-but-mythic tale of Hami and Dou told to the children; it ends with the villagers (visually) representing their experiences, and this—real history, rather than myth—is narrated and explained *by* a child. The capacity for making small but crucial shifts in attitude or social practice, for "doing things differently"—including tradition—is the source to which Flora Gomes returns time and again in his films. It is a source of hope, embodied above all in children, but also in a faith in people, in his own people, as Cabral taught.

Nha Fala (My Voice), Gomes's latest film, is in many ways the opposite of *Po di Sangui* (though, in one respect at least, it is a direct outgrowth of it). For instance, while the latter is a serious examination, in the shape of an allegorical quest, of a traditional society grappling with modernity, the former is a light-hearted treatment, in the shape of a musical, of contemporary society grappling with tradition. As the most recent of his films, *Nha Fala* marks the latest stage in Gomes's chronicling of the postcolonial history of his country, and in this respect, if in no other, is the most modern. The other face of this modernity is, however, that *Nha Fala* looks rather like that most traditional of narrative modes, a fairy story—though a fairy story for twenty-first-century Africa. The events of the film are also simultaneously grounded in the traditional and the modern: the context is the problematic state of contemporary post-independence society in Guinea-Bissau—the corruption, the profiteering, the consumerism. The motor of the plot is, however, traditional, in the shape of a potentially fatal curse affecting the central character Vita and her family, and everything hinges on how this traditional belief is interpreted and dealt with, by her and others.

The question of return (to the source, or perhaps not) resonates through the film in various ways. For Vita, the story is one of departure and return (to Paris and back), though her return to Africa also signals a different kind of departure, in this case, freeing herself from the constraints of tradition, as she prepares to face up to the consequences of her rejection/defiance of the curse. The importance of a careful assessment of the value of traditional culture is something stressed by Cabral, as noted earlier, since "all culture is composed of essential and secondary elements, of strengths and weaknesses, of virtues and failings, of positive and negative aspects, of factors of progress and factors of stagnation or regression."[20] Vita is brought to see how the curse is part of the "factors of stagnation or regression" in her culture, and how she, in the words of the final song of the film, has to learn to "dare," in order to overcome its effects. The daring, in Vita's case, consists of, once again, doing tradition differently, as she—flagrantly, transparently artificially—stages her own traditional wake and funeral, and her "death" and rebirth, her return to and from the source, liberates more than just herself. The obvious counterpart to this is doing modernity (especially its capitalist variant) differently, and by the time Vita returns home to Africa, her sharp-suited, mobile-phone-wielding, would-be boyfriend has abandoned his shady profiteering deals and, in a way reminiscent of Vicente, is involved in business with a social conscience. If, for Flora Gomes, the answer to the opposition (apparent or actual) between modernity and tradition is neither one nor the other but both, then that syncretic resolution is for him only the sign of a larger reality: "L'avenir de cette planète c'est le métissage. Personne ne peut l'interdire."[21] Perhaps no one can, though achieving that all-important mixture may still require courage: in the words of the song from *Nha Fala*, "What do we have to do to be together and different? We have to dare!"

The other significant return in the film—ironic, in many ways, given his position as theorist of the return to the source, but also entirely appropriate—is that of Cabral himself. As the film opens, a truck brings what turns out to be the first statue of Cabral to be erected in the town. This is an additional irony—or condemnation—namely that, a quarter of a century after independence, there is still no monument to the father of that independence. The irony/condemnation is further compounded by the fact that a number of people are unable to recognize the statue, and yet further by their inability to decide where to put it. The problem of "Where do we put Cabral?" is clearly one with more than local or merely rhetorical significance, but in the absence of any initial decision on that in the film, the statue is wheeled around town in a baby's stroller. Although in one sense this reduces Cabral to an almost ridiculous level, as the film progresses so the stroller's following grows, becoming part religious procession, part political march, and part carnival—a mass/popular event, bringing all types of people together in a manner of which Cabral would have heartily approved. In the final section of the film, problems (the curse included) are overcome, wounds are healed, the alienated petty bourgeoisie—capitalist profiteers—see the light, and a place is found for Cabral's statue. Or rather, Cabral's statue finds its own place, as in the last scene it somehow ascends to a position of rightful prominence on an empty plinth. This is not terribly realistic, but then that is not something this film worries about very much.

The title of Flora Gomes's first short film, made in 1976, was, significantly, *Regresso de Cabral* (The Return of Cabral). One of the implications of his latest film is that the return is not a once-and-for-all event, that it needs to be repeated in order to achieve its full meaning—the return not so much *to* the source, as *of* the source, perhaps. It is also an important reminder that, just as in Benjamin's words quoted at the beginning, where tradition must be repeatedly defended against the powers of conformism, so here the lessons and the legacy of Cabral must be repeatedly defended against the threat of oblivion, and restored to the present where they offer the possibility of doing things very differently—the necessary condition for a better, "modern" future: "The cultures that defenders of tradition look back to with such nostalgia are the dream-form of the societies that gave them birth. Precisely for that reason, in their time they functioned ideologically. . . . If the Left returns to the past, it is not to redeem some sort of original ideal world from which we have been banished . . . so the nostalgia is really for *the possibility of something else today*."[22]

NOTES

1. Trotsky, *Literature and Revolution*, 131.
2. Benjamin, "Theses on the Philosophy of History," 257.
3. Trotsky, *In Defence of Marxism*, 222.
4. Cabral, "National Liberation and Culture," *Return to the Source*, 43.
5. Cabral, "National Liberation and Culture," 42.
6. Said, *Culture and Imperialism*, 276.
7. Diawara, *African Cinema*, 160.
8. Diawara, *African Cinema*, 160.
9. Taylor, "Searching for the Postmodern in African Cinema," 139.
10. Boughedir, "African Cinema and Ideology," 119.
11. Cabral, "National Liberation and Culture," 50–51.
12. Cabral, "Identity and Dignity in the Context of the National Liberation Struggle," *Return to the Source*, 61.
13. Cabral, "Identity and Dignity," 63.
14. Gomes, "Interview," *Africultures*, 21 October 2002. http://www.africultures. com/index.asp?menu=revue_affiche_article&no=1282&rech=1.
15. Gomes, "Interview," *Africultures*, 21 October 2002.
16. Gomes, "Interview," *Africultures*, 4 October 2002. http://www.africultures. com/index.asp?menu=affiche_article&no=2187&rech=1.
17. Said, *Culture and Imperialism*, 272.
18. Said, *Culture and Imperialism*, 273.
19. Spivak, *Imaginary Maps*, 198.
20. Cabral, "National Liberation and Culture," 50–51.
21. Gomes quoted in Chérifa Benabdessadok, "Nha Fala. Une comédie musicale de Flora Gomez." *Altérités*, 16 July 2003. http://www.alterites.com/cache/center_cinema/id_332.php.
22. Buck-Morss, *Thinking Past Terror*, 104, 125.

10 Ghosts of Memories, Spirits of Ancestors
Slavery, the Mediterranean, and the Atlantic

Cristina Lombardi-Diop

Whether in literary expression or in real experience, slavery has never been as present as it is in today's Europe. The discovery of forced labor conditions of clandestine immigrants in the South of Italy has brought back the issue of slavery from the depth of European history and memory. Migration is in many ways different from slavery, yet the link between the two phenomena becomes obvious when one considers the contemporary cases of enslavement and trafficking of illegal migrants across Europe's borders. While modern slavery is a global phenomenon and is certainly not limited to Italy, its implications bear important consequences for the exploration of a discourse around contemporary African diasporic literary production in the peninsula. The historical role of Italy at the outset of the Atlantic slave trade is only one of the many connections between the Mediterranean and the Atlantic. Recent scholarly works on the Atlantic slave system have attempted to internationalize this subject by adopting a global perspective on this complex phenomenon.[1] In their effort to explore the distant origins of New World slavery, historians have investigated the many features of medieval and Renaissance Europe that anticipated colonial slavery in the New World. David Brion Davis has argued that there are "strong sequential links" between the Atlantic slave system and the Italian Renaissance.[2] Robin Blackburn has affirmed that sugar production in late medieval Sicily and Andalusia, which had adopted Arab techniques, employed slaves for the cultivation and the processing of sugar cane. Blackburn also noted that "the powers that successfully colonized the Americas had their roots in medieval kingdoms,"[3] while Charles Verlinden has demonstrated that medieval entrepreneurs in Venice and Genoa had established slaveholding colonies in the eastern Mediterranean and on the coasts of the Black Sea.[4]

After the conquest of Constantinople by the Turks in 1453, Black Sea markets closed to the Genovese and the Florentine merchants. It is around this time that "white" slaves were replaced with black Africans transported north by Arab caravans along the trans-Saharan trading routes which passed by important commercial centers, such as Sijilmasa, Fez, and Gha-dames.[5] This turn from an eastern Mediterranean slave trade to a Western Atlantic one was made possible also thanks to the maritime activities of Genovese merchants, who began to trade slaves from sub-Saharan Africa into Lisbon and Seville. In the fifteenth century, ports in Aragon's southern Italian dominions—above all Naples and Palermo—were slave ports.[6] In the middle of the sixteenth century, Paolo Caggio, a writer from the Sicilian capital, published a moral operetta entitled *Iconomica sul governo della casa e della famiglia* (An Economy of Household and Family Governance). In Palermo, he affirmed, slaves were "the worthiest, most appreciated, and most excellent possession."[7] In 1470 the young Bartolomeo Marchionni, after relocating from Florence to Lisbon, began to invest in sugar plantations established in Madera. He also obtained authorization from the Portuguese to trade in slaves.[8] The example of the Marchionni family of Renaissance Florence sheds light, according to David Brion Davis, on the Mediterranean-Atlantic continuity.

The role of Italian merchants and bankers, who furnished capital and technology that enabled the Portuguese to establish a commercial empire in the Mediterranean—thus setting the base for the Atlantic slave trade—awaits further investigation. Nonetheless, the new scholarly works I mentioned create the basis for a discourse on the interconnections, as well as the historical and cultural links, between the Atlantic and the Mediterranean. In the cultural and literary realm, the re-contextualization of Shakespeare's *The Tempest* from its most obvious Mediterranean setting to a New World and Atlantic setting must be seen in light of this effort to trace the many links that have existed between these two cultural systems since the Renaissance.[9] In a parallel move, my investigation of the links between African literary texts created within the context of contemporary African migrations across the Mediterranean and memories of the Atlantic Middle Passage belongs to the same effort. In what follows, I examine how the many different forms of invisibility that illegal immigrants take in Italian society are evoked in African Italian literature by the circulation of images of shadows, ghostly presences, and post-mortem narrative voices that embody ancestor spirits. I argue that the circulation across the Mediterranean of African migrants, as well as their enslavement and trafficking, activates a parallel circulation of images and memories of the Atlantic Middle Passage. These spectral presences stand for a warning about contemporary forms of slavery and dehumanization, and constitute a trace of the cultural memory of the oceanic crossing. Moreover, they are the embodiment of future voices in literary form and a possibility of political awareness and agency in the present.

In my analysis of literary texts, I follow the tripartite analytic structure ("the three things of *the thing*") which, as indicated by Jacques Derrida in his cogent reading of Shakespeare's *Hamlet*, composes a spirit: mourning, the voice and naming, and the power of transformation.[10] *Hamlet*, as

.1 by Derrida, becomes the new textual framework for my reading .e Mediterranean-Atlantic connection. By following Derrida's chase of .nlet's spirit, I read the meaning of these spirits as threefold. First of a.., the analysis of works by Tahar Ben Jelloun, Feven Abreha Tekle, and Giovanni Maria Bellu shows how ghosts return from the past to keep alive a process of remembering and mourning. The act of mourning is initiated through the finding of bodily remains and the sediment of history buried under the depth of the Mediterranean sea. Mourning implies the necessity of knowing who and where these bodies are in order to name them. Secondly, I look at how the power of transformation of literary models is activated by the inscription of the presence of an afterlife in works by writers of West African origin such as Saidou Moussa Bâ and Mbacke Gadji, and how this power is encoded within the specific role of ancestors in the cultures of sub-Saharan Africa. The finding of ancestral presences points to the birth of narrative voices distant from Western literary canons and genres. This function of spectral presences also provides a link between contemporary African Italian literature and its African and African American precedents.

MODERN SLAVERY

An article published in *Le Monde* in the summer of 2006 opened with the shocking title, "Esclaves en Italie." A French reporter had traveled to the southern fields of Puglia where Italian and Polish prosecutors had discovered a system of forced labor of clandestine immigrants that had been functioning for over two years.[11] Before the *Le Monde* article, Italian journalist Fabrizio Gatti of *L'Espresso* had witnessed in the area the presence of at least five thousand, maybe seven thousand, illegal migrants forced to pick tomatoes from dusk to dawn for 15 or 20 euros a day in the farm fields that produce for the tomato-canning industries of southern cities.[12] The disenfranchised migrants, mostly men from countries such as Rumania, Bulgaria, Poland, Nigeria, Mali, Burkina Faso, Uganda, Senegal, Sudan, and Eritrea, lived in makeshift shacks, drank water contaminated by sewage, and ate the meager food provided by their guards. Gatti observed that the migrants worked under threat of physical violence and could not leave the field freely. Those who tried to run away were chased with unleashed dogs. Their human rights were constantly violated by physical threats, humiliations, and psychological abuse. By Kevin Bales's broad definition of a modern slave as "a person held by violence or threat of violence for economic exploitation,"[13] the migrant captives of Puglia are, in every way, "modern slaves."

The Puglia case involves economic, political and social factors that may be found in other parts of the world: globalization's demand for cheap labor, the corruption and complicity of a weak government, and the collaboration of highly developed local and international criminal organizations. But what are the possible socio-historical preconditions implicated in the Puglia case that may be specific to Italy? In his study on the social and legal forms of exclusion of migrants in Italy, sociologist Alessandro Dal Lago argues that the concomitant action of political forces, media representations, and social mechanisms of exclusion have all concurred to create an image of all clandestine migrants as "non-persons."[14] This category is made of people who, unlike Italian citizens, are stripped of all formal protections and rights. Dal Lago reconstructs how, with the implementation of the 1995 Dini Decree, Italian immigrant legislation has established a double juridical system which, for the first time since the Italian Fascist regime, has created inequality between Italian and foreign citizens.[15] The exclusion of certain categories of foreigners (*illegali, clandestini, extracomunitari*) from fundamental civil rights created the premises for their transformation from full persons into non-persons. The events in Puglia seem to indicate that illegal immigrants are reduced to slavery also because they are perceived as "non-persons."

In the early 1990s, a precedent to the Puglia case unleashed a heated debate on Italy's violent new racism against immigrants. In the summer of 1989, a gang killed the black South African Jerry Essan Masslo, who was working in the tomato fields of Villa Literno, near Caserta. Italians began to question their past and links were made between Italy's new forms of racism and its Fascist legacy. In Paul Bakolo Ngoi's 1995 short story "Visto da Kalo," male Moroccan and Senegalese seasonal workers pick tomatoes in the same fields where Masslo was killed. Kalo, the protagonist of the story, manages to escape the fields once he obtains his visa through the early 1990s general immigration amnesty.[16] The killing of Masslo had also inspired Moroccan writer Tahar Ben Jelloun's short story "Villa Literno," included in his *Italian Tales*, and published in collaboration with the Italian journalist Egi Volterrani. The story is told from the perspective of Antonio, a retired Italian man who is a witness of, and participant in, the economic decay and social corruption of this small farming town south of Caserta. Antonio suffers from boredom and insomnia, and one night he sees "shadows" of "tall, slim, black"[17] African migrants slowly emerging from the obscurity of the dark night to occupy the city's main square in search of a place to sleep. The men who lie on the ground in silence sleeping, one next to the other, are "anonymous bodies" that seem dead but are in reality dreaming. Antonio walks among them and imagines the city of Villa Literno transformed into a ship put to sea by the fragments of their dreams.

Ben Jelloun's sleeping Africans are the new "wretched of the earth,"[18] subject to a new form of slavery that is made possible also because, according to Ben Jelloun and Volterrani, the Italian State is absent and has abandoned the South and its inhabitants. They are like the Africans Fabrizio Gatti meets seventeen years later in Puglia. Not much has changed in Italy. As migrants without papers, they become easy prey for local organized crime and their destiny is the underworld of *lavoro nero* (illegal work) and inhuman exploitation. They are, in Dal Lago's terms, non-persons, humans who no longer have human substance; in short, they are ghosts.

DEATH AT SEA

> The radical estrangement of foreigners from the world of real persons is revealed by the destiny of those who die at sea.
>
>   Alessandro Dal Lago[19]

Villa Literno's literary shadowy presences reveal how the radical estrangement of illegal migrants in Italy in the 1990s announced their current enslavement in the southern farms. But their anonymity is not only an effect of their invisible status as illegal foreigners. It is also a consequence of historically determined conditions that have affected migrant Africans since the inception of modernity. In Ben Jelloun's story, these uncountable bodies lie next to each other on the ground and seem forever gone from sight, like the dead. At this very moment, the square becomes a ship that stands for the Middle Passage slave ship, but also for one of the many boats which cross the Mediterranean from Tunisia or Libya to the Sicilian coasts. This crossing is as dangerous and fatal as the Middle Passage.[20] In Libya, those who intend to enter Italy across the Mediterranean wait for days, even months, for their passage to Lampedusa. It is in the Libyan town of Al-Zwara that Asserid, a Nigerian man interviewed by Gatti, heard of the possibility of finding work in the tomato fields of Puglia. Eritrean Feven Abreha Tekle,[21] instead, escaped the military draft and from Asmara reached Ethiopia first, and then the Sudan and Libya. Here, she waited for almost a month in a camp where living conditions were very similar to the ones Gatti saw in Puglia, before being able to find a passage to Italy. In her *Libera* (2005), published in collaboration with Raffaele Masto, Abreha Tekle describes the crossing of the Mediterranean:

> Zwara has a very small harbor. We arrived there in the middle of the night. . . . We were over a hundred, perhaps a hundred and thousand people. After the guards selected us and ordered us to follow them, the camp was almost emptied. . . . I looked around: we were a silent crowd, like timorous and dreamy nightly ghosts, all immersed in their own thoughts. I had never sailed before and the sea, that infinite stretch of water, had always fascinated me.[22]

Once at sea, the phantasmagoric nature of the crossing and the stink of bodies crowded on deck reawaken memories of the Middle Passage: "I was reminded of having read somewhere that the slave ships of two centuries earlier that were used to transport African slaves to America were impregnated with a characteristic smell that was impossible to erase and which was felt at a distance of many miles. On that fishing boat it was the same thing."[23] Alongside the retrospective projection of her current Mediterranean crossing onto the historical event of the Atlantic slave trade, Abheha Tekle also constructs her narrative as an ascent movement from detention to freedom. Her celebratory tones cannot be overlooked. In another passage of her book, Abreha Tekle describes the fascination she experiences while seeing the Mediterranean sea for the first time as "a kind of euphoria."[24] Her feeling of liberation—whose promise inspires the text's title—is fulfilled when, by the end of the narrative, the protagonist is at last safely settled in Italy. She declares: "At last, yes, the dream came true."[25] In the second part of this essay, I will look at the utopian drive of other types of narratives which build on the dystopic memory of the Middle Passage in order to transform the experience of bondage into a promise of emancipation.

MOURNING

> Nothing could be worse, for the work of mourning, than confusion or doubt: one has to know who is buried where—and it is necessary (to know, to make certain) that, in what remains of him, he remains there. Let him stay there and move no more!
>
> Jacques Derrida[26]

Abheha Tekle's *Libera* constitutes one of the few testimonies of the crossing of the Mediterranean. The narration of this successful journey is, as Tekle affirms, "endless" unless memory is given to those who did not end their journey. In his *I fantasmi di Portopalo* (The Ghosts of Portopalo, 2004), Italian journalist Giovanni Maria Bellu's objective is to offer testimony and vindication to those who died during the crossing. Significantly, the book's back cover reproduces the identity card photo of Anpalagan Ganeshu, one of the victims of the most tragic shipwreck in the history of the contemporary Mediterranean. Bellu painstakingly reconstructs Anpalagan's life before the shipwreck, which occurred on Christmas night of 1996 in the Sicilian Channel. In their attempt to disembark on Italy's shore, almost three hundred people of Indian, Pakistani, and Tamil origin died within a few hours. Bellu's retrospective reconstruction of the young Tamil's life makes Anpalagan the real protagonist of his narration, so much so that he is often addressed in the narrative as if he were still present, in the same fashion in which one addresses a ghost. Moreover, Bellu describes the tragedy as "a ghost shipwreck,"[27] one that needed to be silenced and forgotten. At first, the Italian authorities refused to acknowledge the incident. When Sicilian fishermen began to find the remains of corpses entangled within their fishing nets, many of them preferred to keep silent. Adopting a journalistic and a narrative literary style,

Bellu reconstitutes the events by digging into the police files and press articles, and by interviewing people in the Sicilian coastal town of Portopalo, as well as family members of some of those who died:

> It is a day at the beginning of January 1997. At the center of the shining lump of fish there is something strange, big and dark. Nobody is surprised because all sorts of things are found in the smack: Punic amphora and plastic tanks, tires and equipment discarded by cruise ships, as well as, when all goes well, bigger preys such as swordfish and tuna fish. But that thing does not look like a fish, nor like an amphora, nor like a boat relic. A jet of water liberates "the thing" of mud and seaweed. It is the body of a man. A dark-skinned man.[28]

The marine sediments Sicilian fishermen dig out of the bottom of the Mediterranean sea are fragments of its layered history: Punic amphora, plastic tanks, and migrants' dead bodies are a metonymic embodiment of the past and present of Europe's late modernity. The bodies are already dark "things," presages of their return as ghosts.

The contemporaneousness of the presence of such bodily remains with fragments of the material life of the past poses the issue of their surfacing as a meditation on the seeming homogeneity of Mediterranean life. The sea, in its spatial dimension, is a flat and homogeneous stretch of water. Yet, in its depth, it reveals the discontinuities of real time events. In his reflections on historiography Fernand Braudel suggested that, despite the retroactive illusion created by the work of historians—who recompose historical time from the fragments of human events in order to produce seemingly homogeneous periods—human time is always multiple, only falsely monotonous. In reality, human structures imperceptibly and slowly change through a *work* of demolition and creation that never stops and keeps the structures alive: "Events never really disappear; they leave residues, traces, consequences. They are like noises in the background we must deal with in the present. They are a living presence of the past."[29] Like ghosts returning from the past, these corpses of migrants are a "living presence of the past"; they are alive through the *work* they do by changing themselves (decomposing or posing themselves) to transform the present. Like the work of historians, Bellu's work strives towards reconstructing the wholeness of these fragments of anonymous bodies entangled in the fishermen's nets in order to name—as a whole living body—those who did not survive the crossing of the Mediterranean. Naming them and reconstructing their lives is Bellu's work.[30] Yet, the labor of mourning is a collective work and is shared by all his readers.

COLONIAL LEGACIES

Many of those who attempt the Mediterranean crossings come to Italy seeking political asylum. Most of them are young men from the ex-Italian colonies of Eritrea, Ethiopia, and Somalia who are escaping from army conscription, military regimes, and civil wars.[31] Abheha Tekle's "dreamy nightly ghosts" return from a past that is much closer to us than the Renaissance period. Racial discrimination and segregation were imposed against Jews in Italy and against Africans in the ex-colonies of Eritrea, Ethiopia, Somalia, and Libya with the 1938 racial legislations passed by Mussolini's regime. This controversial aspect of Italy's recent past constitutes a heavy legacy for contemporary Italy. In recent years, a renewed scholarly interest in Italian colonialism has shown how post-war Italian society had repressed the memory of this experience. Historians who have studied Italy's colonial past argue that today's Italy is far from having reckoned with it.[32] "The obstinate survival of the legend of Italian colonialism as different, more tolerant, and more humane"[33] is being addressed with forceful historical evidence that proves its flawed and constructed nature. Silenced in the public domain, the colonial legacy continues nonetheless to have an impact on contemporary issues.[34] As Alessandro Triulzi aptly argues, the arrival of new African migrants in the last twenty years has reawakened memories of colonial and imperial history, and yet it has also unleashed new representations of national pride in a revisionist approach to that history.[35]

As Italy reckons with its sense of cultural roots and identity within a unified Europe, current re-examinations of national identity can also be seen as a reaction to the fast-paced demographic changes brought about by immigration and globalization. Yet these nationalist revisions of past and current identity are oblivious to the appalling events such as the ones discovered in Puglia in summer 2006. The formation of master gangs (the so-called *"caporalati"*) by immigrants who decided to collaborate with the Italians points to the fact that ethnic hierarchies were reconstructed in Puglia according to racialist distinctions. A clear example is given by dwelling and working arrangements: individuals within a certain national group were placed in the farming fields in a position of control over their co-nationals, with the only exception of black Africans, who lived segregated from the others and were not given any form of control over their own group or the other national groups. Gatti reports that migrant workers were lodged in dwellings separated according to national groups, except for black Africans, who lived all together. Notwithstanding these forms of segregation, the Puglia case shows that clandestine immigrants from Poland, the Balkans and Africa were all subject to the same exploitative system of captivity and forced labor because of their status as illegal and disenfranchised migrants. Their condition of illegality constituted the main factor that led to their enslavement.

VISIBILITY AND WRITING

One should not rush to make of the clandestine immigrant an illegal alien or, what risks coming down to the same thing, to domesticate him. To neutralize him through naturalization. To assimilate him so as to stop frightening oneself (making oneself fear) with him. He is not part of the family, but one should not send him back, once again, him too, to the border.

Jacques Derrida[36]

In the early 1990s, affirming a voice through writing was for the first generation of African Italian writers a way to satisfy a primary need, a need similar to what African American writers felt in pre-abolitionist America. Writing in Italian meant to affirm the very possibility of their existence, as well as the essential humanity of that existence. What Henry Louis Gates writes in reference to early African American texts easily applies to early African Italian texts: "What was at stake for the earliest black authors was nothing less than the implicit testimony to their humanity, a common humanity which they sought to demonstrate through the very writing of a text."[37] Senegalese writer Pap Khouma, author of *Io, venditore di elefanti* (I, Seller of Elephants, 1990), the very first autobiography published by an African in Italian, explains: "The most important thing was not to demonstrate something. I wanted instead to begin speaking. Italians were talking about us, they would ask questions and they would provide the answers. We who were present began to speak in order to interrupt this monologue among Italians and establish a dialogue. This was the goal of the book."[38] To become visible within Italian society by speaking and affirming a voice also meant, for Khouma, coming out of the gray zone of invisibility where Africans were being represented exclusively as illiterate, dejected, and victimized. Khouma's text is indeed of great interest because it narrates the many incidents and troubles of a protagonist whose "success story" has become somehow a model for future generations of African Italian writers. The transformation of the writing subject Khouma who, from being a seller of African souvenirs becomes an author, reminds us of the trajectory of early African American authors who, through the autobiographical genre, gained authorial control and ultimately freedom from bondage. Khouma's text narrates not only what may be one of many possible stories of migration in Italy; it also narrates the discovery of a subjectivity which can look at the past of suffering and struggle with the awareness of being beyond that past. Yet Khouma's, as well as other early autobiographies, were all co-authored by Italian editors, who recorded the immigrant's testimony and turned it into standard Italian. I have argued elsewhere that this act of linguistic mediation, at times highly controversial, often erased the traces of the original language and the authors' direct literary expression, thus jeopardizing his/her authorial control and agency.[39]

For second generation writers, who are now mastering the language, the issue is today more subtle and yet daunting: how to make their presence visible not only within Italian society, but also within the text, in order to escape the accusation of mimicry of Italianness. The issue of the critical reception of Italophone literature is at the center of Alessandro Portelli's comparative analysis of African Italian and early African American texts.[40] Although Portelli is aware of the historical and geographical distance between the Mediterranean and the Atlantic, he nonetheless highlights some of the crucial issues that African American early writers had to face and which still haunt African Italian authors today: the splitting of authorship between the migrant and his/her co-author; the question of literacy and writing; the issue of language; the dialectical relationship between mobility and invisibility; the ambiguous forms of reception that such writings have so far received. Most significantly, Portelli's acute analysis of French Algerian writer Nassera Chohra's autobiography—significantly titled *Volevo diventare bianca*—stresses how African identity in today's Italy is still haunted by the constant ambiguity of racial double consciousness. The parallel between the Atlantic and the Mediterranean is not for Portelli an idle academic exercise in comparative literary analysis; it is a political gesture by which the critic is able to shed light on the pervasive new racism of contemporary Italy. As writers deal with the different forms that nationalist legacies of racism still assume today, racial difference does indeed appear to be ambiguously enmeshed in the contested terrain of, on the one hand, a desire to contain difference and assimilate it by making it invisible, and on the other, a desire to identify such difference, isolate it, and refuse to incorporate it within the national, supposedly homogeneous, whole.

ANCESTOR SPIRITS, GUARDIAN ANGELS

> What does it mean to follow a ghost? And what if this came back to being followed by it, always, persecuted perhaps by the very chase we are leading? Here again what seems to be out front, the future, comes back in advance: from the past, from the back.
>
> Jacques Derrida[41]

If the ghosts of Italy's colonial past return to visit the living in order to remind them of the legacy of past racism, the migrant's ancestor spirits return to recount another history. After his return from a brief visit home in Senegal, Mor, the narrator/protagonist of Senegalese writer Mbacke Gadij's 1999 novel *Lo spirito delle sabbie gialle* (The Spirit of Yellow Sands) finds himself followed night and day by a presence which reveals itself by engaging in a dialogue with him.[42] The voice introduces itself as a "guardian angel" who belongs to the "invisible world, the world of shadows, a spirit." Mor, who is incredulous, challenges the spirit to reveal itself. The spirit, defiant and provocative, accuses Mor of leading a life limited by linear time and space and by his "Cartesian scientific spirit."[43] The spirit lectures Mor, still incredulous, on the boundless possibilities of a perpetual life without death. The spirit's philosophy challenges Mor's linear conception of temporality in order to affirm a continuous cycle of transformation of the self through a series of lives within an uninterrupted sequence of transformations. Mor falls asleep and, when he wakes up, he is no longer sleeping in a squalid dormitory at Adrara San Rocco, in the north of Italy, nor is he a young immigrant from Senegal working in a factory. He is now transformed into his ancestor Mamour,[44] a young blacksmith originally from Ferlo, Senegal, who travels from village to village outside of his region selling or repairing utensils. His story, embedded within Mor's story, begins when Mamour decides to marry a Peul woman from Bakel and to settle there. When he finally returns home, he is ostracized by his family and his community for having married outside of his caste. Mamour's traveling and his eventual return home with a foreign wife are the reasons for his sudden disappearance. A guardian spirit is sent to chase him and bring him back.

Mbacke Gadij informs us that in precolonial times (more or less when Italian merchants offered the Portuguese the means to begin trafficking with the Atlantic West African countries), the trading activities of Portuguese and Spanish merchants first, and French and Dutch later, had brought about the gradual degradation of the social fabric of the Mabo people in the Northern regions of Ferlo. The importation of more modern and functional utensils had pushed the blacksmiths to diversify their activities by dedicating themselves to sedentary agriculture. This was considered a degrading activity, heralding ill-omened events. In this predicament, guardian spirits were conjured up in order to protect the caste from ruin. According to its historical role, the guardian spirit of the blacksmiths of Ferlo began to protect the wanderings of nomads, exiles, and migrants. In Mbacke's text, the visitation of the spirit in Mor's room conjures up another historical epoch, the experience of Senegalese *tirailleurs* who fought for France during World War I. After being brought to the battlefield, the black soldier, ancestor of Mamour, is stationed in what appear to be German cities. Here, he experiences "a different life, based on the materialistic pleasures that money can generate."[45] At the end of the war, he is back in his native village, where the French authorities appoint him governor of his county. In exchange for his service, he receives horses and farming machines; his existence unfolds thereafter at the service of the colonialists.[46] The colonial and precolonial events lead back to contemporary times. The spirit who appears in a Northern Italian village at the beginning of the twenty-first century has been there since precolonial times. It has now been sent by the elders as a remedy against Mor's spiritual departure from his people. His migratory experience in Italy is the major cause of his changed habits: eating at fixed times of the day with a spoon, wearing tight clothes instead of large *bou-bous*, and his persistent fixation with hygiene.

Mbacke's layered structure of narratives within narratives linked by the continuum of the societal role of the spirit functions in the present because it is based on the sequential historicity of animism. As Caroline Rooney poignantly argues, the concept of animism, along with other terms such as *primitivism* and *nativism*, has always been laden with prejudices. The question whether such thinking had the status of a philosophy or of a system of thought has always been highly debated in anthropological discourse. Animism is a stigmatized term whose origin concerns the concept of crossing over from life to death and life again, as well as crossing species.[47]

The idea of crossing boundaries between different dimensions and realms aptly fits my discussion of animated spirits within a discourse around African diasporic movements across the Mediterranean. I will then retain the concept of animism in order to explain the apparition of ancestor spirits in works by contemporary West African writers. By retaining this concept, I endorse Rooney's contention that animism does not belong to a primitive past but it continuously re-creates itself in different forms. The spirits that return from the past are alive and always present in the present: they affirm over and over again their continuous actuality. In works by West African writers, the spirits of the ancestors show the productive futurity of a circular approach to narrativity and historical time. Such spirits show that "the thing *works*, whether it transforms or transforms itself, poses or decomposes itself: the spirit, 'the spirit of the spirit' is *work*."[48] In this sense, these ancestral spirits are no longer a non-presence to be mourned, but a presence to come, in the future, as a present and living reality.[49] As in Braudel's vision of the transforming work of human structures by the corroding action of time, the transformative work of spirits makes and remakes the future.

Mbacke signifies this role of the guardian spirit by setting young Mor a test of some sort. As the embodiment of a spirit who knows the past, present, and future of events, he is made aware of a murderous scheme at the expenses of Pap, a Senegalese friend. By anticipating the place and modality of the killing, the spirit guides all the actors involved in the scene, this time set in Nice, to act differently from what had been predetermined. Pap is saved, and the spirit returns among the living, as a person and, specifically, as the father of a young girl.

ASCENTS AND CROSSINGS

The spectral embodiment of ancestors in Mbacke's novel allows its protagonist to move back and forth through different spatial and temporal dimensions. Such freedom of movement signifies an emancipatory stance rarely seen in earlier works by African Italian writers. In many early autobiographies, immigrants wander from city to city, in a movement that is usually a northbound ascent from Sicily to Lombardy, and from rural to urban landscapes. Moroccan writer Mohamed Bouchane and Senegalese writer Pap Khouma describe the wanderings of African street vendors from one Italian city to the next, or from one selling location to the next.[50] In Rome and

Milan, the railroad station is the main pole of attraction. Here, immigrants have mapped their own alternative urban itineraries, a new cartography that is imagined in terms of Fredric Jameson's "cognitive mapping,"[51] that is, as a space where immigrants can experience a sense of place and orient themselves mentally. As a cognitive site, the urban space is indeed a site of strong identity formation. The railroad station, and other transitional and clearly marked sites of Rome's or Milan's urban spaces, may provide a sense of familiarity within the unfamiliar. Yet, they are spaces enclosed within invisible walls which fence other parts of the city off from immigrant city dwellers. The Italian historic centers (the Duomo, Piazza Venezia), symbols of Italy's cultural history and national identity, are closed off to immigrants by internal borders that are one more extension of the nation's external super-border. For some of them, as is the case with Pap Khouma, the spatial movement from South to North reproduces the ascent movement of African Americans from slavery to freedom, authorial control and literacy. For Khouma, this spatial movement leads to socioeconomic emancipation but also to authorial control and freedom of expression. For writers who managed to get their books published, this recognition is most often found in the literary self that results from the writing process.

As we have seen, the northbound movement from Africa to Europe across the Mediterranean also evokes a new Middle Passage, in ways that are tragically known through the chronicles of the Mediterranean shipwrecks and the ghastly computations of death by sea. Like the movement of waves, the Mediterranean border rejects or accepts with no apparent logic those who intend to cross it. In Saidou Moussa Bâ's novel *La promessa di Hamadi* (Hamadi's Promise, 1991) the fluxes of the sea reproduce the unpredictable destiny of those who are at the mercy of visa inspectors who, rather randomly, may decide "to tighten the mesh of the net."[52] Random is also the movement of migrants from one Mediterranean port to the next, where they hope to be able to disembark. At the beginning of Bâ's novel, the Islamic *marabout* suggests the offering of water as harbinger against the fear of departure. Semba embarks in Dakar on a ship to the Tunisian harbor of La Goulette, and from there on a *Tirrenia* ship to Mazara del Vallo, in Sicily. On the ship, Semba meets Tunisians, Moroccans, Algerians, and two Senegalese friends. Here they exchange stories and plans, suggestions and dreams. While the stories of migrant men and women travel on the sea, unbound from land, the Mediterranean appears no longer as a limit, but as a fluid multiplicity where all the cultures living on its shores can finally be rejoined. It is indeed the *medias terrae of* antiquity, which unites all the people of its diaspora. Saidou Moussa Bâ describes the ship filled with Africans as "a huge petal that carried all those stories, pains and hopes over the waves, and then summed them up and melted them together into one, to finally spill them onto the land, week after week, month after month."[53]

Paul Gilroy's adoption of the image of the ship as the trope of the Atlantic Middle Passage may serve as a reference for our understanding of a new diasporic Mediterranean model. According to Gilroy, the ship is the emblem of the black Atlantic disengagement with fixed and essentialist models of national and ethnic identity, a chronotope that embodies the relationship of the slave trade to both industrialization and modernity.[54] In many African Italian narratives, ships sailing across the Mediterranean sea are indeed a microcosm of relations which embody the link between Africa and the utopian and dystopic tension of European modernity. The Mediterranean sea is the very first foreign space, at the same time barrier and passageway, frontier and bridge, which must be crossed to reach the other side. Moroccan writer Mohamed Bouchane looks at the Mediterranean Spanish shores from the historical perspective of Tariq Ben Zayad, the Arabian warrior who embarked on the conquest of Spain. The story says that the warrior, after setting fire to his boats, said to his men: "Behind us is the sea, in front of us the enemy. What do you decide to do?" Bouchane adds: "I have also burned my boats and now must move ahead at any cost."[55] Also for Pap Khouma the choice to migrate is ineluctable. His panoptical view of Italy from the plane high in the air yields a peculiar perspective: "I feel like I am abandoning a sinking ship and that our leaders are the prime cause of the shipwreck."[56] For Khouma, Africa is a sinking ship that no longer offers organic communities or future hope. Burning your boats, abandoning a sinking ship are both metaphors for the act of border crossing that imply a violent break with past geographies and time, and the uncertainty of the future. And yet, for immigrants whose stories are told in narrative form, literature has been the ship on which the many shores and cultures of the Mediterranean joined. In Saidou Moussa Bâ's words, literature is the "huge petal that carried all those stories over the waves."[57]

THE PROMISE OF THE FUTURE

The ship, as well as the island, are both historically determined spaces and literary topoi that unify the Mediterranean and the Atlantic.[58] In *La promessa di Hamadi*, the narrator is visiting the island of Gorèe, off the coast of the Senegalese capital Dakar, before embarking onto a ship across the Mediterranean to Europe. The Atlantic Middle Passage is evoked here as a "one-way journey."[59] Yet, contrary to the Middle Passage, the Mediterranean migratory passage is referred to as a journey with a return home. This return is not anything we could possibly imagine. As we learn at the end of the novel, the narrator is murdered for having dared to speak out against exploitative working conditions of seasonal migrant laborers in the Southern tomato fields. The return is in reality the narrator's *post mortem* presence, which goes back among the living to tell the story of his brother Semba and, most importantly, of his own death at the hands of Italian criminal organizations involved in the trafficking and exploitation of illegal immigrants. It is therefore the very possibility of narration, an after life of voice and presence that, faithful to the *griot* tradition, serves to bear witness to moments of historical change.

The novel narrates the story of Semba who decides to leave Dakar for Italy in search of his brother Hamadi, who left Senegal and disappeared. Hamadi has left behind in Dakar a young wife who is pregnant with his son. Hamadi appears in the tale as a first-person narrator who reconstructs Semba's travels across the Mediterranean, his stay in the Casertano tomato fields, and his life in an occupied building, called *kër Vittorio*, in Milan. In one of the final scenes of the novel (reminiscent of Luchino Visconti's dramatic scene in *Rocco and His Brothers*) Semba finally meets Hamadi among the steeples of the Milan cathedral. The brothers soon separate again, this time forever. At the end of a frantic chase, Hamadi is shot and dies. In the last scene, Semba's ascent from the crowded piazza of the *duomo* to the top levels of its roof—where he finally finds his brother—is tragically inverted: Hamadi's death is a final descent into a maze of abandoned buildings plastered with gigantic billboards, one of which, ironically, shows the smiling black and white faces of a famous Benetton advertisement, a mocking reminder of a promise of multiculturalism gone sour. It is a descent into the hellish dimension of urban Italy, where Hamadi's life ends among piles of rubbish and industrial waste.

The invisible presence of Hamadi as narrator, who is able to see and reconstruct Semba's unrelenting quest for his kin, overturns the linear logic—as well as the ascent and descent movement—of the narration, while it highlights its circularity. It is no longer Semba who follows in Hamadi's tracks, but it is Hamadi's ghost, by recounting his story, who chases the unfolding of Semba's events. How can Hamadi, who is dead, talk to us? His omniscient position is not a reproduction of the narrative technique a Western reader is familiar with. It is rather a *post mortem* voice that knows all because it is still present. It is a voice embedded in the animistic tradition, and the novel is a (post)modern embodiment of this tradition. In a song Bâ places in the prologue of the novel, Hamadi's voice says: "Now, once I have reached port, I know all the stories/of those who travelled,/I know all the languages of the world/And this is the story of Semba, my brother."[60] Hamadi, as a guiding spirit of all those who travel to migrate, moves from the invisibility of non-personhood to the visibility Bâ confers onto him through the narrative expedient of the voice. Since the story of Hamadi and Semba cannot be lost, it is narrated through this post-mortem voice which, by turning the prologue's song into writing, activates the oral tradition and incorporates it within its narrative structure.

The prologue, following the *griot* tradition, reconstructs the history of the brothers' family. The song of the prologue is dedicated to Maali, an elderly soothsayer Semba visits before leaving Dakar for Europe. To her, who knows the past and the future and who can communicate with the ancestors, the author entrusts the story. She will give it to the *griot* who will then recount it and pass it on from generation to generation. The song of the prologue, dedicated to Maali, returns on various occasions in the narration and, most significantly, in the last chapter, but with a variation. Here the author introduces within the song some lines of Birago Diop's famous poem, entitled "Souffle," a hymn to the animistic tradition: "Those who died never departed/they are in the brightening shadow and in the darkening shadow/They are in running water and in still water."[61] Caroline Rooney reads Birago Diop's verse as a manifesto of animism. Animism, as we have seen, is the expression of a principle of creativity always made relevant in the present and therefore a principle of an unrelenting modernity: "It [animism] is creativity as the composition or writing of being in a living world that must necessarily continue to be written or inscribed. . . . It is a question of how creativity and living realities are not opposable, where a creative drive is bound up with survival instincts and the desire to transmit and perpetuate life."[62]

Bâ's polyglot text, which mixes Pulaar, Wolof, Arabic, and French oral and written narrative techniques, as well as poems and songs, belongs to an African diasporic sensibility. The creative principle of animism, by which the past is constantly embedded within the present, highlights the diasporic modernity of this Senegalese writer. At the end of Bâ's novel, Hamadi's voice suggests to Semba what his destiny will be: "You will take my place, you will work hard and you will send money home. Perhaps you will resume your studies. And whenever possible, you will fight for a fairer society, where nobody will be excluded on the basis of the colour of their skin."[63] This is the ultimate message of Hamadi's spirit to Semba. This final political message shows that, once ancestors are included within a diasporic narrative, their performative function, as John McCall argues, contributes to the "construction and reproduction of historical consciousness and identity."[64] Spirits are living bodies that indicate self-identity and the overcoming of physical and cultural borders; in this sense, they counteract the death-giving principle of non-personhood with a promise of perpetual presence and absolute futurity. They thus offer identity models that are alternative to the danger of post-slavery consciousness and victimization.

After this suggestion Semba has a vision sent to him by the old Maali: he sees a crowd advancing, as in a march. In the crowd Semba recognizes the many immigrants, characters in the novel who, as if in a Pirandellian scene, are coming to meet their author. Among them is Hamadi's child, symbol of the promise that gives the novel its title. The child's promise, projected onto the future, embodies the performative role of the ancestor's apparition onto future generations. At the very end of the novel, a second generation of children of migrant parents symbolically takes over Hamadi's spectral testimony in order to remember it and pass it on.[65] Bâ's message stands both as a warning against discrimination and exploitation, and as a text whose complex narrative structure offers a model for African Italians who are now writing in Italy and have not forgotten their past.

NOTES

1. See for instance Blackburn, "The Old Background to European Colonial Slavery"; Davis, "Looking at Slavery from Broader Perspectives."
2. Davis, "Looking at Slavery," 459.
3. Blackburn, "The Old Background," 65.
4. Verlinden, *L'esclavage dans l'Europe médiévale*.
5. Pétre-Grenouilleau, *Les traits négrières*.
6. Thomas, *The Slave Trade*.
7. Bonaffini, "Corsari, schiavi siciliani," 1.
8. Pétre-Grenouilleau, *Les traits négrières*; Davis, "Looking at Slavery."
9. See, for instance, the critical apparatus of the new St. Martin's edition of *The Tempest*; Hulme's re-assessment in *The Tempest and Its Travels*; Warner's rewriting of the play in her novel *Indigo* (1992); and Zabus, *Tempests after Shakespeare*.
10. Derrida, *Specters of Marx*.
11. J. Bozonnet, "Esclaves en Italie," *Le Monde*, 22 September 2006.
12. F. Gatti, "I Was a Slave in Puglia." *L'Espresso*, 5 September 2006.
13. Bales, *Disposable People*, 280.
14. Dal Lago, *Non-persone*, 220.
15. The 1995 Dini Decree consisted of a set of provisions that regulated immigrant entrance and stay in Italy. It introduced new rules for seasonal workers, established stricter deportation conditions, as well as severe sanctions for people-smugglers and foreigners without papers. Moreover, the decree allowed deportation of migrants guilty of misdemeanors without possibility of appeal.
16. Bakolo Ngoi, "Visto da Kalo."
17. Ben Jelloun, "Villa Literno," 23. Except where explicitly stated, all translations from Italian and French are my own.
18. Ben Jelloun, "Villa Literno," 34.
19. Dal Lago, *Non-persone*, 224.
20. The geographical coincidence of ancient slave routes with modern migrant routes in the Sahara reinforces the link I am attempting to set up between the Atlantic and the Mediterranean. In Puglia, Gatti interviewed twenty-eight year-old Asserid, from Tahoua in Niger, who crossed the Sahara desert on foot and by catching rides on old four-wheel drive vehicles. The route that Asserid took from Niger to Libya was established by the Tuaregs for the trans-Saharan trade of commodities, including slaves, in the fifteenth and sixteenth centuries. Along this route is the Niger town of Agadez, a prominent center of Arab and Berber commerce and Islamic scholarship in medieval times and now the crossroads of migrant routes from Central Africa toward Libya and therefore Europe. For further details see Rasmussen, "Tuareg: Takedda and Trans-Saharan Trade."
21. Feven Abreha Tekle is a pseudonym used to maintain anonymity and thus avoid possible repercussions for herself and members of her family who are still in Eritrea. The use of one's own name is a privilege even for those who made the crossing of the Mediterranean and achieved public visibility through the publication of their testimony.
22. Tekle, *Libera*, 180.
23. Tekle, *Libera*, 3.
24. Tekle, *Libera*, 183.
25. Tekle, *Libera*, 205.
26. Derrida, *Specters of Marx*, 9.
27. Bellu, *I fantasmi*, 14.

28. Bellu, *I fantasmi*, 33.
29. Braudel, "Introduction à l'empire espagnol," 160.
30. This is also the function of literary works written on the Middle Passage by African American writers. The most illustrious example is Toni Morrison's *Beloved* (1987), which thematizes the impossibility of naming those who did not survive it and the desire to create a memorial to their unknown names. I endorse Itala Vivan's reading of *Beloved* as a text in which "the African cosmology surfaces in absolutely hybrid characters; the concept of the continuity existing between the world of the living and the world of the non-living takes shape in inevitably tragic motions, and whose sense and explanation is found only within their condition of interstitial creatures." Vivan, "Ibridismi postcoloniali," accessed through *El-Ghibli* 2, http://www.el-ghibli.provincia. bologna.it/testi-online/in-010302.html.
31. See Delle Donne, *Un cimitero chiamato Mediterraneo*; Caritas/Migrantes, "Richiedenti asilo e rifugiati," 143.
32. See Labanca, "History and Memory of Italian Colonialism Today."
33. Del Boca, "The Myths, Suppressions, Denials, and Defaults of Italian Colonialism," 20.
34. See Andall and Duncan, "Memories and Legacies of Italian Colonialism."
35. Triulzi, "Odore di colonia."
36. Derrida, *Specters of Marx*, 174.
37. Gates, *The Signifying Monkey*, 171.
38. Parati, "Intervista," 115.
39. See Lombardi-Diop, "Selling and Storytelling," and "Dall'oralità alla scrittura e dalla scrittura all'oralità."
40. Portelli, "Le origini della letteratura afroitaliana." The translation from Italian is the author's.
41. Derrida, *Specters of Marx*, 10.
42. Mbacke Gadji was born in Nguith, Senegal, which he left in 1986. After living in the South of France, in 1994 he moved to Milan. He is the author of a collection of African folk-tales, titled *Numbelan: Il regno degli animali* (1996), and of three other novels, *Pap, Ngagne, Yatt e gli altri* (2000), *Kelefa: La prova del pozzo* (2003) and *Nel limbo della terra: Una vita dai luoghi senza tempo* (2006).
43. Mbacke, *Lo spirito*, 13.
44. In Wolof, *mam* means elderly, or ancestor. The name *Mam-mour* is thus a composite name meaning "the ancestor of Mor."
45. Mbacke, *Lo spirito*, 24.
46. Mbacke Gadij evokes here the destiny of many West Africans, co-opted by the colonial authorities. These include the literary figure of Thiemoko Keita, as described in Birago Diop's tale "Sarzan," included in his *Les contes d'Amadou Koumba* (1961).
47. Rooney, *African Literature, Animism, and Politics*.
48. Derrida, *Specters of Marx*, 9.
49. According to Derrida's *Specters of Marx*, this is the role that, in the *Manifesto* of 1847–1848, Marx confers to the specter of communism.
50. Bouchane, *Chiamatemi Alì*; Khouma, *Io, venditore di elefanti*.
51. Jameson, *Postmodernism*, 52.
52. Bâ, *La promessa*, 94.
53. Bâ, *La promessa*, 93.
54. Gilroy, *The Black Atlantic*.
55. Bouchane, *Chiamatemi Alì*, 56.
56. Khouma, *Io, venditore di elefanti*, 58.
57. Bâ, *La promessa*, 93.

58. Moving from his reading of Shakespeare's *The Tempest* and Olaudah Equiano's autobiography, William Boelhower argues that the *figura* of the ocean-going ship, in its figurative fluidity, is instrumental in creating and representing an Atlantic space. In Boelhower's analysis, Equiano's Atlantic is, in many ways, similar to the Mediterranean I discuss here; Equiano's ships, as "figurative vectors for the sixteenth century's major genres, utopia and *naufragium*," are very similar to Abheha Tekle's, Giovanni Maria Bellu's, and Saidou Moussa Bâ's wrecks. See Boelhower, "'I Will Teach You How to Flow,'" 42.
59. Bâ, *La promessa*, 91.
60. Bâ, *La promessa*, 10.
61. Bâ, *La promessa*, 146.
62. Rooney, *African Literature*, 23.
63. Bâ, *La promessa*, 150.
64. McCall, "Rethinking Ancestors in Africa," 258.
65. There are many important *post mortem* voices and ghostly apparitions in the work of second-generation African Italian writers. For example, Igiaba Scego, in her first novel, *Rhoda* (2004), makes Rhoda, one of her female protagonists, speak from the grave with a post-mortem voice. In *Verso la notte BAKONGA* (2001) Jadelin M. Gangbo makes Mika, his young protagonist, go through a transformative experience during which he meets a guiding spirit, called the Master of the Knife. The spirit shows Mika the power and the regenerating forces of nature, as well as the devastating effects of history, including the nightmarish experience of the Atlantic slave trade.

11 Transatlantic Minstrelsy

Performing Survival Strategies in Slavery and Hip-Hop

Venus Opal Reese

Hip-hop culture operates as a form of global youth culture via its mass transmission on MTV, BET, movies, and advertisements. Does hip-hop teach the youth around the world how to be "a real nigga" (read "black buck") or "a good trick" (read "Jezebel")? This chapter examines the historical roots of hip-hop culture from the context of antebellum slavery. It considers how hip-hop artists embody the rhetoric, posture, and survival strategies of enslaved people in the southern plantation, which would become the basis for the social types evolved in Atlantic minstrelsy. These evolved social types would then become the template for the popular representation of women of African descent as "mammy" or "Jezebel" or "tragic mulatto." There is a similar process with regard to men of African ancestry, represented as "bucks" or "sambos" or "coons." I explore the extent to which it is useful to think about hip-hop performance as a contemporary form of "coon" show. In this reading of hip-hop as minstrelsy, Lauryn Hill features as "mammy," 50 Cent as "buck," Puffy/Puff Daddy/P. Diddy/Diddy as "coon," and Lil' Kim as "Jezebel." I focus my examination on the semiotic inheritance of Atlantic slavery through Lauryn Hill's lyrics, interviews, hair styles, body image, and marketing strategies.

The Antebellum Plantation and Contemporary Music Industry Production: Some Parallels

PLANTANTION	RECORD COMPANY
Antebellum plantation master The owner of slaves and all products produced by slaves.	*Record company president* The owner of the company and of its products.
Cotton gin Eli Whitney's 1793 improved-upon invention "more easily separated the seeds from the strands of cotton" thereby ensuring that "production	*Major distributors* The distribution of a CD is the *only* means of export for any record label and, by extension, the recording artists. A record company ships a CD

that had formally been confined to home use could now be grown for commercial export."[1]

Overseer

Responsible for the "overall day-to-day and management of all season to season strategy of plantation work" utilizing "any means necessary" to ensure that all deadlines were met.[2]

Driver

Usually a black male responsible for the "on-the-spot" discipline of the slaves; he ensured that the "work got done" using "any means necessary."[3]

Cotton

"Cotton was the crop that dominated the plantation economy of the nineteenth-century South becoming this country's principal export crop. . . . Short-staple cotton was in demand throughout the world, especially in England, where textile manufactures never seemed to get enough . . . by 1820 output amounted to 334,378 bales, accounting for more than half of the nation's agricultural exports."[4]

Patroller

Slave patrols were "usually a group of white males, usually of the lower class," called together to find "runaways, to prevent slave gatherings . . . ensure the general safety of the

to wholesalers, which function as "gigantic distribution networks that move records from manufacturing plants" into retail stores.[8]

Product manager

Responsible for the overall management of the "other departments (sales, marketing, promotions, etc.)" to ensure that all departments in the record company, "work together to push your records."[9]

Personal manager

The "general manager and chief operating officer" of an artist's career, who decides "which company to sign with . . . which songs to record, hiring band members, selecting photographs . . . coordinating concert tours, working with . . . agent to make the best deals with promoters, . . . implementing budget, etc."[10]

Hip-hop music

In 1999 "the United States still dominates the global market with a 37% share of world sales."[11] Hip-hop music, second only to rock in sales, between 1982 and 1987 increased by 5%,[12] and from 1990 to 1999 increased by 2.3%, while rock decreased in sales by 10.9%.[13] While hip-hop trails rock in record sales, it "has unquestionably become the dominant force in contemporary American" and global youth culture.[14]

A&R person

Artist and Repertoire persons are "executives of record companies who . . . find, sign, and guide talent, including matching songs to the singers . . . matching producers with white community . . . and to enforce the system."[5]

Sharecropping

After the Civil War ended in 1865, people of African descent began to work for wage as sharecroppers. Sharecropping involved "a planter paying his workers a part of the crop, up to as much as half for their labor. The planter generally provided the tools and seed . . . Since sharecroppers bought their food, clothing, and other items from the plantation, they often finished the year in debt or with very little profit."[6]

Transatlantic slaves

"African slaves occupied the lowest rank in the social order of the colonial societies. Imported as human property, their sole function was to work for those whom had purchased them . . . Arriving as involuntary workers, African slaves confronted the challenge of helping to build societies in which they were and continued to be persons with few if any rights."[7]

Historical crop

Modernity; North America; wealth via cotton production furnished by slave labor.

artists . . . and running the recording sessions."[15]

Royalties

The division of profit between the artist and the company on CDs sold is the royalty. "The record company will agree to pay all recording costs . . . including payment to the artist, the arranger, the copyist, and the musicians. These costs shall be advanced against and recoupable out of royalties which might other otherwise become due to the artist. Companies usually include studio rental editing cost . . . packaging (artwork, wrapping and sales appeal) which are recoupable out of artists royalties."[16]

Recording artists

A recording artist is considered an employee of the record company. The artist "is employed to render personal service as a recording performer on an exclusive basis for the purpose of manufacturing"[17] recordings.

Hip-hop crop

World culture; wealth via recordings furnished by hip-hop artists.

There is something to say for the past. You know, the past—that past. The past that circulates as truth dressed in cheap clothing, three-inch-high fuck-me pumps, and a cigar dangling from the corner of a justified mouth. Truth like "blackness" throughout the Atlantic. There are two forms of circulation of blackness framed as truth that are separated by over two hundred years and that I will address in my analysis: Atlantic minstrelsy and North

American hip-hop culture. In very simple terms, these two entertainment forms have the same momma: North American plantation slavery. Momma, as North America plantation slavery, nurtured, fostered, suckled, and perpetuated the buying and selling of gestures, practices, and products of the "black body," the performance of "self" for the sake of survival (be it real or imagined, physical or financial), and the assimilation of these marginal practices, gestures, and rhetoric into popular culture. Yes, Atlantic minstrelsy and North American hip-hop culture have the same momma, but it's the daddy that makes them different. Papa was indeed "a rolling stone," and "wherever he laid his hat" was not simply "his home"—it became his market. Papa's market was global. Atlantic minstrelsy was the vehicle by which Papa rolled his stone from North America to Africa and Europe. As early as 1848, blackface minstrels visited Capetown, South Africa, and inspired former Javan and Malaysian slaves to create an event that came to be known as the annual Cape Coon Carnival.[18] The Netherlands' *Zwarte Piet* became a classic darky icon in the mid- to late nineteenth century, contemporaneous with the spread of darky iconography.[19] The worldwide circulation of "darky" or "blackness" was conducted primarily through minstrel performance, flyers, posted theater bills, posters of minstrel types, players, and stars that represented the "true" (read authentic) Negro on the North American plantation. The stone rolls. It beeps. It bops. It hips and it hops.

The Papa in minstrelsy becomes the Daddy in hip-hop culture—Pimp Daddy, that is. Pimp Daddy has a bunch of tricks to peddle his wares nationally and abroad: MTV, VH1, commercial advertisements, mixed tapes, bootleg copies of concerts, tours, endorsements, underground house parties, books, sampling, remixes, TV, radio, the Internet, My Space, mp3s, and such. Think quick, easy, accessible circulation and dissemination of "blackness" sold as "truth" (read "real," as in "keepin' it real" and authentic) to youth around the world looking for a way to buck the system, have their say, and have style. They are much like the working-class youth who put on blackface in New York in the 1820s to defiantly separate themselves from the bourgeois as well as snub the norms, expectations, and conventions of control.[20] Youth around the world—from the Netherlands to Asia—have used and embraced hip-hop in similar fashions. But let's get back to Momma. Whether Atlantic minstrelsy or North American hip-hop, the images, gestures, postures, and rhetoric are based on real-life folk from the North American plantation "acting" out survival. These acts of survival—be it a smile, a jig, or silence—once observed and mimicked by people (read northerners) became divorced from the survival for which the acts were created. The gestures, images, posture, and rhetoric then traveled in place of the people. Blackness traveled, black folk stayed on the plantation. W.T. Lhamon Jr. names this circulation of blackness "lore":

> Lore is composed of the basic gestures of all expressive behavior, from moans to narratives, signs to paintings, steps to dances. Part of this

lore acquires a special status. Certain gestures were separate from other gestures. These particular motions of the hands or mouth represented a group to itself and to outsiders and they are recognized for their representation.[21]

Atlantic minstrel lore traveled the world, representing blackness in fetishized gestures, separate from the conditions and function from which the gestures originated. That lore then became the template on which people of African ancestry were/are able to occupy highly visible space in popular culture. Hip-hop uses this lore and traffics in it, while youth around the world bear witness to the lore's effectiveness: just look at the purchase of clothes, CDs, and the mimicry of North American hip-hop cultural attributes (language, posture, poses, attitude, and dance moves) by youth in Africa, Europe, and Asia. But hip-hop does more. Hip-hop may circulate through Daddy but it always goes back to Mama. Hip-hop bitch slaps momma across the face regularly. Here's how: Hip-hop cites and samples the survival strategies on the North American plantation. As both performance and performative act, hip-hop refers, references, and draws from the life-or-death negotiations of enslaved people on the antebellum plantation, ingests the strategies, and then re-sells them as cultural capital in exchange for social existence. While Atlantic minstrelsy ignored the source of the gestures and related to them as separate from its source, hip-hop purposefully uses the roles, the acting out on the antebellum plantation, to make that paper. Let's turn to actual people to illustrate hip-hop artists' use of historical signifiers and signs to produce social existence and recognition. I will direct my analysis to North American examples, but we must keep in mind that the reach of hip-hop culture and music is global. My intention is to examine what hip-hop is teaching our youth globally. I shall use performativity as citationality to articulate my arguments.

HISTORICAL ROLES IN HIP-HOP CULTURE

Because performance is fluid and because time brings change, the historical roles from the plantation—by the time they reemerge in hip-hop culture—have mutated and in some cases conflated with each other. The hip-hop artists I examine are representative of the larger context of hip-hop culture, and by extension, society at large.

During the era of institutionalized slavery on the plantation in the antebellum South, four primary roles were performed within the plantation household: the mistress, the maid, the slave, and the master. Each of the bodies that occupied these roles used various tactics to survive and was based on a social ethos of that era. The survival strategies were demonstrated in various actions, speech acts, or silences. The mistress as "lady" and the master as "gentleman" have their roots in English genteel society, re-created and reconfigured for the antebellum planters' elite society. The maid as "mammy" or "Jezebel" or "tragic mulatto" has its roots in the social ethos that females of African ancestry were chattel, promiscuous, or tainted, which thus justified the reproductive role black women had in the institution of slavery. The male slave as "Sambo" or "Buck" or "Nat" has its roots in the social ethos that males of African ancestry were either non-threatening, docile buffoons, oversexed studs who kept the population of nigger babies a-coming, or violent insurrectionists whose sole desire was/is to kill all white people. Each of these roles is the radical antithesis of its racialized counterpart to some degree.

mistress = submissive, morally pure, esteemed, "Lady"	maid = domineering mammy, sexually loose "Jezebel," tainted, "tragic mulatto"
master = gallant, refined, civilized, "Gentleman"	slave = crass Sambo, oversexed buck, barbaric Nat

Each of these roles was created on a plantation to ensure survival.

Within hip-hop, all of the roles from the plantation reappear, albeit in reconfigured forms. The archetypes of the mistress, maid, slave, and master actually mutated into three types of "maid" and three types of "slave," and in so doing they were transformed from archetypes to stereotypes that are regarded within hip-hop culture as icons, undistinguished as such. The mistress and the master's survival strategies actually became conflated with two of the four types examined here, which are regarded as icons within hip-hop culture. The double consciousness of the mistress as both present and absent appears in hip-hop culture as the standard of beauty, status, and leisurely lifestyle exemplified by the "Jezebel" icon, Lil' Kim. The survival strategies employed by masters on the plantation—ownership, recognition, and domination as measures of masculinity—is clearly demonstrated in hip-hop's "Sambo" icon, P. Diddy. The pious, asexual, nurturing mother—who is also able to talk back while managing business with a hand of steel—to the hip-hop nation manifests itself in Lauryn Hill. The triflin' dog nigga, who is only useful for his sexual prowess is demonstrated in hip-hop's latest "buck," 50 Cent. Each of these artists occupies a role in society via popular culture that was created long before hip-hop was even conceived. The historical roles currently occupied by these artists are not unique to hip-hop culture. Literature, politics, film, television, churches, schools, business and universities have these social-geographical spaces as well. The hyper-visibility of hip-hop culture makes it ideal to examine these social positions critically through the lens of performance.

The roles the hip-hop artists occupy were already in existence prior to the birth of hip-hop in the 1970s. Just as Halle Berry stands in for Dorothy Dandridge in our collective social-geographical psyche, someone else will come along and replace, for example, hip-hop's current "buck," 50 Cent, much as he replaced hip-hop's all-time beloved "buck," Tupac. My point is that while these roles existed prior to hip-hop culture, the artists within hip-hop utilize the roles, the language of these roles, and the survival strategies created by these historical roles in order to "make it" in the hip-hop music industry. What is more, unlike their predecessors, who performed these roles as a means of survival, these artists live the roles as if the roles were themselves. This is made evident in their lyrics, marketing angle, and interviews. While no role is pure (Mariah Carey can just as easily be read as a "Jezebel" or as a "tragic mulatto"), the dominant tenor of each artist's historical predecessor supersedes the lesser timbre of the other roles.

There are many more historical roles I could use to demonstrate the current residue of the institution of slavery in hip-hop culture. Will Smith is the ideal "clown," while Old Dirty Bastard was the quintessential "buffoon." Kalis is a great "Topsy" figure. In contrast, Chuck D from the rap group Public Enemy, with his militant lyrics and Afrocentric philosophy, is hip-hop's "Nat" icon, the insurrectionist who is considered a real threat to society. Another type, turned icon, resides in the woman of biracial heritage who does not fit into either world. The woman who seems to be desperately confused about her place in the world, willing to pass to ensure a better life, yet unable to let go of her nigger roots, is exemplified by hip-hop's "tragic mulatto," Mariah Carey. I will not examine these roles further in this chapter. I have chosen instead to examine one of the four most pervasive types of the antebellum era—the Mammy—for the sake of clarity and focus.

In my analysis of hip-hop, I will use the term *performative* as a "citation" of the historically regulated, punitively consequential roles embodied and acted out on the southern plantation. To state that something has evolved implies the presence of vestiges of its original form, traces of its evolved past which simultaneously demonstrate fresh rifts on the theme from which it began. Hip-hop, as a performative distinction, "cites" or "samples" the historical past, undistinguished as such. Jacques Derrida clearly articulates the way in which that performativity can be regarded as citationality. He writes: "Could a performative utterance succeed if its formulation did not repeat a 'coded' or iterable utterance, or, in other words, if the formula I pronounce in order to open a meeting, launch a ship or a marriage were not then identifiable in some way as a 'citation'?"[22] Hip-hop "cites" the "identifiable" historical past as a performance through the medium of performance—at live concerts, sales of CDs, magazine interviews, and so on. Hip-hop is the performance of the enactment of survival. Hip-hop musical artists—specifically the rap artists—are being performative in that they are sampling, that is, "citing," the rhetoric and posture employed as performative roles on the plantation for the sake of survival. While there are significant parallels between the plantation and the record industry, the context of survival is not the same. History has evolved and so has society. Yet the residue of the roles still lives on in the psyche of the American character and what it means to be American. Hip-hop implodes and exploits the social-geographical spaces people of African ancestry can and are allowed to occupy in popular, highly visible representations.

Hip-hop is currently the most visible popular cultural medium. One could argue that hip-hop teaches the youth globally how to be "a real nigga" (read "black buck") or "a good ho" (read "Jezebel") History re-emerges in hip-hop performatively by "citing" the rhetoric and posture of the plantation roles and the performance of these roles for the purchase of the American Dream. Mammy, Jezebel, Sambo, and Buck re-emerge—"niggafied"—in hip-hop gear for a contemporary context. Unlike the plantation in the nineteenth century, where the roles were alive, breathing, and functional for the sake of survival, in hip-hop the roles are dead forms. They read like masks: ersatz postures and practices and empty rhetoric that no longer work for the function they were originally constructed, yet are evoked to garner a response or a product. Now these bastardized roles have become the means by which North American hip-hop recording artists realize societal recognition by way of material success. Performativity resides in and produces various degrees of materiality through language, societal regulation, and social recognition. That is to say, the selling of the black body, its labor, and "culture" is part of what it means to be American. Hip-hop cites this historicity and pimps it for its own swing at the American Dream.

PERFORMATIVE NARRATIVE

Hip-Hop is the sOcial reVolutioN of this millennium Era Much like the Harlem Renaissance Civil Rights Movement the Black Art's MoVement and the Feminist Moment bOth the fIrst and second wavE Hip-Hop is the voice of a people wHo without obvious advantages CHANGED THE WORLD in the words of lesbian prophet Me'shell NdegèOcello
"Hip-hop is the world the slaveholder made, sent into niggafide future shock."[23]

Let the church say amen. Wellllll, come on now. Preach, preacher. Me'shell continues
"Hip-hop is the black aesthetic by-product of the American dream

machine, our culture of consumption, commodification and subliminal seduction . . ."[24]

She's not finished . . .
"hiphop has no morals no ecological concerns for the scavenged earth or the scavenged American minds wrecked in the pursuit of new markets."[25]

hip-hop RiPs ofF the hUsks that hide the devastation three hundred years of RAPe cASStration and sodomy can do to a country do to a world

benjamins
bucks bangin' gangbangin'
PIMPED AS REAL sold as cool, hip, and down to suburb boys born

with blue contacts for eyes you are
thaT NeW MARKet

fuck a stigma

Jigga
Wha/
Jigga
who
Fuck a
Nigga?
Naw man
Fuck you!@#$%^&*()_)(*&^%$#@!~
the STIGma of being born of
African ancestry in North America
and what that has been positioned
to mean
good black folk
have attemPted to counterbalance
the stigMA
by
being
well
good black
folk.

Be a positiVe role model don't
Dwell on the paSt focus bright-
eyed and optimisticALLy on a
more equitable tomoRrow

But Hip-Hop is different

The artists within Hip-Hop have
an entirely different relationship to
our stigmatized past Hip-Hop cul-
ture, specifically the musical artists
ARE
THE
SURVIVAL
STRATEGIES
THAT
WERE

CREATED
OVER
TWO
HUNDRED
YEARS
AGO

codified even unto itself
let those with ears to hear over-stand

Hip-Hop does not "overcom'" our
ignoble past it uses it—to extreme
in excess
WheREAs perSONalities within
televisiOn Politics histories film
education Jazz plays and opera
Divas try to "overcome" our
pained roots Hip-Hop thriVes on
them Hip-Hop performs surViVal
in subject matter deliVery of the
word and perSONal testiMONIES
of the hardSHIP of being alive.
Hip-Hop does not try to ignore,
apOlogize eXplain or sweetLy
frame
its existence
or its past
it relishes in our tortured HIStory
as a meanS of making it to the
neXt day

In short Hip-Hop performs its
own surViVal

title:
?
HIPHOP
MAN
I
FEST
O
(ode to leroi jones)

Judith Butler states, "Performativity is . . . not a singular 'act,' for it is always a reiteration of a norm or set of norms, and to the extent that it acquires an act-like status in the present, it conceals or dissimulates the conventions of which it is a repetition."[26] The antebellum South was a performative context. The roles donned in the antebellum South were performative to the extent that they reiterated "a norm or set of norms" that concealed or dissimulated "the conventions" of which they were a "repetition." Those norms were managed, maintained, and facilitated by the threat of punitive consequence—the threat of death. These roles originated on the plantation and were circulated globally through minstrelsy. Or, said another way, the survival strategies employed on the plantation would become the basis for the social types evolved in Atlantic minstrelsy. While we are no longer on the plantation, performativity is alive and breathing in present-day hip-hop culture, in an evolved stage. An examination of Lauryn Hill as "hip-hop's mammy" bears witness to this evolution.

DO YOU THINK I'M PRETTY? THE
MAMMIFICATION OF LAURYN HILL

I will examine Lauryn Hill in relationship to the historical roles that stem from the survival strategies of folk from antebellum southern plantations. I have chosen to examine Lauryn Hill and her work because she clearly demonstrates the historical role she occupies. Her heightened visibility and popularity, and her own personal and public accounts demonstrate how she equates herself with the historical role of mammy she resides inside of and performs on and off of stage.

The physical attributes which are associated with the mammy, as popularized by the movie *Gone with the Wind*, are a full figure, dark skin, full lips, big bosom, and general unattractiveness in a sexual sense. Oprah Winfrey, when she was full-figured during the 1980s, fit the physical description of a historical mammy better than Lauryn does in the second millennium. My reading of Lauryn as a mammy figure is a hip-hop read and hip-hop, in its essence, is postmodern. Nelson George considers hip-hop a "postmodern art in that it shamelessly raids older forms of pop culture—kung fu movies, chitlin' circuit comedy, '70s funk, and other equally disparate sources—and reshapes the material to fit the personality of an individual artist and the taste of the times."[27] Hip-hop culture, and by extension Lauryn Hill, have contemporized historical stereotypes, transforming them into cultural icons. Lauryn Hill's reappropriation of the mammy role is no exception. Lauryn's dark skin, full lips, head rags, and pickaninny styled locks—minus the full figure—fit into and cut a hip, stylin', glamorized mammy figure.

While historically mammies have been perceived, at least in literature written by people who were not of African descent,[28] as passive and content, mammies have also been associated with a take-charge manner[29] and the propensity to speak up and talk back.[30] The most famous mammy was, and remains, Vivien Leigh's maid in the epic movie *Gone with the Wind*, performed by Hattie McDaniel. In Scarlett O'Hara's house,

Hattie's character is truly the head nigger in charge. She cooks, cleans, practically runs the plantation,[31] keeps Scarlett in line, and is completely loyal to her white "baby." Hattie, in and out of character, is not passive at all—she speaks up and talks back, using the mammy role for her own purposes. In hip-hop, Lauryn speaks up and talks back in both her lyrics and in her live performances. She spits out lyrics about her emancipation from the tyranny of overbearing bandmates and their hostile resistance regarding her desire to go solo: "My emancipation don't fit your equation/ I was on the humble, you—on every station/Some wan' play young Lauryn like she dumb/ . . . I know all the tricks from Bricks to Kingston/ . . . Now understand L-Boogie's nonviolent/But if a thing test me, run for my gun/ . . . You might win some but you just lost one."[32] In fact they did lose one: the Fugees stopped recording together for eight years after the success of Lauryn's solo project.

Mammies, historically, have been very religious.[33] Lauryn's song, "Forgive Them Father," opens like this: "Forgive us our trespasses as we forgive those that trespass against us/Although then again we will never, never, never trust."[34] Her words cite the Lord's Prayer, Matthew 6:12, "And forgive us our trespasses as we forgive those who trespass against us." Lauryn uses the sample to her advantage by finding a loophole concerning forgiveness, which is made clear in Bible verses 14–15, "For if you forgive men their trespasses, your heavenly father will forgive you. But if you do not forgive men their trespasses, neither will your Father forgive your trespasses." Lauryn's line, "Although we again will never, never, never trust," honors God's instruction, but provides room to protect oneself. Her most maternal song, "Zion," besides bearing the name of her son, refers to Mount Zion, another biblical reference. Lauryn equates her son with the "prince of peace" who graciously bore the "perils" that came because he was the Messiah. Another biblical parallel Lauryn makes with the virgin Mary is the birth announcement. The angel Gabriel came to Mary and told her: "Do not be afraid, Mary, for you have found favor with God. And behold, you will conceive in your womb the birth of a son, and shall call his name Jesus."[35] Lauryn approximates this same visitation and mandate with regard to her conception of her son Zion. She sings: "Unsure of what the balance held/I touched my belly overwhelmed/By what I had been chosen to perform/But then an angel came one day/Told me to kneel down and pray/For unto me a man child would be born/Woe this crazy circumstance/ I knew his life deserved a chance/But everybody told me to be smart/Look at your career they said,/"Lauryn, baby use your head"/But instead I chose to use my heart.[36] Lauryn, like the Virgin Mary, chose to use her "heart" instead of reason.

Moving from the biblical to the maternal, the historical mammy was defined by her loyalty to her white children. This is where time, performance, and hip-hop collide and reinvent the past. "Please perceive me as a mother. I've always tried to be perceived as a mother of someone—a mother of a nation, a mother of people, a mother of love," declares Lauryn.[37] By virtue of her self-proclaimed "mother"-status, figuratively and literally, Lauryn positions herself in a recognizable and non-threatening position—as mammy to the "nation." It is important to note that the hip-hop nation is global. Unlike the mammy of the antebellum plantation, hip-hop's mammy has more advertisement. Hip-hop's global visibility extends Lauryn's scope beyond the "white" children nurtured historically at her breast, to multicultural "hip-hop heads" who are now nurtured globally by her lyrics.

Implicit in the mammy role is nurturance. Sociologist Patricia Hill Collins illuminates this point, stating that female leaders of African descent in corporations "are hampered by being treated as mammies and penalized if they do not appear warm and nurturing."[38] Collins's assertion highlights the issue of appearance. If females of African descent in the corporate world do not "appear warm and nurturing," they are reprimanded in some form. To appear is a performance, an act, a pretense. If they do not play the mammy role, they are "penalized." Lauryn Hill performs nurturance. A staff writer for *Rolling Stone* Magazine, Tiarra Mukherjee, comments: "Hill's brand of maternal affection and devotion to kids extends beyond her music." Tiarra's evidence for this declaration is Lauryn's (tax-deductible) charity work: "She's founded Camp Hill, in upstate New York, and Refugee Camp, in New Jersey, which are both outreach and education programs for underprivileged inner-city kids."[39] Lauryn states that throughout her world travels, she has discerned that "what distinguishes one child from another is not ability but access; access to education, access to opportunity, access to love."[40]

To remedy this, in 1998, Lauryn created a not-for-profit organization, The Refugee Project. This initiative is designed so that people can make financial contributions, which Lauryn uses to "create social programs for young people to provide access to opportunities that might be otherwise unavailable."[41] The advent of the summer programs, Camp Hill (New York) and Refugee Camp (New Jersey), as well as the Refugee Project—which includes the Circle Mentoring Program, the National Youth Initiative, and local, national and global community outreach—performs and commodifies Lauryn's nurturance and positions her squarely in the role of mammy.

The last strand that ties Lauryn to the mammy role is sexuality—or the lack thereof. One can be a mother and not be perceived as sexual. When Lauryn became with child, a virtual "manhunt" for "Lauryn's baby's daddy" was adeptly facilitated by Wendy Williams, former New York radio station WQHT Hot 97 "gossip jock."[42] The fever of the conversation concerning Lauryn's pregnancy was not lost on Lauryn. When asked by the interviewer from *Vibe* magazine in 1998, "Was it hard for the public to see you as a woman? As a real woman?" Lauryn responded: "Yeah. [She laughs] I'm allowed a personal life. [Long pause]."[43] Lauryn, according to this account, is perceived as an icon, a symbol, a sign. She is not perceived as a "real woman," meaning a sexually active female. Lauryn's sexuality was being policed by the hip-hop nation. In short, by becoming pregnant, Lauryn had transgressed. She was criticized as a bad role model for teen-aged females of African decent, as well as advised, via Wendy Williams's call-in phone line, to abort the child and return to the road to finish touring with the Fugees. She was also encouraged not to give up her blossoming career for a baby. The need to police Lauryn's sexuality indicates the need to have her fit into a particular role where having sex is a transgression with "punitive consequences."[44]

The last piece of the mammification of Lauryn Hill involves marriage. Mammies, historically, were wedded to their jobs, which was the sphere of the plantation household. Collins writes: "The mammy image buttresses the ideology of the cult of true womanhood, one in which sexuality and fertility are severed . . . the mammy image is one of an asexual woman, a surrogate mother in blackface whose historical devotion to her White family is now giving way to new expectations. Contemporary mammies should be completely committed to their jobs."[45] Lauryn can have as many babies as she wants; mammies on plantations had many children too. She can have a handsome, doting "boyfriend" that satisfies the romantic notions of love perpetuated in popular culture. As long as she is not married, without "official" sanction, she will be positioned as a mammy. Until that "commitment," the image of Lauryn as asexual and surrogate mother to millions worldwide was secured. It is important to note that once Lauryn married Rohan Marley and mothered two more children, her record sales dropped to the point of annihilation. In 2002, Lauryn released a double disk CD, *Lauryn Hill: MTV Unplugged 2.0*. On this CD she acknowledges that she had created a public persona, a public illusion that kept her hostage. She also talked at length about her husband and their children. In this album Lauryn completely rejects and denounces the role she had played for the world. And she was duly punished—with low records sales. Lauryn wouldn't play the game right and was penalized with social erasure. I am of the opinion that if Oprah ever married her career would alter drastically because she, like Lauryn, would have transgressed her role—Lauryn in hip-hop, Oprah in daytime television—as mammy in the social-geographical psyche of North America and the world.

The loss of financial compensation is minuscule in comparison to the *loss of self—as a socially recognized, societally celebrated being*. Imagine the impact on Lauryn, or Mariah Carey (hip-hop's tragic mulatto), or Hattie McDaniel (the prototype mammy) of going from being a "somebody" to a "nobody" because you would no longer subscribe to the role expected of you. One becomes a social non-being, very much like an enslaved person on a plantation in the antebellum South. That is to say, all of one's efforts, contributions, and gifts to the world are erased or disappear or are hidden or denied as a direct result of one's status as a social non-being. Trying to find information on Lauryn nowadays is like trying to find a needle in a haystack. Once the most celebrated woman American musical artist of African descent, now Lauryn as a hip-hop icon and social being only exists in repetition from her past as hip-hop's mammy. Lauryn—if her commentary on the 2002 *MTV Unplugged* CD is a true indication of her own growth and development as a woman, mother, wife, person, and artist—seems to be happy with her choice to lay down the mask of mammy, and let mammy take a load off—until the next mammy fits the role (Queen Latifah? Nah. Too light.)

On the flip side, the very good news about Lauryn's reinvention of the mammy role is that she defines herself—albeit within the positionality she occupies both publicly and societally. Perhaps recreation would be the more apt term. Collins writes: "no matter how oppressed an individual woman may be, the power to save the self lies within the self . . . the ultimate responsibility for self-definitions and self-valuations lies within the individual woman herself."[46]

And on that note, I leave you with Lauryn's—sweet, magical, beautiful Lauryn—words of self-definition/re-creation. The words, which have inspired and continue to inspire as well as change, through hip-hop, the course of history and, indeed, the world: "My world it moves so fast today/ The past it seems so far away/And I squeeze it so tight, I can't breathe/And every time I try to be/What someone has thought of me/So caught up, I wasn't able to achieve/But deep in my heart the answer it was in me/And I made up my mind to find my own destiny."[47]

NOTES

1. Kelly and Lewis, *To Make Our World Anew*,153.
2. Kelly and Lewis, *To Make Our World Anew*, 178.
3. Kelly and Lewis, *To Make Our World Anew*, 178.
4. Kelly and Lewis, *To Make Our World Anew*, 152–153, 169, 170–172.
5. Kelly and Lewis, *To Make Our World Anew*, 193. It was illegal for a slave to move away from the plantation without a pass from the master, so "a principal task of the patrols was to enforce the pass system."
6. Kelly and Lewis, *To Make Our World Anew*, 260–261.
7. Kelly and Lewis, *To Make Our World Anew*, 27.
8. Passman, *All You Need to Know*, 82.
9. Passman, *All You Need to Know*, 82.
10. Passman, *All You Need to Know*, 47–48.
11. Recording Industry Association of America, Market Data, http://www.riaa. com/MD-World.cfm.
12. Krasilovsky and Shemel, *This Music Business*, xix.
13. Recording Industry Association of America, Market Data, http://www.riaa. com/MD-Cons-2.cfm.
14. Light, *The Vibe History of Hip-Hop*, v.
15. Passman, *All You Need to Know*, 134–135.
16. Krasilovsky and Shemel, *This Music Business*, 3. New artists receive approximately 10% royalties from every 85, not 100, CDs (units) sold at retail price, minus 20% packaging cost. Another 15% are given away for promotion of CDs. Artists, thereby, do not receive royalties on this 15% because artist roy-

alty is based on retail sales (see Passman, *All You Need to Know*, 88–94, for a detailed breakdown of royalty computation).

17. Passman, *All You Need to Know*, 88–94.
18. The name was changed to the Cape Town Minstrel Carnival in 2003, so as to avoid offending tourists.
19. Zwarte Piet, or "Black Peter," is a character in Dutch and Flemish Sinterklaas lore.
20. "Disempowered young workers applied blackface as a defiant measure of their own distance from those arguments among enfranchised interests. Youth in blackface were almost as estranged from the bourgeois inflections of the slavery quarrel as were the blacks whom they therefore chose to figure their dilemma and emphasize their distance. . . . The minstrel show . . . allowed youths to resist merchant-defined external impostures and to express a distinctive style. . . . Abstracting themselves as blacks allowed the heterogeneous parts of the newly toiling young workers all access to the same identity tags. . . . Precisely because middle-class aspirants disdained the black jitterbug in every region, the black figure appealed all across the Atlantic as an organizational emblem for workers and the unemployed. Hated everywhere, he could be championed everywhere alike." Lhamon, *Raising Cain*, 43–44.
21. Lhamon, *Raising Cain*, 69. Black gestures are fetishized and continually embedded in further iterations. W.T. Lhamon argues that the basic stance of "black" street dancers at Catharine's Market in 1820 would then become Daddy Rice's "Jump Jim Crow" and later part of the basic architecture of hip-hop dance.
22. Derrida quoted in Butler, *Bodies That Matter*, 13.
23. NdegèOcello, *Plantation Lullabies*, CD jacket.
24. NdegèOcello, *Plantation Lullabies*, CD jacket.
25. NdegèOcello, *Plantation Lullabies*, CD jacket.
26. Butler, *Bodies That Matter*, 13.
27. George, *Hip-Hop America*, viii.
28. "Black women intellectuals have aggressively criticized the image of African-American women as contented mammies. Literary critic Trudier Harris's volume *From Mammies to Militants: Domestics in Black American Literature* (1982) investigates prominent differences in how Black women have been portrayed by others in literature and how they portray themselves." Collins, *Black Feminist Thought,* 73.
29. "No servant, however senior or accomplished, could realistically pretend to assume the mistress's place, but many could realistically try to take the management of the house into their own hands, leaving their mistresses with the pretense of supervision." Fox-Genovese, *Within the Plantation Household,* 163.
30. "Drucilla Martin recalled that her mother was in full charge of the house and all 'Marse' children. Her mother . . . insisted on their cleanliness and made each white child pass a daily inspection. When white boys came to court, her mother would inspect them with the same attentiveness: 'Do you think my daughta is gwin' to marry any por' white trash', she would say. Be gone, don' come back.'" White, *"Ar'n't I a Woman,"* 48.
31. "So respected was Mammy that she often served as friend and advisor to master and mistress." White, *"Ar'n't I a Woman,"* 48.
32. Hill, "Lost Ones," in *Miseducation of Lauryn Hill.*
33. See Fox-Genovese, *Within the Plantation Household.*
34. Hill, "Forgive Them Father," *Miseducation of Lauryn Hill.*
35. Bible, "Luke," 1:30–31.
36. Hill, "To Zion," in *Miseducation of Lauryn Hill.*

37. Article in *Vibe* magazine, August 1998, http://www.angelfire.com/ab/lauryn/vibe.html. Accessed 12 May 2007.
38. Collins, *Black Feminist Thought,* 73.
39. Tiarra Mukherjee, "Education Is Everything." *Rolling Stone Magazine,* 9 September 1998, http://www.rollingstone.com/news/story/5924885/education_is_everything. Accessed 12 May 2007.
40. Hill, *Miseducation of Lauryn Hill,* CD jacket cover.
41. Hill, *Miseducation of Lauryn Hill,* CD jacket cover.
42. Article in *Vibe* magazine, August 1998, http://www.angelfire.com/ab/lauryn/vibe.html. Accessed 12 May 2007.
43. Article in *Vibe* magazine, August 1998, http://www.angelfire.com/ab/lauryn/vibe.html. Accessed 12 May 2007.
44. Butler, "Performative Acts," 405.
45. Collins, *Black Feminist Thought,* 74.
46. Collins, *Black Feminist Thought,* 119.
47. Hill, "Miseducation of Lauryn Hill," *Miseducation of Lauryn Hill.*

12 Transbodied/Transcultured
Moving Spirits in Katherine Dunham's and Maya Deren's Caribbean

Dorothea Fischer-Hornung

As the site of the first black republic and the center of the African diasporic culture of voodoo, the island of Haiti undoubtedly plays a central role in the African American imagination. Robert Ferris Thompson, in *A Flash of the Spirit,* notes that Haiti was the site of a deep synthesis of the classical religions of the Yoruba, the Dahomeans, the Bakongo, and the saints of the Roman Catholic Church. Voodoo became, "formally speaking, one of the richest and most misunderstood religions of the planet."[1] Katherine Dunham and Maya Deren, each in turn, attempted to decipher the meaning of voodoo for the community of practitioners, outsiders, and their personal lives.[2] Deren's *Divine Horsemen: The Living Gods of Haiti* and Dunham's *The Dances of Haiti* can be counted among founding texts on the anthropology and aesthetics of voodoo. Certainly the cultural richness of voodoo, with its mixture of African and European cosmology and aesthetics, explains in part their attraction, but I would like to attempt a more detailed description of why African diasporic culture had such a powerful attraction for Dunham, an African American, and Deren, a Russian immigrant, in the exploration of their scholarly, spiritual, and artistic lives.

In their mixture of African and European religious and cultural traditions, African diasporic religions—be it voodoo, santeria, or *candomblé*—cast an intricate and complex cultural web over much of the Atlantic space. Antonio Benítez-Rojo elaborates that Caribbean cultures are based on "syncretic artifacts" that are not a synthesis, but rather signifiers made of differences: "[I]n the melting pot of societies that the world provides, syncretic processes realize themselves through an economy in whose modality of exchange the signifier of *there*—the Other—is consumed ('read') according to local codes that are already in existence; that is, codes from *here*."[3] The dancing body is certainly such a "syncretic signifier," one of the most universal yet simultaneously specifically physical forms, with the body speaking directly from and to the cultural context in which it is performed. As one of the most significant avant-garde filmmakers of the 1940s and 1950s, Deren textually documents this imaginary in her book *Divine Horsemen* and visually in her film footage, parts of which were released posthumously by her husband, Teiji Ito, under the same title.[4] The use of experimental film technique, with conscious technical manipulation of time and space, enabled Deren to convey the spiritual reality of voodoo across temporal and spatial dimensions.

Katherine Dunham's career as dancer, anthropologist, choreographer, and leader of America's largest independent dance company in the 1940s and 1950s, also has its origins in the modernist period with its fascination with cultural "primitivism." Choreographers and dancers such as Mary Wigman[5] in Europe and Martha Graham in the United States explored new avenues of class, race, and gender as performed by the (usually white) dancing body on the concert stage.[6] Dunham's work has clear modernist sources as well, but never loses sight of the rootedness of her own dancing body in the African diaspora of the Americas. This conscious rootedness has enabled the contextualization of her dance theory with her verbal and performed protests against racism throughout her career, for example her protests in cities where her dance company was forced to perform in seg-regated theaters and to stay in segregated hotels.[7] Later, in the politically polarized context of the 1960s and after the end of her career as a dancer, she moved to East St. Louis to open the Performing Arts Training Center, where the youth of the community was instructed in African diasporic art forms to combat poverty and urban unrest, and in 1993, at the age of 82, she went on a 47-day hunger strike to protest against the treatment of Hai-tian refugees in the United States.[8]

Despite the artists' very different cultural backgrounds, Haitian Voo-doo forms the central premise of both Deren's and Dunham's theories at the crossroads of cultures in the Atlantic space. For Deren, religious and mythic systems of belief transcend everyday matter, and she defines voodoo as "facts of the mind made manifest in a fiction of matter."[9] The definition could well be transferred to much of what she has written about film. These "facts of the mind" (aesthetics, philosophy, religion—even meaning per se) enable both the creation of art, and a theory of a spiritual connection with the ancestor spirits, who are made "manifest in a fiction of matter" (film, dance, material culture). Hence, her films, and especially her film technique, visualize voodoo's belief that behind everyday reality we experience a deeper reality on the spiritual level (the mind/soul) expressed in ritual action of the body (matter). In Deren's words, the *loa*, or divine spirits, enable us to "stretch our hand back to that time and to gather up all history into a solid, contemporary ground beneath one's feet."[10] It is through the potential of film to manipulate time and space, as well as the body's transcendence of the parameters of race and gender, that Deren's interest in voodoo and her work as a filmmaker intersect in cultural and artistic syncretism.

Katherine Dunham, the daughter of a French Canadian mother and a father of Malagasy background who grew up in Joliet, Illinois,[11] per-formed as a dancer and choreographer in the 1943 stage and subsequent film versions of *Cabin in the Sky* and the film *Stormy Weather*. By that time she had also successfully established the Katherine Dunham School of Dance in New York, where she developed a holistic approach to performance education. Butterfly McQueen, Marlon Brando, James Dean, and Shelley Winters, for example, were among the students; dancers such as José Limon and Livinia Williams, actor and teacher Lee Strasberg, and anthropologist Margaret Mead were among the teachers. Dunham's career as an anthropologist started during her graduate work at the University of Chicago, where she studied primarily with Robert Redfield. She studied briefly at Northwestern University with Melville J. Herskovits, who helped train her for her research in dance anthropology. Using his work on African cultural retentions in the diaspora, which anticipated the contemporary discussion surrounding not only African retentions but also the interconnectedness of black and European Atlantic cultures, Herskovits explored various types of African diasporic performance, especially dance performance in the Caribbean. Having done studies on dance himself, he recognized the potential of an African American dancer for this type of research and helped train Dunham in research techniques, preparing her for her field trip to the Caribbean, in particular Haiti, on a grant from the Julius Rosenwald fund.[12] Just at the point when she was about to be firmly established in the world of anthropology and the world of dance, Herskovits forced a decision between her two potential careers—dancer or anthropologist—and the two potential locations for her degree—University of Chicago or Northwestern University. Despite his clear recognition of Dunham's talent in both research and performance, for Herskovits it was either/or and never both—either scholarship or performance. Dunham chose performance, ending her formal career as a scholar. Nevertheless, she wrote and published in the field throughout her life.

Dunham left the United States to tour Europe in 1948. Her first engagement was planned as a three-week booking in London; however, this first European tour stretched into three months. Over the following fifteen years the Katherine Dunham Dance Company toured over fifty countries as the largest non-subsidized, independent U.S. dance troupe of its day.[13] She also established moderately successful schools of dance in Paris, Stockholm, and Rome.

In her *The Dances of Haiti* (originally published in Spain in 1947, in French ten years later, and in English almost four decades after its original publication in Spanish), Dunham states the following:

> In Haiti, more than any of the other islands of the Caribbean, the peasant priesthood acknowledges the blood relationship of all people whose ancestors hailed from Nan Guinin ("from faraway Guinea"). When the stigma of being an American had worn off, there was great and protective interest in the recognition of "Guinea" blood ties and great concern for my ancestors, who had not received the proper ritual attention because that group of slaves taken farther north had been cut off from their brothers in the Caribbean and had forgotten these practices.[14]

As an African American and a dancer, the culture of voodoo must have felt very much like coming home for Dunham; this is not as evident for Deren on first examination. Nevertheless, both Deren and Dunham tried—each in their own embodiment of voodoo—to transcend what Anna Grimshaw in *The Ethnographer's Eye* calls "ocularcentrism," the particular vision and knowledge in Western discourse that until modernism had regarded the sense of sight as the most elevated of all our senses: "The slitting of the eye with a razor in Luis Buñuel's surrealist film, *Un Chien Andalou*, is perhaps the most stark and shocking expression of the modernist interrogation of vision."[15] Both artists contributed to moving our manner of seeing beyond the immediate material impressions to a simultaneously specific yet universalized meaning. They were persistent in their emphasis on transcultural influences and in many ways anticipated contemporary discussions of the racialization of the black body in dance and film.

Today, many scholars see the history and analysis of black diasporic dance forms as a necessary, but merely additional pursuit in the discussion of the dominant history of "white" dance, while others, such as Brenda Dixon-Gottshild and recently Susan Manning, digging deeper, maintain that there has been a blackening of dominantly white dance culture in more subtle and significant ways.[16] George Balanchine, for example, availed himself of Africanist diasporic dance forms throughout his career, integrating African dance techniques such as body isolation, polyrhythms, and grounded posture with ballet movement. Balanchine worked with Dunham on the film choreography of *Cabin in the Sky*, yet in the film credits he is listed and she is not.[17] The separation of African diasporic and Euro-American concert dance, modern dance, and even ballet may not be as distinct as it has appeared for many years but, as in the realm of music, appropriations of black style are frequently obscured. Film footage of Dunham teaching Africanist dance technique in the Euro-American production *Mambo* illustrate the profound cultural influence these dance forms had on African American and European concert and ballroom dance.

In 1954 Italian film producer Dino De Laurentiis was looking for a vehicle to showcase Silvana Mangano, his wife, and to present her talent as a dancer and singer. The result was the Carlo Ponti-Dino De Laurentiis production *Mambo*, released in the spring of 1955. This film contains the only known footage of Dunham actually teaching "Dunham technique"—a systematic, rigorous system of instructions of body isolation and polyrhythmic Africanist technique—while at the peak of her career. The complex presentation of Dunham technique as portrayed in *Mambo* enables the exploration of the racialized implications of the staging of a black woman dancer/choreographer teaching "primitive dance"[18] to a white European film diva. On the one hand, the footage visualizes and fundamentally challenges the tenet that the black racialized subject performs and dances "naturally" in that it stages rigorous dance training conducted for black dancers. On the other hand, the footage also suggests that the white subject can learn African diasporic dance techniques and "primitive dance," from a teacher who demands serious, hard work and dedication to a performance style with its roots in Africa.

The film was made with great hopes for filling both the Dunham company's and director Robert Rossen's bank accounts, by exploiting the mambo craze of the 1950s.[19] Rossen had been blacklisted into two years of inactivity because he refused to name names when first called to testify before the McCarthy committee. When called again he testified and left for Europe immediately thereafter.[20] The film in general, and the studio dance training scene in particular, received poor reviews when the film was released. It is Rossen's "arty," modernist refusal to stick to straight shots, using available light, mirror reflection and refraction, and sudden, short cuts in the dance class scenes that rubbed against the Hollywood grain. These are the very scenes that we, today, consider positively hybrid and innovative. This footage is particularly important since, like Dunham's erased work on *Cabin in the Sky*, it is clear from archival material that Dunham had a strong influence on all dance footage she was involved in either as dancer or choreographer—and this footage is no exception. The scenes have a definite Dunham signature and reflect the question of the changes necessary when staging concert dance in the attempt to express the "authenticity" of folk cultures on stage.[21]

The scene illustrates the process of Mangano's "possession" of her talent, possession meant both literally and synecdochically. The scene opens in the studio where the girl is to receive her dance instruction, with Mangano and Shelley Winters watching a ballet-like lift of Dunham in the foreground. After introducing Mangano to Dunham, Winters puts Mangano in her instructor's capable hands, invoking Dunham: "Make a dancer of her." We then see Mangano in a series of short cuts showing formal training at the bar in a ballet studio. Although she is initially an outsider to the racially mixed group, Mangano is slowly integrated in the group during free progression on the training floor. Noticeably, she is positioned next to the only white male dancer, who also seems to be a beginner and equally an outsider. Induced by the strain of overwork, the driving rhythm of the drumming, and the frantic motion of the other dancers, Mangano collapses. It is unclear if her collapse is caused by strain and exhaustion or if we are intended to interpret her collapse as a visual enactment of possession. Complying with 1950s racial and gender sensitivities, it is the only other white dancer who lifts her from the floor, after he himself has been shown as disconcerted to the point of attempting to flee from the demonic, driving power of the dancing and drums.

The African Caribbean singing and dancing style we see involves a good amount of twirling of the head and body, with undulation and spinning technique used in many cultures to induce trance states. In accordance with her theory that culturally specific behavior must be adapted to enable understanding in a different cultural context, Dunham uses spinning, twirling, and motion citations, rather than specific dances from voodoo, to indicate trance-inducing behavior. The undulating motion of Mangano's head and neck while Dunham guides Mangano's motion, forming her movements much like the artist forms clay, is taken from the Yonvalou, a dance dedicated to the most powerful snake deity Damballah. With each cut, the vocalization and drumming become more intense; disorientation for the viewer is increased through the reflection and refraction in the studio's mirrors. As a staging of traditional African diasporic culture—that is, voodoo possession—the highly disorienting camera work reflects Dunham's firm belief that a literal depiction of traditional African diasporic dance would not be adequate for comprehension by an audience outside the culture being depicted. Uniting her stage and cultural theories, in a 1955 interview she maintains that she is a "scholar with a flair for showmanship" and that her intention "is not to reproduce an actuality but to get across the meaning behind the things seen and studied."[22]

Throughout her career, Dunham countered the idea that dancing comes "naturally" to any dancer in her lectures and interviews. The racialized concept that physical talent and skill are necessarily associated with peoples of African descent, to whom rhythm and bodily motion come "naturally," stands in contrast to the necessity of rigorous training for peoples of European descent—a perception which was rejected by Dunham from the onset of her career.

Already in her early work, *Dances of Haiti*, Dunham maintains that Haitian dances are "not just accidental outgrowths of an urge for personal expression; they are group dances according to a set pattern, and they necessitate a certain amount of skill in execution." Haitians, according to Dunham, are "interested in perfection of technique" and Haitians "admire an exceptionally well-executed dance or a dancer of obviously superior training or ability."[23] In scenes depicting Mangano subject to the formalized training of Dunham technique in a racially integrated group of performers, *Mambo* depicts how professional dancers are formally taught the techniques that Haitians learn informally in situations of their everyday lives, as well as formally during voodoo initiation.[24]

In her book *Samba: Resistance in Motion*, Barbara Browning, reflecting on her own experience as an outsider learning samba culture in Brazil, notes that "[w]hen an outsider chooses to go through another culture's motions, she may believe hotly in her actions, but the possibility of translating them means they 'are and are not' the same. The translation divides the experience. And yet the act is what one hopes will heal it."[25] Clearly cultural clues are tied to the bodies which perform them, but dancers can attempt to resist these markers, challenging essentialized interpretations.[26] Unfortunately, Mangano's talent does not live up to the potential of the performance. She does not pull it off successfully, and the interpretive split between black body and white mind is reestablished despite the attempt at deconstruction of this very paradigm: what the viewer sees is "white girls can't dance." If one posits the transbodied, transcultured nature of dance it becomes a challenge to objectify this in the practice of two culturally very different artists, Dunham as an African American, on the one hand, and Mangano as an Italian, on the other.

Moira Sullivan's comments on Deren's ethnographic documentation of Haitian Voodoo and on stylistic elements of her film technique could easily refer to Rossen's filming of Dunham technique: "The profound theorem of the Haitian footage is the arrangement of principled dance movement. . . . The purpose was not simply to 'record' rituals but to capture the mobile body involved in dancing, gesture, drumming, and other ceremonial motion and to blend this into a cohesive whole through panning and change of focal lengths."[27] Maya Deren, who worked for some time as Dunham's secretarial assistant while Dunham was preparing the publication of *Dances of Haiti*, is more often known for her three earliest films: *Meshes of the Afternoon* (1943), *At Land* (1944), and *Rituals in Transfigured Time* (1945–46), all of which she produced, directed, and appeared in. In *Anagram of Ideas on Art, Form and Film*, her 1946 manifesto on film theory, Deren elaborates her theories of filmic horizontal motion (time) and vertical components (space), clearly positioning herself as a visual poet who composes her texts with the camera rather than the pen. And according to Deren, film, dance, and poetry are the forms that most resemble each other in their simultaneous specificity and abstraction. This is directly reflected in her experimental films, which explore the technical potential of the medium to transcend narrative and visual linearity. Her modernist aesthetics, which constantly strives to achieve a deeper filmic and psychological reality, marks these moments of (trans-)personal truth by her use of specific filmic effects. Her vertical movement into an epistemology of depth, which interrupts the horizontal movement of the film narrative, enables the viewer to look beneath the surface of the material reality portrayed, thereby achieving a unique and poetic filmic reality. This immersion into recognition—the moment of trance-like altered reality—is effected in a process comparable to the structure and function of human memory or trance.

Eight years younger than Katherine Dunham, Maya Deren was born in Kiev in 1917 as Eleanora Derenkowsky. She came to the United States at the age of 4 when her mother, Marie Fiedler Derenkowsky, and father, Solomon David Derenkowsky, left Russia to escape the pogroms against Jews, the negative repercussions of her father's earlier association with Trotsky, and the ravished economy of Russia in general. Uprooted at the age of 4, throughout her life Deren often felt like an outsider to U.S. culture. When her parents anglicized their name—like so many immigrants to the Unites States before and after—she became Eleanora Deren. After her parents' separation, she was again uprooted when she attended the League of Nations International School in Geneva, Switzerland, as a boarding student between 1930 and 1933. In 1942 while working as Dunham's assistant, Deren met Alexander Hackenschmied, the celebrated Czech émigré filmmaker, who himself had undergone a nominal metamorphosis in the United States, changing his name to Sasha Hammid. It was during her marriage to Hammid that Deren began her career as a filmmaker and began to create her own identity, taking the name Maya Deren. Her last husband, Teiji Ito, a drummer, accompanied her on her trips to shoot in Haiti. After Deren's very early death in 1961 of a brain hemorrhage at the age of 44, Ito posthumously edited and released the footage filmed on three separate trips in 1947, 1949, and 1951. Deren was unsuccessful in getting funding to edit the film because of her insistence on control of the material and also because many anthropologists, despite the support of scholars like Margaret Mead, Gregory Bateson, and Melville Herskovits, refused to accept the legitimacy of the material since she was not a trained anthropologist.[28] Ito selected the material, which represents only a small part of Deren's largely unresearched film footage, and added a musical soundtrack and a voiceover consisting of quotes from Deren's book of the same title, *Divine Horsemen*.

Deren never felt totally an American, having been torn from her Russian home at an early age and always "having a terrible sense of not belonging . . . my family always seemed in my eyes to be foreigners—with my father having a beard and both my parents having an accent, and both, incidentally, being Jews and not having Xmas trees or Easter eggs like all my friends did."[29] She spent much time reading Russian literature to recover her sense of a national identity. Ito maintains that "Maya was always a Russian"—even as late as 1955 in Haiti: "Although she spent eight years in America before going to Geneva, as a national identification, 'American' remained foreign to her."[30] In addition to her alienation from the United States, she felt she had inherent "racial traits of Slavic temperament."[31] With the nostalgia that is so frequently found among migrants, she relates how she once found herself singing a Russian folksong that was "familiar beyond memory." She felt that she was "like a vine trying to spread over the universe, for I love everything, but the roots are sunk in one spot in that universe. Through all my searching tendrils runs the life of the roots."[32] Deren shares this concept of "blood memory" and the impact of Jungian thought with other modernists such as Martha Graham, whose autobiography was entitled *Blood Memory*, a term she used in a more general mythical and Jungian sense; Alvin Ailey, whose choreographies express his own blood memories, representing the culture of all African Americans in a more specifically diasporic and historical sense;[33] and Dunham, whose own feeling of coming home to "Nan Guinan" enabled her to connect to her diasporic roots in Africa via Haitian culture.[34]

Yet if Deren was so very Russian, not so very U.S.-American, and certainly not Haitian, wherein lies the attraction of voodoo? On a personal level, one can certainly speculate that the radical integration of the individual in the community that is so essential in voodoo rituals would have attracted Deren—a way to overcome her deep sense of personal and cultural isolation. In her essay "Religious Possession in Dance," published in 1941, well before she had actually gone to and filmed in Haiti, and during her "nine months' association with Katherine Dunham and her dance group,"[35] she specifically emphasized the intimate connection between the individual and the community in the process of voodoo possession:

> For the possessed individual, the suggestion power of the community is manifested in a three-fold manner. First, the active cooperation of the community confirms and strengthens his own impression. Secondly: the authoritative weight which both the priest and community opinion have intensifies their power to suggest. And thirdly, the social cohesion involved in such uniformity of action is a powerful factor in mass ideology and activity everywhere.[36]

But beyond her personal search for a spiritual and artistic community where she felt she could belong,[37] her film work always tried to visualize a space where contact with a deeper reality behind the material one could be realized, liminal spaces in our conscious and unconscious experience. At certain moments in her films—and these moments are always marked by some special camera effect—there is a vertical movement into depth that enables the viewer to look beneath the surface, creating a new, exclusively filmic reality. Each moment of recognition is marked when the horizontal movement of the film is stopped with vertical immersion into recognition—and this moment of altered reality is effected in a process comparable to the embodiment of a deity, a *loa*, in a voodoo practitioner, a process often described as being ridden by the deity like a horse. This moment is not only visible in the physical performance of the practitioner, but is also indicated by a short disruption in the drumming rhythm, marking the ritual connection between the dancer, the drummers, and the voodoo community, who are familiar with the ritualized practice of trance embodiment. It is this creative imaginary of the individual in the community that marks the difference between everyday activity and creative motion in both dance and film.[38]

Given Deren's early interest in voodoo documented by her writing on Haitian cosmology in the period just before she ventured into filmmaking, we might well interpret her use of the cinematic cut as a kind of formal "crossroads," a concept central to Haitian ritual and cosmology. In voodoo, the crossroads represents an intersection of the material and the spiritual worlds—precisely the same spatial and temporal powers Deren felt she could harness and in turn release through the use of slow motion, varied lenses and depth of field, and film editing.[39] Benítez-Rojo, in imagery very similar to Deren's description of her own intentions for film work, describes the Caribbean as a unique space where, in the creolization process, the foreign reacts with the traditional "like a ray of light with a prism; that is, they produce phenomena of reflection, refraction, and decomposition. But the light keeps on being light; furthermore, the eye's camera almost always induces pleasure, or at least curiosity."[40] Change in reflection, refraction, and decomposition interact with the foundational material, producing a newly aestheticized reality.

But it is not only in the realm of light and lenses that she explored diasporic aesthetics. Deren choreographed a polyrhythmic foundation in her films, where creativity is marked and measured in time and space—what John Chernoff refers to as the "metronome sense"[41] inherent in African music and culture in general. In African and African diasporic music this strict sense of marked time enables our minds and bodies to maintain an additional rhythm to the one we hear. Chernoff refers to Richard Waterman's breakthrough recognition that the polyrhythmic structure of African music has expansive implications for the arts:

> From the point of view of the listener, [metronome sense] entails habits of conceiving any music as structured along a theoretical framework of beats regularly spaced in time and of co-operating in terms of overt or inhibited motor behavior with the pulses of this rhythmic pattern whether or not the beats are expressed in actual melodic or percussive tones. Essentially, this simply means that African music, with few exceptions, is to be regarded as music for the dance, although the "dance" involved may be entirely a mental one.[42]

Deren's films, like Africanist dance and music, have a rhythmic structure that is strictly choreographed to enable viewers to enter into just such a polyrhythmic dialogue with her films, enabling access to a reality behind matter, the facts of the mind she embodied in the matter that was her films.

Voodoo certainly provided a very specific cultural context to the vision she tried to realize but she, like Dunham, was stubbornly insistent on the universalized and modernist interpretation of her art. In a letter to Talley Beatty, a former Dunham dancer who performed in Deren's short experimental dance film *Choreography for a Camera* (1945) and had inquired about an increase in wages, Deren responded with a rather self-serving but nonetheless remarkable response in its modernist universalizing aesthetic transcending racial categories: "I thought it important that this was one of the rare cases when a Negro was presented, not as and because he was a Negro, but purely and simply because he was an artist."[43]

Both voodoo and the world Deren creates in her experimental films all hold true within themselves without losing their cultural specificity. As Shelley Rice, the cocurator of *Inverted Odysseys*, an exhibition which explored Deren's work in the context of the performance of self in the work of Claude Cahun and Cindy Sherman, states, Deren's films have "the capability of manifesting multiple facets of the collective history of the race, allowing all of us to transcend the limited gender, racial, historical, or cultural backgrounds into which we are born. Hardly a nihilistic splintering of identity, such a vision is a massive expansion of the normal Western concept of the human experience."[44] Both Deren and Dunham were voodoo initiates, making of them not only observers but practitioners. Voodoo was, in Shelley Rice's words, an "enduring leitmotif of [Deren's] artistic vision [and] was not, therefore, tangential to her avant-garde film work but central to it. . . . [T]his artist found nourishment in the concepts of the metaphysical and the physical, of space and time, of life and death manifested in African-based religions, ritual, and dance."[45] For Dunham, as well, Caribbean culture became the center of her scholarship, her teaching, and most prominently her professional career as dancer and choreographer. Beyond the aesthetic of performance, Dunham intentionally attempted to intellectually and emotionally convey the deep structure and meaning of diasporic African culture in the Americas to insiders and outsiders as well.

The social milieu in which Dunham and Deren worked was a very special segment of society, a liberated space in many respects. For both women, the dancing body clearly interacts dynamically with the sociocultural matrix of which it is a part, although as an art form they felt dance projected creative images, not simply mirrored them.[46] In their melding of materiality and representation both Deren and Dunham were engaged in a deeply ethical project in their insistence that radical cross- and intercultural understanding were possible in and through the dancing body in motion. Deren's camera, in that it maintains the rhythm and movement of Haitian dance, undercuts the objectivity and ocularcentrism of the static camera of anthropology, moving from outside the group to inside the performing community. Dunham, in her own commitment to cultural transfers, in her move from within black Atlantic culture to an international audience, knew that shifts and modifications were necessary to mediate "authenticity" for an audience located outside the group of origins.

Deren and Dunham developed a philosophy of life and art, each in her own way. In *An Anagram of Ideas on Art, Form, and Film,* Deren maintains: "Art is the dynamic result of the relationship of three elements: the reality to which a man has access—directly and through the researches of all other men; the crucible of his own imagination and intellect; and the art instrument by which he realizes, through skillful exercise and control, his imaginative manipulations."[47] Deren characterized her project as *metaphysical* in its thematic content, the reality of the mind in meaning; *poetic* in the artist's attitude toward meaning, the logic of ideas and qualities; *choreographic* in the design and stylization of movement; and *experimental* in the use of the medium in creating the "accurate metaphor for the meaning."[48] Dunham expresses similar ideas in her own three-part model of the embeddedness of dance in its social and communal context. First, *form and function* define how dance relates to the overall cultural patterns inherent in a particular culture's belief system. Second, dance enables *intercultural communication,* because through dance information about other cultures can be gathered. Third, *socialization through the arts* can enhance the quality of one's life.[49]

In the spirit world, ancestors—be they European, Haitian, or African—
can move freely and interact in the aesthetics of embodied art forms, in film
and dance and the combination of the two where they share the same kin-
aesthetic vocabulary. The spirits may be historically distinct but can meld
into each other in a new syncretistic reality, in what Éduard Glissant has
called a "poetics of relation,"[50] the root identity of a people melding into
a relational identity where is it is no longer necessarily what you say, but
how you say it, a question of style in the creolized aesthetic of something
new.[51] In their radical deconstruction of the dichotomous mind/body split
of Western tradition, and their focus on the body rooted yet transformed in
motion and its position in the time and space of the community, Deren and
Dunham generated a unique and deeply ethical corpus of specific meanings
about diaspora in the Americas.

NOTES

1. Thompson, *Flash of the Spirit*, xvi, 163–191.
2. Zora Neale Hurston, who, because of the particular concerns in this chapter,
   will not be a part of my discussion, also researched voodoo culture in Haiti
   and published her research in *Tell My Horse*. See my "An Island Occupied"
   for a discussion of Hurston's analysis of Haitian culture and the U.S. occupation. For a different interpretation of the same material see Rowe, "Afro-
   Caribbean Politics."
3. Benítez-Rojo, *The Repeating Island*, 21.
4. The footage that Deren shot during her six trips to Haiti was compiled and
   released in 1986 with a voiceover taken from her book *Divine Horsemen*. See
   Jackson, *Modernist Poetics*, 145 n. 35.
5. Dunham was surely aware of Wigman's work because she studied ballet with
   Olga Speranzeva, who had studied with Mary Wigman in Germany. See Perpener, *African American Concert Dance*, 134.
6. Manning, *Modern Dance, Negro Dance*, xxi.
7. See Clark and Wilkerson, *Kaiso!* 88. For an analysis of Dunham's choreography
   addressing lynching, "Southland," see Hill, "Katherine Dunham's *Southland*."
8. Katherine Dunham Centers for Arts and Humanities, "Biography of Miss
   Dunham, http://www.eslarp.uiuc.edu/kdunham/bio.htm. Accessed 12 February 2006.
9. Deren, *Anagram*, 21.
10. Deren, *Divine Horsemen*, 116.
11. Dunham devotes her memoirs, *A Touch of Innocence*, to the influence of her
    childhood in Illinois.
12. This is the same period when Zora Neale Hurston, under the guidance of
    Franz Boas at Columbia University, was pursuing her folklore research in
    the Caribbean. Dunham's research predates Hurston's by several months and
    they were competitors for the meager funding available during the 1930s (see
    Fischer-Hornung, "An Island Occupied," 163 n. 18). Dunham was given let-
    ters of introduction to Haitian scholars such as Jean Price-Mars, J C. Dorsa-
    inville, and Camille Lhérisson; see Dunham, *Dances of Haiti*, xxiii, and *Island
    Possessed*, 3.
13. See Long, *The Black Tradition*, 94–100.
14. Dunham, *Dances of Haiti*, xxiv. For Dunham's description of the U.S. occu-
    pation of Haiti, the problems it caused in her attempts at integration into

Haitian society during the course of her research, and the resolution of these issues in Haitian Voodoo culture see Fischer-Hornung, "An Island Occupied," 161–167.

15. Grimshaw, *The Ethnographer's Eye*, 5.
16. See Dixon-Gottschild, *Digging the Africanist Presence*, and Manning, *Modern Dance, Negro Dance*.
17. For a more detailed description of Balanchine's work with black dancers and choreographers see Perpener, *African American Concert Dance*, 145–146.
18. Dunham used the term *primitive* throughout her career in a non-pejorative sense to denote unadulterated folk culture as opposed to staged culture.
19. For discussion of the international advance of the mambo craze over time and space, see Thompson, "Teaching the People."
20. See Casty, *Robert Rossen*, 20.
21. For a detailed analysis of the footage see Fischer-Hornung, "The Body Possessed," 98–110; for a discussion of Dunham's struggle to claim to cultural ownership of the dance scenes in *Mambo*, see Fischer-Hornung, "Giving Voice and Vent," 105–109. In the same period, the question of authenticity in staged folklore performance was also being addressed in Haiti in reference to government sponsored folklore research and performance. See Wilken, "Spirit Unbound," 116–118.
22. Quoted in Aschenbrenner, *Katherine Dunham*, 56.
23. Dunham, *Dances of Haiti*, 38, 46–47.
24. Around thirty years after Dunham first started to theorize the social implications of dance, she moved to East St. Louis to open The Katherine Dunham Centers for Arts and Humanities to provide a training center for the youth of the troubled urban center. Her conclusions in 1968 are the ultimate consequence of her artistic, scholarly, and political theories from the onset of her career: "After many efforts to arrive at some conclusive decision when thinking of dance, I have decided upon this, that dance is not a technique but a social act and that dance should return to where it first came from, which is the heart and soul of man, and man's social living." Quoted in Aschebrenner, *Katherine Dunham*, 70.
25. Browning, *Samba*, xviii.
26. See Goellner and Murphy, *Bodies of the Text*, 34–35. The debate surrounding African body proportions as unsuitable to the performance of classical ballet is another expression of racial theories of "naturalness." For an extensive elaboration of this debate, see Dixon-Gottshield, *Digging the Africanist Presence*, 65–68.
27. Sullivan, "Maya Deren's Ethnographic Representation," 217.
28. See M. Sullivan, *An Anagram of the Ideas of Filmmaker Maya Deren* (1997); excerpts in Maya Deren Forum, http://www.algonet.se/~mjsull/anagram.html. Accessed 2 February 2006.
29. Clark and Wilkerson, *Kaiso!*, 301.
30. Clark and Wilkerson, *Kaiso!*, 29–96.
31. Clark and Wilkerson, *Kaiso!*, 230. Certainly her intense political activism on the Left also contributed to her alienation in the conservative 1940s and 1950s.
32. Clark and Wilkerson, *Kaiso!*, 473.
33. For a detailed discussion of the concept of "Blood Memory" and its significance for modernist dance, see Manning, *Modern Dance, Negro Dance*, 179–222.
34. Dunham, *Dances of Haiti*, xxiv.
35. This (perhaps consciously) vague formulation led to the often incorrect assumption that Deren herself was a dancer with the company rather than

Dunham's personal assistant and secretary, who assisted with the editing of much of Dunham's own Haitian research (Clark, *Kaiso!*, 476). Deren had sought out Dunham because of their mutual interest in cross-cultural studies, in dance, and in practices of possession and trance. As Dunham's secretary, Deren accompanied the Dunham company's stage production of *Cabin in the Sky* to Hollywood, where she met Sacha Hammid. During this period Deren published her essay "Ritual Possession in Dance." According to Clark and Wilkerson, Dunham's "'Thesis Turned Broadway' was published . . . in August of 1941. The essay 'The Negro Dance' appeared in the classic anthology of black writing, *The Negro Caravan* (1941), edited by Sterling Brown. Eleanora was editorial assistant for both of these articles" (Clark and Wilkerson, *Kaiso!*, 418). In her films, Deren later worked with a number of black dancers who had worked with Dunham early in their career, for example, Tally Beatty in *A Study in Choreography for a Camera* (1945) and Rita Christiani in *Rituals in Transfigured Time* (1945–46).

36. Deren, "Religious Possession in Dancing," 488.
37. Erika Bourguignon speculates on the attraction of trance-inducing dance in the United States:

> What is the basis of the appeal of this material for the choreographer, the dancer and the American audience? There are surely aesthetic considerations at work here, as well as the intrinsic appeal of the exotic. One may wonder whether there is not also a desire for vicarious identification by American audiences with the intense experience of the supernatural that is presented to them in stylized and polished form. To what extent are we faced by a reversed process here? We have seen the development of ritual into drama and ballet. Do we now witness the development of drama and ballet into ritual? (Bourguignon, "Trance Dance," 56)

38. Susan Langer was one of the first theorizers of the aesthetics of motion in dance and film as well. See Langer, *Feeling and Form*, 172–175.
39. See Fischer, "'The Eye for Magic,'" 200.
40. Benítez-Rojo, *Repeating Island*, 21.
41. Deren used a metronome during shooting, which enabled structuring while shooting and restructuring while editing. See Holl, "Moving the Dancers' Soul," 165.
42. Chernoff, *African Rhythms*, 49–50.
43. Quoted in Franko, "Aesthetic Agencies in Flux," 146.
44. Rice, "Maya Deren and Haiti."
45. Rice, "Maya Deren and Haiti."
46. Manning, *Modern Dance*, xiii, 34. According to Manning, "It was Dunham's productions that undid the critical conundrum of natural talent versus derivative artistry that white critics had scripted for African-American choreographers. Dunham did this by confronting critics with a paradox of her own: her dual identity as anthropologist (complete with university degrees and publications) and theater artist (complete with sex appeal and a vibrantly theatrical company)." Manning, *Modern Dance*, 143.
47. Deren, *Anagram*, 17.
48. See Jackson, *Modernist Poetics*, 209.
49. Rose, *Dunham Technique*, 12, 16.
50. Glissant, *Poetics of Relation*, 32.
51. Here Betsy Wing's translator's note provides the interesting contrast of *langue* and *langage* in Glissant's concept of creolized Caribbean languages. Despite differences in imposed colonial languages, the Caribbean is connected beyond Francophone or Anglophone language and culture:

For Glissant, when these two words are set in contradistinction to each other, *langue* is the language one speaks and *langage* is how one speaks it. A *langue* may be a national language (French, Spanish, etc.) or an imposed language (French in Martinique) or a dominated language (Creole). A *langage* is a way of using language that can cross linguistic borders. Glissant shares a *langage* with writers who do not write in French: Derek Walcott, José Maria de Heredia, and Kamau Brathwaite, among others. (Glissant, *Poetics of Relation*, 217 n. 1)

FILMOGRAPHY

Mambo. Dir. Robert Rossen. Prod. Carlo Ponti, Dino De Laurentiis. Screenplay by Guido Piovene, Ivo Perilli, Ennio de Concini, Robert Rossen. Cast: Silvana Mangano, Michael Rennie, Vittorio Gassman, Shelly Winters, Katherine Dunham. Paramount Pictures, 1954. B&W, 94 minutes. VHS Dist. Hen's Tooth Video, 1991.

At Land. 1944. Dir. Maya Deren. Cast: John Cage, Maya Deren, Alexander Hammid. Silent, 15 minutes. VHS: Mystic Fire Video 1986.

A Study in Choreography for a Camera. 1945. Dir. Maya Deren. Cast: Talley Beatty. Silent, 3 minutes.

Meshes of the Afternoon.1943. Dir. Maya Deren (with Alexander Hammid). Silent, 14 minutes. 1959 (sound), with Teiji Ito, VHS: Mystic Fire Video 1986.

Ritual in Transfigured Time. 1945–46. Dir. Maya Deren. Cast: Rita Christiani, Maya Deren, Anaïs Nin, Frank Westbrook. Silent, 15 minutes. VHS: Mystic Fire Video 1986.

Divine Horsemen: The Living Gods of Haiti. 1985; original footage shot by Deren, 1947–1954. Reconstruction by Teiji Ito and Cherel Ito.

13 Venture Smith and James Baldwin
Two Strangers in the Village

Ginevra Geraci

A Narrative of the Life and Adventures of Venture, a Native of Africa
(1798) by Venture Smith and the essay "Stranger in the Village," included
in *Notes of A Native Son* (1955), by James Baldwin are two examples of
that double consciousness Du Bois defines as the warring presence of the
two intimate souls of black folk. Although two centuries stand between
Smith and Baldwin, their texts can be jointly read as representative examples of a transatlantic displacement—one from Africa to America and the
other from America to Europe—showing how the concept of doubleness,
and consequently of black diasporic identity, works in two different yet
closely related spheres: economy and culture.

The concept of diasporic identity as described by Paul Gilroy's *Black
Atlantic*—where Du Bois's double consciousness is identified as a central
notion in order to understand black cultures in post-ethnic terms[1]—provides
another element of the methodological framework used in this chapter to
analyze the ways in which the dominant white culture is affected by American black subjects. The African American historical and cultural identity
represents one of the most evident manifestations of what Homi Bhabha
calls "interstices," those "in-between spaces" where subjectivity and selfhood are elaborated and "the intersubjective and collective experience of
nationness, community interest or cultural values are negotiated."[2]

In Baldwin's and in Smith's case displacement is a critical event in which,
not only is adaptation on the part of the displaced subject necessary, but
radical transformation on the part of the politically and culturally dominant
subject is also involved, resulting in a wider process of dislocation. Smith's
narrative and Baldwin's essay provide some meditations on American society at two critical points: the moment when economic contradictions highlight the hypocrisy of the system concerning slavery and the moment when
that hypocrisy can be tolerated no more. Venture circumspectly suggests
that American social organization is unfair; Baldwin openly exposes white
America's genetic injustice. Their texts mark the process through which
black-white relationships evolve, notwithstanding their fundamental diversity as to the authorial voice. In fact, Venture's narrative only concerns
his achievements as a "homo economicus," leaving out most details of his

inner life; Baldwin lavishly describes the main paths and by-roads of his thinking, filtering everything through his emotional experience. Yet, with all their differences, Baldwin's discourse has one of its historical sources in the former slave's speech act. Venture's *Narrative* and Baldwin's essay can be read as distinct but related chapters of an African American transnational and diasporic macro-text, having some specific characteristics in common: exile, cultural disruption, revision of the autobiographical canon, a shifting of roles, and an extremely modern statement concerning the multiple nature of individual and collective cultural and national identities.

As in Venture Smith's *Narrative*, in "Stranger in the Village" the Middle Passage is the triggering factor of the author's communicative act, despite obvious distinctions to be made. In fact, Baldwin does not cross the Atlantic Ocean on a slave ship but voluntarily chooses to live in Europe. Still, his narration is a delayed and problematic response to slave narratives such as Venture's, as in the Old World he undergoes a process of identity reconstruction which is analogous to Venture's in the New World. The terms of their development are very different of course. Venture's autobiography obsessively focuses on money, Baldwin's essays on what it takes to become not "merely a Negro; or, even, merely a Negro writer"[3] but, more extensively, an American. Venture's Middle Passage and Baldwin's self-imposed European exile are useful to trace the effects produced by their ambivalent position within the white body politic, as the two of them are, at the same time, inside and outside society. Their central and equally peripheral position has a deep impact on their self-perception, but consequences are also meaningful for both slaveholders and the whole American white society. In fact, diasporic writers challenge the supposed homogeneity of communities while black counterdiscourse on the subject "is not only directly engaged with those European discourses of the white subject and the Black Other but in fact subverts and revises some of their most central tenets."[4]

In terms of double consciousness, Venture Smith's narrative provides some interesting elements for consideration from its very title. He defines himself as a "Native of Africa But Resident in the United States of America,"[5] which only indirectly alludes to his former condition of slavery. His narrative shifts back and forth from Africanness to Americanness just to show that, in the end and at least in the case of slaves or former slaves, those two worlds and cultures are perhaps less estranged from each other than they might seem. His moving across cultural boundaries marks his identity as diasporic, which is a trait affecting different levels in the narrative, namely themes, rhetorical strategies, and genre. The process through which he articulates his identity is a process of unceasing metaphorical migration from one pole to another. More specifically, at a thematic level, through insistence on money and hard work, it takes the form of constant negotiation between apparently irreconcilable ethic systems. Concerning a rhetorical level, through the use of irony and ellipsis, the negotiation is between the sphere of the "said" and that of the "unsaid." At a genre level, through the choice of the autobiographical canon the author tries to find a balance between the tradition of the Western individualistic *Buildungsro-man* that will be represented by Benjamin Franklin's *Autobiography* and the African autobiographic tradition, based on a communal perspective on the individual's achievements.[6]

Baldwin's situation is one of constant displacement, too. He feels he is a stranger, not only in the small Swiss village he describes, but also in the West as a whole. He admires and at the same time hates what the West represents in terms of culture, yet his feeling of estrangement allows him to have deeper insight into the true nature of things. However, some relevant shifts and reversals can be detected in comparison with Venture's narrative. Firstly, instead of the pursuit of entrepreneurial objectives, his attention focuses on the pursuit of another typical American goal, namely the pursuit of happiness, which in his specific case coincides on the one hand with the fulfillment of his literary ambitions, on the other with the disclosing of the mystery of his identity as well as of the American identity. Secondly, the strategy of irony and ellipsis becomes, in Baldwin's text, a tortuous progression of statements and denials, which reflects the problematic nature of his stance as a black person, as an American intellectual, and as the embodiment of a cultural paradox. All these elements provide a sort of discontinuous continuity between Africa and America, slaves and slaveholders and, ultimately, between blacks and whites.

Venture moves from one geographical and cultural hemisphere to another, and in doing so he disrupts the Western pursuit of cultural homogeneity. In the West he adopts the bourgeois cultural and ethical code, but when he remarks that the two more evident icons of that code—namely, money and hard work—characterize both the African and the American society, the supposed distinctiveness of being a Westerner ceases to be so distinctive after all. This does not mean that, in the end, everything is smashed into undifferentiated mush, but that white people's alleged superiority, based, among other things, on entrepreneurial ability and bourgeois morality, has no reason to be at all.

As concerns a strictly textual level, notwithstanding evident differences between two cultures and forms of social organizations, Venture's narrative is not structured around an obvious pattern of oppositions. In fact, the strategy is far more subversive, suggesting, as it does, that certain values do not belong exclusively to white Americans and do not consequently entitle anyone to a feeling of racial superiority. An initial hint of this is one of the very first and basic threads linking Africa and America: money. After Venture's village is taken by the enemy tribe, his father prefers to be tortured to death rather than reveal where he keeps his money, which might seem quite an extreme form of stubbornness or of attachment to money on the part of the old king. The dramatic irony here lies in the fact that Venture's father dies voluntarily exchanging his life for his money, while his son will have to do exactly the opposite, earning every little penny to pay for his freedom so as to become socially alive.[7] Furthermore, this scene can be confronted with the one in chapter two in which little Venture is in charge of his master's trunk keys and proves to be so reliable that, in his master's words, "he should not fear to trust him with his whole fortune, for that he had been in his native place so habituated to keeping his word, that he would sacrifice even his life to maintain it" (12). This, by contrast, leads directly to his being particularly exposed to treachery and greediness on the part of his several masters in particular, and to "unfair play" on the part of white people in general.[8]

The strong focus on money can lead to quite disturbing statements, as when Smith apparently quantifies his family's value in terms of dollars and pennies or when he laments the loss of his daughter along with the expensiveness of the bills for the doctor's assistance that her illness had made necessary (21). But isn't this what white people do? Do not slaveholders weight human bodies as they would gold coins? Moreover, if one puts apparently heartless statements and cold remarks in the perspective of the ironic strategy at work in the text, the sense of all of them changes. If the whole text is ironic, the equation between slave and money is being subtly challenged, as a closer analysis of the rhetorical strategies that Venture employs will show. Diligence is the other element in the text stressing the continuity between the Old and the New World. Despite his being the son of a prince, Venture is used to hard work. At the age of six, when his mother leaves him at a rich farmer's house, he is put to tend sheep. From this moment on and all through the time he is a slave until he becomes a small entrepreneur, the reader is constantly informed of the tasks he performs and of the objectives he achieves. His work is described in terms of earnings, as well as in terms of exceptional zeal and industriousness. In embracing so readily the bourgeois ethics, Venture exposes himself to criticism, as when he tells how he has become a slave master.

All in all, Venture shows no particular moral qualms about buying people. Yet his crossing of another boundary, that between master and slave, on the one hand highlights a trait shaping his selfhood as a migrating, diasporic construct, and on the other enables him to proceed further in challenging the very foundation of slave society. When Venture, in his habitual nonchalant way, defines himself as a slaveholder, he disrupts a whole (un)ethical, cultural, and political system. In proving his ability as an economic subject, as well as in embracing and then reshaping the autobiographical canon based on bourgeois ethics, he undermines the separation of roles and races on which America is founded. He also unmasks the contradictory nature of the American economic system, which on the one hand relies on slaves as commodities and on the other allows them, although only partially, to somehow take part in it as actors.[9] Interestingly enough, the slave system made black people a caste of peculiarly untouchable objects. A whole economic system was built upon their "dark" presence and notwithstanding their being reduced to socially dead subjects—according to Orlando Patterson's definition—they were so deeply and threateningly in the American grain as to make it necessary for whites to erase them as a presence.[10] Venture's narrative embodies a complex process of "erosion" and deconstruction which is made all the more effective by the close connections linking the Franklinian bourgeois autobiography, the narrative of emancipation, and the unstable metaphors of money and master-slave dialectics: once one element is questioned, the others inevitably are, too.

While Venture aims at disrupting the pattern of racial supremacy by constantly referring to bourgeois ethics, Baldwin employs a strategy based on aesthetics. In fact, his discourse on the West and on the meaning of whiteness pivots around cultural and artistic expression. Consequently, for him freedom has less to do with economic independence than with spiritual emancipation. He does not have to face the basic problem of buying his freedom, yet he still finds himself in the predicament of acquiring full citizenship. In this new context, however, he still follows the traditional pattern of slave narratives. The canon undergoing significant redefinition is not only the one dictated by the "literature of exile," but also the slave narrative canon. As a literary form, the slave narrative usually follows an established pattern, some fundamental moments of which are: (a) the encounter with the white man; (b) the slave market; and (c) the final escape or liberation. Within this pattern, the specific moment when Africans and Europeans or Americans meet for the first time is a key one. Olaudah Equiano ironically mistakes the white man for the devil;[11] Venture Smith receives as a first salute "a violent blow on the head" (8). In any case, the white man is certainly a "sight," as Baldwin is in reverse in the tiny Swiss village, where people have never seen a black person before. Thus, it is not the white man who arrives among savages, this time the black man does. Such a shift of perspective is further reinforced by Baldwin's description of the village as an "uncivilized" place: "In the village there is no movie house, no bank, no library, no theatre, very few radios, one jeep, one station wagon; and, at the moment, one typewriter, mine, an invention which the woman next door to me here had never seen."[12]

The shift in perspective is not limited to a simple reversal of roles between the first white man and the first black man. The experience of slavery and segregation stand between the two, so that their attitude toward the people observing them is dramatically different: "But there is a great difference between being the first white man to be seen by Africans and being the first black man to be seen by whites. The white man takes the astonishment as tribute, for he arrives to conquer and convert the natives" (155).[13] Yet, while it is certainly true that the "white world," as Baldwin often calls it, has a coactive power in terms of cultural space and definition, the relationship involving African Americans and white Americans is more complex than mere oppression and defense, as Baldwin himself will argue just a few pages later.

Going back to the slave narrative pattern mentioned before, in Baldwin's essay one can even find something resembling a slave market in the villagers' custom of "buying" Africans in order to convert them to Christianity. The third element in the slave narrative pattern is liberation: in Baldwin's case it consists in the emancipation from a sense of inferiority and estrangement,[14] leading him to that dissociation of personality that W.E.B. Du Bois describes as "two warring ideals in one dark body."[15] This does not mean that the black man is doomed to a perpetual lack of identity, but survival requires a special talent on his part, an element of which is exactly his ability to dissemble, as Venture Smith's *Narrative* had already shown.

Venture is a resident in the United States, no longer a slave, not truly a citizen, but somebody whose ambiguity in status affects his language. This becomes evident through the specific rhetorical strategies he uses, ellipsis and irony. These mark his identity as diasporic in that he oscillates between two forms of subjectivity: the persona he creates in the autobiography and the real person who governs the whole autobiographical reconstruction process. As in the case of the Middle Passage, the only way in which the unmentionable can be actually related is by means of elliptical writing. Therefore, flesh-and-blood Venture imposes silence upon the ink-and-paper version of himself. Furthermore, by saying the opposite of what he really means, Venture enacts an analogous form of displacement through irony. In this context, doubleness in the sense of duplicity becomes the mark of African American double consciousness.

Between his childhood in Africa and his present life in America there seems to be a void—that is, slavery—going initially unmentioned. The same indirectness occurs in the titles introducing the three parts of which the autobiography is comprised. In fact, chapter one opens with the subheading, "Containing an account of his life, from his birth to the time of his leaving his native country," and chapter two with the following: "Containing an account of his life from the time of his leaving Africa, to that of his becoming free." Since the verb "to leave" implies a voluntary action on the part of the subject, one would think that Venture, who certainly did not have a chance to have his say when captured and sold as a slave, is adopting a quite reticent attitude.[16] He is certainly in a very delicate position, being dependent on white liberals for his opportunity to speak out. Furthermore, Venture relates his account, but does not write it himself, which might explain some of the communication strategies he chooses to adopt.[17] In choosing ellipsis as a strategy he cannot but define the Middle Passage as "an ordinary passage, except great mortality from small pox" (11), which also proves his ability in terms of irony. The abduction of slaves is referred to as "the business . . . on the coast of Africa" (11) and, significantly enough, no detail is provided concerning the conditions on-board or the supposedly harsh treatment slaves would receive from the crew. The rhythm of the narration is often discontinuous and, if it is true that autobiographic writing embodies a process of identity construction resulting in the ultimate coincidence between author and narrator, then the fragmentary nature of Venture's narration is telling us something.

One element to be considered here is his need to prove a point: a slave can be endowed with alacrity, ingenuity, and intelligence but this means nothing if certain basic rights are not granted to him. The other element is the psychological—one could also say existential—outcome of such an ambiguous status as that of a former slave, who participates in the productive and social system he lives in as a "limited" actor, who is at the same time denied a political subjectivity and given at least basic economic capability. The other rhetorical means by which Venture plays on his double status/consciousness is irony. It is useful to remember that slave narratives posed as a model and an inspiration for some slaves who could have access to them, but they mainly addressed a white audience who would in most cases share the master's point of view rather than the slave's. Accordingly, the author had to represent himself as respectable and truthful. It was strategically wise not to scare the white reader, which could be done by quietly and meticulously pointing out the contradictions the slave system implied.[18]

The text offers at least three clear examples of irony, but the whole text is in itself a deeply ironic act, which covertly undermines established structures and patterns. The first instance occurs when Venture Smith is captured together with the other members of his family: "Then they came to us in the reeds, and the very first salute I had from them was a violent blow on the head" (8). But this is only preparatory to the first masterly blow coming a few pages later, with his remark on the Atlantic passage as being "ordinary" (11). After a fight with his mistress and master he is handcuffed and, half-humorously, half-bitterly, he informs us: "I presented myself before my mistress, shewed [*sic*] her my hand-cuffs, and gave her thanks for my gold rings" (15). The ironic hints recurring in the text finally introduce what could be considered an effective resumé of his predicament. After being unfairly persecuted and compelled to refund a white merchant—a "conscientious gentleman" (22)—for a loss with which Venture had nothing to do, he spiritlessly concludes: "But Captain Hart was a *white gentleman*, and I a *poor African*, and therefore it was *all right, and good enough for the black dog*" (23).

From a wider point of view, the whole narrative is an ironic statement aiming not simply at conveying a meaning that is opposite to the literal meaning, but at disrupting a hierarchy of values. In a different context, Baldwin mentions irony as a cognitive tool in the hands of black people who still choose dissimulation in their relationship with white people. The discrepancy between what appears on the surface and what is hidden behind "the black mask" also reveals much of the beholder's nature: "What one's imagination makes of other people is dictated, of course, by the laws of one's own personality and it is one of the ironies of black-white relations that, by means of what the white man imagines the black man to be, the black man is enabled to know who the white man is" (158).

Baldwin's writing is not free from contradictions, which are an expression of his own doubleness. He cannot reach a peaceful compromise between blackness and whiteness and, similarly, between his overt cultural affiliation to the West and his enraged rejection of western ideas of superiority. While Baldwin laments that complex of rage, contempt, and dissimulation threatening the black man's sanity, he also affirms that "the battle for his identity has long ago been won" (163). Perhaps Baldwin's thought is not perfectly clear here, since just a few lines earlier he writes that the battle dividing the white man trying to protect his identity and the black man trying to establish his identity is by no means finished (163). Such a problematic attitude makes the text—and a large part of Baldwin's work—difficult to handle. There seems to be a constant process of re-elaboration at work, with the author shifting from optimism to despair, from pride to shame, from the Africa he does not know and cannot really connect with to the America he is familiar with yet at the same time estranged to. Even while he so detachedly sets the white world as completely separate from himself as a black man, despising it for its culpable naïveté, he still looks at white cultural icons with envy and hate, calling himself "a suspect latecomer, bearing no credentials" (156).[19] What a difference, in perspective, from the sense of familiarity and entitlement Du Bois displays in producing *The Souls of Black Folk* as a narrative of the interconnections between Africa, Europe and America, a narrative where full access to Western cultural legacy is claimed as a right.[20]

Baldwin is again contradictory when he boldly claims, just a few pages later, that the black man "is not a visitor to the West, but a citizen there" (163), but contradiction is perhaps inevitable when African American identity is still linked to a sense of estrangement and dispossession. White culture cannot be escaped because it is dominant within the Western canon at large. It must be faced, even though only to undermine it, which proves to be not entirely possible, as the black man is a cultural hybrid and historical oxymoron.[21] Having acknowledged that, Baldwin feels entitled to write, in the last paragraph of "Stranger in the Village," that he is "not, really, a stranger any longer for any American alive" (165). The disruption of accepted hierarchies of value is also specifically pursued through the use of the white canon, whether this is represented by the bourgeois Bildungsroman pattern or by James's literature of exile. In both cases canon revision implies history revision, with the inclusion of the black man as one of the actors involved in national history and identity, which has finally to be considered a composite mosaic of cultural heritages and identities. As one has to acknowledge the presence of a black counterpart to Benjamin Franklin—"Franklin . . . in a state of nature" (4)—it is also necessary to accept a rewriting of history, as Baldwin will make clear.

Baldwin's effort to "survive the fury of the colour problem"[22] causes him to physically cross the United States' boundaries and to symbolically transcend a purely racial essence. The new national identity Baldwin is thus formulating is less nationalistic than cosmopolitan.[23] The kind of exile Baldwin chooses is not just from the white world in which he knows he cannot live anymore, but also from the black world he is not yet able to come to terms with.[24] Being exiled from oneself as a result of that sense of alienation that the individual brings within himself, due to political or racial oppression and exclusion, also becomes central to define modernity. If the modern subject is not whole, but inevitably divided and hybrid, then figures like Baldwin—or Venture, all differences considered—can be interpreted as en epitome of modernity exactly because they harbor in themselves a heterogeneous cultural identity.[25] Exile in Europe adds another element to Baldwin's search for a place in the world of men and in the realm of letters. He left for Paris in 1948: Richard Wright had already chosen that city as his elective homeland, while Chester Himes would arrive in 1953.[26] He also seems to follow the American tradition of exile as eminently represented by Henry James.[27] In *The Politics of Exile*, B.R. Washington traces a parallel between James and Baldwin referring to, among other elements, "the famous litany of America's cultural absences emitted in James's *Hawthorne* ('no Oxford, nor Eton, nor Harrow; no literature, no novels, no museums, no pictures, no political society . . . ')" and to the second paragraph of "Stranger in the Village" ("no movie house, no bank, no library, no theater," 151),[28] in which the situation of cultural inadequacy of the United States described by James is conversely ascribed to Europe by Baldwin. The latter's choice is complicated by issues of race and color, yet Europe still provides a context against which it is possible to articulate not just an African American identity but, more extensively, an American identity, especially because of its usually problematical relationship with the past.[29]

In fact, Baldwin writes in a context of displacement, thus employing a device James had already identified as a key feature in the process leading his "innocents abroad" to awareness and experience. Their condition as human beings and artists could not be more different and yet their relationship to Europe serves a similar purpose: showing what the New World is by contrast with the Old. It is exactly such juxtaposition that prompts Baldwin to write. With exile and relocation as a vantage point of view, Baldwin adopts and finally changes the assumptions on which canonical categories are based.[30] While he acknowledges "Dante, Shakespeare, Michelangelo, Aeschylus, Da Vinci, Rembrandt, and Racine" as outstanding figures in the white cultural pantheon—which certainly includes James—he contributes to alter it by inscribing himself into it. Baldwin's literature of exile does not and cannot concern white upper-class disgust for American philistinism; it tells a story of slavery ad racial violence instead, while firmly asserting that all-white America is nothing but mere illusion.

The black man's presence can prove to be of vital importance in the white man's coping with reality, because it provides a more articulate perspective, revealing the inherent doubleness of all things. An example of this heightened vision is Baldwin's perception of the cathedral of Chartres, which is dramatically different from that of the villagers, who metonymically represent an overall—and often undifferentiated—white perspective on the world: "Perhaps they are struck by the power of the spires, the glory of the windows. . . . I am terrified by the slippery bottomless well to be found in the crypt, down which heretics were hurled to death, and by the obscene, inescapable gargoyles jutting out of the stone an seeming to say that God and the devil can never be divorced" (164).

Thus, dealing with the black man and with the past becomes a metaphorical path to awareness, as the obstinate dismissal of history has imposed to white America a tremendous cost in terms of identity, and pretended innocence has led to schizophrenia and racial madness. Having learned to reinvent and adapt themselves, African Americans know how to cope with a complex world, which is not just black or white. On the other hand, the white man seems to be loosing the same battle because he stubbornly clings to the all-American myth of innocence, preventing him from coming to terms with reality: "it was impossible for Americans to accept the black man as one of themselves, for to do so was to jeopardise their status as white men. But . . . the strain of denying the overwhelming undeniable forced Americans into rationalisations so fantastic that they approached the pathological" (163).

Such national predicament implies Europe as a third party which, in Baldwin's terms, is innocent because it has not been "tainted" with the presence of the black man and the necessity on the part "of the American white man to find a way of living with the Negro in order to be able to live with himself" (163). Consequently, it has not been affected with that "insanity which overtakes white men" (163). However, Europe is not just a land of sanity and innocence, it is also the place where healthy displacement is possible for the divided subject, which can eventually lead to a complex awareness that, despite their reciprocal reluctance, blacks and whites are inextricably bound together: "no matter where our fathers had been born, or what they had endured, the fact that Europe had formed us both was part of our identity and part of our inheritance."[31]

Europe helps Baldwin embrace his experience as a black man to finally become not just a black writer, but a Western writer.[32] He would not accept to be confined to a fixed conception of literature in racial terms, nor to be trapped in definitions such as "minority" and "majority," which are too often prescriptive and mutually exclusive. What he is more interested in is the crisis of identity, which is not confined to minorities but affects mainstream culture too. The notion of crisis is certainly more productive for African Americans, in that trying to define black culture simply in opposition to the white mainstream or as African culture would be useless because "any American Negro wishing to go back so far will find his journey through time abruptly arrested by the signature on the bill of sale which served as the entrance paper for his ancestor" (160).[33]

Baldwin has to face a final paradox: the impossibility to write while in the United States, as he realizes upon returning to America in 1957, a fact that causes him to travel back and forth from France. Almost all of his major works were written in Europe, thus confirming his existential condition of perpetual diaspora[34] as a fact enabling him to be creative precisely because of—and thanks to—continuous negotiation and displacement. Displacement and estrangement are the key to gain renewed insight into the black intellectual's role, as well as into the black-white experience as the space where both whiteness and blackness are being reconstructed in a post-racial perspective. American history contains in itself both the horror of racial war and the promise of a perpetual challenge that is also perpetually met. Such a process—"the inter-racial drama acted out on the American continent" (165)—has resulted in a new black man as well as in a new white man. Only thus can they cope with modernity, where cultural difference and heterogeneity must be finally recognized: "It is precisely this black-white experience which may prove of indispensable value to us in the world we face today. This world is white no longer, and it will never be white again" (165).[35] Whiteness does not just stand for color: it is a metaphor for the systematic erasure of multiple identities, of migrant bodies as well as of open and fluid cultural spaces. Conversely, both Venture in the New World and Baldwin in the Old World provide an example of diasporic identity as they repeatedly cross boundaries, whether these are embodied in the economic structures of the country or in its system of cultural values. Where Venture is obsessed with money, Baldwin is frantically driven to ask himself "what it means to be an American"; where the former articulates his social persona by means of bourgeois hard work and diligence, the latter molds his political role by means of a reflection on literature and culture.

Their quest is the effort to solve the historical riddle concerning the nature of American identity. In fact, as Baldwin's suggests, "the very word 'America' remains a new, almost completely undefined and extremely controversial proper noun. No one in the world seems to know exactly what it describes, not even we motley millions who call ourselves Americans."[36]

NOTES

1. Gilroy, *The Black Atlantic*. See chapter 4 on Du Bois and the "Politics of (Dis)placement."
2. Bhabha, *The Location of Culture*, 2.
3. Baldwin, "Discovery," 17. This collection can be used as a useful counterpart to *Notes of a Native Son*, in particular as concerns issues of national identity and culture.
4. Wright, *Becoming Black*, 13.
5. Smith, *A Narrative of the Life*. Further references to this work are included in the text.
6. Concerning the African autobiographic tradition see Alabi, *Telling Our Stories*, 2, 5.

7. With regard to the notion of slavery as a condition of "social death" see Patterson, *Slavery and Social Death*, 5.
8. On the relationship between money and African Americans in the context of the bourgeois revolution see Portelli, *Canoni Americani*, 60–61.
9. Venture openly affirms his belonging to the West, which makes it impossible for him to think about Africa as his motherland. Never indulging in any sentimentalism about homeland, Venture is absolutely determined in his sense of belonging to the New World, however provisional that may be. During one violent confrontation, his master threatens to send him to the West Indies but Venture gives a ready reply: "I answered him I crossed the waters to come here, and I am willing to cross them to return" (15).
10. Toni Morrison analyzes the fundamental traits of American literature as a series of responses to a "dark, abiding, signifying Africanist presence." Morrison, *Playing in the Dark*, 5–6.
11. Equiano, *The Interesting Narrative*, 55. Equiano defines the first white men he sees as "bad spirits."
12. Baldwin, "Stranger in the Village," 151. Further references to this work are included in the text. On this passage echoing Henry James's famous essay on Hawthorne, see Washington, *The Politics of Exile*, 99.
13. Fanon makes an analogous point when he underlines that white colonizers, even when they are a numerical minority, never feel inferior to black people and when he stresses how the colonized subject's sense of inferiority is the correlative of the colonizer's sense of superiority. See Fanon, *Peau Noire, Masques Blancs*, 94–95.
14. Sylvander, *James Baldwin*, 17.
15. Du Bois, *Souls of Black Folk*, 364–365.
16. In an analogous circumstance, Phillis Wheatley chooses a similar course of action by entitling one of her poems "On Being Brought to Africa to America." In this poem there is not a word openly referring to slavery and its brutality and the passive form "being brought" is a rather solitary clue concerning it. See Wheatley, *Collected Works*, 18.
17. See Lee, *Designs of Blackness*, 31. With regard to the dissembling strategies adopted especially by early authors, Lee identifies some characteristics of slave narratives, considered as the founding phase of black autobiography: "They tell a collective story: encapturement, Atlantic transportation, field or house servitude, brutalism as not only labour but sexual property, religiosity, living always on one's wits by double-talk and 'putting' on massa,' together with the sustaining dips into Brer Rabbit, Jack the Bear, 'flying Africans,' High John and each associated figure of black folklore and tricksterism."
18. See Accardo, "Forme e funzioni dell'ironia nelle slave narratives," 131–132, 141–142. Accardo points out the apparent naiveté of Venture's factual and descriptive narration, which initially seems to adhere to the ideology of slavery. However, behind a very subtle use of oppositions, a certain irony can be detected that becomes more and more overt until it is finally unmasked in the contrast the narrator traces between himself—"a black dog"—and a "white gentleman."
19. Eldridge Cleaver criticizes Baldwin's uneasiness concerning his Africa heritage, which he certainly perceives as inaccessible and which shapes his intent of appropriating the white man's heritage and make it his own. See Cleaver, "Notes on a Native Son," 68.
20. Gilroy, *The Black Atlantic*, 121.
21. On the necessity to negotiate with the canon see Washington, *The Politics of Exile*, 18–21. For a discussion of hybridity and, in particular, the problematic nature of cultural heritage see Fabre, "James Baldwin in Paris," 48.

22. Baldwin, "Discovery," 17.
23. Posnock, *Color and Culture*, 220–238.
24. Baldwin is very explicit with regard to this: "I was isolated from Negroes as I was from whites, which is what happens when a Negro begins, at bottom, to believe what white people say about him." Baldwin, "Discovery," 17.
25. See Johnson-Roullier, *Reading on the Edge*, 3–7.
26. See Davis, *Paris without Regret*, 12, 83.
27. See Newman, "The Lesson of the Master," 52–54. The author identifies a specific relationship between James and Baldwin in "the amphibian elegance of . . . syntax," which is only natural for an artist haunted by dualities and paradox: "The Atlantic Ocean separated James's mind into opposed hemispheres, and the gulf of color so cleaves Baldwin" (52). In "The Discovery of What It Means to Be an American" Baldwin openly admits that "it is a complex fate to be an American," thus quoting James's *The Art of Fiction*. See Washington, *The Politics of Exile*, 17, 100, 109.
28. Washington, *The Politics of Exile*, 17.
29. Johnson-Roullier, *Reading on the Edge*, 136–138. See also O'Daniel, *James Baldwin*, 130.
30. See Washington, *The Politics of Exile*, 105.
31. Baldwin, *Nobody Knows My Name*, 18.
32. See Fabre, "James Baldwin in Paris," 47.
33. See Johnson-Roullier, *Reading on the Edge*, 127–128. Baldwin further stresses this concept in discussing the conference of Negro-African Writers and Artists taking place in Paris in 1956: "What *is* a culture? . . . Is it possible to describe as a culture what may simply be, after all, a history of oppression? . . . for what, beyond the fact that all black men at one time or another left Africa, or have remained there, do they really have in common?" Baldwin, "Princes and Powers," 35. For a discussion of the essentialist approach, see Lemelle, "Politics of Cultural Existence," 341. The author criticizes an essentialist approach relying on Afrocentrism as a means to finally acquire an autonomous identity.
34. See Davis, *Paris without Regret*, 22, 23, 27.
35. See Sylvander, *James Baldwin*, 18. Also Ro, *Rage and Celebration*, 78.
36. Baldwin, "Discovery," 17.

14 The Iconic Ship in the Atlantic Dialogue of Black Britain

Itala Vivan

In 1998 Britain celebrated the fiftieth anniversary of the landing at Tilbury Docks of the *Empire Windrush*, a ship that brought from Jamaica to London 492 Caribbean immigrants accepted as British citizens under the provisions of the British Nationality Act passed in 1947 by the Labour government of Clement Attlee. The 1948 event has since become, in retrospect, a momentous happening and the founding icon of a new course in British social history, marking the beginning of what is now called Black Britain, while the Windrush people have become the avant-garde of an army that has changed the face of the country, modifying its perception of identity and converting old-time Englishness into Britishness.[1]

The *Empire Windrush* was a rusty old boat that had previously been used to transport Commonwealth recruits to the U.K., troops for World War II. Again in 1948, most of her passengers were former soldiers, former Royal Air Force servicemen discharged at the end of the conflict who had gone back to their island and found they could not make a decent living there. The old ship then took up the role of a vessel of desire, a means to "return" to English shores, as if England were some sort of "homeland." The image of the ship looms large in the collective imagination of the migratory experience, where the historical vessel is transformed into a vehicle of multiple, ambiguous meanings that in their polymorphous nature are subsumed as mirrors of existential histories. The present essay asks how and why this specific element in the narrative of the black migrants—the ship itself—became a signifier in history.

The theme of this volume, which engages with Atlantic crossings and cultural exchanges, throws new light on the portentous image of our ship and projects it onto a wide backdrop where the history and individual stories of the transatlantic diaspora merge into a blurred silhouette, a vessel of life and death, of discovery and both possible and impossible return(s). The ship that sails from one side of the Atlantic Ocean to the other, carrying its human cargo without any promise of return, is both a metaphor of human life and death and a repetition of historical journeys—a ship of desire as well as a ship of history. But it is also a symbol of the dialogue flowing between the two sides of the Atlantic and creating a triangle with the shores of the African continent, a concrete and consistent container of meanings.

The essential role of the ship as a means of travel, a locus of exchange and communication in itself, and a carrier of human destinies within what Paul Gilroy called the Black Atlantic, has been widely discussed, not only by Gilroy himself, but also by James Clifford and others.[2] The definition of "traveling culture" given to the black world within the Atlantic area is validated by documentary and literary texts from the black diaspora, beginning with slave narratives and ending with contemporary fiction and autobiography. Caribbean authors have focused their attention on the black—African, Caribbean, African American—roots of such culture, without any particular emphasis on the ethnic connotations of each voice, while British scholars in their narrations of imperial history have given paramount importance to the role of the (British) nation, as Gilroy has remarked. These traveling worlds, the ships of slave and general commercial trade, as well as the military ships, all belonged to European imperial powers and were subjected to their interests and governed by their rules. They are relevant objects of analysis because they were the original in-betweens in a by-now long history of (post)colonial in-betweens, and a source of hybrid culture and political discourse. Ships were also the chief places where revolt broke out and systematic repression and massacre were perpetrated by the colonizers. In imaginative representations, both visual and literary, the ship looms large in the history of the anti-imperial struggle.

THE VESSEL OF DESIRE

The medieval world of the Mediterranean, where journeying by sea meant organizing not only commercial exchange but also territorial exploration, had a counterpart to these material aspects in the poetic icon of the ship of desire adopted by courtly love. The profile of the enchanted vessel evoked by Dante Alighieri in *La Vita Nova* is perhaps the best known example:

> Guido, i' vorrei che tu e Lapo ed io
> fossimo presi per incantamento
> e messi in un vasel, ch'ad ogni vento
> per mare andasse al voler vostro e mio;
> sì che fortuna od altro tempo rio
> non ci potesse dare impedimento,
> anzi, vivendo sempre in un talento,
> di stare insieme crescesse 'l disio. . . .
> e quivi ragionar sempre d'amore,
> e ciascuna di lor fosse contenta,
> sì come i' credo che saremmo noi.[3]

This imaginary boat is a coffer or casket of pleasure and love, and bears little, if any, resemblance to the cruel ships of imperial exchange that would soon follow in European history. Yet even this enchanted vessel is taken as an example of dialogue by the poet—a dialogue of love and joy meant to enhance the refinement of life and enjoyment. The ship appears in Dante as an image of isolation in perfection, so as to create a perfect society of the happy few. The dialogue here takes place inside the vessel, and does not flow outward; it is limited within a journeying group of selected people who move through space and time, a chronotope in a blissful state of oblivion and self-indulgence. This gentle side of life, sophisticated and hedonistic, could only exist if the other side, practical and utilitarian, helped it to survive, providing the economic means for such luxury.

THE SHIP OF IMPERIAL CONQUEST
AND COLONIAL LOOTING

With the flourishing of Renaissance splendor, commerce and trade, exploration and exploitation had to increase and develop in order to fuel the sophistication of Europe's upper classes. Territorial conquest, colonization of remote lands, subjugation of "other" societies, properly otherized and classified as inferior, had to grow in proportion with the growing demands of the dominant classes in the Old World. The discovery of the Americas, the invasion of the new continent, went along with systematic raids into the interior of Africa in order to capture men and women to be sold as slaves into the colonies. The ships of discovery first—Christopher Columbus's three caravels—and then the heavily militarized ships of conquest started their voyages from Europe to the Americas, carrying soldiers and explorers, and were soon followed by ships transporting missionaries and traders.

A parallel route of discovery and migration was followed by the ship that brought the Puritans to the shore of the land that was to be called New England. In 1620 the *Mayflower* became a symbol of the dream of founding a new society, and in 1630 the *Arbella* carried the men for a government of the New Canaan, with John Winthrop delivering his speech *A Modell of Christian Charity* on board the ship. These ships were vehicles for a new kind of migration, marking the diaspora of Europe toward the outer boundaries of the known world—a movement of formidable expansion and dissemination of the Christian word, of the Christian sword. England gave life to New England, not a twin sister but a new subject, America.

Soon after the landing of the Pilgrims in Massachusetts, the slave ships of the great powers of Europe—Portugal, France, Spain, and especially England—entered a transatlantic dialogue by unloading all over the Americas huge numbers of Africans who were captured, uprooted from their homes, and unable ever to escape their tormentors because of dislocation and distance. The wide ocean prevented them from running away from their captors and owners. In spite of numerous rebellions and insurrections, slaves had to stay, and create a new life wherever they were sold. The image of the slave ship became a symbol of horror and fear, a dark memory in the minds of many who experienced the fatal crossing of the Atlantic. The ship bristling with the guns of imperial and colonial looters developed a warlike transatlantic dialogue, with a one-way flow of weapons and soldiers directed toward the margins of the European empires.

THE DREAMSHIP OF IMPOSSIBLE RETURN

The million slaves transferred and sold in the Americas carried with them their memories and stories; theirs was a journey of no return. Yet the world of slavery saw the recurrent emergence of the icon of the dreamship, which was supposed to carry the slaves back home in a backflow of redemption and salvation: the slave narratives, the stories passed on through generations of oral storytellers, the work songs, and the spirituals echoed with invocations to a mysterious ship of salvation, which was occasionally called "Jesus." The whites thought their slaves were praying to the Christian savior, while in fact the slaves were invoking the name of an imaginary "supership" that would take them back home.

But where was home by then? What was home? At one point it became evident that home was no longer identifiable and was nowhere except in the grieving minds of the suffering slaves. When Marcus Garvey fantasized about a Black Star Line whose ships should carry the Africans back to their continent—Africa to the Africans! Back to Africa! were the mottos of the Universal Negro Improvement Association and "The Negro World"—the dream soon proved to be impossible. It was just impossible to go back. The dialogue of loss and deprivation, of nostalgia and search for one's own roots, had to continue across the Black Atlantic, during and after the long centuries of slavery. It was a dialogue where identities were confused and juxtaposed, and the dream of Africa became an American icon, the icon of those blacks who had been orphaned of Mother Africa.

THE SHIP OF MIGRATION: BACK TO
THE MOTHER COUNTRY?

The twentieth century brought great changes in the cultural area of the Black Atlantic. The voyage across the Atlantic—the Middle Passage—which had been a journey of no return for the Africans transported into the Americas, inverted its direction and turned back toward Europe. But this was an illusionary return. It was seen by many as a return to a mother country dreamed of in the provinces of the British empire: in fact there was no such return, for there existed no mother country at all for the people of

African descent, for the people of color who landed at Tilbury in 1948, and subsequently at other ports in Britain, coming from the British West Indies. The 1948 expedition was the signal and the beginning of a wave of migrations which became particularly important in the 1950s, after the McCarran Act of 1952 severely limited migration from the West Indies to the U.S. These new migrants who left the Caribbean in the assumption they would be accepted as fellow citizens in Britain, were in fact disowned and rejected by a stepmother Britain. There emerged a fundamental difference between the newcomers and the English people, a difference that these migrants had not foreseen and which made them "strangers" in a land they thought would receive them as sons and daughters.

What has then happened, between that momentous landing of the *Windrush* and the present day, to make the migrants remain in the inhospitable mother country (in fact, a stepmother), and cause England to become what people now call Britain—a land where all are British citizens, but some of these citizens have an added value, and call themselves Black British? What kind of new and multiple identity is this, and what connection is there between the migration, the famous ship, and the Black British subject? What epic history is hidden beneath the fabric of society as we see it now, that gives such vibrant tension to the image of the ship and the power of representation filtering through the social performance of Black Britain?[4]

THE FABRIC OF TRANSLATION AND THE FABRICATION(S) OF THE WRITER

The slaves were African bodies transferred—transported—from Africa to the Americas, human beings transferred into subhuman conditions and deprived of the freedom to return home. Together with people, imperial colonization also translated words, languages, stories. The spider of African folktales, the Ananse of Ashanti tradition, metamorphosed into Nancy, the black slave, nanny, and storyteller, who like the spider of tradition drew the thread of stories from her own belly and went on spinning tales in the South of the United States. Such tales and folktales were constructed into a plot, a fabric, a story, a history. The double consciousness represented and plotted in the tale of the signifying monkey (collected by Roger Abrahams and analyzed by Henry Louis Gates)[5] is the same double consciousness identified by Gilroy as the constitutive feature of modernity itself, and playing at the beginning and the end of the black writer's redemption song. It is a tale of melancholia and displacement, but also of recognition of one's own identity in the compulsive use of the mask and the necessity of performance.

Toni Morrison's *Beloved* (1987) and *Jazz* (1992) and Caryl Phillips's *Cambridge* (1991), *Crossing the River* (1993), *The Nature of Blood* (1997), and more explicitly, *Dancing in the Dark* (2005) are examples of narratives where the underlying plot is derived directly from the translation of slavery. In this context, the iconic ship also splits into a double image: on the one side we have the evil cargo ship loaded with captured bodies and tortured minds; on the other sails the boat of liberation and imagination. But the ship becomes a symbol of impossible return also for a writer who would certainly not like to be defined as postcolonial, V. S. Naipaul, as signaled in the story inscribed into *The Enigma of Arrival* (1987)—a title derived from a painting by Giorgio de Chirico that is a *mise en abîme* of the novel and a representation of impossible return and postcolonial displacement, loss, and melancholy.[6]

The black migration that started in 1948 had in itself the structural dimension of slavery, a history that was not finished and that asked to be played over and over again, to be repeated and translated in a compulsive repetition of performances. The theme of *Beloved*—a retelling of old slave narratives—and its language of mute and disconnected despair; the reenactment of the "Negro" role as an art form in *Dancing in the Dark;* and the *abiku* nature of the main character in Ben Okri's *The Famished Road* (1991), which is clearly reminiscent of Amos Tutuola's *Palm-Wine Drinkard* (1952), are beautiful and moving instances of hybrid translations of transatlantic crossings that still continue in the writing of Black Britain and Black America. The postcolonial writer is a translated man, says Salman Rushdie, whose Gibreel Farishta, in *The Satanic Verses* (1988), threatened imperial London with change: "'City,' he cried, and his voice rolled over the metropolis like thunder, 'I am going to tropicalize you.'"[7]

NARRATIVES MASKING A PRIMARY, UNSPOKEN WOUND

The *Empire Windrush* in Andrea Levy's *Small Island* (2004) and in the narratives of Mike and Trevor Phillips figures as the disquieting icon of an old tale reenacted in the epos of migration. Again, we have human bodies transported from one side of the Atlantic to the other, and lost in translation. This new crossing does not compensate for the ancient tragedy of slavery, but it is rather a new wound that somehow reenacts it. The impossibility of real compensation is due to the lack of words and the inadequacy of language: only gestures, songs, and music could express the wound and perhaps heal it. Performance is a necessary element in this kind of artistic expression, and this is why the historical reconstruction by the Phillips brothers and the dynamic novelization enacted by Andrea Levy work so well with all kinds of readers. Mike and Trevor Phillips create a fabric out of many individual histories taken from real documents, while Andrea Levy makes up an engaging story and positions it on an underlying structure of historical facts and family memories. In both instances we have a reenactment of the epic trip of the *Windrush* in 1948, and a dazzling performance of multiple masks.

Black Britain managed to face the frightening confrontation of difference on the stage of imperial and post-imperial society through a game
of performance, a play of masks. Such masks do not hide the underlying
wound, they only veil it and occasionally do not even seem to remember
it—at least not consciously. But the unforgettable, unforgivable wound
of slavery, transportation, and translation is the origin of the writing
game also when the latter might appear like a show, or a spectacle. Is it a
coincidence that spectacularization appears to be a necessary feature of
modernity, and hybridity an unavoidable element of our contemporane-
ity? Modernity was born in the immense belly of the Middle Passage, in
the mixing and re-mixing, the enacting and reenacting of the Black Atlantic, as many observers of our modernity say. In any case, the strength and
extraordinary vitality of the culture that emanates from Black Britain
speak to the world and have managed to force themselves upon Englishness, breaking it up to give birth to new ethnicities and to new ways of
being British.

THE SHIP ON THE HEAD OF THE
BLACK BRITISH SUBJECT

A very famous beggar in early nineteenth-century London, Joseph Johnson, was known for his eccentric outfit, a sort of mask he used to wear all
the time. He was portrayed, in an illustration published in 1817 by John
Thomas Smith in *Vagabondiana*,[8] as a black man with stereotyped Negro
features and a hat "topped by a fairly sizable replica of a ship complete with
mast and sails with all their meticulous rigging."[9]

Johnson's taste reflected a style that was and still is common in Western
Africa, but, as Dawes appropriately remarks,

> one cannot help recognizing in this act a profoundly symbolic ges-
> ture. . . . He literally wore the badge of his migrant status—his sense
> of alienation and difference—on his head. The ship was his instan-
> taneous narrative of journey. . . . The hat Johnson wore represented
> an ironic apology to white British society for his presence as a Black
> man in that country. . . . an apology in the sense of an explanation,
> a rationale for his presence, his existence and his condition. . . . He
> was brought there on the very ship of abuse, enslavement and ad-
> venture that he carried on his head. . . . The extent to which Black
> people in Britain have worn their ships on their heads speaks to the
> character and nature of British Blackness and the dialogue it has had
> with British whiteness. For Johnson's hat does not simply reflect his
> own perception of himself, but certainly speaks to his understanding
> of the white world that was looking at him, reading him, and defin-
> ing him.[10]

Figure 14.1 Joseph Johnson as portrayed in *Vagabondiana* (1817).

The ship of transportation here becomes a sign and an ironic message to imperial London. The secret reference it contains, its clownlike yet somehow sinister allusive quality, elicits attention, and it takes a special and secret code to read it in its multilayered meaning and detect the pain and the revolt hidden beneath the masquerade. As it took George Lamming's sharp insight to deconstruct Caliban's statements and show their revolutionary purport, to make him the prototype of the Caribbean man in *The Pleasures of Exile* (1960). *The Tempest* was "prophetic of a political future which is our present," Lamming writes. "Moreover, the circumstances of my life, both as a colonial and exiled descendant of Caliban in the twentieth century, is an example of that prophecy." Again, in the Shakespearean tale as it was analyzed by Lamming, the ship has a relevant yet ambiguous role as a vessel which first meant exile, and then revenge and reconciliation. Caribbean writers took upon themselves the task of continuing Caliban's revolt and struggle against the imperial master and enacted their war through language, the ideal vessel of meaning. In *The Tempest*, Shakespeare's Caliban ends by refusing his earlier position of revolt and becomes a mute witness of Prospero's triumph, but his twentieth-century descendant, the Caribbean writer, resurrects and extends his role, and shouts his anger. Lamming's rereading of *The Tempest* starts from a fundamental discovery in the history of postcoloniality, the right of the postcolonial subject to stick to "one man's way of seeing." The act of *seeing* becomes the beginning of a new era and the foundation of a new canon. The ship exhibited on the head of the Victorian beggar is accepted as a viable medium of communication and is finally seen as a challenge and a threat by the Black British writer in his exile and/or return to England: "My subject is the migration of the West Indian writer, as colonial and exile, from his native kingdom, once inhabited by Caliban, to the tempestuous island of Prospero and his language."[11]

THE SHIP OF BLACK DIASPORIC IDENTITIES ON AN ARTIST'S CANVAS: JEAN-MICHEL BASQUIAT

The African diaspora, with its repeated transatlantic crossings, its voyages out and back, its impossible returns to a home elsewhere, generates a geography of its own and marks our globe with a crisscross of scars inscribed on land and water. New and multiple identities were and still are born and reborn in the process, and their marks can be traced in the tormented visions of many artists, whose insight continues the journey undertaken in the remote or near past by listless postcolonial subjects.

Jean-Michel Basquiat was from Haiti and became a star artist in New York's cosmopolitan scene, but never forgot his African and diasporic ancestry, which he translates into an ambiguous message coming from both colonizer and colonized, and playing as both cultured and primitive. African spiritual powers, Exu and Oshoosi, enter his canvas and bring disorder and wrath, but also heroism and resistance. The ship is a frequently recurring element in his paintings, where it suggests ambivalence and conflict. There is a work of his which appears particularly meaningful in the present context, for it conveys a multilayered message, a polysemic vision. *Untitled (History of Black People)*, painted in 1983, shows a huge ship of ancient Egyptian style led down the river Nile by a rigid, mummified Osiris (an uncanny presence) and surrounded by symbols of slavery: the sickle used by slaves in sugar-cane plantations, grinning African masks, inscriptions hinting at slavery, various images of subjugation and oppression.

The critic Andrea Frohne comments that "just as ancient Egypt has been extracted from Africa and adopted by the West, Basquiat's African and African diasporic identities have been ignored, altered, or erased."[12] In fact, the career and life history of this artist, a true *peintre maudit*, reveal a pattern of enslavement and colonization that played a role in his own untimely death. His vision of a phantasmagoric and polysemic ship, inherited through his Haitian voodoo culture but reinterpreted in order to "paint" back to the world, to throw his anger in the face of Western capitalism, stands as a desperate attempt to plan an impossible voyage back home.

Visual artists from the culture of the black diaspora may become strong and powerful interpreters of hybridity and creators of new ironies through their unique ability to see things, as Basquiat did in his brief and meteoric life.[13]

YINKA SHONIBARE AND THE NEW BLACK HYBRIDITY: STEREOTYPES AND DISTANCING IRONY

The artist Yinka Shonibare comes from a family of Nigerian descent but was born in London where he lives and works. He is an important figure in the world of Black British contemporary art and is relevant to the present discourse for his constant use of stereotypes derived from the cultural tradition of Englishness, treated with distancing irony. His final effect of hybridity is obtained by mixing British stereotypes with elements (materials, fabrics, patterns, and his own physical presence portrayed or photographed) meant to ensure an ironic pretension of African authenticity. Shonibare's stereotypes are Victorian or middle class, or both, and are meant to convey the dangers and absurdities of a culture where categories are presented as clear cut, very definite, and based on dichotomies and binary oppositions. Their imaginative role aims to offer analogies with racist thought, while their hybrid character (for instance, a Victorian manikin dressed up in Victorian dress made of an African *ankara* printed cloth, or wax fabric) defeats the very stereotype through humor and creates a conceptual shock. The fact that the author's effigy often enters the work reveals the author's intention to create a narrative of the self, a typically postcolonial viewpoint when applied to canons and stereotypes and/or inserted within the frame of popular and established English authorship (Hogarth, Dickens, Wilde, James, etc.).

Yinka Shonibare is not part of the transatlantic triangle that connects such a great part of the African diaspora. There is no visible ship in his background imagination, and the intense dialogue he establishes between cultures travels via patterns, colors, and manikins put together with audacity, distancing irony and a sort of cold rage. To say it in Manthia Diawara's words, Shonibare

> has to identify with the stereotype as the source of his creativity, make it go through all the violent reviews of history, before finding in it new signifiers and connotations for his art. Just as he deconstructs the meaning of the wax print in Africa by bringing it to a museum in Europe, Shonibare creates a seductive and yet ambivalent relation with the stereotype in his art—through the embrace not only of an elegant way of presenting the stereotype, but also through a constant recourse to repetition and violence as his rhetoric of representation.[14]

Shonibare's serial narratives—photographic sequels (e.g., "Dorian Gray," "Diary of a Victorian Dandy"), installations (e.g., "Gallantry and Criminal Conversation," "Alien Obsessives"), and other compositions (e.g., "Double Dutch," "Line Painting," "Maxa," etc.)—engage the observer with all sorts of questions on identity and identification, point at the hidden miscegenation that lies at the heart of English pretence, and connect with the work done by other Black British artists or writers of the diaspora—such as David Dabydeen, Kamau Braithwaite, George Lamming, Mike Phillips and others—in order to locate and ascertain the place of blacks in English society through history. And he does it with ferocity and humor at the same time.[15]

THE ARCHITECTURE OF HYBRIDITY: DAVID ADJAYE

David Adjaye, who was born in Dar-es-Salaam and has been living in London since 1979, is of Ghanaian descent and represents a meaningful example of hybridity between Africa and the West not because of his ethnic origin but for the language of his architecture, the way he uses space and conceives public buildings. Making public buildings in modest public spaces while giving them the role of mediators and the capacity to engage—whether positively or confrontationally—with communities, he achieves the object of opening such spaces to new practices and roles. His museums, libraries, and art pavilions are not monumentalized, nor are they ritualized, and at the same time they avoid the splendid isolation and self-referentiality of many current public buildings designed by international star architects such as Frank Gehry (Guggenheim Museum in Bilbao), Daniel

Liebeskind (Ground Zero Tower project in New York), Santiago Calatrava (Auditorium in Santa Cruz de Tenerife and Auditorium of the Palace of Arts in Valencia, Spain), and Norman Foster (Chesa Futura Apartments in St. Moritz, Switzerland). Chesa Futura deserves to be mentioned here, although it is a private building, because it is emblematic of this architect's quest for the spectacular. Adjaye's buildings are meant to become sites of engagement through practices and movements inside and across the buildings themselves. These movements result in an effort to recover the possibility of strengthening urban public spaces, while leaving wide interstices for easy, fluid exchange, and communication.

The presence of Africa in Adjaye's buildings is conceptually interesting and shows the intention "to write the world from Africa or write Africa into the world" by reading contemporary Africa in its tradition of design and urban practices, but also in its imbrication of city and township.[16] This approach suggests the necessity of a different kind of encounter with Africa, where the latter is no longer an object apart from the world, anthropologically relevant but finally intractable and other-worldly, but becomes a relevant interlocutor and suggests new narratives and interpretations of social forms and their dwelling spaces.

Works such as the Public Library in Whitechapel, London, and the pavilion for the 2005 Venice Biennale are good specimens of Adjaye's work. His library, located in a narrow space in the middle of the bustling multiethnic neighborhood of Whitechapel, close to the now famous Brick Lane, exalts the multicultural character of the site instead of evading it. The library is not a secluded temple of scholarship and authority imposing respect and distance, but an open and vibrant structure where people enter and visit with complete informality. Inside, one has the startling impression of looking at the world as if from a book, or rather, from many books aligned upright, as it were, in an ideal shelf. Books and people share a communality of life through space, light, and structures. Easiness and familiarity characterize the relationship between building and visitors, and the library turns out to be not so much a neutral zone of worship and respect, but an intensely popular crossroads: Adjaye's metaphor avoids abstraction and is inserted in the vibrant atmosphere of the street. The African inspiration comes here from a public space typical of Dogon architecture, the palaver house, which is always located at the center of villages, entirely open to people and plunged into the middle of everyday life.[17]

YOUNG BLACK BRITISH GENERATIONS
AND THE MEMORY OF THE SHIP

In contrast to the Victorian black beggar carrying a ship on top of his head, one sees that the young generations are more likely to be rid of the eccentric African headgear and tend either to forget it altogether or to transform it into a conceptual element, a locus of the mind. The struggle for identity is no longer hidden by prejudices and made impossible by social taboos, but has become an ongoing battle for the survival of ideas and the recognition of one's own right to freedom of representation. From this viewpoint, Britain offers an interesting scenario in our contemporary world, although one should not indulge in superficial optimism and pass too positive a judgment on the outcome of British multiculturalism. The recent tragic events caused by an Islamic fundamentalist backlash, and increased after the war unleashed by Western countries in Iraq, and the confusion and deception revealed by new and unprecedented versions of terrorism leave a wide-open space for new analyses of society and culture in a context marked by a long history of imperialism and colonialism that created all kinds of affiliations and disaffections, passions and hatreds, and that, most of all, still involves all kinds of economic interests and unfathomable connections.

NOTES

1. See M. Phillips and T. Phillips, *Windrush: The Irresistible Rise of Multi-Racial Britain.*
2. See Gilroy, *The Black Atlantic*; Clifford, "Travelling Cultures"; Baker, Diawara, and Lindeborg, *Black British Cultural Studies*; Hall, *Representation*; Procter, *Writing Black Britain*; Sesay, *Write Black Write British*; Vivan, "The Impact of Postcolonial Hybridization."
3. "Guido, I'd like that you, Lapo and I/Were taken by enchantment/And put into a vessel that with all winds/Would journey by sea at my will and yours;/So that chance or other bad times/Could not be of impediment to us,/But, in a harmonious common life/We would desire to be together forever and ever. . . . /and there reason of love endlessly/so that they [the women] would be happy/ as I think would we." Dante, *La vita nova.* My translation.
4. See Baker, Diawara, and Lindebord, *Black British Cultural Studies*; Sandhu, *London Calling.*
5. Gates, *The Signifying Monkey*; Abrahams, *Afro-American Folktales.*
6. Naipaul, *The Enigma of Arrival.*
7. Rushdie, *The Satanic Verses*, 354.
8. Smith, *Vagabondiana*, 33ff.
9. Dawes, "Negotiating the Ship on the Head," 255.
10. Dawes, "Negotiating the Ship on the Head," 255–256.
11. Lamming, *The Pleasures of Exile*, 13.
12. Frohne, "Representing Jean-Michel Basquiat," 449.
13. On Basquiat see also Castria Marchetti, "New York da Pollock a Basquiat."
14. Diawara, "Independence Cha Cha," 21.
15. On Shonibare's aesthetics see also Guldemond and Mackert, *Yinka Shonibare*; and Oguibe and Enwezor, *Reading the Contemporary.* On the aesthetics of hybridity, see Cossa, *IbridAFrica*; Deepwell, *Art Criticism*; Njami, *Africa Remix*; Vivan, "Ibridismi postcoloniali."
16. See Mbembe and Nuttall, "Writing the World from an African Metropolis."
17. See Adjaye and Eshun, "Learning from Lagos."

15 Lost in Transit
Africa in the Trench of the Black Atlantic

Oyekan Owomoyela

"What's that smell?" I asked. . . ."The smell?" said Neil . . ."Hell, that's Africa!"

Keith Richburg, *Out of America*

Odò kì í sàn kó gbàgbé ìsun (A river does not flow and forget its source)

Yorùbá proverb

THE DILEMMA THAT IS AFRICA

The epigraph from Keith Richburg expresses a sentiment not uncommon among non-Africans as a reaction to any suggestion of close involvement with Africa. It is a sentiment that even some Africans share, especially Africans who have had experiences on the continent horrid and powerful enough to make them flee their native lands and rue their African identity. Watching the recurrent images of Africans wasted by famine and AIDS, or Africans waging inter-ethnic wars that are reminiscent of Pol Pot's murderous excesses, or seeing the obscenely corpulent figures of corrupt presidents-for-life who count their fortunes stashed in foreign banks in the billions (of dollars) while their people suffer owing to the state's inability to provide them with drinking water or other basic necessities, one can easily excuse the non-Africans who want nothing to do with the continent and its people, and the disaffected Africans who wish to renounce their identity.

In the context of an exploration of the processes and implications of migrations across the Atlantic, the enriching possibilities of the commingling of cultural, ethnic, linguistic, national, and other particularities that rim the ocean, I wish to examine some of the consequences for the possibility of Africa's involvement in the circumatlantic exchanges in the face of sentiments like Richburg's. I also wish to raise the question of the location of the contact points, the ease and uniformity of access to them by the agents (or representatives) of the different Atlantics, but in particular

African agents, and, indeed, the fashioning and orientation of those agents. This last issue is crucial because as far as Africa is concerned, quite often what at first glance looks like inclusion turns out on closer examination to be exclusion in a deceptive guise.

A "BLACK" ATLANTIC WITHOUT
AFRICA: AWAY WITH ROOTS!

I want to begin by invoking a concept that is closely related to the circumatlantic world envisaged by this volume, namely Paul Gilroy's familiar "Black Atlantic," with its severely restricted opening to Africa. I refer specifically to his discussion of the plight of the people he variously describes as "Britain's black citizens," "the contemporary black English," and "Anglo-Africans," who are "striving to be both European and black," and of "blacks in the West" in general.[1] Gilroy is dismayed by the limits that white English "cultural insiderism" and its "essential trademark . . . [which] is an absolute sense of ethnic difference and its restricted construction of what constitutes Englishness," places on their sense of belonging in the society in which they live. It is a phenomenon, he notes, that "distinguishes people from one another and . . . acquires an incontestable priority over all other dimensions of their social and historical experience, cultures, and identities." It has a bearing on "national belonging or the aspiration to nationality and other more local but equivalent forms of cultural kinship"; it "sanctions constructs of the nation as an ethnically homogeneous object and invokes ethnicity a second time in the hermeneutic procedures deployed to make sense of its distinctive cultural content" (3). Pre-modern division of peoples into "primitive" and "civilized" categories on the basis of ethnic difference, he adds, has evolved into the modern situation "in which Englishness, Christianity, and other ethnic and racialised attributes" have given way to "the dislocating dazzle of 'whiteness'" (9). The alignment of "race" with the idea of national belonging, Gilroy continues, generated a new racism in which "blackness and Englishness appeared suddenly to be mutually exclusive attributes" (10).

The trauma of exclusion forced on people who consider themselves full members of their society, but whose presence and difference complicate their compatriots' presumption and preference of homogeneity (to somewhat paraphrase Edward Said), ill disposes Gilroy toward the notion of ethnicity and its operations. He speaks therefore of "fractal patterns of cultural and political exchange and transformation" that go by designations "like creolization and syncretism [which] indicate how both ethnicities and political cultures have been made anew in ways that are significant not simply for the peoples of the Caribbean but for Europe, for Africa, *especially Liberia and Sierra Leone*, and of course for black America" (15; emphasis added).

To reinforce the foregoing qualification he appends to Africa Gilroy further specifies that "the Black Atlantic can be defined, on one level, through this desire to *transcend both the structures of the nation state and the constraints of ethnicity* and national particularity" (19; emphasis added). And, lastly, he expresses his disinclination to see identity as related to "roots and rootedness," but he rather sees it "as a process of movement and mediation that is more appropriately approached via the homonym of routes" (19).

Gilroy finds a model for his preferred attitude toward the pull of roots or ethnicity in the experiences of the nineteenth-century African American luminary Martin Robison Delany, "the principal progenitor of black nationalism in America" (20). Gilroy points out that despite Delany's travels in Africa, his determination to work for the uplift of the continent, to work for "the regeneration of our race and restoration of our father-land from the gloom and darkness of our superstition and ignorance" (20), and despite his pledge to return to Africa with his family, he chose never to return to Africa, settling instead in Chatham, Ontario (24). The reason for his Canadian exile was, of course, American racism, the same reason that explains some black scholars' hostility to the involvement of race in questions of identity. For, as Kwame Anthony Appiah has argued, "the disappearance of a widespread belief in the biological category of the Negro would leave nothing for racists to have an attitude toward" (39).[2]

OSTRACIZING AFRICA: RICHBURG, GATES, ET AL.

Gilroy's elision of Africa from his Black Atlantic however seems comparatively benign when viewed alongside some more frankly hostile regards of the continent and its peoples, and adamant desires to do away with them in intercultural, international transactions. I refer to sentiments apparently provoked by convictions of African malignancy, a malady that manifests itself in various ways and makes ostracizing the continent from global contexts prudent. A case in point is the African American journalist Keith Richburg, who spent three years as the Bureau Chief of the *Washington Post* in Nairobi and returned to America to write about what he describes as "the insanity of Africa."[3] He had the misfortune of being witness to one of the unfortunate inter-ethnic brutalities that have plagued the continent in recent years—the 1991 massacre of the Tutsi in Rwanda—having arrived on location in Tanzania just in time to see the gruesome harvest of this particular bloodshed in the form of bloated human corpses floating down the river under the Rusomo Falls bridge. As he watched the bodies float by, he recalls, he was so disgusted with Africa and Africans that he came to a radical reassessment of the significance and meaning of the Atlantic slave trade for those Africans who were enslaved and their descendants. The capture and enslavement of his ancestor was providential, he concluded, for, he told himself, "if things had been different, I might have been one of them [the victims whose bloated corpses floated past him]—or might have met some similarly anonymous fate in one of the countless ongoing civil wars or tribal clashes on this brutal continent. And so I thank God my ancestor survived that voyage [on the slave ship]." Later, having returned to the safety of America, he confesses: "I still recoil in horror whenever I see another television picture of another tribal slaughter, another refugee crisis. But most of all I think: Thank God my ancestor got out, because, now, I am not one of them [Africans]. . . . In short thank God that I am an American."[4]

Richburg's reaction to his African experience is substantially of a kind with the belated revelation some African American would-be returnees to Africa experienced, as documented by Henry Louis Gates in a sequence of his television program, *Wonders of the African World* (2000). Gates opens the third of the six-program series with a sequence titled "The Slave Kingdoms." With a panorama of a Ghanaian beach as his backdrop, Gates comments on Ghana's role as one of the major sources of slaves during the transatlantic slave trade and identifies himself as a descendant of one of the slaves. When Kwame Nkrumah became president of Ghana in 1957, he continues, so great was the new president's love for African Americans that he invited them all to come back to Ghana, to think of Ghana as their home. "Some actually came," Gates says, "but not everybody stayed." Then with a smirk he launches into what he says is "the funniest story" Ghanaians tell "about the relationship between Africans and African Americans." In 1960, he relates, many African Americans arrived in Accra in response to Nkrumah's invitation. At midnight soon after their arrival, they went to the beach and after reciting some "magic ritualistic words from the Ashanti threw their passports way out to sea beyond the barriers. Then they smacked their hands, saying they had got rid of American racism and were back on the mother continent."

Six weeks later, Gates continues, the people who lived close to the beach noticed shadows under the full moon and wondered if they were being invaded. They got their torches and went to investigate, and what did they find? He answers with a chuckle, "Those same Black Americans out beyond that barrier [he gestures toward some rocks] searching for those passports." They had obviously seen the reality of Africa (or "the insanity of Africa" as Richburg put it), and wanted no part of it. Gates, the W.E.B. Du Bois Professor of the Humanities at Harvard University, neglects to say that W.E.B. Du Bois was one of Nkrumah's invitees, and that he spent the rest of his life in Ghana, where a research center (in Accra) honors his memory to this day.

Incidentally, Gates devotes a significant chunk of time, space, and effort in the same series to recriminating against Africans who, he stresses, bore a huge share of the responsibility for the slave trade, and to raising questions about the nature of people who would sell their own kinsmen and women into slavery, knowing full well the fate that awaited them. For him, at least, enslavement was not providential or salvational.

Richburg's, then, is only one of the more recent, more vehement, and more unabashed rejections of African roots, for expressions similar to his, though less strident, date as early as the earliest African American writing. In her 1773 poem, "On Being Brought from Africa to America," Phillis Wheatley writes "'Twas mercy brought me from my *Pagan* land;/Taught my benighted soul to understand/That there's a God, that there's a *Savior* too."[5] Alice Walker has argued, with some merit, that Wheatley has been "most misunderstood," for she was a slave girl "who owned not even herself," let alone a room of her own, and who could therefore not write her real mind.[6] Another African American woman writer, though, wrote in much different circumstances. The Harlem Renaissance writer Zora Neale Hurston (whom Walker also champions) considered slavery the prize she paid for "civilization." She considered it "a bully adventure and worth all that I have paid through my ancestors for it." She declares, *"No one on earth ever had a greater chance for glory. The world to be won and nothing to be lost."*[7] Africa was no loss to be missed; it was in fact antithetical to civilization, and slavery was a godsend.

In view of the foregoing one might be permitted to harbor misgivings regarding some suggested correctives to the tendency to sideline Africa in circumatlantic and other supra-national transactions.

REPRESENTING "AFRICA ITSELF": THE TALENTED TENTH

In his introduction to a special issue of *Research in African Literatures* devoted to Gilroy's book, the guest editor, Simon Gikandi, calls attention to the existence of "some uneasiness about the haunting shadow of Africa in the making of modern culture, a feeling that the continent is both within the grand narrative of modernity [and] outside it," and wonders if one can speak of an African diaspora in Europe and the Americas, one that has made significant contributions to the cultural productions of the modern world, and at the same time avoid "some concrete intellectual encounter with Africa itself."[8] In the same journal issue the South African Ntongela Masilela, for his part, expresses the view that Gilroy's exclusion of Africa seriously attenuates "the Africanness or Africanity of the 'Black Atlantic.'" He also sees in Gilroy's book "an unremitting disdain for Africa, for things African, and for things that come from our 'Dark Continent,'"[9] and goes on to suggest better alternatives to Gilroy's treatment of Africa.

But had Gilroy followed Masilela's prescription the problem would not have been solved, inasmuch as the engagement Masilela envisages would amount to an "intellectual encounter," certainly, but not necessarily with "Africa itself." Masilela would be satisfied if Gilroy acknowledged connections among intellectuals from Africa and the Americas going as far back as the times of Edward Blyden, Martin Delany, Alexander Crummell, and others, whose historical project, he asserts, was "the liberation of Africa" (89). In the view of those men who were intent on remaking Africa in the image of the West, however, "liberation" was not only from colonialism but also from "superstition" and "savagery," their characterization of the African difference from the West. Writing from Liberia in 1860, Crummell had the following to say about the continent:

> Africa lies low and is wretched. She is the maimed and crippled arm of humanity. Her great powers are wasted. Dislocation and anguish have reached every joint. Her condition in every point calls for succor—moral, social, domestic, political, commercial, and intellectual . . . Africa is the victim of her heterogeneous idolatries. Africa is wasting away beneath the accretions of civil and moral miseries. Darkness covers the land, and gross darkness the people.[10]

In their discussion of Crummell in *An Enchanting Darkness: The American Vision of Africa in the Twentieth Century*, Dennis Hickey and Kenneth Wylie concede that Crummell was not plagued by a sense of racial inferiority; they quote his biographer Wilson Moses to the effect that he was, however, pessimistic about Africans' ability "to develop a culture on their own terms," and that indeed "he had a pessimistic view of primitive humanity. All good in the world came from submission to Christian institutions."[11]

Masilela stresses that the "intellectual bridge of trans-Atlanticism" with which they connected Africa and its diaspora was "not because of racial ontologies or the myth of the search for origins, but rather because of political solidarity, intellectual affiliations, cultural retainments, and historical appropriations" (90). He thus shies away from concepts that have become bugaboos for contemporary thinkers: "racial ontologies" and "the search for origins," or roots, although he is willing to embrace "cultural retainments."

Masilela focuses his discussion mostly on the role that African American intellectuals played in the formation of South African modernity. The "New African intelligentsia," he says, "modeled themselves on the New Negro Talented Tenth," and in his view the advent of South African modernity "is inconceivable without the example of American modernity: the New Africans appropriated the historical lessons drawn from the New Negro experience within American modernity to chart and negotiate the newly emergent South African modernity: the Africans learned from African Americans the process of transforming themselves into agencies in or of modernity" (90). The African Americans who wished to transcend, or believed they had transcended, the difference between themselves and white America, presented themselves as proof that African Americans could be *improved* to such a state that would make them acceptable to white America for absorption into its bosom, a state that would, in other words, enable them to pass. Charles W. Chesnutt offers a telling portrait of the bourgeois African American in the members of the Blue Vein Society he features in the short story "The Wife of His Youth." Its membership is made up of "individuals who were, generally speaking, more white than black," and it earned its name because "some envious outsiders made the suggestion that no one was eligible for membership who was not white enough to show blue veins."[12] Mr. Ryder, the hero of the story and "dean of the Blue Veins," thus describes the racial location of the society's members: "Our fate lies between absorption by the white race and extinction in the black. The one doesn't want us yet, but may take us in time. The other would welcome us, but it would be for us a backward step . . . we must do the best we can for ourselves and those who are to follow us. Self-preservation is the first law of nature."[13]

Masilela explains the attraction of the Talented Tenth model for South African intellectuals by pointing out that the country was subjected to "'forced' modernization," which meant Westernization: "We encountered European modernity as a process of the colonial system and imperialist projection." He continues,

> The fundamental historical question became: what is it that enabled Europeans to defeat Africans militarily, and consequently hegemonically impose themselves on us? The only serious response on our part could only be through the appropriation of that which enabled Europeans to triumph: modernity. Hence the obsession with Christianity, civilization, and education by the new African intelligentsia, from Blaise Diagne in Senegal through Harry Thuku in Kenya and Nnamdi Azikiwe in Nigeria to Walter Rubusana in South Africa. (90)

That reasoning recalls the African professional philosophers' rationale for recommending westernization for Africa—the need to "try to discover not our unrecognized greatness or nobility *but the secret of our defeat by the West.*"[14]

LOCATION, AND RIVERS MINDLESS OF THEIR SOURCES

The idea of circumatlantic movement and transformation taken together with Gilroy's proposal that we focus on routes instead of roots calls attention to a crucial fact—that the crucibles and the laboratories dedicated to the alchemical sea-change process are located in places well removed from Africa (or from "Africa itself"), places only accessible through a sea crossing, both real and metaphorical. I speak of locations where people from the different Atlantics commingle—places more likely to be in Europe and the Americas, and even if they are on the African continent, then in the cosmopolitan centers, places, in other words, that Masilela has described as "the imperialized capitals on the African continent" (89). Such places are by and large, extensions of the overseas locations, and not really "Africa itself." That fact entails another inevitability: the Africans in a position to participate in these comminglings are the ones who have already undergone a measure of sea-change, having taken a metaphoric cultural voyage *out of Africa* and into the bosom of the West. These are the Africans who navigate around and across borders and margins, who operate in the interstices of cultures, and to whom terms like hybridity, creolization, and *métissage* have meaning and relevance. Wendy Griswold describes the Nigerian members of this group as possessing an "extraordinary level of education relative to their fellow Nigerians—relative to anyone!" and wonders about their relevance to Nigeria "since they are so unrepresentative of the populace."[15] Gates admits the same point, I believe, when he calls for a closer dialogue between African intellectuals and their African American counterparts, saying that "while peasants in Tanzania, peasants in Nigeria, and peasants in Georgia might not share a common culture, *intellectuals* and artists in Pan-Africa . . . share a common *intellectual* culture, just as surely as European intellectuals did in the Latin Middle Ages and the Renaissance, when the average person in those societies knew virtually nothing about a common European heritage."[16]

Much has been written about the making of the modern African intellectual class, its deliberate fashioning during the colonial period by forward-looking colonial policy makers intent on creating a cadre of westernized Africans on whom they could rely to continue, after the colonies became independent, the "civilizing" work the colonizers had begun.[17] The famous Macaulay Minute on Education of 1835 spelled out the colonialists' intention with regard to India (where the policy/strategy was designed to facilitate the cooption of Indians in consolidating colonial rule): "We must," it states, "do our best to form a class who may be interpreters between us and the millions we govern,—a class of persons Indian in blood and colour, but English in tastes, in opinions, in morals and in intellect."[18]

The thoroughness of the Western conditioning of African intellectuals found one of its most eloquent expressions in the determined assault that Western-trained African philosophers mounted against African traditional thought, habits, and institutions during the latter part of the last century. For example, the Ghanaian Kwesi Wiredu mocked the intellectual and ideational capabilities of "aged peasants or fetish priests or [traditional] court personalities," reserving the ability to engage in philosophical thought to "individual thinkers," preferably those able to communicate "in print";[19] the Kenyan Henry Odera for his part ridiculed Africans who expected "the white world" to accept as "African religion" what he described as "superstition," and "the white culture" to accept as "African philosophy" what he dismissed as "mythology";[20] and the Beninois Paulin Hountondji considered it "a mockery" to place "African systems of thought" alongside the "ambitious philosophies and . . . scholarly surveys of the history of philosophy" produced by Western thinkers like Spinoza, Hegel, and company.[21] And he aligned himself with his fellow philosopher Marcien Towa, whose wish for traditional African institutions was that the Christian missionaries' assault on them would be resumed and their eradication completed: Africans, he recommended, should engage in "'revolutionary iconoclasm,' a 'destruction of traditional idols' which will enable us to 'welcome and assimilate the spirit of Europe.'"[22] And the Nigerian Abiola Irele has argued, adopting a familiar concept, that for Africans the colonial experience "marked a sea-change . . . [that] effected a qualitative re-ordering of life [and] . . . rendered the traditional way of life no longer a viable option for our continued existence and apprehension of the world." He concludes, therefore, that "as a matter of practical necessity, we have no choice but in the direction of Western culture and civilization."[23]

Colonial officers writing on colonial education well after Macaulay and with regard to other colonial territories had vastly different opinions from Macaulay's about the most advisable form of education for colonial subjects. Lord Frederick D. Lugard, as though anticipating the dangers of creating a class of intellectuals out of sync with their peoples and cultures, argued that colonial education should enable the "exceptional individual" to "use his abilities for the advancement of the community and not to its detriment, or to the subversion of constituted authority," and that it should produce "a generation able to achieve ideals of its own, without a slavish imitation of Europeans." He went further to observe:

> The impact of European civilisation on tropical races has indeed a tendency to undermine that respect for authority which is the basis of social order. The authority of the head, whether of the tribe, the village, or the family, is decreased, and parental discipline is weakened . . . so that [quoting Lord Macdonnell] "the younger men view with increasing impatience the habits, traditions, and ideas of their elders."[24]

He believed that what he called the "purely literary type of education" that had been adopted for India had already proved disastrous in that colony by the end of the nineteenth century, when educated Indians were perceived to have lost all respect for authority. He cited complaints by others, including a British officer in Nigeria, a Nigerian who was acting as director of education, and a Sierra Leonean chief, to show that the same sort of education (as had discredited itself in India) was producing a "very unsatisfactory result" in West African colonies—products who were "unreliable, lacking in integrity, self-control, and discipline, and without respect for authority of any kind," whose vanity was intolerable, and who had been taught "to despise their elders." The educated people, Lugard concluded, "have lost touch . . . with their own people."[25]

As for the Francophone African elite, Eugène Schaeffer has documented their alienation from their roots and their attachment to French ways and institutions. The considerable influence of French culture on them, he observes, resulted from an education which "in the case of the first generation of independence, went right from primary school to university, and even to a seat in the National Assembly" (255). With specific reference to their behavior in designing legal education for their independent nations, Schaeffer observes:

> Any suggestion that the courses should be changed to adapt them to conditions in the developing countries has long been regarded by Africans as a form of discrimination, and as training for an intermediate rather than an advanced technology. Also, *the recipients of this training, who have been uprooted at an early age, have seldom got the African social background which would enable them to know about or be able to preserve an authentic African attitude to the customs and traditions of their country.* They cannot therefore study French law from the comparative angle.[26]

Among the factors he cites as likely to keep the countries concerned "within the French zone of influence" is "the defence by African legal experts of their modern knowledge against traditional law, which they consider retrograde." Tellingly, he notes that they do not know traditional law, anyway, because it has the disadvantage compared to French law of being unwritten, and therefore difficult to know, "whereas it is easy to get access to French doctrine and precedents." He adds that "the westernisation of the elites of these new states has been so complete that no African has even questioned the advisability of economic development on the model of the industrialised countries."[27]

We can blame the persistence and intensification of the alienation of African intellectuals, to some extent at least, on the inhospitable, anti-intellectual conditions that prevail in many African countries and that induce increasing numbers of disaffected members of the elite to migrate abroad, mostly to the West, and not simply for temporary residence. Not surprisingly, writers who began their careers lambasting the West for the havoc it wreaked on the African space and African institutions now find themselves dependent on the kindness and hospitality of the West: Chinua Achebe and Ngugi wa Thiong'o occupy distinguished chairs at American universities, as do Wole Soyinka (who has however never really been critical of the West), Syl Cheney-Cocker, Buchi Emecheta, and Ben Okri, while others like Ayi Kwei Armah and Kole Omotoso, although remaining in Africa, live in exile in countries other than their native lands.

One of the more glaring examples of the combination of exile location with sheer opportunism to render a presumptive voice of Africa suspect is Buchi Emecheta's propagation of damning representations of African (specifically Igbo) gender relations, representations that ingratiate her to her Western (feminist) fans. I will approach her via an observation her fellow Igbo writer Achebe makes in his foreword to Nade da Obradovi 's *The Anchor Book of Modern African Stories*. I refer to his sarcastic comment on F. J. Pedler's admonition in his 1951 book, *West Africa*, that "It is misleading . . . when

Europeans talk of Africans buying a wife." Pedler's book, Achebe writes, "was in some ways remarkably advanced for its time" because "he told his readers the startling news that African men did not buy their wives . . . and thus assailed a pet notion *which Europeans had invented* and cherished and recycled again and again in popular as well as serious literature."[28] Achebe implies that the exchange of gifts as part of the marriage transaction in African societies, usually from the groom and his family to the bride and hers, is often misunderstood and misrepresented even by some Africans. Contrary to what the English terms for the practice (bride price or bridewealth) would suggest, the real value of the gifts involved was generally inconsiderable, until, that is, the distortions of modern commoditization set in.[29] Achebe wrote the foreword in 1994, by which time he surely must have read Buchi Emecheta's repetition of this cherished notion in her novels. For example, in *Second Class Citizen* (published in 1974), she speculates about a wife being "bought" for Francis, and later in the same novel she says that Igbo wives are "bought, paid for[,] and must remain . . . obedient slaves."[30] In a later work, *The Joys of Motherhood* (1979), she repeats the notion, writing about Nnu Ego's first husband's need of money "to pay for" another wife. A little later in the same novel, Nnu Ego's second husband asks her rhetorically, "Did I not pay your bride price? Am I not your owner?"[31] Emecheta happens, of course, to be one of the most sought-after African writers and interpreters of Africa to the world, and it goes without saying, I aver, that representations like hers command more hearing in the Western world than those representing Africa in a more favorable light.

Emecheta is only one of a slew of African intellectuals who fit Edward Said's description of "professional" intellectuals, intellectuals, that is, who are dedicated to making themselves "marketable and above all presentable, hence uncontroversial and . . . 'objective.'"[32] Objectivity in this case meaning, of course, subscribing to (and seizing every opportunity to trumpet) the conventional wisdom about Africa, corroborating what the colonizers had said all along about Africans, and, lately, chastising Africans for blaming all their problems on colonialism and its long-term effects, on neo-colonialism and economic imperialism, instead of accepting the fact of their own incompetence and moral corruption. They share the traits of the Arab professional intellectuals Said describes as "Arab Second Thoughters," erstwhile critics of the United States and the West who after the U.S. established itself as the power to reckon with in the Middle East opportunistically switched from critics to anti-Arab U.S. worshipers. Arabs, the "Second Thoughters" say, "should try to be more like the West, should regard the West as a source and a reference point. Gone is the history of what the West actually did. Gone are the Gulf War's destructive results. We Arabs and Muslims are the sick ones, our problems are our own, totally self-inflicted."[33]

To reiterate, given the likely sites of cultural interactions, the agents of the purported African contribution are most likely to be the highly educated, highly Westernized, and highly mobile African intellectuals. That being the case, if these spokespersons have become for all practical purposes mimic Europeans (or Westerners), the question inevitably arises, how *African* would (or could) their input into the dialogue of cultures be? Would what passes for dialogue between Africa and the West (for instance) not amount to a Western exchange with its mirror reflection, or to Western utterance answered by its echo representing itself as interlocution?

A "YORUBA ANCESTOR" ABROAD

At this point I wish to turn my attention, by way of clarification (or illustration), to a recent effort to effect a dialogue between Africa and Europe, which in my view failed to achieve its end precisely because of the mistaken choice of an African voice. I refer to late Nigerian (Yoruba) writer Amos Tutuola's 1990 visit to Italy. I have discussed the ironies of Tutuola's career at length in *Amos Tutuola Revisited* (1999). The major one, I believe, is reflected in the fact that although he had not experienced the thoroughgoing Westernization through education that had been the fate (or misfortune) of such compatriots of his as Achebe or Soyinka, and, although his fluency in Yoruba had therefore not been impaired while his ability to express himself in English was severely limited, he nevertheless opted to adopt English for his writing. His career brings to mind the character Apo, the legendary ancestor of the flamboyant Ras Jomo Quince Equiano in Ayi Kwei Armah's *Osiris Rising*. At the height of the transatlantic slave trade, Armah's Apo found it expedient to insist that the European slavers who rescued him from the sea take him aboard their slaving vessel instead of returning him to his native shore as they wished to. The bemused slavers found his behavior utterly incomprehensible: they did not want him but he insisted on being added to their human cargo![34]

Toward the end of his Italian visit, Tutuola was interviewed by Claudio Gorlier, a scholar from the University of Turin. The interview offers some insight on the difficult dialogue between Africa and the West, and for that reason I quote somewhat extensively from the transcript. Asked about his becoming a storyteller Tutuola explained: "at the age of thirty or so, I noticed that our young men had no interest in our culture or customs. Then I wrote all the folktales and the other riddles and so on which I had collected, in order to revive, or to wake up, or to change the minds of these young people who had left our traditional things. To bring their mind back to their things, I wrote some of the folktales, riddles, and so on."[35] The Italian scholar, presumably sensing some discrepancy in relating intention to practice, turned to the question of language and tradition:

GORLIER: Why did you decide to write your first book in English and not in Yoruba? Your tales were in Yoruba, not in English. So how did you arrive at this decision?

TUTUOLA: Well, that was how it came to my mind at that time. At that time, we were under the British. So many people did not read Yoruba books so much. We'd take English to read something important—or what people who could speak English thought very important. That influenced me to write my first book in English.

GORLIER: What does the word "tradition" mean to you? How have you been faithful to your tradition?

TUTUOLA: When I wrote *The Palm-Wine Drinkard*, this was the main improvement which the book gave to our tradition. I mean, my writing also improved our tradition and customs much. Because so many in my town, so many Yoruba people—like Wole Soyinka, Kole Omotoso, and many others—so many writers like them began to write stories about our tradition, customs, and so on. So, by the time, our tradition continued to exist and maybe to improve. (160)

Because Tutuola repeatedly used the word "civilization" to characterize the effect of colonization on himself and his people, and because he described the European concept of time as "superior" to the African, Gorlier asked him what he meant by "civilization." He answered, "The civilization which Europeans brought to us helped Africa much—not only Nigerian people, the whole African country. It helped us a lot" (162). He had said earlier that one aspect of the "civilization" the colonizers brought was the inculcation of the habit of diluting palm-wine with water, making it less "genuine." Gorlier wanted him to clarify the statement, and Tutuola obliged by saying, "Now, as I talked about the palm-wine, which is diluted with water and so on, not genuine as before, that does not affect us much. Even, many people do not drink palm-wine anymore in Nigeria or in Africa, except from beer, wine, and so on. They never taste palm-wine" (162).

My purpose in letting Tutuola's own voice come through is not to point out the weaknesses in his English, but rather to emphasize the substance of what he had to say: his unsatisfactory response to the question how his abandoning Yoruba for English reflected his faithfulness to his tradition; his superior valuation of European concepts vis-à-vis African ones; and his unequivocal positive assessment overall of the impact of colonization on the continent and its people.

GRAMSCI AND INTELLECTUALS: THE APOSTATIC AND THE FAITHFUL

The scholarly attempt to engage with African tradition through Tutuola failed for the same reasons that the sort of African representation Masilela (for example) would have liked to see in Gilroy's book would not in fact have been a real representation of Africa: one cannot engage with "Africa itself" by dealing with agents who are only nominally African but have in fact gone over to the Western side in those regards that really make a difference, Africans, that is, who fit Macaulay's prescriptions to a tee or aspire to that end. Nor can Africa derive any benefit from extra-African contacts through the agency of such Africans, who have no real connection or commitment to "Africa itself." Here, I believe that the considerations that matter are precisely those that many of our apologists for Westernization would avoid: culture, group identities and their obligations, or the "constraints of ethnicity."

One of the attractions of Westernity for many African intellectuals is, I have pointed out, its synonymousness (in their minds) with empowerment and "development." Africanity, being for them the obverse of Westernity, is thus also antithetical to power and progress. There is historical evidence, however, to explode the assumption that adherence to traditional habits or ethos is necessarily inimical to development or even to technological modernization. Antonio Gramsci has pointed out that the Russian elites were successful in transforming their nation for the better by appropriating progressive influences from abroad *without abandoning their Russian character*. According to him,

> an *élite* consisting of some of the most active, energetic, enterprising and disciplined members of the society emigrates abroad and assimilates the culture and historical experiences of the most advanced countries of the West, *without however losing the most essential characteristics of its own nationality, that is to say without breaking its sentimental and historical links with its own people*. Having thus performed its intellectual apprenticeship, it returns to its own country and compels the people to an enforced awakening, skipping historical stages in the process.[36]

The Russian intellectuals imbibed the West's technical culture and an understanding of the social change it entailed, but without being de-Russified. Gramsci states that the contrast between this elite and "that imported from Germany (by Peter the Great, for example) lies in its essentially national-popular character." They could moreover not be assimilated by the "inert passivity of the Russian people, because they were themselves "an energetic reaction of Russia to her own historical inertia."[37] The achievement of the Russian elite, as Gramsci describes it, translates to "healthy glocalization," which Thomas L. Friedman defines as "the ability of a culture, when it encounters other strong cultures, to absorb influences that naturally fit into and can enrich that culture, to resist those things that are truly alien and to compartmentalize those things that, while different, can nevertheless be enjoyed and celebrated as different."[38] It is possible, then, for the intellectuals among a people to absorb technical expertise from other cultures, along with the allied knowledges necessary to put it to work, and to absorb compatible influences, without losing the "most essential historical links to [their] people" or their essential national-popular character, regardless of whatever form of lassitude might afflict the people in general. The failure of the African intellectual class, or at least of far too many in it—the most mobile, most vocal, and most celebrated—is its internalization of the notion that difference (from the West) amounts to backwardness, non-development, or some sort of pathology.

GLOBALISM AND THE NATION

Before I conclude I want to return to Gilroy's minimization of the importance of national borders, his chiding reminder that "neither political nor economic structures of domination are still simply co-extensive with national borders." Ergo, it seems, we should acknowledge the new porousness of borders and act in conformity to it. But that view is insufficiently circumspect, despite the insight his phrasing—"economic structures of domination"—suggests, inasmuch as it seems to recommend embracing the status quo. We cannot simply accept the reality of globalization (which is what I believe he has in mind) as a fact of life and live with it despite its huge problems. Precisely because it is, in William Greider's words, "an economic system of interdependence designed to ignore the prerogatives of nations, even the most powerful ones,"[39] it deserves to be subjected to continuous and thorough debate in all its aspects, especially from the point of view of the less powerful nations, with a view to eliminating as much as possible its inequities. Beset already by the difficulties of restoring some modicum of coherence to African social organizations after the rampages of colonialism, the continent can ill afford to unquestioningly acquiesce in a global economy that "divides every society into new camps of conflicting economic interests . . . undermines every nation's ability to maintain social cohesion . . . [and] mocks the assumption of shared political values that supposedly unite people in the nation-state."[40]

The crux of my argument is that while there are certain benefits to the world becoming a village, there are also drawbacks, like the weakening of local capacities for self-preservation, and the freedom of particular groups to pursue particular interests and to adopt particular approaches to achieving particular aims. The arguments marshaled against ethnicity often rely on occasions on which its influences have caused great havoc, like the atrocities that made Richburg thank God that his ancestors were captured and sold into slavery. But it is possible to compare those instances of its abuse to cancerous growths, when normally beneficial cells, on being exposed to certain deleterious elements or situations, begin to behave abnormally and then go out of control. Just as the lung is not in itself a bad organ because it is susceptible to cancer, so also ethnicity is not in itself a bad thing simply because it is prone to manipulation and abuse.

Much of the pervasive antisocial behavior in modern African states, which is at the root of what appears to many as an African malignancy, can in fact be explained as resulting from the destruction of clan and cultural institutions, the most influential of which were designed to enforce behavior conducive to group harmony and collective welfare. The Nigerian academic ashimuneze k. heanacho provides an educative illustration of what happens when such institutions are rendered irrelevant. He spent his early years, he testifies, among his Igbo people who had been transplanted to Lagos, then Nigeria's capital city situated in the Yoruba part of the country. There they maintained their ethnic associations and kept their traditions alive by meeting regularly. He recalls that the elders who at the meetings poured the libations to the ancestors accompanied them with an invocation that included the words: "guide us, as we seek and attain possession of our share of wealth from the public space and *orun beke* (white man's employment); may the 'white' man be blind to and inept at interdicting our scheming; may we be successful at bringing the loot home; may our home become prosperous therefrom; and may our ancestors be honored by our triumph." The invocation, he explains, indicates "an assumption, which may be powerful in African consciousness, that employment outside the homeland, is forced, unrequited, and exploitive labor; that it favors the employer, so much more than the laborer, that employee counteraction, such as pilfering, is justified chivalry; a bold, risk-taking, to sabotage an enemy's machinery of exploitation!" (USA/Africa Dialogue, No. 958: "Kenyan Minister and the Morality of Corruption"). Unfortunately, that attitude has been transferred to the successors of the white colonizers and their employment—the national governments and their assets. The commitment to the ethnic group trumps fidelity to the Nigerian nation and its institutions; the nation's coffers can therefore be looted for the greater good of the ethnos.

But commitment to the ethnic group was a positive force before colonial distortions. Active group identity, whether ethnic or otherwise, proved its value in Africa's past and continues to do so in its present. Kwame Anthony Appiah witnesses to the intervention of a "proliferation of non-state organizations" in Ghana, among them the traditional, the modern, the religious, and the professional, during a period of state withdrawal, when the government failed to provide the necessary services for its citizens. He observes:

> it has always been true that in large parts of Africa, "tribalism"— what, in Ivory Coast, is half humorously called geopolitics, the politics of geographical regions, the mobilization and management of ethnic balancing—far from being an obstacle to governance, is what makes possible any government at all. And we can see this new role as facilitator—acknowledging the associations of society rather than trying to dominate to ignore or to eradicate them—as an extension of this established pattern.[41]

Tribalism, in other words, is not necessarily a force for evil, an inciter of people to murder and mayhem, although it could be and has been manipulated to such ends. "Clearly," Appiah, continues, "if the state is ever to reverse recent history and expand the role it plays in the lives of its subjects, it will have to learn something about the surprising persistence of these 'premodern' affiliations, the cultural and political fretwork of relations through which our very identity is conferred."[42]

TOWARD AN INCLUSIVE CIRCUMATLANTIC INTERACTION

The desire to do away with (or at least deemphasize) concepts that facilitate inter-group antagonisms and exclusionary impulses—color, culture, ethnicity, race—might make good sense for people who have had to endure, as members of some "outgroup," the prejudices of the "ingroup" people they had to interact with. It does not for Africans who have experienced the security of membership in a traditional community. For African participation in the circumatlantic discourse to be inclusive of (and beneficial for) all concerned, therefore, those who carry Africa's brief must effectively advocate what has proved itself of value in Africa, and what the continent has to offer, instead of demonstrating how much like the West Africa can be. At the very least, they should actively disabuse the Western world of its misconceptions regarding practices and institutions that have played and do play salutary roles in society, instead of joining detractors in tarring things African with the brush of "nativism," "primitivism," "traditionalism," and so forth.

To reiterate, in conclusion, instead of contributing to the choruses that undermine African institutions and practices that work, African intellectuals' participation in the dialogue with the West should rather point out their beneficial potentials and thus help non-Africans achieve a better understanding of the African world. That way the Black Atlantic will not be blackened simply because it leeches the blackness off every bit of Africa that traverses it.

NOTES

1. Gilroy, *The Black Atlantic*, 1. Further references are included in the text.
2. I have discussed Appiah's views on this question in my *The African Difference*, 171–173.
3. Richburg, *Out of America*, xv.
4. Richburg, *Out of America*, xvi, xviii.
5. Wheatley, "On Being Brought," 219.
6. Walker, "In Search," 24–32.
7. Hurston, "How It Feels," 1031; emphasis added.
8. Gikandi, "Introduction," 2, 5.
9. Masilela, "The 'Black Atlantic,'" 88. Further references are included in the text.
10. Crummell quoted in Hickey and Wylie, *An Enchanting Darkness*, 243.

11. Hickey and Wylie, *An Enchanting Darkness*, 244.
12. Chesnutt, "The Wife," 624.
13. Chesnutt, "The Wife," 626. Arthur Davis and Saunders Redding describe the so-called Talented Tenth as "raceless," adding that the coinage of the notion and the expectation of the designee's social role vis-à-vis the Negroes exposed its author W.E.B. Du Bois to accusations that he was class-conscious and concerned only with the "dicky" middle class of Negroes. They add that "by 1910 the idea of a 'talented tenth' no longer seemed defensible or viable even to some members of the talented tenth" (Gates and McKay, *Norton Anthology*, 231). Du Bois himself, it is fair to point out, described the talented tenth as having "no traditions to fall back on, no long established customs, no strong family ties, no well defined social classes," all things which, he added, "must be slowly and painfully evolved" (Gates and McKay, *Norton Anthology*, 54).
14. Hountondji, *African Philosophy*, 172; emphasis added.
15. Griswold, *Bearing Witness*, 45.
16. Gates, "On the Rhetoric of Racism," 17.
17. See Lloyd, *The New Elites of Tropical Africa*; and Morris-Jones and Fischer, *Decolonisation and After*, in particular Section 1, "The Transfer of Power."
18. Macaulay in Curtin, *Imperialism*, 190.
19. Wiredu, "How Not to Compare African Thought with Western Thought," 157.
20. Odera in Hountondji, *African Philosophy*, 60.
21. Hountondji, *African Philosophy*, 74.
22. Hountondji, *African Philosophy*, 172.
23. Irele, "In Praise of Alienation," 207, 215. I have discussed this issue at some length in my book, *The African Difference*, 17–41.
24. Lugard in Curtin, *Imperialism*, 234, 235.
25. Lugard in Curtin, *Imperialism*, 235–237.
26. Schaeffer, "Private Law," 255–256; emphasis added.
27. Schaeffer, "Private Law," 256–257.
28. Achebe, Foreword to *The Anchor Book of Modern African Stories*, xiii; emphasis added.
29. On this issue see S. J. Tambiah, "*Bridewealth* and *Dowry* Revisited"; and Owomoyela, *The African Difference*, 140, 148–151.
30. Emecheta, *Second Class Citizen*, 112, 156.
31. Emecheta, *Joys of Motherhood*, 48.
32. Said, *Representations of the Intellectual*, 74.
33. Said, *Representations of the Intellectual*, 116, 119.
34. Armah, *Osiris Rising*, 123, 174–178, 266–269.
35. The Tutuola interview appears in Di Maio, *Tutuola at the University*. Further references are included in the text.
36. Gramsci, "The Intellectuals," 19–20; emphasis added.
37. Gramsci, "The Intellectuals," 20.
38. Friedman, *The Lexus and the Olive Tree*, 295.
39. Greider, *One World*, 17.
40. Greider, *One World*, 18.
41. Appiah, *In My Father's House*, 170.
42. Appiah, *In My Father's House*, 171.

Part III
Black Bodies, Global Voices

16 I Sing the Black Body Electric
Transnationalism and the Black Body in Walt Whitman, Alain Locke, and Paul Robeson

Jeffrey C. Stewart

With the popularity of Atlantic narratives of black modernity launched in the wake of Paul Gilroy's 1993 publication, *The Black Atlantic*, a tendency emerged to see the American racial situation as essentially an extension of Great Britain's.[1] This is unfortunate. Every transatlantic black identity is both a circumlocution of the Atlantic and a burrowing into the particularities of a place where Africans settled and which they were forced to call home. Unlike Britain, the United States of America owes its very existence to the labor of black bodies, since, as Edmund Morgan noted in *American Slavery, American Freedom*, the American Revolution could not have succeeded without the goods traded to France during the war, goods produced by black bodies. African American slavery gave white American subjectivity its freedom and its identity.[2] From the seventeenth to the twentieth centuries, America wrestled psychologically and politically with the consequences of this fact, specifically the existence of a large internal black population amid a white majority; and this struggle over the meaning of the American subject occurred long before the West Indian immigrations of the twentieth century caused dramatic changes in British identity.

The British Empire's "abroad" problem of race was lived as a "domestic" race problem in the bosom of America, precisely at that historical moment when America emerged as the most attractive example of capitalism and representative democracy in the West. The United States' success at reaching the highest stage of agricultural capitalism, its relentless advertisement of its democratic exceptionalism, and its continued bondage to millions of black bodies spawned a schizophrenic American discourse that denigrated black bodies, but also desired and adored them. Indeed, a powerful counternarrative of adulation of the black body emerged in American culture that was co-produced by culturally rebellious white artists and progressive-minded black artists and intellectuals, who dug themselves out of the avalanche of racist black body discourses in the United States to fuse an "electric" counternarrative of the black body as heroic and beautiful.[3] This counternarrative emerged out of contradictory and contested discourses of the body, racial nationalism, American democracy, aestheticism, homoeroticism, and socialism to enable a selected group of modernist African American intellectuals to begin to see the black body as a symbol of liberation, not only for African peoples, but also for all mankind.[4]

Our story begins with Alain Locke, the African American philosopher, Rhodes Scholar, and editor of *The New Negro: An Interpretation*. In 1927 Alain Locke wrote a review of the scandalous Harlem Renaissance magazine, *FIRE!!*, edited by the gay black writer Wallace Thurman. The magazine, which only managed to get out one beautiful, pricey issue, declared sexual and intellectual freedom as the goal of the Young Rebels of the Negro Renaissance. Locke applauded the magazine's explicit rejection of black bourgeois control of Negro creative freedom, the editorial control exercised by the National Association for the Advancement of Colored People's *Crisis*, which had published much of the early writing of the movement. But Locke also chastised the young black artists for their "too hectic imitation of Oscar Wilde and Aubrey Beardsley."[5] Wilde and Beardsley were, as historian Richard Powell has pointed out, transatlantic inspirations for some artists of the Harlem Renaissance. But Locke rejected these British decadents as a fitting inspiration for the movement. He rejected what he saw as the overly feminine image of the black male body communicated by some of the magazine's artists, such as Bruce Nugent, whose drawings and short story were frank homosexual imaginatives. While Locke could understand how such frankness might be liberating for some who wished to create images more consistent with their homosexual desire, he believed that such imagery played into stereotypes already rampant in American culture, perhaps best expressed by the sociologist Robert Park, who called the Negro the "female of the races." Better to follow in the footsteps of Walt Whitman, Locke suggested, thereby recommending, in effect, a more masculine image of the black male body revealed in Whitman's poetry.[6]

Why did Locke say this? Because he was aware that a feminized British gay representation of the black body would not work in the United States, as it would not counter or even contest the dominant racist representation of the Negro in American culture. Robert Park's description of the Negro as "the female of the races," while meant as a sign of the inner character of Negro people, was more accurate as an analysis of the presence of the Negro in America, a presence circumscribed by how the black body had been *seen* and used by whites in American culture. Art historian John Berger explains the dynamic of such presence in his discussion of the similar if still different way in which that dynamic structures the representation of women in Western culture:

> According to usage and conventions which are at last being questioned but have by no means been overcome, the social presence of a woman is different in kind from that of a man. A man's presence is dependent upon the promise of power which he embodies . . . a power which he exercises on others. By contrast a woman's presence expresses her own attitude to herself. . . . To be born a woman has been to be born, within an allotted

and confined space, into the keeping of men. The social presence of women has developed as a result of their ingenuity in living under such tutelage . . . but this has been at the cost of a woman's self being split into two. A woman must continually watch herself. She is almost continually accompanied by her own image of herself. From earliest childhood she has been taught and persuaded to survey herself continually. And so she comes to consider the *surveyor* and the *surveyed* within her as the two constituent yet always distinct elements of her identity as a woman.[7]

This dynamic, while doubly poignant for black women, who struggle against such surveillance of both black and female bodies, is particularly interesting to me when applied to the black male body. For in American discourse the black body, especially when it is male, is always seen as something which never exercises power over others, which is never, in a word, heroic.

This leads us to Whitman. Now, Whitman has never struck me as a philosopher of black liberation, so initially I chalked up Locke's reference to him as merely a move to pivot the young artists of the Harlem Renaissance away from flamboyant homosexual display. But as I reread Whitman's *Leaves of Grass*, the 1855 edition, I came across the poem he later titled "I Sing the Body Electric," which crafts a democratic politics out of a homoerotic embrace of the body, and includes a heroic representation of the body of the African American slave. First, of course, Whitman is committed to establishing in that poem what J. M. Coetzee argues is Whitman's notion of democracy, "a civic religion energized by a broadly erotic feeling that men have for women, and women for men, and women for women, but above all that men have for other men."[8]

> The bodies of men and women engirth me, and I engirth them,
> They will not let me off nor I them till I go with them and respond to them and love them.[9]

But then Whitman startles with an embrace of the slave based on the equality of all American bodies:

> The man's body is sacred and the woman's body is sacred . . . it is no matter who,
> Is it a slave? Is it one of the dullfaced immigrants just landed on the wharf?
> Each belongs here or anywhere just as much as the well off . . . just as much as you.[10]

I say "startles" because the central discourse of antebellum America on the black body had been established by another Democrat, Thomas Jefferson (Whitman was a Democrat, not an Abolitionist or even a Republican), who argued in *Notes on the State of Virginia* that blacks should not be incorporated into the American body politic because of their black bodies:

> It will probably be asked, Why not retain and incorporate the blacks into the state, and thus save the expense of supplying, by importation of White settlers, the vacancies they will leave? [instead of expatriating freed people outside the United States, as Jefferson proposed] Deep rooted prejudices entertained by the whites . . . the real distinctions which nature has made . . . will produce convulsions. . . . To these objections, which are political, may be added others, which are physical and moral. The first difference which strikes us is that of colour . . . the difference is fixed in nature. . . . And is this difference of no importance? Is it not the foundation of a greater or less share of beauty in the two races? Are not the fine mixtures of red and white . . . preferable to that eternal monotony, which reigns in the countenances, that immoveable veil of black which covers all the emotions of the other race? Add to these, flowing hair, a more elegant symmetry of form, their own judgment in favour of the whites, declared by their preference of them, as uniformly as is the preference of the Oranootan for the black women over those of his own species.[11]

It was clear to Jefferson that blacks were inferior because of the "difference" of black bodies. Jefferson had added to the American colonial discourse of the black body—that it smelled, that it was stupid—one more facet, that it was undesired, because it was not beautiful. But Whitman, writing almost sixty years later, reverses that judgment, and, continuing in "I Sing the Body Electric," almost as an answer to Jefferson's prior description, portrays the black body as not only beautiful but noble:

> Do you know so much that you call the slave or the dullfaced
>   ignorant?
> Do you suppose you have a right to a good sight . . . and he or she
>   has no right to a sight?[12]

And even more dramatically:

> A slave at auction!
> I help the auctioneer . . . the sloven does not half know his business.
>
> Gentleman look at this curious creature,
> Whatever the bids of the bidder *they cannot be high enough for*
>   *him*,
> For him the globe lay preparing quintillions of years without one
>   animal or plant,
>
> In that head the all baffling brain,
> *In it and below it the making of the attributes of heroes.*[13]

This last line is crucial for our purposes here, because, as we noted earlier, Jefferson's descriptions of the black body as hopelessly different and inferior occurs in his discussion of politics in *Notes*, as his answer to the question: why can't the Negro be admitted to the political body of America as an equal participant? And it bears remembering that Whitman is reconstructing the presence of the heroic black body as part of a radical democratic political vision, in which the lowliest of Americans—the Negro—symbolizes what is heroic about American democracy. For Whitman, the people, the common people, are the heroes of this land. For Whitman, the bodies are the anchors of the spiritual equality promised by democracy, "whose history, I suppose, remains unwritten, because that history has yet to be enacted"—a yet to be realized triumph of the "human spirit, rooted in eros," as Coetzee puts it.[14] Here is the last, crucial element in seeing the black body as heroic: Whitman sees it as desirable, as *desired*, in marked contrast to Jefferson, who characterizes desire as always tending toward the white body, even among blacks. But through eros, Whitman, obviously much more public with his desire than the Sally Hemings–obsessed Jefferson, is able to reconstruct the American people as a body that includes the black spirit. Whitman is able to accomplish in *Leaves of Grass* in 1855 what Michael Hardt, the radical literary historian, recently called for: to fuse eros and agape into a language that creates a new politics, that looks forward to one day when all of the dispossessed will become a politically and poetically self-conscious collective movement, a multitude that includes the dispossessed.[15]

Even more telling for Locke, however, is Whitman's depiction of the black body as *heroic* and *masculine*. Whitman links the black body to a noble character that is almost always characterized as male in Western culture, as Berger points out. Therefore, in choosing Whitman to reconstruct the image of the Negro as a black male body, with the "presence" accorded to it within Western culture, Locke is not so much overthrowing the regime of sexism in Western culture as seeking to reclaim its patriarchal presence for the black males. Locke's maneuver reflects his awareness of the particular problematic of exerting power as a black male in American society. A narrative emerged in America to circulate throughout the Atlantic world that black male bodies were fundamentally threatening, backward, and worthy of dismemberment. Perhaps the pressure felt by whites of living in closest proximity with large numbers of blacks for four centuries created a barely suppressed panic among the white elite and masses. Perhaps the Christian fundamentalism of what became the United States of America, rooted in a Protestantism committed to recognizing sin and punishing the sinner, provided early British colonists with a need to find a victim, a black Adam, as a scapegoat for their own sense of evil.

Theorists have quite rightly focused attention on the treatment of the black female body and especially the perverted gaze and dismemberment visited on such victims as Saartjie Baartman, the so-called Hottentot Venus. But we should not forget that for much of the nineteenth and twentieth centuries, black male bodies elicited the greatest amount of viciousness from whites, as witness the lynching parties of the Jim Crow South, where the violence toward and spectacle made of black male bodies played an important, perhaps pivotal, role in constructing late nineteenth-century notions of whiteness. And yet, while white fear is often mentioned to explain lynchings, burnings, and castrations of black men, these spectacles also exhibit black bodies as sites of sexual and social desire.[16] The black male body often symbolized the attractions of whites for alterity. And sometimes, if rarely, eros for the black body opened a space where, for the first time, some whites transcended the racial consciousness blocking the development of a truly transracial multitude in America. Whitman's willingness to embrace the black body as heroic proved that the meaning of the black body was not fixed, immutable, or unchanging, but alterable in the face of the democratic romanticism of the enlightened artist. By recommending Whitman to young black artists, Locke is saying that this is where a powerful revision of the black body can *begin*.

It is good to stop here and assess what Whitman and Locke had achieved and what lay ahead. Just as *Leaves of Grass* gave an identity to the body called American, so too *The New Negro* gave an identity to the body called Negro. What made these books pivotal—one a collection of poems by one author, the other a collection of poems, essays, fiction, and drawings by several authors—is that they were internally generated self-representations that said, "I love myself," as in "Song of Myself," the title Whitman later gave to the first and most powerful poem in the 1855 edition of *Leaves*. Recall John Berger's analysis of the debilitating attitude the woman in Western society is encouraged to take toward her own body. She must always adopt toward it the attitude of a man, surveying it, and judging it, through the eyes of the male beholder. America had adopted a similar attitude, had viewed itself through the eyes of the European, had looked at the cultural body of America through the judging eyes of European aesthetics. Even Emerson had been a victim of this surveying America with the gaze of a European Romantic. Whitman saw the Romantic in the American. Whitman's "Preface" declares: "The Americans of all nations at any time upon the earth have probably the fullest poetical nature."[17] Locke announced something similar in *The New Negro*, a re/vision to overcome what W.E.B. Du Bois described as the usual attitude of the Negro towards him/herself, that of a "double consciousness," which, understood now in its true meaning in *The Souls of Black Folk*, was "this peculiar sensation" of "looking at one's self through the eyes of others"—the eyes of the white man.[18] As Berger puts it: "A split is created in the woman [read American, read Negro] who must take the attitude of seeing herself as two—the beholder and the beholden." Locke offered *The New Negro* as a transcendence of that dualism, the crafting of a self-image by the Negro out of the "poetical nature" of the race. While *Leaves of Grass* changed the valuation of the black body and allowed it to be beholden, and internalized, as beautiful and noble, *The New Negro* generated a self-image from within that was self-conscious, and self-loving, no longer simply an object of another's—however loving in

Whitman—gaze, but a body aware of its Romanticism, a poem called the New Negro.

Yet failure lurked inside the whole enterprise. Even the supremely confident author of *The New Negro* suffered from an intense dislike of his own body. Victimized as a child by a grandmother who counseled him to "stay out of the sun, you're black enough already,"[19] Alain Locke struggled throughout his life with the sense of hurt, the sense of difference, and the sense of ugliness that that experience—and others—bequeathed to him. That sensitivity gave him a peculiar awareness of the ways that, even with the ecstatic triumph of *The New Negro*, the counternarrative of black self-love was not enough to overcome all of the damage done by the internalization of the white beholder in the Negro self-consciousness. Locke acknowledged as much when he answered criticism of his choice of a German artist, Winold Reiss, to create the most powerful images of the New Negro in the anthology—the pastel portraits of individual black people reproduced in color in the first edition of the book. Even among educated Negro artists, Locke confided in "To Certain of Our Philistines," most suffered from an alienation from his/her own body, such that there were no black American artists sufficiently accomplished in Negro portraiture to illustrate the book with powerful renderings of the Negro.[20] The Negro artist still surveyed him or herself with the eye of the beholder, having internalized through upbringing a discouraging Jeffersonian image of the Negro body. And that self-image was weak, disfigured, ugly, and unheroic.

Of course, as a caveat, we must acknowledge that there were some artists, such as Meta Warrick Fuller, who had broken out of this trap. But she was a sculptor, and the best African American painter, Henry O. Tanner, was unavailable in 1925, having expatriated to France and refused, according to what Locke later affirmed, to take up leading a New Negro movement in Negro portraiture. Locke had turned to a German—not a Brit—to create what he needed, a romantic image of the Negro that would visually convey something even more modern than Whitman's Negro bodies—a group of self-conscious, alive, dignified, and beautiful African American subjects embarking on the most dangerous of careers—a career of self-fashioning a healthy, productive, self-affirming life in a racist, debilitating America. A latter-day Whitman, Locke's vision of the New Negro was as silent about the pain and protest of black life as *Leaves of Grass* was silent about the suffering and labor protest of industrializing America. But while "negative" characterizations of the Negro self-image were rigorously excluded from the writings in *The New Negro*, Reiss's poignant portraits hinted at the pathos of the Negro's journey towards freedom.

Whitman helped to further the process of self-healing Locke envisioned, but only as a beginning. His romanticism delivered a beautiful portrait of the black body, but it remained a nineteenth-century body, contained by its labor under slavery. That may be part of the charm the black body held for Whitman: the fact that these glistening, sweating bodies laboring on the docks in New Orleans or New York were bound objects of desire to his homoerotic gaze. But when such Negroes began to get outside of their "allotted and confined space," out of the "keeping of whites," as Berger might put it, after the Civil War, they lost their charm for Whitman, who, according to Coetzee, referred to political rule by Negroes under Reconstruction as an "abomination." That Locke looked back to Whitman as a model for black artists suggests how romantic Locke's vision was, but also how compelling the body of the heroic slave was for 1920s black intellectuals. Paul Robeson, for example, made a very successful concert career out of singing the spirituals, and achieved his greatest commercial success as an actor performing the role of Jim, a Sambo-like character, in the stage and film versions of *Show Boat*. Yet Locke and Robeson did not want to stop there. They wanted the black common man to come alive, to become not just an American artifact, but also a cultural subject, a new Whitman, who could "sing the [black] body electric," and transform the black body as artifact into an aesthetics. It was one thing to see American civilization as composed of the black, but another to see America itself as a black civilization. To do the latter required black intellectuals to become transnational in ways that Whitman never imagined.

Locke, therefore, could begin his transnationalist vision of the New Negro by paraphrasing Whitman—that the Negroes "of all nations at any time upon the earth have probably the fullest poetical nature"—but could not end there. Whitman celebrated America uncritically in *Leaves of Grass* and was rewarded for it. He need not leave America, because American self-love is confirmed and reified by Americans. That is why the American poet most loved by Europeans is also the one who is most prized by American Studies programs. But similar self-love was problematical for black Americans in America, because there could be only one dominant male image in America—the white man. That's why Whitman's image of the black body was always aesthetic—encoded with an objectification that made it appear beautiful but unable to exert power as a political male. Locke had to go beyond Whitman because Locke's aspirations were always larger than that—to create a Negro body as subject with political as well as cultural efficacy. If the black body remained primarily an object of aesthetic admiration, as it was in Whitman, then the black body would be contained and denied the role Locke envisioned for himself and the black body in American culture—to be its leader.

To celebrate the Negro as America's leader, therefore, required the African American intellectual to step outside prevailing, even liberal, opinion in Whitman's America—or Locke's 1920s America. It forced the African American intellectual to be transnational and to conceive of the Negro as something more than a minority within the American contours of nationality. For only in the diaspora could the black body emerge as the *vanguard* of a majority, since in America the prevailing self-conception was that the white body was not oppressed. Locke went outside of America to find recognition for the fecundity of black culture, as when he journeyed to Haiti in 1943 and delivered lectures on the powerful presence of African cultural forms in the "Three Americas." But for Locke the key transnational importance of the black body was that wherever the slave trade had deposited the black body, it opened up a *political* space that tested whether democracy—Whitman's metaphor for America—was a reality in these New World societies.

> In every one of the countries where he constitutes a considerable pro-
> portion of the population, the Negro represents a conspicuous index by
> which the practical efficiency and integrity of that particular country's
> democracy can readily be gauged and judged. For the same high visibility
> [of the black body] which internally makes possible ready discrimination
> against Negroes makes the domestic practices of race externally all the
> more conspicuous and observable in the enlarging spotlight of interna-
> tional relations. Here the American treatment of the Negro can have and
> already has had serious repercussion on enlightened Asiatic and African
> public opinion and confidence. Or, for that matter, so will our treatment
> of any racial minority such as the treatment of the American segments of
> the Hindu or the Chinese resident among us.[21]

While the Negro culturally led outward to Africa, the West Indies, and Latin America as complementary locations of the "Aframerican" (Locke's term), the black body's political "visibility" made it a sign not only for how black bodies were treated, but also for how the multitude—who were not buttressed against recognition of their oppression by whiteness—were treated and repre-sented in so-called democratic societies.

Of course, the Negro could never be simply a national success, trying to acquire what white Americans wanted so desperately to keep Negroes from obtaining—simple, mindless membership in the *corpus Americanus*. The New Negro promised something different for America—a life in which a revolution in ways of seeing the black body would usher in a transformation in how Americans saw themselves and their lives in a global perspective. For the heroic black body was always a critique of hegemonic Americanism— that swagger white Americans exuded as they strode the world and claimed, implicitly if not explicitly, that their freedom and nation was created inde-pendently *by them*. But there was also something fundamentally American about the New Negro—for the process of making the Negro in America had melded a unique black consciousness out of the tempering of modern American capitalism with the formation of modern racism and modern democracy. Something in the scarification of the black American body after centuries of whippings, torture, disfranchisement, and segregation gave it a countervision on the whole American enterprise, a vision that informed African American views of how freedom looked from the bottom up. And something of the ability to wring a love for oneself and for humanity out of the pain of seeing humanity at its worst colored the unique modern-ism that emerged in the culture of twentieth-century American Negroes—a grace under pressure that captivated the rest of the world. For it was in the daily life of places like Harlem that Locke found the vibrancy that Whitman defined as quintessentially American—"Their manners speech dress friend-ships—the freshness and candor of their physiognomy—the picturesque looseness of their carriage . . . their deathless attachment to freedom—their aversion to anything indecorous or soft or mean . . . the fierceness of their roused resentment—their curiosity and welcome of novelty—their self-esteem and wonderful sympathy—their susceptibility to a slight"[22]—these were, in fact, the quintessential qualities of the New Negro of the 1920s in places like Harlem, Chicago, Los Angeles, St. Louis, but also spreading out and infecting other black nurseries of self-conscious bodies in Paris, London, Haiti, and Cairo.

Locke knew, as Gayatri Spivak put it in *A Critique of Postcolonial Reason*, that the "body can never be its own sign."[23] The particularity of symbolic regimes in the diaspora shaped how black bodies were received and resisted as representative of the "particular country's democracy," as Locke put it. When Whitman balked at the post-slavery political power of the Negro, who might be the white man's ruler as well as his peer, the term "abomination" represented the dominant white American reaction to the late nineteenth- and early twentieth-century black body. Within the United States, the former slave of the 1870s became the feared enemy and lynching victim of the 1890s, as the Negro as feared beast replaced the softer, more domesticated, more dominated image of the Negro as Aunt Jemima and Uncle Tom. Subjection to such schizophrenic stereotypes in American popular culture gave the black body a dual status as both the white American's gravest threat and best friend. What was most distinctive, of course, was the emergence of the black body as violent primitive, epitomized perhaps by the success of the African American boxer Jack Johnson, who turned Social Darwinist discourses about the Negro as the "missing link" between man and animal into the possibility that the black body was the "fittest." To redress the psychic imbalance caused by Jack Johnson's body dominating all those white bodies brought into the boxing ring, white men rioted and burned black neighborhoods after Johnson beat heavyweight champion Jim Jeffries in 1910. But this weak show of white male dominance merely publicized the impression that the black body was not only primitive, but superior.

Ironically, the ascendancy of this feared big black body in the white American imagination coincided with a broader shift in the iconic American body, when the slender, gentleman, middle-class body of Victorian America gave way to the masculine ideal of Teddy Roosevelt's "Rough Riders," the aggressively physical, muscle-bound male—the body, Marx might add, of the late nineteenth-century industrial laborer, whose unskilled brawn was the cog in America's emerging industrial empire.[24] The big, physically powerful black body became iconic of a violent, undomesticated New Negro who migrated out of the South and replaced white bodies going off to Europe for World War I with a chip on his or her shoulder. This New Negro would fight back when attacked in the white race riots of 1919, the so-called Red Summer, when, suddenly, the docile, acquiescent, all-forgiving Negro body of Uncle Remus stories was a memory. The new black body incorporated a white fascination and begrudging respect for the "primordial" Negro, who might just be the strongest and most dangerous of men.

But Locke was suspicious of this masculinist turn in the early twentieth–century black body politics, for when America rejected the lean, disciplined, middle-class gentleman as an icon of masculinity, it rejected, in effect, him. Locke viewed this fetishized black body as a trap, a step back from the balance Whitman accorded to the black body as beautiful and noble, strong and poetic. Moreover, Locke's own body politics shaped his reaction, since, as a mere 4'11" and weighing only 98 pounds, his diminutive body was one of the impediments to his becoming the kind of heroic black American leader he wished to be. In general, in America, but especially in twentieth-century black America, the man, the strong man, is most often tall and imposing, and the turn to football heroes and athletes as representative Americans made it even more difficult for Locke to be perceived as a hero.

Indeed, Locke manipulated his image as a man to gain the Rhodes Scholarship, and at Oxford he had transformed himself into the image of the middle-class, sophisticated gentleman that was in decline in the United States when he returned in 1912. Throughout his life, Locke exemplified a genius for creating, in words and in commissioned photographs, an image of himself as larger, taller, and more imposing than he was. Yet such strategies did not protect him from derision from those who resented what they considered to be his inflated estimation of himself as "God Locke," as some called him, even while confined to a tiny physique. Some, such as Owen Dodson, the gay, black, mid-twentieth-century dramatist and novelist, linked his size and his sexual orientation. When I interviewed Dodson, he said that he once asked Locke, "What sport did you play at Oxford as a Rhodes Scholar?" Locke, he said, answered, "A coxswain!"[25] Dodson laughed and laughed, he told me, because he thought it so perfect. "Locke steered the rowers of boats and sucked cock!" This kind of crudity, which Locke suspected behind the laughter, I am sure, bothered him, since it implied he was not a representative American because of his diminutive size and his sexual orientation. Other Rhodes Scholars at Oxford must have felt the same, for Cecil Rhodes's Trust imagined that only Americans of brawn and brains could qualify. But Locke had disguised his body image, directed attention to his brain, and been so successful at it that he received the scholarship. Yet Locke could not escape the blues of not having the right kind of black body. His lack of fit with the big brawny, heterosexist body stereotype of the American marginalized him and his attempt to be the representative American.

Of course, all such figures—Locke, Dodson, Robeson, and Whitman—defined the American body representativeness in gendered terms, as male. To be "representative" as a body meant to represent the best that the nation had to offer, which, of course, was always male, a reification of American identity heightened in turn-of-the-century American politics by the rise of imperialism and the need for more bodies, male bodies, as soldiers in the nation's quest for national and international glory. Black thinkers like Locke were just as immersed in a sexist conception of racial liberation, by the very way they framed the race issue as a problematic of the *male* body image. Locke was a well-known misogynist; and yet, ironically, Owen Dodson, another black homosexual, enjoyed linking Locke's small body type and sexual orientation to male femininity. Here was another example of the internalization of the surveyor, though this time it was a patriarchal observer, which fused blackness and lack of a powerful presence with physique. Dodson invokes a discourse that renders Locke inappropriate as a black body, which means he does not qualify as a *real* representative of the African American, a maneuver that anticipates Black Panther Party spokesperson Eldridge Cleaver's legendary dismissal of James Baldwin in the 1960s as unrepresentative of black manhood because he was gay.[26] Here was another incentive to Locke's transnationalism—his sexual and physical misrepresentativeness of heterosexist nationalism.

Alienated by the inability to reproduce the nation as a transgenerational eros, Locke found a way out of the American dichotomy of genteel femininity on the one hand, and primordial masculinity on the other. He embraced a non-American masculine alternative—the body of the African, especially the Ethiopian men he met on his first trip to Africa in 1922. These were not the "wild savages" of colonialist imagination, but the epitome of the sophisticated, slender, refined, and beautiful elite, who also had the advantage of not having been colonized by the Europeans. In going outside of America for a model of the beautiful unconquered black body, Locke echoes earlier "body missionaries," such as the Rev. Charles Morris, who, on a "civilizing mission" for the Colored Baptists of America in the 1890s, was transformed by the "'bontee,' manhood . . . muscularity and intelligence of the warrior Zulu," whom he met and whom he praised precisely because Zulus had never been enslaved.[27] Locke also was intoxicated by his version of the African body—the lean physical strength and gentlemanly figures of the West African intellectuals he met, such as Nnamdi Azikiwe, a six-foot-tall Igbo scholar who became Nigeria's first president. Indeed, Locke's transnational worship of the African body can be seen in his collection of West African art, which he collected, exhibited, interpreted, and celebrated, not only for its cultural heritage, but also for its representation of the African body as a transnational sign of racial dignity and efficacy. Collecting African art became a clandestine way of celebrating his love for a certain kind of man, a certain kind of body—not the hypermasculine, heterosexist black body of

Du Bois's Pan-African Congress or Marcus Garvey's Back-to-Africa movement, but the svelte, homoerotic, transatlantic black body that still retained its ancestral bisexuality and dignity. For Locke, the black body functioned as a sign of the thinking black man, whose deliberative, transnational, and self-conscious manhood was still preserved in West African art.

Art, finally, allowed Locke to register blackness in the world of representation rather than simply in the world of the physical. West African art created a space where the black body was an archive of lost knowledge of how to be heroic and powerful before the reification of the black body as a sign of weakness took root in Western racist iconography. By seeing the black body as an archive instead of an essence, Locke opened up the black body as a field of deliberative exploration rather than a private property available only to black people. As he put it in 1940, "In contemporary American art of this generation, both the Negro and the white artist stand on common ground in their aim to document every phase of American life and experience," including the face and form of the Negro. Of course, opening the black body up to such discursive meditations also opens the possibility of manipulation and misrepresentation; but, as a progressive, Locke felt the march of history would produce—especially if led by self-conscious black and white artists—more accurate and compelling representations of the black body that would trump, ultimately, the more inept.[28]

Before leaving Locke for Robeson, I must ask: did Locke ever find, locate, or self-fashion the iconic black body that did not marginalize him? I think the answer is yes, although in an unusual way. Instead of in literature, Locke found its closest American transcriptions in the sculpture of Richmond Barthé, a more talented and more indulgent protégé than Owen Dodson, and a native-born New Orleans artist. For Barthé imbibed Locke's advice to Negro artists in the 1930s to use African principles of design, such as elongation and abstraction of forms, to visualize poetically and truthfully black masculinity in three-dimensional space. In a series of creations, some of black women, others of black men, Barthé forged ideal types of the Negro physique. Again, while this project might be called essentialist, I believe it was no more essentialist than the Greek search for the ideal in the Venus de Milo, for, as classicists, both Locke and Barthé studied the Greeks and their quest for the classic in all forms.

In his "Male Torso" (1932) Barthé sought to create such an ideal for the Negro male, one Locke collected and adored, in part because of its lean physique, its combination of female and male elements, and its representation, perhaps, of Locke's ideal in a lover as much as in the self-fashioning he did to make the New Negro an object of beauty for America.

When we turn to Robeson and *his* black body politics, we confront once again the conflict that Gail Bederman points out about American masculinity at the turn of the twentieth century. For Robeson fits into both traditions about the body and masculinity—he was the quintessential gentleman, having made himself into that nineteenth-century icon by the

Figure 16.1 Richmond Barthé, *Male torso* (1932). Painted plaster, Gallery of Art, Howard University.

time he graduated summa cum laude from Rutgers College. He had also become a football hero, becoming the first black player to be chosen to the All-American Team in 1917. If we were catty, we could say that Locke and Barthé could have saved themselves a lot of time looking for the ideal body by simply carving Robeson's. Actually, an Italian sculptor, Antonio Salemme, produced a life-size sculpture of the nude Robeson, in part, I suspect because he saw something of the classical ideal in Robeson's body. Here Salemme achieves something beyond what Barthé had done—he renders a black man as a self-conscious hero, a culture bearer, who, in his uplifted hands, communicates a universal spiritual message that everyone can embrace.[29]

Well, almost everyone embraced it. The Philadelphia committee rejected it as an outdoor sculpture, claiming it might incite a riot. But by the time Salemme produced this sculpture in 1927, Nickolas Muray had already photographed Robeson's body in the nude. Here, again, we sense something of classical iconography—the discus thrower, Atlas, the Christ figure. But that Robeson is black frames (and reframes) these icon images into a more modernist fascination with the big black body. When Muray published a book of his photographs of celebrities and included Robeson, Robeson's photograph was one of the few of men in the nude.

Some of the nude Robeson photographs were made into postcards and exchanged among friends in elite New York. I found some, for example, in the collection of famed Robeson friend and homosexual rake, Carl Van Vechten. Such images contrast with others of Robeson that do not construct him as a homoerotic object of desire, but as the epitome of the gentleman, whose poise, calm, and self-possession cast him in a different discourse from that of the equally physically imposing Jack Johnson. When Robeson turned to acting on the stage, he met a different but related gaze—that of Mary Tuborg and Eugene O'Neill, white playwrights who also were fond of placing Robeson in scenes where he was naked. In *Taboo*, Tuborg cast him as an African; but instead, in the London production of the work, he looked more like a fool. And in *Emperor Jones* and then *The Hairy Ape*, O'Neill cast Robeson in roles that represented him as the anti-hero, the barbarian, the bare-chested man, who was a threat to himself and the social order.

Robeson, who shared Locke's infatuation with Africa, sought to escape from this representational tension in the 1930s by starring in motion pictures about Africa, and especially in films made outside of the United States, predominantly in Britain. Yet, in such films as *Sanders of the River* (1935), *King Solomon's Mines* (1936), and *Jericho* (1937), Robeson learned a difficult lesson—that the representation of Africans from the British imperial viewpoint was as compromising as being the Emperor Jones in America. In *Sanders of the River* Robeson is undressed again, but this time he is not the feared other, but a willing servant of British power. Once again, he seems the fool. While *Solomon's Mines* provides us with more authentic images, Robeson still must remain a servant of white power. What begins to creep

Figure 16.2 Paul Robeson, photo by Nickolas Muray. Gelatin silver print, George Eastman House. © Nickolas Muray Photo Archives.

into some of the stills from these movies is a sense of frustration and pathos, which, while tied to the character he plays, begin to be emblematic of his own consciousness as an artist. In some respects, Robeson cannot be as successful as Locke or Barthé in crafting an alternative image because, as an actor in the motion picture industry, he cannot "sing the black body electric" all by himself.

Figure 16.3 Paul Robeson on stage of *Black Boy* with Otto Liveright and son (1926). Gelatin silver print, New York Library for the Performing Arts.

The popular culture industry is both a source of his power, and his pain. For the international film industry will not allow him to be a hero to his people, since that contradicts for a majority of the audience their dominant representation of the black body as a sign of subservience.

Robeson confronted the predicament of being just a dependent body in the film representation of the Negro by using his body as a weapon in the political upheaval of the 1930s. He becomes a revolutionary in reaction to the containment of his mind and agency by the dominant discourse of the black body. And he does so by going beyond Locke's racialized politics to forge a transatlantic body based on the figure of the international worker. Even in his later films, he enacts a politics in his choice of roles, such as in *The Tunnel* (1940), a story of a black man among the Welsh miners, whose cause he takes up as his cause and for which he gives his life. For by embracing the worker's internationalist cause, Robeson forges a larger corporate body for the New Negro—as a socialist imaginary that encompasses the American, the African, the European, the Russian, the Australian, including the aboriginal peoples, within his large body. By traveling broadly, Robeson internationalizes his body and makes the black body a representative symbol of the aspirations of all oppressed workers of the world, not just black ones in Africa and America. He merges his body with that of the international worker oppressed wherever capitalism exists.

Here, Locke and Robeson may have parted company. Robeson was Whitmanesque in a different way than Locke—more comfortable with the common people, the people Whitman loved; his socialism was more optimistic than the American brand of socialism, built on a profoundly democratic faith in the black, white, Hispanic, and other workers, who would overthrow the Big White Folks (as Robeson called them in his autobiography, *Here I Stand)* in America.[30] Locke, always suspicious of the hyper-masculine black body image, was also suspicious of Robeson as a dupe of Communists. He resisted Robeson as body and leader because, as a small black man, Locke was suspicious of all physically and politically dominating men and their discourses. Locke favored, instead, a new black personality and a new American body politics in the present that left behind the masculinist dichotomies that excluded him. Yet in the end, Locke was hampered by the fact that destiny had given him a body that was never going to be perceived as the body of a leader, especially a leader of black *men*. And Robeson remained suspicious of Locke because of his own experience with the homoerotic gaze as objectifying and containing. He also came to believe that Locke's mainly racial paradigm hampered him as a potentially transnational leader of humanity.

But Robeson's largeness of vision—his socialist internationalism, and his largeness of body—also exposed him to attack. Pushing his body out into the anti-capitalist public space he came to occupy as a heroic transnational black leader made him a highly visible target of Cold War witch-hunting. In a sense, Robeson was attacked by the American right wing as much because of his threatening, commanding black body as for his Communist sympathies. His asset—that his black body could become a symbol of the black leader of the multitude—also meant that he could elicit the white fear—the Jack Johnson effect—as much as the admiration needed

Figure 16.4 Alain Locke and Paul Robeson (ca. 1942). Gelatin silver print, Alain Locke Papers, Moorland-Spingarn Research Center, Howard University.

to be a transnational hero. Moreover, Robeson's abundance of sexuality, like Locke's homoeroticism, complicated his aspirations for transformative leadership. For just as Robeson broke with Locke's primarily race-based notion of cultural politics, he also rejected, in practice, the unwritten rule that black leaders should never put themselves in a position to be accused of interracial womanizing. As Martin Duberman's biography pointed out, almost obsessively, Robeson responded actively to the sexual attention he attracted from white women. That made Robeson problematical for black nationalists, who believed that black people should embody the sexual racial loyalty that whites claimed but never practiced.

I want to suggest, however, that Robeson's sexual availability, like Locke's sexual rakiness, may have contributed to his ability to be a compelling leader. Eros may have been one of the reasons for Robeson's charismatic appeal as a singer, actor, and political activist. Robeson's sexual energy may have contributed the "electricity" coursing through audiences at his rallies, concerts, and performances which transformed them into a new kind of political community. After all, Whitman's poetic love of the black body in *Leaves of Grass* seemed to be fixated on black bodies in New Orleans that resembled Robeson's. The tragedy for Locke's politics is that he can never generate a similar eros in his audiences with his body or his presence at his lectures. Something about the erotic love of the black body funnels through Robeson and enables him to pull the white masses of Wales, England, Germany, Russia, and elsewhere into a new orbit of consciousness behind him as their leader. It also allows them to transcend the numbing quality of their own oppression and see their struggle for liberation as connected with that of other people who do not look like them.

While lacking Robeson's black body magnetism, Locke possessed a quality as a black gay male that was effective in advancing a different kind of politics. As a small, effeminate man, Locke never would allow himself to be as politically and sexually public as Robeson was. As a black gay male, Locke was a master of disguise, adapting to and performing a variety of poses in such a way as to protect himself while effectively transforming the social cultural discourse of the American. Locke's "femininity," as Owen Dodson described it, contained a deeper truth: Locke's ability to pose as a powerful American—a Rhodes Scholar—and a representative American during the apogee of hypermasculinist images of the American circulating in popular culture was an act of black bodily genius. By contrast, Robeson's presentation of blackness as heroic masculine body lacked a similar finesse. Back to Whitman, Locke would have admonished, especially since Whitman had "no great faith in any specific scheme of social reconstruction," as Nathan Scott, Jr., put it.[31] The essence of Whitman's message, which both Locke and Robeson embodied in different ways, was that a "new beginning" was possible through the transformative love of the body.

Locke's and Robeson's struggles reveal something profound about the black male body as a site of transnational liberation. Locke and Robeson epitomized a tension in the black body between its gay, feminine presence and its heterosexist, hypermasculine presence—the ability of the black male body to function as both an object and subject of male desire. And that duality, that implicit bisexuality, makes the black male body an "electric" sign for the multitude of racial, class, ethnic, gender, and sexual communities seeking freedom. There is a sexual "doubleness" to the representation of the black male body that, perhaps, explains why it remains so controversial and also so powerful a sign of the potential for a "new beginning" for humanity.

Interesting contemporary realities are upon us in the light of this discussion: in America, the black body and black music (hip-hop and rap) appeal as much to suburban white youth as to black inner-city dwellers, or more. The black body (especially the sense of alterity and subversiveness associated with the black body as threat to the social order) is once again desired. But now the desire and consumption of the black body is more broadly based, and not exclusive to the avant-garde as in the 1920s. Moreover, while the fool and the clown remain part of hip-hop iconography, some black bodies have emerged who articulate a subversive politics, claim the role of leader, spokesperson, critic, and can imagine themselves as transnational heroes.

For example, Kanye West became a hip-hop star in 2005, after his Grammy-winning album, *The College Dropout*, sold 2.6 million copies. But he has also used his stardom to create a fiery political song, "Diamonds from Sierra Leone," that he turned into a video to bring attention to the grotesque realities of Africa's diamond trade. The second verse of the song goes like this:

> Take your diamonds and throw them up like you bulimic
> Yea the beat cold but the flow is anemic.[32]

Whitman, it is not. But it does do something Whitman did—capture the language of the street of his time, and turn it into a subversive vision of the Now. West is also more overtly political, which brings him closer to Robeson. He became internationally famous when he spoke out in the aftermath of Katrina, saying, "George Bush doesn't care about black people. America is set up to help the poor, the black people, the less well-off as slow as possible" (3 September 2005). Evidence of his power was that President George W. Bush had to get secretary of state Condoleezza Rice to say she did not believe that race was a factor in the federal government's slow response to the poorest of the hurricane victims.[33] That the secretary of state—which Jefferson was when he wrote *Notes on the State of Virginia*—had to answer a "college dropout" suggests some of the voice and agency the black male body has today that it never had in Locke's and Robeson's time, in part, I believe, because thanks to contemporary media the audience for such critique is both larger and more global than it was in the first half of the twentieth century.

Locke and Robeson are linked to Kanye West by a willingness to undermine the status quo by *bringing it*—the body of submerged black realities—into the face of world opinion. If transnationalism is to be more than an endless circumlocution of bodies and signs across borderless borders, if it is to become the inspiration if not the basis for a new sense of global democracy, it must examine whether the ideologies of transnationalists contribute to the formation of what Hardt and Negri call a multitude, a global community in which all are represented and all differences are preserved. From the eighteenth to the twentieth centuries, the black body was the site of the production of Western capital, but also the body most dramatically alienated from the social benefits of its labor. The black body symbolized those without property, indeed, those who had been property, those who produced the wealth of the West, and those who were denigrated and dehumanized in terms of their bodies by the likes of Thomas Jefferson. But Whitman's eros for the black body restored its heroism as central to the identity of the American. The most heavily policed of bodies became the most desirable. As Locke would argue in *Race Contacts and Inter-racial*

Relations, the more the races were separated, the more desire was produced across color lines.

Locke's faith was that cultural production could organize people of color throughout the world in a commonality of art. Those who listened to Robeson sing and loved him and one another in new ways because of it could form the new multitude. For the black body became more than an object of desire—it became, especially in the twentieth century, a counternarrative to the objectification of global capitalism, and thus a speaking subject with a social conscience. Kanye West, thus, on the one hand resonates with Locke in his concern with seeing the black subject as the prime subject of black art, while on the other he represents Robeson's interrogation of the system of abuse and oppression from inside American cultural production—the American music industry configured by hip-hop music. West's transnational *reach* is powerful, because immaterial labor is hegemonic in the West, and hip-hop artists are dominant in global popular culture production.

Kanye West is an heir, therefore, to the new cultural labor energy just emerging during the time of Locke and Robeson. What remains to be seen is whether hip-hop can take its unique embrace of the black body at the center of global cultural production and turn its language into the lingua franca of the new multitude. For black bodies retain their potential to be the only true flag of the multitude, the bringer of conscience to the world, the bringer of a still fetishized eros hidden under foot, their anguished souls belying a global democracy whose history, still, as Whitman saw, is yet to be written.

NOTES

1. I wish to thank Anna Scacchi, E. Curmie Price, Fath Davis Ruffins, Ben Carton, Alison Landsberg, Alan Trachtenberg, Dan Green, and Michael Hardt for their suggestions.
2. Morgan, *American Slavery, American Freedom*, 5.
3. As will be clear later in the chapter, I am referring here to Walt Whitman and his poem "I Sing the Body Electric."
4. See Locke, *The New Negro*, 9–14.
5. Locke, "*Fire!!* A Negro Magazine," 563.
6. See Kim, "Invisible Desires," for the full quote and an excellent explication of its impact on Ralph Ellison and African American thinking.
7. Berger, *Ways of Seeing*, 45–46.
8. Coetzee, "Love and Walt Whitman," 26.
9. Whitman, *Leaves of Grass*, 119.
10. Whitman, *Leaves of Grass*, 123.
11. Jefferson, *Notes on the State of Virginia*, 264–265.
12. Whitman, *Leaves of Grass*, 124.
13. Whitman, *Leaves of Grass*, 124; italics mine.
14. Whitman, quoted in Coetzee, "Love and Walt Whitman," 26.
15. Michael Hardt, "Love in the Multitude," lecture presented at the Berkley Center for Religion, Peace, and World Affairs at Georgetown University, Washington, D.C., 20 April 2006.

16. See Frederickson, *The Black Image*; Wallis, "The Slave Daguerreotypes of Louis Agassiz," 102–106; Wells, *Southern Horrors*. I am inspired in my use of the term "multitude" by Michael Hardt and Antonio Negri's *Multitude*.
17. Whitman, *Leaves of Grass*, 7.
18. Du Bois, *Souls*, 364.
19. Locke, Letter to Charlotte Mason, 8 September 1931, Alain Locke Papers, Moorland-Spingarn Research Center, Howard University, Washington, D.C.
20. Locke, "To Certain of Our Philistines," 155–156.
21. Locke, "The Negro in the Three Americas," 461.
22. Whitman, *Leaves of Grass*, 8.
23. Spivak, *A Critique of Postcolonial Reason*, 193.
24. See Bederman, *Manliness and Civilization*.
25. Author interview with Owen Dodson (1981).
26. See H. L. Gates, "The Fire Last Time: A Reconsideration of James Baldwin," excerpt from *The New Republic*, 1 June 1992; http://www.nathanielturner. com/firelasttime.htm. Accessed 20 April 2007.
27. Carton, "'We Are Made Quiet by This Annihilation,'" 99–100. Charles S. Morris expressed his views in the *Cleveland Gazette*, 31 March 1900, and *Voice of Missions*, 1 December 1900.
28. Locke, "Exhibition of the Art of the American Negro (1851 to 1940), July 1940," quoted in Ittmann, *Dox Thrash*, xiii.
29. For images and biographical information mentioned here, see Stewart, *Paul Robeson*.
30. Robeson, *Here I Stand*, 95.
31. Scott, *Three American Moralists*, 21.
32. http://www.lyricstop.com/d/diamondsfromsierraleone-kanyewest.html.
33. "Look, I find it very strange to think that people would think the President of the United States would sit deciding who ought to be helped on the basis of color, most especially this President," Rice said. "It's just—it's (a) not true and it's (b) poisonous that somebody would say that. And I hope that people would be challenged on the assumption if they're going to say it. Now, what evidence is there that this is the case? Why would you say such a thing? What makes you think so?" *New York Times,* 13 September, 2005.

17 W.E.B. Du Bois and the Black Intellectual Abroad

Anna Scacchi

One three centuries removed
From the scenes his fathers loved,
Spicy grove, cinnamon tree,
What is Africa to me?

Countee Cullen, "Heritage" (1925)

An inveterate transatlantic traveler who lived, studied, and lectured world-wide, W.E.B. Du Bois has recently come to prefigure the contemporary cosmopolitan intellectual, who rejects essentialist notions of identity and chooses instead to be a citizen of the world. This is a radical departure from the conventional portrait of Du Bois as the last of the Victorian "race men," devoted to the uplifting of African Americans and committed to the fight against American racism, which was popularized by the Harlem Renaissance and is still commonly accepted. Some contemporary scholars who are growing skeptical of multiculturalism, identity politics, and the focus on difference that characterized the humanities in the last three decades of the twentieth century—Paul Gilroy and Ross Posnock are prominent examples of this trend—tend to emphasize Du Bois's cultural affiliation with a *communitas* transcending national borders and ethnic particularities over his life-long devotion to racial solidarity.[1] They find in his worldwide *flânerie*, belief in the catholic power of culture, support of anticolonialism across racial boundaries, and penchant for genre hybridity in his writings, instances of the diasporic subject's rejection of authenticity and inclination to cultural crossovers. They place him, as a consequence, at the beginning of a line of nonconformist African American universalists which would later include the likes of James Baldwin and Ralph Ellison.

Contra Du Bois's timely enrolment in both the "beyond identity politics" movement and cosmopolitanism, this chapter argues that while Du Bois's political activism was never confined to the United States and his racial group, his sense of his own position in the world was firmly rooted in his being an American of African descent. Scholars interpreting Du Bois's life commitment to the international fight against imperialism and racism as a breaking free of the strictures of national and racial identity erase the complexity of his notion of double consciousness, turning it into a "neither . . . nor," instead of a "both . . . and." Du Bois's critique of the United States—which soon became a complex understanding of the interconnectedness of capitalism, imperialism and racism and of the role of the slave trade in the making of modernity—was founded on the belief that the struggle for full citizenship, though it had to become a global, transracial movement, was to have the nation-state as its interlocutor.

DU BOIS AND THE TURN FROM IDENTITY POLITICS

Eventually Du Bois's nomadic life produced a literal change of motherland. When he died in 1963, on the eve of the march on Washington, he died an African in Accra. Having accepted President Kwame Nkrumah's invitation to move to Ghana in 1961, he had renounced American citizenship a few months before his death. Blacks in both countries claimed him, whatever Du Bois's intentions in his decision to become a citizen of Ghana. Celebrated by the African Americans assembled in front of the Lincoln Memorial in Washington, D.C., as the "father" of the Civil Rights Movement in the U.S., he was saluted as an "African Prophet" in the front page obituary of *The Ghanaian Times*, which bluntly stated that he was sleeping "the long sleep in a spot that symbolizes his true return to the home of his ancestors."[2] His funeral was indeed a highly symbolic event, celebrating postcolonial Africa and its fight for nationhood.

Was Du Bois's move to Africa really meant to stress the African over the American in his double identity? Or was it rather an extreme challenge to the U.S. within the American tradition of protest? Or was it, as some scholars maintain, a final declaration of unbelonging in the nomadic life of a cosmopolitan intellectual who had been astonished by German patriotism when he was in Berlin as a young man and, half-regretfully, had realized that the Germans' unmixed feeling of identification with their native country was denied to black Americans?[3]

In "The Uncompleted Argument: Du Bois and the Illusion of Race" Kwame Anthony Appiah—whose claim that W.E.B. Du Bois's early racial essentialism extends well beyond "The Conservation of Races" (1897) is an exception in a scholarly panorama that tends to celebrate Du Bois's understanding of race as social and cultural construct[4]—reads Du Bois's death in Accra as an inevitable outcome of "the dream of Pan-Africanism."[5] Appiah seems to imply that Du Bois's choice of Ghana as motherland is further evidence that his notion of race was based on biology rather than common history and culture. Choosing Africa as motherland—albeit at the very end of his life—might indeed seem to place Du Bois among those black nationalists, from Paul Cuffe to Martin Delany, Marcus Garvey, and the Rastafarians, who had no faith in integration and believed that only a journey "back to Africa," either literal or metaphorical, would ensure freedom and nationhood for the offspring of slaves.[6]

For many who had known him Du Bois's renunciation of American citizenship made his move to Africa the last act in his life-long protest against the U.S. for the betrayal of its black sons and daughters, an act stating that he no longer hoped that African Americans would ever be successful in their fight to become full citizens. They believed, to use David Levering Lewis's words, that "Du Bois had finally concluded that [the] promised land was a cruel, receding mirage for people of color. And so he had chosen to live out his last days in West Africa."[7] So many shared the opinion that by moving to Ghana he had given up the fight for African American liberation that in 1993 Herbert Aptheker, Du Bois's protégé and literary executor, felt compelled to write a short article where he rejected the notion of Du Bois's turn toward political pessimism and put his last journey in the historical context of the witch-hunt.[8]

According to Aptheker the denial of passports to communists and communist sympathizers forced Du Bois to anticipate a project, the Encyclopedia Africana to be based in Accra, that he had agreed to head in 1960 and had had in mind for several decades. Once in Accra the Du Boises applied for the renewal of their passports but they were told that they should immediately return to the U.S. because their traveling documents were invalid. Only then did they inquire of President Nkrumah if they might become citizens of Ghana. For Aptheker, then, Du Bois's change of citizenship was rather an extreme act of protest against his native country, than a return to the ancestral home.

Unlike Appiah, Paul Gilroy and Ross Posnock, who have both argued for the dismissal of race as a useful category for sociopolitical and cultural analysis, have found in W.E.B. Du Bois's transatlantic crossings—or, as Gilroy writes in *The Black Atlantic*, "his lack of roots and the proliferation of routes in his long nomadic life"[9]—and final landing in Accra evidence enough to enroll Du Bois in the ranks of the "beyond identity politics" movement or, to use Posnock's words, to turn him from a prophet of black nationalism into a champion of post-ethnicity *avant la lettre*.[10] According to Gilroy,

> Du Bois's travel experiences raise in the sharpest possible form a question common to the lives of almost all these figures who begin as African-Americans or Caribbean people and are then changed into something else which evades those specific labels and with them all fixed notions of nationality and national identity. Whether their experience of exile is enforced or chosen, temporary or permanent, these intellectuals and activists, writers, speakers, poets, and artists repeatedly articulate a desire to escape the restrictive bonds of ethnicity, national identification, and sometimes even "race" itself.[11]

Gilroy both emphasizes Du Bois's sense of race as social construction and self-creation and underlines his growing estrangement with the United

States, which soon ceases "to be the locus of his political aspirations,"[12] to be replaced by a transnational stage for political action. In other words, Gilroy—*contra* Du Bois's own narrative of his life as progress from elit- ist individualism to race and class consciousness[13]—depicts Du Bois's life route as an emerging from, rather than an immersion into, racial and national identity. Ross Posnock adds to traveling another escape route from the strictures of race and nation, namely the "world elsewhere" of art, "the promise of aesthetic freedom—that art and culture can be practices resis- tant to racial identity."[14] Both scholars refer time and again to the spatial dynamics of Du Bois's self-fashioning and find in his continuous displace- ments and relocations a reason to make of him an early example of the (black) intellectual who rejects the primacy of identity and racial authentic- ity in favor of universalism.[15]

Addiction to travel does not make one necessarily a cosmopolite, of course, but Gilroy and Posnock have had no difficulty at substantiating their portraits of a Du Bois transcending American—and African Ameri- can—exceptionalist nationalism with apt citations from his works. They depict Du Bois as a cosmopolitan flâneur who refused to be pinned down to a provincial sphere by his skin color and American racial prejudice and so claimed his rightful membership in a "kingdom of culture" with neither color nor national borders. Against studies reading Du Bois's Pan-African- ism as black nationalism or, on the contrary, emphasizing the integrationist stance of his work within the National Association for the Advancement of Colored People (NAACP), they both maintain that these were critical stages in his evolution toward universalism and the elaboration of transna- tional, interracial modes of affiliation, which the contemporary turn from identity politics is now making easier to discern.[16]

Du Bois's back-to-Africa move cannot be satisfyingly read as a yielding to the seduction of roots, if only because it came so late in his life and after he had expressed his anger at the United States' betrayal of its ideals of freedom in a most eloquent manner: he had applied for membership in the U.S. Communist Party, which, according to the McCarran Internal Security Act, whose constitutionality was upheld by the Supreme Court in 1961, would lead to his loss of citizenship in a short time. But can we read Du Bois's self-exile as a final yielding to the temptation of routes, as an act claiming world citizenship on the part of an intellectual whose experiences of dislocation had carried him beyond the nation-state and racial identity?

Gilroy and Posnock build much of their argument on Du Bois's rejec- tion of nationalism and ethnic absolutism around *Dark Princess*, a novel with an obvious autobiographical slant, which opens with "a transatlan- tic crossing"[17] and deals with exile, racial identity, and political activism at a number of levels.[18] *Dark Princess* was one of the most neglected among Du Bois's works until a few years ago because its wedding of the aesthetic and the political appeared decidedly archaic and its style an odd hodgepodge of genres, from romance to political pamphlet, from sociological document to exotic Baedeker and erotic fantasy. To Posnock, on the contrary, the novel is "self-consciously embedded within the international matrix of high modernism," and Matthew Towns, its protagonist, an embodiment of the archetypical modernist icon, "the expatriate aesthete abroad."[19] While in his book's introduction Posnock declares that *Dark Princess* was Du Bois's fantasy of an "escape from race responsibility through erotic obsession,"[20] Gilroy finds in the final scene of *Dark Princess* an epiphany of the Black Atlantic as a diasporic community embracing "hybridity and intermixture" against national belonging and racial purity.[21]

They read the novel, in other words, as an autobiographical narrative where Du Bois projects his own desires for release from the burden of race and the duty of representativeness on his alter ego. For Gilroy, however, Matthew Towns's rejection of political compromise in Chicago is not a retreat from politics but rather a path towards a superior political level, "entirely appropriate to troubled anti-colonial times,"[22] where the United States loses its dominant position on the novel's geopolitical map and the stage for action stretches from Virginia to Asia. Du Bois, in Gilroy's opinion, imagines a transnational community founded on "the meeting of two heterogeneous multiplicities" who resist any neat classification by race or culture[23]—Matthew, the African American exile born of the black laboring class, who though uncultivated has a natural appreciation for beauty and soon develops into a connoisseur of contemporary art, and Kautilya, the Indian princess with communist sympathies, whose urge toward the real turns her into a worker and union organizer and even exposes her to rape. Posnock, on the contrary, reads Matthew (and Du Bois, of course) as torn between his duties as "race man" and his objects of desire, namely the princess, aesthetic bliss and the freedom of individuality. Matthew's withdrawal from the Chicago political scene, then, signals that he has chosen a "free-floating subjectivity" over political responsibility.[24]

What follows is an attempt to argue that *Dark Princess* is not a fantasy of release through erotic desire, where "the burden of exemplarity" is thrown off together with "the burden of masculinity,"[25] but rather a utopian text where the erotic opens up new political prospects for the African American male subject reduced to impotence by U.S. racism, and allows his remasculinization. Neither is it an untroubled paean to hybridity and intermixture. Though Du Bois was certainly committed to the idea of an international fight against capitalist imperialism, his novel's prejudiced representation of Eastern people demonstrates—to quote one of the few essays underlining the Orientalism of Du Bois's vision of Asia—"the difficulties of global solidarity."[26] His ideal revolutionary unit is an interracial couple in *Dark Princess* less because it embodies heterogeneous multiplicity than because he had difficulty at imaging an African American woman in the role played by princess Kautilya.

DU BOIS'S EXPERIMENT WITH ART FOR SOCIAL CHANGE

After a long period of disregard, *Dark Princess: A Romance*, Du Bois's second novel sporting a protagonist that, like its author, travels in Europe, has a penchant for modern art and shows a dandyish care for his appearance, seems to be on the verge of a reevaluation. Posnock and Gilroy are only two of a considerable number of scholars who in the last few years have turned their attention to *Dark Princess* and its global scenario for the fight against white supremacism, drawn to the novel by its remarkably prophetic vision that "[i]n 1952 the Dark World goes free."[27] After its publication to little acclaim by Harcourt, Brace and Company in 1928, the novel was out of print until Aptheker's 1974 edition and then disappeared for more than twenty years, to become available again in 1995, in a volume edited by Claudia Tate.[28] Du Bois's contemporaries, according to Tate, were dismayed by his second novel and privately expressed their disappointment with what in their eyes was a problematic mélange of the personal and the political which graphically exposed the limits of Du Bois's theory of the ideological function of art.[29]

Later commentators, such as Arnold Rampersad and David Levering Lewis, have shared their perplexity towards *Dark Princess*, which they regard, in Rampersad's words, as "a queer combination of outright propaganda and Arabian tale, of social realism and quaint romance."[30] In other words, they seem to consider the novel an old man's indulging in nostalgia and romantic reverie, rather at odds with Du Bois's "serious" writing. But not only did Du Bois take seriously his literary experiments: he believed that literature was a powerful instrument in the fight against racism and had always combined the sociological and the political with the literary in his writing practice, as one can easily see in *Souls* or *Darkwater*.

Dark Princess, which Du Bois probably started to write on his way back from the Soviet Union in 1926, when he was musing in amazement at the social dream of the Bolshevik revolution, was completed under the urge to provide an aesthetic alternative to such Harlem Renaissance novels as Claude McKay's *Home to Harlem* and Carl Van Vechten's *Nigger Heaven*. He dismissed the latter as "a blow in the face" in *The Crisis*, outraged at Van Vechten's description of Harlem as a bohemian paradise unfettered from bourgeois morality. Two years later he would criticize McKay as harshly for catering "for that prurient demand on the part of white folk for a portrayal in Negroes of that utter licentiousness which conventional civilization holds white folk back from enjoying."[31]

This was a problem Du Bois felt keenly—how to write about Negro life in the United States and create a national market for African American literature without falling into the trap of minstrelsy.[32] *Dark Princess* was his aesthetic experiment with art as "part of the great fight" of African Americans to create a better world or, in other words, with art as a political weapon "to set the world right."[33] "That somehow, somewhere eternal and perfect Beauty sits above Truth and Right I can conceive," he had written in 1926 against those artists advocating art for art's sake, "but here and now and in the world in which I work they are for me unseparated and inseparable."[34] In the context of racist U.S., that is, what the white world upholds as universal aesthetic criteria may just be, after all, "racial pre-judgment" confining blacks to "Uncle Toms, Topsies, good 'darkies' and clowns."[35] *Dark Princess* was not his first attempt at writing fiction about Negro life in the United States—in 1911 he had published *The Quest of the Silver Fleece*, a remarkable portrait of the cotton industry and southern racism set as a backdrop to the love story between Bles and Zora, representing the ideal wedding of a rising black middle class and the folk—but this time he turned decidedly from romantic realism to the utopian mode in order to join Art and Propaganda.

One of the reasons why *Dark Princess*, with its odd montage of heterogeneous narrative registers and sudden shifts to sociological commentary, is now attracting the attention of scholars might be our growing appreciation of stylistic hybridity and generic mixing, but the real pivot of the contemporary interest in this novel is the fact that it deeply resonates with the current debates on transnationalism, multiculturalism and postmodern politics of difference. At the beginning of the novel, when he meets the seductive princess of Bwodpur in a Berlin café, the novel's protagonist writes his address in Kautilya's memorandum book as "Matthew Towns, Exile, Hotel Roter Adler," and at the end of the story he is the proud father of a multiracial child destined to be the messiah of the Darker Worlds. No wonder that he seems to be on the way to become the literary hero of contemporary transnationalism, and that both the erasure of Africans in the novel and Matthew Towns's decidedly Orientalist vision of Asians as mysterious, scheming and archaic tend to be overlooked. The novel's incipit, with Matthew on-board a ship to Antwerp, fleeing U.S. racism, places him squarely among the displaced heroes of modernity and, as Gilroy writes, it is not long "before he becomes the proto-typical black flaneur sipping his tea on the Unter den Linden."[36]

Yet the novel can hardly be defined a celebration of the freedom of cosmopolitanism and modern flânerie, and even less, in my opinion, a fantasy of release from the burden of racial responsibility or national belonging. Matthew's exilic condition has nothing in common with the proto-typical flâneur's invisibility, detachment and ability to perform roles at will. As a bright medical student at the University of Manhattan Matthew believed in the power of individual talent to rise above racism, was convinced that "[p]rejudice was a miasma that character burned away" (12), and felt that he belonged to a universal elite of the endowed rather than to a mass of black people complaining of "no chance." But then "the blow fell," as he tells the Indian princess he meets in Berlin (13): since a "nigger doctor" cannot touch white women's bodies and deliver their babies, he was refused admittance to the required course in obstetrics and denied graduation.

Matthew's realization that talent will not exempt him from racial discrimination is a veritable heroic fall in his life route, leading to racial awareness. His self-exile is only a temporary flight from the United States, which follows a crisis in the identity of a young African American man whose pragmatic "theories of race and prejudice" (14)—skin color doesn't matter if you work hard—have been shattered. A temporary flight that serves as a prelude to his coming back as a political activist, with a completely different outlook on "race and prejudice."

In the context of contemporary discussions of transnational identities and cosmopolitanism it is important, then, that the transatlantic section of the novel and Matthew's experience "above the veil" of color are only one tenth of an over 300-page novel. In spite of its flirting with the idea of a joint movement of the dark peoples of the world, most of the novel is set in the United States and deals with American racial prejudice and lynching, the pitfalls of African American emergent political activism and the social dangers of a receding dream of democracy. To put it bluntly, *Dark Princess* can be read as a cosmopolitan journey beyond the color line only if our reading is very selective. I wonder if such a turning of a profoundly political novel, complexly embedded in the racial situation of the 1920s United States, into an easy dismissal of racial and national identity says something about the ideological framework behind some contemporary versions of cosmopolitanism, which do not seem to be aware of its past problematic coincidence with empire or Americanism.

Asia, or better India, it is true, provides Matthew Towns with a powerful imaginary geography of liberation, while the novel's revolutionary couple hides away from Chicago's corrupted political scenario in their romantic Orientalist nest, but, as Dohra Ahmad has shown, Du Bois's interest in India was limited to having it function as a convenient spiritual counterpoint to the barrenness of African American institutionalized politics.[37] Strangely enough for one with such a profoundly sociological mind, it never prompted him to gather facts and figures about it. While India remains a mysterious, bizarre, and exotic site, sufficiently nondescript so as to merge easily with a mythical U.S. south on the basis of their common nurturing quality to humanity, Du Bois's geopolitical map of African America is very detailed and in the know about the emerging sites of black political activism in the 1920s.

As a matter of fact, after the 30-page section entitled "The Exile" comes the much longer "Pullman Porter" part, where Matthew, who had shunned menial jobs as "bad for the soul" and because he might meet his white fellow students not as a peer (13), becomes part of the first unionized labor movement of African America. In the third part he enters the political scene of Chicago, where the first black congressman after Reconstruction—the much-gossiped-about Oscar DePriest—was elected in 1928. In the fourth section, which is mainly set in Chicago though evocatively titled "The Maharajah of Bwodpur," he joins the ranks of black labor. He starts digging the Chicago subway and raves about "the sense of reality in this work" while dreaming "to reunite thought and physical work" ("Brain and Brawn," 264–266, 282).

But length is not the only reason why we should question the quality and implications of the novel's transnationalism and, since it is one of the texts that figure prominently in Gilroy's theory of the Black Atlantic as embodying the diasporic deconstruction of race and nation, use the occasion to rethink the theory itself. As Matthew writes in a letter to Kautilya, Chicago is the site from which their regeneration of the world will have to start. America, in other words, though playing the part of the enemy continues to be the center dictating timing, strategies and locations to the internationalist struggle against white supremacism. Considering that Matthew's invaluable contribution to the Committee of the Darker Peoples led by the princess—who had excluded Africans and African Americans from the struggle for liberation on a racial basis, revealing that there is a color line within the color line—is to change their aristocratic politics based on blood and lineage into a democratic doctrine based on merit and fair opportunities for all, it is not surprising that America still looms large in the narrative as the stage for political action.

Meritocratic democracy is a doctrine that Matthew loudly declares as belonging to the United States and one which, in spite of his disillusionment with American racial politics and even though he knows it does not apply to African Americans, he identifies with: "America is teaching the world one thing and only one thing of real value, and that is, that ability and capacity for culture is not the hereditary monopoly of a few, but the widespread possibility for the majority of mankind if they only have a decent chance in life" (26). Democracy, for Matthew, extends to women. In spite of their superior culture and manners and their dream of overturning white supremacism, the committee is, after all, a bunch of patriarchal aristocrats imbued with class, race and gender prejudices. Not only do they deny Africans and African Americans cultural and political agency, they also infantilize women, in the person of the princess, who is venerated for her royal blood but carefully guarded upon like a child. Matthew's defense of the princess's right to self-determination, then, coming as it does immediately after he reveals his identification with the American ideology of fair opportunities for all, is also part of his Western identity, opposing him to the racial and gender politics of a patriarchal, archaic Eastern aristocracy.

A closer look at the transatlantic section of the novel, in addition, reveals that Matthew's experience of a life beyond the color line is not only brief but doomed from the start. Ever since the shattering of his belief in a color-blind realm of higher education in New York he has become conscious of living in a white supremacist world. Not only does his transatlantic passage expose him to the curious gaze of traveling companions and to racial segregation—being the only black passenger on board, he is shunned by other

Americans at first and then he willingly avoids them, especially American women. His whole traveling experience, even after the U.S. is left behind, seems to be haunted by American racism, and Du Bois's second novel is, in this respect, less a free-floating journey above the veil of color than a cautionary tale to white and black America—a warning that the closing down of democratic horizons will only produce terrorists like the Garveyesque Perigua and corrupted politicians like Sammy Scott—and a utopia where black political agency successfully breaks free from a racist context which dooms it to failure.

Even while the novel's protagonist is enjoying racial freedom in a Berlin café—class and not race is what counts in Europe, he muses, and since he is elegantly dressed and looks well-off he will be waited upon without question—he is aware that such freedom is going to last only as long as his money and would probably fail more serious testing: "What would they say if he asked for work? Or a chance for his brains? Or a daughter in marriage?" Matthew wonders, feeling lonesome and homesick (7). His exhilaration at this new colorblind environment is doomed to end soon. Unfortunately, Americans are everywhere, as Du Bois himself had to realize while in Germany, when an American lady interfered in his youthful romance with a German girl.[38] Matthew is violently brought back to his racial identity by an American tourist's insulting behavior toward a beautiful dark woman who is sitting alone in the Viktoria Café. His duty to the race—to the women of the race and to black men's gender identity—compels him to act. The same cold rage he was burning with on the ship leaving the U.S. comes suddenly back (a textual index of the fact that the Berlin café episode is symmetrical to the maiming of his manhood in New York), but this time Matthew finds space for action and hits the white American on the face.

Matthew Towns's, then, is no romantic act of chivalry but a profoundly political action that marks the beginning of his remasculinization. Kautilya, in other words, is not a promise of erotic release from the burden of race but rather erotic desire that enables Matthew to recover political agency as a black man, after he has been deprived of his virility by U.S. racism.[39] As he muses upon the chance encounter that will change his life, while he is in the princess's hotel waiting for the conference to begin, he realizes that somehow the event has appointed him as a black leader: "For the first time since he had left New York, he felt himself a man, one of those who could help build a world and guide it" (18). Kautilya herself seems to read Matthew's protective behavior in these terms, connecting resistance to emasculation with erotic desire and political activism: "It had never happened before that a stranger of my own color should offer me protection in Europe. I had a curious sense of some great inner meaning to your act—some world movement" (17). Matthew's love for Kautilya, then, ignites the process of recovering male patriarchal authority that will culminate in the final fathering of a son.

Du Bois was deeply aware that white supremacism used gender identity as an instrument to control African Americans' access to power, emasculating black men and excluding black women from the ideology of womanhood. For Du Bois not only was racial oppression predicated upon gender, the abuse of black women was the epitome of racism. Rape is the primal scene of the United States as a nation, he seems to imply in *The Souls of Black Folk*, when he describes the "gray-haired gentleman . . . with hate in his eyes" and the black woman who "at his behest had laid herself low to his lust" (383) as typifying the age of slavery. Black men, in other words, are rendered impotent and turned into half-men by the degradation of black women. In *Souls* he had described both voting rights and higher education as practices able to restore African American manhood, against Booker T. Washington's advocacy of vocational training. But in *Dark Princess* Matthew Towns's academic talents and diligent work as a medical student can do nothing to prevent his metaphoric castration by institutionalized racism.

In "The Damnation of Women" (*Darkwater*, 1920) Du Bois celebrates black women in mythic terms, defending their moral purity in spite of abjection, but also perceptively puts them at the head of modernity for their economic independence and freedom from the strictures of contemporary gender ideology. The essay has been rightly praised for its remarkable feminism, especially when he advocates women's self-determination in motherhood and their right to have a career, yet it stops short of acknowledging women's right to an autonomous sexuality. When Du Bois connects the economic independence of black women to the higher ratio among them of divorces and single motherhood, moreover, he is laying the basis for the infamous 1965 Moynihan Report, blaming African American women's nonstandard behavior for the problems of the black family. In "The Damnation of Women" Du Bois pronounces the Southern abuse of black women the vilest of insults, the one racial offense that cannot be forgiven. He does so, he writes, out of anger at the hypocrisy of men who debase black womanhood while declaring it immoral and unworthy of respect, but at a deeper analysis his outrage seems to be caused, as Hazel Carby has convincingly argued in *Race Men*, by the burden that racial rape imposes on black men: "Du Bois clearly believed that women . . . could become the mediators through which the nation-state oppressed black men."[40]

Hence his difficulty at imagining an African American woman as an agent in the remasculinization of black men. In *The Quest of the Silver Fleece* Zora—the powerful, imaginative and defiant child of the swamp, endowed with an uncommon ability to see through the self-serving moral principles of the whites—is an obstacle in Bles's path towards emancipation, because of her lack of a (white) moral conscience. Even though she is a much more interesting character than the conformist Bles, the text is deeply ambivalent about Zora at the ideological level and its ambivalence produces a flawed structure from a narratological point of view. In order to become an acceptable partner for the black hero she has to undergo an "uplifting process," but seems to lose a large part of her vitality and capacity for action in the while and all of her African roots, precisely what makes her the real hero of the narrative.[41] In *Dark Princess* African American women are either assigned a symbolic function but deprived of agency—Matthew's mother, for example, represents the nurturing qualities and dignity of black women who have fought hard against poverty and oppression but never speaks nor has a name—or turned, like Sara Andrews, Sammy Scott's secretary and Matthew's wife, into bossy, domineering, opportunistic viragos who capitalize on their virginity.

While the blues singer Matthew meets in a Harlem cabaret and has an affair with threatens his political commitment, as shown by Perigua's comment: "You're having a hell of a time, ain't you! Prostitutes instead of patriotism" (70), Sara's political cynicism quenches his idealism. But the "'colored' and yet not at all colored" Kautilya (14)—she smokes in public and generally behaves with the freedom of white women—triggers in him "a longing for action, breadth, helpfulness, great constructive deeds" (42). Yet, as an almost white woman of royal blood, the princess does not fit into the novel's political landscape once Europe is left behind for the United States. Her cosmopolitan allure needs to find a strategic location within racist America. While it is not my intention to deny the importance of Du Bois's pioneering attention toward Asia's, and in particular India's, emerging role in the fight against imperialism, I think that in the textual economy of *Dark Princess* Kautilya's ethnic and class identity needs to be analyzed against her rebirth as a black working-class woman in the United States. Not until she is "blackened" through her own experience of black women's oppression, including the danger of rape, is Kautilya fit to become the mother of a black Messiah. Since her identity is finally subsumed under the archetypical black womanhood symbolized by Matthew's mother, the hybridity of Du Bois's revolutionary couple appears less radical than Gilroy would like it to be.[42]

AN AFRICAN AMERICAN INTELLECTUAL ABROAD

"I was in Harvard but not of it," wrote Du Bois in a passage of *Dusk of Dawn* (1940), where he described his Harvard years as racially segregated.[43] His words emphasize the detached stance which marked his participation in the life of one of the most elitist institutions in the U.S. and, as characteristically happens with him, read as self-congratulatory. Since he continues, "and realized all the irony of 'Fair Harvard.' I sang it because I liked the music," he qualifies his detachment as a conscious resistance on his part to being co-opted by a "temple of learning" where all the academics and most of the students were white, and an overwhelming majority of both were staunch believers in white supremacy.[44]

"I was in Harvard but not of it": the phrase rings familiar for the Du Bois reader, because it plays on the spatial dynamics at the heart of the well-known trope of the veil—a figure built on the opposition within/above, where the horizontal axis within/without merges with the vertical axis below/above, positing culture and traveling as ways to rise above, and to escape, racial prejudice. W.E.B. Du Bois left his country sixteen times heading for Europe, the U.S.S.R. and other nations behind the Iron Curtain, Africa, the Caribbean, Japan, and China. Long trips most of them, lasting years that—as he repeatedly wrote in his autobiographies—enlarged his mind and carried him, albeit temporarily, beyond the "veil" of American racism.

Du Bois took his first journey abroad in 1892, when he left for "Friederich Wilhelm," now Humboldt University, Berlin. In Europe he first experienced a freedom from the American color line that in "The Shadow of Years," a mythopoeic autobiographical essay included in *Darkwater*, he describes in spatial terms as a broadening of his horizon:

> On mountain and valley, in home and school, I met men and women as I had never met them before. Slowly they became, not white folks, but folks. The unity beneath all life clutched me. *I was not less fanatically a Negro, but "Negro" meant a greater, broader sense of humanity and world-fellowship.* I felt myself standing, not against the world, but simply against American narrowness and color prejudice, with the greater, finer world at my back urging me on.[45]

Of his European journey, he wrote retrospectively almost seven decades later: "Of greatest importance was the opportunity which my Wanderjahre in Europe gave of looking at the world as a man *and not simply from a narrow racial and provincial outlook*."[46] In both passages he describes his European experience as cosmopolitanizing, yet the fact that he also qualifies it in respect to race is not to be overlooked: "Negro" does not disappear as a symbol of identity, but its meaning changes from the predetermined, confining badge of difference it was in the United States to a broader sign which can convey distinctiveness as well as commonality. In other words, double consciousness can be changed from "unreconciled strivings" to "self-conscious manhood" and the black subject can aspire at representativeness beyond racial particularity. Du Bois's building of universal brotherhood on ethnic identity seems to point in the direction of the contemporary debates questioning both the assumed fixity of cosmopolitanism and its radical opposition to identity politics and arguing for the possibility of a cosmopolitics based on the discourses of minorities.

In his writings Du Bois repeatedly credits his traveling as instrumental for him to connect American racism to colonial imperialism and see the exploitation of Africa "as part of my problem of race,"[47] and, above all, to get beyond the parochial sphere African Americans are forced to live in by white supremacism. Yet, such an emphasis on the opening of the spiritual and intellectual sphere is increasingly accompanied, in Du Bois's life-writing, by the detailed description of the concomitant closing down on him of opportunities and freedom of movement. The opposition between America as confinement for blacks—who are forced into a narrow definition of their identity which pinpoints them to their color and are expected to reduce their aspirations to menial labor performed for sheer survival—and the world, where they are free to be human beings with a dark skin, is a recurrent rhetorical structure in Du Bois's works. The mythology of American mobility and fair opportunities for all is repeatedly deconstructed in detailed descriptions of how white expectations about African Americans confine them economically, socially, politically and culturally.

Du Bois chronicles his progress through life, however, less as an ever-widening flânerie, either literal or metaphoric, than as a deepening awareness of the fundamental role of race in determining his and all black subjects' destiny. Rather than breaking free of race responsibility and enjoy the liberality of culture, as Posnock suggests, he came to realize that "one could not be a calm, cool, and detached scientist while Negroes were lynched, murdered and starved."[48] As a young man, Du Bois seemed to view optimistically his possibilities as an individual to rise above the racial veil through culture but his autobiographies, the last one in particular, tell a different story, one that resonates with Matthew Towns's realization that intellect and determination are not enough against racism and that the American Dream does not hold true for black people.

In *The Autobiography*, which he tellingly subtitled *A Soliloquy on Viewing My Life from the Last Decade of Its First Century* as if to underline its "deathbed speech" character, Du Bois crafts a life narrative that obsessively records the closing down of horizons for the black hero who had thought of himself as unique, talented and destined to excel in spite of white supremacism. The early elation of the narrated self at his intellectual superiority which wins him the freedom of higher learning and European traveling—"I dreamed and loved and wandered and sang"[49]—turns into disillusionment and awareness that what he had called "Will and Ability was sheer Luck."[50]

Traveling did more for Du Bois than provide an escape route from the problem of the color line in the U.S., especially since after his early affair with Europe he soon came to understand the global dimensions of the color line and the connections between American racism and European imperialism. Traveling seems to have furnished Du Bois with a framework to interpret his own life as an individual and as a member of an oppressed group on a global scale. *The Autobiography*, as Kenneth Mostern has perceptively written, is more "a narrative of international travel, in which Du Bois looks at the rest of the world as an outsider, a privileged observer" than a narrative of personal identity.[51] The text is peculiarly structured in three parts, with the first—a fifty-page account of his 1958–1959 trip to

Europe, the Soviet Union and China which describes in detail the social conditions of the countries he visited—constructing Du Bois's narratorial persona as a cosmopolite, someone whose value judgments are legitimized by his traveling experience.

His status as a detached observer, then, is merely a strategy to give authority to his belief in the communist nation-state as the only available course to social justice and an alternative to America's racist democracy.[52] "Fifteen times I have crossed the Atlantic and once the Pacific. I have seen the world," writes Du Bois at the beginning of the concluding paragraph, before pronouncing the People's Republic of China a miracle nation and going on to state in the Interlude—a short insert preceding the life narrative proper—"I believe in Communism."[53] While race is what unsettles Du Bois's early naive identification with the mainstream and forces him to become a stern critic of the American status quo, traveling is what enables him to add economy to the picture, which inscribes American racism as a national phenomenon into a global matrix, and to envision a universal brotherhood of the oppressed that is to achieve social justice through communism.

In the 1950s Du Bois experienced severe restriction of his freedom of movement because it was not "to the best interests of the United States" that he went abroad. He had fought hard to preserve his double consciousness as an American and an African, but it was not easy to take his citizenship for granted when mobility, a quintessential American right—and a most symbolic badge of Americanness—was refused to him on the basis of his wishing to exert another right standing for American freedom, the right to dissent. Paul Robeson, who also had his passport revoked in 1950 because of his political activism, devotes a whole chapter of his 1958 political manifesto, *Here I Stand*, to discussing what "the best interests of the United States" are—and he tellingly titles it "Our Right to Travel." Interestingly, Robeson's defense of African Americans' right to travel—and to speak out against racism—is not framed in cosmopolitan terms. Or better, the identity he shares with all other human beings comes as a crescendo after his racial and national identity. "This is my right—as a Negro, as an American, as a man!" he writes, and then proceeds to illustrate how African Americans, from fugitive slaves to those who went north during the Great Migration, from David Walker to Frederick Douglass, Louis Armstrong and W.E.B. Du Bois, have used traveling as a means to fight against U.S. racism and for American democracy.[54]

He ends the chapter quoting Frederick Douglass's vindication of his right to criticize the U.S. as true patriotism—"for he is a lover of his country who rebukes and does not excuse its sins."[55] Likewise, two years later Du Bois would end his last fierce assault on the United States asserting his right as an American of African descent to criticize America. He did so, like other American dissenters before him, speaking from within the typically American tradition of the jeremiad:

I know the United States. It is my country and the land of my fathers. It is still a land of magnificent possibilities. It is still the home of noble souls and generous people. But it is selling its birthright. It is betraying its mighty destiny . . . this is a wonderful America, which the founding fathers dreamed until their sons drowned it in the blood of slavery and devoured it in greed. Our children must rebuild it.[56]

As Sacvan Bercovitch argues in *Rites of Assent*, appropriating the jeremiad is a dangerous move that co-opts dissent into American exceptionalism. Du Bois's celebration of the founding fathers certainly comes as a surprise from such a merciless analyst of the links connecting slavery and freedom since the founding of the United States. It is an indication, however, that in 1960 Du Bois still thought of the U.S. as the main interlocutor of his fight for social justice.

NOTES

1. This is an unproblematized version of cosmopolitanism that both Gilroy and Posnock, in my opinion, seem to uphold, if only because they oppose it to "multiculturalism." The debate on whether we can speak of a single notion of cosmopolitanism without endorsing a problematic Western idea of the universal is very intense, as we can gather from the fact that the term is now often used in the plural and/or qualified by an adjective pointing to its opposite, such as "rooted," "vernacular," "comparative," or "discrepant." See, as an introduction to current revisions of cosmopolitanism, Cheah and Robbins, *Cosmopolitics*.
2. Quoted in D. L. Lewis, "Exit Strategy." *The Crisis*, July–August 2003; http://findarticles.com/p/articles/mi_qa4081/is_200307/ai_n9240656. Accessed 18 October 2006.
3. Du Bois narrates the episode in his *Autobiography*, comparing the patriotism of German students to the impossibility for African Americans, though they revered some white Americans, to have similar feelings "for the nation which held their fathers in slavery for 250 years" (168–169). While in *Dusk of Dawn* the narrator seems to admire Germany as a strong nation and propose it as a model for black nationalism, the issue appears much more complex in the later text, where Du Bois, focusing on the double consciousness that characterizes African American identity, writes that, while listening to German students sing the national anthem, he had realized that he would never experience this kind of untroubled patriotism: "I began to feel that dichotomy which all my life has characterized my thought: how far can love for my oppressed race accord with love for the oppressing country? And when these loyalties diverge, where shall my soul find refuge?" (*Autobiography*, 169).
4. Among the many essays devoted to refuting Appiah's argument, see Outlaw, "'Conserve' Races?"; Gooding-Williams, "Outlaw, Appiah, and Du Bois"; and Taylor, "Appiah's Uncompleted Argument."
5. Appiah, "The Uncompleted Argument," 35.
6. In pre-Emancipation times and well after the Civil War, though the American Colonization Society appeared to African Americans a way well-meaning and less well-meaning white Americans had devised to get rid of free blacks, the colonization project seemed the only viable alternative to racism and economic exploitation. Unlike stern integrationists like Frederick Douglass,

whose response to Harriet Beecher Stowe's initial endorsement of black migration to Liberia was, "The truth is, dear madam, we are here, and here we are likely to remain" (F. Douglass, Letter to Harriet Beecher Stowe. March, 8, 1853; http://teachingamericanhistory.org/library/index.asp?document=771), they believed that separatism was the basis on which to build equality and full citizenship for African Americans. Although early colonization schemes envisioned the U.S. West, Mexico, or other areas in the Americas as likely places to found a black nation, Africa was soon preferred to other sites in the American continent because it carried the mythical connotations upon which nationalisms are to feed.

7. Lewis, *Biography of a Race*, 3.

8. H. Aptheker, "On Du Bois's Move to Africa." *Monthly Review* 45 (December 1993): 36–40; http://findarticles.com/p/articles/mi_m1132/is_n7_v45/ai_14693264. Accessed 20 October 2006.

9. Gilroy, *The Black Atlantic*, 117.

10. Posnock, *Color and Culture*, 45. I am aware that Gilroy's and Posnock's positions on the issue of race are by no means identical—while Gilroy is concerned with the collusion of ethnic absolutism and fascistic/misogynistic representations of blackness in mass culture, for example, and advocates the rejection of "race" as a corrupted notion that cannot be salvaged, Posnock seems to have little interest in what is behind the history of ideas. Yet, since they reach similar conclusions regarding Du Bois's position on race and national identity, I will not use my allotted space to analyze them separately.

11. Gilroy, *The Black Atlantic*, 19.

12. Gilroy, *The Black Atlantic*, 114.

13. In his autobiographical writings, Du Bois repeatedly distances the narrator's awareness of race and class from his younger narrated self's candid belief in the power of talented individuals to fight against prejudice. I deal with this issue in the last part of this chapter.

14. Posnock, *Color and Culture*, 6.

15. Gilroy, in *The Black Atlantic*, titles the chapter devoted to Du Bois "'Cheer the Weary Traveller': W. E. B. Du Bois, Germany, and the Politics of (Dis)placement," and in the first chapter he underlines the significance of Du Bois's choice of Kaiser Wilhelm II as an icon on which to model his own dandyish style (17). Posnock, on the other hand, builds much of his argument on Du Bois's witnessing the Dreyfus Affair while in Europe (*Color and Culture*, 53ff.), but he forgets that Du Bois himself, reporting his trip to Paris in the *Autobiography*, commented that the Dreyfus affair "gained only my passing attention." Like a true aesthete, he had little time for politics and was "fascinated by the glory of French culture in painting, sculpture, architecture and historical monument. I saw Sarah Bernardt; I haunted the Louvre" (*Autobiography*, 177). In the context of the *Autobiography*, however, this is no celebration of his aesthetic taste, even though in the text Europe does indeed play the role of the Old World awakening the racially oppressed to beauty. The passage is one of many where Du Bois's narrative highlights the fact that the younger narrated self still had a naively egocentric approach to the world and, dazzled by European cultural superiority to America, had not yet realized the full import of European racism.

16. Posnock, *Color and Culture*, 91–92 and passim; Gilroy, *The Black Atlantic*, 123.

17. Gilroy, *The Black Atlantic*, 140.

18. The novel's protagonist, Matthew Towns, is an African American medical student who leaves the U.S. in anger and contempt because his registration for an obstetrics course has been rejected due to his race.

19. Posnock, *Color and Culture*, 161.
20. Posnock, *Color and Culture*, 9.
21. Gilroy, *The Black Atlantic*, 144.
22. Gilroy, *The Black Atlantic*, 144.
23. Gilroy, *The Black Atlantic*, 144.
24. Posnock, *Color and Culture*, 173.
25. Posnock, *Color and Culture*, 84.
26. Ahmad, "'More than Romance,'" 792.
27. Du Bois, *Dark Princess*, 297. Further references to this work are included in the text. Between 1951 (Egypt) and 1969 (Guinea-Bissau) most of Africa became independent. As for the emerging interest in *Dark Princess*, see, for example, Rampersad, "Du Bois's Passage to India"; Gregg and Khale, "*The Negro* and *Dark Princess*"; Warren, "An Inevitable Drift?"; Mullen, "Du Bois, *Dark Princess*"; Miller, "W.E.B. Du Bois and the Dandy."
28. Tate's introduction and her later work on the novel (*Psychoanalysis and Black Novels*) marked the beginning of what seems to be a new critical trend moving the analytical focus from Du Bois's sociological and political writings and especially *The Souls of Black Folk*, the work which has attracted most of the critical attention so far, to his more explicitly fictional and autobiographical production. There were a few scholars, however, who anticipated the current interest in Du Bois as a writer, notably Arnold Rampersad, who devoted a volume to Du Bois's "art and imagination" in 1976, and later Richard Kostelanetz (*Politics and the African American Novel*) and Keith Byerman (*Seizing the Word*).
29. Tate, Introduction to *Dark Princess*, xxiii–xxv.
30. Rampersad, *Art and Imagination*, 204. David Levering Lewis considers *Dark Princess* "a complicated propaganda novel" written as "a literary experiment and an antidote to [Harlem] Renaissance excesses" and deems it a failure if compared to other contemporary works such as *The Great Gatsby* and *The Sun Also Rises* (Lewis, *Fight for Equality*, 220). Rampersad does not revise his negative opinion of the novel as "a work of art" in his later essay, "Du Bois's Passage to India" (161), and remains skeptical of Du Bois's theory of literature, but he also adds that "*Dark Princess* is much more than a statement about aesthetics" (162), thus rescuing the novel as a uniquely rich index to Du Bois's thinking.
31. Du Bois, "Book Reviews," *Writings*, 1217; Du Bois, "Two Novels."
32. In 1926, together with Jessie Fauset, he had organized a symposium on "The Negro in Art: How Shall He Be Portrayed?" in *The Crisis*, where artists were asked to interrogate themselves on the criteria by which to evaluate art by or about black people. His own speech, delivered at the Chicago NACCP convention of 1926, "Criteria of Negro Art," argues for the interconnectedness of literature and ideology and deems the notion of art for art's sake an illusion that might become real in a far future, but is a danger for black artists who naively reject utilitarian theories of art in the context of racism. The speech rings quite differently from the famous paragraph he had written at the end of the sixth chapter of *Souls*, "I sit with Shakespeare and he winces not. Across the color line I move arm in arm with Balzac and Dumas, where smiling men and welcoming women glide in gilded halls," which Posnock reads as a paean to the colorblindness of culture. The passage from *Souls* acquires different overtones, however, when read together with "Criteria of Negro Art," where he states that "all Art is propaganda and ever must be, despite the wailing of purists" (Du Bois, "Criteria," 1000). While in 1903 Du Bois certainly believed that culture was a powerful tool to defeat prejudice, the passage, coming as it does at the end of "Of the Training of Black Men," seems more to advocate

the right of the Negro "to be a co-worker in the kingdom of culture" (Du Bois, *Souls*, 365), against Booker T. Washington's idea of a vocational training for African Americans, than a fusion of "aesthetic experience and the erasure of the color line" (Posnock, *Color and Culture*, 104).

33. Du Bois, "Criteria," 993, 995.
34. Du Bois, "Criteria," 995. Du Bois's belief in the power of art to defeat prejudice and stereotypes led him to experiment with different artistic media. On his use of the pageant as a tool to forge a "usable past" for African Americans and help them envision utopian possibilities for the future, see Lorini, "'The Spell of Africa.'"
35. Du Bois, "Criteria," 1001, 999.
36. Gilroy, *The Black Atlantic*, 140.
37. Ahmad, "'More than Romance.'"
38. Du Bois mentions his romantic attachment with Dora Marbach in both *Dusk of Dawn* and the *Autobiography*, but while in the earlier text he devalues the role played by the American couple who warned the Marbach family against interracial marriage—he remarks that the warning was unnecessary because he had already told the girl that marriage between them was impossible (187)—in the *Autobiography* the American woman is the one who sees to it that "no entanglement between me and Dora took place" (161).
39. I have dealt elsewhere with the reason why this role cannot be performed by an African American woman. See Scacchi, "Esuli, principesse e maragià."
40. Carby, *Race Men*, 33.
41. Her mother Elspeth, voodoo woman who lives in a cabin in the swamp and brags she is the granddaughter of a king, is the possessor of the powerful cotton seed coming from Africa.
42. Kautilya, it can be objected, pronounces Matthew's mother an avatar of Kali, so the reverse could hold true as well. But while this can be read as a metaphoric homage in tune with Kautilya's predilection for a highly imagistic style, their hands, equally gnarled and knotted, are literally the same.
43. Du Bois, *Dusk of Dawn*, 581.
44. About twenty years later—when his experience of American racism included an eight-year refusal on the part of the government to grant him a passport on the allegation that it was not in the best interest of the United States that he traveled abroad—he would repeat those words unchanged, but added a phrase which carried his detachment further: "and not from any pride in the Pilgrims" (*Autobiography*, 136).
45. Du Bois, *Darkwater*, 9; my emphasis.
46. Du Bois, *Autobiography*, 159; my emphasis.
47. Du Bois, *Autobiography*, 209.
48. Du Bois, *Dusk of Dawn*, 603; Du Bois, *Autobiography*, 222.
49. Du Bois, *Autobiography*, 183.
50. Du Bois, *Autobiography*, 183.
51. Mostern, *Autobiography*, 76.
52. As William Cain has noted, "Du Bois's grand endorsement of Communism represents his own implacable verdict upon America" ("W.E.B. Du Bois's *Autobiography*," 304).
53. Du Bois, *Autobiography*, 53, 57.
54. Robeson, *Here I Stand*, 64ff.
55. Robeson, *Here I Stand*, 73.
56. Du Bois, *Autobiography*, 419–422.

18 Re-mapping Caribbean Land(Sea)scapes

Aquatic Metaphors and Transatlantic Homes in Caryl Phillips's *The Atlantic Sound*

Elvira Pulitano

> But can't you even imagine what it must feel like to have a true home?
> Toni Morrison, *Paradise*

In a pivotal passage in *The Atlantic Sound*, Caryl Phillips is confronted with the historically charged question, "Where are you from?" The question, fired by Phillips's traveling companion on a plane headed to the West Coast of Africa, inevitably triggers reflections on home and belonging. Phillips writes: "Does he mean, who I am? Does he mean, do I belong? Why does this man not understand the complexity of his question? I make the familiar flustered attempt to answer *the* question. He listens and then spoils it all. 'So my friend, you are going home, to Africa. To Ghana.' *I say nothing.* No, I am not going home."[1]

Home and belonging are indeed highly contested terrain for diasporic subjects forced for one reason or another to migrate. In *Cartographies of Diaspora*, Avtar Brah argues that "the concept of diaspora places the discourse of home and belonging in creative tension, inscribing a homing desire while simultaneously critiquing discourses of fixed origins."[2] Regardless of the kind of diaspora we might want to consider, the notion of home haunts diasporic subjects inhabiting the borderless territory of exile. Born in the Caribbean, Phillips left his native island of St. Kitts as a four-month-old infant when his parents, following the path of many post-World War II West Indian subjects migrating to the "mother country," crossed the Atlantic to take up residency in England. "This migration has had an incalculable effect on who I am," Phillips states, to the extent that a rich layering of transatlantic journeying (British, African diasporan, Caribbean) has become part of his complex, multifaceted sense of self.[3]

Refusing to confine his identity to one single place or, more specifically, to one single idea of home, Phillips cultivates a plural notion of home symbolically dis/located in the Atlantic, "at a point equidistant between Britain, Africa, and North America."[4] Phillips has found in the Atlantic a "watery crossroads" able to give him a sense of belonging while powerfully undermining Western notions of nationality and identity strictly linked to territorial borders. Undoubtedly a powerful trope to reconfigure ethnocentric visions of home, Phillips's Atlantic home, I argue, does not ultimately suggest a flight from the land by affirming a fluid, free-floating seascape in perfect sync with contemporary theorizations of global circulation and travel.[5] With all its aquatic rhizomes, the Atlantic, for Phillips, stretches out to the three symbolic locations that have shaped the history and predicament of his ancestors: England, Africa, and North America (including the Caribbean). And it is such a triangular spatial configuration that Phillips re-maps in *The Atlantic Sound*, in journeys that become at once physical, historical, and psychological. Liverpool (England), Accra (Ghana), and Charleston (South Carolina) are the three major cities associated with the transatlantic slave trade across which Phillips travels in the attempt to understand the meaning of home for the descendants of the African diaspora. Reading through the richly layered narrative of Phillips's travelogue, we realize how the author is bound to land as much as he is to sea and that the two elements are powerfully yoked together in what could be termed a geography of land(sea)scapes.

TIDALECTIC MOVEMENTS

In her reading of *The Atlantic Sound*, Bénédicte Ledent emphasizes the "ternary topography" of the book, but overlooks the importance of an additional location in Phillips's transatlantic cartography: the Caribbean. *The Atlantic Sound* opens with a prologue titled "Atlantic Crossings," which describes Phillips's journey from the French-Caribbean island of Guadeloupe to England aboard a banana boat. Reenacting his parents' migration from St. Kitts to England as well as the migration of so many other West Indian subjects of the *Windrush* generation, Phillips realizes how different his travels are from that first generation of West Indian migrants: "I realize that I do not feel the sense of nervous anticipation that almost forty years ago characterized my parents' arrival, and that of their entire generation. . . . I have traveled toward Britain with a sense of knowledge and propriety, irrespective of what others, including my fellow passengers, might think" (21–22). That such a sense of propriety cannot give Phillips a kind of closure or, more significantly, as Ledent suggests, a sense of "home" in England becomes evident upon considering the obsessive presence of the word "home" in each of the three main narrative sections.[6] But the importance of the prologue, I argue, goes beyond problematic theorizations of home and belonging.

Phillips's departing point is not his native St. Kitts but Guadeloupe, the island that retains more than any other the strongest links with Europe and

European culture. By choosing such an important strategic location Phillips foregrounds his migrant trajectories in the spatiotemporal complexity of the Caribbean region, a crosscultural dynamic entity combining island space and open sea in an intricate system of closed insularity and incessant traveling. Critical of notions of roots clearly reflected in nostalgic feelings and anachronistic attempts to return to mother Africa, Phillips looks at the Caribbean as the most tangible example of the fact that what history has broken cannot be made whole. "Africa cannot cure. Africa cannot make anybody feel home. Africa is not a psychiatrist" (216), Phillips writes in the section of the book set in Ghana and titled, "Homeward Bound."

In his theoretical study of the Caribbean, Antonio Benítez-Rojo characterizes the region as a meta-archipelago, a dynamic entity having "neither a boundary nor a center."[7] As a meta-archipelago, the Caribbean contours stretch out toward Africa, Europe, India, and North America, its intricate history of travels, migrations, and creolization providing a perfect model for our twenty-first-century transnational world order. Crucial in Benítez-Rojo's vision is the presence of the sea as a space of uncharted historiography, an element in flux that defies national and territorial boundaries therefore providing a perfect unifying trope to the chaotic scattering of the islands. Drawing from post-structuralist theorists Gilles Deleuze and Félix Guattari, as well as on the scientific discourse of chaos theory, Benítez-Rojo conceives of the Caribbean as an aquatic rhizome, a problematic concept that, as has been noted, conveniently avoids the entanglements with history and ultimately contributes to "dehistoricizing" the region.[8] As attractive as it might appear in a Caribbean context, Deleuze's and Guattari's poetics of travel as a model for postmodern subjectivity raises some doubts when applied uncritically to any discourse of displacement. According to Caren Kaplan, "Deleuze and Guattari are suggesting that we are all deterritorialized on some level in the process of language itself and that this is a point of contact between 'us all.' . . . Theirs is a poetics of travel where there is no return ticket and we all meet, therefore, en train."[9]

Kaplan goes on to argue that it is important, when considering theoretical positions that advocate discourses of mobility, to ask whether people "*choose* deterritorialization or whether deterritorialization has chosen [them]."[10] Questions such as these have been also investigated by Martinican writer and critic Édouard Glissant. Glissant criticizes Deleuze and Guattari for silencing the discourse of *other* cultures, whose "errantry is in effect immobile" since "they have never experienced the melancholy and extroverted luxury of uprooting."[11] What these theorists are at pains to demonstrate is that a postmodern approach to theories of travel and nomadism inevitably reveals its ethnocentric bias in the denial of the importance of "place" and "history."[12]

Glissant's *Poetics of Relation* opens with a chapter entitled "The Open Boat," in which the critic evokes aquatic origins for the dislocated people of the African diaspora. "The entire ocean, the entire sea, gently collapsing in the end into the pleasures of sand, make one vast beginning, but a beginning whose time is marked by these balls and chains gone green."[13] Although materially unmarked by monuments or gravestones, the sea for Glissant "is History" in the sense suggested by Derek Walcott's eponymous poem: "a grey vault" locking up the battles, martyrs, and tribal memory of the millions of people traveling the (in)famous routes of the Middle Passage.[14] In Glissant's formulations, the sea then is a powerful trope to reconfigure the spatiotemporal complexity of the Caribbean region, at the same time as it is a powerful site of historical violence. In this sense, I concur with Elizabeth Deloughrey's assertion that "the sea enters history" and w/rites the innumerable stories/voices silenced by colonial historiography.[15]

The crucial role that the sea plays in *The Atlantic Sound* clearly suggests Phillips's awareness of a tradition of Middle Passage narratives with which his own travel book inevitably conducts dialogue. Once aboard the MV *Horncap*, the vessel that will transport Phillips across the Atlantic, he abandons himself to the rhythms and sounds of the ocean while undergoing the various moods that a long journey by water ultimately projects: freedom, boredom, depression, anxiety. "I have actually come to like the rhythm of life on the Atlantic Ocean. I want to see land; I want to go home, I definitely want to leave this banana boat, but I have a feeling that I will miss the sea" (20). While in Liverpool, Phillips finds himself "looking for the sea" since he closely associates the city with the maritime activities that made it one of the most active ports during the transatlantic slave trade. During his sojourn in Ghana, in which he encounters various figures of the pan-Africanist movement, he often finds himself sitting in front of the sea, "looking out at the rough Atlantic breaking over the rocks and then surging up the beach."[16] Ironically, the Atlantic provides the background to places such as Elmina Castle, a fort built by the Portuguese in the fifteenth century which would be transformed into a storage place for slaves. As one of the repatriated African Americans puts it, "If the Atlantic Ocean was to dry up there would be a double highway from the Cape to Jamaica paved with African bones" (153).

A landmark in the history of Middle Passage narratives, Elmina castle houses the (in)famous "door of no return," the last stop for captives before boarding the slave ship, the last connecting point with the continent before the diaspora.[17] In the consciousness of blacks, the door has become a spiritual location, a place of pilgrimage for Africans in the diaspora to visit in the attempt to come to terms with the burden of history. Phillips's account of the encounter with Elmina, however, is narrated in that distinctively detached and "always too controlled"[18] tone that characterizes most of the writing in *The Atlantic Sound*, a tone that ultimately betrays his profound skepticism toward the ideology of return. Focusing on the encounter between the Portuguese captain-general Azambuja and the African king Caramansa, Phillips meditates on the complicity of Africans in the overall machinery of European trade in human beings. And yet, Phillips's refusal to adopt a rhetoric of victimization by demonizing whites *tout court* does not prevent him from voicing a severe critique against the collective historical amnesia that pervades white Anglo-European and American cultures. In Charleston, Phillips visits Sullivan's Island in search of the "pest houses" where slaves used to be "quarantined" before being transferred to the mainland. Unable to find any trace of such haunting sites since nobody ever bothered to erect a monument or a plaque, Phillips reflects: "It should, after all, be one of the most significant sites in the United States: the place where over 30 per cent of the African population first landed in the North American world. The black Ellis Island" (257).

Discussing the structure of *The Atlantic Sound*, Ledent detects "a wave-like movement . . . that constantly flows forward and backward, like the sea," a formal technique reminiscent of the diasporic quality of most of Phillips's novels.[19] To Ledent's commentary, I would add that such an ebb and flow movement, as well as Phillips's personal Atlantic crossings, are to be envisioned within a tradition of Caribbean discourse that has drawn attention to the dynamic relationship between land and sea. Barbadian poet and critic Kamau Brathwaite has conceptualized the notion of "tidalectics" to describe the cyclic movement of water backward and forward. With the obvious play on the term *tide* and the prefix *-dia, tidalectics*, for Brathwaite, involves the rejection of the notion of Hegelian dialectic and points instead to an ebb and flow process that is circular and repetitive (rather than linear and progressive).[20] Similarly, for Glissant, *tidalectics* calls attention to the dynamic relationship between beach and ocean reinscribing thus the landscape within the fluidity of the sea. Crucial to such tidalectic movements is the process of reclaiming history or histories and of digging deep into the collective memory that in the Caribbean, according to Glissant, was "broken up by sterile barriers."[21] For Glissant, "history as a consciousness at work" and "history as lived experience" are not the terrain of investigation of historians only. The creative writer has as much to say as the historian in the archeological process of excavating the past.[22]

In *The Atlantic Sound* Phillips takes on the role of the historian as much as he does that of the non-fiction creative writer. History, and particularly the obliterated history of the slave trade, is once again the true protagonist of the book. According to Ledent, the "sound" of the title evokes the voices of the various protagonists populating the English port of Liverpool, Elmina, and Charleston, the three cities linked to the slave trade toward which Phillips is bound to travel.[23] But the Atlantic sound refers also to the innumerable voices silenced during the Middle Passage—when it was common practice to prevent slaves from speaking their mother tongues—as well as to those endless floating bodies dissipated in salt water for whom the sea became inexorably "home," as D'Aguiar's novel powerfully reminds us.[24] Redolent with the voices of history, the sound of the ocean inevitably refers to contemporary travelers such as Phillips himself, who now revisit those same places in the attempt to come to terms with the horrors of the past. Backward and forward like the endless movement of the sea, *The Atlantic Sound* resonates with a polyphony of voices that account for the complex experience of the African diaspora. Like in *Crossing the River*, Phillips opposes a series of private, intimate stories reflecting the complexity and diversity of the human condition and the tension permeating individuals whose lives and circumstances are torn apart by incomprehensible historical forces. Discussing the indictment of large-scale oppression such as slavery and colonialism on the one hand, and acceptance of personal complicity on the other, Phillips states:

> I've never really been able to accept the fact that one should regard slavery, or something like colonial incursion into Africa or the Caribbean, as being something to be just condemned in the way that a historian or a sociologist might condemn it. To me, individuals are ultimately much more complicated than historical forces or historical events. There is a tension because the individual is often mired in an ambiguous situation that historical narratives don't capture. As long as I'm writing about individuals whose lives are torn apart by events and circumstances that are out of their control, and who find themselves powerless to respond, there will inevitably be a tension. Those individuals who are washed ashore and find themselves marooned in a very strange place by history are often the people that interest me the most.[25]

The three main sections that comprise *The Atlantic Sound* stage this tension quite effectively. Woven within the historical accounts linked to the slave trade—particularly the role of the three major cities in the trading triangle—are the narrated lives of isolated individuals including the author himself, whose ambivalent feelings cannot be captured by the dry accounts of officialized discourse. The first section, "Leaving Home," tells of the lonely trip to Liverpool of John Ocansey, the Fulani adopted son of a prominent African trader, who, in the last part of the nineteenth century, traveled to the British port in order to investigate the financial loss of his father. In the attempt to convey the spiritual and cultural transformation produced by the diaspora experience on isolated individuals, Phillips projects his novelist's sensitivity onto a historical character, probing Ocansey's mind with the same imaginative vision he displays in his fiction and ultimately blurring the line between fiction and non-fiction. A pious Christian and devoted son, Ocansey is soon confronted with the entanglements of the British justice system and with his ambivalent feelings toward his own identity as an African assimilated into Christian beliefs. He certainly finds insulting certain preconceived notions toward the African still prevailing in the city of Liverpool; and yet, the narrator tells us, "he had no desire to put himself in a position where he had either to defend his people, or chastise his hosts for their uncivilized behavior" (65).

To further enhance Ocansey's alienation, Phillips punctuates his story with brief, lyrical passages hinting at the complicity of Africans in the slave trade: "*The African dispatches the money to the white man and his African heart swells with pride. . . . Time passes. The white man is silent. African voices begin to whisper. . . . And then he discovers himself to be floundering in a place of despair. . . . The African has dispatched money to the white man. And now his heart is heavy with grief*" (23). Functioning almost like a chorus, such italicized passages remind us of the voice of the transhistorical father figure in *Crossing the River*, who, in 1752, sold his children to an eighteenth-century slave trader, "a desperate foolishness" that would haunt him two hundred fifty years later. Again and again Phillips avoids falling into the trap of binary thinking by pitting Africa against Europe, blacks against whites, and probes instead the psychological complexity of historical economic contingencies and the way they blur the line between enslavers and slaves, oppressors and victims.[26] In *The Atlantic Sound*, the "historical voices" contribute to John's confusion in what is already a "complex" relationship with his "father." John's sojourn in Liverpool lasts a few months, long enough, however, for him to reflect on the emotional effects that the forced separation from one's homeland ultimately produces on isolated subjects. More importantly, he realizes that something about the "complexity of Liverpool" will not ease his return trip to Africa.

The complexity of Liverpool weighs heavily across the centuries. The transition to Phillips's personal account of his trip to the city is signaled with a quotation from Richard Wright's *Black Power*: "Yet, how calm, innocent, how staid Liverpool looked in the June sunshine! What massive and solidly built buildings! From my train window I could catch glimpses of a few church spires punctuating the horizon. Along the sidewalks men and women moved unhurriedly. Did they ever think of their city's history?" (93–94). Phillips's first impressions of Liverpool seem to counteract such a forceful desire to forget the past. He is struck by "the satanic quality of the station," and he first senses "something disturbing about Liverpool" (94–95). Despite the fact that the inner-city violence of the 1970s and 1980s seems to have declined and that the city (by the early 1990s) does show "a suspiciously multiracial quality"—to the extent that the captain of the Liverpool football team is a black man—Phillips is never at ease in this place. Sitting on a bench overlooking the Albert Dock, he goes back to his childhood, when upon reading *Wuthering Heights* he had been struck by the dirty, ragged, black-haired child that Mr. Earnshaw, most certainly "motivated by a sense of charity," had brought back from Liverpool. Although no textual evidence in Brontë's novel suggests that Heathcliff might have had "Negro blood," upon looking around the docks, Phillips thinks that it must have been in this area that "the dark apparition" named Heathcliff was first spotted. He writes: "not for the first time in my life, I close my eyes and try to solve the puzzle of this seven-year-old boy's origins" (115). Having visited the landmark monuments linked to the slave trade—the Grand Town Hall and the Maritime Museum permanent exhibition—Phillips is ultimately relieved that he is living, for, as he puts it, "it is disquieting to be in a place where history is so physically present, yet so glaringly absent from people's consciousness" (117). One of the main goals of Phillips's travelogue (and, I would argue, of his entire oeuvre) is precisely to make history, and in this case the history of the Middle Passage, "physically present" in people's consciousness, for it is only through an understanding of what really happened in the past that we can come to terms with some of the anxieties around issues of race as they confront us today, in this increasingly transnational and transcultural world we all live in.

TRANSATLANTIC HOMES

In a poem titled "Postlude/Home," included in his 1967 collection *Rights of Passage*, Brathwaite poignantly asks: "Where then is the nigger's/home? In Paris Brixton Kingston/Rome?/Here?/Or in Heaven?"[27] As complex as the "Where are you from?" question Phillips is asked by the Ghanaian man while traveling to Africa, Brathwaite's question suggests that for the Africans in the diaspora home might ultimately reside elsewhere, everywhere and nowhere. In the second section of *The Atlantic Sound*, titled "Homeward Bound," Phillips undertakes Brathwaite's search for a home in painfully obsessive terms. The longest and richest section of the book when it comes to the layering of intertwined stories and narrative voices, it presents Phillips's own voice and dispassionate commentary much more strongly than in the previous section. Phillips's envious feelings for Ben, his fellow passenger who is *truly* returning home, comfortably secured in his Ghanaian identity, allow him to investigate the significance of Africa as home for the descendants of the diaspora.

In the story of Mansour Nassirudeen, a friend of a friend expelled from England for being an illegal immigrant, a man forced to return to his native Ghana without having fulfilled his aspirations to become a writer, Phillips perceives a slightly different version of his own life story: "Perhaps, it was wrong that I should be in any way judging this man who had not had the opportunities that I had" (139). Mansour's dream is to leave Ghana to go to America and get the famous degree that would allow him to move up in the economic and social sphere. Upon Phillips's suggestion that he should work his way up within the Ghanaian society, Mansour responds by saying that "the only way up in Ghana is out" (197). One in the long line of "(un)belonging citizens"[28] produced by the African diaspora, Mansour seems to have fallen into the trap of a nationalistic consciousness that in Frantz Fanon's terms "demands solid investments and quick returns."[29] Despite his sympathy and willingness to help, Phillips does not spare a note of criticism to his Ghanaian chauffeur friend. He writes: "Mansour

who has not even bothered to apply for jobs since returning t
country. A democratic country of eighteen million people wi
economy. Mansour who has spent all of his time looking fo'
Mansour, African supplicant. . . . Able-bodied, smart Mansou., ,
himself as 'third-world' victim" (197–198).

All the more critical is Phillips of the African Americans who have
returned "home" to settle in the mother country. Kohain Halevi is one such
man. Having bought two plots of land in Elmina, he has dedicated himself to establishing "a whole infrastructure" so that all African Americans
in the diaspora can return. He has also been working on "a sensitization
programme," hoping to turn the recently purchased Abanze Castle into the
equivalent of the Wailing Wall for the Jews, a place of pilgrimage where
Africans can "cleanse their spirits." Phillips writes:

> I listen to Kohain, but I remain somewhat unconvinced. As he tells me
> that slavery happened because the Almighty ordained it for those who
> disobeyed his commandments, I bite my tongue. . . . I look at Kohain
> as he convinces himself. Suddenly, he seems a long way from home.
> Wayne Boykin from Mount Vernon [Kohain's place of birth, north of
> New York city]. Already it has been a long journey. (207)

How does one "go back" to the past, Phillips asks a renowned Ghanaian
Pan-Africanist earlier in the narrative (144). The answer triggers a whole
conversation on slavery, history and responsibility. Dr. Ben Abdallah firmly
believes that "one does not go back" at all, but that "it is all moving forward." Whereas cultures from all over the world have always adapted and
changed naturally to the influence of other cultures, abandoning what is
no longer of use to them and borrowing from the other, Africa has been
denied this process. As a consequence, the best way toward the future,
for Dr. Abdallah, is to look into the past and see what of any value Africans can still bring to the present (144–145). Admiring his interlocutor's
passion, Phillips nonetheless soon discovers that even the most liberal and
forward-looking pan-Africanist thinker is not free from the traps of ethnocentric biases. Discussing the importance of African holocaust shrines such
as Elmina and Cape Coast Castle, Dr. Abdallah posits that these places
"should be given to those in the diaspora to look after" (149). Clearly
drawing a line between who is African and who is not, he argues that
Africans do not need to be reminded of their history because they know.
"*For us*," he says, "[these places] do not mean the same thing as they do
for you people." Shaking his host's hands at the end of the discussion, a
disillusioned Phillips meditates: "So much for Pan-Africanism, I thought.
'You people?'" (149).

The more Phillips becomes involved in the pan-African spirit in the
attempt to unpack the mystery and complexity of the "return home" question, the more he realizes the differences binding the descendants of the

African diaspora. He sympathizes with Kate, the hotel manager, who is fighting a lost battle against a contingent of Jamaican "pilgrims" who, she tells him, smoke dope and cook in their hotel bedrooms, in the belief that "if they dress down and filthy then they are being African" (215). He attends the Panafest celebrations at Elmina and Cape Coast, advertised as the "biggest gathering of the African family to celebrate our cultural unity" (143). Wondering as to the significance of these events, Phillips skeptically meditates: "Welcome to Panafest. Prepare to be swept away by the romance of home" (168). As he moves backward and forward, alternating narrative sections chronicling the Panafest events along with the historical account of Elmina Castle, Phillips becomes all the more convinced of the absurdity of the "Panafesting" concept. To the Panafest feeling of cultural unity and brotherhood, Phillips forcefully responds with a highly fragmented narrative and polyphonic text clearly, suggesting that the strength for the descendants of the African diaspora is to be found in fracture and dispersal rather than in a utopian mythic return to a lost homeland. Within this context, the most symbolic narrative of "Homeward Bound" remains the story of Philip Quaque, the eighteenth-century African minister educated in London who decided to turn a blind eye to the horrors of slavery.

Strategically placed after the historical section on Elmina and in the middle of the Panafest celebrations, Quaque's story becomes symbolic of the complexity of historical forces and events Phillips mentions in the interview excerpt quoted earlier. Upon reading the minister's letters, Phillips realizes that Quaque's ambivalence betrays one more story of loss: "Loss of home, loss of language, loss of self, but never loss of dignity" (180). The story of the minister who "lived and worked through the height of the slave trade" without, however, ever referring to "'his brothers and sisters' in the dungeons beneath his feet" (179) makes very clear, Phillips maintains, why slogans such as "One Love" and "One Africa" ultimately remain a pure illusion and a merely touristic attraction.

In the concluding essay in *A New World Order*, titled "The High Anxiety of Belonging," Phillips writes how he wishes his ashes to be scattered in the middle of the Atlantic Ocean, at a point equidistant from Britain, Africa, and North America, a site which he has come to identify as his "Atlantic home." He writes:

> Across the centuries, countless millions have traversed this water, and unlike myself, these people have not always had the luxury of choice. They have felt alienated from, or abandoned by, the societies that they have hitherto known as "home." They have hoped that somewhere, over the horizon, there might be a new place where they might live and raise their children. These are the people that I have written about during the course of the past twenty years, and as one book has led to another, I have grown to understand that I am, of course, writing about myself in some oblique, though not entirely unpredictable, way.[30]

Phillips's conceptualization of the Atlantic Home comes at a point when passionate debates surrounding the scholarship of Atlantic Studies increasingly call for a reconceptualization of the field. As various critics—including some of the contributors to the present volume—have clearly pointed out, Paul Gilroy's study of transatlantic modernity, as influential as it has been, ultimately reveals its ethnocentric biases by revolving around a North European/North American cartography that excludes Africa, the Caribbean, and South America.[31] Reinscribing the discourse of Africa (and the Caribbean) back into the triangular equation that marked the transatlantic slave trade (an equation connecting Europe, Africa, and the Americas) has been one of the main goals of Phillips's writing and teaching.[32] Within this context, it could be argued that all the stories narrated in *The Atlantic Sound* (as well as all his other works displaying a "ternary topography") mark an important step in the on-going redefinition of Atlantic Studies and ultimately provide a significant corrective to Gilroy's theories of transatlantic modernity.

Like Gilroy, Phillips is rather skeptical of essentialist definitions of identity and would argue that any conception of black identity as ethnically and racially homogeneous is absolutely untenable in light of the transnational and intercultural network of routes that the transatlantic slave trade opened up. Whereas Gilroy takes the image of the ship—the quintessential symbol of the Black Atlantic economy and "a living micro-cultural, micro-political system in motion" in itself[33]—as the starting point of his critical investigation, Phillips in *The Atlantic Sound* uses his journey aboard the MV vessel from the Caribbean back to England as a means to reinscribe the Caribbean land(sea)scape in the transatlantic routes of the African diaspora. Whereas Gilroy cites black figures such as Equiano, Phillis Wheatley, Martin Delany, Marcus Garvey and Bob Marley as significant examples of historical travelers who would challenge identitarian politics linked to territory or blood, Phillips focuses on less known but equally emblematic historical figures such as John Ocansey and Philip Quaque, and extends his analysis to include contemporary diasporic citizens such as Mohammed Mansour Nassirudeen, who travels from Ghana to England and back to Ghana in a sort of reversal of the first leg of the triangular trade routes used by European merchants. Whereas Gilroy embraces the notion of diaspora as a valuable alternative to reassess "nationalist and raciological thinking,"[34] forcefully reminding us that neither Equiano (despite his scheme to repatriate eighteenth-century London blacks to Sierra Leone) nor Wheatley ever went back to take up residence in the African homelands from which their original journeys through slavery had started, and that not even Bob Marley went to Africa to make a home, Phillips presents us with human stories of diaspora experience that hardly ever get recorded in historical official records. The protagonists of Phillips's fiction and non-fiction articulate in painful but powerful terms some of Gilroy's theorization around the concept of diaspora as "a concept that problematizes the cultural and historical mechanics of belonging." Diaspora, Gilroy further states, "disrupts the fundamental power of territory to determine identity by breaking the simple sequence of explanatory links between place, location, and consciousness."[35]

Phillips's approach to notions of home and belonging as well as his forceful critique to ideas of pure origins and true self would find him in perfect agreement with Gilroy's critical construct. Phillips nevertheless goes beyond Gilroy's "cartography of celebratory journeys" in which the Middle Passage, Joan Dayan notices in a forceful critique of *The Black Atlantic*, "becomes a metaphor anchored somewhere in a vanishing history."[36] She argues that, by focusing on the "transcultural circulation" and "nomadism" of "a minority of educated elites" (Delany, Douglass, DuBois, and Wright to mention just a few), Gilroy conveniently blurs the difference between "choice" and "forced migration."[37] Whereas history, in Gilroy's theoretical construct, is fashionably turned into a transnational, diasporic narrative of black modernity and the Middle Passage conveniently subsumed within the current transnational circulation of global forces, history, in Phillips's transatlantic narratives, is articulated in the stories of the innumerable individuals (both victims and perpetrators) whose lives have been disrupted by forces beyond their control. More importantly, according to Ledent, Phillips is always alert to the effects of history on the descendants of the African diaspora.[38] All the stories of displacement and fragmentation that make up *The Atlantic Sound* inevitably point to the fact that homelessness and (un)belonging are ultimately a painful experience for the descendants of the African diaspora; they are indeed, Ledent suggests, "a far cry from the glamour and adventurousness that one sometimes associates today with trans-national living."[39]

A transnational, diasporic subject himself, one for whom, we might say, traveling and migration are ultimately inscribed within the pleasures of mobility and surplus characterizing twenty-first-century migrant intellectuals, Phillips has embraced travel as a way of constantly reinterpreting and reinventing his multifarious, composite self. That such reinterpretation might ultimately present the most complex, and by no means comfortable, turns is what his writing is all about. When, during his first West African visit, a hotel waiter, upon hearing the news of the death of Lady Diana, expresses his sincere sympathy for what he thinks is a deeply tragic event for any British citizen, Phillips replies:

> These days we are all unmoored. Our identities are fluid. Belonging is a contested state. Home is a place riddled with vexing questions. . . . I want to tell Daniel that this boy has had to understand the Africa of his ancestry, the Caribbean of his birth, the Britain of his upbringing, and the United States where he now resides, as one harmonious entity. He has tried to write in the face of a late-twentieth century world that has sought to reduce identity to unpalatable clichés of nationality or race.[40]

That a British passport does not make a person necessarily "belong" to the place that issued such a passport is something that Daniel, the hotel waiter, seems to overlook, bound as he is to preconceived Western notions of nationality and race. Along with countless other individuals comfortably secured in their rooted identity, Daniel seems to forget that for some people caught in-between, for migrants, asylum seekers, and refugees created by the forces of history, the question of where to belong is ultimately an existential dilemma.

As stated above in relation to Phillips's account of his trip to Elmina, one of the most recurrent criticisms against the narrative in *The Atlantic Sound* has been his analytical distance and sharply humorous tone, which at times turns into mocking irony. Especially in the second and third sections of the book, Phillips has been accused of distancing himself, becoming "an indifferent even dispassionate observer" à la V.S. Naipaul.[41] And yet I argue that Phillips's analytic distance betrays a much more complex relation with its subject of investigation. As he puts it in *A New World Order*, he is "of, and not of, this place" (whether Africa, North America, and/or England), belonging and at the same time not belonging to the strategic locations that have marked the transatlantic geography of the African diaspora. Each of the three points of the triangle cannot constitute *home* for Phillips, if we consider *home* from within the traditional Aristotelian conception of place as bounded locality. Phillips's notion of home in *The Atlantic Sounds* comes close to bell hooks's definition, according to which "home is no longer just one place. It is locations. . . . One confronts and accepts dispersal and fragmentation as part of the constructions of a new world order that reveals more fully who we are, who we can become."[42]

Ironically, "Home" is the title of the last section of *The Atlantic Sound*, which, however, significantly disrupts the readers' expectations in terms of tone and content. Despite the fact that Phillips has now been living in the United States for more than fifteen years, is a resident there, and America constitutes the subject of his most recent writing,[43] America cannot provide him with a feeling of home as it is testified by his incessant traveling à la recherche of "a sense of belonging somewhere."[44] Phillips's last chapter focuses on the story of J. Waties Waring, a white judge in Charleston, champion of equal rights for blacks, who in 1947 opened white Democratic primaries to "Negro voters." Waring's story is, once again, a story of isolation and loss. Ostracized by the conservative Charlestonian community for his anti-slavocratic ideals, chastised by the same community for divorcing his Southern belle wife to marry a Detroit-born, independent, and outspoken woman who befriended blacks, Judge Waring would also experience the psychological wounds of exile. "In 1952 Judge Waring was a seventy-two-year-old man who was unhappy with the insults, the ostracization, and the mental anguish of being a pariah in the land that he loved. He was painfully out of tune with his home, and he decided that he had no choice but to leave. It was simply too burdensome to be among those who openly hated you in a place you called home" (255). Judge Waring and his second wife, Elizabeth, would take up residency in New York, but "New York," Phillips writes, "was not home" (263).

Though considerably shorter compared to the other sections of the book, "Home" is structured in similarly polyphonic terms. An epigraph from Robert Frost, stating that "Home is the place where, when you go, they have to take you in," further conveys Phillips's ambiguous feelings about home. For all the romance usually attached to the very meaning of the term, Phillips suggests that home, in the disrupted world of the colonial space, can indeed be a slippery concept. It can be "a mythic place of desire,"[45] as Brah puts it, a place where diasporic subjects know that they will never be able to return. But home in the diasporic imagination can also *become* a place re-created again and again to coincide with the kinds of fictions Salman Rushdie has envisioned in portraying the condition of writers such as himself, diasporic individuals who can retrieve the lost homes only as "imaginary homelands."[46] Interwoven within Judge Waring's story are excerpts of newspaper articles, letters, legal documents, Phillips's own historical account of the role of Charleston as a gateway city "between Philadelphia and the Caribbean," a city "reaching across the Atlantic to Africa and Europe" (232), fragments upon fragments nicely shored up within Phillips's attempt at remembering a collective memory. The section relating Judge Waring's feelings of alienation and displacement is juxtaposed with Phillips's visit at Sullivan's Island. Individual exile triggers images of a historical collective dispersion:

> Sullivan's Island is an eerie and troubled place. Flat, marsh, grassland. An arrival in America. Having crossed the Atlantic in the belly of a ship. An arrival. Here, in America. Step ashore, out of sight of Charleston. To be fed, watered, scrubbed, prepared. To be sold. Back home, a similar fate. Different vegetation. Different birds. Family. An arrival. Low, low land. Water. The mainland lying low in the hazy distance. Charleston. Farewell Africa. Welcome to America. (257–258)

Passages such as these clearly show that Phillips's main interest in *The Atlantic Sound* is always for human complexity and for individuals in search of an elsewhere that can be called home. Ledent suggests that *The Atlantic Sounds* (as well as Phillips's fiction in general) provides a pragmatic counterdiscourse to abstract theorizations of diaspora.[47] As a writer, Phillips is more interested in probing the psychological implications of the diaspora phenomenon, bringing human stories of dispersion and fragmentation to the foreground of what is often conceived of as a purely social-scientific and theoretical concept. Against visions of diaspora evoking "imagery of traumas of separation and dislocation,"[48] which he obviously acknowledges as an important aspect of the migratory experience, I would argue that

Phillips looks at diasporas as "potentially sites of hope and new beginning," contested sites "where individual and collective memories collide, reassemble and reconfigure."⁴⁹ As he watches an African dance performed by five young African black women, Phillips meditates:

> Here in this city which "processed" nearly one-third of the African population which arrived in the United States, a population who were encouraged to forget Africa, to forget their language, to forget their families, to forget their culture, to forget their dances, five young women try to remember. Five young black women attempt to liberate their souls and their spirits. Sandy? Margaret? Joan? Susan? Kim? I imagine that they have already taken an African name for themselves. They do not share it. Their sinewy bodies weave invisible threads that connect them to the imagined old life. (264)

Against the pervasive amnesia that characterizes the cities linked to the slave trade, Phillips constantly reminds us that the healing process can only occur with a courageous act of remembering.

DIASPORIC JOURNEYS

In an article published in *The Guardian* titled "Necessary Journeys," Phillips has discussed the importance of travel for writers of Afro-Caribbean origins in the West:

> The gift of travel has been enabling for me in the same way it has been enabling for those writers in the British tradition, those in the African diaspora tradition, and those in the Caribbean tradition, many of whom have found it necessary to move in order that they might reaffirm for themselves the fact that dual and multiple affiliations feed our constantly fluid sense of self. . . . As a young writer, travel enabled me to understand the importance of constantly reinterpreting and, if necessary, reinventing oneself is an admirable legacy of living in our modern culturally and ethnically fluid world.⁵⁰

The Atlantic Sound ends, in line with most of Phillips's fiction, en route. Phillips travels to Israel, where two thousand African Americans are attempting to create a utopian community of "Black Hebrews" in the Negev desert. The desert landscape appears hostile and entrapping. Phillips describes it as "sudden, unpredictable and rash" (267), a land that regardless of the season conveys stasis and stagnation, in stark contrast with the borderless fluidity of the sea conveyed in "Atlantic Crossings." Phillips's tone is all the more dispassionate and detached as he observes these Hebrew Israelites firmly convinced that all Africans must return "home." While they find inspiration in biblically based beliefs passionately rekindled by Bob Marley and the Rastafari movement, Phillips wonders why he does not/cannot understand their cause. Perhaps the answer is to be found in the final passages of the book, in which Phillips recounts his experience at an evening performance in the desert town of Dimona. Upon his minister's friend invitation to take a look at the desert landscape, to observe its astonishing beauty, Phillips redirects his gaze thinking that there is nothing he can say. His "gaze" is directed to a different kind of landscape, to that layering of journeys by land and sea that compels him to incessant travel in search for those homes that, as a repository of history, might give him a sense of "diasporic belonging."⁵¹

Written in the second person voice, the final paragraph clearly suggests that Phillips's quest is not over, that there is no ultimate promised land, no "closure" to soothe the wandering spirit of the Africans in the diaspora:

> You were transported in a wooden vessel across a broad expanse of water to a place which rendered your tongue silent. Look. Listen. Learn. And as you began to speak, you remembered fragments of a former life. Shards of memory. Careful. Some will draw blood. You dressed your memory in the new words of this new country. Remember. There were no round-trip tickets in your part of the ship. Exodus. It is futile to walk into the face of history. (275)

Phillips's voice here merges the personal and the historical, his story moving along and across the collective stories of his African ancestors, for whom, once they stepped beyond the door of no return onto the ship, a metamorphosis into something different would inexorably begin. With his triple heritage of journeying, Phillips keeps traveling across the Atlantic bridging land and sea, past and present, feeling of, and not of, these places but ultimately and paradoxically creating a sense of "home" in what he terms "my increasingly precious, imaginary, Atlantic world."⁵²

NOTES

1. Phillips, *The Atlantic Sound*, 125. Further references to this work are included in the text.
2. Brah, *Cartographies of Diaspora*, 192–193.
3. D. Morrison, "A Writer of Wrongs." *Time Europe*, May 19, 2003; www.time.com/time/europe/magazine/article/0,13005,901030519–450955,00.html. Accessed 30 September 2005.
4. Phillips, *A New World Order*, 304.
5. See Appadurai, "Disjuncture and Difference," 328–329. Appadurai has found in the suffix "scape" a useful trope to conceptualize the fluid, irregular landscapes which characterize international capital and global circulation today. My use of the term *land(sea)scape* in this chapter is to a certain extent indebted to Appadurai—it certainly reflects ongoing debates on contemporary transnational circulations of people and ideas—but is also and

more importantly perhaps, inscribed within a Caribbean historical context. I clarify this point later on in my discussion.

6. Ledent, "Ambiguous Visions of Home," 202.
7. Benítez-Rojo, *The Repeating Island*, 4.
8. Deloughrey, "Tidalectics," 27. Deloughrey also draws attention to the ways in which Benítez-Rojo perpetuates the gendered dualism typical of early colonialist discourse. By conceptualizing the Caribbean within feminized fluidity and mother imagery, Benítez-Rojo, Deloughrey suggests, ultimately fixes the region into a masculinist tradition that opposes travelers versus islanders ironically undermining his overall critical apparatus that privileges (at least in theory) maritime routes and rhizomorphic structures.
9. Kaplan, "Deterritorialization," 361.
10. Kaplan, "Deterritorialization," 361.
11. Glissant, *Poetics*, 19.
12. In *In Praise of New Travelers*, Isabel Hoving discusses the ways in which black women writers have been frequently and consistently excluded from such ethnocentric theories of travel. See the chapter, "Tropes of Women's Exile: Violent Journeys and the Body's Geography," 29–76.
13. Glissant, *Poetics*, 6.
14. Drawing from both Walcott and Glissant, Fred D'Aguiar, in *Feeding the Ghosts* (1998), expands the vocabulary of the sea by writing that "the sea is slavery" (3). The novel reconstructs the 1783 infamous episode of the slave ship *Zong*, whose crew threw 132 sick "livestock" in the Atlantic as they would be more valuable as "goods lost at sea" than at the auction block. I am indebted to Anna Scacchi for bringing to my attention the connection with D'Aguiar's novel.
15. Deloughrey, "Tidalectics," 24. For a contemporary version of the Middle Passage journey as experienced by Haitian refugees en route to Miami, see Edwidge Danticat's "Children of the Sea." For Deloughrey, Danticat's story exemplifies the sea as "a tautological history of the middle passage." See her discussion in "Tidalectics," 22–24.
16. Phillips, *The Atlantic Sound*, 174.
17. The topos of the door as both a physical location and spiritual condition of (un)belonging is the central theme of Dionne Brand's evocative non-fiction narrative, *A Map to the Door of No Return* (2001), a book that would make an interesting comparison with Phillips's travelogue. As Brand puts it, "This door is not mere physicality. It is a spiritual location. It is also perhaps a psychic destination. Since leaving was never voluntary, return was, and still may be, an intention, however deeply buried. There is as it says no way in; no return." Brand, *A Map*, unnumbered page.
18. Alibai-Brown, "Three Sides to the Story," 12.
19. Ledent, "Ambiguous Visions," 204.
20. Mackay, "An Interview with Kamau Brathwaite," 14.
21. Glissant, *Caribbean Discourse*, 65.
22. Glissant, *Caribbean Discourse*, 64–65.
23. Ledent, "Ambiguous Visions," 201.
24. D'Aguiar, *Feeding the Ghosts*, 4.
25. Schatteman, "Disrupting the Master Narrative," 94–95.
26. Along with the African father in *Crossing the River*, Maria Lourdes López Ropero draws attention to the governor figure in the "Heartland" section in *Higher Ground* as an example of how both victims and oppressors are mired in historical circumstances beyond their control. See her brief discussion in "Travel Writing and Postcoloniality," 60.
27. Brathwaite, *Rights of Passage*, 78.

28. I borrow this phrase from Sarah Lawson Welsh who uses it to discuss tropes of "belonging" and "unbelonging" in contemporary black British literature. Contextualizing her discussion within on-going contested debates of what defines black British identity, Lawson Welsh suggests that what is being contested is ultimately "the nature of British national culture and literary praxis" now being powerfully re-mapped by "the discordant new voices" of black British writers. See "(Un)belonging Citizens, Unmapped Territory," 60–61.
29. Fanon, *The Wretched of the Earth*, 155.
30. Phillips, *A New World Order*, 305.
31. For additional criticism of Gilroy's study, see the special issue on *The Black Atlantic* in *Research in African Literatures*, edited by Simon Gikandi (1996).
32. Phillips, "Caryl Phillips on His Writing," Video 2, "The Literature of the Middle Passage," course at Barnard College, Fall 2005; http://www.barnard. columbia.edu/middlepassage/bios.html. Accessed 13 December 2006.
33. Gilroy, *The Black Atlantic*, 4.
34. Gilroy, *Beyond Camps*, 11–53.
35. Gilroy, *Against Race*, 123.
36. Dayan, "Paul Gilroy's Slaves, Ships, and Routes," 7. See also the introduction by Simon Gikandi, "Africa, Diaspora, and the Discourse of Modernity," 1–6.
37. Dayan, "Paul Gilroy's Slaves, Ships, and Routes," 7.
38. Ledent, "Ambiguous Visions," 206.
39. Ledent, "Ambiguous Visions," 207.
40. Phillips, *A New World Order*, 6.
41. Ledent, "Ambiguous Visions," 208.
42. hooks, "Choosing the Margin as a Space of Radical Openness," 151.
43. Phillips's novel *Dancing in the Dark* (2005) reimagines the tragic, and relatively obscure life of Bert Williams, the first black entertainer in the U.S. who used "to black up to go on stage." Williams's story, Phillips explains in an interview discussing the genesis of the novel, brings him to make connections with hip-hop performers and the way they are presenting themselves (and being presented) to the wider American audience. Once again, through the complexity and depth of a single life, Phillips reflects on the tragedies of race and identity, this time however keeping his focus on the U.S. See http://www. randomhouse.com/knopf/catalog/display.pperl?isbn=9781400043965&view =qa.
44. Williams, "'A State of Perpetual Wandering.'"
45. Brah, *Cartographies of Diaspora*, 192.
46. Rushdie, "Imaginary Homelands," 10.
47. Ledent, "Ambiguous Visions," 200.
48. Brah, *Cartographies of Diaspora*, 193.
49. Brah, *Cartographies of Diaspora*, 193.
50. Phillips, "Necessary Journeys." *The Guardian*, December 11, 2004; http:// books.guardian.co.uk/review/story/0,,1370289,00.html. Accessed 13 December 2004.
51. Ledent, "Ambiguous Visions," 208.
52. Phillips, *A New World Order*, 308.

19 Strike a Pose
Capitalism's Black Identity

Paulla A. Ebron

Something ironic happened on the way to black revolution: it became the leading edge of U.S.-based global capitalism.[1] The stylish opposition of black athletes and performing artists has become, arguably, the best asset of U.S.-based product commodification. Black style[2] attracts consumer attention around the world: advertisers thrive on images of youthful oppositional young men, many of whom are African American. The presence of these advertising icons changes the nature of politics as black style configures political commentary on both sides of the Atlantic and indeed around the world. This chapter explores how this surprising situation came about, while also offering reflections on the consequences and possibilities for cultural politics on a global scale.

My analysis suggests that the ambivalent triumph of black oppositional consciousness as a marketing tool is not just a matter of "co-optation." Instead, it points to the role of contingency in creating new structures of culture and political economy. By tracking the "articulations" and "friction" of black cultural politics, my chapter shows how struggles over the representation of black people in the United States made a global advertising industry reach even greater potential than could have been foreseen. As consumers around the world have connected to images of black pride, black style has become intrinsic to many forms of oppositional politics. Such politics, on the one hand, spread the hegemony of U.S.-based advertising culture. Yet, on the other hand, even while endorsing U.S.-sanctioned "universals" of style, such politics of pose also take on locally distinctive forms of political charge.

What follows is divided into four sections. In the opening section, I introduce the predicament: the rhetoric and symbolism of black struggle have become harnessed to consumerism. I use ethnographic anecdotes to show how imagery from the Civil Rights era has been expanded to speak to new challenges—and particularly those that mark the stylish progressivism of entrepreneurs and consumers. I recount the story of a Civil Rights-charged political mobilization for, of all things, a hand-held computer device! This vignette opens my argument: our moment in history is marked, as Néstor

García Canclini's book title *Consumer and Citizen* (2001) provocatively suggests, by the conflation of consumerism and human rights; furthermore, our politics, for better or worse, confuses spectacle and empowerment.

The second section turns to theoretical tools that allow for an appreciation of the role of contingency in history, and particularly in the development of new forms of politics under late capitalism. I consider Stuart Hall's approach to emergent political identities. I then discuss Anna Tsing's notion of friction, a concept used for the ethnographic analysis of global connections and social movements within uneven global sociopolitical processes.

The third section of the essay looks at the history in which Civil Rights struggles in the United States focused attention on the representation of African Americans in the media. My argument is that the success of struggles over representation allowed the spectacular rise of black imagery in U.S. media, which, in turn, has produced the ironic conjunction between consumerism and black pride, that is at the heart of my chapter. I begin with the Civil Rights campaign's promises to achieve equal rights, access to public institutions, and entrance into mainstream jobs and businesses. The Civil Rights movement is best known for its opposition to racial segregation laws and its demands for equal treatment under the law. Yet another significant feature of the movement was the attention it brought to the representation of black people in the media. This attention brought black cultural styles generated in community interactions, the arts, and political struggles into a new forum: advertising. Meanwhile, imagery from the Civil Rights era became a powerful resource for all kinds of struggles, in the United States and around the world. The political charge of Civil Rights became coupled with black entertainment and arts in producing a politically salient "black style."

After this discussion of the changing significance of the Civil Rights moment, I turn to a more focused discussion of the U.S. history of black struggles for equal representation in advertising. I argue that it is the success of the struggles over representation of African Americans, ironically, that made it possible for black style to become one of the foremost products of American capitalism. This conjuncture was in part made possible because of a historical link: black advertising arrived into its own just as U.S.-based capitalism, jolted into a new forced profitability by the "shareholders' revolution," cast off production to specialize in marketing—indeed in the manufacturing of—style. Black stylized poses turned out to be the most successful American style product, and, given the worldwide respect for U.S. black struggle that developed through the twentieth century, they traveled across the world with alacrity.

Black style gained its power because of the spirit of opposition consumers read into them. This reading created its own political trajectories as it engaged oppositional causes of many kinds in many different political climates. My discussion of commodity culture and its intimate link to a U.S.-American oppositional style takes inspiration from Thomas Frank's analysis of the development of a commercial youth niche as opposition. I look then at how black oppositional style becomes a movable sign that is able to travel globally.

In the fourth and final section of my chapter, I bring youth opposition and style into a discussion about the performance genre of hip-hop, to illustrate the global circulation and its "local" engagements with youth around the world. Rap music offers the kind of attraction that has made black style so successful as both commerce and politics. Its musical "hook" articulates brilliantly with advertising objectives: it both catches and creates audiences. Rap interpellates subjects, catching listeners up in the possibilities of the pose. Rap has traveled successfully, both refiguring oppositional consciousness as style and reconfiguring the pose itself for distinct political challenges. In my brief discussion I show how African hip-hop artists self-consciously mimic the styled poses of U.S. rap stars. At the same time, I show that this transnational community of artists and listeners offers locally engaged African political commentary through a medium that appears ubiquitous.

I must offer a proviso here, given the ubiquity of studies on hip-hop.[3] This is not a history of hip-hop. I leave aside questions about the origins of hip-hop and its various transformations. My discussion of hip-hop is to illustrate the ways oppositional culture and consumer culture circulate together and to open questions about the ironic bringing together of commercial potential and oppositional politics in the figure of the young black man.

FIGHTING FOR OUR (CONSUMER) RIGHTS

Several years ago, I received an urgent e-mail message with the header, "Make Your Voices Heard." Shortly after, the message was followed by a phone call requesting that I join, along with numerous other owners of a hand-held computer called Newton, in a march of protest on Apple Computer headquarters to express our dismay at Apple's decision to discontinue manufacturing the Newton product. At that time, Newton was touted as the most sophisticated of the hand-held computing devices; it was considered ahead of its time. Upon learning of its discontinuation my correspondent said, "As loyal customers, we deserved better." The rally was designed to "raise awareness of the plight of the Newton community" and, as my correspondent suggested, "we demand a dialogue."

As I followed the campaign of support for continuing the life of Newton, what struck me was the rhetoric of this movement in its efforts to build coalition and the strength it drew from previous social movements of different kinds.[4] At the demonstration, a gathering of somewhere between one hundred and one hundred twenty-five participants, activists were treated to a catered lunch. Participants were offered door prizes, which included plastic replica Newtons, distributed to ralliers who were then instructed to collectively smash the fake models at the right moment. The speeches by the organizers offered much to think about. One of the coordinators of the "demonstration" spoke during the rally and offered a connection to earlier protest moments. To recount the sentiments the spokesperson for the protest implied that although this protest was not the same as the more famous protests of an earlier generation, protests like this have ended segregation, the Vietnam War, and Nixon's presidency. An earlier message made an even more explicit connection to the Civil Rights movement.

In the summer following the march on Apple, a radio news report recounted a reunion of Civil Rights leaders who were convened in Washington, D.C., to pass the torch of the movement to a younger generation. One of the students interviewed at the conference was asked what she thought about the shift in the power of the movement; what it would mean to her generation. The young woman replied that she thought it was a good idea because what the Civil Rights movement had offered was really important: the movement had laid the groundwork so that now African Americans could build successful businesses.

These two accounts, in their particular ways, draw attention to the successful effects of campaigns for civil rights and multiculturalism in the United States. Racial subjects have been drawn into the public sphere and noticed not just as entrepreneurs and consumers but also as models for capitalist subjectivities. The triumph of the U.S. Civil Rights and other protest movements of identity could also become immortalized in the advertising campaigns of a computer company that even now continues to advance socially aware and forward-looking marketing strategies in its product design. These two accounts are coupled in my analysis of the commercial sign-value of social protest movements of identity, where U.S. corporations and producers/consumers began to see the lucrative possibilities of building profit-generating rhetorics of alliance. Both corporate marketing strategies and the dreams of the successors of the early Civil Rights movement find exchange value in their use of the past, albeit at radically different scales. These come together most strikingly in the condensed iconography of "black style," understood both as political struggle and as model subjectivity for entrepreneurs and consumers.

THE "FRICTION" OF GLOBAL POLITICS

To understand the contingent histories in which Civil Rights politics and black oppositional style have come to circulate globally, innovative forms of theory are required. How have struggle and style come to evoke multiple political and commercial objectives? How do struggles and styles travel across the gap of national cultures? Two analytic terms become central in the development of my analysis. To understand emergent political and cultural identities, the notion of "articulation" as used by Stuart Hall links different social elements in a temporary but transformative relationship:

> the form of the connection can make a unity of two different elements, under certain conditions. It is a linkage that is not necessary, determined, absolute and essential for all time. You have to ask, under what circumstances can a connection be forged or made? The so-called "unity" of a discourse is really the articulation of different, distinct elements that can be rearticulated in different ways because they have no necessary "belongingness." The "unity" which matters is a linkage between the articulated discourse and the social forces with which it can, under certain historical conditions but need not necessarily, be connected.[5]

The notion of a temporary alliance is attractive for it does not require that one completely ignore the often-contradictory elements in social relations that might prevent the formation of political alliances. Drawing upon the legacy of Antonio Gramsci, Hall effectively uses the concept of articulation to analyze social formations. Articulation can insert questions of class, for example, into an otherwise unmarked discussion.

Hall uses this idea to track changes in English public culture. Yet how does this notion expand beyond national cultures to track global political eruptions? How might we consider the connections across youth cohorts from various global regions? The lyrics of many hip-hop songs indicate that the marginal sense youth feel within their particular nation-state is pervasive. To address such concerns about global movements, the concept of "friction," as coined by Anna Tsing,[6] is productive to my argument.

As "the resistance to relative motion between two bodies in contact," the metaphor of friction is a reminder that global connections do not simply slide into place without a process of engagement. Tsing uses the term to refer to "awkward—grinding, grasping, sticky, tripping, slipping—engagements through which global connections are made."[7] Friction thus has the capacity to provide ethnographic tools for studying the circulation of global phenomena. Friction can recognize difference beyond local social interactions. In contrast to the common ways articulation is summoned, friction can be applied to a more expansive arena, an entity larger than the national social context.

> Friction offers attentiveness to uneven social relationships within global encounters interrupting the notion that culture flows in only one direction.
>
> On the one hand, this work can avoid the idea that new forms of empire spring fully formed and armed from the heads of Euro-American fathers. On the other hand, this work avoids too eager a celebration of a southern autonomy capable of absorbing and transforming

every imperial mandate. Instead, a study of global connections shows the grip of encounter: friction. . . . Friction reminds us that heterogeneous and unequal encounters can lead to new arrangements of culture and power.[8]

In sum, friction then allows for the dynamic exchange between global subjects who at times find themselves involved in cultural practices and even movements that are inspired and inspiring beyond their "localized" directions.

Both articulation and friction help me interpret the global politics of oppositional black style. In considering the youth cohorts who enact black style, differences need not be ignored or collapsed into a homogenous project in order to recognize commonalities, but can be understood as loosely formed partnerships. These concepts show us processes of engagement that at some points link and at other points offer disengagements, transformations, and contradictions. As we will see in the next section, articulation and friction help bring into view the contingent and linked histories of current global deployments of black style.

FROM CIVIL RIGHTS TO BLACK STYLE

Bus boycotts, sit-ins, and protest marches: these campaigns framed the public imagination about the Civil Rights movement in the United States of the 1960s, a social movement that sought to eliminate racial segregation and discriminatory practices in the U.S. Acts of civil disobedience pressed upon the governing bodies the necessity for legal sanctions to guarantee voters' rights and to end school segregation, as well as provide general access to the public sphere. Despite the view of a popular poem, turned song, of the 1970s, Gil Scott-Heron's "The Revolution Will Not Be Televised," it is precisely television that showed the country and the world the plight of African Americans. Images of social persecution and protest circulated beyond regional and national boundaries. They formed a critical turn in stereotyped representations of African Americans as subservient. The televised accounts of Civil Rights struggles would allow black people to become icons for the downtrodden. Blacks came to represent a kind of moral authority, a kind of ethical subject whose oppression via the U.S. state could move other globally oppressed groups. The critical place of television and related advertising focused attention on representation and the media.

Thus, in addition to struggles for public access, also integral to the movement for change was the Civil Rights turn toward a more expansive set of images of African Americans. Television played a critical role in portraying the daily struggle of blacks against southern tyranny. Scenes of ferocious dogs, armed police, and water hoses turned on black protesters drew the nation's attention to the mid-century political struggle for rights. Other campaigns also changed the racial landscape of the media by changing the visibility of African Americans.

At the beginning in the movement for political enfranchisement, racial uplift organizations understood the significance of turning around the pervasively negative images of African Americans in the public sphere. The theatre was one such institution that the National Association for the Advancement of Colored People (NAACP) targeted. As Leonard Archer's history of the fight waged by the NAACP around the entertainment industry reveals, public performance and image were significant to the Civil Rights campaign from the first:

> Among the factors that have created a more favorable and acceptable attitude of white people toward Black people in America has been the success stories of Black performers in music, sports, on radio and television and other performing arts. With this goal in mind the NAACP early turned some of its attention toward the commercial theatres, hoping to gain entrance to the mainstream mass media as well as gain more economic opportunities for Black performers. The Association, in its desire to use the theatre for creating favorable racial impressions, offered objections and requirements in the form of criticism and points-of-view as to what is desirable for Negroes, from Negroes and about negroes. And at the same time, the NAACP enlisted the cooperation of Black performers in behalf of its major protest campaigns.[9]

Yet the lobbying of mass media industries, including radio and television, and by extension the advertisers associated with these media, would soon become part of the challenge to correct the denigrating representations of blacks. The NAACP launched a campaign over a popular radio and subsequent television show, "Amos 'n' Andy" described in an often-cited essay, "Why the Amos 'n' Andy TV Show Should Be Taken Off the Air."[10] The NAACP's bulletin emphasized the role of the image in building racial pride. It listed the organization's reasons for their disapproval of the show:

> [It] tends to strengthen the conclusion among uninformed and prejudiced people that Negroes are inferior, lazy, dumb and dishonest.

> Every character in this one and only TV show with an all Negro cast is either a clown or a crook.

> Negro doctors are shown as quacks and thieves.

> Negro lawyers are shown as slippery cowards, ignorant of their profession and without ethics.

Negro Women are shown as cackling, screaming shrews, in big mouthed close-ups, using street slang, just short of vulgarity.

All Negroes are shown as dodging work of any kind.

Millions of white Americans see this Amos 'n' Andy picture of Negroes and think the entire race is the same.[11]

Critics of this campaign argued that both blacks and whites enjoyed the program. However, the organization's disapproval offers a key component of Civil Rights thinking, in which respectable representations were a necessary element of the political repositioning that might allow black people to fight for equal rights.

It would be incorrect, however, to make the NAACP and like groups appear as the collective outlet for black protest. Equally visible during the 1960s were groups described as militant and separatists. Black nationalists also emphasized race pride, but they contrasted their self-representations with what they saw as the mainstream incorporative goals of liberal rights groups. Masculine poses of opposition became popular to promote radical cases. Groups such as the Nation of Islam and the Black Panthers, though rather different in their philosophies, used masculine poses to symbolize a radical stance that moved beyond black integrationists.

The pressure from Civil Rights groups yielded greater visibility of African Americans in the media by the 1970s. Yet, in a swing of the pendulum from stereotypic depictions of difference to the other end, African Americans were cast in "respectable" roles that made them seem just like one of the U.S. citizen groups. Such respectable representations happened co-temporally with an emerging sense of class differences within the black community and an associated blurring of the sharp representational divide between blacks and whites. Yet even the most mainstream Civil Rights groups were not able to relax. They remained vigilant, pressing for more and better representations of black people. As recently as 1999, for example, the NAACP led a protest against the major television network stations for the relative absence of blacks in their fall line-up. The president of the NAACP, Kweisi Mfume, alerted the networks that Civil Rights groups would monitor them and take legal actions against them in case they didn't include programs with diverse actors.[12]

The interplay between the fight for respectability and the fight for radically independent black manhood shaped an emergent politics of style, in which the ability of black men to represent "cool" became seen as politically charged. This history, in turn, shaped the emergent black presence in advertising. By the turn of the century, black people increasingly appeared in advertisements to depict youthful, risky, and politically oppositional consumers. In a study of television advertisements, Henderson and Baldasty argue that black people in ads became figures to attract a youthful audience: "These ads focus on being 'hip,' 'cool,' 'risky,' and 'powerful'— all attributes teens crave. For example, the McDonald's campaign urges its audience to play the Code name game because 'winning is cool.' Nike's admonition to 'Just Do It,' and Powerade's encouragement to 'keep playing' both support these youth attitudes."[13] Henderson and Baldasty further argue that people of color are visible in television advertising in marketing low-cost products including fast food and soft drinks, sports and equipment, and lower-cost clothing ads. They represent entrepreneurs and consumers from the bottom—and thus come to embody the possibilities of global capitalism for everyone.

The new visibility of black people in the media shaped the political subjectivities of post-Civil Rights generations of black—as well as white—Americans.[14] Cultural critic Nelson George describes the period beyond the pervasive protests of the Civil Rights and Black Power movements as being "post-soul". He speaks particularly of the period between 1979 and 1989:

> The term "post-soul" defines the twisting, troubling, turmoil-filled, and often terrific years since the mid-seventies when black America moved into a new phase of its history. Post-soul is my shorthand to describe a time when America attempted to absorb the victories, failures, and ambiguities that resulted from the soul years. The post-soul years have witnessed an unprecedented acceptance of black people in the public life of America. As political figures, advertising images, pop stars, coworkers, and classmates, the descendants of African slaves have made their presence felt and, to a remarkable degree considering this country's brutal history, been accepted as citizens, if not always as equals.[15]

The new acceptance of black America allowed black people to speak as models for the future—and particularly the future of enterprise, understood as radical innovation. Black "badness" became a desirable icon suited for commercial promotion and for the spread of U.S. consumerism to the rest of the world. Black people could even help define the new "generations" of entrepreneurial consumers that would mark the aspirations of a newly unfettered global capitalism.

The Source, a popular hip-hop magazine, started using the term "hip-hop generation" to refer to a cohort of black youth born between 1965 and 1984, people whose parents would have been a part of the Civil Rights/Black Power era. The hip-hop generation would bring stylish innovations, not just for black Americans, but also for the world. Bakari Kitwana argues that the hip-hop generation are those who move beyond the supposedly "traditional" values of their parents into a brave new cosmopolitanism: "For our parents' generation, the political ideas of Civil Rights and Black power are central to their worldview. Our parents' generation placed family, spirituality, social responsibility, and Black pride at the center of their identity as Black Americans. They, like their parents before them, looked to their elders for values and identity."[16] The new generation would turn to world-making media productions, not parochial traditions:

> Today the influence of these tradition purveyors of Black culture has largely diminished in the face of powerful and pervasive technological advances and corporate growth. Now media and entertainment such as pop music, film, and fashion are among the major forces transmitting culture to this generation of Black Americans. At the same time, the new Black youth cuts across class lines, so that whether one is middle class, coming of age in suburban or rural settings, college-bound, or a street-wise urban dweller, what it means to be young and Black has been similarly redefined.[17]

Blackness could transcend local and national communities, then, and take over the world with oppositional "style":

> We live in an age where corporate mergers, particularly in media and entertainment, have redefined public space. Within this largely expanded public space, the viewing public is constantly bombarded by visual images that have become central to the identity of an entire generation. Within this arena of popular culture, rap music more than anything else has helped shape the new Black youth culture. The irony in all this is that the global corporate structure that gave young Blacks a platform was the driving force behind their plight.[18]

Black social and political aspirations, then, can no longer be separated from corporate globalization itself. "In fact, the face of globalization that emerged in the 1980s and 1990s is itself a critical factor that has significantly influenced the worldview of hip-hop generationers. In short, the transnational corporations of the 1970s evolved into the mega-corporations of the 1980s, 1990s, and beyond."[19]

COMMODIFICATION AND THE POLITICS OF OPPOSITIONAL STYLE

The connections between oppositional style and capitalist expansion are not entirely new. Thomas Frank, in *The Conquest of Cool* (1997), persuasively argues that there were much earlier connections between commercialism and political protests. The "bad boy" image as a marketing strategy began in the 1950s, Frank argues, and he traces the roots of this bad-boy rebellion to Madison Avenue advertisers. In the United States, he explains, the bad boy became a powerful figure bringing together rebellion and commercial appeal. As a condensed symbol of the ambivalent status of non-conformity, bad boys rebelled and thus ushered in hopes for the end of corrupt hierarchies. Bad boys strutted, selling their energies as "rebels without a cause,"[20] and thus made themselves available as icons of style, if not substance. Moreover, bad boys sold well, inspiring stylish product. Thus bad boys emerged as figures of contradiction, both sympathetic and evil. They captured the spirit of popular culture as icons of both corporate power and popular spirit. The significant development at present is the centrality of young urban African American men as iconic representatives of U.S. capitalism.

This contemporary articulation draws from the success of a number of highly visible commercial campaigns. As I have argued thus far, since the 1960s, Civil Rights and Black Power movements have pressured advertisers to include "positive" images of African Americans. Some of the new advertisements were targeted particularly at the African American market. Here advertisers tried out "black" themes. Surprisingly, these black-themed advertisements attracted large cross-over audiences of all races. It was the success of these campaigns that changed the face of U.S. advertising. Furthermore, black-themed ads proved effective in bringing in new consumers outside of the United States. This success, in turn, made black advertising the leading edge of U.S. marketing, offering African Americans the opportunity to represent U.S. capitalist aspirations to the world.

One important company is McDonalds fast food chain. After years of self-promotion as a wholesome all-American company, the corporation found it needed to include African Americans, who after all formed an important segment of its core customers. The company hired Chicago-based Burrell Advertising Agency, one of the largest African American advertising agencies. In the 1990s Burrell suggested a promotional idea that would gesture directly to African American loyalties. McDonald would sponsor a series of tours for U.S. Americans, imagined as black, to visit the African homeland. The promotion was explicitly imagined as a gesture to improve relations with African American communities.[21] Yet this plan, it also turned out, produced good advertising for the company in all its range.

This successful strategy of target marketing to African American communities by stressing links with Africa was soon adopted by other prominent companies in the 1990s. Heineken beer company, for example, also sponsored a "homeland" trip to Africa for winners of a contest. The company's ad contrasted with the reverent tone of the McDonald's contest advertisement in that commercial actors staged a conversation where they were deciding which "home" was best for the fourth of July: a U.S. home eating American hot dogs or an African home. The advertisement strategy, in the end, suggested the multiplicity of American homes and thus gestured beyond the African American community. Similarly, another beer company, Budweiser, joined in the multicultural act offering poster images of African civilizations and kings to consuming audiences during African American history month.

Perhaps the most successful campaign in the 1990s, however, is that of the sneaker industry, where the use of African Americans in a number of capacities offers an important site for my analysis. As consumers and product endorsers, African Americans are intimately intertwined in the story of the growth of the sneaker industry. Nike is one such prominent company. In 1996 Nike comprised 42.1% of the sneaker business. The company was centrally associated with African Americans in important ways.[22] The sneaker industry thrives on image and possibility. African American sports celebrities such as Tiger Woods and Michael Jordan became icons that helped promote the global capitalism aspirations of the U.S. sports clothing industry.

Nike's success formed a model for entrepreneurship and advertising in a number of ways. Nike never produced shoes; the success of the company was a success of marketing. Nike showed the world the advantages of a new form of capitalism in which profits could be made by eliminating manufacturing and instead focus on the production of style as a marketing tool. Black style was the product Nike chose to promote. In the process, the company opened an avenue for black style to represent the future of capitalism—especially as it traveled around the "emerging markets" of the post-Cold War world.

YOUTH, IDENTITY, AND THE PERFORMANCE OF STYLE

> Now, the media play a crucial role in defining our experience for us. They provide us with the most available categories for classifying out the social world. It is primarily through the press, television, film, etc. that experience is organized, interpreted and made to cohere in contradiction as it were.
>
> Dick Hebdidge, *Subculture*

Dick Hebdige's classic work on youth and the meaning of style analyses the culture of white British working-class youth. His study focuses on the politics of the British nation-state and the alienation of working-class youth. Yet Hebdige's unit of analysis is much smaller than what is required for an investigation of global processes. What is necessary for an examination of global cultural practices is for analysts to track back and forth between the different kind of niches—both productive and non-productive, laboring and non-laboring, sectors under the regime of late capitalism. These varying niches link youth across geographies often in a politics of opposition, and embrace an expressive commentary about the world many feel has left them out. Hip-hop, as a genre initially associated with urban youth, provides a vehicle for staging youth cultural politics while being a successful promoter of products, in part, because it engages with other legacies in the articulation of politics and performance.

In this final section, I analyze hip-hop as it circulates in African urban centers including Nairobi, Dakar, and Soweto. As many artists are quick to comment, there is no shortage of groups across the continent, as well as other places in the world, who do rap. Successful hip-hop artists from most countries provide their thoughts on the unique choices they make in form and, most of all, content. Hall's notion of articulation comes through clearly in these artists' discussions, where stylistic forms at times parallel with and at other times seek a departure from particular kinds of U.S. rap styles. The second analytic concept, Tsing's notion of friction, comes into play as well in the kind of communicative global energy that surrounds hip-hop.

But before I proceed with my argument, it is important to comment on a precursor to the omnipresence of hip-hop, one part of this being television and mass-mediated music. Some youths on the continent rework their image through the increasingly available image repertoire of U.S. television and advertising. The shifts towards a more positive image of American blacks in American advertisements and television shows, for example, circulated beyond U.S. borders and offered a vocabulary of "blackness" with some influence on identities. A graduate student now living in the United States, but who grew up in Kenya during the 1980s, recounted for me the ways old American television programs framed a major part of his adolescence in Nairobi.[23] Television docudramas such as *Roots* and the *North and the South* provided ideas, he said, about America to African school children. But equally significant were U.S. popular television programs such as *Sanford and Sons*, *Good Times* and *The Fresh Prince*, that brought television portrayals of African Americans to African youth. These shows combined with global music promoters including MTV and BET to generate popular images of a globally empowered blackness for a transnational audience. Not to be left out of this cross-continental exchange, the influence of an imagined Africa worked in the other direction to inspire African Americans to adopt certain clothing, particular ceremonies, such as taking "African" names, and learning of performance styles, all in an effort to build a counter version to the mass culture of the U.S. In these efforts, the circulation of "Africa" allows one to move outside of an explicitly U.S. and corporately controlled context.

A noticeable image of the Senegalese hip-hop group Daara J appears in the folk/World music magazine *Froots*. The picture can also be found on the group's latest CD cover, *Boomerang*. Promoted as "The best Hip-Hop album of the new century" by the London-based newspaper *The Observer*, the picture offers an instance where the iconic circulation of the "bad boys with attitude" quite clearly moves across continents. In most circles, the loose and baggy clothes hanging off young men's bodies that are sometimes excessively adorned with gold jewelry—coupled with a performance style that combines spoken word and "in-your-face" gesturing—are some of the pervasive images of transnational hip-hop artists. One of the artists wears Timberland boots, a Carolina shirt, and a bandana. At first glance, in addition to the clothes, the pose immediately brings to mind a familiar site associated with hip-hop artists from Los Angeles and New York.

From the webpage of the record company that produced Daara J's latest record, Wrasse, the group makes a distinction between themselves and the stereotypical images of U.S. hip-hop artists. "We need a new term for a new kind of hip-hop that is not about bitches, bragging and bling, and Boomerang will do nicely. The word conveys perfectly the sense of a music that thrives on two-way influences flying back and forth."[24] Quick to stress their own style that emerged from their sampling of African diasporic music, they produced a form known as "Sene-rap." One of the group's performers, Aladji Man, states in an interview: "There were rap groups, soul groups, and reggae groups before us, but we were the first to consistently bring those three styles together. I had already started learning toasting, Ndongo was into rap, and Faada Freddy knew how to sing those harmonies. We united all those skills in one outfit, and thought we'd better use that to our advantage."[25] Despite the pervasive image of hip-hop artists in the United States, brought to audiences by global media producers, the members of Daara J want to distinguish themselves from the crass materialism of some artists. But, in this, also form imaged alliances with those across the Atlantic who have rejected the commercial appropriations of hip-hop by the corporate music industry. Again group member Aladji Man states: "Daara J means 'school of life.' With every production, we want to give an education to our listeners." And in a press release available on the website "Rock Paper Scissors" appears another statement about the group's purpose:

> In the vein of De La Soul, Public Enemy, and Blackstar, *Boomerang* strays from the typically machismo [*sic*] and materialistic subject matter permeating America's mainstream rap scene. Joining the likes of Positive Black Soul and MC Solaar as one of Senegal's elite hip hop crews, Daara J uses their words as a positive force. Proudly earning their name, the trio focuses on the ills of globalism, the perils of a traditional society, the threatened environment, and on spirituality.[26]

The category of youth and hip-hop are neither transhistorical nor determined by U.S. standards of what counts as oppositional. Many hip-hop artists in Africa have used their art for global-local commentary. Young men in Africa are increasingly alienated from dreams of modernization and the hope of nationalism. They lack schooling, formal employment, and access to public sphere opportunities. Many feel left outside social planning, and they use their sense of marginalization to turn their reactions and reflections into poetry. In this new movement for social justice, masculinity and the image of "ultra bad" are resources for taking a position from which to be heard. Global hip-hop style makes it possible for them to speak out. This is true across the Atlantic as poor education, joblessness, prison futures are what scripts the lives of many rappers.

African youth in some countries on the continent must live between African gangs, militias, armies, and revolutionary movements and as such youth have become identified with the ambivalence of the future.[27] Another popular rap artist now living in Kenya, Emmanuel Jal, lived on both sides of the line. After the death of his mother when he was seven years old, Jal was taken by the Sudan People's Liberation Army to be a child soldier. For much of his early childhood the war between the north and south raged, and children were used to scout out enemy camps. After five years as a soldier, Jal found his way to a refugee camp. He was adopted and smuggled into Kenya. Jal now sings of peace and unification across linguistic, religious, and ethic lines. His song "Elengwen" speaks to a different future:

> All my men, if you ask Taban Deng Gai
> The house of Nyatue Deng and Nyaruob Deng
> If you don't forgive each other
> You are the ones that will destroy us
> Here peace has come—don't mess it up
> All the people from that side are going to Juba
> Please listen to what I am saying
> Let's hold on, if you are an Anyuak
> Nuer or Nuba, it doesn't matter where you come from
> We are one, please let's not plan to kill each other
> Let's enjoy this wonderful, blessed land of ours
> Let's live together as God decreed
> *Chorus*
> Why are people killed every day?
> Why can't people live together?[28]

The words to this song are hardly reminiscent of corporate U.S. hip-hop's message. In a radio interview, Jal explained how he came to his version of hip-hop. He relates that initially he started out singing gospel rap songs much to the dismay of the people around him. But then they realized that the message he was promoting was one of peace and unity and they became a bit more accepting. Emmanuel Jal uses traditional Sudanese forms that are a part of the songs he remembered hearing when he was a child. He also addresses, with Abdel Gardir Salim, the linguistic diversity of the Sudan by providing the words to his songs on their CD *Ceasefire* in four languages.

The last illustration is of *kwaito*, a genre of music often compared to hip-hop. Young black residents in South Africa's ghettos are said to imagine *kwaito* as a life style. Like Sene-rap's fusion of multiple sounds *kwaito* combines jazz, house music, and local sounds. People make a distinction between *kwaito* and U.S. rap music, with the former rejecting the latter's misogyny. In a radio interview with South African poet, musician, and actor Zola, he spoke about the content of his message: "I talk about HIV and AIDS, I talk about women abuse. I talk about male abuse because men get abuse too. I talk about the guns, I talk about cocaine. I talk about vulgar."[29] Zola's concern is to distinguish himself from those who might promote empty lyrics. Rather his work draws inspiration from the Black Consciousness Movement and the fight against apartheid in South Africa. South African novelist Niq Mhlongo continued in the vein offered by Zola:

> This is the real *kwaito*. How do you go about fighting crime. How do you go about fighting poverty. How do you go about solving crime. These are the things that are relevant at the moment. The generation that is no longer focusing on the past ration—not focusing on the past trying to build a future. Apartheid cliche. Young people in South Africa can't afford to divide themselves by the past, can't afford to define themselves by the past—how do you go about fighting poverty, crime.

These problems form a set of challenges for black youth on both sides of the Atlantic.[30] Yet black oppositional style, I have argued, addresses them in locally particular ways.

CONCLUSIONS

Recognizing the ties between Africa and its diaspora is critical for tracking alliances and departures. Again Katharina Lobeck comments on the appeal of hip-hop in the imaginations of African youth:

> Historical connections, racial relations and cultural affinities between African-Americans and Africans have undoubtedly played their part in the warm reception hip-hop has received on African shores. Rap's potential as a tool of outspoken criticism against society's injustices has clearly been another reason. Yet American hip-hop culture has exerted a strong pull due to the powerful economic promise it holds. Flash trainers, glitzy jewelry and designer labels are as much a part of hip-hop Africa as anywhere else in the world, even though the grand devotion to bling bling culture has never taken the same hold. Hip-hop not only represents black culture, it also represents America and its fortune, which continuously attracts young Africans in search of a better future.[31]

This chapter examines the sign value of social protest movements of identity where U.S. corporations and producers/consumers see the lucrative possibilities of building symbolic alliances for generating profit. I have taken as a point of entrance the themes of the business of identity and politics of style and linked these to the ubiquitous circulation of a performance genre known as hip-hop. Through this, I have asked how transnational connections across the Atlantic articulate global capitalism's cultural production.

The ubiquity of this form, or way of life as some refer to hip-hop, has created an imagined community that potentially forges a generational alliance across national boundaries. Strikingly, the pervasive image associated with hip-hop draws upon a performative stance, a masculinist style, that pulls from the archive of images of bad black men who pose as the quintessential oppositional figure always at odds with the dominant order. This figure produces a symbolic currency where representations of blackness link U.S. urban youth to youth in other world centers.

Capitalism, these days, thrives on developing distinctive niches of consumers with their distinctive "needs" invented and then catered to—and youth is one such consumer niche. Yet, the significance of what global capitalism produces has far more potential than its own commercial agenda can contain. One of the project of the 1960s Civil Rights movement was to insist upon social justice. So may this potential exist for youth transnationally.

NOTES

1. My sincere appreciation goes to all who contributed to this chapter in a number of ways. Special thanks go to Thomas Biolsi, Claudia Engel, Frank Holmquist, Joanie McCullum, Curtis Njue Murungi, Robert Sammett, Marcyliena Morgan, Dawn-Elissa Fischer for her assistance with the collection in the Hip-Hop Archive at Stanford University, Anna Tsing, E. Frances White, and finally to the editors, Anna Scacchi and Annalisa Oboe.
2. I use the term *black* in ways that were once common practice in the 1980s by the British Cultural Studies, a term that collectively included diverse marginal subjects, groups commonly thought of as marginal because of the national politics of the British nation-state. Yet I also draw upon a history that appears particular to the African American history in the United States. I want the idea of black style to move within and at the same time beyond essentialized notions of blackness. Still essentialized notions are often in play as media agencies attempt to make an object out of ethnic/racial identities.
3. With nothing short of 132 officially catalogued books in the United States library system and countless other sources including books, articles, and audiovisual texts that have not made their way to libraries, it is reasonable to leave this area aside. One recent book is worth noting, for it contains extensive interviews with hip-hop artists: Spady, Alim, and Meghelli, *Tha Global Cipha*.
4. My account of the Newton demonstration owes a great deal to the research notes of Joanie McCollum, who kindly allowed me to use her observations and comments.
5. Hall, "On Postmodernism and Articulation," 53.
6. Tsing, *Friction*.
7. Tsing, "Contingent Commodities."
8. Tsing, *Friction*, 5.
9. Archer, *Black Images in the American Theatre*, 45.
10. NAACP, "Why the Amos 'n' Andy TV Show Should Be Taken Off the Air."
11. NAACP, "Why the Amos 'n' Andy TV Show Should Be Taken Off the Air."
12. Mifflin, "N.A.A.C.P. Plans to Press For More Diverse TV Shows," 10; Torres, *Black White and in Color*.

13. Henderson and Baldasty, "Race, Advertising, and Prime-Time Television," 105–106.
14. Latinos, Asian Americans, and Native Americans were also very much affected by the rhetorics and strategies of the Civil Rights movement. Fights for representation in the media and advertising also marked these minority communities. See, for example, Davila, *Latinos, Inc.*
15. George, *Post-Soul Nation*, x.
16. Kitwana, *The Hip Hop Generation*, 7.
17. Kitwana, *The Hip Hop Generation*, 7.
18. Kitwana, *The Hip Hop Generation*, 9.
19. Kitwana, *The Hip Hop Generation*, 9.
20. *Rebel without a Cause* was a popular film in the 1950s United States that depicted the life of a teenager who rebels against his parents authority. He joins a gang and actively carves out an oppositional identity to that of mainstream America.
21. For an in-depth analysis of this tour see Ebron, *Performing Africa*.
22. Vanderbilt, *The Sneaker Book*, xi.
23. Many thanks go to Curtis Njue Murungi for his comments during an informal conversation in February 2007, where he talked about the presence of U.S. media and their having great appeal to him and members of his cohort of youth.
24. http://www.wrasserecords.com/Daara_J_50/biography.html. Accessed 24 April 2007.
25. Lobeck, "Dakaration," 39.
26. "From the South Bronx to Goree, Hip Hop Boomerangs Back to Africa: Senegal's Daara J Keeps It Positive on American Debut"; http://www.rockpaper-scissors.biz/index.cfm/fuseaction/current.press_release/project_id/179.cfm. Accessed 24 April 2007.
27. See Hecht and Simon, *Invisible Governance*; Abbink and van Kessel, *Vanguard or Vandals*.
28. Text by Emmanuel Jal Jak Gatwitch, in his English translation.
29. N. Conan, "The Voice of South African Kwaito: Zola." March 7, 2006. *Talk of the Nation*. http://www.npr.org. Accessed 26 April 2007.
30. S. Cole, "South Africa's Kwaito Generation." *Inside Out Documentaries* WBUR. http://www.insideout.org/documentaries/kwaito/. Accessed 24 April 2007.
31. Lobeck, "Dakaration," 39.

20 "Nothing but a Feeling of Brotherhood"

The Interracial Question and the Return to Africa in Pauline Hopkins's *Of One Blood*

Simone Francescato

Charlie Vance was inconsolable . . . He spent money like water in his endeavor to find the secret passage, believing that it existed, and that in it Reuel was lost.[1]

The end of the nineteenth and the beginning of the twentieth centuries were hard times for black people in the United States, characterized by extremely dreadful events—the infamous case of Plessy vs. Ferguson (1896), the promulgation of the Jim Crow laws, and the incredible rise of lynching among others—and many blacks feared the repealing of the civil and social achievements gained after the Civil War. The black intelligentsia was certainly aware of such a backlash and fought hard to contrast it, both by preserving the memory of black Americans' oppression, and by fostering a political and cultural awareness in black people's minds. In their commitment to put an end to the discriminations, however, some African American thinkers began to conceive the return to Africa as the only possible solution to the oppression of their people. In the late 1910s–early 1920s, the clash between "integrationists" and "separatists" culminated in the famous ideological dispute of two great African American thinkers, Marcus Garvey—leader of the separatists and advocate of the back-to-Africa movement—and W.E.B. Du Bois, the integrationist philosopher and a believer in the cooperation between blacks and whites in the struggle for civil rights.

It is important to notice, however, that since much earlier—at least since the beginning of the nineteenth century—any reference to the African past or to the experience of the diaspora in the black literature of the period more or less had reflected the authors' views on the larger debate about emigration and integration in the United States. Not unlike other important theorizers and writers at that time, Pauline Hopkins firmly believed in the possibility of integration, but thought that the deepest and most lasting transformations of American society could only be obtained through the progressive acculturation of the emerging black middle class. She was one of the first to realize that the easiest way to spread counternarratives of world history among black Americans was the magazine format.[2] Between 1900 and 1905 Hopkins worked as the literary editor of the Boston-based *Colored American Magazine (CAM)*, a publication specifically conceived for the uplift and education of the black middle class. There she was incredibly prolific, producing a heterogeneous body of work that aimed at contrasting the power of white supremacist ideology.

This chapter focuses on *Of One Blood, or the Hidden Self*—serialized in *CAM* between 1902 and 1903—the last of Hopkins's four novels. Although influenced by the fiction of Poe, Hawthorne and Twain,[3] *Of One Blood* can be more fruitfully read as a distinctive African American rewriting of those popular fantastic narratives supporting the imperialist politics of the Western countries on the black continent, such as H. Rider Haggard's novel *She* (1887).[4] In her study of late nineteenth-century African American novels, Maria Giulia Fabi argues that novels like *Of One Blood* are to be intended as "resocialization texts" (a definition that the Italian scholar borrows from Claudia Tate), since they have the important function of creating an African American middle-class awareness, through the recovery of a largely discarded African heritage.[5] This political and social goal shapes the whole of Hopkins's production, and culminates in her meticulous rewritings of biographies of famous African Americans. If we analyze such rewritings, we may agree with C. K. Doreski, who reads them as "participatory, exemplary texts,"[6] characterized by an explicitly allegorical and pedagogical framework deriving from a distinct Northern American (Puritan) tradition. But the emphasis on the participatory element is also traceable in all of Hopkins's fiction and in *Of One Blood* in particular—which is indeed, as Hazel Carby remarks, "a journey towards the knowledge of a black heritage [both] for the protagonist and the reader."[7]

The title of the novel, however, reveals an important ambiguity. As Deborah McDowells points out in her introduction to the latest edition of the book, the novel's "'back to Africa' plot, as some have termed it, has consistently baffled critics. . . . If we [blacks and whites] are all of 'one blood,' critics ask, how can the novel logically conclude, as it does, with a recuperation of distinct bloodlines . . . of an 'originary' African identity, existing in its own state of imaginary purity before Anglo-Saxon contamination[?]"[8] *Of One Blood* in fact offers two kinds of contrasting but juxtaposed readings, which can be roughly described as *intraracially* and *interracially* focused: the novel can be read as a sort of manifesto of black racial pride *and/or* as a demystification of the very concept of race, which questions (but also allows) the possibility of integration and interracial/universal brotherhood in the United States. The hypothesis I would like to advance is that Hopkins makes use of the back-to-Africa theme as a sort of mythical genealogy for the survival of black people in the United States, rather than conceiving it as an actual solution to the problems of race in America. Moreover, a close reading of the novel also allows us to find evidence of Hopkins's belief in the possibility of interracial brotherhood in the United States. In fact, although half of the novel takes place in a fantastic African landscape, the relations among the characters continuously reflect the writer's interest in the development of the interracial situation in America.

The juxtaposition of intra- and interracial readings, in my viewpoint, can be better investigated through the analysis of the characterization in the novel: if we describe the interactions of its principal male characters as *dialectic* or *symmetric* in a *positive* or *negative* way, we can better understand the complexity of the text's allegorical message. As a premise, I would argue that the allegorical/pedagogical "intraracial" function expressed by the protagonist's adventure—the *good mulatto,* Reuel Briggs, who turns into the *good black character* by recovering his black heritage—relies on three main elements: the punishment of his antagonist—the *bad mulatto* Aubrey Livingston, who believes he is white and through his adherence to white southern (im)morality reveals himself as the *bad white character*; the punishment of the *bad black character,* Jim Titus, a black man who betrays his African origins by carrying out his white master's racist, evil plan; and, more interestingly, the moral growth of the *good white character,* Charlie Vance, and his conversion to the value of interracial/universal brotherhood.

To anticipate briefly, my argument is that the *good black male character* (Reuel Briggs) and the *bad white male character* (Aubrey Livingston) are the two poles of a *dialectic* which sees them in opposite positions regarding the female characters (the unfortunate mulatto singer Dianthe Lusk and the ghost of the black slave Mira),[9] who represent the symbolic pivot of the story, coinciding with the survival of the African heritage. Their different attitude towards such pivotal characters thus constitutes the measure of their allegorical/pedagogical value as positive or negative. On the other hand, the *symmetry* which characterizes the relation between the *good black character* (Reuel) and the *good white character* (Charlie Vance)—which we may call "positive interracial relation" or "universal brotherhood"—is allowed because they are *not* "of one blood": namely, there is no female character who actually links them together—so that any specter of rape, incest, or miscegenation is banished;[10] and, more interestingly, because they share some positive "Yankee" values.

Incest and miscegenation are linked to another central theme in the novel, that is to say the contrast between appearance and reality. The social chaos generated by these practices seems to be conceived by Hopkins as an overwhelming force which is undermining the whole country and its democratic principles. Although such contrast is mainly built on the tragedy of the two protagonists, the "passing mulattoes" Reuel and Aubrey, it also relies, to a lesser but significant degree, on the characterization of the other two male characters, Jim and Charlie. The interesting fact is that in the novel *no one is what he seems to be,* and—as we will see—identity changes, as do relations to the other characters. Since the question of race (and that of identity) significantly intersects with the question of morality in the novel, we may think that the author aimed at emphasizing identity as the result of social construction, with the purpose of stimulating or reinforcing agency in her readers.

In order to analyze the interaction among the four characters, I will start by outlining the protagonist of the novel. Reuel Briggs is a distinguished student at the faculty of medicine of Harvard, very intelligent and serious. At the beginning of the story we read that "Briggs could have told you that the bareness and desolateness of the apartment were like his life, but he was a reticent man, who knew how to suffer in silence" (1). Reuel suffers from a strange kind of neurasthenia and his psychic torment increases after reading an article entitled "The Unclassified Residuum," dealing with the scientific treatment of issues like supernatural phenomena and multiple personality. Being a mulatto who has successfully managed to "pass" as white, Reuel is obsessed with the clash between the world of supernatural powers (linked to his African heritage and his mother)[11] and that of philosophical/scientific thinking (conceived as the major achievement of Western culture). In this conflict, in fact, he recognizes the tragedy of his ambiguous identity, suspended between black and white.

Reuel Briggs's mulattoism is one of the most interesting and complex elements in the book. By somehow embodying the enlightened thinker of the turn of the century, the medicine student can be seen as an allegory of the "new man," a kind of Du Boisian/Jamesian philosopher[12] who can elucidate real knowledge by going beyond the rigid categories of black/white, myth/science, man/woman, and so on. In the construction of Reuel's character, in fact, Hopkins attempts a synthesis of the two different "visions of the world" exposed in William James's article "The Hidden Self" (1890), which the novelist used as a main source of inspiration for this work. James writes that "the scientific-academic mind and the feminine-mystical mind shy from each other's facts, just as they fly from each other's temper and spirit. . . . [H]e who will pay attention to facts of the sort dear to mystics, while reflecting upon them in academic-scientific ways, will be in the best possible position to help philosophy."[13] Thus, as a successful scientific student interested in supernatural phenomena, Reuel embodies the possible reconciliation between the "male side" (the hegemonic scientific discourse of white, patriarchal academia) and the "female side" (the repressed power of black folk rituals transmitted through matriarchal line), in a captivating rewriting of William James's text.

Reuel's task in the novel is to rebalance the black side of his identity and to recover the values of spiritualism and collective responsibility toward his people, which Hopkins sees as distinctive African American traits.[14] But since he is a respectable member of a white intellectual caste, this goal clashes with Anglo-American materialism and individualism, which Reuel has passively accepted as his own values. The push toward recovering his black identity finally comes from his disinterested (let us say, highly moral) love for the unfortunate black singer Dianthe Lusk, who has lost her memory of her past and her identity as a black woman. Through the sleight of hand of the archeological expedition to Africa, Hopkins solves the problematic evolution of the love story between Reuel and Dianthe (who turns out to be his sister) and at the same time completes the tragic story of incestuous seduction between Dianthe and her half-brother Aubrey. But Reuel's original decision to marry Dianthe *in spite of* her blackness is indeed the element demonstrating the protagonist's moral superiority, as he is willing to recover his black identity, in the face of his possible loss of respectability among the whites. In this key passage, Reuel states:

> *"I will marry her in spite of hell itself!* Marry her *before* she awakens to consciousness of her identity. I'm not unselfish; I don't pretend to be. There is no sin in taking her out of the sphere where she was born. *God and science* helping me, I will give her life and love and wifehood and maternity and perfect health. . . . What do you know of a lonely, darkened life like mine? I have not the manner nor the charm which wins women. Men like me get love from them which is half akin to pity, when they get anything at all. It is but the shadow. This is my opportunity for happiness; *I seize it.* Fate has linked us together and no man and *no man's laws shall part us."* (43–44, italics mine)

In this highly dramatic moment, Reuel reveals himself as the *good black character.* He advocates both "God and science" against "[white?] man's laws," and confessing all his deep humanity ("I'm not unselfish; I don't pretend to be"), finally commits himself to "seizing" his (and Dianthe's) "opportunity for happiness." Reuel's revelation is thus centered on the revalorization of the black family and, in particular, of the figure of the black woman (embodied by Dianthe Lusk), which—as already pointed out by feminist scholars[15]—symbolizes the continuity of African heritage in the book.

Reuel's direct antagonist is another medicine student, the rich Aubrey Livingston. At the beginning of the novel, he is presented as Reuel's best friend. He is not aware of being a mulatto and both Reuel and Dianthe's half-brother. Aubrey is what I have called the *bad white character,* because he appears as a sort of prototypical white southern villain, being extremely idle, dishonest, racist and sexist.[16] In chapter one, Hopkins introduces him as "a tall man with the beautiful face of a Greek god, but the sculptured features," she remarks, "did not inspire confidence" (6). In contrast to Reuel, who is portrayed as a man "of superior physical endowments, but as yet he had never had reason to count them blessings"(3), Aubrey bears the concrete mark of recognition by his own community,

which individuates in Greek aesthetics the canons of physical and intellectual perfection. Hopkins insists on this point, underlining for instance
Aubrey's use of Greek mythology in his speech ("you son of Erebus . . .
it's as black as Hades," 6). But the aura of classicism that affects both
Aubrey's physical traits and his language will have to be read differently
later, in an ironical reversal: in the novel, in fact, the reader discovers that
the seeds of the knowledge that flourished in ancient Greece came—via
the Egyptians—from the Ethiopians, that is to say, from the black race
that Aubrey so much despises.[17]

In portraying the contrast between Aubrey and Reuel, Hopkins makes
use of stereotypes that were generally attached to black people and operates a successful reversal, by representing them as the prototypical vices
of southern aristocracy.[18] A trait which strongly puts Aubrey in contrast
to Reuel, for instance, is his extreme idleness: as Reuel tells his friend that
he hopes he will never experience the hardness of toil he has undergone,
Aubrey replies full of contempt: "Shades of my fathers, forbid that I should
ever have to work" (7).[19] Moreover, while Reuel has an incredibly strong
moral restraint in sex matters, Aubrey is obsessed by it, and, most noticeably, in contrast to Reuel he talks of black women only as objects for white
men's pleasure (see 7–13). While Reuel is capable of "complete self-sacrifice" (58), Aubrey is associated with a form of extreme individualism which
lays down spiritual values for materialistic self-interest. In fact, he recognizes the existence of supernatural powers—persistently associated in the
novel with the African heritage—but tries to exploit them for his own purposes, in the same way his father, a Virginian doctor and planter, used the
powers of his slave/lover Mira to "perform tricks of mind-reading for the
amusement of visitors" (50). Aubrey is totally incapable of true emotional
response and his extreme superficiality emerges during one of the most
moving parts of the novel—the jubilee concert—as he claims to understand
Negro music just because he grew up in the South (8).

Besides the above discussed elements, what makes Aubrey the *bad white
character* is his direct involvement in the suppression of the black heritage
by perpetrating forced miscegenation and incest—the same black heritage
of which he himself, a mulatto, is ironically part of. In fact, while Reuel
wants to help Dianthe recover the memory of her true black identity, Aubrey
diabolically prevents her from regaining it, in order to seduce her.[20] The
stark contrast which characterizes Reuel's and Aubrey's behavior toward
Dianthe—and, symbolically, toward the other women of the story victim
of incest and miscegenation, like their own mother Mira—is the element
which makes them form what I have called a *negative dialectic*.

Besides his extreme dishonesty toward his best friend Reuel (he plans
his voyage to Africa in order to kill him), even Aubrey's other relations are
entirely negative. At the beginning he and Charlie Vance apparently are
friends, because Aubrey is Charlie's sister's fiancée. But then they become
fierce enemies because Aubrey murders the girl, when he no longer desires

or needs her. Moreover, Aubrey finds an initial partner in crime in his black servant, Jim Titus. Eventually, however, Aubrey becomes the servant's worst enemy, because he basically uses him to kill a man of his own race and then causes his death in Africa. The wicked allegiance between Aubrey and Jim represents what I would call a *negative symmetry*.

Jim Titus embodies the *bad black character*. His figure is rapidly sketched in chapter ten: "Jim was proving himself a necessary part of the expedition. He was a Negro of the old regime who felt that the Anglo-Saxon was appointed by God to rule over the African. He showed his thoughts in his obsequious manner, his subservient 'massa,' and his daily conversation with those about him" (78). Jim's essential duplicity gets manifested in the episode of Reuel's aggression by a leopard, when he, supposed to be Reuel's guard, pretends not to hear him call for help. At the end of the novel, Jim tells Reuel that he agreed to obey Aubrey because he could not refuse him anything, since Aubrey is his foster brother. In spite of this, Hopkins's emphasis is still on Jim's being a sort of prototypical submissive slave, punished for the betrayal of his own people: by serving the evil plans of the white master and accepting money for it, in fact, he becomes complicit with a racial fratricide (since he knew that Reuel and Aubrey were both mulattoes and half-brothers).

Jim's only positive interaction is the dialectic one linking him to the other white character of the novel, Charlie Vance. Critics have tended to neglect the figure of Charlie Vance, but I think that the study of this character is essential in order to reassess previous understandings of racial relations in the novel. Introduced as the portrait of the thoughtless youth, Charlie is a rich northern young man who always makes jokes about everyone and everything. He does not seem to care much either for the racial problems of his country or for the mysteries of the human psyche—and he even ridicules Reuel's incredible accomplishment in saving Dianthe from her state of apparent death (he apostrophizes his friend saying "Briggs is our 'show man,'" 48). Charlie shares with Aubrey an apparent tendency to idleness, self-interest, and racism. Unlike Aubrey, however, he is allowed a final conversion which reveals him as the *good white character*, the perfect symmetric mate of the black protagonist.

At first, Charlie joins the party of the expedition just "as a tourist for the sake of the advantages of such a trip" (63) and, as the enterprise reveals itself to be more serious than it originally seemed, he reaffirms his careless attitude ("Well, I'm only travelling for pleasure, so . . . I intend to get some fun out of this thing," 98). In Charlie Vance's initially superficial attitude, Hopkins seems to blame both the consumerist and the capitalistic views of Africa[21]—two aspects of Western self-interest which appear in the two references Charlie makes to Barnum's circus. In the first one, Charlie compares Africa to a great show ("it promises to be better than anything Barnum has ever given us even at a dollar extra reserved seat," 77). In the second one, he even discusses a plan of exploitation:

> "It's business this time. . . . the sight of a camel always makes me child again. The long-necked beast is inevitably associated in my mind with Barnum's circus and playing hookey. Pop wants me to put out my sign and go in for business, but the show business suits me better. For instance . . . Arabs, camels, stray lions, panthers, scorpions, serpents, explorers etc., with a few remarks by yours truly, to the accompaniment of the band . . . a sort of combination of Barnum and Kiralfy. The houris would do Kiralfy's act, you know. There's money in it." (81)[22]

Although he does not seem to be very serious, Charlie even ponders the idea of bringing some Arabians to the United States to organize a big show, like Barnum's, and profit by them. And what is more interesting, Charlie makes fun of the *houris*—supernatural female creatures in the Muslims' afterlife, similar to angels—thus adhering to a form of racial sexism, which echoes Aubrey's father's "impious" exploitation of his slave Mira's supernatural powers. But what Hopkins seems to stress here is that Charlie's lack of serious interest in his African experience derives from his indifference to the crucial problem of race in his own country. Because he is not familiar with the "Southern exuberance" of his own country, the young man is unable, for instance, to understand that the disorder of the world which surrounds him in Tripoli is only apparent ("what a jostling, what a noise," 78). That disorder, in fact, only consists of his superficial perception of a deeply structured culture.

But as he witnesses the conversations between Reuel and the archaeologist of the group, Professor Scott, Charlie undergoes an intellectual shock which paves the way for a deeper emotional change. As Scott explains the intellectual and technical attainments accomplished by black people in Asia and Africa, Charlie is incredulous and exclaims: "Great Scott! . . . you don't mean to tell me that all this was done by *niggers?*" (99, italics mine). This change is clearly underlined in another passage of the text, where we read that Charlie "had suffered so many shocks from the shattering of *cherished idols* since entering the country of mysteries that the power of expression had left him" (101, italics mine), and it is quite easy to grasp that the most "cherished idol" here is the supposed cultural superiority of the Anglo-Saxon race.

Charlie's conversion from his tendency to self-interest and racism is realized in his *positive dialectic* interaction with the black servant Jim—whom Charlie gets better acquainted with after Reuel's disappearance in the underground city of Telassar. Hopkins writes that "Charlie was glad of Jim's lively conversation. Anecdotes of Southern life flowed glibly from his tongue, illustrated by songs descriptive of life there. It really seemed to Vance that *a portion of the United States had been transported to Africa*" (150, italics mine). In these brief anticipatory passages, we learn that Jim's company allows Charlie to be introduced to African Americans in a context which is not their own. His conversion, however, is completed only in the passage describing his and Jim's entrapment in the labyrinth (157–159). As they realize that it is impossible to escape, the two men are left alone with each other and their despair. Hopkins writes:

> [Charlie] spoke in jest, but the tears were in his eyes, and as he clasped Jim's toil-hardened black hand, he told himself that Ai's [Telassar's prime minister] words were true. *Where was the color line now? Jim was a brother; the nearness of their desolation in this uncanny land, left nothing but a feeling of brotherhood.* He felt then the truth of the words, "Of one blood have I made all races of men." (159, italics mine)

In this highly emotional and intense passage, we find out that Charlie's witty temper hides a truly sympathetic disposition, which allows him to overcome his superficial prejudice toward black people.

Signs of Charlie's essential goodness appear from the beginning of the African journey as well. In chapter ten, for instance, he is described as a kind-hearted man, capable of Christian self-sacrifice, a quality which positively links him to Reuel. In fact, not only did he save the protagonist from the leopard (83–86; thus acting the opposite way to Jim Titus), but he also "suppressed his own feelings" over the lack of news and letters from his father and sister to "comfort" his friend, who also hears nothing from his beloved Dianthe in America (107). Nevertheless, it is important to mention that Charlie is *not* aware that Reuel is a mulatto until the final chapters of the novel, and the details of his discovery have been left untold by the author. As my reading suggests, Hopkins's portrayal of the interaction between Reuel and Charlie is symmetrical and not dialectic. This means that, interestingly, any direct confrontation on the racial issue between the two good characters is avoided. What, then, is the nature of their relation?

My argument is that, in the novel, symmetry individuates a clear process of identification. After Reuel's disappearance in the kingdom of Telassar, Charlie undergoes a real change: he dismisses both superficiality and idleness, and acquires those positive intellectual and moral traits which Hopkins had previously underlined in Reuel Briggs. We read, in fact, that after his friend had disappeared Charlie was "no longer the spoiled darling of wealth and fashion, *but a serious minded man of taciturn disposition*" (149, italics mine). Charlie's striking identification with Reuel is even more underlined as he and Jim are taken prisoners by the soldiers of Telassar. Wishing to understand the unknown tongue of his warders, "Charles wished then that he had spent more time in study and less in sport . . . *he was of a philosophical nature*; if he had been poor and forced to work for a living, he might have become a *learned philosopher*" (152, italics mine), like his friend Reuel.

The positive symmetrical relation of Reuel and Charlie, however, poses a new question, dealing with their uncritical acceptance of certain American "Yankee" values. At the beginning of chapter twelve, Charlie is already undertaking a gradual departure from the superficial image of the "show business man," and is slowly acquiring that of the American entrepreneur. Hopkins writes that Charlie's gaze wandered with curiosity on the desolation of the African landscape and "his *healthy American organization* missed the march of progress attested by the sound of hammers on unfinished buildings that told of a busy future and cosy modern homeliness" (93, italics mine). This passage echoes another one, where Reuel contemplates the wealth and fertility of the African kingdom of Telassar and "with an *American's practical common sense* bewailed this *waste* of material" (134, italics mine). As we can see from these passages, Hopkins's emphasis on industriousness or pragmatism as positive "interracial" American values, linking the two good American protagonists in their African enterprise, seems to suggest an implicit ideological adherence to those American imperialist views that the writer herself tried to condemn. The presence of this uncriticized "American's practical common sense" in *Of One Blood* could then be intended as another sign of the tension between a radical racial essentialism and an interiorization of the dominant ideology, that has been already identified in the novel by various critics, such as Martin Japtok or Marla Harris.[23]

In spite of such "ideological symmetry," however, Hopkins underlines that the similarity between the two men's experience is limited. After the death of Jim Titus—who finally tells Reuel that Aubrey is his half-brother—the two good characters are left to face a situation which is comparable only in part. Reuel and Charlie in fact have been both offended by a sororicide (Reuel/Dianthe, Charlie/Molly), but Hopkins emphasizes that they experienced "very different degrees of feeling. Charlie Vance held to the old Bible punishment for the pure crime of manslaughter, but in Reuel's wrongs lay something beyond the reach of punishment by the law's arm; in it was the accumulation of years of foulest wrongs heaped upon the innocent and defenceless women of a race, added to this last great outrage" (164). Reuel's pain is very different from Charlie's, because it is complicated by the burden of violence that along the centuries has been perpetrated—through forced miscegenation and incest—against the women of his race and against his race itself. Thus, the feeling of universal brotherhood that links these two characters gets partially smothered by the old injustices which haunt American history. Commenting on the end of the novel, Hazel Carby has underlined that

> it is dominated by the impossibility of resolving *Of One Blood* within the framework of popular forms. . . . The social relations of the institution of slavery determine the relations of contemporary society, and Hopkins offers *no possibility that these contradictions can be resolved within the boundaries of the United States.* The social and moral order of American society is revealed to be based on incest, and thus no happy endings are possible. The tangle of incestuous relationships

represents Hopkins's vision of a hell in which the "laws of changeless justice bind oppressor and oppressed."[24]

Eric Sundquist does not seem to agree with such interpretation, and writes instead that Hopkins's "intent was less to promote back-to-Africa philosophy than to draw from it a popularized basis for pride in black history and, more important, a theoretically complex way to understand African-American double consciousness."[25] As I hope to have shown, the analysis of the novel's characterization allows us to make some remarks that slightly contradict Carby's fitting but peremptory conclusion. At the same time, it also adds a new dimension to Sundquist's more optimistic reading. In my opinion, the novel does not dismiss American society as a whole; rather, it seeks to revitalize those *positive* interracial relations which flourished in the North of the country during the abolitionist era, and stemmed—as Carby herself has pointed out—from "a neglected New England tradition of radical politics."[26] Although complicated by the questions of incest and miscegenation, the influence of abolitionist thinking in Hopkins's novel can be traced in the emphasized allegorical contrast between the two main "white" characters, the *bad southerner* Aubrey Livingston and the *good northerner* Charlie Vance, and in their different interactions (*negative dialectic* or *positive symmetrical*) with the "black" characters, Reuel Briggs and Jim Titus. Such interactions finally show that the possibility of positive interracial relations in the novel intersects with the protagonists' different moral positions toward the essential problem of race both in their own lives and the history of America.

NOTES

1. Hopkins, *Of One Blood*, 149. Further references to this work are included in the text.
2. As C. K. Doreski has pointed out, "the shadow of a compromised citizenship cast by Plessy vs. Ferguson (1896) necessitated an urgent commitment to the recovery and perpetuation of race history. Hopkins transcended the journal's arts context by writing for 'those who never read history or biography.' She hoped that, through the imitative commodified culture of the magazine, ideas of the marketplace could become a marketplace of ideas." Doreski, "Inherited Rhetoric and Authentic History," 72.
3. Hopkins's only partial adherence to such literary models has been read by Hazel Carby as "reveal[ing] the limits of these popular American narrative forms for black characterization" (Carby, *Reconstructing Womanhood*, xxix). The similarities of *Of One Blood* with the above-mentioned American classics have been pointed out by various scholars (see Kassanoff, "'Fate Has Linked Us Together'," 173; Otten, "Pauline Hopkins and the Hidden Self of Race," 235; and McDowell, Introduction to *Of One Blood*, xi).
4. For a discussion of Hopkins's deconstruction of Haggard's novel, see for example Allen, *Black Women Intellectuals*.
5. Maria Giulia Fabi locates the novel at the source of a specific tradition of "African American Utopian texts," pointing out that

both on a formal and on a thematic level, [such works, of which *Of One Blood* is a forerunner,] are informed by the intersections between the tropes of miscegenation and passing. On one hand, miscegenation and passing are symptoms of a dystopian contemporary world where whiteness as normative utopia makes the rejection of blackness a tempting option. On the other, race travel operates on a fictional level as an ideological reversal of racial hierarchies that is eventually epitomized in the passer's choice to forsake passing and belong to the African American community. According to Fabi, we have "race travel" when "the voluntary passer frees himself from the cultural hegemony of white America, develops greater pride in his black heritage, [and] acquires the ability to read the signs of this powerful heritage even in the United States." Fabi, *Passing*, 47–48.

6. Doreski, "Inherited Rhetoric and Authentic History," 74.
7. Carby, Introduction to *The Magazine Novels*, xliv.
8. McDowell, Introduction to *Of One Blood*, xv.
9. But also by the old Aunt Hannah, the "voodoo" doctor, and Queen Candace of Telassar. For a detailed analysis of the relations among these female characters see Allen, *Black Women Intellectuals*, 41.
10. Kassanoff has remarked that in the novel universal brotherhood is always threatened by a fear of contamination, explaining that "although *Of One Blood* explicitly argues for a brotherhood of man, subtexts of incestuous blood (fraternalism run amok) and black eugenetics (brothers biologically united against a perceived contaminant) dispute this claim." Kassanoff, "'Fate Has Linked Us Together,'" 171.
11. For an analysis of the importance and the use of the fantastic element in the novel, see Otten, "Pauline Hopkins and the Hidden Self of Race," 230.
12. See Sundquist, *To Wake the Nations*, 565.
13. James, "The Hidden Self," 362.
14. See for instance Schrager, "Pauline Hopkins and William James," 190.
15. See for instance Carby, Introduction to *The Magazine Novels*, xlvi.
16. I would like to suggest that Hopkins's concern here is not much that of providing a "psychological" portrait of the mulatto who identifies with the "white father." Rather she "insists on the presence of intermixed blood in the Southern white aristocracy as a historical fact of oppressive social relations under slavery" (Schrager, "Pauline Hopkins and William James," 196), but also as an ironical defiance of the image of purity often associated with southern whiteness.
17. The early twentieth-century debate on the origins of Western culture had erased the links between the Egyptians and Africa. See Young, *Colonial Desire*.
18. As a matter of fact, these prejudices were the same ones northerners had against southern aristocracy.
19. Hopkins had previously underlined that Reuel "lived and paid his way at the expense of the dull intellects or the idle rich, with which a great university always teems" (4).
20. As Thomas Otten has remarked, "Aubrey's domination of Dianthe is based on a racial purity he turns out not to possess and on the failure to recognize the origins he and Dianthe share." Otten, "Pauline Hopkins and the Hidden Self of Race," 350.
21. Hopkins writes that the expedition included "artists, savans and several men—capitalists—who represented the business interests of the venture" (75). The issue of consumerist views of Africa in the novel has been previously analyzed by Marla Harris. See her article "Not Black and/or White."
22. Phineas Taylor Barnum (1810–1891) was a famous American showman, known for having made the American circus a popular and gigantic spectacle,

the so-called "Greatest Show of Earth." Imre Kiralfy was another American Jewish showman of Hungarian descent who actually collaborated with P. T. Barnum from the 1890s.

23. See Japtok, "Pauline Hopkins's *Of One Blood*," and Harris, "Not Black and/ or White." The latter has significantly remarked that even "the final image of Reuel, teaching his people all that he has learned in years of contact with modern culture, . . . provides not so much an alternative to Western patriarchy but a continuation in a benign form of the paternalism of white slave-owners and missionaries" (387–388). My opinion is that Hopkins's uncritical description of the two good characters sharing common American values should not be left unquestioned; rather it should be taken as a further element to analyze the ideological ambiguities of the text.

24. Carby, "Introduction," xlvii; italics mine.

25. Sundquist, *To Wake the Nations*, 573.

26. According to Carby, Hopkins's political aim was to "revive a neglected New England tradition of radical politics. . . . In Hopkins's imagination, the city of Boston could be recreated as the center of *black and white* political agitation that it was at the height of abolitionism." Carby, Introduction to *The Magazine Novels*, xxxii; italics mine.

21 Marine Origins and Anti-Marine Tropism in the French Caribbean
André and Simone Schwarz-Bart

Antoinette Tidjani Alou

THE SYMBOLIC ATLANTIC

For the people of the Caribbean, the Atlantic Ocean and the Caribbean Sea are charged with symbolic power. They are not merely the generic "Ocean Sea" of certain literary or cinematic fantasies. Such fantasies continue to exist and thrive, from Baudelaire to Walt Disney. But if we believe Claude Lévi-Strauss, such "innocent" imaginary treasures of fictional and poetic magic have been forever tainted by the "half corrupted memories" of a "proliferating and overexcited civilization [that] troubles forever the silence of the seas."[1] In the literal, scientific or symbolic sense, this original silence is of course debatable. At any rate, since Columbus, if ever the sea was silent, it now speaks, multifariously, and the subjects of its enunciations are not necessarily mythical adventures, neat hybridity, or exotic memories.[2]

In fact, the postcolonial counterdiscourse of the "Other Americas"[3] casts Latin America and the Caribbean as the legacy of the marine obsessions of the Middle Passage, of transatlantic crossings, and of a second coming out of the sea. The region is viewed as the nucleus of a prolific New World whose marine origins imprint on Caribbean experience creative creolization and diversity, but also roaming, "sea-sickness" and instability. Far removed from exotic fantasies, such analyses and interpretations highlight the positive and negative marine influences on Caribbean reality and their symbolic representations. Similarly, regarding the archipelago, Glissant's essays—engaged in a poetical and philosophical construction of pan-Caribbean unity, in the context of a world marked by complex historically situated relations—optimistically construct the idea of an invisible submarine rhizomic link connecting the islands.[4] The sea-root/route is a metaphor of profound, hidden, submarine unity in the face of apparent fragmentation and valorized chaos. As a corollary to submarine unity, Glissant's novels also propose openness to the call of "the two seas," the Caribbean Sea and the Atlantic Ocean, one calm, the other rough, as a welcoming of life in a multidimensional global world in which the regional reconstructions of identity wrought by cultural and racial intermingling (*métissage*) encounter doubts (suggested in terms like *opacité*) concerning the means of achieving sovereignty, economic viability, dignity, and recognition in a world shaped by the global market forces originating in the North.[5]

In addition to these historical, political, and economic factors, the geographic reality is also important, as long as we admit that in the present case, as in others, the geography of maps is doubled by a geography of the soul. In strictly geographical terms, the Atlantic Ocean washes the shores of Africa, North and South America, and Europe. The Caribbean Sea forms the acute angle of the triangle of trade which linked these continents and the Antillean archipelago through chains of profit, blood, madness—and change. The Caribbean Sea is not really separate and apart from the Atlantic. But the island chain of the Antilles describes a partial enclosure, formed by fragile land masses encircling the warm currents of marine waters named after the Carib people, one of the first American populations to experience genocide due to the European lust for gold. Many but not all of the islands are washed by both the marine masses and currents of the Atlantic Ocean and those of the Caribbean Sea. But this detail is of no major importance, for the Atlantic we are concerned with here does not merely involve the geography of maps; it is, moreover, infused with a far-reaching symbolic meaning, related to the embodied and gendered trope of *crossing*. Expressed through a symbolic constellation, it comprises effective oceanic and other metaphors for global and local New World dialogue, literary and otherwise.

Finally, there is also a psychosomatic Atlantic, as represented by the Caribbean as an experienced and phantasmal space. The sea, in Caribbean literature and in literature on the Caribbean, also symbolizes trauma, madness, and embodied chaos (as in Shakespeare's *The Tempest*, Césaire's *Cahier d'un retour au pays natal*, André Schwarz-Bart's *La Mulâtresse Solitude*, Glissant's *Case du commandeur*, Maryse Condé's *Moi, Tituba, sorcière*). Textually inscribed as the route of alienating temptations (Césaire's *Discours sur le colonialisme*, Zobel's *Rue cases-nègres*, Fanon's *Peau noire, masques blancs*), the sea also symbolizes the last frontier of life (Simone Schwarz-Bart's *Pluie et vents sur Télumée Miracle*) and the executor of poetic justice (Glissant's novel *La Lézarde*), and is often associated with death by shipwreck or drowning.

This perspective of marine brooding interlaced with hope belongs to the trope of the "tainted Atlantic." It is, by and large, the product of a certain academic, postcolonial, or anticolonial discourse, of Caribbean, "alter-American" or "global" orientation. This discourse coexists alongside living, past or contemporary, expressions of Ocean-Sea dreaming. In fact, well into the nineteenth century, when the immense profits from the plantation economy had already set about radically changing the configuration and the imagination of European society, even after the Enlightenment and its mixed messages regarding the slave trade and plantation economy as part of the question of human rights and equality, poets like Baudelaire still found themselves in a position to instill into marine metaphors dreams of freedom, exotic flights of fancy, and sublime sensuality. Walt Disney films like *Pocahontas* or *The Little Mermaid* provide contemporary examples of Ocean-Sea fantasies of a different type. They have little or nothing to do with post-slavery trauma or post-plantation mythopoeia, though they incorporate musical rhythms (Trinidad) and speech rhythms (Jamaica) of the Caribbean.

In the context of literature and criticism, the Atlantic evokes and subsumes symbolically all that the history of European imperialism, and the Triangular Trade in particular, brought into existence or raised to an unprecedented plane. As we know, this includes slavery, global traffic and global crossings, racial intermingling, and economic globalization, at one level. At another, these can be read as consecutive radical political, economic, social, cultural, and psychic changes and discourses. In short, these historical dynamics produced a whole "New World," not only on the sites of the Caribbean and on American slave plantations, but all over the world and for peoples everywhere.[6] However, this chapter will focus on certain aspects of these circumatlantic "events" and their symbolic representations from the perspective of the Caribbean, as seen in two related novels. For various reasons, as we will see, André Schwarz-Bart's *La Mulâtresse Solitude* and Simone Schwarz-Bart's *Pluie et vent sur Télumée Miracle*, taken together, provide an interesting point of departure for a discussion of sea changes, body, language, and memory in Caribbean literature and in certain literary works on the Caribbean. But these two novels, linked to each other in several ways, some of them obvious, others less so, are also part of a larger alter-American New World discourse.

It is true that, with the exception of a secondary character like Elie in *Pluie et vent sur Télumée Miracle*, they do not feature marine bodies and explicit marine obsessions like those of Anne Hébert's novelistic universe in *Les Fous de bassan*. However, in both novels, featuring a common character, Solitude, the sea/ocean trope seems to form an overarching signifier, crowning the initial and terminal poles delimiting the narratives, whose global time-space is contained between the painful historical origin of slavery, and the ultimate, if still future, annihilation of the last in line of a matriarchy, staunchly awaiting death. But this is not all; other binaries, like land/sea, ocean/river, or coast/mountain, feature among the paradoxical subcodes of an ongoing Caribbean discourse on history, cultural identity, and "worlding." The rhythms of crossing (*traversée*) and roaming (*errance*) are central to the dynamics of this discourse, which is neither linear, nor necessarily coherent, in which life is flux and reflux, inscribed within a metaphysics of unsettledness and uncertainty that marks and limits even (literary) heroism.

I will argue that the experiences of Atlantic crossing have left in the other Americas, and, indeed, on either side of the Atlantic, deep symbolic and psychic inscriptions. These are etched in both novels and in their interstices, triggering apparently paradoxical sociocultural orientations.

Benítez-Rojo refers to these as the "processes, dynamics, and rhythms that show themselves within the marginal, the regional, the incoherent, the heterogeneous or, if you like, the unpredictable that coexists with us [peoples of the Caribbean] in our everyday life."[7]

READING *LA MULÂTRESSE SOLITUDE* AND *PLUIE ET VENT SUR TÉLUMÉE MIRACLE* AS INTERTEXTS

Simone and André Schwarz-Bart collaborated both as a couple and as writers. Their novels that concern us here were published the same year: 1972. André Schwarz-Bart was born in France in 1928 in a family of Polish origin, deported by German Nazis in 1942. In 1943, he joined the French Resistance. His novel *Le Dernier des Justes,* written in 1959, won the Prix Goncourt and was a great commercial success. *La Mulâtresse Solitude* was intended as a follow-up. The introduction notes that it was written "in collaboration with his wife Simone," whose name does not appear as co-author, but who was at the same time busy with the writing of her own novel, *Pluie et vent sur Télumée Miracle* (translated into English as *The Bridge of Beyond*). Earlier, the couple had co-authored another novel, *Un Plat de porc aux bananes vertes* (1967). Simone Schwarz-Bart was born in Guadeloupe in 1938, when this island was not yet a French *département d'outremer*. She studied in the capital, Pointe à Pitre, then in Paris and Dakar. She met André Schwarz-Bart in 1959. These scant biographic details are in themselves evocative of yet another type of transatlantic dialogue, focused on the Caribbean experience.

The following line, quoted from Oruno Lara's *Histoire de la Gaudeloupe* (1921), serves as an epigraph to *La Mulâtresse Solitude*: "The mulatto woman Solitude was on the point of becoming a mother; arrested and imprisoned, she suffered capital punishment after delivery." The epigraph inserts the novel in the "true history" of Guadeloupe by drawing on a mythified heroine "who really existed," while underlining the fatal arrest of the female protagonist's possibilities. Set in the period 1769–1802, this short novel narrates the experiences of Bayangumay, the heroine, in her native Casamance (in today's Senegal), prior to her capture, deportation, and sale as a slave in Guadeloupe, near the end of the slave trade. Child of the meeting of three waters, the Atlantic Ocean, the great river Casamance, and the village pond, Bayangumay was born near 1750, when slave-hunting expeditions had gained the interior of the African continent, signaling the end of peace for the affected populations.

In 1973, Simone Schwarz-Bart's *Pluie et vent* won the Reader's Prize of the well-known French women's magazine, *Elle.* The following lines from a poem by Paul Eluard serve as an epigraph to *Pluie et vent*: "Beautiful without solid earth/Without floor without shoes without sheets."[8] These lines penned by one of the fathers of the Dadaist movement zero in on the novel's peculiar epic perspective, which makes beauty out of pain and heroines out of destitute figures. It further places the emphasis on the miracle of standing up to be counted as a "femme debout" in the early post-slavery context of Guadeloupe, where lack of footing and drifting were overarching tropes of black people's experience.

The character Solitude, a slave of mixed blood, forms a bridge between these two novels, on the one hand, and links Africa and Europe to each other and both to the Caribbean, on the other. In André Schwarz-Bart's novel, Solitude, born in Guadeloupe to Bayangumey (dubbed Bobette on her arrival) and an unknown white sailor, was conceived aboard the slave ship, fruit of the ritual of violence and sexual abuse meted out to black women by their white jailers, near the end of the Atlantic crossing. This ritual rape, called "la Pariade,"[9] is also featured at the very beginning of Maryse Condé's novel *Moi, Tituba, sorcière*. Self-named Solitude, the character is called Rosalie at birth, in keeping with the colonial ritual of the Duparc plantation's system of lending and recycling names: "the names of the dead went to the living who gave them up, when the time came, along with their souls."[10] Other similarities between the novels include, within the trope of crossing and of the imperial gaze: the centrality of the female point of view; the focus on individual survival versus the community *and* within the community; the spotlighting of female and mother-child relationships, on the one hand, and male-female heterosexual relations, on the other; the concern with African identity and with Antillean madness ("la folie antillaise"); the emphasis on naming and ritual, and on mapping landscapes of resistance.

MARINE ORIGINS

Several passages of both novels serve as interesting points of entry into their interrelated New World/Atlantic discourse. The opening of *La Mulâtresse Solitude* affords the reader a glimpse into the "other [African] side of the Atlantic," from whence "all America and the West Indies took slaves."[11] The opening site of the narrative is Casamance, just before and in the immediate aftermath of "tainting": "Once upon a time, on a strange planet, there was a little negro girl called Bayangumay. She came in the world near 1750, in the calm and complicated landscape of a delta, in a country in which the clear waters of a river, the green waters of the ocean and the black waters of a pond flowed into one another, and where the soul—it is said—was still immortal" (*M* 11). The reconstruction of Solitude's story begins with the fairytale formula "Il était une fois" ("once upon a time"), initially evoking mythical time. But, in fact, Solitude's mother, Bayangumay, a little Negro girl from "a strange planet," is situated within the hybrid time of myth/history. For, here, "once upon a time" is an identifiable period, "around 1750." This ambivalent time frame ultimately gives way to a preference for historical and post-mythical time. Since the advent of slave hunting, the "soul" is no longer "immortal"; the era of simple certitudes is over.

Later, the narrative frame shifts from a historical time frame to an inscription in space: "When Bayangumay was born, the big town on the banks of the river, a luxurious place of shadows and tranquility, was still called Sigi, which means: Sit down" (*M* 33). The space in question is a complex one, simultaneously "calm" and "complicated": the collecting space of a delta, a meeting place of the fresh waters of the great river with the salty waters of the ocean and the alluvium-invaded dead waters of the village pond. This is the time/space of an "immortality" from which the narrator distances himself by citing the authority of popular belief. History and myth, time and space, are drawn together in an unobtrusively multifaceted writing of New World experience, engraved in a space where water is a prominent trope of origin, and the ocean already foreshadows the route outwards and away. The spatial and temporal complexity is doubled by the intricacy of evoked New World spaces on "Old World" sites. These are engendered by the slave trade, its attendant relationships, and their evolution.

Unwittingly no doubt, André Schwarz-Bart's description of the untainted town of Sigi echoes Baudelarian exoticism. In fact, the town's character is summed up in a trilogy of epithets with a familiar ring. Admittedly, "ombre . . . luxe . . . tranquillité" is not quite the same as the "calme, luxe et volupté" of Baudelaire's dream of exotic adventure and evasion. But the "calme" is evoked at the outset of the narrative; "luxe" is the invariant, and "tranquillité" a possible phonic substitute for "volupté" that maintains the post-romantic rhythm.[12] If this reading is plausible, then André Schwarz-Bart's anti-colonial discourse is unconsciously counterdiscursive. Be that as it may, the advent of slave hunting in the region provokes a change in the name of Solitude's native land. The town named Sigi, meaning "sit down," becomes Sigi-Thyor, meaning "sit down and weep." This renaming underlines the collective agency of the disrupted population; it is not a colonial palimpsest of defining the other through remapping. However, it responds to a confrontation with, and an inscription of, new meanings, initially imposed from the outside, violently impinging on settled collective self-representations, acknowledged as a change for the worse. It remains an expression of the residual power of self-definition, "a symbolic . . . act of mastery and control."[13]

But, to move forward in history, the colonial corruption "Ziganchor" is the name by which this space has entered the geography of the contemporary world, through a further, colonial overwriting. This colonial "universalizing" results in a misfit between space and place. It introduces place as "a trope of difference."[14] Symbolic dislocation (for those who escape deportation and exile) and psychological and social alienation (for those who do not) respond, across the Atlantic, to capture, and palimpsest as related concepts evoking historical processes of colonialism as lived experiences. (Re)naming responds (on the part of the subject of colonization) to the tragic imperatives of entering the "world." This is indeed a "New World" beyond the comforting shadows of previous ignorance of the West.

ATLANTIC AND OTHER CROSSINGS

In the trans-Atlantic move from continental Sigi-Thyor to the island of Guadeloupe, crossing begins as a trek over land to the slave pens of the coast, prior to descent to the ocean: "They herded the people into the stone house . . . the whips, the irons, bludgeons and gun butts pressed them into a corridor which descended to the ocean. A three-master rolled at their feet" (M 39). Suffice it to say that the first step of the ocean crossing, a movement of descent, subtly foreshadows the horrors to come, comprising violent symbolic death and rebirth to a short and wretched life.[15] The Atlantic passage dramatizes the violence of the colonial encounter; featuring capture, murder, suicide, revenge and the instruments through which such violence is accomplished: whips, guns, iron bludgeons, sharks, ship, and ocean. Understandably, a major motivation of the rejection of the sea in Caribbean novels like *Pluie et vent* is a refusal of the traumatic memory of the holds of the slave ship.[16]

The fictional reconstruction of the Atlantic crossing in *La Mulâtresse Solitude* is followed by a description of the island debarkation and difficult installation in the New World. It foregrounds a new life of slavery in the plantation economy of Guadeloupe, constructed, once again, around the tropes of naming and mapping:

> The mulatto woman Solitude was born during slavery near 1772: French island of Guadeloupe, Duparc Plantation. . . . The Duparcs employed the system of the perpetual Register. . . . If an old slave called Rosalie happened to die, she was buried on the fallow ground of a roving, temporary cemetery, which would embellish the sugarcane lances of the future. And a new Rosalie took the place of the old with a soft cry on the Great Book of the Plantation. (M 49)

This New World mapping paradoxically employs the trope of stability as part of the "master's narrative": the master's "perpetual Register," containing a limited set of recycled names, and the fixed system of plantation management employed by the Duparcs, where everything is ordained "once and for all." From the point of view of the slave, however, it is a universe of approximation (without the exactitude of historical records; Solitude is "born near" 1772), of dehumanization (the slave is no different from a horse), of interchangeability (a slave dies, another is born to replace her), of impermanence (even the slave cemetery is not permanent and will one day become fertile land for planting sugarcane). This is a system of utter exploitation, to the bitter end, and even after (the slave's remains become manure for the master's future harvests), where one owns nothing, neither oneself nor one's "name."

MISCEGENATION AND PSYCHOSOMATIC DEGENERATION

Solitude's "true name" on the slave register is Rosalie. She is an emblematic, hybrid New World fruit, the child of "colonial desire," rape and miscegenation, an embodiment of sexual boundary transgressions and of non-belonging; a living symbol of conflict, schizophrenia and anxious "in-betweenness." Ocean and slave ship are sites of a ritual enacting of a rite of passage, prolonged on the anchored boat of the slave-island, in which the female slave endures a double share of torture. Interestingly, this narration of ritualized rape is refracted through the narrator's situated gaze. Drunken "white sailors" assault "black bellies," brought on deck to be disinfected by cold seawater, prior to arrival. The result of the sailors' "folly" and of the women's rape are mulatto "seeds" ready to sprout into pain and madness, "black meat" destined for continued "consumption" by the master, fond of such hybrid delicacies. The narrator cites the authority of old *bossales*, Africa-born plantation slaves (called "salt water" slaves, as opposed to "superior," "fresh water," island-born slaves), not that of the planter or overseer. According to these local experts, the physical and psychic indeterminacy of the slave of mixed blood is due to the nature and site of the sexual encounter at her origin: violence instead of love, un-housed copulation sites like the wayside, the borderline, the ditch, and the deck of the slave ship.

What further layers of meaning does this textualization reveal, if we take into consideration the author's identity and "affiliations"? A European of Jewish origin, having suffered from and "resisted" Nazi racism, married, at the time of writing, to a black Guadeloupean woman, a spiritual descendant of Solitude, proud of maroon resistance, and who, moreover, was closely involved in this fictional reconstruction. As suggested earlier, the author is of necessity informed and inspired by tropes derived from European literary representations, ideology, and aesthetics. How are these unavoidable interferences translated in this narration of miscegenation? In my view, translation includes an unwitting evocation of power as possession by violence, as dehumanization and dismembering of the female slave's body. For the sailors, notwithstanding the backing of "quoted" slave authority, are not demoted from the human status, whilst the slave women they rape are only "black bellies" forcefully possessed.

Moreover, the subtext seems to be that the rapists, in their ritual, act under the double (and perhaps related) influence of alcohol and madness (*égarement*). Notwithstanding, we are still in the presence of a writing of power, "racial hierarchy" and "difference" inscribed in the black female body,[17] constructed here as an exploitable and exploited "thing." This is a rung lower than familiar constructions of the female slave as temptress, endowed with animal or diabolic sexiness that, added to tropical heat and idleness, inveigled white planters into sexual depravity.[18] The sailors are not cast as responsible persons; their act of ritual rape is mildly defined as "strange." This is not to censure, but rather to underline the polysemic complexities and contradictions involved in writing the colonized body, for all stakeholders, be they champions, well-wishers, or exploiters.

Finally, housed in an incoherent body whose "features flee in all directions, hesitant eyebrows, eyes between two worlds," Rosalie is torn between two universes, situated on either side of the Atlantic Ocean, and alienated from both: "She knew that her mother came from the other side of the ocean, that she was a savage, according to the Whites, an African devil, according to the island-born Blacks. . . . Yet, without being a fresh water slave, Mama Bobette was not really a salt water Negress: her filed teeth excepted, there was nothing ignoble about her" (*M* 54). Rosalie's reflection is all about M-Other as a writing of difference/ambivalence.[19] Three ideological positions are voiced in this text: Rosalie's, that of "les Blancs" and that of "les Noirs." Rosalie's situation as a slave of mixed blood is expressed through a reading of her mother's identity—and implicitly of her own—as a "neither . . . nor" answer to a racialized plantation hierarchy. Her effort at personal definition, suggesting residual agency in the secret of the individual consciousness,[20] is built around binary pairs of terms. It quotes and "talks back" to two sets of interrelated, homogenizing discourses. In terms of place, these are: *l'autre côté de l'océan/le pays* (the other side of the ocean/the country), also expressed as *Afrique/Habitation* (Africa/Plantation), and *eau salée/eau douce* (sea water/fresh water). People pairs read like this: *les Blancs/les Noirs, nés au pays/Congo-Congo* (Whites/Blacks, born in the country/Congo-Congo). Other terms have no explicit correspondences: *figure incisée, forme curieuse d[es] incisives, parler de bêtes, les inquiétantes manières d'eau salée* . . . Overall, black sets pair off in equivalents as follows: the other side of the ocean = Africa = Blacks = Congo-Congo, along with their attributed characteristics quoted above. These, placed at the bottom of the plantation hierarchy, conflate the African, the slave, the primitive, the savage and the colonized as one and the same: ugly, bestial, uncivilized; belonging to another place, not *here*. This definition is that of the slave owner and of the island-born slave who accepts dominant categories in exchange for a rung higher on the classificatory ladder (as civilized/creolized slave). At the top of the pyramid we find *le pays, les Blancs, [l']Habitation*, which, comprising *the* standard, have no need for defining epithets of quality, being quality per se. Somewhere in between are fresh water, island born slaves, racially and/or culturally *métisse*, tamed and evolved locals who do not sport primitive facial marks, filed teeth, savage language, and behavior likely to disturb the master. Overall, this is also a discourse of the colonizer as plantation owner/manager and as *créole*.

FRESH WATER IS SUPERIOR: VALORIZING THE
ISLAND, CASTING THE SEA AS ENEMY

The island as a creole space is valorized, while Africa is maligned as the "other" (wrong) side of the Atlantic. Finally, Rosalie's disclaimer posits similarity and rejects denigration: "Mama Bobette was like all the other old women; except for the strange shape of her (certainly filed) teeth, there was nothing ignoble about her." Implicitly, Rosalie herself sees this dental aesthetics as an "ignoble trait." Hence, she is, if only marginally, self-identified as a fresh water slave, having internalized, to some extent, the definition of the Other. Rosalie's sole personal reference of origin is her Africa-born mother, torn between love and hate of her child. The mother-origin-Africa connection is the object of two opposing discourses. Solitude's discourse "talks back" to the "master's narrative" of difference, not without an underlying ambivalent counterdiscourse revealing a split identity. Her predicament results in the alienation that inspires her self-renaming as Solitude and, finally, her public execution, aided by the violent hierarchies of plantation society and the forces of French colonial history. But all is not loss in this biography. Thanks to her ultimate acceptance by a group of Maroons, she experiences the solace of healing and community, and even a certain distinction, despite the precariousness and perils of resistance. Finally, community acceptance is of vital importance to this character as it reestablishes her sense of belonging, or in spatial terms, her sense of finding a home. This rehousing takes the form of tenuous island roots, a metaphysical and cultural bridge that draws both *La Mulâtresse Solitude* and *Pluie et vent sur Télumée Miracle* together.

Solitude, mentioned in passing near the end of the Guadeloupean writer's novel, figures as a mythical ancestor whose experience of "lost victories" significantly mirrors the ambivalent quality of resistance and the margins of agency that marked early post-slavery island life, for the most resilient. If the island is home, it is certainly not paradise; it is not the exotic *there* that fuels Baudelairian dreams of evasion. In fact, as Mannoni points out, such exotic daydreams are poetic equivalents of spatial "othering" in terms of primordial purity and radical difference.[21] To the contrary, in *Pluie et vent sur Télumée Miracle* Simone Schwarz-Bart's territorialization is a complex, multilayered electing of the island space as garden, home, and country. But this insecure island refuge is the site of incessant inland crossings. As Ileana Rodríguez rightly remarks, the female protagonists' "yoking" to the land establishes territory mainly as geography (as opposed to politics).[22] It is a liminal space of orality,[23] with (maternal) ancestry and popular resistance as key elements.

However, I will argue counter to Rodríguez, this treatment of space is not only a "fencing off" and does not entail an entirely "ethno-tragic" representation of the souls of black folks. For, while Rodríguez is correct in underlining the Guadeloupean writer's realistic approach to the description

of island life, she downplays the writing of beauty, the self, joy, and defiance, which are far from insignificant. Moreover, while she rightly comments on the importance of inland sites like "the mountain, the jungle, the
hillside, the swamp as referent, symbol, and sign of the construction of a
new nation,"[24] she does not question the silencing of the sea, that is, the
inscription of the sea as presence-in-absence.

In the rest of this chapter, I will reflect briefly on some of these aspects
of this "woman's book." To borrow from Rodríguez's apt summary, *"Pluie
et vent sur Télumée Miracle* or *Bridge of Beyond . . .* is the story of the
Lugandor [*sic*] family and its ancestry. . . . The central figures are the
grandmother, Queen without a Name, and her granddaughter Télumée.
The novel tells the story of . . . undaunted, enduring and resilient love."[25]
The opening lines of this novel feature Télumée's discourse on self, island,
and history: "A man's country may be cramped or vast according to the
size of his heart. I've never found my country too small, though that isn't
to say that my heart is great. And if I could choose it's here in Guadeloupe
that I'd be born again, suffer and die. Yet not long back my ancestors were
slaves on this volcanic, hurricane-swept, mosquito ridden, nasty-minded
island" (*P* 3). This is clearly a metaphorical and ontological writing of
agency and centrality from the perspective of the individual experience of
a wise old woman. Descended from a line of exceptionally resilient fore-
mothers, Queen without a Name (as Reine sans Nom is called in the English translation of the novel) has weathered the storms of life and managed
to escape with her "heart" (joy) intact. Her discourse presents a Russian
doll-like interlocking of microcosms—heart, person, garden and island. Of
these miniature spaces, the heart, and even the heart of hearts, or "second
heart," is the key. It is the secret center of strategic resistance, the site of
concealed agency. On its grandeur depend individual and universal significance or insignificance. The heart symbolizes the concealed power of the
creative imagination and spiritual wealth strategically deployed in the face
of life's inevitable vicissitudes. This is the key to "joy," despite everything,
including death, which the heroine staunchly awaits with good humor and
defiant spunk.

These spaces also fit inside one another as a writing of the "middle," of
centrality: Télumée's philosophical testimony is delivered as she stands in
the middle of her garden, her invincible heart well anchored in the middle of her self, her self in the island, the island in the metaphysical and
"real" world. For Guadeloupe is, in the same breath, identified as an ex-
slave island, mosquito-ridden, subject to earthquakes and hurricanes, not
only to the joys and ills of community life. Notwithstanding this realistic
outlook, the island is irrevocably chosen as home in the same breath that
affirms that joy is an individual creation and a question of vision. While the
physical spaces mentioned above symbolize and define moral positioning,
aquatic metaphors evoke the eventful and relentless flow of existence. These
also insist on a peculiar type of marginal agency: the enduring resistance of

dominated but strong and resourceful characters, whose coping strategies shrewdly oppose attempts to enslave the soul along with the body.

Yet, part of this novel's Caribbean discourse on resistance is a deliberate avoidance of heroic self-portraiture by its prominent female characters. Though the reader's interpretation inevitably counters this refutation, this posture is important for an understanding of the moral economy of the novel. Télumée, unlike the victims of the ritual rape called "la Pariade," is able to escape sexual abuse at the hands of M. Desaragne, the master of the white creole household where she works as a maid at one point. Yet she has a deliberately prosaic reading of her success, sold as neither a "victoire de négresse" nor a "victoire de femme," but another current in the sea of life, before the ultimate "drowning." Here, victory, downplayed with ruthless lucidity, is another hard-learned application of a survival strategy. Thus resistance here corresponds neither to Rodríguez's reading of tragedy nor to Anthea Morrison's interpretation of *Pluie et vent* in terms of a "redeeming certainty."[26] In fact, this sea metaphor, threaded throughout the entire novel, consistently underlines the limits to heroic achievement in the specific, historic situation the novel evokes. Ultimately, the novel's philosophical and sociocultural perspective is closer to Campbell and Frickey's conception of powerlessness as "the inability to overcome, not the inability to fight and struggle."[27] In its complex writing of resistance, realistic clairvoyance complements strategies of spiritual marooning (*marronage*). As in the case of the "lost victories" (Maroon battles) of their foremother Solitude, those of her female lineage in the *Pluie et vent* occur both within the landscape and within the fastness of the self. They address the larger issues of resistance and acceptance, explored in destinies characterized by the ebullient rhythms of crossing and drowning.

Between the parentheses of birth and death, biographies are written with their backs to the sea as inland crossings, as retreat to the secret garden of the inner self and to the ritual space of the hills. They are poetically evoked through fluvial and other metaphors of passage as control-in-the-present, a piloting of one's boat on the river of life, as far and as long as possible. Near the opening of *Pluie et vent*, the narrator focuses on Télumée's precocious entry into adulthood. At age fourteen, she has moved beyond the parentheses of school, a protected "pool" beyond the "torrential rains" of the real world of adult life. But school is also a privileged site for the inscription of dominant discourses of racial hierarchy. According to its pedagogically enforced ideology, France is origin, goddess-mother, and the epitome of civilization, whereas black Guadeloupean pupils are improvable savages. Parenthetical space of childhood innocence, subjected nonetheless to colonial assimilation, school is powerless to bar indefinitely the "floodgates" of adult strife.

The following quotation, narrating Télumée's anxieties at the prospect of school-leaving, is ominously tinged with marine brooding, over and beyond the river metaphor: "All rivers, even the most dazzling . . . all rivers go down to and are drowned in the sea. And life awaits man like the sea awaits the river. You can take meander after meander, twist, turn, seep into the earth—your meanders are your own affair. But life is there, patient, without beginning or end, waiting for you, like the ocean" (*P* 74). As the sea is an inimical force, it is logical that Télumée and her female forbears, all descendants of Solitude, choose to evolve in accordance with fresh water images like the Blue Pool of childhood innocence, of washerwomanly chores, of lustral influence and of the fusional emotions of first love. Good women are associated with fresh water: from the buckets carried on the head for domestic purposes, to the herbal waters of balmyards (where women treat and heal physical and psychic disorders). Sorrow precipitates the pathetic fallacy of rainfall, while light showers of blessing signal the passing of strong women like Reine sans Nom.

Water is everywhere in this "woman's book," but only fresh water is valorized. Women of evil influence, whose words breed pessimism, fear and mental dislocation, are likened to marine flotsam, to huge shipwrecked whales that the sea rejects. Finally, it is interesting to note the evolution of the concept of "fresh water" associated with black Guadeloupean females, already underlined in relation to André Schwarz-Bart's *La Mulâtresse Solitude*. Simone Schwarz-Bart's writing of *créolisation*, before the invention of the term, elects the Caribbean island as home through an implicit rejection of "salt water" (the ocean). No longer synonymous with a rejection of Africa or with an introjection of the Other's gaze, it still distances itself from origin, interpreted in marine terms. Notwithstanding, marine rhythms are hard to evade since they infuse the subconscious and therefore the imagination. Thus the island itself becomes an anchored boat battered by marine winds and waves. Island "housing" is not synonymous with "settlement."

This point of view is summed up in the concluding lines of the novel, spoken by Télumée in her final testimonial: "I've moved my cabin to the east and to the west; east winds and north winds have buffeted and soaked me; but I am still a woman standing on my own two legs, and I know that a Negro is not a statue of salt to be dissolved by the rain" (*P* 245–246).

CONCLUSION

The perpetual rhythm of crossing seems to be written into the cultural genes of the children of the Middle Passage. This is certainly the case of the protagonists of both novels. Solitude's crossing starts on land, in her native Casamance where she is captured. It continues over sea to the Caribbean island of Guadeloupe she claims as home. And her immediate descendants do not find rest in their New World environment, where permanence is an unattainable dream and where moving house can mean literally picking up one's hut and moving with it to another place.

So, in *Pluie et vent sur Télumée Miracle*, the Atlantic crossing also gives way to inland crossings, to "sites," "places" and "municipalities," "named following heartfelt mandates,"[28] evoking mental trauma, dire misery, marginality, and a sense of rejection. But if home is not inherently sweet, it is sweetened by "attitude," in the positively charged African American sense of the word. These novels reflect on resistance, from the perspective of a gendered writing of the self, the country and the world. Here, agency is a shrewd and creative exploitation of a limited room for maneuver. It involves "hanging in there" as long as possible, that is, not "going under" at the first tidal wave of misery and misfortune. In both novels, claiming the island as home is hard work, as confirmed by other French Caribbean writings of crossing and roaming, like Césaire's *Cahier d'un retour au pays natal*, Glissant's novels, Simone Schwarz-Bart's *Ton beau capitaine* and Maryse Condé's *Moi, Tituba, sorcière*, among other works. It involves incessant moving, a phenomenon which, at a broader level, surfaces as a fundamental element of the Caribbean and New World experience of unsettledness, ambivalence and roaming.

Paradoxically, the sea/ocean trope is simultaneously liminal, overarching and interspersed throughout this writing of the inevitable: suffering and death where both resistance and resignation are part of the agenda, aspects of the coping mechanisms of the female lineage these works celebrate. The sea is a misanthropic demiurge, ensconced in the cyclic eternity of mythical time, patiently observing the lives of poor black people, until the fatal snip, in the last scene. But this does not preclude a celebration of the joys of the interim as an inalienable human right to be fought for, preferentially evoked in fresh water and hinterland images. In *Pluie et vent* the writing of the self and of the community, set in a time gone by, communicates with larger spaces and questions, essentially in philosophical and humanistic terms. The novel affirms the wealth of all human experience, lived even in the most wretched conditions. Its memory work, like that of *La Mulâtresse Solitude*, reconstructs and valorizes the effaced history of the children of the Middle Passage, of those who "came from the Atlantic." But it does more than that to the extent that it addresses, over and beyond Caribbean experiences of a specific period, the problem not just of surviving but of *living* in troubled times.

NOTES

1. Lévi-Strauss, *Tristes Tropiques*, quoted in Bongie, *Exotic Memories*, 1.
2. Bongie, *Exotic Memories*, 1. Bongie's quotations from Giacomo Leopardi's "Ad Angelo Mai" and from Claude Levi Strauss's *Tristes Tropiques* figure as introductory emblems to the futurelessness of exoticism.
3. Dash, *The Other America*, and Benítez-Rojo, *The Repeating Island* (inspired by C.L.R. James, drawing inspiration from José Marti, Aténor Firmin, Alejo Carpentier, Édouard Glissant), deserve mention.
4. Glissant, *L'intention poétique*, 1969; *Le discours antillais*, 1981; *Poétique de la relation*, 1990.
5. See, in particular, *La Lézarde, Le Quatrième siècle, La Case du commandeur*.

6. For an Enlightenment and obviously Eurocentric perspective on this, which still retains a certain relevance today, see G. T. Raynal, *L'Histoire philosophique et politique des Deux Indes*, 13. As C.L.R. James writes in *The Black Jacobins*, "Christopher Columbus landed first in the New World at the island of San Salvador, and after praising God, urgently enquired for gold" (6). Later, European planters aimed at instilling self-hatred into the chattel population, by calling them "by every opprobrious name . . . unjust, cruel, barbarous half-human, treacherous, deceitful, thieves, drunkards, proud, lazy, unclean, shameful, jealous to fury, and cowards" (17). Coping for the slave majority involved fatalism and feigned stupidity (15). Moreover, Benítez-Rojo puts the Caribbean and its "People of the Sea" center-stage of "the map of world history's contingency" as the "painfully delivered child of the Caribbean" (*Repeating Island*, 5), whose psychic trauma is explored by Fanon's *Peau noire, masques blancs*.

7. Benítez-Rojo, *Repeating Island*, 3.

8. Schwarz-Bart, *Pluie et vent*. Further references to this work are included in the text as *P* followed by page number. Translations are quoted from the English version, *The Bridge of Beyond*.

9. As Christine Chivallon reminds us, "for Édouard Glissant, the rape of the African woman forms the origin of this decomposed family," which began "in the absolutely insane universe of the slave ship" (*La Diaspora noire des Amériques*, 120–121). Thus, Glissant writes, "there is no Martinican who does not count at least one violated woman among his ancestors" (*Le Discours antillais*, 297; my translation).

10. Schwarz-Bart, *Mulâtresse*, 49. Further references to this work are included in the text as *M* followed by page number. This and following translations of passages from the novel are mine.

11. James, *The Black Jacobins*, 9.

12. I am, of course, referring, here and above, to poems in the *Spleen et ideal* section of *Les Fleurs du mal*, like "L'homme et la mer," "Le beau navire," and, obviously, "L'invitation au voyage," which André Schwarz-Bart echoes here, perhaps unconsciously. The dreamlike elsewhere that forms the refrain of this poem reads: "Là, tout n'est qu'ordre et beauté/ Luxe, calme et volupté."

13. Ashcroft, Griffiths and Tiffin, *Post-Colonial Studies*, 32.

14. Ashcroft, Griffiths and Tiffin, *Post-Colonial Studies*, 177.

15. See James, *The Black Jacobins*.

16. See James, *The Black Jacobins*.

17. O'Callaghan, *Women Writing the West Indies*, 149.

18. O'Callaghan, *Women Writing the West Indies*.

19. See Gayatry Spivak, quoted in Ashcroft, Griffiths and Tiffin, *Post-Colonial Studies*, 171.

20. See James, *The Black Jacobins*.

21. Mannoni, *Prospero and Caliban*, 21.

22. Rodríguez, *House/Garden/Nation*, 132–140.

23. See Bhabha, *The Location of Culture*.

24. Rodríguez, *House/Garden/Nation*, 140.

25. Rodríguez, *House/Garden/Nation*, 133.

26. As opposed to the more "unsettling, even tragic" tale in Simone Schwarz-Bart's later work, *Ton beau capitaine*. Morrison, "The Caribbeanness of Haiti," 117.

27. A definition I gladly share with Elaine Campbell and Pierrette Frickey in their introduction to *The Whistling Bird*, 4.

28. Rodríguez, *House/Garden/Nation*, 136.

22 Narratives of Traversal

Jamaica Kincaid and the Erasure of the Postcolonial Subject

Paul Giles

Over the past generation, academic formulations of postcolonialism have been organized, albeit often covertly, around a mythic idea of transformation, a displacement of A into B. My contention here is that these kinds of conceptual equation have become increasingly problematical in an era of what Benedict Anderson calls "long-distance nationalism," where inhabitants of one country often keep in touch with their former places of domicile through e-mail and the Internet, so that they might in many cases be said to live concurrently in two places at once.[1] Rather than the older, modernist idea of exile, which was based upon an epic narrative of the journey involving a difficult quest for knowledge and liberation, more recent configurations under the rubric of globalization have involved narratives of traversal, a two-way process involving reciprocal interactions between different territories. This has served consequently to problematize the autonomy of the postcolonial subject, both the academic subject and the individual agent which emerge instead as a split and hybrid phenomenon. This chapter will trace how some of these postcolonial paradoxes can be seen to have entangled themselves textually in the work of the Antiguan American writer Jamaica Kincaid.

Neil Lazarus and many other critics have commented recently on how "postcolonial studies has tended," in Lazarus's words, "to be overly schematic, restricted—not to say attenuated—in its coverage, range of reference, and field of vision."[2] One reason for this, as Dipesh Chakrabarty has acknowledged, is because postcolonial scholarship has been "committed, almost by definition, to engaging the universals—such as the abstract figure of the human or that of Reason—that were forged in eighteenth-century Europe and that underlie the human sciences."[3] The idea of emancipation from tyranny, in other words, is based upon an Enlightenment notion of the freedom of the subject, involving a metamorphic capacity, the power to regenerate both oneself and society. In its weaker forms, as Jenny Sharpe has observed, postcolonial discourse seeks to reconstitute the margins in the metropolitan center, so that through the simple expedient of inverting established hierarchies it morphs into a form of "liberal multiculturalism," one that effectively "obfuscates" the more obdurate category of race.[4] Alternatively, as most notably in the work of Robert Young and Aijaz Ahmad, postcolonialism relegates its epistemological premises to something of secondary interest and positions itself firmly as an "interventionist methodology" that is committed, in Young's words, "towards political ideals of a transnational social justice."[5] The strength of this latter approach lies in its clarity, the way in which it identifies the subject of postcolonialism specifically with the colonial struggles of the 1950s and 1960s and the kind of writing that attempted subsequently to negotiate the political power struggles of the late twentieth century. Its potential weakness, though, could be said to lie in its instrumentalism and its epistemological flimsiness, in particular the way it failed to account for questions of oppression and freedom in anything other than social and economic terms. There was a contradiction, in other words, between postcolonialism as an intellectual discourse and postcolonialism as a mode of political praxis, something that became very obvious in Ahmad's savage critique of Salman Rushdie and what he called Rushdie's "aesthetic of despair."[6] Ahmad complained, basically, that Rushdie's fiction was simply not politically progressive enough, that the celebrated author did not press his postcolonial imagination into the service of a politics of emancipation.

I want to argue that these contradictions in the theory of postcolonialism manifest themselves most overtly in the general failure of the discourse to deal convincingly with U.S. culture. There has been some interesting recent work, from Lawrence Buell and others, on the ways in which nineteenth-century American literature might be seen as postcolonial, and Edward Watts in particular has written convincingly about how the United States after the revolution developed a complex, paradoxical position, "both colonizer and colonized at once."[7] For Robert Young, however, the United States can only be "technically" a postcolonial society, while in her 1995 book *Colonial and Postcolonial Literature* Elleke Boehmer declares: "The United States is excluded because it won independence long before other colonial places, and its literature has therefore followed a very different trajectory."[8] But why should it have followed a different trajectory? If, as Young suggests, postcolonialism is concerned with ways in which "colonial history . . . has determined the configurations and power structures of the present," then surely the trajectory of U.S. society over the past two hundred years should be susceptible of examination within a postcolonial framework, albeit one in which the contours would be mapped very differently from conventional treatments of the subject today.[9] That the entanglement of the United States in a cultural rhetoric of race, liberty and rights can be traced back to the Enlightenment era is clear enough, and many scholars have written about ways in which John Locke, for example, influenced the colonial administration of Virginia and the Carolinas. Another important angle, as Anne McClintock has pointed out, is the whole question of Native American culture and the extent to which that indigenous environment might still be classified as postcolonial. It is hard to avoid agreeing with McClintock's conclusion that postcolonialism today signifies mainly a term of academic convenience, a discourse of "linear, historical 'progress'" that is "prematurely celebratory and obfuscatory in more ways than one."[10] Moreover, to exclude the United States from the matrix of postcolonialism altogether is to relapse into the largely discredited theoretical model of American exceptionalism, the idea that the "special conditions" of the United States rendered that culture immune from the kinds of tensions and pressures that permeated the rest of the world.[11]

One way through this dilemma, I think, is to attempt to bring the discourse of postcolonialism much more into dialogue with theories of transnationalism and globalization. Although of course it operates unevenly and unequally, the dynamic of transnationalism is globally pertinent now, so that locations all around the world, not just in the United States, should be recognized as sites of multiple crosscurrents where international capital and social formations intersect in what Boehmer and Bart Moore-Gilbert, writing in 2002, called the "zig-zag" fashion "which perhaps more accurately characterizes transverse forms of anticolonial nation-making and resistance."[12] Nowadays, as Bruce Robbins has said, "global culture" is ordinary; the big beasts of colonialism are now of less pressing significance than the complex and often barely identifiable intertwining of local and global cultures.[13] Within this context, the United States can no longer be categorized simply as a mythical melting pot, a realm into which immigrants are assimilated and integrated; instead, as Arjun Appadurai has written, the country functions as "yet another diasporic switching point," a refractive location through which various flows of ideological, capital and human resources pass.[14] The immersion of the United States itself in global economics has been well described by Immanuel Wallerstein, who has pointed out how the United States is simultaneously the object of such processes rather than simply the imperial puppeteer pulling all the strings. Wallerstein has also written of how, in his terms, the relative "decline of U.S. hegemony" in the twenty-first century is guaranteed because of the more complicated, post-Cold War structure within which the political and economic system of the United States will necessarily be engaged.[15]

All of this will tend further to complicate the binary opposition of colonizer and colonized, oppression and emancipation, upon which political rhetoric in the mid-twentieth century tended to depend. It is, therefore, not entirely true to say, as Neil Lazarus has suggested, that the world since 1989 can be said to have operated merely under the shadow of a unipolar "pax Americana"; since the exceptionalist model no longer appertains, the United States itself cannot be immune from the dislocating forces of transnationalism.[16] Instead, we will find ourselves moving towards the kind of situation brilliantly described by Judith Butler in *The Psychic Life of Power*, where she formulates a theory of the incoherence of identity for what she calls these "postliberatory times," in which an attachment to subjection becomes part of the psychic condition of the formation of the subject.[17] This does not involve, as Butler points out, merely a masochistic acquiescence in the exercise of power, but rather an active capacity to rework and unsettle through resignification that passionate attachment to subjection without which subject formation and reformation cannot succeed. Butler of course describes a realm of the split subject, and my contention would be that the development of globalization has opened up creative fissures within social and aesthetic identity, split as it now is between local, national, and transnational attachments. Postcolonial conditions in the twenty-first century do not involve epic voyages or transformations so much as putting the near and the remote into closer proximity. This in turn serves to complicate the spatial and temporal mapping which formerly preserved colonial and postcolonial zones as discretely bounded geographic zones and academic territories.

I want to use as an example of these developments the work of Jamaica Kincaid, which furnishes a particularly interesting example of the ways in which globalization has impacted upon the study of national literatures. Kincaid herself was born in 1949 as Elaine Potter Richardson on the island of Antigua, a British colony until it became self-governing in 1967. Kincaid lived in Antigua until 1965, when she went to Scarsdale, New York, to work as an au pair, having (so she said in 1976) prayed to go to the United States since the age of nine because she was so struck as a child with American popular culture, which she thought "funny and great and attractive and smart."[18] She subsequently wrote "Talk of the Town" pieces for the *New Yorker*, changed her name in 1973—choosing "Jamaica" to retain a flavor of the Caribbean—and is now settled in the United States, where she lives in Vermont and teaches writing at Harvard. Even though she declared in 1991 that she would "never become an American citizen," considering herself "a citizen of Antigua" and so "Caribbean," she in fact subsequently took U.S. citizenship in 1993, largely, so she said, "because of Bill Clinton," whom in 2006 she still thought to be "as great an American President as I can expect in my lifetime."[19]

Yet the British colonial context has been erased too frequently from discussions of Kincaid's work, and, as Michael Bérubé has remarked, her "success in mainstream American venues" has led to her being "widely considered to be 'almost' an American writer."[20] In this sense, it is important to acknowledge how a postcolonial theoretical framework would open up for the reader of Kincaid significant questions of identity and cross-affiliation that might otherwise have been occluded. However, it is also clear that Kincaid cannot be safely categorized within a conventional postcolonial rubric, since she is one of those writers for whom the question of national identity has become reversible: she herself has said that when she is in the United States she feels her home is in Antigua, and vice versa.[21] Caryl Phillips, a writer born on the Caribbean island of St. Kitts but brought up in Britain, objected to Kincaid's inclusion in the *Norton*

Anthology of African American Literature on the grounds that this tended to obliterate the significance of her Antiguan upbringing, and certainly it is true that in her early books it is the British colonial inheritance with which the author wrestles most forcibly.[22] *Annie John,* published in 1985, chronicles the development of a girl in Antigua under the leaden sound of "the Anglican church bell" and the ominous shadow of an English head-mistress who "looked like a prune left out of its jar a long time." The heroine is denounced as "arrogant" and "blasphemous" by her teacher for her antipathy toward Columbus, said to have "discovered" Antigua in 1493, but who is deemed by Annie John to be a prototype of the colonizing mentality, and for her insubordination she is made as punishment to copy out the first two books of Milton's *Paradise Lost.* Kincaid's first novel thus engages intertextually with English literature in order to valorize the heroine's insurrectionary manner; she mentions a painting entitled *The Young Lucifer,* which "showed Satan just recently cast out of heaven for all his bad deeds," and the reference at the beginning of *Annie John* to the heroine's childhood in Antigua as a "paradise" exemplifies her self-conscious affiliation with a mode of satanic transgression.[23]

The Prince of Darkness is also the inspiration for the name of the central protagonist in the 1990 novel, *Lucy*: her mother says she named her "after Satan himself, Lucy, short for Lucifer." This is another literate Caribbean heroine who has read *Paradise Lost* as part of her colonial education, along with Wordsworth's famous poem on daffodils, ensuring that, despite her subsequent removal to the United States, she can never see daffodils as other than "a scene of conquered and conquests."[24] One crucial theme pervading Kincaid's early works, then, is the incorporation of her fictional protagonists into an English cultural imaginary. The heroine of *Annie John* cites Charlotte Brontë's *Jane Eyre* as her "favorite novel," testifying again to her empathy with a spirit of rebellion; but such rebelliousness is always set in counterpoint to a rigid framework of patriarchal authority that is associated with an English tradition.[25] Concomitant with this is the gap between authority and autonomy, a gap within which Kincaid's bipolar narratives oscillate, playing off a theoretical map of Englishness against her native experience, but simultaneously refracting that experience through ancestral expectations. Whereas the fictional Lucy says that although she was forced to memorize the Wordsworth poem at the age of ten, she never saw an actual daffodil until she was nineteen, Kincaid, as she herself recalled in 1994, "had never read a West Indian writer when I started to write. Never. I didn't even know there was such a thing until I met Derek Walcott."[26] Kincaid's fiction thus resonates with the ghosts of Shakespeare, of the King James Bible, even of the traditionalist English children's writer Enid Blyton, whom Kincaid herself read and who is cited in *Annie John*. The British context here functions as a social and intellectual milieu from which there is no obvious escape; the narrator records how her Brownie troupe "swore allegiance to our country, by which was meant England," and in the final chapter of *Annie John* the heroine boards a ship to England to train as a nurse.[27]

The inevitable sense of anger against such colonial conditioning is most apparent in Kincaid's scathing account of Antiguan history, *A Small Place* (1988), which led her for a while to be "informally banned" from the island.[28] Here the wrongs of empire are plentifully enumerated, with the English denounced as a "bad-minded people" who used the Caribbean for the trading of slaves and other kinds of economic exploitation. The author points out how the Barclay brothers, who started Barclays Bank, were prominent slave-traders, and how many streets in Antigua are named after "English maritime criminals": Nelson, Hood, Hawkins, Drake, and others. This is clearly a revisionist version of history which seeks to demystify picturesque local legends of the slaves as a "noble and exalted people" and of slavery itself as "a pageant full of large ships sailing on blue water." The anger here might be said to derive partly from an American attitude, from a newly energized sense of outrage against the old colonial oppressor that stems from a transformed position of secure independence. Kincaid herself was of course safely domiciled in the United States by this time, and she records here that while "the Antigua I grew up in revolved almost completely around England," the young people on the island now look more toward "North America" for their cultural values; indeed, Kincaid said in 1994 that the West Indies by that time was no longer a British colony but "a suburb of America."[29] But the anger in *A Small Place* is directed not just against the English but also against the Antiguans, herself included, for what she takes to be their gullibility and willingness passively to subscribe to colonial myths. In this sense, it suggests how postcolonialism signifies a realm of the split self: not a mythical transition from A to B, but a legacy of rupture and violence turned back against the self.

This sense of an irascible New Yorker attempting to exorcise the ghosts of her own past is also conveyed in the bizarre essay "On Seeing England for the First Time" (1991), which violently deconstructs the mental image of England as a celestial "Jerusalem" that had been handed down from her youth. It is, perhaps, not surprising that when she encounters "the real England" it loses its fairy-tale qualities, but it might seem odd that she should be moved to exclaim so virulently: "I hate England; the weather is like a jail sentence, the English are a very ugly people, the food in England is like a jail sentence, the hair of English people is so straight, so dead looking, the English have an unbearable smell so different from the smell of people I know." Intellectually, she justifies this aversion in terms of a general English rudeness and obsequiousness to royalty, along with their collective blindness to the legacy of slavery and the fact that in commemoration of this inglorious history they have "monuments everywhere."[30] In the introduction to a collection of her *New Yorker* pieces, Kincaid observes how much she detests English aristocrats and recalls feeling "sympathetic to the IRA when they blew up Lord Mountbatten's yacht" in 1979.[31] There can be no doubt, then, about the genuineness of Kincaid's political hostility toward Britain, but the way this antipathy is expressed stylistically through a poetics of traversal—inverting the stereotypes applied historically to black people and turning them against the English—suggests how Kincaid's rhetoric characteristically aspires not to transcend such forms of objectification but to stand them on their head.

In this sense, Kincaid's narrative method self-consciously abjures a progressive or redemptive spirit. Instead, it rotates upon an axis where positions of domination can be exchanged but not eradicated. The prevalence of this circular structure illuminates also the strain of self-loathing in Kincaid's writing, the sense of a woman now metamorphosed into an American citizen seeking to avenge a former self which had been imprisoned within this English world. "On Seeing England for the First Time" starts with memories of sitting at school in Antigua looking at a map of England that had been pinned on the blackboard—the mother country in Kincaid is typically represented through simulations, copies—and it proceeds to play off those pedagogical assumptions against the darker knowledge brought about by adulthood. In this sense, Susie O'Brien is right to suggest that Kincaid's novels imply how dreams of liberation are symbiotically intertwined with the more sinister compulsions of violence, and how these images of entanglement serve to problematize not only "the Old Americanist trope of national redemption, whereby the emancipation of a people is figured as a process of individual self-discovery," but also the "disturbing persistence" of this assumption in New Americanist critical narratives, which, despite their overtly revisionist emphasis (in terms of gender, race, and so on) too often replicate the method of aligning the teleology of liberation with an idea of American national destiny.[32] Kincaid's work, by contrast, is predicated upon a philosophically less comfortable system of transgression and reversal. It is often the very subversion of a protected state that gives her subjects their energy, and in this sense it is the memory of this circumscribed colonial condition which lends her work its peculiar iconoclastic resonance.

This is why Kincaid's work cannot be said to fit unproblematically within a U.S. context. She argued in 1994 that American black women have a "much different sensibility" from their Caribbean counterparts, particularly in their belief that "being black is a predestination in some way": since racial categories in the West Indies appear much more fluid, she suggested, Americans "have a kind of nationalism about it that we don't have." This means that for Kincaid racial politics is connected less to identity than to questions of social power: "an obsessive theme" of her work, she acknowledged in this same interview, is "the relationship between the powerful and the powerless."[33] In line with this meditation on the theoretical premises of colonialism, *My Garden (Book)* (1999) draws analogies between the tending of her private garden in Vermont and the actions of a colonial conqueror reshaping a landscape according to his own will, as it discusses

both the specific nature of locality and the ways in which particular places
become part of the human mind. Kincaid said in 1989 that she still loves
"to read about the history of England," and her work is concerned intertextually to revise received accounts of an English cultural tradition which
attempted "to erase any knowledge of another history" through its institutional exclusions and silences.[34] *My Garden* interweaves its treatment of
horticulture with discussions of such works as Thomas Jefferson's letters
on England and William H. Prescott's *Conquest of Mexico*, thereby trick-
ily alternating the impulse of territorial possession through a minimalist
model of gardening and a maximalist model of empire.

Kincaid's texts thus effectively demystify national narratives by turning
back reflexively on their own ingrained assumptions about native families
and the motherland. As Kincaid herself has acknowledged, her work fuses
attitudes to colonialism with attitudes towards her own family, returning compulsively to scenes of the Antiguan past from a supposedly more
emancipated American perspective. But the perennial sense of split loyalties ensures that her writing does not seek simply to "redress the balance of colonial mystification" and dissolve "the economy of domination,"
as Moira Ferguson somewhat pedantically argued; less formulaically, it
also creates a hybrid style which blends a mood of feminist independence
with an immersion in repetitious streams of the unconscious.[35] Lucy, like
Kincaid's other fictional protagonists, has an awkward relationship with
her mother, who makes conventional assumptions about gender which the
heroine finds exasperating, but in the end Lucy and the others find themselves inescapably bound to the matrilineal cord. Louise Bernard has written that the title of *The Autobiography of My Mother* (1996) "playfully"
echoes Gertrude Stein's *The Autobiography of Alice B. Toklas* (1933); but
this association is more than just playful, for the circular idiom of Kincaid's
book follows Stein's style of patterned repetitions in the way it implies the
traumas of memory, both personal and collective, and how the present is
linked inexorably to the past.[36] *My Brother* (1998) similarly chronicles the
slow death of the author's brother from AIDS, with Kincaid presenting
herself as being pulled back into the orbit of her childhood as she shuttles
between her home in Vermont and the hospital in Antigua. "The dead never
die" is one of the key phrases in this book, whose rhetorical repetitions and
reliance on non-sequential conjunctions reflect a recursive structure where
logical exposition is superseded by the return of a primordial fate, as her
brother regresses at the end and calls out for his mother: "And my brother
died, for he kept dying; each time I remembered that he had died it was as
if he had just at that moment died, and the whole experience of it would
begin again." This book is very good at recording the shock of death, both
a "worn-out thing" and something "new" each time.[37]

Rather than merely promulgating identity politics, then, Kincaid's
recent work reads more like that of a postcolonial Gertrude Stein, where
the elemental truths of death, time and generation serve to pare down the

questions of cultural formation and self-definition by which her earlier works were riven. *Mr. Potter* (2002) is on one level an elegy to her own absent father—Frederick Potter, an Antiguan taxi driver, who was not part of the Richardson family unit—but it displaces him from a social to a much more abstract context, focusing not on any personal relationship but on his ontological status as a human being within the physical world. While Potter "had no private thoughts," Kincaid says, his body was an integral part of the Caribbean landscape: "So too would his life be unimaginable without that water, that land, that sky." In some sense this is not so much an autobiography as an anti-autobiography, a hollowing out of her father's personal identity so that he appears in a kind of minimalist perspective, as a blank space who becomes part of the "very shape of the earth."[38] All of this indicates the way Kincaid has been influenced by the stylistics of modernism: she admits to admiring Virginia Woolf and James Joyce as well as the anti-anthropomorphic mode of Alain Robbe-Grillet, and she has also expressed a particular interest in Chris Marker's film *La Jetée* (1962), an experimental work consisting of a sequence of still black and white photographs, set in a post-apocalyptic Paris where a soldier is used as a guinea pig in time travel experiments which ultimately lead him back to the moment of his own death, as if to exemplify how, as the film puts it, there is no way out of time. Kincaid first tried out this kind of avant-garde literary mode in various early short stories published in *The New Yorker*, which attracted the favorable attention of Susan Sontag and were brought together in *At the Bottom of the River* (1984). The author later repudiated the style of this first book, saying it was too "unangry, decent, civilized" to be effective, and again blaming her English education for smoothing off her rough edges into "their version of a human being."[39] However, such formal complexity is not incidental to her most original work, for it is clear that Kincaid's most provocative texts do not simply promulgate American identity politics but refract issues of colonization, memory and time travel through narratives which consciously intermingle hypotheses about the ontology of subjectivity with a broader historical awareness.

Kincaid, then, has little interest in multiculturalism or diversity per se, what she dismissed as pedagogical "themes of cultural and racial identity" centered around "how to be me, whatever that is." Instead, she deploys the *métissage* of the Caribbean, its imbrication in multiple "rhizomatic" relationships (to use Édouard Glissant's term), in order to break away from regulated structures of whatever kind, whether those associated with Britain, the United States, or Antigua.[40] This means her work does not fit in comfortably with standard forms of the postcolonial dialectic. In the twenty-first century era of globalization, the emphasis on how political power and subalternity have been consolidated through discursive formations and fictions, which was the focus of so much of the work of Homi Bhabha and Gayatri Spivak in the 1980s and 1990s, now seems of less compelling significance than the various contradictions associated with the figure of the body in space. One of the most striking aspects of Kincaid's *Among Flowers* (2005) is the way it deliberately traverses and traduces global mapping through a counternarrative foregrounding the unavoidable nature of bodily incarnation. *Among Flowers* is a non-fiction account of a hike in the Himalayas, with Kincaid deliberately leaving her home in Vermont to get "far away from everything I had known." The narrative turns upon a structure of alienation, with the protagonist recording her "love of feeling isolated, of imagining myself all alone in the world and everything unfamiliar"; but, more than this, the Himalayan mountains function for Kincaid as an "ontological laboratory," within which conventional notions of time and distance seem no longer to apply.[41] In *Among Flowers*, the maps through which we normally position ourselves in relation to global space seem peremptorily to have dissolved; even the time differences in Nepal, where time zones are fifteen minutes out of kilter with the rest of the world, seem both "confusing" and "magical," and this disequilibrium fits with the narrator's peculiar sense of moving from the everyday horizontal world, where time and space are measured in terms of the landscapes around you, to a world that unfurls instead in a vertical direction, "an unending series of verticals going up and then going down." There is a meditation here on grids and boundaries, on how it is a natural tendency of human beings "to think of every place in which you find yourself for longer than a day as home, and to make it familiar," so that the explorers meticulously set out their knife and fork for dinner in a tent half-way up the mountain; but there is also consciousness of how topographic perspectives are constantly shifting, how geographic coordinates appear illusory, how when she looks back on where she's come from, as she says, "I did not recognize what I saw."[42]

There is, then, a principled emphasis in Kincaid's texts on disorientation, on the suspension of traditional boundaries of custom and security. In *Among Flowers*, such boundaries are associated not just with the familiar comforts of home but also with protection from a global state of terror; at the outset, the narrator records with portentous capital letters how "The Events of September 11th" delay her planned trip by a year, and the expedition to the Himalayas is itself shadowed by the presence in the background of a group of Maoist terrorists, who do in fact attack the airport at Kanchenjunga just a few days after her party has passed through it.[43] The point here, though, is as much metaphysical as political: *Among Flowers* is about the stripping away of illusory states of security, the disruption of epistemology, the uncovering of the human condition in its abject nakedness and absurdity. Although this condition of terror is given a particular historical dimension in the months after 9/11, the political situation also illuminates a more general state for which it stands as a metonymic figure. This is why the philosophy of Kincaid's narrative is intertwined with self-mockery—"huge cackling and laughter," as she puts it—and also with scatology, as she details how her body reacts to sleeping and urinating outdoors. As so often with the surrealists, this kind of toilet humor is presented as a deliberate form of vulgarity which functions in an adversarial way to undermine the polite conventions upon which established codes of polite society are grounded.[44] *Among Flowers* is predicated upon a rhetoric of desublimation and trick perspectives, where corporeality traverses abstract global designs and resists their allegories of emancipation: "Not ever did I get used to this—the deceptive nearness of my destinations—not ever did I become accustomed to the vast difference between my expectation, my perception, and reality; the way things really are."[45]

In his 2001 essay, "Turn to the Planet: Literature, Diversity, and Totality," Masao Miyoshi takes the fact of a "transnational and deterritorialized" world to be a fait accompli, and he seeks to consider human culture in terms of its common bonds to the planet, looking in particular at issues of the environment and natural resources. "Literature and literary studies now have one basis and goal," Miyoshi concludes: "to nurture our common bonds to the planet—to replace the imaginaries of exclusionist familialism, communitarianism, nationhood, ethnic culture, regionalism, 'globalization,' or even humanism, with the idea of planetarianism. Once we accept this planet-based totality, we might for once agree in humility to devise a way to share with all the rest our only true public space and resources."[46] There are several things to be wary of here: one is the explicit moralistic injunction in relation to planetarianism, another is the dogmatic insistence that literature and literary studies now have only "one basis and goal." Nevertheless, this formulation is interesting when placed alongside the familiar postcolonial paradigm of the dominant and the subaltern. It is not, of course, that planetarianism serves simply to depoliticize the environment; indeed, Miyoshi talks specifically about the malign influence of transnational corporations in a borderless world. What is important, though, is that human culture is situated here explicitly within a framework where the abstractions of language cannot be regarded as autonomous and where the larger concern is with the body, both the human body and the social body, in physical space.

In the era of globalization, then, it is no longer so easy to partition the world in terms of discrete social and political zones, to disentangle the oppressor from the oppressed. Part of the cathectic charge of Kincaid's writing involves its admission of psychic fragmentation, where a spirit of emancipation finds itself turning back sharply but disturbingly upon another version of the self. Kincaid's writing thus speaks above all to a condition of psychological and physical confinement, which is quite unlike the older, expansive notion of radical transformation. Such comforting myths of a world elsewhere, predicated upon distinct contrasts between discrete and circumscribed territories, appear now difficult to sustain. This is not to relapse into philosophical fatalism; it is, though, to suggest that postcolonialism in the twenty-first century needs urgently to address the issue of a common heritage, a common planet, and to modify the kind of fetishization of political difference that such myths of radical transformation implicitly underwrite. The postcolonial myth of transformation is indebted ultimately to an Enlightenment promise of utopia, but it is one of the strengths of Kincaid's writing to complicate this theoretical dialectic by describing ways in which abstract ideas of regeneration are immersed in, and inexorably circumscribed by, the tangled conditions of bodily incarnation.

NOTES

1. Anderson, "Exodus," 327. For an empirical study of this phenomenon in relation to Dominicans living in Boston, see Levitt, *The Transnational Villagers*.
2. Lazarus, "Indicative Chronology," xii.
3. Chakrabarty, *Provincializing Europe*, 5.
4. Sharpe, "Is the United States Postcolonial?" 108.
5. Young, *Postcolonialism*, 58.
6. Ahmad, *In Theory*, 155.
7. Watts, *Writing and Postcolonialism*, 2.
8. Young, *Postcolonialism*, 3; Boehmer, *Colonial and Postcolonial Literature*, 4.
9. Young, *Postcolonialism*, 4.
10. McClintock, "The Angel of Progress," 254, 260.
11. On this topic, see Kammen, "The Problem of American Exceptionalism," 11–13.
12. Boehmer and Moore-Gilbert, "Postcolonial Studies and Transnational Resistance," 14.
13. Robbins, *Feeling Global*, 16.
14. Appadurai, *Modernity at Large*, 172.
15. Wallerstein, *Decline of American Power*, 1.
16. Lazarus, "The Global Dispensation since 1945," 38.
17. Butler, *Psychic Life of Power*, 18.
18. Kincaid, *Talk Stories*, 57.
19. Birbalsingh, "Jamaica Kincaid: From Antigua to America," 143; Kincaid, letter to author, 18 June 2006. Kincaid says that she tried to take U.S. citizenship, with its ancillary voting rights, "in time for the 1992 presidential election."
20. Bérubé, "Introduction: Worldly English," 13.
21. Paravisini-Gebert, *Jamaica Kincaid*, 13.
22. Phillips, "Literature: The New Jazz for Black America?" 17.
23. Kincaid, *Annie John*, 13, 36, 82, 94, 25.
24. Kincaid, *Lucy*, 152, 30.
25. Kincaid, *Annie John*, 92.
26. Ferguson, "A Lot of Memory," 169.
27. Cudjoe, "Jamaica Kincaid," 398; Kincaid, *Annie John*, 51, 15.
28. Bernard, "Countermemory and Return," 129.
29. Kincaid, *A Small Place*, 23, 24, 80, 54, 31, 44; Ferguson, "A Lot of Memory," 174.
30. Kincaid, "On Seeing England for the First Time," 32, 37, 40.
31. Kincaid, *Talk Stories*, 13.
32. O'Brien, "New Postnational Narratives," 71.
33. Ferguson, "A Lot of Memory," 164, 176.
34. Cudjoe, "Jamaica Kincaid," 403; Ferguson, "A Lot of Memory," 168.
35. Ferguson, *Jamaica Kincaid*, 4, 6.
36. Bernard, "Countermemory and Return," 120.

37. Kincaid, *My Brother*, 122, 148, 193.
38. Kincaid, *Mr. Potter*, 130, 37, 40.
39. Cudjoe, "Jamaica Kincaid," 402–3; Paravisini-Gebert, *Jamaica Kincaid*, 28–29.
40. Ferguson, "A Lot of Memory," 175; Glissant, *Poetics of Relation*, 11.
41. Kincaid, *Among Flowers*, 3, 7. The phrase "ontological laboratory" is applied to Caravaggio's paintings by Leo Bersani and Ulysse Dutoit, *Caravaggio's Secrets*, 59.
42. Kincaid, *Among Flowers*, 11, 77, 106, 129.
43. Kincaid, *Among Flowers*, 5, 186.
44. Kincaid, *Among Flowers*, 89–91. The most famous example of toilet humor in surrealist art is Marcel Duchamp's urinal, *The Fountain* (1917).
45. Kincaid, *Among Flowers*, 143.
46. Miyoshi, "Turn to the Planet," 292, 295–296.

Bibliography

Abastado, Claude. "Introduction à l'analyse des manifestes." *Littérature* 39 (Oct. 1980): 3–11.

Abbink, Jon, and Ineke van Kessel, eds. *Vanguard or Vandals*. Leiden and Boston: Brill, 2005.

Abrahams, Peter. *Tell Freedom* [1954]. London: Faber, 1981.

Abrahams, Roger D., ed. *Afro-American Folktales: Stories from Black Traditions in the New World*. New York: Pantheon Books, 1985.

Accardo, Anna Lucia. "Forme e funzioni dell'ironia nelle slave narratives." In *Identità e scrittura: Studi sull'autobiografia nord-americana*, edited by A. L. Accardo, M. O. Marotti, and I. Tattoni. Roma: Bulzoni, 1988.

Achebe, Chinua. *Arrow of God*. London: Heinemann, 1964.

Achebe, Chinua. Foreword to *The Anchor Book of Modern African Stories*, edited by Nade da Obradovi. New York: Anchor, 2002.

Adams, Mark B., ed. *The Wellborn Science: Eugenics in Germany, France, Brazil, and Russia*. Oxford and New York: Oxford University Press, 1990.

Adjaye, David, and Kodwo Eshun. "Learning from Lagos: A Dialogue on the Poetics of Informal Habitation." In *David Adjaye. Making Public Buildings: Specificity, Customization, Imbrication*, edited by P. Allison. London: Whitechapel, 2006.

Adorno, Theodor. *Minima Moralia: Reflections from Damaged Life*. London: Verso, 1987.

Agamben, Giorgio. *La potenza del pensiero. Saggi e conferenze*. Vicenza: Neri Pozza Editore, 2005.

Ahmad, Aijaz. *In Theory: Classes, Nations, Literatures*. London: Verso, 1992.

Ahmad, Dohra. "'More than Romance': Genre and Geography in *Dark Princess*." *ELH* 69 (2002): 775–803.

Alabarces, Pablo. "Boundaries and Stereotypes (or What Is the Use of Football, If Any Indeed?)." Translated by Marta Ines Merajver. *Sociedad* (2006): 1–12.

Alabi, Adetayo. *Telling Our Stories: Continuities and Divergences in Black Autobiographies*. New York: Palgrave Macmillan, 2005.

Albright, Ann Cooper. *Choreographing Difference: The Body and Identity in Contemporary Dance*. Middletown, CT: Wesleyan University Press, 1997.

Allen, Carol. *Black Women Intellectuals: Strategies of Nation, Family and Neighborhood in the Works of Pauline Hopkins, Jessie Fauset and Marita Bonner*. New York: Garland, 1998.

Allison, Peter, ed. *David Adjaye. Making Public Buildings: Specificity, Customization, Imbrication*. London: Whitechapel, 2006.

Amado, Jorge. *Tenda dos Milagres*. São Paulo: Martins, 1969.

Andall, Jacqueline, and Derek Duncan. *Italian Colonialism: Legacy and Memory*. Bern: Peter Lang, 2005.

Andall, Jacqueline, and Derek Duncan. "Memories and Legacies of Italian Colonialism." In *Italian Colonialism: Legacy and Memory,* edited by Jacqueline Andall and Derek Duncan. Bern: Peter Lang, 2005.

Anderson, Benedict. "Exodus." *Critical Inquiry* 20 (Winter 1994): 314–327.

Anderson, Benedict. *Imagined Communities: Reflections on the Origin and Spread of Nationalism.* London: Verso, 1983.

Andrews, George Reid. *Blacks and Whites in São Paulo Brazil, 1888–1988.* Madison: University of Wisconsin Press, 1991.

Appadurai, Arjun. "Disjuncture and Difference in the Global Cultural Economy." In *Colonial Discourse and Post-Colonial Theory: A Reader,* edited by Patrick Williams and Laura Chrisman. New York: Harvester Wheatsheaf, 1993.

Appadurai, Arjun. *Modernity at Large: Cultural Dimensions of Globalization.* Minneapolis and London: University of Minnesota Press, 1996.

Appiah, Kwame Anthony. *In My Father's House: Africa in the Philosophy of Culture.* Oxford and New York: Oxford University Press, 1992.

Appiah, Kwame Anthony. "The Uncompleted Argument: Du Bois and the Illusion of Race." *Critical Inquiry* 12, no. 1 (1985): 21–37.

Archer, Leonard C. *Black Images in the American Theatre: NAACP Protest Campaigns—Stage, Screen, Radio and Television.* Brooklyn, NY: Pageant-Poseidon Ltd., 1973.

Archer-Shaw, Petrine. *Negrophilia: Avant-Garde Paris and Black Culture in the 1920s.* London: Thomas & Hudson, 2000.

Archetti, Eduardo P. *Masculinities: Football, Polo and the Tango in Argentina.* Oxford: Berg, 1999.

Archetti, Eduardo P. "Masculinity and Football: The Formation of National Identity in Argentina." In *Games without Frontiers: Football, Identity, and Modernity,* edited by Richard Giulianotti and John Williams. Aldershot: Arena, 1994.

Archetti, Eduardo P. "Playing Football and Dancing Tango: Embodying Argentina in Movement Style and Identity." In *Sport, Dance, and Embodied Identities,* edited by Noel Dyck and Eduardo P. Archetti. Oxford: Berg, 2003.

Arjomand, Said Amir and Edward A. Tiryakian. Introduction to *Rethinking Civilizational Analysis,* edited by S. A. Arjomand and E. A. Tiryakian. London: SAGE, 2004.

Armah, Ayi Kwei. *Osiris Rising: A Novel of Africa Past, Present and Future.* Popenguine, Senegal: Per Ankh, 1995.

Aschenbrenner, Joyce. *Katherine Dunham: Reflections on the Social and Political Contexts of Afro-American Dance.* New York: Dance Research Annual 12, 1981.

Ashcroft, Bill. *Post-Colonial Transformation.* London and New York: Routledge, 2001.

Ashcroft, Bill, Gareth Griffiths, and Helen Tiffin. *Post-Colonial Studies: The Key Concepts.* London and New York: Routledge, 2002.

Bâ, Saidou Moussa, and P. A. Micheletti. *La promessa di Hamadi.* Novara: De Agostini, 1991.

Baker, Houston A., Manthia Diawara, and Ruth H. Lindeborg, eds. *Black British Cultural Studies: A Reader.* Chicago and London: University of Chicago Press, 1996.

Bakolo Ngoi, Paul. "Visto da Kalo." In *Le voci dell'arcobaleno,* edited by Roberta Sangiorgi. Santarcangelo di Romagna: Fara Editore, 1995.

Baldwin, James. "The Discovery of What It Means To Be an American." In *Nobody Knows My Name* [1961]. London: Penguin, 1995.

Baldwin, James. "Princes and Powers." In *Nobody Knows My Name* [1961]. London: Penguin, 1995.

Baldwin, James. "Stranger in the Village." In *Notes of a Native Son* [1955]. London: Penguin, 1995.

Bales, Kevin. *Disposable People: New Slavery in the Global Economy*. Berkeley: University of California Press, 1999.

Balibar, Étienne. *La crainte des masses. Politique et philosophie avant et après Marx*. Paris: Galilée, 1997.

Bartlett, Andrew. "Airshafts, Loudspeakers, and the Hip Hop Sample: Contexts and African American Musical Aesthetics." *African American Review* 2, no. 4 (Winter 1994): 639–652.

Bederman, Gail. *Manliness and Civilization*. Chicago: University of Chicago Press, 1996.

Bell, Bernard W., Emily Grosholz, and James B. Stewart, eds. *W.E.B. Du Bois on Race and Culture: Philosophy, Politics and Poetics*. London and New York: Routledge, 1996.

Bellos, Alex. *Futebol: The Brazilian Way of Life*. London: Bloomsbury, 2002.

Bellu, Giovanni Maria. *I fantasmi di Portopalo. Natale 1996: La morte di 300 clandestini e il silenzio dell'Italia*. Milano: Mondadori, 2004.

Benítez-Rojo, Antonio. *The Repeating Island: The Caribbean and the Postmodern Perspective*. Translated by James E. Maraniss. Durham, NC: Duke University Press, 1996.

Ben Jelloun, Tahar. "Villa Literno." In *Dove lo Stato non c'è. Racconti italiani*. Torino: Einaudi, 1991.

Benjamin, Walter. "Theses on the Philosophy of History." *Illuminations*. London: Fontana, 1982.

Bercht, Fatima, and Lelia Coelho Frota. *House of Miracles: Votive Sculpture from Northeastern Brazil*. Exhibition catalogue. New York: Americas Society Art Gallery, 1989.

Bercovitch, Sacvan. *The Rites of Assent: Transformations in the Symbolic Construction of America*. London and New York: Routledge, 1992.

Berger, John. *Ways of Seeing*. New York: Viking, 1973.

Bernard, Louise. "Countermemory and Return: Reclamation of the (Postmodern) Self in Jamaica Kincaid's *The Autobiography of My Mother* and *My Brother*." *Modern Fiction Studies* 48 (Spring 2002): 113–138.

Bersani, Leo, and Ulysse Dutoit. *Caravaggio's Secrets*. Cambridge, MA: MIT Press, 1988.

Bérubé, Michael. "Introduction: Worldly English." Special Issue on Postmodernism and the Globalization of English. *Modern Fiction Studies* 48 (Spring 2002): 1–17.

Bhabha, Homi. "The Manifesto." *Re-inventing Britain: A Forum. Wasafiri* 29 (Spring 1999): 38–39.

Bhabha, Homi K. *The Location of Culture*. London and New York: Routledge, 1994.

Birbalsingh, Frank. "Jamaica Kincaid: From Antigua to America." In *Frontiers of Caribbean Literature in English*, edited by Frank Birsbalsingh. New York: St. Martin's Press, 1996.

Bittencourt, J. Bastos. *Ouro Preto: Aleijadinho, Monumentos, Outras Cidades*. São Paulo: Sebastian, 1976.

Blackburn, Robin. "The Old World Background to European Colonial Slavery." *William and Mary Quarterly* 54, no.1 (1997): 65–102.

Blier, Suzanne. "African Art and Architecture." In *Microsoft Encarta Africana Third Edition*, edited by Kwame Anthony Appiah and Henry Louis Gates. CD-ROM. Encarta Reference Suite, 2003.

Boal, Augusto. *Hamlet and the Baker's Son: My Life in Theatre and Politics*. Translated by Adrian Jackson and Candida Blaker. London and New York: Routledge, 2001.

Boal, Augusto. "Notas de um diretor de Sortilégio." In *Teatro Experimental do Negro: Testemunhos*, edited by Abdias do Nascimento. Rio de Janeiro: Edições GRD, 1966.

Boehmer, Elleke. *Colonial and Postcolonial Literature: Migrant Metaphors*. Oxford and New York: Oxford University Press, 1995.

Boehmer, Elleke. *Empire, the National, and the Postcolonial*. Oxford and New York: Oxford University Press, 2002.

Boehmer, Elleke, and Bart Moore-Gilbert. Introduction to special issue, "Postcolonial Studies and Transnational Resistance." *Interventions: International Journal of Postcolonial Studies* 4, no.1 (2002): 7–21.

Boelhower, William. "'I Will Teach You How to Flow': On Figuring Out Atlantic Studies." *Atlantic Studies* 1, no. 1 (2004): 28–48.

Boelhower, William. *Through a Glass Darkly*. Venezia: Edizioni Helvetia, 1984.

Bohleber, Werner. "Die Entwicklung der Traumatheorie in der Psychoanalyse." *Psyche* 9/10 (2000): 797–839.

Bok, Christian. "An Untellable Desire: Dionne Brand's Characters Orbit an Empty Space." *Calgary Herald*, 22 January 2005: G-3.

Bonaffini, Giuseppe. "Corsari, schiavi siciliani nel Mediterraneo (Secoli XVIII–XIX)." *Cahiers de la Méditerranée*, 65: xxxx.

Bongie, Chris. *Exotic Memories: Literature, Colonialism, and the Fin de Siècle*. Stanford, CA: Stanford University Press, 1991.

Botkin, B. A. *Lay My Burden Down: A Folk History of Slavery*. Chicago: University of Chicago Press, 1945.

Bouchane, Mohamed. *Chiamatemi Alì*. Edited by C. De Girolamo and D. Miccione. Milano: Leonardo, 1991.

Boughedir, Ferid. "African Cinema and Ideology: Tendencies and Evolution." In *Symbolic Narratives/African Cinema*, edited by June Givanni. London: BFI, 2000.

Bourdieu, Pierre, and Loïc Wacquant. "On the Cunning of Imperialist Reason." *Theory, Culture & Society* 16, no. 1 (1999): 41–58.

Bourguignon, Erika. "Trance Dance." *Dance Perspectives* 34 (Autumn 1968): 1–61.

Bozonnet, Jean-Jacques. "Esclaves en Italie." *Le Monde*, 23 September 2006.

Brah, Avtar. *Cartographies of Diaspora: Contesting Identities*. London and New York: Routledge, 1998.

Braidotti, Rosi. *Metamorphoses: Towards a Materialist Theory of Becoming*. Cambridge: Polity Press, 2002.

Brand, Dionne. *A Map to the Door of No Return: Notes to Belonging*. Toronto: Doubleday Canada, 2001.

Brand, Dionne. *Inventory*. Toronto: McClelland & Stewart, 2006.

Brand, Dionne. *thirsty*. Toronto: McClelland & Stewart, 2002.

Brand, Dionne. *What We All Long For*. Toronto: Alfred A. Knopf Canada, 2005.

Brathwaite, Edward Kamau. *Contradictory Omens: Cultural Diversity and Integration in the Caribbean*. Mona: Savacou, 1974.

Brathwaite, Edward Kamau. *Rights of Passage*. Oxford and New York: Oxford University Press, 1967.

Braudel, Fernand. "Introduction à l'empire espagnol." In *Autour de la Méditerranée*. Paris: Editions de Fallois, 1996.

Brennecke, Allan, Alberto C. Amadio, and Júlio C. Serrao. "Parâmetros dinâmicos de movimentos selecionados da Capoeira." *Revista Portuguesa de Ciências do Desporto* 5 (Maio 2005): 153–159.

Broschke Davis, Ursula. *Paris without Regret: James Baldwin, Kenny Clarke, Chester Himes, and Donald Byrd*. Iowa City: University of Iowa Press, 1986.

Browning, Barbara. *Samba: Resistance in Motion*. Bloomington: Indiana University Press, 1995.

Brydon, Diana. "Detour Canada: Rerouting the Black Atlantic, Reconfiguring the Postcolonial." In *Reconfigurations: Canadian Literatures and Postcolonial Identities*, edited by M. Maufort and F. Bellarsi. Brussels: P.I.E. Peter Lang, 2002.

Buck-Morss, Susan. *Thinking Past Terror*. London: Verso, 2003.

Buell, Lawrence. "American Literary Emergence as a Postcolonial Phenomenon." *American Literary History* 4 (Fall 1992): 411–442.

Butler, Judith. *Bodies That Matter: On the Discursive Limits of "Sex."* London and New York: Routledge, 1993.

Butler, Judith. "Performative Acts and Gender Constitution: An Essay in Phenomenology and Feminist Theory." In *Writing on the Body: Female Embodiment and Feminist Theory*, edited by Katie Conboy, Nadia Medina, and Sarah Stanbury. New York: Columbia University Press, 1997.

Butler, Judith. *Precarious Life: The Powers of Mourning and Violence*. London and New York: Verso, 2004.

Butler, Judith. *The Psychic Life of Power*. Stanford, CA: Stanford University Press, 1997.

Byerman, Keith E. *Seizing the Word: History, Art, and Self in the Work of W.E.B. Du Bois*. Athens: University of Georgia Press, 1994.

Cabral, Amilcar. *Return to the Source: Selected Speeches*. New York: Monthly Review Press, 1976.

Cain, William E. "W.E.B. Du Bois's Autobiography and the Politics of Literature." *Black American Literature Forum* 24, no. 2 (1990): 299–313.

Campbell, Elaine and Pierrette Frickey. *The Whistling Bird: Women Writers of the Caribbean*. Kingston, Jamaica: Ian Randle Publishers, 2003.

Camboni, Marina. "Networking Women: A Research Project and a Relational Model of the Cultural Sphere." In *Networking Women: Subjects, Places, Links Europe-America: Towards a Re-Writing of Cultural History*, edited by Marina Camboni. Roma: Edizioni di storia e letteratura, 2004.

Canclini, Néstor García. *Consumer and Citizen: Globalization and Multicultural Conflicts*. Minneapolis: University of Minnesota Press, 2001.

Caplan, Marc. "Nos Ancêtres, Les Diallobés: Cheikh Hamidou Kane's Ambiguous Adventure and the Paradoxes of Islamic Negritude." *Modern Fiction Studies* 51, no. 4 (2005): 936–957.

Capoeira, Nestor. *The Little Capoeira Book*. Berkeley, CA: North Atlantic Books, 2003.

Carby, Hazel. Introduction to *The Magazine Novels of Pauline Hopkins*. Edited by Hazel Carby. Oxford and New York: Oxford University Press, 1988.

Carby, Hazel. *Race Men*. Cambridge, MA, and London: Harvard University Press, 1998.

Carby, Hazel. *Reconstructing Womanhood: The Emergence of the African American Woman Novelist*. Oxford and New York: Oxford University Press, 1987.

Caritas/Migrantes. "Richiedenti asilo e rifugiati: il Sistema di protezione italiano." *Immigrazione 2006. Dossier Statistico*. Roma: Centro Studi e Ricerche IDOS, 2006: 136–144.

Carter, Dan T. *Scottsboro: A Tragedy of the American South*. Baton Rouge: Louisiana University Press, 1984.

Carton, Benedict. "'We Are Made Quiet by This Annihilation': Historicizing Concepts of Bodily Pollution and Dangerous Sexuality in South Africa." *International Journal of African Historical Studies* 39, no. 1 (2006): 85–106.

Castria Marchetti, Francesca. "New York da Pollock a Basquiat." In *La pittura americana*, edited by Roberta Bernabei, Francesca Castria Marchetti, and Stefano Zuffi. Milano: Electa, 2002.

Castro, Ruy. *Garrincha: The Triumph and Tragedy of Brazil's Forgotten Footballing Hero*. London: Yellow Jersey Press, 2004.

Casty, Alan. "Robert Rossen: A Retrospective Study of His Films." *Cinema (US)* 4, no. 3 (1968): 18–22.

Cavarero, Adriana. *A più voci. Filosofia dell'espressione vocale.* Milano: Feltrinelli, 2003.

Cavarero, Adriana, and Judith Butler. "Condizione umana contro 'natura.'" *Micromega* 4 (September–October 2005): 135–146.

Caws, Mary Ann, ed. *Manifesto: A Century of Isms.* Lincoln: University of Nebraska Press, 2001.

Césaire, Aimé. *Cahier d'un retour au pays natal.* Paris: Présence Africaine, 1962.

Césaire, Aimé. "Cahier d'un retour au pays natal." In *The Collected Poetry of Aimé Césaire.* Translated by Annette G. Smith and Clayton Eshleman. Berkeley: University of California Press, 1983.

Chakrabarty, Dipesh. *Provincializing Europe: Postcolonial Thought and Historical Difference.* Princeton, NJ: Princeton University Press, 2000.

Cheah, Pheng and Bruce Robbins, eds. *Cosmopolitics: Thinking and Feeling beyond the Nation.* Minneapolis: University of Minnesota Press, 1998.

Chennells, Anthony. "Narrative in Sol Plaatje's *Mhudi.*" *English in Africa* 24, no. 1 (May 1997): 37–58.

Chernoff, John Miller. *African Rhythms and African Sensibility: Aesthetics and Social Action in African Music.* Chicago: University of Chicago Press, 1979.

Chesnutt, Charles. "The Wife of His Youth." In *The Norton Anthology of African American Literature*, edited by H. L. Gates and N. Y. McKay. New York: Norton, 2004.

Chivallon, Christine. *La Diaspora noire des Amériques: Expression et théorie à partir de la Caraïbe.* Paris: CNRS, 2004.

Chrisman, Laura. *Postcolonial Contraventions: Cultural Readings of Race, Imperialism and Transnationalism.* Manchester: Manchester University Press, 2003.

Chrisman, Laura. *Rereading the Imperial Romance: British Imperialism and South African Resistance in Haggard, Schreiner, and Plaatje.* Oxford: Clarendon Press, 2000.

Clark, VèVè A., and Margaret B. Wilkerson, eds. *Kaiso! Katherine Dunham: An Anthology of Writings.* Berkeley: University of California Institute for the Study of Social Change, 1978.

Cleary, David. "Race, Nationalism, and Social Theory in Brazil: Rethinking Gilberto Freyre." [Unpublished] Working Paper. David Rockefeller Center for Latin American Studies, Harvard University. Available from http://www.transcomm. ox.ac.uk/working%20papers/cleary.pdf. Accessed 3 March 2007.

Cleaver, Eldridge. "Notes on a Native Son." In *A Collection of Critical Essays*, edited by Kenneth Kinnamon. Englewood Cliffs, NJ: Prentice-Hall, 1974.

Clifford, James. "Diasporas." *Cultural Anthropology* 9, no. 3 (August 1994): 302–338.

Clifford, James. *The Predicament of Culture: Twentieth-Century Ethnography, Literature, and Art.* Cambridge, MA, and London: Harvard University Press, 1988.

Clifford, James. *Routes: Travel and Translation in the Late Twentieth Century.* Cambridge, MA, and London: Harvard University Press, 1997.

Clifford, James. "Travelling Cultures." In *Cultural Studies*, edited by L. Grossberg et al. London and New York: Routledge, 1992.

Coetzee, John M. "Love and Walt Whitman." *The New York Review of Books* 52, no. 14 (22 September 2005).

Collins, Patricia Hill. *Black Feminist Thought: Knowledge, Consciousness, and the Politics of Empowerment.* Boston: Unwin Hyman, 1990.

Condé, Maryse. *Moi, Tituba sorcière . . .* , Paris: Gallimard, 1986.

Conrad, Robert. *Children of God's Fire: A Documentary History of Black Slavery in Brazil.* Princeton, NJ: Princeton University Press, 1983.

Cossa, Egidio, and Guido Schlinkert, eds. *IbridAfrica*. Roma: Gangemi, 2002.

Cotkin, George. *Reluctant Modernism: American Thought and Culture, 1880–1900*. New York: Twayne, 1992.

Couzens, Tim. *The New African: A Study of the Life and Work of H.I.E. Dhlomo*. Johannesburg: Ravan, 1985.

Couzens, Tim and Stephen Gray. "Printers and Other Devils: The Text of Sol T. Plaatje's *Mhudi*." *Research in African Literatures* 9, no. 2 (1978): 198–215.

Cudjoe, Selwyn R. "Jamaica Kincaid and the Modernist Project: An Interview." *Callaloo* 39 (Spring 1989): 396–411.

Cunard, Nancy. *Black Man and White Ladyship*. London: Utopia Press, 1931.

Cunard, Nancy. *Negro: An Anthology* [1934]. Edited and abridged with an introduction by Hugh Ford. New York: Continuum, 2002.

Cunard, Nancy. "Scottsboro appeal and petition with signatures" [1933]. Nancy Cunard Papers. Harry Ransom Humanities Research Center at the University of Texas, Austin.

Cunard, Nancy. "White Lies" [1932]. Nancy Cunard Papers. Harry Ransom Humanities Research Center at the University of Texas, Austin.

Curtin, Philip D., ed. *Imperialism*. New York: Walker and Company, 1971.

D'Aguiar, Fred. *Feeding the Ghosts*. London: Vintage, 1997.

Dal Lago, Alessandro. *Non-persone. L'esclusione dei migranti in una società globale*. Milano: Feltrinelli, 1999.

Da Matta, Roberto. *Carnivals, Rogues, and Heroes: An Interpretation of the Brazilian Dilemma*. Notre Dame, IN: University of Notre Dame Press, 1991.

Da Matta, Roberto and Luiz Felipe Baêta Neves, eds. *Universo do Futebol: Esporte de Sociedade Brasileira*. Rio de Janeiro: Pinakotheke, 1982.

Danticat, Edwidge. "Children of the Sea." In *Krik? Krak!*. New York: Vintage, 1996.

Danticat, Edwidge. *The Dew Breaker*. New York: Alfred A. Knopf, 2004.

Danticat, Edwidge. Introduction to *The Butterfly's Way: Voices from the Haitian Diaspora in the United States*, edited by Edwidge Danticat. New York: Soho, 2001.

Dash, J. Michael. *The Other America: Caribbean Literature in a New World Context*. Charlottesville: University of Virginia Press, 1998.

Dash, J. Michael. "Postcolonial Eccentricities: Francophone Caribbean Literature and the *fin de siècle*." In *The Francophone Caribbean Today: Literature, Language, Culture*, edited by Gertrud Aub-Buscher and Beverly Ormerod Noakes. Kingston, Jamaica: University of the West Indies Press, 2003.

Daurio, Beverley. "Writing It." In *The Power to Bend Spoons: Interviews with Canadian Novelists*, edited by B. Daurio. Toronto: Mercury, 1998.

Davila, Arlene. *Latinos, Inc.: The Marketing and the Making of a People*. Berkeley: University of California Press, 2001.

Davis, Arthur P., and Saunders Redding, eds. *Cavalcade: Negro American Writing from 1760 to the Present*. Boston: Houghton Mifflin Co., 1971.

Davis, Darién. *Avoiding the Dark: Race and the Forging of National Culture in Modern Brazil*. Aldershot: Ashgate International Center for Research in Ethnic Studies, 1999.

Davis, David Brion. "Looking at Slavery from Broader Perspectives." *The American Historical Review* 105, no. 2 (April 2000): 452–466.

Dawes, Kwame. "Negotiating the Ship on the Head: Black British Fiction." In *Write Black Write British: From Post Colonial to Black British Literature*, edited by K. Sesay. Hertford: Hansib, 2005.

Dayan, Joan. "Paul Gilroy's Slaves, Ships, and Routes: The Middle Passage as Metaphor." *Research in African Literatures* 27, no. 4 (1996): 7–14.

de Certeau, Michel. *The Practice of Everyday Life*. Berkeley: University of California Press, 1988.

De Frantz, Thomas F. *Dancing Many Drums: Excavation in African American Dance*. Madison: University of Wisconsin Press, 2002.

Degler, Carl N. *Neither Black nor White: Slavery and Race Relations in Brazil and the United States*. Madison: University of Wisconsin Press, 1971.

Del Boca, Angelo. "The Myths, Suppressions, Denials, and Defaults of Italian Colonialism." In *A Place in the Sun: Africa in Italian Colonial Culture from Post-Unification to the Present*, edited by Patrizia Palumbo. Berkeley: University of California Press, 2003.

Deloria, Vine. "Civilization and Isolation." *North American Review* 236, no. 1 (1978): 11–14.

Deloughrey, Elizabeth. "Tidalectics: Charting the Space/Time of Caribbean Waters." *SPAN* 47 (1998): 18–38.

Deren, Maya. "An Anagram of Ideas on Art, Form and Film" [1946]. In *Maya Deren and the American Avant-Garde*, edited by Bill Nichols. Berkeley: University of California Press, 2001.

Deren, Maya. *Divine Horsemen: The Living Gods of Haiti* [1953]. New York: McPherson, 1983.

Deren, Maya. "Religious Possession in Dancing." In *The Legend of Maya Deren: A Documentary Biography and Collected Works*, Vol. 1, Part 1: Signatures (1917–42), edited by VèVè A. Clark *et al.* New York: Arthouse, 1984.

Derrida, Jacques. *Specters of Marx: The State of the Debt, the Work of Mourning, & the New International*. Translated from the French by Peggy Kamuf. London and New York: Routledge, 1994.

Desmond, Jane C. "Embodying Difference: Issues in Dance and Cultural Studies." In *Meaning in Motion: New Cultural Studies of Dance*, edited by Jane C. Desmond. Durham, NC: Duke University Press, 1997.

Diawara, Manthia. *African Cinema: Politics and Culture*. Bloomington: University of Indiana Press, 1990.

Diawara, Manthia. "Independence Cha Cha. The Art of Yinka Shonibare." In *Yinka Shonibare*, edited by J. Guldemond and G. Mackert. Rotterdam: NAi Publishers, 2004.

Di Maio, Alessandra, ed. *Tutuola at the University: The Italian Voice of a Yoruba Ancestor*. Roma: Bulzoni, 2000.

Diop, Birago. "Sarzan." In *Les contes d'Amadou Koumba*. Paris: Présence Africaine, 1961.

Dixon-Gottschild, Brenda. *Digging the Africanist Presence in American Performance Dance and Other Contexts*. Westport, CT: Praeger, 1998.

Doreski, C. K. "Inherited Rhetoric and Authentic History: Pauline Hopkins at the *Colored American Magazine*." In *The Unruly Voice: Rediscovering Pauline Elizabeth Hopkins*, edited by John Cullen Gruesser. Urbana: University of Illinois Press, 1996.

Douglas, Ann. *Terrible Honesty: Mongrel Manhattan in the 20s*. New York: Farrar, Straus and Giroux, 1995.

Du Bois, W.E.B. "The African Roots of War." *Atlantic Monthly* 115 (May 1915): 707–714.

Du Bois, W.E.B. *Autobiography: A Soliloquy on Viewing My Life from the Last Decade of Its First Century* [1968]. New York: International Publishers, 1991.

Du Bois, W.E.B. "The Color Line Belts the World." *Collier's Weekly*, 20 October 1906: 30.

Du Bois, W.E.B. "Criteria of Negro Art." *The Crisis* (October 1926). In *Writings*, edited by Nathan Huggins. New York: The Library of America, 1986.

Du Bois, W.E.B. "The Damnation of Women." In *Darkwater: Voices from within the Veil* [1920]. New York: Dover, 1999.

Du Bois, W.E.B. *Dark Princess: A Romance* [1928]. With an introduction by Claudia Tate. Jackson: University Press of Mississippi, 1995.

Du Bois, W.E.B. *Darkwater: Voices from within the Veil* [1920]. Introduction by Manning Marable. New York: Dover, 1999.

Du Bois, W.E.B. *Dusk of Dawn: An Essay toward an Autobiography of a Race Concept* [1940]. In *Writings*, edited by Nathan Huggins. New York: Library of America, 1986.

Du Bois, W.E.B. *The Quest of the Silver Fleece: A Novel* [1911]. Introduction by Arnold Rampersad. New York: Harlem Moon, 2004.

Du Bois, W.E.B. *The Souls of Black Folk* [1903]. In *Writings*. Edited by Nathan Huggins. New York: Library of America, 1986.

Du Bois, W.E.B. "The Talented Tenth" [1903]. In *Writings*, edited by Nathan Huggins. New York: Library of America, 1986.

Du Bois, W.E.B. "Two Novels." *The Crisis* (June 1928). Available from http://edtech.tennessee.edu/itc/grants/twt2000/modules/ebledso1/documents.htm. Accessed 14 September 2006.

Du Bois, W.E.B. "Van Vechten's 'Nigger Heaven'" [1926]. In *Writings*, edited by Nathan Huggins. New York: Library of America, 1986.

Duke, Vic and Liz Crolley. "*Fútbol*, Politicians, and People: Populism and Politics in Argentina." In *Sport in Latin American Society: Past and Present,* edited by J.A. Mangan and P. LaMartine DaCosta. London: Frank Cass, 2002.

Dunham, Katherine. *The Dances of Haiti.* Los Angeles: University of California at Los Angeles Press, 1983. Revision of "Las Danzas de Haiti." *Acta Anthropologica* II.4 (1947) and *Les Danses de Haiti.* Paris: Fasquel Press, 1957.

Dunham, Katherine. *Island Possessed* [1969]. Chicago: University of Chicago Press, 1994.

Dunham, Katherine. *A Touch of Innocence: Memoirs of Childhood* [1959]. Chicago: University of Chicago Press, 1994.

Dyck, Noel and Eduardo P. Archetti. "Embodied Identities: Reshaping Social Life through Sport and Dance." In *Sport, Dance, and Embodied Identities*, edited by Noel Dyck and Eduardo P. Archetti. Oxford: Berg, 2003.

Dyer, Richard. *White.* London and New York: Routledge, 1997.

Ebron, Paulla. *Performing Africa.* Princeton, NJ: Princeton University Press, 2002.

Edwards, Brent Hayes. *The Practice of Diaspora: Literature, Translation, and the Rise of Black Internationalism.* Cambridge, MA, and London: Harvard University Press, 2003.

Edwards, Brent Hayes. "The Uses of Diaspora." *Social Text* 19, no. 1 (Spring 2001): 45–73.

Eisenstadt, Shmuel N. "The Civilizational Dimension of Modernity." In *Rethinking Civilizational Analysis*, edited by S. A. Arjomand and E. A. Tiryakian. London: SAGE, 2004.

Emecheta, Buchi. *The Joys of Motherhood* [1979]. Oxford: Heinemann, 1988.

Emecheta, Buchi. *Second Class Citizen* [1974]. New York: Braziller, 1983.

Equiano, Olaudah. *The Interesting Narrative and Other Writings* [1789]. Edited with an introduction by Vincent Carretta. New York: Penguin, 1995.

Fabi, Maria Giulia. *Passing and the Rise of the African American Novel.* Urbana: University of Illinois Press, 2001.

Fabre, Michel. "James Baldwin in Paris: Hardships and Romance." In *James Baldwin: His Place in American Literary History and His Reception in Europe*, edited by Jakob Kollhöfer. Frankfurt am Main: Peter Lang, 1991.

Fair, Laura. "Ngoma Reverberations: Swahili Music Culture and the Making of Football Aesthetics in Early Twentieth-Century Zanzibar." In *Football in Africa: Conflict, Conciliation, and Community*, edited by Gary Armstrong and Richard Giulianotti. Basingstoke: Palgrave, 2004.

Fanon, Frantz. "Algeria Face to Face with the French Torturers." In *Toward the African Revolution*, translation of *Pour la révolution africaine*, 1964, by Haakon Chevalier. New York: Grove Press, 1988.

Fanon, Frantz. *Peau Noire, Masques Blancs*. Paris: Seuil, 1952.

Fanon, Frantz. "This Is the Voice of Algeria." In *A Dying Colonialism*, translation of *L'an cinq de la révolution algérienne*, 1959, by Haakon Chevalier. New York: Grove Press, 1967.

Fanon, Frantz. *The Wretched of the Earth*. Translation of *Les damnés de la terre*, 1961, by Constance Farrington. New York: Grove Press, 1963.

Ferguson, Moira. *Jamaica Kincaid: Where the Land Meets the Body*. Charlottesville: University Press of Virginia, 1994.

Ferguson, Moira. "A Lot of Memory: An Interview with Jamaica Kincaid." *Kenyon Review* 16, no. 1 (Winter 1994): 163–188.

Fernandes, Floristan. *The Negro in Brazilian Society*. New York: Columbia University Press, 1969.

Fiedler, Leslie. *Love and Death in the American Novel*. Harmondsworth: Penguin, 1984.

Filho, Mário. *O Negro no Futebol Brasilero*. 2nd ed. Rio de Janeiro: Civilização Brasileira, 1964.

Fischer, Lucy. "'The Eye for Magic.'" In *Maya Deren and the American Avant-Garde*, edited by Bill Nichols. Berkeley: University of California Press, 2001.

Fischer-Hornung, Dorothea. "The Body Possessed: Katherine Dunham Dance Technique in Mambo." In *EmBODYing Liberation: The Black Body in American Dance*, edited by Dorothea Fischer-Hornung and Alison D. Goeller. Hamburg: Lit Verlag, 2001.

Fischer-Hornung, Dorothea. "Giving Voice and Vent to African American Culture: August Wilson's Black Aesthetics and Katherine Dunham's Fight for Cultural Ownership in *Mambo*." In *August Wilson and Black Aesthetics*, edited by Sandra Shannon and Dana Williams. New York: Palgrave Macmillan, 2004.

Fischer-Hornung, Dorothea. "An Island Occupied: The Marine Occupation of Haiti in Zora Neale Hurston's *Tell My Horse* and Katherine Dunham's *Island Possessed*." In *Holding Their Own: Perspectives on the Multi-Ethnic Literatures of the United States*, edited by Dorothea Fischer-Hornung and Heike Raphael-Hernandez. Tuebingen: Stauffenburg Verlag, 2000.

Fonsêca, José Palo Moreira da. "Nota sôbre 'Sortilégio' e alguns dos problemas que envolveu." In *Teatro Experimental do Negro: Testemunhos*, edited by Abdias do Nascimento. Rio de Janeiro: Edições GRD, 1966.

Ford, Hugh, ed. *Nancy Cunard: Brave Poet and Indomitable Rebel*. Philadelphia: Chilton Books, 1968.

Foucault, Michel. *The Will to Knowledge: The History of Sexuality*, vol. 1. London: Penguin, 1998.

Fox-Genovese, Elizabeth. *Within the Plantation Household: Black and White Women of the Old South*. Chapel Hill: University of North Carolina Press, 1988.

Franko, Mark. "Aesthetic Agencies in Flux." In *Maya Deren and the American Avant-Garde*, edited by Bill Nichols. Berkeley: University of California Press, 2001.

Fredrickson, George M. *The Black Image in the White Mind*. Middletown, CT: Wesleyan University Press, 1987.

Fredrickson, George M. *Black Liberation: A Comparative History of Black Ideologies in the United States and South Africa*. Oxford and New York: Oxford University Press, 1995.

Freyre, Gilberto. *Brazil: An Interpretation*. New York: Alfred A. Knopf, 1945.

Freyre, Gilberto. *Casa Grande e Senzala. Formação da família brasileira sob o regime de economia patriarcal*. Rio de Janeiro: Maia and Schmidt, 1933. Reprint. São Paulo: Global, 2003.

Freyre, Gilberto. *Interpretação do Brasil.* Rio de Janeiro: José Olympio, 1947.

Freyre, Gilberto. *The Gilberto Freyre Reader.* Translated by Barbara Shelby. New York: Alfred A. Knopf, 1974.

Freyre, Gilberto. *New World in the Tropics: The Culture of Modern Brazil.* New York: Alfred A. Knopf, 1959.

Freyre, Gilberto. *Ordem e progresso: processo de desintegração das sociedades patriarcal e semipatriarcal no Brasil sob o regime de trabalho livre, aspectos de um quase meio século de transição do trabalho escravo para o trabalho livre e da monarquia para a república.* 2 vols. Rio de Janeiro: José Olympio, 1959.

Freyre, Gilberto. *Order and Progress: Brazil from Monarchy to Republic.* Translation of *Ordem e progresso,* 1959, by Rod W. Horton. Berkeley: University of California Press, 1986.

Freyre, Gilberto. *Sobrados e mocambos: decadência do patriarcado rural e desenvolvimento do urbano.* São Paulo: Companhia Editora Nacional, 1936.

Freyre, Gilberto. *The Mansions and the Shanties: The Making of Modern Brazil.* Translation of *Sobrados e mocambos,* 1935, by Harriet de Onís. New York: Alfred A. Knopf, 1963.

Freyre, Gilberto. *The Masters and the Slaves: A Study in the Development of Brazilian Civilization.* Translation of *Casa Grande e Senzala* by E. Bradford Burns and Frank Tannenbaum. Los Angeles: University of California Press, 1986.

Freyre, Gilberto. *The Masters and the Slaves: A Study in the Development Brazilian Civilization.* 2nd ed. New York: Alfred A. Knopf, 1966.

Freyre, Gilberto. *Vida, forma e cor.* Rio de Janeiro: José Olympio, 1962.

Friedman, Thomas L. *The Lexus and the Olive Tree.* New York: Anchor, 2000.

Frohne, Andrea. "Representing Jean-Michel Basquiat." In *The African Diaspora: African Origins and New World Identities,* edited by I. Okpewho, C. B. Davies, and A. Mazrui. Bloomington: Indiana University Press, 1999.

Frye, Northrop. *The Secular Scripture: A Study of the Structure of Romance.* Cambridge, MA, and London: Harvard University Press, 1976.

Gabaccia, Donna. "A Long Atlantic in a Wider World." *Atlantic Studies* 1, no. 1 (April 2004): 1–27.

Gadji, Mbacke. *Kelefa: La prova del pozzo.* Monza: Edizioni dell'Arco, 2003.

Gadji, Mbacke. *Lo spirito delle sabbie gialle.* Monza: Edizioni dell'Arco, 1999.

Gadji, Mbacke. *Nel limbo della terra. Una vita dai luoghi senza tempo.* Monza: Edizioni dell'Arco, 2006

Gadji, Mbacke. *Numbelan: il regno degli animali.* Monza: Edizioni dell'Arco, 1996.

Gadji, Mbacke. *Pap, Ngagne, Yatt e gli altri.* Monza: Edizioni dell'Arco, 2000.

Gandhi, Leela. "Sketch for an Ethics of Cosmopolitanism." In *Modernist Women, Race, Nation: Networking Women 1890–1950, Circum-Atlantic Connections,* edited by Giovanna Covi. London: Mango, 2005.

Gangbo, Jadelin. M. *Verso la notte BAKONGA.* L'Aquila: Portofranco, 2001.

Garvey, Johanna X. K. "'The place she miss': Exile, Memory, and Resistance in Dionne Brand's Fiction." *Callaloo* 26, no. 2 (Spring 2003): 486–503.

Gates, Henry Louis, Jr. *Figures in Black: Words, Signs, and the "Racial" Self.* Oxford and New York: Oxford University Press, 1987.

Gates, Henry Louis, Jr. "On the Rhetoric of Racism in the Profession." *ALA Bulletin* 15, no. 1 (Winter 1989): 11–21.

Gates, Henry Louis, Jr. *The Signifying Monkey: A Theory of African American Literary Criticism.* Oxford and New York: Oxford University Press, 1988.

Gates, Henry Louis, Jr. and Nellie Y. McKay, eds. *The Norton Anthology of African American Literature.* New York: Norton, 2004.

George, Nelson. *Hip-Hop America.* New York: Penguin, 1998.

George, Nelson. *Post-Soul Nation.* New York: Viking, 2004.

Geppert, Alexander C.T., Jean Coffey and Tammy Lau. "International Exhibitions, Expositions Universelles and World's Fairs, 1851–1951: A Bibliography." *Wolkenkuckucksheim: Internationale Zeitschrift fur Theorie und Wissenschaft der Architektur* (Special Issue, 2000). Available from http://www.tu-cottbus .de/theo/Wolke/eng/Bibliography/ExpoBiblioqraphy.htm. Accessed March 15, 2002.

Gibson, Nigel C. "Jammin' the Airwaves and Tuning into the Revolution. The Dialectics of the Radio in *L'an cinq de la révolution algérienne.*" In *Fanon: A Critical Reader*, edited by L. R. Gordon, T. Denean Sharpley-Whiting, and R. T. White. Oxford: Blackwell, 1996.

Gibson, Nigel C. "Radical Mutations. Fanon's Untidy Dialectic of History." In *Rethinking Fanon: The Continuing Dialogue*, edited by N. C. Gibson. New York: Humanity Books, 1999.

Gikandi, Simon. "Introduction: Africa, Diaspora, and the Discourse of Modernity." Special Issue on *The Black Atlantic. Research in African Literatures* 27, no. 4 (Winter 1996): 1–6.

Gikandi, Simon. "Picasso, Africa and the Schemata of Difference." *Modernism/ modernity* 10, no. 3 (2003): 455–480.

Gilroy, Paul. *Against Race: Imagining Political Culture Beyond the Color Line.* Cambridge, MA, and London: Harvard University Press, 2000.

Gilroy, Paul. *The Black Atlantic: Modernity and Double Consciousness.* London: Verso; Cambridge, MA: Harvard University Press, 1993.

Giulianotti, Richard and Gary Armstrong. "Constructing Social Identities: Exploring the Structured Relations of Football Rivalries." In *Fear and Loathing in World Football*, edited by Richard Giulianotti and Gary Armstrong. Oxford: Berg, 2001.

Giulianotti, Richard. *Football: A Sociology of the Global Game.* Cambridge: Polity Press, 1999.

Givanni, June, ed. *Symbolic Narratives/African Cinema.* London: BFI, 2000.

Glissant, Édouard. *Caribbean Discourse. Selected Essays.* Translation of *Le discours antillais*,1981, by J. Michael Dash. Charlottesville: University Press of Virginia, 1996.

Glissant, Édouard. *La case du commandeur.* Paris: Seuil, 1981.

Glissant, Édouard. *Le discours antillais.* Paris: Seuil, 1981. Translated as *Caribbean Discourse* by J. Michael Dash. Charlottesville: University Press of Virginia, 1989.

Glissant, Édouard. *L'Intention poétique.* Paris: Seuil, 1969.

Glissant, Édouard. *La Lézarde.* Paris: Seuil, 1958. Translated as *The Ripening* by J. Michael Dash. London: Heinemann, 1985.

Glissant, Édouard. *Le quatrième siècle.* Paris: Seuil, 1964. Translated as *The Fourth Century* by Betsy Wing. Lincoln: University of Nebraska Press, 2001.

Glissant, Édouard. *Poétique de la relation.* Paris: Seuil, 1990. Translated as *Poetics of Relation* by Betsy Wing. Ann Arbor: University of Michigan Press, 1997.

Goellner, Ellen W., and Jacqueline Shea Murphy. *Bodies of the Text: Dance as Theory, Literature as Dance.* New Brunswick, NJ: Rutgers University Press, 1995.

Gooding-Williams, Robert. "Oulaw, Appiah, and Du Bois's 'The Conservation of Races'." In *W.E.B. Du Bois on Race and Culture: Philosophy, Politics and Poetics*, edited by Bernard W. Bell, Emily Grosholz, and James B. Stewart. London and New York: Routledge, 1996.

Goodman, James. *Stories of Scottsboro: The Rape That Shocked 1930s America and Revived the Struggle for Equality.* New York: Pantheon Books, 1994.

Gordon, César C. "História Social dos Negros no Futebol Brasileiro." *Pesquisa de Campo* 3/4 (1995): 71–90.

Gordon, Cesar, and Ronaldo Helal. "The Crisis of Brazilian Football: Perspectives for the Twenty-First Century." In *Sport in Latin American Society: Past and Present*, edited by J.A. Mangan and LaMartine P. DaCosta. London: Frank Cass, 2002.

Gramsci, Antonio. "The Intellectuals." In *Selections from the Prison Notebooks of Antonio Gramsci*, edited by Q. Hoare and G. Nowell Smith. London: Lawrence and Wishart, 1971.

Gray, Stephen. "Sources of the First Black South African Novel in English: Solomon Plaatje's Use of Shakespeare and Bunyan in *Mhudi*." *Munger Africana Library Notes* (Dec. 1976): 6–28.

Gregg, Robert and Madhavi Khale. "*The Negro* and *Dark Princess*: Two Legacies of the Universal Races Congress." *Radical History Review* 92 (Spring 2005): 133–152.

Greider, William. *One World, Ready or Not: The Manic Logic of Global Capitalism*. New York: Simon and Schuster, 1997.

Grimshaw, Anna. *The Ethnographer's Eye: Ways of Seeing in Anthropology*. Cambridge and New York: Cambridge University Press, 2001.

Griswold, Wendy. *Bearing Witness: Readers, Writers, and the Novel in Nigeria*. Princeton, NJ: Princeton University Press, 2000.

Guerreiro Ramos, Alberto. "O Museu como sucedâneo da violência." In *Relações de Raça no Brasil*, edited by A. Guerreiro Ramos. Rio de Janeiro: Edições Quilombo, 1950.

Guerreiro Ramos, Alberto. "O Negro desde dentro." In *Teatro Experimental do Negro: Testemunhos*, edited by Abdias do Nascimento. Rio de Janeiro: Edições GRD, 1966.

Guldemond, Jaap, and Gabriele Mackert, eds. *Yinka Shonibare*. Rotterdam: NAi Publishers, 2004.

Gunn, Janet Varner. *Autobiography: Toward a Poetics of Experience*. Philadelphia: University of Pennsylvania Press, 1982.

Hall, Stuart. "On Postmodernism and Articulation: An Interview with Stuart Hall." Edited by Lawrence Grossberg. *Journal of Communication Inquiry* 10, no. 2 (1986): 45–60.

Hall, Stuart, ed. *Representation: Cultural Representations and Signifying Practices*. London: Open University and SAGE, 1997.

Hamilton, Aidan. *An Entirely Different Game: The British Influence on Brazilian Football*. Edinburgh: Mainstream Publishing, 1998.

Hanchard, Michael. "Black Cinderella: Race and Public Sphere in Brazil." In *Racial Politics in Contemporary Brazil*, edited by Michael Hanchard. Durham, NC: Duke University Press, 1999.

Hardt, Michael and Antonio Negri. *Multitude*. New York: Penguin: 2004.

Harris, Marla. "Not Black and/or White: Reading Racial Difference in Heliodorus's *Ethiopica* and Pauline Hopkins's *Of One Blood*." *African American Review* 35, no. 3 (Fall 2001): 375–390.

Harrison, Paul Carter. "Form & Transformation: The Immanence of the Soul in the Performance Modes of Black Church and Black Music." In *Black Theatre: Ritual Performance in the African Diaspora*, edited by Paul Carter Harrison, Victor Leo Walker II, and Gus Edwards. Philadelphia: Temple University Press, 2002.

Hebdige, Dick. *Subculture: The Meaning of Style*. London and New York: Routledge, 1987.

Hebert, Anne. *Les fous de bassan*. Paris: Seuil, 1982.

Hecht, David, and A.M. Simone. *Invisible Governance: The Art of African Micro-Politics*. Brooklyn, NY: Automedia 1994.

Helal, Ronaldo. "Idolatria e Malandragem: a cultura brasileira na biografia de Romário." In *Futbologías, Fútbol, Identidad y Violencia en América Latina*, edited by Pablo Alabarces. Buenos Aires: CLACSO, 2003.

Helal, Ronaldo and Cesar Gordon, Jr. "Sociologia, história e romance na construção da identidade nacional através do futebol." In *A Invenção do País do Futebol*, edited by Ronaldo Helal, Antonio Jorge Soares, and Hugo Lovisolo. Rio de Janeiro: Mauad, 2001.

Henderson, Jennifer Jacobs, and Gerald Baldasty. "Race, Advertising, and Prime-Time Television." *Howard Journal of Communication* 14, no. 2 (2003): 97–112.

Herschmann, Micael, and Kátia Lerner. *Lance de Sorte: O Futebol e o Jogo do Bicho na Belle Époque Carioca*. Rio de Janeiro: Diadorim, 1993.

Hickey, Dennis, and Kenneth C. Wylie. *An Enchanting Darkness: The American Vision of Africa in the Twentieth Century*. East Lansing: Michigan State University Press, 1993.

Hill, Constance Valis. "Katherine Dunham's Southland: Protest in the Face of Repression." In *Dancing Many Drums: Excavations in African American Dance*, edited by Thomas F. DeFrantz. Madison: University of Wisconsin Press, 2001.

Holl, Ute. "Moving the Dancers' Soul." In *Maya Deren and the American Avant-Garde*, edited by Bill Nichols. Berkeley: University of California Press, 2001.

Holloway, Thomas H. "'A Healthy Terror': Police Repressions of *Capoeiras* in Nineteenth-Century Rio de Janeiro." *Hispanic American Historical Review* 69 (November 1989): 637–676.

hooks, bell. "Choosing the Margin as a Space of Radical Openness." In *Yearnings: Race, Gender, and Cultural Politics*. Boston: South End Press, 1990.

Hopkins, Pauline. *The Magazine Novels of Pauline Hopkins*. Edited by Hazel Carby. Oxford and New York: Oxford University Press, 1988.

Hopkins, Pauline. *Of One Blood* [1902–1903]. Edited by Deborah E. McDowell. New York: Washington Square, 2004.

Hountondji, Paulin. *African Philosophy: Myth and Reality*. Translation of *Sur la philosophie africaine*, 1976, by H. Evans & J. Rée. Bloomington: Indiana University Press, 1983.

Hoving, Isabel. *In Praise of New Travelers: Reading Caribbean Women's Writing*. Stanford, CA: Stanford University Press, 2001.

Hughes, Langston. *Scottsboro Limited: Four Poems and a Play in Verse*. New York: Golden Stair Press, 1932.

Hulme, Peter and William H. S. Herman, eds. *The Tempest and Its Travels*. Philadelphia: University of Pennsylvania Press, 2000.

Hurston, Zora Neale. "Characteristics of Negro Expression" [1933]. In *Negro: An Anthology*, edited by Nancy Cunard. Edited and abridged with an introduction by Hugh Ford. New York: Continuum, 2002.

Hurston, Zora Neale. "How It Feels to Be Colored Me" [1928]. In *The Norton Anthology of African American Literature*, edited by H. L. Gates and N. Y. McKay. New York: Norton, 2004.

Hutchinson, George. *Harlem Renaissance in Black and White*. Cambridge, MA, and London: Harvard University Press, 1997.

Hyatt, Marshall. *Franz Boas, Social Activist: The Dynamics of Ethnicity*. Westport, CT: Greenwood Press, 1990.

Inglis, Fred. *Clifford Geertz: Culture, Custom and Ethics*. Cambridge: Polity Press, 2000.

Irele, Abiola. "In Praise of Alienation." In *The Surreptitious Speech*: Présence Africaine *and the Politics of Otherness 1947–1987*, edited by V. Y. Mudimbe. Chicago: University of Chicago Press, 1992.

Ittmann, John. *Dox Thrash: An African American Master Printmaker Rediscovered*. Seattle: University of Washington Press, 2001.

Jackson, Renata. *The Modernist Poetics and Experimental Film Practice of Maya Deren (1917–1961)*. Studies in History and Criticism of Film, vol. 5. Lewiston, NY: Edwin Mellen Press, 2002.

James, C.L.R. *The Black Jacobins: Toussaint L'Ouverture and the San Domingo Revolution.* New York: Random House, 1963.

James, William. "The Hidden Self." *Scribner's Magazine* 7, no. 3 (January–June 1890): 361–373. Available from http://cdl.library.cornell.edu/cgi-bin/moa/moa-cgi?notisid=AFR7379-0007-37. Accessed 12 December 2006.

Jameson, Fredric. *Postmodernism or, The Cultural Logic of Late Capitalism.* Durham, NC: Duke University Press, 1991.

Japtok, Martin. "Pauline Hopkins's *Of One Blood*, Africa, and the 'Darwinist trap.'" *African American Review* 36, no. 3 (Fall 2002): 403–415.

Jefferson, Thomas. "Query 14. 'Laws' The administration of justice and description of the laws?" In *Notes on the State of Virginia.* Electronic Text Center, University of Virginia Library. Available from http://etext.virginia.edu/etcbin/toccernew2?id=JefVirg.sgm&images=images/modeng&data=/texts/english/modeng/parsed&tag=public&part=14&division=div1. Accessed 20 April 2007.

Johnson-Roullier, Cyraina E. *Reading on the Edge: Exiles, Modernities, and Cultural Transformation in Proust, Joyce, and Baldwin.* Albany: State University of New York Press, 2000.

Julien, Eileen. "Terrains de Rencontre: Césaire, Fanon, and Wright on Culture and Decolonization" *Yale French Studies*, no. 98 (2000): 149–166.

Jung, C. G. "Prefazione." In *I Ching. Il Libro dei mutamenti*, edited by R. Wilhelm, translated by B. Veneziani and A. G. Ferrara. Milano: Adelphi, 2005.

Kammen, Michael. "The Problem of American Exceptionalism: A Reconsideration." *American Quarterly* 45 (March 1993): 1–43.

Kant, Immanuel. *The Philosophy of Law: An Exposition of the Fundamental Principles of Jurisprudence as the Science of Right* (1796). Translated by W. Hastie. Edinburgh: Clark, 1887.

Kaplan, Caren. "Deterritorialization: The Rewriting of Home and Exile in Western Feminist Discourse." In *The Nature and Content of Minority Discourse*, edited by Abdul JanMohamed and David Lloyd. Oxford and New York: Oxford University Press, 1990.

Kaplan, Caren. "Resisting Autobiography: Out-Law Genres and Transnational Feminist Studies." In *De/Colonizing the Subject*, edited by Sidonie Smith and Julia Watson. Minneapolis: University of Minnesota Press, 1992.

Karush, Matthew B. "National Identity in the Sports Pages: Football and the Mass Media: Football and the Mass Media in 1920s Buenos Aires." *The Americas* 60 (July 2003): 11–32.

Kassanoff, Jeannie A. "'Fate Has Linked Us Together': Blood, Gender, and the Politics of Representation in Pauline Hopkins's *Of One Blood.*" In *The Unruly Voice: Rediscovering Pauline Elizabeth Hopkins*, edited by John Cullen Gruesser. Urbana: University of Illinois Press, 1996.

Kelley, Robin D. G. *Hammer and Hoe: Alabama Communists during the Great Depression.* Chapel Hill: University of North Carolina Press, 1990.

Kelley, Robin D. G. "'We Are Not What We Seem': Re-thinking Black Working-Class Opposition in the Jim Crow South." *Journal of American History* 80 (June 1993): 75–112.

Kelley, Robin D. G., and Earl Lewis, eds. *To Make Our World Anew: A History of African Americans.* Oxford and New York: Oxford University Press, 2000.

Khouma, Pap. *Io, venditore di elefanti. Una vita per forza fra Dakar, Parigi e Milano.* Edited by Oreste Pivetta. Milano: Garzanti, 1990.

Khouma, Pap. *Nonno Dio e gli spiriti danzanti.* Milano: Baldini Castoldi Dalai, 2005.

Kim, Daniel Y. "Invisible Desires: Homoerotic Racism and its Homophobic Critique in Ralph Ellison's *Invisible Man.*" *NOVEL: A Forum on Fiction* 30 (Spring 1997): 309–328.

Kincaid, Jamaica. *Among Flowers: A Walk in the Himalaya*. Washington, DC: National Geographic, 2005.

Kincaid, Jamaica. *Annie John*. New York: Farrar, Straus, Giroux, 1985.

Kincaid, Jamaica. *Lucy* [1990]. London: Picador, 1994.

Kincaid, Jamaica. *Mr Potter*. London: Chatto and Windus, 2002.

Kincaid, Jamaica. *My Brother* [1997]. London: Random House-Vintage, 1998.

Kincaid, Jamaica. *My Garden*. London: Random House-Vintage, 2000.

Kincaid, Jamaica. "On Seeing England for the First Time." *Transition*, no. 51 (1991): 32–40.

Kincaid, Jamaica. *A Small Place*. London: Virago, 1988.

Kincaid, Jamaica. *Talk Stories*. London: Random House-Vintage, 2001.

King, Richard C., ed. *Postcolonial America*. Urbana: University of Illinois Press, 2000.

Kitwana, Bakari. *The Hip Hop Generation: Young Blacks and the Crisis in African-American Culture*. New York: Basic Books, 2002.

Kostelanetz, Richard. *Politics in the African-American Novel: James Weldon Johnson, W. E. B. Du Bois, Richard Wright and Ralph Ellison*. Westport, CT: Greenwood Press, 1991.

Krasilovsky, William M., and Sidney Shemel. *This Music Business*. New York: Billboard, 1990.

Kuhl, Stefan. "Eugenics in Brazil, 1917–1940." In *The Wellborn Science*, edited by Mark Adams. Oxford and New York: Oxford University Press, 1990.

Kuhl, Stefan. *"The Hour of Eugenics": Race, Gender, and Nation in Latin America*. Ithaca, NY, and London: Cornell University Press, 1991.

Kunene, Mazizi. Review article on Sol Plaatje. *Research in African Literatures* 11, no. 2 (Summer 1980): 244–247.

Kuper, Simon. *Football against the Enemy*. London: Orion, 1994.

Labanca, Nicola. "History and Memory of Italian Colonialism Today." In *Italian Colonialism: Legacy and Memory*. Edited by Jacqueline Andall and Derek Duncan. Bern: Peter Lang, 2005.

Lacey, Josh. *God is Brazilian: Charles Miller, the Man Who Brought Football to Brazil*. Stroud: Tempus Press, 2005.

Lamming, George. *The Pleasures of Exile* [1960]. Ann Arbor: University of Michigan Press, 1984.

Langer, Susan. *Feeling and Form: A Theory of Art Developed from Philosophy in a New Key*. London: Routledge and Kegan Paul, 1953.

Lazarus, Neil, ed. *The Cambridge Companion to Postcolonial Literary Studies*. Cambridge and New York: Cambridge University Press, 2004.

Lazarus, Neil. "The Global Dispensation since 1945." In *The Cambridge Companion to Postcolonial Literary Studies*, edited by N. Lazarus. Cambridge and New York: Cambridge University Press, 2004.

Lazarus, Neil. "Indicative Chronology." In *The Cambridge Companion to Postcolonial Literary Studies*, edited by N. Lazarus. Cambridge and New York: Cambridge University Press, 2004.

Ledent, Bénédicte. "Ambiguous Visions of Home: The Paradoxes of Diasporic Belonging in Caryl Phillips's *The Atlantic Sound*." Available from http://www.brunel.ac.uk/faculty/arts/entertext/Ledent.pdf. Accessed 29 July 2005.

Lee, Andrew, ed. *Scottsboro Alabama: A Story in Linoleum Cuts by Lin Shi Khan and Tony Perez*. New York: New York University Press, 2003.

Lee, Robert A. *Designs of Blackness: Mappings in the Literature and Culture of Afro-America*. London: Pluto Press, 1998.

Leiris, Michel. *L'Afrique fantôme*. Paris: Gallimard, 1934.

Leite Lopes, José Sergio. "A vitòria do futebol que incorporou a *pelada*." *Revista USP* 22 (June–August 1994): 64–83.

Leite Lopes, José Sergio. "Success and Contradictions in 'Multiracial' Brazilian Football." In *Entering the Field: New Perspectives on World Football,* edited by Gary Armstrong and Richard Giulianotti. Oxford: Berg, 1997.

Leite Lopes, José Sergio. "The Brazilian Style of Football and Its Dilemmas." In *Football Cultures and Identities,* edited by Gary Armstrong and Richard Giulianotti. London: Macmillan, 1999.

Lemelle, Sidney J. "The Politics of Cultural Existence: Pan-Africanism, Historical Materialism and Afrocentricity." In *Imagining Home: Class, Culture and Nationalism in the African Diaspora,* edited by Sidney J. Lemelle and Robin D. G. Kelley. London: Verso, 1994.

Lever, Janet. *Soccer Madness.* Chicago: University of Chicago Press, 1983.

Lever, Janet. "Sport in a Fractured Society: Brazil under Military Rule." In *Sport and Society in Latin America: Diffusion, Dependency, and the Rise of Mass Culture,* edited by Joseph L. Arbena. Westport, CT: Greenwood Press, 1988.

Lévi-Strauss, Claude. *Tristes Tropiques.* Paris: Seuil, 1955.

Levitt, Peggy. *The Transnational Villagers.* Berkeley: University of California Press, 2001.

Levy, Andrea. *Small Island.* London: Review, 2004.

Lewis, David H. P. Maybury. Introduction to *The Masters and the Slaves: A Study in the Development of Brazilian Civilzation,* by Gilberto Freyre. Los Angeles: University of California Press, 1986.

Lewis, David Levering. *W.E.B. Du Bois: Biography of a Race (1868–1919).* New York: Henry Holt & Co., 1993.

Lewis, David Levering, ed. *W.E.B. Du Bois: A Reader.* New York: Henry Holt & Co., 1995.

Lewis, David Levering. *W.E.B. Du Bois: The Fight for Equality and the American Century (1919–1963).* New York: Henry Holt & Co., 2000.

Lewis, J. Lowell. *Ring of Liberation: Deceptive Discourse in Brazilian Capoeira.* Chicago: University of Chicago Press, 1992.

Lhamon, W.T., Jr. *Raising Cain: Blackface Performance from Jim Crow to Hip-Hop.* Cambridge, MA, and London: Harvard University Press, 1998.

Light, Alan, ed. *The Vibe History of Hip-Hop.* New York: Three River Press, 1999.

Limb, Peter. "The 'Other' Sol Plaatje: Rethinking Plaatje's Attitudes to Empire, Labour and Gender." Paper presented on 27 July 2001 at a RAU Sociology Seminar. http://general.rau.ac.za/sociology/limb.pdf.

Lipsitz, George. "Midnight's Children: Youth Culture in the Age of Globalization." Foreword to *Youthscapes: The Popular, the National, the Global,* edited by Sunaina Maira and Elisabeth Soep. Philadelphia: University of Pennsylvania, 2005.

Lloyd, P. C., ed. *The New Elites of Tropical Africa.* Oxford and New York: Oxford University Press, 1966.

Lobeck, Katharina. "Dakaration." *Froots Magazine* no. 239 (May 2003): 37–39.

Locke, Alain. "*Fire!!* A Negro Magazine." *Survey Graphic* 58, nos. 10–12 (15 August–15 September 1927): 563.

Locke, Alain. "The Negro Contribution to American Culture." *Journal of Negro Education* 8 (July 1939): 521–529.

Locke, Alain. "The Negro in the Three Americas." In *The Critical Temper of Alain Locke: A Selection of His Writings on Art and Culture,* edited by Jeffrey C. Stewart. New York: Garland Publishing, 1982.

Locke, Alain, ed. *The New Negro: An Interpretation.* New York: Albert and Charles Boni, 1925.

Locke, Alain. *Race Contacts and Inter-Racial Relations.* Washington, DC: Howard University Press, 1992.

Locke, Alain, "To Certain of Our Philistines." *Opportunity* 3 (May 1925): 155–156.

Lombardi-Diop, Cristina. "Dall'oralità alla scrittura e dalla scrittura all'oralità." In *Parole parlate: comunicazione orale fra tradizione e modernità*, edited by Annalisa Oboe. *Afriche e orienti* 4 (2005): 98–108.

Lombardi-Diop, Cristina. "Selling and Storytelling: African Autobiographies in Italy." In *Italian Colonialism: Legacy and Memory*, edited by Jacqueline Andall and Derek Duncan. Bern: Peter Lang, 2005.

Long, Richard. *The Black Tradition in American Dance*. London: Prion, 1989.

López Ropero, Maria Lourdes. "Travel Writing and Postcoloniality: Caryl Phillips's *The Atlantic Sound*." *Atlantis* 25 (2003): 51–62.

Lugard, Frederick Dealtry, Lord. "Lord Lugard on Educational Planning for Nigeria." In *Imperialism*, edited by Philip D. Curtin. New York: Walker and Company, 1971.

Lyon, Janet. *Manifestoes: Provocations of the Modern*. Ithaca, NY, and London: Cornell University Press, 1999.

Macaulay, Thomas Babington. "Thomas Babington Macaulay on Education for India." In *Imperialism*, edited by Philip D. Curtin. New York: Walker and Company, 1971.

Mackey, Nathaniel. "An Interview with Kamau Brathwaite." In *The Art of Kamau Brathwaite*, edited by Stewart Brown. Bridgend, Wales: Seren, 1995.

Manning, Susan. *Modern Dance, Negro Dance: Race in Motion*. Minneapolis: University of Minnesota Press, 2004.

Mannoni, Octave. *Prospero and Caliban: The Psychology of Colonization*. Translation of *Psychologie de la colonisation*, 1950, by Pamela Powesland. New York: Fredrick A. Praeger Publishers, 1964.

Marcus, Jane. *Hearts of Darkness: White Women Write Race*. New Brunswick, NJ: Rutgers University Press, 2004.

Marcus, Laura. *Auto/biographical Discourses—Theory, Criticism, Practice*. Manchester: Manchester University Press, 1994.

Marramao, Giacomo. *Passaggio a occidente. Filosofia e globalizzazione*. Torino: Bollati Boringhieri, 2003.

Marx, Anthony W. *Making Race and Nation: A Comparison of the United States, South Africa and Brazil*. Cambridge and New York: Cambridge University Press, 1998.

Masilela, Ntongela. "The 'Black Atlantic' and African Modernity in South Africa." Special Issue on *The Black Atlantic*. *Research in African Literatures* 27, no. 4 (Winter 1996): 88–96.

Masilela, Ntongela. "New Negro Modernity and New African Modernity." Paper presented to the "Black Atlantic: literatures, histories, cultures" forum in Zurich, January 2003. Available from www.pitzer.edu/New_African_Movement/general/modernity.pdf. Accessed 27 January 2007.

Matory, L. Lorand. "The English Professors of Brazil: On the Diasporic Roots of the Yoruba Nation." *Comparative Studies in Society and History* 41 (January 1999): 72–103.

Maurício, Augusto. "Sortilégio." *Jornal do Brasil*, August 27, 1957. Reprinted in *Dionysos* (número especial sobre o Teatro Experimental do Negro, edited by Ricardo Gaspar Müller), no. 28 (1988).

Mbembe, Achille. "Ways of Seeing: Beyond the New Nativism. Introduction." *African Studies Review* 44, no. 2: 1–14.

Mbembe, Achille, and Sarah Nuttall. "Writing the World from an African Metropolis." *Public Culture* 16, no. 3 (Fall 2004): 347–372.

McCall, John C. "Rethinking Ancestors in Africa." *Africa: Journal of the International African Institute* 65, no. 2 (1995): 256–270.

McClintock, Anne. "The Angel of Progress: Pitfalls of the Term 'Postcolonialism.'" In *Colonial Discourse/Postcolonial Theory*, edited by Francis Barker, Peter Hulme, and Margaret Iversen. Manchester: Manchester University Press, 1994.

McClintock, Anne. *Imperial Leather: Race, Gender and Sexuality in the Colonial Context*. London and New York: Routledge, 1995.

McDowell, Deborah. Introduction to *Of One Blood*, by Pauline Hopkins, edited by Deborah E. McDowell. New York: Washington Square, 2004.

McKay, Claude. "Letter to Nancy Cunard." Tangier, Morocco, December 1, 1931. Nancy Cunard Papers, Harry Ransom Humanities Research Center at the University of Texas, Austin.

McKay, Claude. *A Long Way from Home*. London: Pluto, 1985.

McRae, Donald. *Heroes without a Country: America's Betrayal of Joe Louis and Jesse Owens*. New York: Harper Collins, 2002.

Mifflin, Lawrie. "N.A.A.C.P. Plans to Press for More Diverse TV Shows." *New York Times*, 13 July 1999:10.

Mignolo, Walter. *Local Histories/Global Designs: Coloniality, Subaltern Knowledges, and Border Thinking*. Princeton, NJ: Princeton University Press, 2000.

Miller, Monica. "W.E.B. Du Bois and the Dandy as Diasporic Race Man." *Callaloo* 26, no. 3 (Fall 2003): 738–765.

Miller, Patrick, ed. *Sport and the Color Line*. London and New York: Routledge, 2003.

Miyoshi, Masao. "Turn to the Planet: Literature, Diversity, and Totality." *Comparative Literature* 53 (Fall 2001): 283–297.

Morgan, Edmund. *American Slavery, American Freedom* [1975]. New York: Norton, 2005.

Morrell, Carol, ed. *Grammar of Dissent: Poetry and Prose by Claire Harris, M. Nourbese Philip, Dionne Brand*. Fredericton, NJ: Goose Lane, 1994.

Morresi, Renata. "Racial Shake, 'Jagged Harmony' and Circum-Atlantic Networks: The Correspondence of Claude McKay and Nancy Cunard." In *Modernist Women, Race, Nation: Networking Women 1890–1950, Circum-Atlantic Connections*, edited by Giovanna Covi. London: Mango, 2005.

Morris-Jones, W. H., and Georges Fischer, eds. *Decolonisation and After: The British and French Experiences*. Studies in Commonwealth Politics and History No. 7. London: Frank Cass, 1980.

Morrison, Anthea. "The Caribbeanness of Haiti. Simone Schwarz-Bart's *Ton beau capitaine*." In *The Francophone Caribbean Today: Literature, Language, Culture*, edited by Gertrud Aub-Buscher and Beverly Ormerod Noakes. Kingston, Jamaica: University of the West Indies Press, 2003.

Morrison, Toni. *Beloved*. New York: Alfred A. Knopf, 1987.

Morrison, Toni. *Jazz*. New York: Alfred A. Knopf, 1992.

Morrison, Toni. *Playing in the Dark: Whiteness and the Literary Imagination*. New York: Vintage Books, 1993.

Morton, Patricia. *Hybrid Modernities: Architecture and Representation at the 1931 Colonial Exposition*. Cambridge, MA: MIT Press, 2000.

Mostern, Kenneth. *Autobiography and Black Identity Politics: Racialization in Twentieth-Century America*. Cambridge and New York: Cambridge University Press, 1999.

Moynagh, Maureen. "Cunard's Lines: Political Tourism and Its Texts." *New Formations* 34 (Summer 1998): 70–90.

Moynagh, Maureen. *Essays on Race and Empire: Nancy Cunard*. Peterborough, Ontario: Broadway Press, 2002.

Mullen, Bill V. "Du Bois, *Dark Princess*, and the Afro-Asian International." *positions* 11, no. 1 (Spring 2003): 217–239.

Nadeau, Maurice. *Histoire du surréalisme, suivie de documents surréalistes*. Paris: Seuil, 1964.

Naipaul, V.S. *The Enigma of Arrival*. New York: Viking, 1987.

Nascimento, Abdias do, ed., *O Negro Revoltado*. Rio de Janeiro: Edições GRD, 1968.

Nascimento, Abdias do. "Prólogo para brancos." In *Dramas para negros, prólogo para brancos*. Rio de Janeiro: Edição do TEN, 1961.

Nascimento, Abdias do. "Sortilege (Black Mystery)." Translated by Peter Lownds. *Callaloo* 18, no. 4 (Fall 1995): 821–862.

Nascimento, Abdias do, ed. *Teatro Experimental do Negro: Testemunhos*. Rio de Janeiro: Edições GRD, 1966.

Nascimento, Edson Arantes do. *Pelé: The Autobiography*. London: Simon and Schuster, 2006.

National Association for the Advancement of Colored People. "Why the Amos 'n' Andy TV Show Should Be Taken Off the Air." *NAACP Bulletin*, August 15, 1951.

Needell, Jeffrey D. "History, Race, and the State in the Thought of Oliveira Viana." *The Hispanic American Historical Review* 75, no. 1 (Feb. 1995): 34–48.

Needell, Jeffrey D. "Identity, Race, Gender, and Modernity in the Origins of Gilberto Freyre's Oeuvre." *The American Historical Review* 100, no. 1 (Feb. 1995): 51–77.

Newman, Charles. "The Lesson of the Master." In *James Baldwin. A Collection of Critical Essays*, edited by Kenneth Kinnamon. Englewood Cliffs, NJ: Prentice-Hall, 1974.

Nietzsche, Friedrich. *The Birth of Tragedy from the Spirit of Music*, translated by Douglas Smith. Oxford and New York: Oxford University Press, 2000.

Nixon, Rob. *Homelands, Harlem, and Hollywood: South African Culture and the World Beyond*. London and New York: Routledge, 1994.

Njami, Simon, ed. *Africa Remix. Contemporary Art of a Continent*. London: Hayward Gallery, 2005.

North, Michael. *The Dialect of Modernism: Race, Language and Twentieth-Century Literature*. Oxford and New York: Oxford University Press, 1994.

Oboe, Annalisa, ed. *Approaching Sea Changes: Metamorphoses and Migrations across the Atlantic*. Padova: Unipress, 2005.

Oboe, Annalisa, ed. *Parole parlate: Comunicazione orale fra tradizione e modernità*. Dossier. *Afriche e orienti* 4 (2005): 8–108.

Oboe, Annalisa. *Fiction, History and Nation in South Africa*. Venezia: Supernova, 1994.

O'Brien, Susie. "New Postnational Narratives, Old American Dreams; or, The Problem with Coming-of-Age Stories." In *Postcolonial America*, edited by R. C. King. Urbana: University of Illinois Press, 2000.

O'Callaghan, Evelyn: *Women Writing the West Indies, 1804–1939: "A Hot Place Belonging to Us."* London and New York: Routledge, 2004.

O'Daniel, Therman B. *James Baldwin: A Critical Evaluation*. Washington, DC: Howard University Press, 1977.

Oguibe, Olu, and Okwui, Enwezor, eds. *Reading the Contemporary: African Art from Theory to the Marketplace*. London: Institute of International Visual Arts, 1999.

Okpewho, Isidore, Carol Boyce Davies, and Ali A. Mazrui, eds. *The African Diaspora: African Origins and New World Identities*. Bloomington: Indiana University Press, 1999.

Okri, Ben. *The Famished Road*. London: Cape, 1991.

Olbey, Christian. "Dionne Brand in Conversation." *Ariel* 33, no. 2 (April 2002): 87–102.

O'Neill, Eugene. Letter to Abdias do Nascimento. December 6, 1944. TEN clipping file, FUNARTE, Rio de Janeiro.

Otten, Thomas. "Pauline Hopkins and the Hidden Self of Race." *ELH* 59, no. 1 (Spring 1992): 227–256.

Outlaw, Lucius. "'Conserve' Races? In Defense of W.E.B. Du Bois." In *W.E.B. Du Bois on Race and Culture: Philosophy, Politics and Poetics*, edited by Bernard W. Bell, Emily Grosholz, and James B. Stewart. London and New York: Routledge, 1996.

Owomoyela, Oyekan. *The African Difference: Discourses on Africanity and the Relativity of Cultures*. Lincoln and London: University of Nebraska Press, 1996. Repr. Peter Lang, 2001.

Owomoyela, Oyekan. *Amos Tutuola Revisited*. New York: Twayne, 1999.

Palumbo, Patrizia, ed. *A Place in the Sun: Africa in Italian Colonial Culture from Post-Unification to the Present*. Berkeley: University of California Press, 2003.

Parati, Graziella. "Intervista di Graziella Parati a Pap Khouma." *Italian Studies in Southern Africa* 8, no 2 (1995): 115–121.

Paravisini-Gebert, Lizabeth. *Jamaica Kincaid: A Critical Companion*. Westport, CT: Greenwood Press, 1999.

Parry, Benita. "Resistance Theory/Theorizing Resistance or Two Cheers for Nativism." In *Rethinking Fanon: The Continuing Dialogue*, edited by Nigel C. Gibson. New York: Humanity Books, 1999.

Passman, Donald. *All You Need to Know about the Music Business*. New York: Simon & Schuster, 1994.

Patterson, Orlando. *Slavery and Social Death: A Comparative Study*. Cambridge, MA, and London: Harvard University Press, 1982.

Perpener III, John O. *African American Concert Dance: The Harlem Renaissance and Beyond*. Urbana: University of Illinois Press, 2001.

Pétre-Grenouilleau, Olivier. *Les traits négrières. Essai d'histoire globale*. Paris: Gallimard, 2004.

Phillips, Caryl. *The Atlantic Sound*. New York: Alfred A. Knopf, 2000.

Phillips, Caryl. *Cambridge*. London: Bloomsbury, 1991.

Phillips, Caryl. *Crossing the River*. London: Bloomsbury, 1993.

Phillips, Caryl. *Dancing in the Dark*. London: Secker and Warburg, 2005.

Phillips, Caryl. *The European Tribe*. London: Faber & Faber, 1987.

Phillips, Caryl. "Literature: The New Jazz for Black America?" Review of *The Norton Anthology of African American Literature*, edited by H. L. Gates and N. Y. McKay. *Observer Review*, 6 April 1997: 17.

Phillips, Caryl. *The Nature of Blood*. London: Faber & Faber, 1997.

Phillips, Caryl. *A New World Order*. London: Vintage, 2001.

Phillips, Mike, and Phillips, Trevor, eds. *Windrush. The Irresistible Rise of Multi-Racial Britain*. London: Review, 1998.

Plaatje, Sol T. *Mhudi*. With an introduction by Tim Couzens and woodcuts by Cecil Skotnes, edited by Stephen Gray. London: Heinemann, 1978.

Plaatje, Sol T. *Mhudi: An Epic of South African Life a Hundred Years Ago*. Alice: Lovedale Press, 1930.

Plaatje, Sol. T. *The Mote and the Beam: An Epic on Sex-Relationship 'twixt White and Black in British South Africa*. New York: Youngs, 1921. Reprinted in *Selected Writings*, edited by Brian Willan. Johannesburg: Witwatersrand University Press; Athens: Ohio University Press, 1996.

Plaatje, Sol T. *Native Life in South Africa*. Introduction by Brian Willan, Foreword by Bessie Head. Johannesburg: Ravan Press, 1982.

Plaatje, Sol T. *Selected Writings*. Edited by Brian Willan. Johannesburg: Witwatersrand University Press; Athens: Ohio State University Press, 1996.

Portelli, Alessandro. "Le origini della letteratura afroitaliana e l'esempio afroamericano." In *L'ospite ingrato*. Annuario del Centro Studi Franco Fortini. Macerata: Quodlibet, 2000.

Portelli, Alessandro. *Canoni americani: oralità, letteratura, cinema, musica*. Roma: Donzelli, 2004.

Posnock, Ross. *Color and Culture: Black Writers and the Making of the Modern Intellectual*. Cambridge, MA, and London: Harvard University Press 1998.

Prado, Decio de Almeida. *Seres, Coisas, Lugares: Do teatro ao futebol*. São Paulo: Companhia das Letras, 1997.

Pratt, Mary Louise. *Imperial Eyes: Travel Writing and Transculturation*. London and New York: Routledge, 1992.

Procter, James, ed. *Writing Black Britain 1948–1998: An Interdisciplinary Anthology*. Manchester: Manchester University Press, 2000.

Pulitano, Elvira. "'I Am of, and Not of, This Place': Caribbean Dis/locations in the Work of Jamaica Kincaid and Caryl Phillips." In *The Society For Caribbean Studies Annual Conference Papers*, edited by S. Courtman, vol. 6 (2005). Available from http://www.scsonline.freeserve.co.uk/olvol6.html. Accessed 15 December 2006.

Radway, Janice A. *Reading the Romance: Women, Patriarchy, and Popular Literature*. Chapel Hill: University of North Carolina Press, 1984.

Rampersad, Arnold. *The Art and Imagination of W.E.B. Du Bois*. New York: Schocken, 1976.

Rampersad, Arnold. "Du Bois's Passage to India: *Dark Princess*." In *W.E.B. Du Bois on Race and Culture: Philosophy, Politics and Poetics*, edited by Bernard W. Bell, Emily Grosholz, and James B. Stewart. London and New York: Routledge, 1996.

Rasmussen, Susan. "Tuareg: Takedda and Trans-Saharan Trade." *Encyclopedia of African History*. 3 vols. London and New York: Routledge, 2004. Available from http://www.routledge-ny.com/ref/africanhist/tuareg.html. Accessed 2 May 2007.

Raynal, G. Th. *L'Histoire philosophique et politique des Deux Indes* [1775]. Paris: Maspero, 1981.

Reichmann Rebecca, ed. *Race in Contemporary Brazil: From Indifference to Inequality*. University Park: Pennsylvania University Press, 1999.

Rice, Shelley, ed. *Inverted Odysseys: Claude Cahun, Maya Deren, Cindy Sherman*. Cambridge, MA: MIT Press, 1999.

Richburg, Keith B. *Out of America: A Black Man Confronts Africa*. San Diego, CA: Harcourt Brace & Co., 1998.

Ro, Sigmund. *Rage and Celebration: Essays on Contemporary Afro-American Writing*. Atlantic Highlands, NJ: Humanities Press, 1984.

Robbins, Bruce. *Feeling Global: Internationalism in Distress*. New York: New York University Press, 1999.

Robeson, Paul (with Lloyd L. Brown). *Here I Stand* [1958]. Introduction by Sterling Stuckey. Boston: Beacon Press, 1988.

Rodrigues, Nelson. "Abdias: O Negro autêntico." In *Teatro Experimental do Negro: Testemunhos*, edited by Abdias do Nascimento. Rio de Janeiro: Edições GRD, 1966.

Rodrigues, Nelson. *A Pátria em Chuteiras—Novas Crônicas de Futebol*. São Paulo: Companhia das Letras, 1994.

Rodríguez, Ileana. *House/Garden/Nation: Space, Gender and Ethnicity in Postcolonial Latin American Literatures by Women*. Durham, NC: Duke University Press, 1994.

Rodrigues, Nelson. "Será racista Abdias do Nascimento?" *Ultima Hora*, São Paulo, September 17, 1957. Reprinted in *Dionysos*, no. 28 (1988). Special issue on the Teatro Experimental do Negro, edited by Ricardo Gaspar Müller.

Ronsbo, Henrik. "The Embodiment of Male Identities: Alliances and Cleavages in Salvadorean Football." In *Sport, Dance, and Embodied Identities*, edited by Noel Dyck and Eduardo P. Archetti. Oxford: Berg, 2003.

Rooney, Carol. *African Literature, Animism, and Politics.* London and New York: Routledge, 2000.

Rose, Albirda. *Dunham Technique, 'A Way of Life'.* Dubuque, IA: Kendall/Hunt Publishing Co, 1990.

Rosenfeld, Anatol. *Negro, Macumba e Futebol.* Campinas: Editora Da Unicamp, 1993.

Rowe, John Carlos. "Opening the Gate to the Other America: The Afro-Caribbean Politics of Zora Neale Hurston's *Mules and Men* and *Tell my Horse.*" In *Kontaktzone Amerika: Literarische Verkehrsformen kultereller Übersetzung*, edited by Utz Riese and Doris Dziwas. Heidelberg: Carl Winter Verlag, 2000.

Rowe, William and Vivian Schelling. *Memory and Modernity: Popular Culture in Latin America.* London: Verso, 1991.

Rushdie, Salman. *Imaginary Homelands: Essays and Criticism 1981–1991.* London: Granta, 1991.

Rushdie, Salman. *The Satanic Verses.* London: Viking, 1988.

Said, Edward W. *Culture and Imperialism.* London: Chatto & Windus, 1993.

Said, Edward W. *Representations of the Intellectual.* New York: Pantheon Books, 1994.

Sandhu, Sukhdev. *London Calling. How Black and Asian Writers Imagined a City.* London: HarperCollins, 2003.

Sansone, Livio. *Blackness without Ethnicity: Constructing Race in Brazil.* Basingstoke: Palgrave, 2003.

Scacchi, Anna. "Esuli, principesse e maragià: orientalismo e cosmopolitismo in *Dark Princess* di W.E.B. Du Bois." *Letterature d'America* 22, nos. 93–94 (2002): 55–94.

Scego, Igiaba. *Rhoda.* Rome: Sinnos Editrice, 2004.

Schaeffer, Eugène. "Private Law in the New Francophone States." In *Decolonisation and After: The British and French Experience*, edited by W. H. Morris-Jones and Georges Fischer. London: Frank Cass, 1980.

Schatteman, Renée. "Disrupting the Master Narrative: An Interview with Caryl Phillips." *Commonwealth* 23, no. 2 (2001): 93–106.

Schrager, Cynthia D. "Pauline Hopkins and William James: The New Psychology and the Politics of Race." In *The Unruly Voice: Rediscovering Pauline Elizabeth Hopkins*, edited by John Cullen Gruesser. Urbana: University of Illinois Press, 1996.

Schwartz, Roberto. *Misplaced Ideas: Essays on Brazilian Culture.* London: Verso, 1992.

Schwarz-Bart, André. *La Mulâtresse Solitude.* Paris: Seuil, 1972.

Schwarz-Bart, André and Simone Schwarz-Bart. *Un plat de porc aux bananes vertes.* Paris: Seuil, 1967.

Schwarz-Bart, Simone. *Pluie et vent sur Télumée Miracle.* Paris: Seuil, 1972. Translated as *The Bridge of Beyond* by Barbara Bray. London: Atheneum, 1975.

Schwarz-Bart, Simone. *Ti-Jean l'horizon.* Paris: Seuil, 1979.

Schwarz-Bart, Simone. *Ton beau capitaine.* Paris: Seuil, 1987.

Scott, Bonnie Kime. *The Gender of Modernism: A Critical Anthology.* Bloomington: Indiana University Press, 1990.

Scott, James. *Domination and the Arts of Resistance: Hidden Transcripts.* New Haven, CT, and London: Yale University Press, 1990.

Scott, James. *Weapons of the Weak: Everyday Forms of Peasant Resistance.* New Haven, CT, and London: Yale University Press, 1985.

Scott, Nathan A., Jr. *Three American Moralists: Mailer, Bellow, Trilling*. Notre Dame, IN: University of Notre Dame Press, 1973.

Sembène, Ousmane. *God's Bits of Wood*. Translation of *Les bouts de bois de dieu*, 1960, by Francis Price. Garden City, NY: Doubleday, 1962.

Senghor, Léopold Sédar. "L'esprit de la civilisation ou les lois de la culture negro-africaine." *Présence Africaine* 6, no. 8/10 (June–Nov. 1956): 51–65.

Senghor, Léopold Sédar. *Léopold Sédar Senghor et la revue* Présence Africaine. Paris: Présence Africaine, 1996.

Senghor, Léopold Sédar. *Liberté 3: négritude et civilisation de l'universel*. Paris: Seuil, 1977.

Senghor, Léopold Sédar. *Liberté 5: le dialogue des cultures*. Paris: Seuil, 1993.

Serres, Michel. *Passaggio a Nord-Ovest*. Translation of *Hermes 5: Le passage du Nord-Ouest* (1980) by Edi Pasini and Mario Porro Numeri. Parma: Pratiche Editrice, 1984.

Sesay, Kadija, ed. *Write Black Write British: From Post Colonial to Black British Literature*. Hertford: Hansib, 2005.

Shakespeare, William. *The Tempest (A Case Study in Critical Controversy)*. Edited by Gerald Graff and James Phelan. Boston: Bedford/St Martin's, 2000.

Sharpe, Jenny. "Is the United States Postcolonial? Transnationalism, Immigration, and Race." In *Postcolonial America*, edited by R. C. King. Urbana: University of Illinois Press, 2000.

Sharpe, Jenny. "The Unspeakable Limits of Rape: Colonial Violence and Counter-Insurgency." In *Colonial Discourse and Post-Colonial Theory*, edited by Patrick Williams and Laura Chrisman. London and New York: Harvester Wheatsheaf, 1994.

Sheriff, Robin E. *Dreaming Equality: Color, Race, and Racism in Urban Brazil*. New Brunswick, NJ: Rutgers University Press, 2001.

Shirts, Matthew. "Sócrates, Corinthians, and Questions of Democracy and Citizenship." In *Sport and Society in Latin America: Diffusion, Dependency, and the Rise of Mass Culture*, edited by Joseph L. Arbena. Westport, CT: Greenwood Press, 1988.

Skidmore, Thomas. *Black Into White: Race and Nationality in Brazilian Thought*. Oxford and New York: Oxford University Press, 1974. Reprint Durham, NC: Duke University Press, 1993.

Skidmore, Thomas E. "Bi-Racial U.S.A. vs. Multi-Racial Brazil: Is the Contrast Still Valid?" *Journal of Latin American Studies* 25 (May 1993): 373–386.

Slater, Candace. *Stories on a String: The Brazilian Literatura de Cordel*. Los Angeles: University of California Press, 1980.

Smith, John Thomas. *Vagabondiana*. London: Chatto and Windus, 1817.

Smith, Sidonie. *Subjectivity, Identity, and the Body: Women's Autobiographical Practices in the Twentieth Century*. Bloomington: Indiana University Press, 1993.

Smith, Stephen. *Négrologie. Pourquoi l'Afrique meurt*. Paris: Calmann-Lévy, 2003.

Smith, Venture. *A Narrative of the Life and Adventures of Venture a Native of Africa But Resident Above Sixty Years in the United States of America* [1798]. Kila, MT: Kessinger Publishing, 2005.

Soares, Antonio J. "História e a invenção de tradições no futebol brasileiro." In *A Invenção do País do Futebol*, edited by Ronaldo Helal, Antonio Jorge Soares, and Hugo Lovisolo. Rio de Janeiro: Mauad, 2001.

Soares, Antonio J. "O Racismo no Futebol do Rio de Janeiro nos anos 20: Uma história de identidade." In *A Invenção do País do Futebol*, edited by Ronaldo Helal, Antonio Jorge Soares, and Hugo Lovisolo. Rio de Janeiro: Mauad, 2001.

Sommer, Doris. "Irresistible Romance: The Foundational Fictions of Latin America." In *Nation and Narration*, edited by Homi K. Bhabha. London and New York: Routledge, 1990.

Soyinka, Wole. "Appendix: The Fourth Stage." *Myth, Literature and the African World*. Cambridge and New York: Cambridge University Press, 1990.

Spady, James G., Samy H. Alim, and Samir Meghelli. *Tha Global Cipha: Hip Hop Culture and Consciousness*. Philadelphia: Black History Museum Press, 2006.

Spivak, Gayatri Chakravorty. "Can the Subaltern Speak?" In *Colonial Discourse and Post-Colonial Theory: A Reader*, edited by Patrick Williams and Laura Chrisman. Hemel Hempstead: Harvester Wheatsheaf, 1993.

Spivak, Gayatri Chakravorty. *A Critique of Postcolonial Reason*. Cambridge, MA, and London: Harvard University Press, 1999.

Spivak, Gayatri Chakravorty. *Imaginary Maps*. London and New York: Routledge, 1995.

Stewart, Jeffrey C., ed. *Paul Robeson: Artist and Citizen*. New Brunswick, NJ: Rutgers University Press, 1998.

Stocking George W. Jr., ed. *A Franz Boas Reader: The Shaping of American Anthropology, 1883–1911*. Chicago, IL: University of Chicago Press, 1974.

Strehle, Susan and Mary Paniccia Carden, eds. *Doubled Plots: Romance and History*. Jackson: University Press of Mississippi, 2003.

Stuckey, Sterling. *Slave Culture: Nationalist Theory and the Foundations of Black America*. Oxford and New York: Oxford University Press, 1987.

Sullivan, Moira. "Maya Deren's Ethnographic Representation of Ritual and Myth in Haiti." In *Maya Deren and the American Avant-Garde*, edited by Bill Nichols. Berkeley: University of California Press, 2001.

Sundquist, Eric. *To Wake the Nations: Race in the Making of American Literature*. Cambridge, MA, and London: Harvard University Press, 1993.

Sylvander, Carolyn Wedin. *James Baldwin*. New York: Ungar, 1980.

Tambiah, Stanley J. "*Bridewealth* and *Dowry* Revisited: The Position of Women in Sub-Saharan Africa and North India." *Current Anthropology* 30, no. 4 (August–October 1989): 413–435.

Tate, Claudia. Introduction to *Dark Princess: A Romance*, by W.E.B. Du Bois. Jackson: University Press of Mississippi, 1995.

Tate, Claudia. *Psychoanalysis and Black Novels: Desire and the Protocols of Race*. Oxford and New York: Oxford University Press, 1998.

Taylor, Chris. *The Beautiful Game: A Journey through Latin American Football*. London: Victor Gollanz, 1998.

Taylor, Clyde. "Searching for the Postmodern in African Cinema." In *Symbolic Narratives/African Cinema*, edited by June Givanni. London: BFI, 2000.

Taylor, Paul C. "Appiah's Uncompleted Argument: Du Bois and the Reality of Race." *Social Theory and Practice* 26, no. 1 (Spring 2000): 103–128.

Tekle, Feven Abreha, with Raffaele Masto. *Libera. L'odissea di una donna eritrea in fuga dalla guerra*. Milano: Sperling & Kupfer, 2005.

Thomas, Helen. *The Body, Dance, and Cultural Theory*. Basingstoke: Palgrave Macmillan, 2003.

Thomas, Hugh. *The Slave Trade. The History of the Atlantic Slave Trade, 1440–1870*. London: Picador, 1997.

Thompson, Robert Farris. "An Aesthetic of the Cool: West African Dance." *African Forum* 2 (Fall 1966): 85–102.

Thompson, Robert Farris. *Flash of the Spirit: African and Afro-American Art and Philosophy*. New York: Vintage, 1983.

Thompson, Robert Farris. "Teaching the People to Triumph over Time: Notes from the World of Mambo." In *Caribbean Dance from Abakuá to Zouk: How*

Movement Shapes Identity, edited by Susanna Sloat. Gainesville: University Press of Florida, 2002.

Toledo, Luiz Henrique de. *Lógicas no futebol*. São Paulo: Hucitec/Fapesp, 2002.

Toledo, Luiz Henrique de. *No País do Futebol*. Rio de Janeiro: Jorge Zahar, 2000.

Torres, Sasha. *Black White and in Color: Television and Black Civil Rights*. Princeton, NJ: Princeton University Press, 2003.

Tribe, Tania, ed. *Heroes and Artists: Popular Art and the Brazilian Imagination*, exhibition catalogue. Cambridge, MA: Brazil Connects/The Fitzwilliam Museum, 2001.

Triulzi, Alessandro. "Odore di colonia." *Leggendaria*, no. 55/58 (March–April 2006): 30–33.

Trotsky, Leon. *In Defence of Marxism*. London: New Park, 1966.

Trotsky, Leon. *Literature and Revolution*. New York: Russell & Russell, 1957.

Tsing, Anna Lowenhaupt. "Contingent Commodities." In *Taking Southeast Asia to Market*, edited by Joseph Nevins and Nancy Peluso. Ithaca, NY, and London: Cornell University Press (forthcoming).

Tsing, Anna Lowenhaupt. *Friction: An Ethnography of Global Connection*. Princeton, NJ: Princeton University Press, 2005.

Twine, France W. *Racism in a Racial Democracy: The Maintenance of White Supremacy in Brazil*. New Brunswick, NJ: Rutgers University Press, 1998.

Vanderbilt, Tom. *The Sneaker Book: Anatomy of an Industry and an Icon*. New York: New Press, 1998.

Varvin, Sverre. "Extreme Traumatisierung und Psychotherapie." *Psyche* 9/10 (2000): 895–930.

Verlinden, Charles. *L'esclavage dans l'Europe médiévale*. Vol. 2: *Italie, Colonies italiennes du Levant, Levant latin, Empire byzantin*. Brugge: De Tempel, 1977.

Vivan, Itala. "Ibridismi postcoloniali e valenze estetiche." In *Estetica e differenza*, edited by P. Zaccaria. Bari: Palomar, 2002.

Vivan, Itala. "The Impact of Postcolonial Hybridization on the Britishness of British Literature." In *In That Village of the Open Doors. Le nuove letterature crocevia della cultura moderna*, edited by S. Bassi, S. Bertacco, and R. Bonicelli. Venezia: Cafoscarina, 2002.

Walcott, Derek. "The Sea Is History." *Collected Poems: 1948–1984*. London: Faber & Faber, 1992.

Walcott, Rinaldo and Leslie Sanders. "At The Full and Change of CanLit. An Interview with Dionne Brand." *Canadian Woman Studies* 20, no. 2 (2000): 22–26.

Walker, Alice. "In Search of Our Mothers' Gardens." In *The Norton Anthology of African American Literature*, edited by H. L. Gates and N. Y. McKay. New York: Norton, 2004.

Walker, Keith Louis. "In Quest of the Lost Song of Self: Aimé Césaire and the Problem of Language." *Callaloo* 16, no. 17 (February 1983): 120–133.

Waller, Nicole. *Contradictory Violence: Revolution and Subversion in the Caribbean*. Heidelberg: Winter Verlag, 2005.

Wallerstein, Immanuel. *The Decline of American Power*. New York: New Press, 2003.

Wallis, Brian. "The Slave Daguerreotypes of Louis Agassiz." *The Journal of Blacks in Higher Education* 12 (Summer 1996): 102–106.

Walter, Roland. "Between Canada and the Caribbean: Transcultural Contact Zones in the Works of Dionne Brand." *International Journal of Canadian Studies* 27 (Spring 2003): 23–41.

Warner, Marina. *Indigo or Mapping the Waters*. London: Simon & Schuster, 1992.

Warren, Kennett. "An Inevitable Drift? Oligarchy, Du Bois, and the Politics of Race between the Wars." *boundary 2* 27, no. 3 (Fall 2000): 153–169.

Washington, Booker T. *Up from Slavery. An Autobiography.* New York: Double-day, Page, 1901; Bartleby.com, 2000. Available from www.bartleby.com/1004/. Accessed 18 October 2006.

Washington, Bryan R. *The Politics of Exile: Ideology in Henry James, F. Scott Fitzgerald, and James Baldwin.* Boston: Northeastern University Press, 1995.

Watts, Edward. *Writing and Postcolonialism in the Early Republic.* Charlottes-ville: University Press of Virginia, 1998.

Weinbaum, Alys Eve. "Reproducing Racial Globality: W.E.B. Du Bois and the Sexual Politics of Black Internationalism." *Social Text* 67 (Summer 2001): 15–39.

Wells, Ida B. *Southern Horrors and Other Writings.* Edited by Jacqueline Jones Royster. Boston: Bedford/St. Martin's, 1996.

Welsh, Sarah Lawson. "(Un)belonging Citizens, Unmapped Territory: Black Immigration and British Identity in the Post-1945 Period." In *Not on Any Map: Essays on Postcolonial and Cultural Nationalism,* edited by Stuart Murray. Exeter: University of Exeter Press, 1997.

Wheatley, Phillis. *The Collected Works of Phillis Wheatley,* edited with an essay by John C. Shields. Oxford and New York: Oxford University Press, 1988.

Wheatley, Phillis. "On Being Brought from Africa to America." In *The Norton Anthology of African American Literature,* edited by H. L. Gates and N. Y. McKay. New York: Norton, 2004.

White, Deborah Gray. *Ar'n't I a Woman?: Female Slaves in the Plantation South.* New York: W. W. Norton & Co., 1985.

Whitman, Walt. *Leaves of Grass: First and "Death-Bed" Editions, Additional Poems.* New York: Barnes & Noble, 2004.

Wiens, Jason. "'Language Seemed to Split in Two': National Ambivalence(s) and Dionne Brand's 'No Language is Neutral'." *Essays on Canadian Writing* 70 (2000): 81–102.

Wild, Brendan. "Overhearing Dionne Brand: An Organic Intellectual Project." *Crossing Boundaries* 1, no. 3 (Fall 2002): 144–161.

Wilken, Lois. "Spirit Unbound: New Approaches to the Performance of Haitian Folklore." In *Caribbean Dance from Abakuá to Zouk: How Movement Shapes Identity,* edited by Susanna Sloat. Gainesville: University Press of Florida, 2002.

Willan, Brian. *Sol Plaatje, South African Nationalist, 1876–1932.* London: Heine-mann, 1984.

Williams, Bronwyn T. "'A State of Perpetual Wandering': Diaspora and Black British Writers." (1999) *Jouvert* 3, no. 3. Available from http://152.1.96.5/jouvert/v3i3/willia.htm. Accessed 18 April 2005.

Winkiel, Laura. "Nancy Cunard's *Negro* and the Transnational Politics of Race." *Modernism/modernity* 13, no. 3 (September 2006): 507–530.

Winner, David. *Brilliant Orange: The Neurotic Genius of Dutch Football.* London: Bloomsbury, 2000.

Wiredu, J. E. [Kwasi]. "How Not to Compare African Thought with Western Thought." In *African Philosophy: An Introduction,* edited by Richard A. Wright. Lanham, MD: University Press of America, 1984.

Wisnek, José Miguel. "The Riddle of Brazilian Soccer: Reflections on the Emancipatory Dimensions of Culture." *Review: Literature and Arts of the Americas* 73 (November 2006): 198–209.

Wright, Michelle M. *Becoming Black: Creating Identity in the African Diaspora.* Durham, NC: Duke University Press, 2004.

Wright, Patrick. "Interview with H. Bhabha, S. Nasta and R. Araeen." In "Re-inventing Britain: A Forum." *Wasafiri* 29 (Spring 1999): 40–41.

Young, Robert. *Colonial Desire: Hybridity in Theory, Culture and Race.* London and New York: Routledge, 1995.

Young, Robert. *Postcolonialism: An Historical Introduction.* Oxford: Blackwell, 2001.

Zabus, Chantal J. *Tempests after Shakespeare.* London: Palgrave Macmillan, 2002.

Zackodnik, Teresa. "'I am blackening in my way': Identity and Place in Dionne Brand's *No Language Is Neutral.*" *Essays on Canadian Writing* 57 (1995): 194–211.

Zobel, Joseph. *La Rue cases-nègres.* Paris: Présence Africaine, 1974.

Contributors

Franca Bernabei teaches English and Postcolonial Literature at Ca' Foscari University, Venice, Italy. She has worked on American literature, Caribbean and diasporic writers, and transatlantic themes. Among her publications are a number of essays on Caryl Phillips and Dionne Brand, and the volumes *Jean Rhys e il pensiero del luogo* (2000) and *La storia del romanzo americano e la lezione francese* (1981).

Manthia Diawara is the author of *We Won't Budge: An African Exile in the World* (2003), *Black-American Cinema: Aesthetics and Spectatorship* (1993), *African Cinema: Politics and Culture* (1992), and *In Search of Africa* (1998). He has published widely on the topic of film and literature of the black diaspora. He collaborated with Ngũgĩ wa Thiong'o in making the documentary *Sembene Ousmane: The Making of the African Cinema*, and directed the German-produced documentary *Rouch in Reverse*.

Paulla A. Ebron is Associate Professor of Cultural and Social Anthropology at Stanford University. Her interests include culture as a commodity, memory and history, feminism and difference, and performance. Her book *Performing Africa* (2002), based on her research in The Gambia, traces the significance of West African praise-singers in transnational encounters. A second project focuses on tropicality and regionalism as it connects West Africa and the U.S. Georgia Sea Islands in a dialogue about landscape, memory and political uplift.

Dorothea Fischer-Hornung is Senior Lecturer in the English Department of the University of Heidelberg, Germany, where she specializes in American cultural studies. She is founding co-editor of the journal *Atlantic Studies: Literary, Cultural and Historical Perspectives* and President of The Society for Multi-Ethnic Studies: Europe and the Americas (MESEA). Her research focuses on minority writing and performance cultures in the United States and the Caribbean, especially African diasporic dance, literature, and film.

Richard Follett is Reader in American History at the University of Sussex, Brighton, England. He is the author of *The Sugar Masters: Planters and Slaves in Louisiana's Cane World, 1820–1860* (2005) and of multiple articles on plantation slavery and demography in the American South. He was editor of *Atlantic Studies* (2003–2007) and currently works on black expressive culture in the Americas and the psychology of slavery in the circumcaribbean world.

Simone Francescato is a PhD student in Anglo-American Studies at Ca' Foscari University, Venice, Italy, working on Henry James and the consumption of works of art. His research interests include nineteenth-century aesthetics and American realism, gender studies, and twentieth-century African American literature. He has published "Lost Voices of the Trans-Atlantic Journey: Three Texts by John Berryman, Robert Hayden and J. M. Coetzee" in the e-journal *49th Parallel*.

Ginevra Geraci obtained her PhD in American Studies from the University of Roma 3 with a dissertation on the representation of Jews in Zora Neale Hurston, Chester Himes, and Alice Walker. Her main area of research is twentieth-century African American literature. Her essay "Fear, Flight and Fate: The Transcendental Quest in Richard Wright's 'The Man Who Lived Underground'" is forthcoming in the proceedings of the 2005 AISNA biennial conference.

Paul Giles is Professor of American Literature and Director of the Rothermere American Institute at the University of Oxford. He has published widely on transatlantic themes. His most recent books are *Atlantic Republic: The American Tradition in English Literature* (2006), *Virtual Americas: Transnational Fictions and the Transatlantic Imaginary* (2002), and *Transatlantic Insurrections: British Culture and the Formation of American Literature, 1730–1860* (2001).

Cristina Lombardi-Diop is Assistant Professor in the Department of Italian Studies at the American University of Rome. She has published articles on Italian colonial literature and ideology, and on the African diaspora in contemporary Italy. She is at work on a book on colonial fiction and women's travel writing in Italy (1890–1940) and is also conducting research on Senegalese migrant culture in Italy.

Renata Morresi received her PhD in Comparative Literature from the University of Macerata, Italy, where she now teaches English literature. She has written on Nancy Cunard, transatlantic modernism, literary magazines of the 1930s, African American autobiography, Claude McKay's novels *Home to Harlem* and *Banjo*, translation, and polylinguism. She is the author of *Nancy Cunard: America, modernismo, negritudine* (2007).

Annalisa Oboe is Professor of English and Postcolonial Literature at the University of Padua, Italy. She works on British colonial and twentieth-century literature, postcolonial studies, African and Australian indigenous cultures, and South African and Black Atlantic literatures. Her publications include *Approaching Sea Changes: Metamorphoses and Migrations across the Atlantic* (2005); *Mongrel Signatures: Reflections on the Work of Mudrooroo* (2003); and *Fiction, History and Nation in South Africa* (1994).

Oyekan Owomoyela was the Ryan Professor of African Literatures at the University of Nebraska, Lincoln, and the author of *Amos Tutuola Revisited* (1999), *The African Difference: Discourses on Africanity and the Relativity of Cultures* (1996), and *A History of Twentieth-Century African Literatures* (1993). *Yoruba Proverbs* (2005), on Yoruba folklore, is his most recent work.

Elvira Pulitano is Assistant Professor of Ethnic Studies at California Polytechnic State University. She is the author of *Toward a Native American Critical Theory* (2003) and of various essays on contemporary Native American and postcolonial writing. She is also the editor of *Transatlantic Voices: Interpretations of Native North American Literatures* (forthcoming). Her interests in the field of cross-cultural, global approaches to contemporary Anglophone studies include Caribbean literatures, literatures of the Black Atlantic, transnationalism, diaspora, and human rights discourse.

Venus Opal Reese is a solo performer, playwright, director, choreographer, and poet. She teaches at the University of Texas at Dallas. Her latest solo performance work, *Split Ends*, about the relationship between American women of African ancestry and their hair, had a successful run off-Broadway at La MaMa and other experimental theaters. She has performed nationally and internationally.

Anna Scacchi teaches American Literature at the University of Padua, Her main areas of research are language ideology and multilingualism, gender, and race studies. She has published essays on Benjamin Franklin, Margaret Fuller, Harriet Beecher Stowe, Herman Melville, Charlotte Perkins Gilman, Zora Neale Hurston, W.E.B. Du Bois, and language ideology in the Early American Republic. She is the author of a book on Melville's *Benito Cereno* (2000), and has co-authored a book on American multilingualism (2005). She is the editor of a collection of essays on the mother-daughter relationship (2005).

Jeffrey C. Stewart is Professor of History and Art History at George Mason University, Virginia. He holds a PhD in American Studies from

Yale University. He is currently writing a biography of Alain Locke. He is the editor of *The Critical Temper of Alain Locke* (1983), *Race Contacts and Interracial Relations: Lectures on the Theory and Practice of Race by Alain Locke* (1995), and *Paul Robeson: Artist and Citizen* (1998), and the author of *To Color America: Portraits by Winold Reiss* (1989) and *1001 Things Everyone Should Know about African American History* (1996).

Antoinette Tidjani Alou is Professor of French and Comparative Litera-ture and Literary Criticism at the Université Adbou Moumouni de Niamey (Niger) and a founding member of an interdisciplinary research group on Gender, Literature and Development in Niger. Author of translations in socio-anthropology and literature, she has also published papers in French and on Francophone literature. She is the editor of *Niger: Emerging Litera-ture and Modern Orature: Voicing Identities* (2005).

Itala Vivan, formerly Professor of Cultural and Postcolonial Studies at the State University of Milano, Italy, has published extensively on postcolonial fiction and African cultures, on gender and women's writing, and on con-temporary literary and cultural hybridity. From 1987 to 1995 she edited a series of African and Caribbean fiction in Italian and currently remains a consultant for Italian publishers on postcolonial literatures. Her latest book is *Corpi liberati in cerca di storia di storie: Il Nuovo Sudafrica dieci anni dopo l'apartheid* (2005).

Nicole Waller holds a Junior Professorship for American Studies with spe-cial emphasis on Caribbean and Atlantic Studies at Johannes Gutenberg Universität, Mainz. She has taught at Columbia University, New York, and the City University of New York. Among her research interests are Arab American literature and colonial American history. She has published a book entitled *Contradictory Violence: Revolution and Subversion in the Caribbean* (2005) and is currently working on colonial American literature and slave narratives.

Judith Michelle Williams is a theater historian and teaches Drama at the University of Massachusetts. She earned her PhD from Stanford University with a dissertation on nineteenth-century stage images of black women. Her areas of specialization are African American theater and drama, and theater in Brazil. Her work in progress includes the forthcoming volume, *Neither Blacks nor Blackness: Afro-Brazilian Theatre 1888–1968.*

Patrick Williams is Professor of Literary and Cultural Studies at Notting-ham Trent University, UK. He has published widely on postcolonial theory and writing, cultural theory, and film. His work has been translated into Korean and Turkish. His publications include *Colonial Discourse and Post-Colonial Theory* (ed. with L. Chrisman, 1993); *Post-Colonial Theory. A*

Critical Introduction (with Peter Childs, 1996); *Ngugi wa Thiong'o* (1999); *Edward Said* (2000); and *Post-Colonial African Cinema* (2007).

Marcus Wood is a painter, performance artist, and filmmaker, and is Professor of Diaspora Studies at the University of Sussex. For the last twenty years he has been producing work, as an artist and academic, which addresses the cultural inheritance of Atlantic slavery in England, North America and Brazil. He is the author of *Blind Memory: Visual Representations of Slavery in England and America 1780–1865* (2000) and of *Slavery, Empathy and Pornography* (2003). He is currently working on a comparative study of Brazilian and North American slavery propaganda.

Index